CRIMINAL PROCEDURE

ACCORDING TO

THE LAW OF SCOTLAND

CRIMINAL PROCEDURE

ACCORDING TO

THE LAW OF SCOTLAND

by

ROBERT WEMYSS RENTON

and

HENRY HILTON BROWN

FOURTH EDITION

by

GERALD H. GORDON,
Q.C., M.A., LL.B., Ph.D., LL.D.

Professor of Criminal Law in the University of Edinburgh

EDINBURGH
W. GREEN & SON LTD.
LAW PUBLISHERS
1972

ISBN 0 414 00544 9

Printed in Great Britain by The Eastern Press Ltd., London and Reading

PREFACE TO FOURTH EDITION

RENTON AND BROWN'S *Criminal Law* has served the profession for over half a century, and its style and layout have become familiar to all who practise in the criminal courts. The aim of this fourth edition has been the modest one of bringing the work up to date. I have, therefore, for the most part avoided any alteration of the text which was not necessary for that purpose, although I have occasionally made some alterations in an attempt to achieve greater clarity, particularly in chapter 11, and in those parts of chapter 5 which deal with arrest and search. In the interests of economy the table of forms in the Appendix has been curtailed by the exclusion of forms which are readily available in statutory schedules, or which are issued as printed forms to procurators fiscal or sheriff clerks.

There have been considerable changes in the law since the publication of the third edition in 1956. Most of these have been statutory and have been concerned with the disposal of offenders and particularly of young offenders, but there have also been changes in the common law of evidence, especially in the area of admissibility of confessions. As a result most of Part IV of this edition has been written anew.

I am indebted to many colleagues for help at various stages in the preparation of this edition. Mr. O. J. Brown, Clerk of Justiciary, read the whole work in proof and made many helpful suggestions as well as saving me from numerous errors. Others to whom I am indebted include Mr. W. G. Chalmers of Crown Office, and Dr. E. M. Clive and Mr. St. J. N. Bates of Edinburgh University. The errors and omissions which remain in the book are to be laid at my door alone.

I am indebted also to Mrs. M. A. M. Wedderburn who provided secretarial and other assistance far in excess of what I was entitled to expect from her, and to Dr. G. R. Thomson of W. Green & Son Ltd., and The Eastern Press Ltd., for keeping their accustomed watchful eye on me, and maintaining their high standard of accuracy.

The tables of cases and statutes, which were prepared by my wife and Dr. Ann Smith, and the index, with which my wife also assisted, have been newly prepared for this edition. I am grateful to both ladies for the time they spent on the computer-like drudgery involved.[1]

---

[1] It is monstrous, for example, that in order to describe the modern procedures for dealing with children one has to refer to two Acts of Parliament, three separate Schedules of one of which amend the other, and five statutory instruments. If one wishes to include the relevant legal aid provisions, one must look to yet another Act, two statutory instruments, and a legal aid scheme.

I have tried to state the law as at 1st April 1972, but I have assumed the passing of the Criminal Justice Bill 1972 and the coming into force of the Immigration Act 1971.

Gerald H. Gordon

EDINBURGH UNIVERSITY, *May*, 1972.

PREFACE TO FIRST EDITION

THE passing of the Summary Jurisdiction (Scotland) Act, 1908, following upon the Criminal Procedure Act of 1887 and the Bail Act of 1888, has produced the nearest approach to a code of criminal procedure that Scotland has yet possessed. The time seems, therefore, appropriate for the preparation of a book which should treat of the whole subject of criminal procedure, apart from the principles of crime. Such a book might be expected not only to be of service to the practitioner, but also to be a convenient means of ascertaining where the law is still defective, with a view to its further amendment.

It has seemed natural that we should collaborate in the preparation of a volume of the character suggested, seeing that we have both already written on the subject of criminal procedure, and have also had the honour of assisting to some extent in the drafting of the recent Act.

Our idea has been to provide a work which will be useful in practice. We have accordingly resisted the temptation to discuss the many interesting historical and jural questions which surround the procedure of our criminal courts, or the curious points which occur in practice rarely and at long intervals. These exceptional points can be studied in the pages of Hume, Alison and Macdonald, and in the older treatise of Sir George Mackenzie. We have sought rather to gather together all those matters which have to be considered in daily practice in the prosecution and defence of criminal charges, to state them briefly and concisely, and to arrange them in a form convenient for ready reference. We hope that our efforts may be attended with some measure of success; and as our professional brethren know the difficulties inseparable from such an undertaking, we feel that we can rely upon their kindly consideration.

In the matter of forms, we have been liberal in examples illustrating the various steps of procedure, and we trust that in this branch our work will be found to be fairly complete. We have, however, decided not to suggest Forms of Charges in addition to those furnished in the schedules of the statutes, as it seems more prudent with reference to the new forms introduced by the 1908 Act, to allow some time for experience in actual practice before adapting these to charges not contained in the schedules.

The plan of the book is very simple. It is in three parts—(1) an Introduction applicable to all criminal procedure; (2) Procedure in Solemn Jurisdiction, or trial by jury; and (3) Procedure in Summary Jurisdiction, or trial without a jury. A synopsis of Procedure introduces Parts II and III, and affords a general view of the subject.

A number of illustrative notes have been furnished, containing extracts from important decided cases, with, in many instances, the *ipsissima verba* of the judges. It seemed to us that it would be convenient to have, so far as possible, the exact words of the authorities placed in contiguity to the steps of procedure to which they refer. When a question suddenly arises in court, the prosecutor, or the agent for the defence, is thus able to ascertain readily the decided points. As the 1887 and 1908 Acts have superseded many of the older decisions, we have only referred to such decisions under the former law as seemed still to have a bearing on procedure.

Special pains have been taken with that most necessary portion of a law book—the index. We have sought to make the whole work readily accessible by this means—text, illustrative notes, and appendix. The whole of these have been included in one alphabetical vidimus.

In conclusion, we wish to express our thanks to all those who have assisted us by suggestions or by the use of forms. In particular, thanks are due to Mr. Agnew, Procurator-Fiscal at Dundee, and Mr. Jameson, Procurator-Fiscal at Perth, for furnishing us with various forms of procedure; to Mr. W. J. Lewis, S.S.C., Edinburgh, who has not only revised the proof-sheets but favoured us with many valuable suggestions; and to Mr. Alexander Rae, one of the Depute Clerks of Justiciary, who has given us information on many points of practice.

R. W. R.

H. H. B.

EDINBURGH, *May* 1909.

CONTENTS

TABLE OF CASES

TABLE OF STATUTES

ACTS OF THE PARLIAMENT OF SCOTLAND

STATUTES OF THE PARLIAMENT OF GREAT BRITAIN

lix

LOCAL ACTS

STATUTORY INSTRUMENTS

LIST OF ABBREVIATIONS

(Excluding standard law reports)

Alison — *Principles and Practice of the Criminal Law of Scotland*, by A. J. Alison (2 vols.: vol. i, *Principles*, Edin., 1832; vol. ii, *Practice*, Edin., 1933).

Dickson on Evidence — *A Treatise on the Law of Evidence in Scotland*, by W. G. Dickson, 2nd ed., by P. J. Hamilton Grierson, Edin., 1887.

Gordon — *The Criminal Law of Scotland*, by G. H. Gordon, Edin., 1967.

Hume — *Commentaries on the Law of Scotland Respecting Crimes*, by Baron Hume, 4th ed., by B. R. Bell, 2 vols., Edin., 1844.

Macdonald — *A Practical Treatise on the Criminal Law of Scotland*, by J. H. A. Macdonald (Lord Kingsburgh), 5th ed., by J. Walker (later Lord Walker) and D. J. Stevenson, Edin., 1948.

Mackenzie — *The Laws and Customs of Scotland in Matters Criminal*, by Sir G. Mackenzie, 2nd ed., Edin., 1699.

Moncreiff on Review in Criminal Cases — *A Treatise on the Law of Review in Criminal Cases, etc.*, by the Hon. H. J. Moncreiff (later Lord Wellwood), Edin., 1877.

Trotter on Summary Criminal Jurisdiction — *Summary Criminal Jurisdiction according to the Law of Scotland*, by T. T. Trotter, Edin. and Glasgow, 1936.

Walker and Walker on Evidence — *The Law of Evidence in Scotland*, by A. G. Walker and N. M. L. Walker, Edin. and Glasgow, 1964.

J.C.L. — Journal of Criminal Law
J.R. — Juridical Review
L.Q.R. — Law Quarterly Review
N.I.L.Q. — Northern Ireland Legal Quarterly
S.A.L.J. — South African Law Journal

1887 Act — Criminal Procedure (Scotland) Act 1887
1908 Act — Summary Jurisdiction (Scotland) Act 1908
1921 Act — Criminal Procedure (Scotland) Act 1921
1926 Act — Criminal Appeal (Scotland) Act 1926
1937 Act — Children and Young Persons (Scotland) Act 1937
1949 Act — Criminal Justice (Scotland) 1949
1954 Act — Summary Jurisdiction (Scotland) Act 1954
1960 Act — Mental Health (Scotland) Act 1960
1963 Act — Criminal Justice (Scotland) Act 1963
1968 Act — Social Work (Scotland) Act 1968

Part I

INTRODUCTION

CHAPTER 1

CRIMINAL JURISDICTION

Crimes and offences

1–01 A CRIME is an act or omission punishable by law.[1] The criminality of an act or omission is not dependent upon the degree of moral guilt which it implies. An immoral offence may not be a crime; a crime may not be a breach of the moral law. The element which imposes the quality of criminality is a declaration by the state, either implied in its common law, enacted in its statutes, or made by its courts,[2] that if a person does or omits to do a certain act, he will be liable to punishment. The term " offence " has a similar signification,[3] and is most frequently applied to breaches of statute law designed to regulate the conduct of the citizens in regard to matters of public administration and policy.

Prescription

1–02 The vicennial prescription of crime does not form part of the law of Scotland.[4]

Criminal jurisdiction

1–03 Criminal jurisdiction is a power which the state has vested in a judge, or body of judges, to take cognisance of and determine questions which arise in relation to crimes and offences committed within a specified district or territory. As the term has been extended so as to include proceedings of widely different character, it is sometimes a delicate matter to decide whether the jurisdiction in a particular case is civil or criminal.[5] Where it is necessary to consider such questions, it may be laid down as a general rule that the jurisdiction exercised is criminal:

(1) Where the state authorises proceedings in vindictam publicam, for conviction of an offence, and for sentence inferring imprisonment for a specified time, at the expiration of which the prisoner is entitled to liberation, although he has not paid any penalty, or done any act, prescribed in the judgment; or

(2) Where the state authorises proceedings which are of a criminal character, the person charged to be brought immediately before the court, and the judgment called a conviction.[6]

---

[1] Cf. Summary Jurisdiction (Scotland) Act 1954, s. 77.
[2] *Bernard Greenhuff* (1838) 2 Swin. 236.
[3] See Gordon, 14–15.
[4] *Sugden* v. *H.M. Adv.*, 1934 J.C. 103.
[5] *Moncreiff on Review in Criminal Cases*, Chap. VI.
[6] *Stevenson* v. *Scott* (1854) 1 Irv. 603; *Bruce* v. *Linton* (1861) 24 D. 184.

Solemn and summary jurisdiction

1-04   Criminal jurisdiction is of two kinds—solemn and summary. These
are distinguished mainly by the course of procedure which is followed in
the trial of a case,[7] and the measure of punishment which follows conviction. Any contravention of the criminal law of Scotland must fall into one
or other of these categories, and this distinction is of crucial importance.
In solemn procedure the judge sits with a jury, and cases falling within this
category can be tried only in the High Court of Justiciary and in the sheriff
court. The trial proceeds upon an indictment, and the punishment may
in the High Court extend to imprisonment for life, and even to death, and
in the sheriff court to two years' imprisonment.[8] Summary jurisdiction is
exercised by a judge or judges sitting without a jury and is confined to the
sheriff, justices of the peace, burgh and police courts. The trial proceeds
upon a complaint, and the punishment does not normally exceed a moderate term of imprisonment. The tests to be applied in order to decide
whether a case should be dealt with in a solemn or summary manner are
considered in Chapter 3.

Original and appellate jurisdiction

1-05   All the criminal courts in Scotland possess original jurisdiction, and
are courts of first instance. The High Court of Justiciary, in addition to
its original jurisdiction, exercises an appellate jurisdiction both in solemn
and in summary procedure. In solemn procedure the original jurisdiction
of a single judge sitting with a jury is, in certain circumstances, subject to
an appeal to the High Court of Justiciary sitting as a court of criminal
appeal.[9] In summary jurisdiction there are various methods by which
proceedings in the summary courts may be reviewed in the High Court
of Justiciary.[10]

Territorial jurisdiction

1-06   As a general rule the locus delicti determines the particular criminal
jurisdiction to which a person is amenable. A person charged with a crime
or offence is subject to the jurisdiction of any court which has authority
to deal with it in the place where the act or omission is said to have
occurred. The jurisdiction of the High Court extends to all Scotland, and
in the absence of statutory limitation it can take cognisance of any crime
committed in Scotland. The jurisdictions of the inferior courts are territorially limited.

     As criminal jurisdiction depends primarily on the locus delicti, the
High Court can take cognisance of any crime committed in Scotland,
whether by a British subject or a foreigner.[11] This jurisdiction over the

---

[7] Cf. *Lamb* v. *Threshie* (1892) 3 White 261, L.J.-C. at 270.
[8] Criminal Justice (Scotland) Act 1949, s. 16 (1). See also *Maguiness* v. *MacDonald*, 1953
J.C. 31, L.J.-G. at 34.
[9] Infra, Chap. 11.
[10] Infra, Chap. 16.
[11] Macdonald, 190; Hume, ii. 57; Alison, ii. 81–82.

whole territory of Scotland extends also to the territorial waters within the three-mile limit, and the criminal jurisdiction exercised over ships within these waters appears to be independent of the nationality of the accused or of the ship.[12] So, where an American sailor was charged with assault committed on board an American ship lying in the Clyde, it was held that the sheriff had jurisdiction to try him, as the ship was within the sheriff's territory at the time of the offence.[13]

It is not essential to the jurisdiction of the High Court that the whole of the acts constituting the crime should have been done in Scotland. There is jurisdiction if the main act has been committed there.[14] It has been held that there was jurisdiction in Scotland where money was obtained by an Englishman by means of fraudulent advertisement in Scotland [15]; where a Scots bankrupt uplifted money in England to defraud his creditors,[16] and in forgery cases where uttering has taken place in Scotland.[17] Where an Englishman, by means of false representations contained in letters addressed by him to traders in Scotland and posted in England, obtained from such traders goods, without paying or intending to pay therefor, it was held that the Scottish courts had jurisdiction to try the offence.[18]

In a prosecution for a contravention of section 2 of the False Oaths (Scotland) Act 1933, it was held on appeal that the court which had jurisdiction to try the offence was the court which had jurisdiction at the place where the correct entry should have been made.[19]

Extraterritorial Jurisdiction

The following exceptions to the rule that jurisdiction is based on locus delicti may be noted.

Piracy

1–07   Piracy may be tried by the Scots courts irrespective of the place of the offence or of the nationality of the ship or of the offenders.[20]

Geneva Conventions Act 1957

1–08   Offences against the Geneva Conventions Act 1957 committed outside the United Kingdom may be dealt with by the High Court.[21]

---

[12] Macdonald, 192; *Lewis* v. *Blair* (1958) 3 Irv. 16.
[13] *Lewis* v. *Blair*, supra.
[14] Macdonald, 191; see also Gordon, 83–91; Glanville Williams, " Venue and the Ambit of Criminal Law " (1965) 81 L.Q.R. 518.
[15] *H.M. Adv.* v. *Allan* (1873) 2 Couper 402.
[16] *John McKay* (1866) 5 Irv. 329.
[17] Hume, ii. 53; *Wm. Jeffrey* (1842) 1 Broun 337.
[18] *John Thomas Witherington* (1881) 4 Couper 475; *Wm. Edward Bradbury* (1872) 2 Couper 311.
[19] *Waugh* v. *Mentiplay*, 1938 J.C. 117.
[20] Hume, i. 480; Macdonald, 192; cf. *Cameron and Ors.* v. *H.M. Adv.*, 1971 S.L.T. 333. See Tokyo Convention Act 1967.
[21] Geneva Conventions Act 1957, s. 1 (2), (3).

Treason

1-09   In the crime of treason, jurisdiction is based on allegiance and the Scots courts can try persons charged with treason no matter where the treasonable acts were committed.[22]

Murder and culpable homicide

1-10   Any British subject who in any country outside the United Kingdom does any act or makes any omission which if done or made in Scotland would constitute the crime of murder or of culpable homicide is guilty of the same crime and subject to the same punishment as if the act or omission had been done or made in Scotland.[23]

Such a person may be proceeded against, indicted, tried and punished for his offence in any county or place in Scotland in which he is apprehended or is in custody as if the offence had been committed in that county or place; and the offence is, for all purposes incidental to or consequential on the trial or punishment thereof, deemed to have been committed in that county or place.[24]

Offences by Crown employees

1-11   Any British subject employed under Her Majesty's Government in the United Kingdom in the service of the Crown, who, in a foreign country, when acting or purporting to act in the course of his employment, does any act or makes any omission which if done or made in Scotland would constitute an offence punishable on indictment is guilty of the same offence, and subject to the same punishment, as if the act or omission had been done or made in Scotland.[25]

The procedure in such cases is regulated by the provisions of section 29 (3) of the 1949 Act.

Offences at sea

1-12   Crimes committed on British ships on the high seas, and, where the accused is a British subject, on British ships in foreign ports, are within the jurisdiction of the Scots criminal courts. This matter is now regulated by the Merchant Shipping Act 1894, ss. 680–710, and the Merchant Shipping Act 1906, s. 82. These Acts define the jurisdiction of the courts, but do not appear to extend their common law jurisdictions. By section 684 of the 1894 Act it is provided that, for the purpose of giving jurisdiction under the Act, every offence is deemed to have been committed either in the place of its commission or in the place where the offender may be.[26]

---

[22] Hume, ii. 50.
[23] 1949 Act, s. 29 (1).
[24] Ibid. s. 29 (3).
[25] Ibid. s. 29 (2).
[26] Under a corresponding section in the Merchant Shipping Act 1854, it was held that the sheriff at Greenock had jurisdiction over a British seaman charged there with contraventions of the Act alleged to have been committed in Australia: *Simpson* v. *Board of Trade* (1892) 3 White 167.

Section 685 gives courts jurisdiction over vessels on or lying or passing off any of the coast over which they have jurisdiction, or in or near any bay, channel, lake, river or navigable water on which the territory of the court's jurisdiction abuts or into which it projects.

Under the provisions of section 686, the Scots courts may try (i) a British subject charged with an offence committed on board a British ship on the high seas,[27] or in a foreign port or harbour; (ii) a British subject charged with an offence committed on board a foreign ship to which he does not belong; and (iii) a person not being a British subject charged with an offence committed on a British ship on the high seas.

Fishery statutes, e.g. Herring Fishery (Scotland) Act 1889, may, for a particular purpose, confer jurisdiction upon the Scots courts over areas of sea outwith territorial waters even in the case of foreigners in foreign ships.[28] For the purposes of the Sea Fisheries Acts the fishery limits of the British Isles now extend to twelve miles from the base line from which territorial waters are calculated, and are divided into an exclusive fishery limit extending for six miles from the base line, and an outer belt.[29]

1–13 Under the Coinage Offences Act 1936, the Scots courts may try coinage offences committed at sea on ships registered in Scotland. Offences committed by persons acting in concert in different jurisdictions may be tried in any of these jurisdictions.[30] There is also jurisdiction to try offences committed on a vessel which touches at any part of Scotland.[31] These provisions do not apply to contraventions of section 8 of the Act.

1–14 The provisions of Part I of the Wireless Telegraphy Act 1949, which prohibit the installation or use of any station or apparatus for wireless telegraphy without a licence, apply to " territorial waters," to any sea-going ships or aircraft registered in the United Kingdom wherever they are, and to apparatus released from within the United Kingdom or its territorial waters or from any such ship or aircraft.[32] Offences committed outwith the United Kingdom but within " territorial waters " may be treated as if they were committed anywhere in the United Kingdom.[33] " Territorial waters " for the purposes of the Act are determined by reference to the Territorial Waters Order in Council 1964.[34]

Offences on aircraft

1–15 On common law principles a court has jurisdiction over aircraft which are within or flying over its territory. Section 1 of the Tokyo Convention Act 1967 provides that any act or omission taking place on a British controlled aircraft in flight elsewhere than in or over the United Kingdom,

---

[27] *Cameron and Ors.* v. *H.M. Adv.*, supra.
[28] *Mortensen* v. *Peters* (1906) 5 Adam 121; cf. *Peters* v. *Olsen* (1905) 4 Adam 608.
[29] Fishery Limits Act 1964, s. 1. Special jurisdictional provisions are also made in the Continental Shelf Act 1964, s. 1, and the Antarctic Treaty Act 1967, s. 5.
[30] Coinage Offences Act 1936, s. 15 (3), (4).
[31] Ibid. s. 15 (4).
[32] s. 6 (1) as amended by Wireless Telegraphy Act 1967, s. 9 (1).
[33] Wireless Telegraphy Act 1967, s. 12.
[34] Wireless Telegraphy Act 1967, s. 9 (1).

which if taking place in, or in a part of, the United Kingdom, would constitute an offence under the law in force there, shall constitute that offence.
For the purposes of jurisdiction any offence under such law committed on
an aircraft in flight is deemed to have been committed in any place in the
United Kingdom (or in that part thereof) where the offender may for the
time being be.

Election offences

1–16   Offences against the Representation of the People Act 1949 committed by British or Irish subjects outside the United Kingdom may be
tried before the appropriate court in the United Kingdom having jurisdiction where the accused is for the time being.[35]

Foreign enlistment

1–17   The Foreign Enlistment Act 1870 provides that any offence against
that Act shall, for all purposes of and incidental to the trial and punishment of any person guilty of any such offence, be deemed to have been
committed either in the place in which the offence was wholly or partly
committed, or in any place within Her Majesty's dominions in which the
person who committed such offence may be.[36]

Theft and reset

1–18   A thief or resetter is treated by the common law as continuing to commit his crimes so long as he has the stolen goods in his possession. Thus a
thief, having stolen in England, may, if apprehended in Scotland with the
stolen goods in his possession, be tried there.[37] The law on this matter is
now regulated by the Larceny Act 1916. Section 39 (2) and (3) of the
Act provides that every person who steals or otherwise feloniously takes
property in any one part of the United Kingdom may be tried in any other
part of the United Kingdom where he has the property in his possession
as if he had actually stolen or taken it in that part, and that any person
who receives in any one part of the United Kingdom property stolen or
otherwise feloniously taken in any other part of the United Kingdom may
be tried in that part of the United Kingdom where he so receives the
property as if it had been originally stolen or taken in that part.[38]

1–19   Thefts or attempted thefts of mail in course of transmission as such
between different jurisdictions in the British postal area, and any robbery,
attempted robbery or assault with intent to rob committed in stealing or
with intent to steal mail may be tried in any jurisdiction in Scotland.[39]

[35] s. 155 (1) as amended by Representation of the People Act 1969, s. 21.
[36] s. 16. See also Official Secrets Act 1911, s. 10 (1).
[37] Macdonald, 190; Hume, ii. 54, 55; Alison, ii. 78–79; *J. W. Nicol* (1834) Bell's Notes 149;
cf. *Roy* v. *H.M. Adv.*, 1963 S.L.T. 369; infra, para. 10–42.
[38] This section applies only to Scotland. The corresponding English law is now contained in
the Theft Act 1968, s. 24.
[39] Post Office Act 1953, s. 70, as substituted by Theft Act 1968, 2nd Sched., para. 10.

Visiting forces

1–20   Section 3 (1) of the Visiting Forces Act 1952 excludes the jurisdiction of the Scots courts to try certain offences committed in Scotland by members of visiting forces or their civilian components.[40] The offences excluded are offences arising in the course of the offender's duties, offences against persons associated with a visiting force, and offences against the property of a country to which a visiting force belongs or of a person associated with such a force. The exclusions apply only where the offender is subject to the jurisdiction of the service courts of the visiting force. These provisions do not apply to civilians unless it is shown that the case can be dealt with under the law of the sending country.[41]

A certificate from the Lord Advocate that the sending country has notified him that they do not propose to deal with the offender is sufficient to confer jurisdiction on the Scots courts.[42] Where a court does assume jurisdiction contrary to section 3 (1) but without objection, its proceedings are valid.[43]

Section 4 of the Act provides that where a person has been tried for any offence by a service court of a sending country he shall not be tried for the same crime by the Scots courts. Where he is tried for a different crime arising wholly or partly out of the same facts the Scots court may take the sentence of the service court into account.[44]

The Act applies to the forces of Canada, Australia, New Zealand, India, Pakistan and Ceylon,[45] as well as to those of the United States of America, France, Belgium, Norway and the Netherlands,[46] and to any other countries designated by Order in Council.[47] It may also be applied to the forces of international headquarters or defence organisations set up under arrangements to which the United Kingdom is a party.[48]

Inferior courts

1–21   As the territorial jurisdiction of the sheriff court and other inferior courts is limited, special considerations arise regarding the specification of the locus delicti in indictments and complaints brought therein. Such specification must be sufficient to determine the jurisdiction of the court. Its absence amounts to incompetency within the meaning of section 73 of the 1954 Act and vitiates any conviction.[49]

[40] See R.C.H., " Criminal Jurisdiction over Civilians accompanying United States Force, stationed in Scotland," 1962 S.L.T. (News) 101; M. Friedland, *Double Jeopardy* (Oxfords 1969), pp. 396–403.
[41] s. 3 (2).
[42] s. 3 (3) (*a*).
[43] s. 3 (3) (*b*) (*c*).
[44] s. 4 (2); see M. Friedland, op. cit., loc. cit.
[45] s. 1 (1).
[46] Visiting Forces (Designation) Order 1954.
[47] Visiting Forces Act 1952, s. 1 (3). The Act applies to all Commonwealth countries.
[48] International Headquarters and Defence Organisations Act 1964.
[49] *McMillan* v. *Grant*, 1924 J.C. 13; infra. para. 16–17.

Procedure Where Two Jurisdictions Involved

1–22   Statutory provisions have been made to meet the case of crimes falling within the ambit of two separate jurisdictions and of crimes committed on the boundary of two jurisdictions. They are as follows:

1887 Act, s. 22

1–23   (a) Where a crime has been committed partly in one county and partly in another county; or
         (b) Where one crime following on and connected with another crime has been committed in a different county from that in which the first was committed; or
         (c) Where several crimes which, if committed in one county, could be tried under one indictment are alleged to have been committed by any person in different counties in succession, a person accused may be lawfully indicted to a court to be held in one of such counties as shall be determined by the Lord Advocate, whether for trial in the High Court of Justiciary or in the sheriff court.

1–24   Once an accused has been lawfully indicted in a sheriff court under this section he may be tried for and convicted of charges committed outside the court's jurisdiction even if the charges committed within the jurisdiction are deserted before the jury is empanelled.[50]

1908 Act, s. 77 (2), (4)

1–25   Where there are charges against an accused person in different counties, he may be brought before the sheriff of any one of such counties, at the instance of the procurator fiscal of such county, for examination on all or any of such charges, and may be dealt with on complaint or on indictment in every respect as if such charges had arisen in the county where he is examined, but without prejudice to the power of the Lord Advocate, under section 22 of the 1887 Act, to determine the court before which the accused shall be tried on such charges.

1954 Act, s. 6 (1908 Act, s. 77 (4))

1–26   The following provisions are enacted by section 6 of the 1954 Act regarding crimes committed in different jurisdictions or on the boundary of two jurisdictions or on a moving vehicle or ship or otherwise involving two or more jurisdictions. Similar provisions in section 10 of the 1908 Act are applied to procedure under indictment by section 77 (4) of the 1908 Act, which, along with the enactments mentioned therein [51] as they apply to procedure under indictment, are kept in force by section 78 of and Schedule 4 to the 1954 Act:
         (1) An offence committed in any harbour, river, arm of the sea, or other water (tidal or other) which runs between or forms the

---

[50] *MacKie* v. *H.M. Adv.*, 1969 J.C. 20.
[51] ss. 10, 30, 34 (7), 40, 45, 46 and 47.

boundary of the jurisdiction of two or more courts, may be tried by any one of such courts.

(2) An offence committed on the boundary of the jurisdiction of two or more courts, or within the distance of 500 yards of any such boundary, or partly within the jurisdiction of one court and partly within the jurisdiction of another court or courts, may be tried by any one of such courts.

(3) Where an offence is committed on any person, or in respect of any property in or upon any carriage, cart, or vehicle employed in a journey by road or railway, or on board any vessel employed in a river, lake, canal, or inland navigation, such offence may be tried by any court through whose jurisdiction such carriage, cart, vehicle, or vessel passed in the course of the journey or voyage during which the offence was committed. Where the side, bank, centre, or other part of the road, railway, river, lake, canal, or inland navigation along which the carriage, cart, vehicle, or vessel passed in the course of such journey or voyage is the boundary of the jurisdiction of two or more courts, such offence may be tried by any one of such courts.

(4) Where several offences, which if committed in one county could be tried under one indictment or complaint, are alleged to have been committed by any person in different counties, proceedings may be taken for all or any of those offences under one indictment or complaint before the sheriff of any one of such counties.[52]

(5) Where an offence is authorised by this section to be tried by any court it may be dealt with, heard, tried, determined, adjudged, and punished as if the offence had been wholly committed within the jurisdiction of such court.[53]

1949 Act, s. 38 (as amended by 1954 Act)

1–27   This section, as so amended, provides that the power conferred by section 59 of the 1887 Act to convict a person of an offence other than that with which he is charged in an indictment shall be exercisable by the sheriff court before which such person is tried notwithstanding that that other offence was committed outside the jurisdiction of that sheriff court. This matter is fully dealt with at paragraph 10–42, infra.

Combined counties

1–28   Where counties are combined under the Sheriff Courts (Scotland) Act 1870,[54] the combined counties are for judicial purposes treated as

---

[52] See *Lipsey* v. *Mackintosh* (1913) 7 Adam 182, where it was held that the sheriff-substitute at Dundee had jurisdiction both at common law and under s. 10 (4) of the 1908 Act (now s. 6 (4) of the 1954 Act) to try a Glasgow bookmaker charged with contravening the Betting Acts by sending by post from Glasgow cards to persons in Dundee inviting them to bet.
[53] 1954 Act, s. 6. See also Coinage Offences Act 1937, s. 15.
[54] s. 12.

one sheriffdom, and it is competent to try in one county an offence committed in another county of the combined sheriffdom.[55] A sheriff may try an offence at any place within his sheriffdom where courts are held.[56] A sheriff has jurisdiction in all parts of the sheriffdom for which he is appointed.[57]

---

[55] *Kelso District Committee* v. *Fairbairn* (1891) 3 White 94; following *Tait* v. *Johnston* (1891) 18 R. 606.
[56] *Hendry* v. *Brims* (1889) 2 White 380.
[57] Sheriff Courts (Scotland) Act 1971, s. 7.

CHAPTER 2

CRIMINAL COURTS

2–01   IT has already been pointed out that criminal jurisdiction may be either original or appellate.[1]   Appellate jurisdiction is the prerogative of the High Court of Justiciary, which performs the function of a criminal appeal court in cases falling under solemn procedure, and the function of a court of review in cases falling under summary procedure. These two functions of appellate jurisdiction and of review will be considered subsequently.[2] The present section is devoted to the criminal courts of first instance. Original criminal jurisdiction is exercised in Scotland by six classes of court. These are divided into superior and inferior. The superior court is the High Court of Justiciary. The inferior courts are those of the sheriff, justices of the peace, burgh magistrates, police magistrates (including stipendiary magistrates) and the bailie of the river Clyde.

Constitution of High Court

2–02   The High Court of Justiciary sits in Edinburgh, and also on circuit in various towns in Scotland. It consists of from thirteen to nineteen Senators of the College of Justice, who are, in virtue of their appointment as such, Lords Commissioners of Justiciary in Scotland.[3] As a general rule, only one judge sits at a trial; but in cases of special importance two or more, usually three, may sit.[4] Where points of particular difficulty arise, as to relevancy or as to the effect of verdicts, or the proper sentence to be pronounced, the presiding judge may certify the case for the opinion of the Whole Court. In such circumstances the case is heard before three or more judges.[5]

Sittings of High Court

2–03   The determination and arrangement of circuits is now vested in the Lords Commissioners of Justiciary who, after consultation with the Lord Advocate, may deal with these matters by Act of Adjournal.[6] The Lords Commissioners of Justiciary hold such sittings for the trial of criminal

---

[1] Supra, para. 1–05.
[2] Infra, Chaps. 11 and 16.
[3] 1887 Act, s. 44; Administration of Justice Act 1968, s. 1.
[4] Justiciary Court (Scotland) Act 1868. See, as examples, *H.M. Adv.* v. *Cairns*, 1967 J.C. 37; *H.M. Adv.* v. *McKenzie*, 1970 S.L.T. 81. In both these cases the larger court sat to hear pleas to relevancy.
[5] Macdonald, 194. See, as examples, *H.M. Adv.* v. *Bickerstaff*, 1926 J.C. 65; *H.M. Adv.* v. *Wilson*, 1942 J.C. 75; *H.M. Adv.* v. *Cunningham*, 1963 J.C. 80; *H.M. Adv.* v. *Burns*, 1967 J.C. 15; and, where three judges sat to decide a point of law in the course of a trial in Edinburgh, *Hay* v. *H.M. Adv.*, 1968 J.C. 40.
[6] Circuit Courts and Criminal Procedure (Scotland) Act 1925, s. 1; Act of Adjournal (Sittings of the High Court of Justiciary on Circuit) 1971.

causes as may be necessary, on the requisition of the Lord Advocate.[7] Every sitting of the Lords Commissioners is a sitting of the High Court of Justiciary.[8]

Scotland is divided for judicial purposes into four districts—Home, West, North, and South. These comprehend the following counties:

(1) HOME—Midlothian, East Lothian, West Lothian, and Peebles.

(2) WEST—Lanark, Renfrew, Bute, Stirling, Dumbarton, Clackmannan, Kinross, Argyll.

(3) NORTH—Perth, Fife, Angus, Aberdeen, Banff, Kincardine, Inverness, Ross and Cromarty, Elgin, Nairn, Sutherland, Caithness, Orkney and Zetland.

(4) SOUTH—Ayr, Dumfries, Kirkcudbright, Wigtown, Roxburgh, Berwick, and Selkirk.

For these districts courts are usually held in the following places:

HOME—Edinburgh.
WEST—Glasgow, Stirling and Oban.
NORTH—Inverness, Aberdeen, Dundee, and Perth.
SOUTH—Dumfries, Jedburgh, and Ayr.[9]

Although these are towns in which the High Court has been wont to sit, it is not restricted to these. It may hold a court in any town which may be most convenient for the trial of any crime, in or near the locality in which such crime has been committed.[10] It is also competent to hold trials at Edinburgh, wherever in Scotland the offence was committed.[11]

2–04   On the other hand, it is not necessary that a circuit court should be held when there is not sufficient business to be done. It is not necessary for the High Court of Justiciary to proceed to any town for the purpose of holding any court in use to be held in such town, when there are no cases indicted for the sitting of the court at such town, or when so many of the persons indicted thereto have either pleaded guilty before the sheriff at the first diet or have, between the first and second diets, tendered in writing to the Crown Agent in terms of section 2 of the Circuit Courts and Criminal Procedure (Scotland) Act 1925 pleas of guilty which the Lord Advocate has intimated to the Clerk of Justiciary that he is prepared to accept as to make the holding of a special court inexpedient or unnecessary.[12]

If a number of cases have been set down for the sitting of the High Court of Justiciary, and so many of the persons who have been indicted have either pleaded guilty at the first diet or have, between the first and second diets, intimated and had accepted written pleas under the 1925 Act, as above described, as to make inexpedient or unnecessary the holding

[7] 1925 Act, s. 1 (3).
[8] Ibid. s. 1 (3).
[9] Macdonald, 194; Act of Adjournal (Argyll Circuit Court) 1953.
[10] Criminal Law (Scotland) Act 1830, s. 12.
[11] e.g. *Dewar* v. *H.M. Adv.*, 1945 J.C. 5; *Hay* v. *H.M. Adv.*, 1968 J.C. 40.
[12] 1887 Act, s. 48; 1925 Act, s. 2.

of a separate court for the cases remaining, it is lawful for any Lord Commissioner of Justiciary, on the petition of the Lord Advocate, and in chambers, and without the presence of the prosecutor or person accused, to order the second diets of such cases to be postponed, and to be held at any sitting of the High Court of Justiciary about to be held in any adjacent county, or any county in the same district of the country, or in Edinburgh.[13]

Where any crime is committed in any county of an existing circuit in which no sitting of the High Court of Justiciary falls to be held in ordinary course for some months thereafter, it is competent to cite the person accused to appear before the High Court of Justiciary at any sitting which is to be held sooner in Edinburgh, or in another county being in a circuit district adjacent to the first-mentioned county.[14]

2–05   The High Court now has a regular sitting in Glasgow in every month except April and August.[15]

Powers of High Court

2–06   The High Court, as a court of first instance, exercises solemn jurisdiction only. Its jurisdiction to try all crimes committed within Scotland is practically universal, and is excluded only where a particular court is fixed by statute for the trial of certain offences. The exclusion of the High Court must be expressed or necessarily implied.[16]

The High Court has an inherent power to punish every act which is obviously of a criminal nature, though it be such as in time past has never been the subject of prosecution.[17] The High Court also has the exclusive power of providing a remedy for all extraordinary or unforeseen occurrences in criminal business.[18] This power is similar to the nobile officium of the Court of Session. It has been held that this power can be exercised only by a quorum of the court, and not by a single judge.[19]

The High Court has power to make rules and regulations by Act of Adjournal for the conduct of criminal proceedings.[20]

Exclusive jurisdiction of High Court

2–07   The High Court has exclusive jurisdiction in cases of treason, murder, rape, incest, deforcement of messengers, and breach of duty by magis-

---

[13] 1887 Act, s. 50; Circuit Courts and Criminal Procedure (Scotland) Act 1925, ss. 2 and 4.
[14] 1887 Act, s. 51.
[15] Act of Adjournal (Sittings of the High Court of Justiciary, Glasgow) 1967.
[16] *Robt. Rowet* (1843) 1 Broun 540; *Matthew Robinson or Robertson* (1844) 2 Broun 176; *George Duncan* (1864) 4 Irv. 474; Macdonald, 193.
[17] Hume, i. 12; *Bernard Greenhuff* (1838) 2 Swin. 236; *H.M. Adv.* v. *Coutts* (1899) 3 Adam 50 at 59; *Chas. Sweenie* (1858) 3 Irv. 109; *Strathern* v. *Seaforth*, 1926 J.C. 100; *McLaughlan* v. *Boyd*, 1934 J.C. 19; *Kerr* v. *Hill*, 1936 J.C. 71; *Dewar* v. *H.M. Adv.*, 1945 J.C. 5; *H.M. Adv.* v. *Mannion*, 1961 J.C. 79; Macdonald, 193; Gordon, 21–42.
[18] Alison, ii. 23; Macdonald, 193; *Moncreiff on Review in Criminal Cases*, 264; *Smith* v; *Ritchie & Co.* (1892) 3 White 408; *Wylie* v. *H.M. Adv.*, 1966 S.L.T. 149; *J. P. Hartley*, Petnr. (1968) 32 J.C.L. 191; *Patrick Connelly Meehan*, Petnr., 1969 S.L.T. (Notes) 90. *Patrick McCloy*, Petnr., 1971 S.L.T. (Notes) 32; cf. *MacLeod* v. *Levitt*, 1969 J.C. 16.
[19] *H.M. Adv.* v. *Lowson* (1909) 6 Adam 118; *Milne* v. *McNicol*, 1944 J.C. 151.
[20] 1887 Act, s. 76; Bail (Scotland) Act 1888, s. 10; 1954 Act, s. 76; 1926 Act, s. 15.

trates.[21] Special statutory provision is made for the crime of treason. It has also exclusive jurisdiction in certain statutory offences.[22]

Sheriff Court

2–08   The sheriff court alone exercises both solemn and summary criminal jurisdiction. In solemn procedure the sheriff principal or a sheriff sits with a jury; in summary procedure he sits alone.

The solemn jurisdiction of the sheriff is limited by the fact that he cannot award any higher punishment than imprisonment which is limited to two years.[23] Consequently, cases are not normally sent for trial by sheriff and jury except those for which such a sentence would be adequate.[24]

The limitations of the sheriff's summary jurisdiction are set forth later.[25]

2–09   Territorially, the authority of the sheriff court is limited to the district for which it exists—a county, a combination of counties, or part of a county. There are exceptions in the case of continuous crimes [26] and of crimes in reference to which the sheriff of the place of apprehension has jurisdiction by statute.[27] The special rules laid down in the 1908 Act in regard to crimes involving separate jurisdictions, or to crimes committed on the boundaries of two jurisdictions, have already been mentioned.[28] But the sheriff frequently tries persons who are charged with crimes committed beyond his jurisdiction when they are sent to him for trial by the Lord Advocate under section 22 of the 1887 Act.

The jurisdiction of the sheriff court is further limited by the fact that certain crimes may be tried in the High Court only.[29]

2–10   Apart from these limitations, the jurisdiction of the sheriff court is universal in contradistinction to the other inferior courts, on which jurisdiction must be specially conferred by statute either expressly or by necessary implication.[30] Thus, in *McPherson* v. *Boyd* [31] a Full Bench held that a burgh magistrate had no jurisdiction to try an offence against the Motor Car Act 1903, Lord Justice-General Dunedin remarking: " I have always understood it to be the law of Scotland that, in the case of statutory offences, which are not offences at all until they are created by statute, the jurisdiction must be specially conferred on any courts which have not

---

[21] Macdonald, 193; Hume, ii. 58, 59; Alison, ii. 20, 22, 23.
[22] e.g. Official Secrets Act 1911, s. 10 (3); Geneva Conventions Act 1957, s. 1 (3).
[23] 1949 Act, s. 16.
[24] This is not always the case; see e.g. *Craig*, Aug. 1968, unreported, where an accused tried by sheriff and jury for attempted murder was sentenced to 12 years' imprisonment on remit to the High Court, the proceedings and sentence being upheld on appeal.
[25] *Infra*, paras. 12–15 et seq.
[26] *Supra*, para. 1–06; Macdonald, 190–191.
[27] Macdonald, 195; see e.g. Merchant Shipping Act 1894, ss. 684–686.
[28] *Supra*, para. 1–26.
[29] *Supra*, para. 2–07.
[30] On the elements to be considered in determining whether the sheriff's jurisdiction embraces a statutory offence, see *Clark and Bendall* v. *Stuart* (1886) 1 White 191, Lord McLaren at 206 et seq.
[31] (1907) 5 Adam 247.

universal jurisdiction, and the only courts which have universal jurisdiction are the Sheriff Court and this Court." [32] In one case, however, the court held that the stipendiary magistrate of Glasgow had, by necessary implication, power conferred on him by section 3 of the Stipendiary Magistrates Jurisdiction (Scotland) Act 1897 to entertain complaints brought under the Milk and Dairies (Scotland) Act 1914 despite an express provision in the latter statute for the recovery of penalties imposed thereunder before the sheriff. [33]

2–11　　　The sheriff has, by statute, [34] a concurrent jurisdiction with every other court within his sheriffdom in regard to all offences which can be competently tried in such courts. This was held to include a juvenile court sitting under section 51 of the Children and Young Persons (Scotland) Act 1937. [35]

Justice of Peace Courts

2–12　　　Justices of the peace can only exercise summary criminal jurisdiction, mostly in petty charges at common law and under statute relating to excise, roads, licensing and the like. [36] Their authority extends to the county, or county of a city, for which they are appointed. They are dealt with in a later chapter. [37]

Burgh and Police Courts

2–13　　　The courts established in various royal, parliamentary, and police burghs (including that of the stipendiary magistrates in Glasgow, who are the only holders of this office in Scotland), and also the court of the bailie of the river Clyde, [38] may be grouped together. Their authority is limited to particular boundaries. They exercise summary criminal jurisdiction only, and their powers of punishment are limited. Their cases are also dealt with later in this volume. [39]

2–14　　　It has been held by a Full Bench that the procedure in the dean of guild court is of a civil nature, and a conviction following on a summary criminal complaint in that court was set aside. [40]

2–15　　　The sheriff, justices of peace, burgh magistrates and police magistrates have within burghs to which the Burgh Police (Scotland) Acts 1892 to 1903 apply, concurrent jurisdiction under the Burgh Police (Scotland) Act 1892, ss. 508 and 509, and the 7th section of the 1954 Act. [41]

---

[32] Ibid. at 254.
[33] *Robert Torrance & Son Ltd.* v. *Robertson*, 1946 J.C. 135.
[34] 1954 Act, s. 7.
[35] *Weir* v. *Cruickshank*, 1959 J.C. 94.
[36] e.g. *Tasker* v. *Simpson* (1904) 4 Adam 495—(Licensing Act 1903). They do not have jurisdiction under the Dogs (Protection of Livestock) Act 1953—*Czajkowski* v. *Lewis*, 1956 J.C. 8.
[37] Infra, paras. 12–19 et seq.
[38] The jurisdiction of this court may be exercised by any Glasgow police judge: Glasgow Corporation Act (1907), s. 42.
[39] Infra, paras. 12–24 et seq.
[40] *Jeffray* v. *Angus*, 1909 S.C. 400.
[41] *Cameron* v. *McNiven* (1894) 1 Adam 346.

Lyon Court

2–16   In imposing a statutory penalty for unlawful usurpation of arms the Lord Lyon King-of-Arms is exercising a civil and not a criminal jurisdiction.[42]

[42] *Macrae's Trs.* v. *Lord Lyon King-of-Arms*, 1927 S.L.T 285.

CHAPTER 3

DUTIES OF A PROSECUTOR IN CONSIDERING WHETHER A CRIMINAL CHARGE SHOULD BE MADE

3–01 WHEN considering whether, in any particular case, criminal jurisdiction should be involved, attention ought to be paid by all prosecutors to the following points:

(1) Whether the facts disclosed in the information constitute either a crime according to the common law of Scotland, or a contravention of an Act of Parliament which extends to that country.

(2) Whether there is sufficient evidence in support of these facts to justify the institution of criminal proceedings.

(3) Whether the act or omission charged is of sufficient importance to be made the subject of a criminal prosecution.

(4) Whether there is any reason to suspect that the information is inspired by malice or ill-will on the part of the informant towards the person charged.

(5) Whether there is sufficient excuse for the conduct of the accused person to warrant the abandonment of proceedings against him.

(6) Whether the case is more suitable for trial in the civil court, in respect that the facts raise a question of civil right.[1]

Should the information before the prosecutor appear to warrant criminal proceedings, these must be taken in a court having jurisdiction to try the offence and, in the event of conviction, to impose an adequate punishment.

A defect in jurisdiction is a fatal nullity, and a prosecutor should not institute proceedings if there is doubt as to whether his court has jurisdiction to try the case.[2]

Solemn or summary

3–02 A prosecutor may have to consider whether criminal proceedings in a particular case should be summary or on indictment. " There is no rigorous classification of crimes which the Sheriff may try summarily, and crimes which he may not try without a Jury, and it is not necessary that there should be one, because under our system of public prosecutions, the discretion of determining whether the crimes reported to them should or should not be tried summarily is vested, in the first instance, in the Crown officers. Should a case arise of a crime manifestly unsuited for summary

---

[1] Prosecutors must use their good sense as regards the enforcement of statutory regulations which are out of date and unrelated to modern conditions (*Kirkland* v. *Cairns*, 1951 J.C. 61; cf. *Bego* v. *Gardner*, 1933 J.C. 23).

[2] The inferior summary courts may remit causes which they cannot competently try to higher courts (1954 Act, s. 5), see infra, para. 12–30.

19

trial being tried by the Sheriff without a Jury, there can be no doubt that the Court of Justiciary has power to give redress by quashing the conviction." [3]

In the case of common law crimes, assuming that the offence is not one of the class reserved for trial on indictment in the High Court of Justiciary, the practical test to be applied in determining whether the trial is to take place according to solemn or summary procedure is to consider whether, having regard to the gravity of the offence, an adequate sentence can be imposed by a summary court in the event of conviction.

As regards statutory offences, the Acts which create these usually prescribe the procedure for their trial and must be looked to. Summary procedure will be excluded (a) where it is forbidden by the statute creating the offence, and (b) where its use is inconsistent with the terms of that statute. Where both forms of procedure are open to the prosecutor the gravity of the offence will determine his choice.[4] If the sentence appropriate to the offence is not fixed by statute the prosecutor may proceed upon a summary complaint, restricting his crave for sentence to the appropriate amount.[5] Section 9 of the 1954 Act provides that any statutory offence described as a " misdemeanour " or a " crime and offence " may be tried in the sheriff court summarily or on indictment and that if tried summarily the maximum penalty, unless fixed by the statute, shall be three months' imprisonment.

Lord Advocate's directions

3–03   It is provided by section 12 of the Sheriff Courts and Legal Officers (Scotland) Act 1927 that it shall be lawful for the Lord Advocate, after consultation with the Treasury, by order to direct in the case of any Act of Parliament, that, notwithstanding anything therein contained, all proceedings in the sheriff court under the Summary Jurisdiction Acts for a contravention of or offence against such statute shall be taken by and at the instance of the procurator fiscal.[6]

3–04   Section 33 of the 1949 Act provides that the Lord Advocate may from time to time issue instructions to a chief constable or to chief constables with regard to the reporting, for consideration of the question of prosecution, of offences alleged to have been committed within the area of such chief constable or chief constables, and that it shall be the duty of a chief constable to whom any such instruction is issued to secure compliance therewith.

3–05   Where the accused is a juvenile and there is a children's hearing with jurisdiction over him the procurator fiscal will normally refer the case to the appropriate reporter.[7]

---

[3] *Clark and Bendall* v. *Stuart* (1886) 1 White 191, Lord McLaren at 208–209.
[4] Some statutes provide for sentences of imprisonment exceeding three months on conviction by a court of summary jurisdiction, e.g. The Prevention of Crimes Act 1871 allows 12 months in certain circumstances.
[5] See *Chisholm* v. *Black & Morrison* (1871) 2 Couper 49; *Tague* v. *Smith* (1865) 5 Irv. 192.
[6] So far the only order made under this section is the Sheriff Courts (Prosecutions for Poaching) Order 1938.   [7] See infra, Chap. 19.

Part II

SOLEMN PROCEDURE

CHAPTER 4

PROSECUTORS AND THEIR TITLE

4-01 IN solemn procedure there are two types of prosecutor—the public and the private. Private prosecution on indictment is of very rare occurrence.

Public prosecutors

4-02   The prosecution of indictable crime in Scotland is in the hands of the Lord Advocate and of subordinate public prosecutors acting under his control. The Lord Advocate has the universal and exclusive title to prosecute [1] on indictment, and is the only competent public prosecutor in the High Court, the Solicitor-General and the advocates depute being his deputies.[2] In solemn procedure in the sheriff court the public prosecutor is the procurator fiscal who takes his instructions from the Lord Advocate, the indictment being signed by the procurator fiscal upon the authority of the Lord Advocate.[3] In important cases the prosecution in the sheriff court is taken by one of the advocates depute.

Change of Lord Advocate

4-03   The Lord Advocate and his deputes do not demit office on the resignation of the Lord Advocate, but continue in office until their successors receive their appointments.[4] The Lord Advocate enters upon the duties of his office immediately on receiving his appointment, and takes the oaths of office before any Secretary of State, or any Lord Commissioner of Justiciary.[5] He cannot, however, act until the royal warrant appointing him reaches the Crown Office. Notice of his appointment in the *Edinburgh Gazette* does not entitle him to do so.[6] All indictments which have been raised by a Lord Advocate continue in force and effect notwithstanding his resignation, and may be taken up and proceeded with by his successor.[7]

When the Lord Advocate dies during his tenure of office, or is otherwise removed from office, it is lawful to indict persons accused in name of the Solicitor-General then in office, until another Lord Advocate is appointed. The advocates depute and the procurators fiscal have power, notwithstanding the death or removal from office of the Lord Advocate, to take up and proceed with any indictments already raised in name of such Lord Advocate, and any indictments that may be raised in name of the

---

[1] Macdonald, 212; Alison, ii. 86.
[2] Hume, ii. 130.
[3] 1887 Act, s. 2; infra, para. 6–08.
[4] Ibid. s. 3.
[5] Ibid.
[6] *Halliday* v. *Wilson* (1891) 3 White 38.
[7] 1887 Act, s. 3.

Solicitor-General.[8] Removal from office includes promotion to the Bench. An indictment properly raised in name of the Solicitor-General does not lapse because of his elevation to the Bench before the appointment of the new Lord Advocate.[9]

The Law Officers Act 1944 provides that all the Lord Advocate's functions may be discharged by the Solicitor-General if (a) the office of Lord Advocate is vacant, or (b) the Lord Advocate is unable to act owing to absence or illness, or (c) the Lord Advocate authorises the Solicitor-General to act in any particular case.[10] This Act also provides that, during any period when the office of Lord Advocate is vacant, any certificate, notice, information, intimation, proceedings or other matter or thing whatsoever authorised or required by any enactment to be given, made, directed or done to or against the Lord Advocate may be given, made, directed or done to or against the Solicitor-General.[11]

Private prosecution

4–04   Public prosecution of crime in Scotland has proved so satisfactory that the ancient system of private prosecution at the instance of a party wronged or injured by the crime[12] is practically unknown.[13] Hume mentions two cases,[14] one in 1633 and the other in 1823. In 1909, however, a private party was authorised by a Full Bench to institute a prosecution in the High Court of Justiciary by way of criminal letters.[15]

A citizen desiring to institute a prosecution at common law in the High Court must be in the position that the crime alleged is a wrong to himself [16] and that he has applied to the Lord Advocate for his concurrence in the prosecution.[17] So, where a bill for criminal letters to authorise a private prosecution was presented without the consent of the Lord Advocate having been asked, it was refused as premature and incompetent.[18] But the Lord Advocate does not have an absolute right of veto,[19] and where he refuses his concurrence the citizen may complain to the High Court of Justiciary.[20] That court will not lightly interfere with the discretion of the Lord Advocate,[21] but, if it takes a different view from him, it may either direct him to give his concurrence or authorise the private

---

[8] Ibid.
[9] *S.-G.* v. *Lavelle* (1913) 7 Adam 255.
[10] s. 2 (1).
[11] s. 2 (2).
[12] Hume, ii. 125–126.
[13] *J. & P. Coats Ltd.* v. *Brown* (1909) 6 Adam 19, L.J.-C. at 37; See also *Alex. Robertson* (1887) 1 White 468; *Angus Mackintosh* (1872) 2 Couper 236; *Herbert* v. *D. of Roxburgh* (1855) 2 Irv. 346; *Kennedy* v. *Cadenhead* (1867) 5 Irv. 539; Gerald H. Gordon, " Institution of Criminal Proceedings in Scotland " (1968) 19 N.I.L.Q. 249.
[14] Hume, ii. 126.
[15] *J. & P. Coats Ltd.* v. *Brown*, supra.
[16] *J. & P. Coats Ltd.* v. *Brown*, supra, L.J.-C. at 37.
[17] Ibid.; *Robertson* v. *H.M. Adv.* (1892) 3 White 230.
[18] *Robertson* v. *H.M. Adv.*, supra.
[19] *J. & P. Coats Ltd.* v. *Brown*, supra, L.J.-C. at 38.
[20] *Angus Mackintosh* (1872) 2 Couper 236; *Alex Robertson* (1887) 1 White 468; *J. & P. Coats Ltd.* v. *Brown*, supra.
[21] *Alex Robertson* (1887) 1 White 468; *J. & P. Coats Ltd.* v. *Brown*, supra.

party to proceed without it.[22] The latter is the more practical and less embarrassing course,[23] and was adopted in the case of *J. & P. Coats Ltd.* v. *Brown*,[24] where the Lord Advocate, while admitting that the bill which had been presented praying for criminal letters authorising a prosecution in the High Court was relevant, refused his consent on the ground that, in his view, it was improbable that a conviction would be secured.

In *McBain* v. *Crichton*[25] an office bearer in a union of boys' clubs was refused leave to prosecute a bookseller for selling *Lady Chatterley's Lover* which he claimed to be obscene. The court held that the proposed prosecution was for a public wrong the sole right to prosecute for which lay in the Lord Advocate. The court indicated that they would not inquire into the Lord Advocate's reason for not prosecuting in any case.

In *Trapp* v. *M*; *Trapp* v. *Y*[26] the complainer sought criminal letters for perjury against persons who had given evidence at an inquiry under section 81 of the Education (Scotland) Act 1946 into his dismissal from a post as rector of a school. He alleged that as a result of their evidence he was deprived of his reputation and livelihood. The court refused to allow the complainer to bring a prosecution and referred to a settled practice whereby private prosecutions had fallen into disuse and which would be departed from only in exceptional cases. They held that perjury was essentially a crime against public justice and the right to prosecute for it therefore belonged to the Lord Advocate.

4–05 Private prosecution on indictment is competent only in the High Court.[27] It is incompetent for a private person to prosecute on indictment in the sheriff court, whether with the consent of the Lord Advocate or not.[28] There is no recorded example of private prosecution on indictment in the sheriff courts, and the older writers regard it as incompetent.[29]

4–06 In summary prosecutions at the instance of private prosecutors the concurrence of the procurator fiscal or other prosecutor of the court is required, unless the right to prosecute is conferred by statute on private persons.[30] Where a private person has no interest to prosecute, his title is not validated by the concurrence of the public prosecutor.

[22] *J. & P. Coats Ltd.* v. *Brown*, supra.
[23] Ibid., L.J.-C. at 39.
[24] Supra.
[25] 1961 J.C. 25.
[26] 1971 S.L.T. (Notes) 30; see also *Alex. Robertson*, supra.
[27] *Dunbar* v. *Johnston* (1904) 4 Adam 505.
[28] Ibid.
[29] Mackenzie, II, 19.1.
[30] Infra, para. 13–19.

CHAPTER 5

INITIAL STEPS

5-01 It has already been explained that in Scotland the only courts which exercise solemn criminal jurisdiction are the High Court of Justiciary and the sheriff court. In both these courts procedure is regulated for the most part by the 1887 Act, the Criminal Procedure (Scotland) Act 1921, the Circuit Courts and Criminal Procedure (Scotland) Act 1925, the 1949 Act, the 1963 Act, the Bail Act 1888, and certain sections of the 1908 and 1954 Acts. Procedure in appeals by persons tried on indictment is regulated by the Criminal Appeal Act 1926 as amended by the 1949 Act. From the provisions of the 1887 Act the crimes of treason and rebellion against the Sovereign are specially excepted.[1] The procedure in the prosecution and trial of all cases of treason and misprision of treason is now assimilated to that in cases of murder by the Treason Act 1945.

The present chapter sets out the various steps to be taken by the procurator fiscal in initiating criminal proceedings against accused persons and corporations.

Bodies corporate

5-02 In Scotland procedure on indictment against companies and other bodies corporate was unknown prior to the Second World War, when it was introduced by statute in cases of offences against Defence Regulations and price control legislation. It was subsequently applied to offences against the Companies Act 1948 by section 443 of that statute. This section is repealed by the 1949 Act (section 79 and Schedule 12), section 40 of which now regulates the procedure in cases on indictment against bodies corporate.

Petition

5-03 The initial writ in solemn criminal jurisdiction, whether in the High Court of Justiciary or the sheriff court, is a petition which is presented to a magistrate (in practice a sheriff). This petition sets forth, where the particulars are known, the name, designation, and address of the accused person; states the criminal charge against him; and craves the necessary warrants.

Where the accused is an individual, not a body corporate, these are: (1) to arrest the accused and bring him before the magistrate for examination, (2) to search his person and premises and the place where he is found and to open lockfast places, (3) to cite witnesses for precognition and production of writs or other articles of evidence, (4) after examination, to

[1] 1887 Act, s. 75.

26

commit the accused for further examination or until liberated in due course of law.

5–04 Where the accused is a body corporate the form of the petition requires modification in accordance with the provisions of section 40 (7) of the 1949 Act, which are as follows:

> " If on the application of the procurator fiscal, a sheriff is satisfied that there is reasonable ground for suspecting that an offence has been or is being committed by a body corporate, the sheriff shall have the like power to grant warrant for the citation of witnesses and the production of documents and articles as he would have if a petition charging an individual with the commission of the offence were presented to him."

5–05 It is illegal to apply for a general warrant to arrest all persons suspected of a certain crime, or to search at large for stolen goods or other productions, without making a specific charge against a particular individual,[2] and the execution of the warrant does not prevent its being suspended.[3] If the name of the accused person is unknown, the petition may set forth " that a man to the petitioner unknown," giving such a description as will suffice to distinguish him, had committed a certain offence.[4]

5–06 In stating the charge, the same general principles apply which regulate the statement of the charge in an indictment.[5] Those principles will have to be discussed in treating of the preparation of the latter document, and it will be more convenient to reserve until then what has to be said on the subject.[6] It must be observed, however, that the facts of a case have seldom been fully investigated at this early stage of the proceedings, and consequently the time, place and mode of committing the crime have usually to be described in a tentative manner. The charge set forth in the petition may, and often does, differ materially from the charge ultimately set forth in the indictment. This cannot be avoided. All that is necessary is to indicate, as clearly as circumstances permit, the person accused and the nature of the charge against him.

5–07 It is proper that the petition should be dated; but if the date is inadvertently omitted, the omission can be supplied otherwise.[7]

5–08 Where a petition in ordinary form had been presented and the proceedings against the accused thereafter abandoned, Crown Counsel later ordered his apprehension. The new proceedings were initiated by a minute written on the original petition. This practice was held not to be objectionable,[8] but it would appear the better course in such circumstances to present a fresh petition.

---

[2] Hume, ii. 78; *Bell* v. *Black and Morrison* (1865) 5 Irv. 57.
[3] *Bell*, supra.
[4] Alison, ii. 123.
[5] 1887 Act, s. 16.
[6] Infra, paras. 6–14 et seq.
[7] *McLeod* v. *Buchanan* (1835) 13 S. 1153; *Crawford* v. *Wilson* (1838) 2 Swin. 200.
[8] *McVey* v. *H.M. Adv.* (1911) 6 Adam 503.

Warrant to arrest

5-09   Upon presentation of a duly signed petition, the magistrate usually grants warrant to arrest an accused person as a matter of course. Such petitions, being presented by responsible officials, are assumed to be well founded. In an emergency, warrant to arrest may be granted without a written petition[9]; but this course ought not to be adopted where it is possible to follow the regular practice. Any magistrate may grant warrant to arrest a person charged with a crime committed within his jurisdiction, although the charge is of too serious a character for him to try.[10] In modern practice, however, the initial warrant in solemn criminal jurisdiction is signed by a sheriff of the sheriffdom to which the accused person is amenable.

Arrest

5-10   An accused person may be arrested with or without a warrant. If he has been arrested without a warrant, a petition is presented and a regular warrant obtained as soon as possible,[11] and thereafter the procedure is the same as if a warrant had been granted before apprehension.

Arrest without warrant: common law offences

5-11   It is difficult to state clearly the common law regarding arrest without warrant, partly because the propriety of such an arrest often depends on the precise circumstances in which it is made, and partly because the authorities use vague and untechnical terms like " felony," or " breach of the peace," in endeavouring to distinguish cases where arrest without warrant is proper from those where it is not.[12] There is no distinction in Scots law between felony and misdemeanour, or between arrestable and non-arrestable offences,[13] only a general principle that arrest is more easily justified the more serious the offence.

The general rule is that arrest without warrant is a proceeding which requires to be justified if challenged.[14] But it is by no means a rare occurrence and it is not often challenged. A person should not be arrested without a warrant unless this is necessary in the interests of justice, and more particularly unless it is necessary to prevent the arrestee absconding,[15] committing further crimes, or hindering the course of justice by, for example, interfering with witnesses or disposing of stolen property or of evidence. Whether or not a particular arrest without warrant is wrongful usually depends on whether it was reasonable for the arrester to believe it

---

[9] Hume, ii. 77; Alison, ii. 121; Macdonald, 198.
[10] Ibid.
[11] *Peggie* v. *Clark* (1868) 7 M. 89, Lord Deas at 93.
[12] Cf. Hume, ii. 75: " our law does not seem to have attained as yet to the same maturity and precision as that of England, respecting the manner of an arrest, or the powers enjoyed in that respect."
[13] Cf. Criminal Law Act 1967.
[14] *Peggie* v. *Clark* (1868) 7 M. 89; *Robertson* v. *Keith*, 1936 S.C. 29; *Shields* v. *Shearer*, 1914 S.C.(H.L.) 33, although Lord Shaw of Dumfermline seems to adopt two contradictory views on the question of onus of proof.
[15] Alison, ii. 116, 117; *Peggie* v. *Clark*, supra.

was justified. The arrestee's subsequent conviction or discharge is not in itself conclusive of the propriety or impropriety of the arrest.[16] The reasonableness of the arrester's belief in the existence of justifiable conditions may depend on such things as the arrestee's character,[17] the fixity or otherwise of his residence, or the seriousness of the offence which in some cases, such as murder, may itself justify the arrest.[18] The arrest of a member of the criminal classes or of someone with no means of honest livelihood or fixed abode is easier to justify than that of a respectable householder, of " what, in our justiciary practice, we call a ' law-abiding party '." [19]

It may be said too that arrest without warrant is not justifiable if the interests of justice can be equally served by waiting for a warrant [20] or by proceeding by citation. It is for this reason that arrest without warrant is not normally justified, and warrants are not normally issued, for minor offences. Conversely, arrest without warrant by a police constable will be justified even for a minor offence if the officer has ground for believing it to be necessary to arrest without waiting for a warrant. Arrest without warrant may also be justified as necessary to prevent injury to others such as the arrested person's wife or children where he is charged with assaulting them, or indeed to prevent self-inflicted injury to the arrestee himself. The longer the time which has elapsed since the offence the more difficult it will be to justify arrest without warrant.[21]

All statements about arrest must be read subject to the above general principles.

5–12   A private citizen is entitled to arrest without warrant for a serious crime he has witnessed,[22] or perhaps where, being the victim of the crime, he has information equivalent to personal observation, as where the fleeing criminal is pointed out to him by an eye-witness.[23] He has no power to arrest someone who has committed only a breach of the peace, although he may intervene to prevent the occurrence of such a breach.[24] A person not himself entitled to arrest may assist someone who has such a right.[25]

---

[16] *Wood* v. *North British Railway Company* (1899) 1 F. 562; *Jackson* v. *Stevenson* (1897) 2 Adam 255, 260.

[17] Cf. *Carlin* v. *Malloch* (1896) 2 Adam 98.

[18] *Peggie* v. *Clark*, supra; cf. *H.M. Adv.* v. *McGuigan*, 1936 J.C. 16; *Pringle* v. *Bremner and Stirling* (1867) 5 M.(H.L.) 55.

[19] *Peggie* v. *Clark*, supra, Lord Deas at 93; cf. *Harvey* v. *Sturgeon*, 1912 S.C. 974; *Malcolm* v. *Duncan* (1897) 24 R. 747; *Melvin* v. *Wilson* (1847) 9 D. 1129; *Carlin* v. *Malloch*, supra. *Mill on Police Powers*, 74, points out that persons with criminal records " have their rights—though, to the advantage of the police, they are rarely aware of them," and that the police should not take liberties with them or with persons with no fixed abode.

[20] *Leask* v. *Burt* (1893) 21 R. 32; *Somerville* v. *Sutherland* (1899) 2 F. 185. This is the " golden rule " which is " in practice, it is to be feared, a counsel of perfection "—*Mill on Police Powers*, 66.

[21] Cf. *Mill on Police Powers*, 71, where he suggests rather unrealistically that the right to arrest without warrant flies off after two hours in the case of a trivial assault and within a day for serious crimes, unless the offender is in hiding, or likely to abscond, or his identity cannot be ascertained.

[22] Hume, ii. 76; Alison, ii. 119; Macdonald, 197.

[23] Alison, ii. 119; Macdonald (3rd ed.), 260, notes that Alison has no authority for this statement.

[24] Hume, ii. 76–77; Alison, ii. 119; Macdonald, 197.

[25] Hume, ii. 75–76; Alison, ii. 116–117; Macdonald, 197. See also Burgh Police (Scotland) Act 1892, s. 467; infra, para. 5–17.

5-13   Although the situation is unlikely to arise in practice, it appears that magistrates have certain powers of peremptory arrest. A magistrate may arrest without warrant in the case of a serious crime, riot or breach of the peace, committed within his jurisdiction, which he has witnessed or of which he has received an immediate complaint, provided that the circumstances are such that the offender would escape if there were any delay.[26] He may also in such circumstances issue a verbal order to others to arrest the offender.[27]

5-14   Most arrests nowadays are carried out by police constables. A constable of any Scottish force is entitled to act as a constable throughout Scotland.[28] A constable may arrest without warrant if he witnesses a crime, or breach of the peace, being committed or attempted, or violence being threatened,[29] or if he sees the offender in flight from the crime.[30] He may also arrest on credible information that a serious crime has been recently committed or attempted, at any rate if there is a probability that the offender will abscond.[31] Where the constable is carrying out an arrest for a serious crime, but not for a mere breach of the peace or other minor offence, he may force entry into premises without warrant if refused admission.[32]

A constable has a general power to arrest an offender wherever this is necessary in the interests of justice.[33] He may in pursuance of this power arrest any person found under suspicious circumstances with goods believed to be stolen for the possession of which he cannot satisfactorily account, at any rate if there is a probability of an escape if an arrest is not made.[34]

Arrest without warrant: statutory offences

5-15   It is not clear what common law rights the Scots police have to arrest without warrant for statutory offences. There is no distinction in Scots law between arrestable and non-arrestable offences, or between felonies, misdemeanours and statutory offences. All offences, including statutory offences, are offences against the Queen's peace.[35] It may be that statutory powers of arrest do little more than express implied common law powers; they must certainly be exercised subject to the same general rule that arrest without warrant is not justified unless necessary in the interests of justice.[36] In practice, and because of the general requirements of justifica-

---

[26] Hume, ii, 75; Alison, ii. 117; Macdonald, 197; cf. *Beaton* v. *Ivory* (1887) 14 R. 1057.
[27] Hume, ii. 75; Alison, ii. 117; Macdonald, 197.
[28] Police (Scotland) Act 1967, s. 17 (4). A special constable may act only in emergency, or in preventing or suppressing riot or tumult, unless assigned for duty by the chief constable to gain practical experience: s. 17 (6).
[29] Hume, ii. 75–76; Alison, ii. 117; Macdonald, 197.
[30] *Peggie* v. *Clark*, supra.
[31] *Peggie* v. *Clark*, supra, Lord Deas at 93. According to *Mill on Police Powers*, 67, the information must be corroborated where the offence is a trivial one.
[32] Hume, ii. 76; Alison, ii. 118; Macdonald, 197.
[33] *Peggie* v. *Clark*, supra.
[34] Ibid.; *Mill on Police Powers*, 69.
[35] *McMillan* v. *Grant*, 1924 J.C. 13, Lord Sands at 22.
[36] *Peggie* v. *Clark*, supra. The almost universal power to arrest anyone on suspicion of anything, formerly contained in Police Acts, was restricted in this way—cf. *Shields* v. *Shearer*,

tion for arrest without warrant, arrest without warrant is rare except in the case of statutory offences punishable by imprisonment in the first instance, but such an arrest may not be absolutely excluded, for example, where the offender has no fixed abode, or refuses to give an address.[37] Where a statute gives a more limited power of arrest than would be available at common law any arrest must comply with the statute.[38] A statute may, of course, expressly or impliedly exclude any power of arrest.[39]

5–16   Among the more common statutory provisions for arrest without warrant are the Road Traffic Act 1960, ss. 6, 11, 110 [40] and 217; Road Safety Act 1967, s. 2; Prevention of Crime Act 1953, s. 1 (when the officer is not satisfied as to the suspect's name and address or the arrest is necessary to prevent another offence); Firearms Act 1968, s. 50; Misuse of Drugs Act 1971, s. 24 (where the officer believes with reasonable cause that the suspect will abscond, or cannot ascertain his name and address); Official Secrets Act 1911, s. 6; Protection of Animals (Scotland) Act 1912, s. 11; Public Order Act 1936, s. 7; Deer (Scotland) Act 1959, s. 28; Salmon and Freshwater Fisheries (Protection) (Scotland) Act 1951, s. 12 (which authorises arrest by water bailiffs as well as by police); and Night Poaching Act 1828, s. 2. (which authorises arrest by landowners and gamekeepers).[41] There are also a number of statutes under which police commonly carry out arrests without warrant although the statutes contain no provisions entitling them to do so. This is true of such statutes as the Incest Act 1567, the Criminal Law Amendment Act 1885, ss. 4, 5 and 11, and the Police (Scotland) Act 1967, s. 41[42]. There are also very considerable powers of arrest in relation to many of the offences created by the Burgh Police (Scotland) Act 1892, and by corresponding local legislation.

Where a statute gives a right to arrest on reasonable suspicion, the suspicion must be based on reasonable grounds—it is not enough that the constable bona fide suspected the arrested person.[43] A power to arrest someone committing an offence may be interpreted as a power to arrest someone reasonably suspected of committing the offence, as in the case of the power to arrest someone driving while unfit through drink.[44]

---

infra; *Peggie* v. *Clark*, supra; *Leask* v. *Burt* (1893) 21 R. 32. The power contained in s. 86 of the Burgh Police (Scotland) Act 1892 was repealed by the Police (Scotland) Act 1956, and that contained in s. 88 of the Glasgow Police Act 1866 by the Glasgow Corporation Consolidation (General Powers) Order Confirmation Act 1960.

[37] Cf. *Mill on Police Powers*, 74; *Angus on Police Powers* (2nd ed.), 63. Mill doubts whether there is a common law power to arrest for statutory offences. Angus says that there is power to arrest for any offence which is punishable with imprisonment, and for any offence at all where the offender is drunk, or is not a law-abiding person, or his name and address are unknown. Angus's views probably represent general practice better than Mill's.

[38] See e.g. Prevention of Crime Act 1953, s. 1 (3); *Lundie* v. *MacBrayne* (1894) 21 R. 1085.

[39] Cf. Poaching Prevention Act 1862.

[40] Road Safety Act 1967, s. 30.

[41] All these provisions relate to offences punishable with imprisonment.

[42] Arrest would also be clearly competent under such Acts as the Concealment of Birth (Scotland) Act 1809, and the Criminal Law (Scotland) Act 1829.

[43] *Shields* v. *Shearer*, 1914 S.C.(H.L.) 33; cf. *Melvin* v. *Wilson* (1847) 9 D. 1129; *Harvey* v. *Sturgeon*, 1912 S.C. 974.

[44] *Wiltshire* v. *Barrett* [1966] 1 Q.B. 312.

Arrest without warrant: offences of dishonesty

5–17   In addition to specific statutory provisions the Burgh Police (Scotland) Act 1892 and the corresponding local Police Acts [45] give wider powers of arrest to police constables within the areas affected by the Acts.[46] Section 467 of the Burgh Police (Scotland) Act 1892 provides that any person found committing any offence punishable either on indictment, or upon summary conviction under that Act or any other Act under which the magistrate has jurisdiction, may be taken into custody without warrant by any police officer, or may be apprehended by the owner of the property on or with respect to which the offence is committed or by his servant or any person authorised by the owner or his servant, and be detained until he can be delivered into the custody of a constable, and provides further that the arrested person must then be taken as soon as conveniently may be before a magistrate. The section also provides that the officer in charge of any police station to which such a person is brought may liberate him if satisfied that there is not sufficient proof of his guilt.[47] It is an offence under section 155 (1) of the Glasgow Corporation Consolidation (General Powers) Order Confirmation Act 1960 for any person to be found on any premises for an unlawful purpose, and such a person may be arrested without warrant. The police could presumably arrest an offender on this charge and hold him until they obtained a warrant on the charge in which they were really interested.

5–18   There are also provisions in these Acts giving powers of arrest for theft or other crimes of dishonesty. It is an offence for a known thief, or the associate of a known thief, to be found loitering with intent to commit theft, or in some cases certain other crimes of dishonesty,[48] or to be found in possession of housebreaking implements or of goods for the possession of which he cannot satisfactorily account, and power is given to arrest without warrant for these offences.[49] It is common practice to arrest known thieves found in possession of property and hold them on this charge until sufficient evidence is obtained to charge them with the theft or reset of the property.

Arrest without warrant: offences against children

5–19   In terms of section 24 (1) of the Children and Young Persons (Scotland) Act 1937 a constable may take into custody without warrant any person he sees committing any offences specified in the First Schedule to the Act if he does not know and cannot ascertain his address, and any person who

---

[45] The 1892 Act applies to all Scottish burghs except Edinburgh, Glasgow, Dundee, Aberdeen and Greenock, which each has its own Act, and also to any landward areas of counties which have adopted it.

[46] Although it has been said that provisions of this kind are merely declaratory of the common law—see n. 36 supra.

[47] See also Dundee Corporation (Consolidated Powers) Order Confirmation Act 1957, s. 490.

[48] See Glasgow Corporation Consolidation (General Powers) Order Confirmation Act 1960, s. 155.

[49] Burgh Police (Scotland) Act 1892, s. 409; Glasgow Corporation Consolidation (General Powers) Order Confirmation Act 1960, s. 155.

has, or whom he has reason to believe has, committed any such offences
if he does not know and cannot ascertain his name and address or has
reason to believe he will abscond. The offences in the First Schedule are
offences under the Criminal Law Amendment Act 1885, incest with a
child, any offence involving bodily injury to a child, and certain offences
against the 1937 Act itself.

Execution of warrant to arrest

5–20   The existence of a warrant is sufficient authority to permit a police
officer to arrest the offender and detain him pending the arrival of the
officer who is in possession of the warrant. A warrant should be executed
as soon as possible.[50] When a person is arrested on warrant, the warrant
should be shown to him if he asks to see it, but the officer should retain
possession of it.[51] Where there is a warrant in existence for the arrest of an
offender, but there is no reason to fear that he will abscond if not arrested,
he may be brought before the sheriff without actual apprehension. It is
competent to warn him that there is a warrant against him and to invite
him to attend at a certain time and place [52]: he will normally be asked to
attend at such time and place as will enable the police to carry out the
normal procedure of searching, finger-printing, and otherwise documenting
his appearance.

The officer is not entitled to break open doors, even when he possesses
a warrant, unless he has notified his identity and the purpose of his visit to
those in the premises and has asked for and been refused admission.[53]

Meaning of arrest

5–21   There is no binding Scots authority on what constitutes an arrest.
According to *Mill on Police Powers* a person is under arrest when he has
been effectively deprived of his liberty, but the courts will be slow to hold
that there has been an arrest in the absence of force or of threats making it
clear that the offender has no alternative but to accompany or remain with
the police.[54] This view is based on *Muir* v. *Hamilton Magistrates*,[55] where
the offender was suspected of buying drink illegally and the police insisted
that he go to the hotel ı question so that the barman could identify him.
He was described as having been " marched off," and as going with the
police because of a fear that if he did not, worse might happen. Lord
Salvesen held that as he had agreed to go with the police without the
necessity of force and handcuffing, he had not been arrested. (He was in
fact innocent and the barman confirmed this.) It may be doubted whether
the courts today would go so far as Lord Salvesen. It has been held in
England that a person is arrested " when any form of words is used which

---

[50] *Farquharson* v. *Whyte* (1886) 1 White 26.
[51] Hume, ii. 79; Macdonald, 199.
[52] *Spowart* v. *Burr* (1895) 1 Adam 539.
[53] Hume, ii. 80; Alison, ii. 124; Macdonald, 199, 200.
[54] *Mill on Police Powers*, 75.
[55] 1910, 1 S.L.T. 164.

in the circumstances of the case were calculated to bring to the defendant's notice, and did bring to the defendant's notice, that he was under compulsion and thereafter he submitted to that compulsion." [55a] So the English court were surprised when magistrates believed a driver who said that when told by the constable that he would have to ask him to come to the police station for further tests under the Road Safety Act 1967, he had gone voluntarily to the station without realising that he was under arrest. Blain J. expressed considerable sympathy with the police constable who finds he has failed to arrest " through using words selected with a laudable desire to perform his duties with the maximum of courtesy." He added however that that was of far less importance than the vital right of the subject to know when he is compellable and when he is free.[56] There is no such thing as being " detained on suspicion." A person is either arrested or free.[57]

Procedure following arrest

5-22   When a person has been arrested he must be told immediately of the charge on which the arrest has been made, and the arrest must be justified by reference to that charge, even if it was used merely as a holding charge.[58] Where a citizen makes an arrest he must call in the police as soon as possible.[59]

A person arrested, with or without a warrant, has a right to be brought before a court as soon as possible.[60] Section 17 (1) of the Police (Scotland) Act 1967 obliges the police to bring offenders before the court without detaining them unreasonably or unnecessarily. Section 20 (3) of the 1954 Act provides that a person arrested under a warrant in terms of that Act or by virtue of common law powers or other statutory powers shall wherever practicable be brought before a competent court not later than the first lawful day after being taken into custody, such day not being a public or local holiday.[61] Between arrest and appearance in court, the prisoner may be detained in a police station or cell or other convenient place.[62] An arrested person has a right to have intimation sent to his solicitor, and to the solicitor's advice prior to his appearance in court [63];

[55a] *Alderson* v. *Booth* [1969] 2 Q.B. 217, L.C.J. at 221.
[56] *Alderson* v. *Booth* [1969] 2 Q.B. 217; cf. *R.* v. *Wall* [1969] 1 W.L.R. 400; *Campbell* v. *Tormey* [1969] 1 W.L.R. 189.
[57] Cf. *Chalmers* v. *H.M. Adv.*, 1954 J.C. 66.
[58] *Christie* v. *Leachinsky* [1947] A.C. 573.
[59] *McKenzie* v. *Young* (1902) 10 S.L.T. 231; *John Lewis & Company* v. *Tims* [1952] A.C. 676; cf. *Dallison* v. *Caffery* [1965] 1 Q.B. 348.
[60] Hume, ii. 80; Alison, ii. 129; Macdonald, 200; *Crawford* v. *Blair* (1856) 2 Irv. 511; *Maitland* v. *Douglas* (1861) 24 D. 193; *Kelly* v. *Rowan* (1897) 2 Adam 357; *Peggie* v. *Clark*, supra; *Melvin* v. *Wilson*, supra; *McDonald* v. *Lyon and Main* (1851) J. Shaw 516. According to *Mill on Police Powers*, 69, where a person has been arrested on suspicion and no corroborative evidence is forthcoming within a few hours, he should be released unless the offence is a very serious one: in cases of doubt the prosecutor should be consulted.
[61] A warrant may be executed on a Sunday: *Maitland* v. *Douglas* (1861) 24 D. 193.
[62] Alison, ii. 129–130; Macdonald, 200; 1954 Act, s. 20 (2).
[63] 1887 Act, s. 17; *H.M. Adv.* v. *Aitken*, 1926 J.C. 83; *Cheyne* v. *McGregor*, 1941 J.C. 17; *Ferguson* v. *Brown*, 1942 J.C. 113; *Law* v. *McNicol*, 1965 J.C. 32; Macdonald, 200.

but failure to accord this right is not necessarily fatal to subsequent proceedings.[64] A person charged with murder or culpable homicide also has a right to the services of the duty solicitor under the provisions of the Legal Aid Scheme.[65] Once a person is arrested he is protected from police questioning on the charge for which he has been arrested.[66]

5-23   The fact that a person was not originally lawfully arrested does not of itself render his ultimate trial invalid.[67] The minutes of proceedings on both petitions and summary complaints include warrants to arrest which are signed even where the accused is already in custody. Furthermore, a person may be indicted without being committed for trial at all.[68]

The case of persons under sixteen years of age is dealt with in Chapter 19.

Search
Personal search

5-24   The police are entitled to search the person of anyone they have lawfully arrested with or without warrant.[69] The normal complaint [70] and petition warrants include warrants to arrest and to search the person and premises of the suspect. The search may be carried out on the spot.[71] The police have a duty to investigate by search to find if the information they have is supported by evidence providing a prima facie case against the arrested suspect,[72] but may not normally carry out a search in order to determine whether or not to arrest the suspect.[73] The right to search extends to making a physical examination, including the visual examination of injuries,[74] to taking fingerprints,[75] and to placing the suspect in an identification parade.[76] Nail scrapings,[77] palm rubbings,[78] and bite marks [79] are in the same position as fingerprints.

The police are not entitled at common law to search without warrant the persons of suspects whom they have not apprehended [80] except in cases

---

[64] *Cheyne* v. *McGregor*, supra; cf. *H.M. Adv.* v. *Cunningham*, 1939 J.C. 61; *H.M. Adv.* v. *Fox*, 1947 J.C. 30.
[65] Legal Aid (Scotland) (Criminal Proceedings) Scheme 1964, art. 8.
[66] See infra, paras. 18–36 et seq.
[67] *Sinclair* v. *H.M. Adv.* (1890) 2 White 481; *McHattie* v. *Outram* (1892) 3 White 289; *McHattie* v. *Wyness* (1892) 19 R.(J.) 95; *Lloyd* v. *H.M. Adv.* (1899) 2 Adam 637; cf. 1954 Act, s. 20 (4).
[68] *McVey* v. *H.M. Adv.* (1911) 6 Adam 503; *Orr* v. *Deans* (1902) 3 Adam 645.
[69] *Jackson* v. *Stevenson* (1897) 2 Adam 255; *Adair* v. *McGarry*, 1933 J.C. 72; *Bell* v. *Leadbetter*, 1934 J.C. 74; *Mauchline* v. *Stevenson* (1878) 4 Couper 20.
[70] See 1954 Act, s. 17.
[71] *Jackson* v. *Stevenson*, supra; *Bell* v. *Leadbetter*, supra.
[72] *Adair* v. *McGarry*, supra, L.J.-G. at 77.
[73] *Jackson* v. *Stevenson*, supra.
[74] *Forrester* v. *H.M. Adv.*, 1952 J.C. 28. There are, however, special rules in cases under the Road Traffic Act 1960, s. 6: *Reid* v. *Nixon*, 1948 J.C. 68.
[75] *Adair* v. *McGarry*, supra. This common law right is unaffected by any rights the prison authorities may have under the Prisons (Scotland) Act 1952 to fingerprint convicted prisoners. There is no right to take the fingerprints of a person who is on bail: *Adamson* v. *Martin*, 1916 S.C. 319.
[76] *Adair* v. *McGarry*, supra.
[77] *McGovern* v. *H.M. Adv.*, 1950 J.C. 33.
[78] *Bell* v. *Hogg*, 1967 J.C. 49; (1967) 31 J.C.L. 208.
[79] *Hay* v. *H.M. Adv.*, 1968 J.C. 40.
[80] *Jackson* v. *Stevenson*, supra; *Adair* v. *McGarry*, supra; *McGovern* v. *H.M. Adv.*, supra.

of urgency.[81] Urgency is widely interpreted in favour of the police and extends to the possibility that a suspect detained but not arrested may wash suspicious marks off his hands,[82] or perhaps even that a suspect may visit his dentist and have removed or altered a tooth whose precise shape is of importance.[83]

Warrant to search suspect

5-25   A magistrate may grant a warrant to search the person of a suspect who has not been arrested, including a warrant to take from him impressions of his bite marks, although it may be that the High Court will uphold the legality of such a warrant only in exceptional cases.[84] Presumably such a warrant entitles the persons named to use all reasonable necessary force to carry it out, although there is no reference to the use of force in the standard petition warrant to arrest and search,[85] and no reference was made to force in the warrant in *Hay* v. *H.M. Adv.*,[86] the only specific warrant of this kind granted in a reported case.

Evidence obtained irregularly

5-26   Even where material has been irregularly obtained by improper personal search the court has a discretion to excuse the irregularity and admit it in evidence. Urgency is often thought of as a ground for such excuse, but it may be that it can also render the search itself lawful.[87]

Statutory provisions for personal search

5-27   There are a number of statutory provisions entitling the police to search persons without warrant. Section 467 of the Burgh Police (Scotland) Act 1892 entitles the police to search any person reasonably suspected of having or carrying stolen property or property fraudulently obtained or carried away.[88] Section 493 of the Edinburgh Corporation Order Confirmation Act 1967 entitles the police to stop, search and detain any person reasonably suspected of being in possession of any money or article which has been unlawfully obtained.[89]

There are also a number of specific statutory offences for which personal search is authorised.[90]

---

[81] *Bell* v. *Hogg*, supra; *Hay* v. *H.M. Adv.*, supra.
[82] *Bell* v. *Hogg*, supra.
[83] *Hay* v. *H.M. Adv.*, supra.
[84] Ibid.
[85] See infra, para. 5–31.
[86] Supra.
[87] *Bell* v. *Hogg*, supra; *Hay* v. *H.M. Adv.*, supra; *Crook* v. *Duncan* (1899) 2 Adam 658.
[88] Cf. Dundee Corporation (Consolidated Powers) Order Confirmation Act 1957, s. 490.
[89] Ibid.
[90] See e.g. Deer (Scotland) Act 1959, s. 27; Firearms Act 1968, s. 47—see G. L. Allan, " Right to Search before Apprehension," 1966 S.L.T.(News) 117; Protection of Birds Act 1954, s. 12 (1); Misuse of Drugs Act 1971, s. 23 (2); Poaching Prevention Act 1862, s. 2. There is apparently no right at all to arrest under the last-named Act. The power of search is sometimes expressed as one to detain and search (e.g. Firearms Act 1968, s. 47 (3)). The Road Safety Act 1967 sets up a special and complex procedure for the obtaining of breath, blood and urine specimens from persons suspected of driving with

Search of premises

5-28   The law relating to search of premises is much the same as that relating
to the search of persons. Warrant to arrest includes warrant to search the
suspect's premises for evidence. Search without warrant after the arrest
without warrant of the owner of the premises is irregular except in cases of
urgency.[91] But where a person is arrested with or without warrant in his
house it is probably competent to search the house for stolen property or
any evidence of guilt.[92] Irregular searches may be excused and the result
admitted in evidence whether or not they purported to proceed on a
warrant.[93] The degree of invasion of privacy may be relevant in determining the excusability of an irregular search,[94] as also may be the good faith
of the searcher.[95] It is competent to issue a warrant to search premises in a
case in which no one has yet been charged or arrested,[96] and probably to
search without warrant in such a case in circumstances of urgency.[97] The
procurator fiscal has also a common law right to remove articles such as
motor-cars believed to be connected with a crime, at any rate for the purpose of examining them, even where these articles belong to the ultimate
accused, if the person in whose custody they were consents.[98]

Statutory provisions for search of premises

5-29   There are many statutory provisions entitling magistrates to grant
warrants to search premises and vehicles in the absence of any charge or
arrest.[99]

5-30   There are also statutory provisions giving the police rights to enter and
search premises without warrant. Section 467 of the Burgh Police (Scotland) Act 1892 gives any constable power to search any premises or vessel
on which there is reason to suspect the presence of articles which have been
stolen or unlawfully obtained or fraudulently carried away.[1] Section 496
of the Edinburgh Corporation Order Confirmation Act 1967 gives a right
to search premises where there is reasonable cause to suspect that unlawfully obtained articles are kept or concealed and the case is one of urgency

---

an excess amount of alcohol in their blood. For the law relating to medical examination in
cases of persons unfit to drive through drink or drugs: see *Reid* v. *Nixon*; *Dumigan* v.
Brown, 1948 J.C. 68.

[91] *H.M. Adv.* v. *McGuigan*, 1936 J.C. 16.

[92] Cf. *Ghani* v. *Jones* [1970] 1 Q.B. 693, Lord Denning M.R. at 706; *Dillon* v. *O'Brien &
Davies* (1887) 16 Cox C.C. 245; see also *Butler* v. *Board of Trade* [1971] Ch. 680,
Goff J. at 691.

[93] *Pringle* v. *Bremner and Stirling* (1867) 5 M.(H.L.) 55; *Lawrie* v. *Muir*, 1950 J.C. 19; *Fairley*
v. *Fishmongers of London*, 1951 J.C. 14; *H.M. Adv.* v. *Turnbull*, 1951 J.C. 96; *H.M. Adv.* v.
Hepper, 1958 J.C. 39; *H.M. Adv.* v. *McKay*, 1961 J.C. 47; cf. *King* v. *The Queen* [1969] 1
A.C. 304; J. T. C., "Evidence Obtained by Means Considered Irregular," 1969 J.R. 55.

[94] *Laverie* v. *Murray*, 1964 S.L.T.(Notes) 3.

[95] Ibid.; *Fairley* v. *Fishmongers of London*, supra; *Lawrie* v. *Muir*, supra.

[96] *Stewart* v. *Roach*, 1950 S.C. 318.

[97] Cf. *Laverie* v. *Murray*, supra.

[98] *Watson* v. *Muir*, 1938 J.C. 181.

[99] e.g. Licensing (Scotland) Act 1959, s. 179; Betting, Gaming and Lotteries Act 1963, s. 51;
Public Order Act 1936, s. 2 (5) (warrant must be issued by a sheriff); Misuse of Drugs
Act 1971, s. 23 (3); Salmon and Freshwater Fisheries (Protection) (Scotland) Act 1951,
s. 11; Firearms Act 1968, s. 46.

[1] Cf. Dundee Corporation (Consolidated Powers) Order Confirmation Act 1957, s. 490.

such that the delay necessary to obtain a warrant would be likely to defeat
the ends of justice. There is also a power to stop and search vehicles or
vessels reasonably suspected of carrying unlawfully obtained goods.[2]
There is a right under the various Police Acts to enter licensed premises
and premises of public entertainment, as well as brothels and thieves'
kitchens, either generally or, in some cases, to search for stolen property.[3]

Scope of warrant

5-31   Warrants to search premises must be specific as to the purpose and
limitations of the search. A wide and indefinite warrant is illegal.[4] The
normal petition warrant authorises a search of " the person, repositories
and dwelling house of the said accused, and the house or premises in which
he may be found, and to secure all writs, evidents and articles found therein
tending to establish guilt or participation in the charge aforesaid and for
that purpose to open all shut and lockfast places." [5] But a warrant in the
nature of a " fishing diligence " to search the premises of an unarrested
person (or of an arrested person in relation to offences with which he has
not been charged) may be illegal if it is likely to lead to oppression in
execution. So a warrant to search for documents in the house of a suspect
for evidence of guilt was held to be illegal partly because it would cover
confidential documents which would require to be read before their
relevancy could be ascertained, and because, that being so, the warrant
provided for no safeguard against its oppressive execution, such as the
presence of the sheriff.[6] A warrant may also be granted to search the
premises of a third party before or after any arrest has been made.[7]

Where a warrant is granted to search for specific articles it depends on
the circumstances of the case whether other articles may be removed
which tend to establish guilt of the offence for which the warrant was issued
or of other offences. The general principle seems to be that once the police
are lawfully on premises with a search warrant they may take any suspicious
articles they happen to see, but cannot actively search for articles outwith
the warrant or take away articles which might on further examination
disclose further offences.[8] Where the police obtain permission to enter
a house to search for a specified purpose the position is the same as if they

---

[2] Edinburgh Corporation Order Confirmation Act 1967, s. 495.
[3] See Burgh Police (Scotland) Act 1892, s. 401; Glasgow Corporation (General Powers)
Consolidation Order Confirmation Act 1960, s. 179; Edinburgh Corporation Order Confirmation Act 1967, s. 492; Dundee Corporation (Consolidated Powers) Order Confirmation
Act 1957, s. 489; s. 11 of the Salmon and Freshwater Fisheries (Protection) (Scotland) Act
1951 gives power to search vehicles or persons without warrant in case of urgency.
[4] *Nelson* v. *Black and Morrison* (1866) 4 M. 328; *Webster* v. *Bethune* (1857) 2 Irv. 597.
[5] Cf. *John Porteous* (1867) 5 Irv. 456. A summary warrant to arrest or search implies warrant
to break open shut and lockfast places where necessary: 1954 Act, s. 20 (1).
[6] *Nelson* v. *Black and Morrison*, supra, esp. Lord Ardmillan at 332; *Stewart* v. *Roach*, supra;
see also *Bell* v. *Black and Morrison* (1865) 5 Irv. 57; *Bell* v. *Black and Morrison* (1865) 3
M. 1026.
[7] Cf. *Watson* v. *Muir*, supra.
[8] *Pringle* v. *Bremner and Stirling*, supra; *H.M. Adv.* v. *Turnbull*, supra; *H.M. Adv.* v. *Hepper*,
supra; cf. *Chic Fashions (West Wales) Ltd.* v. *Jones* [1968] 2 Q.B. 299; *Elias* v. *Pasmore*
[1934] 2 K.B. 164.

had a warrant limited to that purpose.[9] Where a warrant had been obtained
to search an accountant's office for documents relating to the affairs of a
particular client, it was held that the removal under the purported authority
of the warrant of documents relating to other clients was illegal, and the
latter documents were not admitted in evidence at the accountant's trial
on charges connected with these clients' affairs.[10] On the other hand,
where police searched the house of a suspect, without a warrant but with
his wife's permission, in pursuance of an investigation unconnected with
the subsequent charge, and found and took away a case bearing the name
and address of another person which was later found to have been stolen,
it was held in the accused's subsequent trial for theft that the removal of
the case had been proper, or at least that the evidence of its finding was
admissible.[11] This case was distinguished from the former one on the
basis that the police in finding the case had " accidentally stumbled upon "
a suspicious article.[12]

Arrest Beyond Jurisdiction

In Scotland, England and Wales

5-32   A warrant of apprehension to which section 25 of the Sheriff Courts
(Scotland) Act 1838 applies, issued by a sheriff, may be executed through-
out Scotland without endorsation.[13] A warrant of apprehension issued in
Scotland may be executed within his police area by any English or Welsh
constable, whether or not it has been endorsed under the Indictable
Offences Act 1848.[14]

In Border counties

5-33   Any constable appointed in a border county, i.e. Berwick, Roxburgh,
Dumfries, Northumberland and Cumberland, may execute in any of these
counties a warrant for the arrest of a person accused or convicted of a
crime committed, or for recovery of any goods alleged to have been
stolen, in the county for which he is appointed.[15]

Conveyance of prisoner

5-34   It is lawful for any officer of the law, while lawfully conveying any
prisoner to any gaol or before any magistrate, to convey such prisoner
through any county adjacent to that over which the magistrate possesses
jurisdiction before whom such prisoner is to be carried for examination,
or to that in which the gaol is situated to which such prisoner is to be

[9] H.M. Adv. v. Hepper, supra.
[10] H.M. Adv. v. Turnbull, supra.
[11] H.M. Adv. v. Hepper, supra.
[12] H.M. Adv. v. Hepper, supra, Lord Guthrie at 40; cf. H.M. Adv. v. McKay, supra; see also
     Chic Fashions (West Wales) Ltd. v. Jones [1968] 2 Q.B. 299; Brian Davis, " John Wilkes
     R.I.P.," 1968 S.L.T.(News) 105.
[13] 1963 Act, s. 41.
[14] 1963 Act, s. 39.
[15] Police (Scotland) Act 1967, s. 18.

committed, in the same way and in all respects as if such officer had been
an officer of the county through which he may so pass, and as if the warrant
under which he is acting had been granted or endorsed by a magistrate of
such county.[16]

Indictable Offences Act 1848

5–35   If the accused is in the United Kingdom, including the Channel Islands,
the provisions of the Indictable Offences Act 1848 may still be invoked.
A warrant issued in Scotland by a judge of the High Court of Justiciary,
a sheriff, a justice of peace, or a burgh magistrate, or a warrant issued
under the 1954 Act, may be endorsed by a justice of the peace who has
jurisdiction at the place where it is to be executed. When it has been
backed, the warrant may be executed either by the person who brings it,
or by any person to whom it was originally addressed, or by a constable
or other officer of the law for the place where it is endorsed.[17] It is now
the practice to convey the prisoner into the jurisdiction from which the
warrant was issued, and take him before a magistrate there, without
previous examination at the place of his arrest.[18]

If a warrant is to be executed under the Indictable Offences Act 1848
by an officer of the court from which it was issued, the officer should see it
signed and be prepared to depone to the signature. He then proceeds to
the jurisdiction where it is to be executed, attends before a justice of peace,
and after being put on oath depones that the signature to the warrant is
the signature of the magistrate. It is then backed by the justice of
peace.

If, on the other hand, it is to be executed by an officer of the foreign
jurisdiction, a declaration as to the signature must be written upon it
before it is dispatched. By means of this declaration the foreign officer
gets his warrant backed.

Fugitive Offenders Act 1967

5–36   The arrest of persons for relevant offences committed in designated
Commonwealth countries [19] and United Kingdom dependencies, and their
return to the place of their offence, is governed by the Fugitive Offenders
Act 1967. The Act also applies to persons unlawfully at large after conviction of a relevant offence. The relevant offences covered by the Act are in
the case of Commonwealth countries offences falling within Schedule 1
to the Act and punishable with at least twelve months' imprisonment, and in
the case of dependencies offences punishable on conviction by a superior
court with at least twelve months' imprisonment, provided that the act or
omission in each case would also be an offence under the law of the

---

[16] Criminal Law (Scotland) Act 1830, s. 6.
[17] Indictable Offences Act 1848, ss. 14 and 15.
[18] *Sinclair* v. *H.M. Adv.* (1890) 2 White 481.
[19] See Fugitive Offenders (Designated Commonwealth Countries) Order 1967, and subsequent Orders.

United Kingdom or any part thereof.[20] There is an exception for political offences, for cases where the true reason for the request for the return of the offender are his prosecution or punishment for reasons racial, religious, national or political, and for cases where if the offender were returned his trial might be prejudiced or his liberty restricted for reasons of race, religion, nationality or politics.[21] The courts will order the return of an offender only where the requesting country has entered into an arrangement undertaking not to take proceedings against him for any offences committed prior to his return other than offences proved by the facts on which his return was requested, except with the consent of the United Kingdom.[21a] Warrants under the Act may be issued on the authority of the Secretary of State by the Sheriff Principal of the Lothians and Peebles,[22] although provisional warrants may be issued by any magistrate. These provisional warrants are subject to review by the Secretary of State who may discharge them, or authorise committal proceedings to be taken on them. Committal proceedings are heard in the sheriff court of the Lothians and Peebles with an appeal to the High Court.[23]

5-37   The return to the United Kingdom of persons accused of offences there who are in other Commonwealth countries or United Kingdom dependencies is governed by the corresponding legislation for the place where the offender is found.[24]

5-38   The Act provides that proceedings may not be taken against returned offenders for offences committed prior to their return which do not arise out of the facts in reference to which they were returned, without the consent of the returning country.[25]

An offender arrested under the Act may be returned only where the committing court is satisfied that there would be sufficient evidence to warrant his trial for the offence if it had been committed within the jurisdiction of that court.[26]

Extradition

5-39   Where the offender has fled to a foreign country outwith the Commonwealth the right to secure his return to Scotland will depend on the terms

---

[20] s. 3. See *R.* v. *Governor of Brixton Prison, ex p. Gardner* [1968] 2 Q.B. 399; *R.* v. *Governor of Brixton Prison, ex p. Rush* [1969] 1 W.L.R. 165; *R.* v. *Governor of Pentonville Prison, ex p. Teja* [1971] 2 Q.B. 274; [1971] 1 W.L.R. 678.

[21] s. 4 (1). The burden of proof is on the fugitive: *R.* v. *Governor of Pentonville Prison, ex p. Fernandez* [1971] 1 W.L.R. 987. A person will not be returned where it appears that if charged in the United Kingdom with the offence in question he would be entitled to be discharged under any rule of law relating to previous acquittal or conviction: s. 4 (2).

[21a] s. 4 (3).

[22] And may be executed throughout the United Kingdom without being backed: s. 6 (4).

[23] ss. 7 and 8. For forms of procedures, see the Fugitive Offenders (Forms) (Scotland) Regulations 1967. The High Court may discharge the offender if to return him to the requesting country would be unjust or oppressive because of the triviality of the offence or its staleness or because the accusation was not made in good faith in the interests of justice: s. 8 (3); see *R.* v. *Governor of Brixton Prison, ex p. Cook* [1970] Crim.L.R. 699.

[24] Legislation in the case of U.K. dependencies being made by Order in Council.

[25] s. 14; Fugitive Offenders (Extension) Order 1967.

[26] s. 7 (5) (*a*); this is a decision which English courts are used to making, but which Scots courts have not been in the habit of making for some time in relation to domestic cases.

of the extradition treaty, if any, between that country and the United
Kingdom, and on the extradition laws of that country made consequent on
such a treaty.[27] A person surrendered under such a treaty can be dealt with
only for offences " proved by the facts on which the surrender is
grounded." [28]

5-40   Extradition from Scotland is governed by the Extradition Acts 1870–
1935. The determination of whether the facts in any case constitute an
extraditable offence is governed by the definition of that offence under the
law of England.[29] There is no extradition for political offences.[30] A provisional warrant for the arrest of a fugitive may be granted by any police
magistrate or justice of the peace in Scotland,[31] but the offender will then
be brought before the metropolitan magistrate at Bow Street in London.
Fugitives are normally arrested on a warrant from the metropolitan
magistrate proceeding on an order from the Secretary of State, and such a
warrant is enforceable in Scotland without endorsation.[32] The extradition
proceedings are thus normally heard at Bow Street, but if the Secretary of
State is of opinion on representations made by the fugitive that it would be
prejudicial to his health to move him to Bow Street, he may order the case
to be heard by the sheriff principal or sheriff of the place of apprehension.[33]

Ireland

5-41   Persons sought on warrant from the Republic of Ireland may be arrested in Scotland, provided the warrant is backed in terms of the Backing of
Warrants (Republic of Ireland) Act 1965.[34] The offences to which the Act
applies and the procedure to be followed are laid down in the Act. The
offence must correspond with an offence under Scots law and must not be
a political or revenue offence. The arrested person is brought before a
sheriff court which will remand him for delivery to the Irish police if the
proceedings are in order.[35] Delivery may be refused if there are substantial
grounds for believing that he would be prosecuted in Ireland " for another
offence . . . of a political character," provided this is an offence he has
already committed.[36] An order made under the Act may be appealed to the
High Court as if it were a summary conviction.[37]

---

[27] For this purpose the Republic of Ireland is now a foreign country.
[28] Extradition Act 1870, s. 19.
[29] Extradition Act 1870, Sched. 1. The courts must issue an extradition order if there is a
prima facie case against the offender: whether it would be oppressive to return him is a
matter for the Secretary of State: *Atkinson* v. *U.S.A. Government* [1971] A.C. 197.
[30] Extradition Act 1870, s. 3.
[31] Ibid. s. 8 (2).
[32] Ibid. s. 13.
[33] Extradition Act 1895, s. 1. For offences at sea see Extradition Act 1870, s. 16.
[34] See also Act of Adjournal (Backing of Warrants) (Republic of Ireland) 1965.
[35] Backing of Warrants (Republic of Ireland) Act 1965, s. 2. There is no provision for inquiry
into the existence of a prima facie case: *R.* v. *Metropolitan Police Commissioner, ex p.
Arkins* [1966] 1 W.L.R. 1593; *R.* v. *Governor of Brixton Prison, ex p.Keane* [1972] A.C. 204
[36] Ibid. s. 2 (2) (*b*); *R.* v. *Governor of Brixton Prison, ex p. Keane*, supra.
[37] Backing of Warrants (Republic of Ireland) Act 1965, s. 3 (2).

Procedure After Arrest

Judicial examination

5-42   Under section 17 of the 1887 Act the accused is entitled, immediately upon his arrest, to have intimation sent to any properly qualified solicitor that his professional assistance is required by the accused and informing him of the place to which the accused is to be taken for examination. The solicitor is entitled to have a private interview with the accused before the examination and to be present thereat.[38] There is no right to the presence of a solicitor at any earlier stage, e.g. at the time when the accused is charged, but a request to have a solicitor at that time will normally be granted, and refusal to grant such a request may constitute oppression.[39] The sheriff or magistrate may delay the examination for a period not exceeding forty-eight hours from the time of arrest in order to allow time for the attendance of such solicitor.[40]

The section imposes no duty upon anyone to inform the accused of his right to summon professional assistance, but this should always be done.[41] If he attends the examination without a solicitor, the officiating sheriff or magistrate should advise him of his right.[42]

As soon as possible after his arrest, the accused is brought before a magistrate for examination. Such examination should, if possible, take place not later than the morning of the day after arrest. Examinations are not now conducted on Sundays. The necessity for avoiding delay arises from the circumstance that the accused cannot apply for liberation on bail until he has been brought before a magistrate.

5-43   A person being dealt with under solemn procedure is entitled to legal aid without any inquiry into his resources up to the stage at which he is admitted to bail or fully committed. This legal aid consists of the services of the duty solicitor in attendance at the time and place of his appearance for judicial examination, in terms of article 8 of the Legal Aid (Scotland) (Criminal Proceedings) Scheme 1964, and includes legal aid in any application for review of bail or any appeal in connection with bail.

5-44   Judicial examination ceased to be of importance on the passing of the Criminal Evidence Act 1898, which entitled the accused to give evidence at his trial, and even formal declarations ceased to be taken in most cases when the 1908 Act provided that if an accused intimated that he did not

---

[38] Cf. 1954 Act, s. 12, formerly 1908 Act, s. 15. In summary proceedings the fact that the accused has been wrongfully refused a private interview with his solicitor to which he is entitled under s. 15 of the 1908 Act (now s. 12 of the 1954 Act) is not, per se, a bar to all further proceedings (*Cheyne* v. *McGregor*, 1941 J.C. 17); see Gerald H. Gordon, " Institution of Criminal Proceedings in Scotland " (1968) 19 N.I.L.Q. 249; J. G. Wilson, " Pre-Trial Criminal Procedure in Scotland: A Comparative Study," 1965 S.A.L.J. 69, for discussions of pre-trial procedure.

[39] *Law* v. *McNicol*, 1965 J.C. 32; *H.M. Adv.* v. *Cunningham*, 1939 J.C. 61; *H.M. Adv.* v. *Fox*, 1947 J.C. 30.

[40] 1887 Act, s. 17.

[41] *H.M. Adv.* v. *Goodall* (1888) 2 White 1; cf. *Ferguson* v. *Brown*, 1942 J.C. 113. In *H.M. Adv.* v. *Goodall* a declaration taken from an illiterate woman who was unattended by a law agent and was not informed of her right to have one was rejected at her trial.

[42] *H.M. Adv.* v. *Goodall*, supra.

wish to make a declaration, it was unnecessary to make one.[43] It is now the exception rather than the rule for a declaration to be made and the judicial examination is now usually only a brief formality. Omission of the examination does not necessarily vitiate a subsequent conviction,[44] but the proper practice is to include in the warrant for apprehension a warrant to bring the accused before a magistrate, even although, when previously apprehended on the same charge, he declined to emit a declaration.[45]

The examination may be conducted before any magistrate, even before one who has not power to try the offence.[46] In practice, a sheriff invariably presides. An honorary sheriff may preside, but the sheriff clerk, although holding a commission to act as sheriff, may not do so.[47]

The proceedings are private. All persons ought to be excluded except the magistrate, the sheriff clerk or his depute, the procurator fiscal or his depute, the accused and his solicitor, and the necessary police officers. The magistrate must be present and attentive during the whole proceedings. The magistrate should interrogate the accused,[48] but it seems that in the past the procurator fiscal often did so.[49] In one case, however, a declaration emitted at an examination by the procurator fiscal was rejected at the trial.[50]

5–45   It is the practice to give a copy of the petition to the accused or his solicitor before he appears in court. When he appears his solicitor will normally merely intimate: " No plea; no declaration," and the accused will then be committed, either for further examination or for trial.

If the accused elects to make a declaration, the magistrate then addresses him in some such formula as this: " You have heard the charge which has been read over to you. You have been brought here for the purpose of being judicially examined in regard to that charge. You are not bound to answer any questions which may be put to you; but if you do answer, what you say will be written down and may be used in evidence at your trial."

If the accused intimates that he does not desire to emit a declaration, the fact is recorded in the warrant of commital.[51] He may thereafter be committed for further examination or until liberated in due course of law, but it is competent for him subsequently to emit a declaration should he intimate to the prosecutor his desire to do so.[52] If he refuses to give any answer, the fact is noted. If he makes a statement, the material substance of it is written down, but it is not necessary to note every word.[53] The

---

[43] 1908 Act, s. 77 (1). This section, so far as relating to procedure under indictment, remains in force (1954 Act, s. 78 and Sched. 4).
[44] Hume, ii. 80; *McVey* v. *H.M. Adv.* (1911) 6 Adam 503.
[45] *McVey* v. *H.M. Adv.*, supra.
[46] Hume, ii. 77; Alison, ii. 566; *Thos. Hay* (1824) Shaw 113.
[47] *Mabon and Shillinglaw* (1842) 1 Broun 201; *John Stewart* (1855) 2 Irv. 614.
[48] *H.M. Adv.* v. *Brims* (1887) 1 White 462.
[49] See Gerald H. Gordon, op. cit., 19 N.I.L.Q. at pp. 256–257.
[50] *Brims*, supra.
[51] 1908 Act, s. 77 (1).
[52] Ibid.
[53] *Andrew Brown* (1866) 5 Irv. 215. See infra, App. C. Form 1.

declaration is written by the sheriff clerk or his depute. No one connected with the prosecution may do so.[54]

A declaration must not be taken unless the accused is in his sound mind and sober senses.[55] If he is intoxicated, the examination will be deferred until he is sober. If there is reason to suspect that he is of unsound mind, he should be examined by a medical man, and the result entered in the record of proceedings. If he is certified to be mentally disordered, the examination is stopped, and he is committed to prison to await further procedure.

The accused's statement must be free and voluntary. No threat or inducement of any kind may be offered to him to make him speak.[56]

At the close the whole is read over to the accused, and he is asked if he adheres to it. If so, he signs the declaration, or if he declares he cannot write, the fact is noted. Reading is an essential step.[57] The declaration is then signed by the magistrate, and two or three of those present as witnesses.

If the accused is a foreigner, an interpreter is employed, who first takes the oath de fideli. He interprets the charge to the accused, and the questions and answers, and reads the declaration to the accused.

5–46   The accused may if necessary be re-examined at any time prior to service of the indictment.[58] Where fresh charges emerge, it is always proper that he should be examined anew upon these on fresh petitions, although this is not essential.[59]

5–47   When there are charges against an accused person in several counties, he may be brought before the sheriff of any one of them for examination on all or any of the charges.[60]

5–48   Statements by an accused after committal other than by way of declaration may be inadmissible as hearsay,[61] unless made against his interest. Authority will not be given for an accused's advisers to have him interrogated under the influence of a truth drug while he is in custody awaiting trial.[62]

Committal

5–49   At the close of the judicial examination, the procurator fiscal moves the presiding magistrate to commit the accused either for further examination or until liberated in due course of law. The latter form is often called "committal for trial," or "full committal." If the first committal is only for examination, the prosecutor must see that the accused is in due course

[54] Galbraith v. Sawers (1840) 3 D. 52.
[55] And not under the influence of a "truth drug": cf. Patrick Connelly Meehan, Petnr., infra.
[56] Hume, ii. 324; Macdonald, 203.
[57] Hume, ii. 330.
[58] Hume, ii. 330, 331.
[59] W. T. Keith (1875) 3 Couper 125.
[60] 1908 Act, s. 77 (2).
[61] Patrick Connelly Meehan, Petnr., 1969 S.L.T.(Notes) 90.
[62] Ibid.

committed for trial unless he has been released on bail. Accused persons who have attained the age of twenty-one years are committed to prison. Those under sixteen will normally be committed to the local authority who are responsible for their safe custody.[63] Persons between sixteen and twenty-one may be committed to prison, but as and when remand centres are available are sent there.[64]

The length of time which may intervene between committal for further examination and committal for trial is not absolutely fixed, but as a general rule does not exceed eight days.[65] This must be particularly observed in those cases where bail cannot be insisted upon till after committal until liberation in due course of law. If the prisoner has been committed for further examination and liberated on bail, it is not necessary to commit him until liberated in due course of law.[66]

The sheriff nowadays commits accused persons for trial on presentation of a petition containing a prima facie relevant charge signed by the procurator fiscal. This petition may be the one on which the accused was originally arrested or on which he originally appeared, or may be one substituted therefor after arrest or continuation for further examination.

5-50   On the same day that the accused person is committed until liberated in due course of law, he is served with a full copy of the petition and warrants signed by the officer or warder who serves it.[67] This service is not required when the committal is merely for further examination. No form of execution of service is provided. Where necessary, it is proved by the oath of the officer; but, in order to prevent errors, it is desirable to preserve a memorandum of the time and place of service, signed by the officer or warder who serves.

5-51   It may be observed that the original warrant of committal until liberated in due course of law remains in force until the accused person is acquitted, or sentenced or liberated in legal form.[68] For administrative reasons, however, modern practice frequently requires the preparation of a new warrant for detention where an accused is remanded in custody after conviction but before sentence.

5-52   Where there are charges against an accused person in different counties, he may be committed on all or any of the charges by the sheriff of any one of such counties before whom he is brought.[69]

5-53   An invalidity in the warrant of committal of an accused person does not vitiate a conviction proceeding on an indictment regularly served and a trial regularly conducted.[70] A bad committal is no more in law than a non-committal. On this ground the court held that subsequent

[63] Infra, para. 19–11.
[64] 1949 Act, s. 28.
[65] See *Arbuckle* v. *Taylor* (1815) 3 Dow's App. 160, 184.
[66] 1887 Act, s. 18.
[67] Macdonald, 205; Hume, ii. 85, Alison, ii. 154; Criminal Procedure Act 1701.
[68] 1887 Act, ss. 31, 34, 52.
[69] 1908 Act, s. 77 (2).
[70] *McVey* v. *H.M. Adv.* (1911) 6 Adam 503; *H.M. Adv.* v. *Keith* (1875) 3 Couper 125, Lord Ardmillan at 130.

proceedings were not vitiated in a case where, instead of a new petition being presented, a minute was written on the original petition and the crave for examination was omitted.[71]

Bail

5-54   All crimes and offences, whether at common law or by Act of Parliament, are bailable except murder and treason.[72] Even in regard to these excepted crimes, bail may be accepted at the discretion of the Lord Advocate, or the High Court of Justiciary.[73] This discretion cannot be exercised by a single judge, but only by a quorum of the High Court.[74] An application for liberation on bail may be made either before or after final committal.

Any person accused of a crime which is by law bailable is entitled, immediately after he has been brought before a magistrate for examination on declaration, to apply to such magistrate or to the sheriff for liberation on his finding caution in common form to appear at any diet to which he may be cited for further examination, or in order to answer any indictment or complaint which may be served upon him.[75] The prosecutor is entitled to be heard against such application, and the sheriff or other magistrate is entitled in his discretion to refuse such application before the accused is committed until liberated in due course of law.[76] When an application for bail is made before committal and refused, it is incompetent for the accused to appeal to the High Court.[77] Appeal before committal is open only to the prosecutor.[78] The statute gives a right of appeal only in cases of refusal of bail after committal.[79]

Offences against Children

5-55   By section 24 of the Children and Young Persons (Scotland) Act 1937 it is provided that where an arrest has been made by a police constable without warrant under the provisions of section 24 (1) of the Act the superintendent or inspector of police or an officer of equal or superior rank, or the officer in charge of the police station to which the person arrested is brought, shall, unless in his belief the release of the person would tend to defeat the ends of justice, or cause injury or danger to the child or young person against whom the offence is alleged to have been committed, release the person arrested on his entering into an obligation to attend at the hearing of the charge or on his finding bail for such amount

---

[71] *McVey* v. *H.M. Adv.*, supra.

[72] Bail (Scotland) Act 1888, ss. 2 and 9.

[73] Ibid. s. 8; Macdonald, 206; Hume, ii. 90; *W. H. Thomson* (1871) 2 Couper 103; *H.M.Adv.* v. *Saunders* (1913) 7 Adam 76; *McLaren* v. *H.M. Adv.*, 1967 S.L.T. (Notes) 43.

[74] *Milne* v. *McNicol*, 1944 J.C. 151.

[75] 1887 Act, s. 18.

[76] Ibid.

[77] *Milne* v. *McNicol*, supra.

[78] Ibid.

[79] *H.M. Adv.* v. *Lowson* (1909) 6 Adam 118; *Milne* v. *McNicol*, supra.

as may in the judgment of the officer of police be required to secure his attendance.[80]

Bail after committal

5–56   In the event of bail being refused prior to committal till liberation in due course of law, the application may be renewed after such committal.[81]

Any sheriff having jurisdiction to try the offence charged, or to commit the accused until liberated in due course of law, may at his discretion admit or refuse to admit the accused to bail.[82]

Bail applications

5–57   Application for liberation is usually made by petition, and ought invariably to be so if there is any prospect of a dispute as to the amount of bail, and of a subsequent appeal or review.[83]   In some cases it may be applied for verbally, and fixed by the sheriff in the warrant of committal. When this is done, a clause is added to the warrant in these terms: " and admits the said A. B. to bail on his finding caution to the extent of . . . pounds sterling."

An application for bail must be disposed of within twenty-four hours after its presentation to the magistrate, failing which the accused is forthwith liberated.[84]   An opportunity must be given to the prosecutor to be heard upon such application.[85]

Grounds for refusal

5–58   Where a person charged with any crime except murder or treason applies for bail, the court to which application is made must grant it unless in the exercise of its discretionary right of refusal it is of opinion that, looking to the public interest and to securing the ends of justice, there is good reason why bail should not be granted.[86]   " In the case of the untried prisoner the presumption of innocence involves . . . that, unless good reasons can be shown to the contrary, the applicant has a right to be released on bail, if the crime with which he is charged is a bailable crime." [87]

This discretionary power to refuse bail is not limited to cases where the court thinks there is a danger of the accused absconding before the trial.[88]   The court is not concerned merely with the duty of preventing the unnecessary detention of an untried person: it must also protect the public and safeguard the interests of justice from the consequences of his being

---

[80] See further, infra, para. 5–19.
[81] Bail (Scotland) Act 1888, s. 3.
[82] Ibid., ss. 2 and 9.
[83] Cf. *Arbuckle* v. *Taylor* (1815) 3 Dow's App. 160.
[84] Bail (Scotland) Act 1888, s. 2.
[85] Ibid.
[86] *Mackintosh* v. *McGlinchy*, 1921 J.C. 75; see Bail Act 1888, s. 2; W. A. Brown, " Bail in Scotland " [1968] Crim.L.R. 70; *H.M. Adv.* v. *Docherty*, 1958 S.L.T.(Notes) 50 in which the High Court upheld a sheriff's decision to release an itinerant gipsy on £100 bail.
[87] *Young* v. *H.M. Adv.*, 1946 J.C. 5, L.J.-C. at 6.
[88] *Mackintosh* v. *McGlinchy*, 1921 J.C. 75.

at large. The well-being and safety of the community might be imperilled by the liberation of a dangerous robber, the life of the victim of a brutal assault might again be menaced through the release of the assailant, and the setting free of an unscrupulous criminal might well result in intimidation of, or tampering with, witnesses in the case. It is neither possible nor expedient to categorise all the classes of case in which the court should refuse bail. The only safe rule is that each one must be considered on its own merits.[89]

5–59　There are, however, three important matters to which, in general, the court will have regard when exercising its discretion regarding bail, viz.: (1) the character of the offence charged, (2) the previous record of the accused, and (3) the attitude of the Crown towards the allowance of bail.

As the gravity of the charge increases, so, presumably, does the probability that the accused, if liberated, may abscond, and so, too, may there be a greater danger to the public interest. Where, therefore, the crime charged is serious, the court will not readily allow bail unless the Crown offers no objection.[90] The court attaches great weight to any statement by the Lord Advocate and will be very slow to do anything contrary to his judgment.[91] So, in a case where the accused was charged with administering poison with intent to murder his wife and the Crown opposed bail the court refused to grant it.[92] On the other hand, where, in a case of rape, the Crown consented to liberation on bail the court granted the application.[93] In *Wilson* v. *McGuire*[94] Lord Justice-Clerk Macdonald expressed the opinion that bail should not be allowed in any case of rape where the Lord Advocate objected to its being granted, but in the later case of *A. B.* v. *Dickson*[95] Lord Justice-General Dunedin declined to take so extreme a view, affirming the existence of the court's discretion in all cases, which opinion coincides with that expressed by Lord Justice-General Clyde in *Mackintosh* v. *McGlinchy*.[96]

The previous record of the accused is a relevant and proper factor for consideration, and is not excluded by section 39 of the 1949 Act.[97] As Lord Stormonth Darling pointed out in *Scott* v. *H.M. Advocate*,[98] an application for bail is largely founded on the presumption of innocence which an untried person enjoys, and anything which weakens or destroys this presumption is material. In that case the charge, which was that of forgery, had been substantially admitted in a declaration emitted by the accused, and this factor, together with the gravity of the crime, induced

---

[89] Ibid.
[90] *A.B.* v. *Dickson* (1907) 5 Adam 372; *H.M. Adv.* v. *Saunders* (1913) 7 Adam 76; *Mackintosh* v. *McGlinchy*, supra.
[91] *Mackintosh* v. *McGlinchy*, supra; *A.B.* v. *Dickson*, supra.
[92] *H.M. Adv.* v. *Saunders*, supra.
[93] *A.B.* v. *Dickson*, supra.
[94] (1889) 2 White 267.
[95] Supra.
[96] Supra.
[97] *Macdonald* v. *Clifford*, 1952 J.C. 22. It is particularly relevant where it is substantial or where the latest conviction is relatively recent: *MacLeod* v. *W. 'ght*, 1959 J.C. 12.
[98] (1890) 2 White 570.

the court to refuse bail. And in *H.M. Advocate* v. *Quinn and Macdonald*,[99] Lord Salvesen drew a sharp distinction between the case of persons who had been law-abiding citizens up to the date of the charge and that of known criminals who, in his opinion, were not entitled to bail.

Amount of bail

5-60   The magistrate who admits a person to bail fixes the bail at such an amount as he may consider sufficient to ensure the appearance of such person to answer at all diets to which he may be cited on the charge.[1] All Acts of Parliament which limit the amount of bail which may be fixed by a magistrate are repealed.[2] There are few matters which require greater delicacy than fixing the amount of bail. A sum ought to be named which there is a reasonable probability that the prisoner can find, yet which will be sufficient to ensure that he will not abscond. It is not easy to combine these two essentials. Circumstances vary in every case, and little assistance can be obtained from a citation of decisions. In one case where the charge was that of scuttling three ships, the value of which, including cargoes, was £3,800, bail was allowed at the amount of £400.[3] On the other hand, bail of £700 was required in the case of a solicitor accused of embezzling £400.[4]

The opinion has been expressed by Lord McLaren [5] that where, after the liberation on bail of an accused person, earlier crimes are discovered and libelled against him, bail, if allowed, should be fixed on an ascending scale as each new crime is discovered and the magnitude of the series of offences for which the accused is to be tried increases.

Review and appeal

5-61   Section 37 of the 1963 Act gives power to any court to review its decision on bail where it originally refused bail, or where it allowed bail but the accused has not found the sum fixed. The court may then allow bail or reduce the amount, as the case may be. An application for review of the court's original decision may not be made before the fifth day after the decision; an application for review of a subsequent decision may not be made until the fifteenth day after such decision. In solemn procedure applications for review are made by minutes on the original bail petition.

These provisions are without prejudice to the right of appeal to the High Court on bail, but once an appeal has been disposed of by the High Court a lower court will not entertain an application for review which must be made to the High Court.[6]

---

[99] 1921 J.C. 61.
[1] Bail (Scotland) Act 1888, s. 4.
[2] Ibid.
[3] *Hobbs* v. *H.M. Adv.* (1893) 3 White 487.
[4] *Sutherland* v. *Brims* (1891) 2 White 576.
[5] *Peters* v. *McDonald* (1893) 1 Adam 72.
[6] *H.M. Adv.* v. *Jones*, 1964 S.L.T.(Sh.Ct.) 50. If the High Court uphold a sheriff's allowance of bail the sheriff can later review the amount: *Ward* v. *H.M. Adv.*, 1972 S.L.T. (Notes) 22.

5–62   As already mentioned,[7] an applicant has no right of appeal on any
question of bail before committal until liberation in due course of law.[8]
Thereafter, however, he may appeal to the High Court of Justiciary (1)
where an application for bail made after such committal is refused by the
sheriff or magistrate, or (2) where he is dissatisfied with the amount of bail
fixed on such application.[9] The court may in its discretion order intimation
of the appeal to be made to the Lord Advocate. In practice this is always
done. The public prosecutor, on the other hand, can appeal to the High
Court both before and after committal.[10] Where an application for bail
is granted, whether before or after committal, the prosecutor, if dissatisfied with the decision allowing bail or the amount of bail fixed, may
appeal in like manner as the accused.[11] The applicant cannot be liberated
except as after-mentioned, until the appeal at the instance of the public
prosecutor is disposed of.[12]

          Written notice of appeal is immediately given to the opposite part by
the party appealing. The appeal is disposed of in court or in chambers,
after such inquiry and hearing of parties as the court deems just. In the
event of the appeal of the public prosecutor being refused, the court may
award expenses against him.[13] No clerk's fees, court or other fees or
expenses are exigible from, or can be awarded against, the accused person
in respect of his application for bail, or of his appeal to the High Court.[14]

5–63   When an appeal is taken at the instance of the public prosecutor, the
accused, if he has found bail, may be liberated after seventy-two hours, or
where the place of application is in any island in the Outer Hebrides, or in
the Orkney and Shetland Islands, ninety-six hours, from the time of his
application being granted.[15] This liberation takes effect whether the appeal
is disposed of or not, unless the High Court grants order for further
detaining him in custody pending consideration of the appeal. Notice by
telegraph to the gaoler of the issue of such order within the appointed time,
bearing to be sent by the clerk of court or by the Crown agent, is sufficient
to justify the applicant's detention until the arrival of the order in due
course of post. In computing the period of hours, Sundays, public fasts,
and public holidays, whether general or court holidays, are not included.

5–64   When bail is found, the accused person and any cautioner sign a bond
which must specify a domicile of citation at which the indictment or
complaint may be served.[16]

Recall of forfeiture

5–65   Where forfeiture of bail has been ordered by any court, it is now competent for that court, if satisfied that it is reasonable to do so, to recall the

---

[7] Supra, para. 5–54.
[8] *H.M. Adv.* v. *Lowson* (1909) 6 Adam 118; *Milne* v. *McNicol*, 1944 J.C. 151.
[9] Bail (Scotland) Act 1888, s. 5.
[10] Ibid.   [11] Ibid.
[12] Ibid.   [13] Ibid.
[14] Ibid. s. 6.
[15] Ibid. s. 7.
[16] Justiciary Court (Scotland) Act 1868, s. 18.

order and direct the bail money to be refunded. Such decision is final and not subject to review.[17]

Legal aid

5–66   The accused's right to the services of the duty solicitor cease once he is admitted to bail or committed for trial.[18] If he wishes to continue to receive legal aid, he must apply therefor to the sheriff before whom he was taken for judicial examination.[19] He may do so at any time after full committal. The application will be granted if the sheriff is satisfied after consideration of the accused's financial circumstances that he is unable without undue hardship to himself or his dependants to meet the expenses of the case.[20] Legal aid will not be made available except on special cause shown where the accused has available rights to facilities making legal aid unnecessary, or has a reasonable expectation of obtaining financial or other help from a body of which he is a member. Persons granted legal aid have no liability to make any contributions to the Legal Aid Fund, except that where a person who obtains legal aid is a member of a body which reasonably might have been expected to give him financial help, he must sign an undertaking to pay to the Law Society any sum received from that body on account of the expenses of his defence.[21]

Legal aid once granted continues until the conclusion of the accused's trial, unless it is withdrawn as a result of a determination by the court disqualifying the accused on the ground of misconduct on his part.[22] Decisions on applications for legal aid are final,[23] but an accused who has been disqualified for continuance of legal aid may appeal against his disqualification by petition to the nobile officium of the High Court.[24]

The accused has the right to nominate any solicitor who is on the appropriate list of solicitors available to take legal aid cases. If no solicitor is nominated the local committee of the Law Society will nominate a solicitor, but in the case of a person charged with murder or culpable homicide, the duty solicitor is deemed to be the nominated solicitor unless the accused requests another solicitor.[25]

The nominated solicitor is also available to prepare the accused's notice of appeal and an application for a legal aid appeal certificate.[26]

Precognition

5–67   The duty of obtaining precognitions of Crown witnesses rests on the procurator fiscal. As these form the material on which a decision is

---

[17] 1949 Act, s. 44.
[18] Legal Aid (Scotland) Act 1967, s. 2 (5) (*a*). But the duty solicitor is required to act in any bail appeal or review proceedings—Legal Aid (Scotland) (Criminal Proceedings) Scheme 1964, art. 8.
[19] Legal Aid (Scotland) Act 1967, s. 2 (2).
[20] Ibid. s. 2 (3) (*b*).
[21] Legal Aid (Scotland) (Criminal Proceedings) Regulations 1964, reg. 6 (2), (3).
[22] Act of Adjournal (Rules for Legal Aid in Criminal Proceedings) 1964, rule 10.
[23] Ibid., rule 9.
[24] *J. P. Hartley*, Petnr. (1968) 32 J.C.L. 191.
[25] Legal Aid (Scotland) (Criminal Proceedings) Scheme 1964, arts. 17 (1) and 8 (3).
[26] Ibid., art. 18 (1). See infra, para. 11–04.

reached as to whether proceedings are to be taken against a suspected person or not and also the basis for examining witnesses at the trial, care must be taken in their preparation.

The circumstances of each case differ so widely that it would serve no good purpose to enter into a statement of the methods of investigation which ought to be adopted. It is necessary, however, to say that all productions should be marked for identification at the trial. With this object, documentary productions are usually initialled by the witnesses who speak to them, and other productions, such as lethal weapons and stolen articles, have a label attached to them and sealed, which is signed by each witness to whom it is shown.

The precognition, having been completed, is reported in due course for consideration by Crown counsel. If they are of opinion that there is no prima facie case against the accused person, an order will be made for his liberation (if in prison), which must be carried out with the least possible delay. If the accused person has been liberated on bail, intimation should be made to the sheriff clerk, in order that the bail bond may be discharged.

If Crown counsel are of opinion that a prima facie case has been established, they will order the accused to be indicted for trial in the High Court of Justiciary, or sent for trial by the sheriff and a jury, or by the sheriff summarily, according to the gravity of the charge. In either of the first two cases an indictment has to be prepared.

5–68 If witnesses refuse to attend the procurator fiscal for the purpose of giving a precognition, their attendance may be enforced. The usual course is to obtain a warrant of citation. This is usually craved in the original petition, but may be obtained at any subsequent stage of the proceedings. As was pointed out by Lord Justice-Clerk Macdonald in the case of *Forbes* v. *Main*,[27] a warrant should be granted prior to the arrest of the accused only in very serious cases or for the purpose of investigating some unascertained crime. In that case a procurator fiscal presented a petition to the sheriff, setting forth that at a certain bazaar a lottery had been carried on in contravention of the Lotteries Act 1823, and that the Chief Constable had endeavoured to get evidence against persons engaged in the lottery from persons able to give information, but that they refused to give it, and praying for a warrant to cite all available witnesses for precognition on oath if necessary. The sheriff granted the warrant. Certain persons were cited and brought suspensions. The court suspended the warrants and citations.

Once a criminal prosecution is in being it is the duty of every citizen to give such information to the Crown or to the defence as he may be asked to give:

"I consider it to be the duty of every true citizen to give such information to the Crown as he may be asked to give in reference to

[27] (1908) 5 Adam 503.

the case in which he is to be called; and also that every witness who is to be called for the Crown should give similar information to the prisoner's legal advisers, if he is called upon and asked what he is going to say." [28]

5-69   Each witness should be precognosced separately and outwith the presence of the other witnesses.[29] The accused is not entitled to be present or to be represented at the examination.[30] Nor is he entitled to see the precognitions, but he may be allowed to see them. An accused person has no right to ask that all the results of the Crown investigation should be communicated to him,[31] but circumstances may be such as to oblige the Crown to disclose to him evidence in its possession which is material to his defence.[32] The precognition is reduced to writing by the procurator fiscal. It is not signed, and is usually not seen, by the witness.

Witnesses may be put on oath when deponing on precognition, but this is now a rare practice.[33] It is illegal for a prosecutor to take sworn precognitions outwith the presence of a magistrate.[34]

5-70   Crown precognitions are very highly confidential. Where their production is refused by the Crown it will be ordered by the court only where it is necessary for the ends of justice in view of some great and overwhelming necessity.[35] Confidentiality of Crown precognitions is, in general, necessary for the successful prosecution of crime. The Lord Advocate is head of the Criminal Department and his views carry great weight with the court.[36] If he declines to produce a Crown precognition on the ground that such an act would be contrary to public policy it will require very strong circumstances to induce the court to ordain him to do so,[37] although that power is inherent in the court.[38] In *Arthur* v. *Lindsay* [39] the pursuer sued a procurator fiscal in the Court of Session for damages on the ground that the defender had defamed him by maliciously inserting in precognitions taken in connection with certain criminal proceedings false and calumnious statements regarding the pursuer which were not made by the witnesses and had shown these precognitions to persons who had no legal right to see them. A motion by the pursuer for a diligence to recover the precognitions and certain communications passing between the defender and the Crown Office was opposed by the Lord Advocate on the ground that it was in the public interest that such documents should be considered confidential, and that the public service would suffer by their production.

---

[28] *H.M. Adv.* v. *Monson* (1893) 1 Adam 114, L.J.-C. at 135.
[29] Hume, ii. 82; *Dickson on Evidence*, paras. 1592–1593; *Reid* v. *Duff* (1843) 5 D. 656.
[30] Hume, ii. 82; Alison, ii. 139.
[31] *Slater* v. *H.M. Adv.*, 1928 J.C. 94.
[32] *Smith* v. *H.M. Adv.*, 1952 J.C. 66.
[33] Hume, ii. 82, 378; *Dickson on Evidence*, para. 1590.
[34] Ibid.
[35] *Donald* v. *Hart* (1844) 6 D. 1255.
[36] *Arthur* v. *Lindsay* (1894) 1 Adam 582.
[37] Cf. *Dowgray* v. *Gilmour*, 1907 S.C. 715, Lord President Dunedin at 720.
[38] Cf. *Sheridan* v. *Peel*, 1907 S.C. 577, Lord President Dunedin at 580; *Rogers* v. *Orr*, 1939 S.C. 492; and see *Glasgow Corporation* v. *Central Land Board*, 1956 S.C.(H.L.) 1.
[39] Supra.

The court (dubitante Lord Kinnear) refused the motion, holding that the circumstances did not warrant their overruling the discretion of the Lord Advocate.

5–71 A person who may himself be charged with the crime under investigation is not precognosced; and where a person is precognosced on oath, he cannot afterwards be charged with the crime.[40] It is not settled whether the same applies when the precognition has not been taken on oath. The question was raised, but not decided, in the case of *Cook* v. *McNeill*.[41] In that case, however, it was held that no person is liable to have brought up in criminal prosecution against him at any time what he said in precognition, " not " as Lord Justice-Clerk Macdonald put it, " because there is any reason to suspect bad faith on the part of the prosecutor, but because the people who take the precognitions are searching for evidence in order to prove a crime, and what they take down or afterwards remember of what has been said to them is apt to be coloured by their desire to make out a good case." [42]

5–72 Despite the wide terms of section 3 of the Evidence (Scotland) Act 1852 [43] it is not competent to use a precognition, or any statement of the nature of a precognition, to discredit a witness.[44]

A witness may competently ask that his precognition be delivered up to him to be destroyed before he can be called on to give evidence.[45]

When a prospective witness dies after precognition it is not competent to prove by the evidence of the precognoscers what he said to them.[46]

---

[40] Alison, ii. 138.
[41] (1906) 5 Adam 47.
[42] Ibid. at 51.
[43] This section is as follows:
   " It shall be competent to examine any witness who may be adduced in any action or proceeding, as to whether he has on any specified occasion made a statement on any matter pertinent to the issue different from the evidence given by him in such action or proceeding; and it shall be competent in the course of such action or proceeding to adduce evidence to prove that such witness has made such different statement on the occasion specified."
[44] Hume, ii. 381; Alison, ii. 504; *Dickson on Evidence*, paras. 265, 1591; *O'Donnell* v. *McGuire* (1855) 2 Irv. 236; *Emslie* v. *Alexander* (1862) 1 M. 209, 210; *Sheridan* v. *Peel*, 1907 S.C. 577, L.J.-G. Dunedin at 579; *Binnie* v. *Black*, 1923 S.L.T. 98; *McNeilie* v. *H.M. Adv.*, 1929 J.C. 50; *Kerr* v. *H.M. Adv.*, 1958 J.C. 14; *Hall* v. *H.M. Adv.*, 1968 S.L.T. 275. See also *Dysart Peerage Case* (1881) 6 App.Cas. 489, Lord Watson at 509; *Lauderdale Peerage Case* (1885) 10 App.Cas. 692, Earl of Selborne, L.C. at 710; *Cook* v. *McNeill*, supra. The contrary cases of *Peter Luke* (1866) 5 Irv. 293; *Inch* v. *Inch* (1856) 18 D. 997; *Alice Robertson* (1873) 2 Couper 495; *H.M. Adv.* v. *Leckie* (1895) 1 Adam 538; *Gilmour* v. *Hansen*, 1920 S.C. 598 and *Shearer* v. *McLaren*, 1922 S.L.T. 158 can no longer be regarded as authoritative: but see *Walker and Walker on Evidence*, 368.
[45] Hume, ii. 381; *Cook* v. *McNeill* (1906) 5 Adam 47, L.J.-C. at 51.
[46] Ibid.; *Bridget Kenny or Lynch* (1866) 5 Irv. 300; *Connolly* v. *N.C.B.*, 1953 S.C. 376. Contra *Francis and Michael Ward* (1869) 1 Couper 186.

CHAPTER 6

THE INDICTMENT

General Form

6-01 IN solemn procedure both in the High Court and in the sheriff court the prosecution proceeds upon an indictment drawn up in accordance with the forms contained in Schedule A to the 1887 Act, as amended by section 39 (1) of and Schedule 12 to the 1949 Act, or as nearly conform thereto as the circumstances permit.[1] The following example follows Schedule A as amended:

> A. B., you are indicted at the instance of N. R. W. (*name of Lord Advocate*), Her Majesty's Advocate, and the charge against you is that on 20th   , 197 , in a shop in George Street, Edinburgh, occupied by John Cruikshank, draper, you did steal a shawl and a boa.

Procedure by criminal letters is now applicable only to private prosecution in the High Court.

Naming accused

6-02 Prior to the 1887 Act a material error in stating the name of the accused person was generally fatal to the indictment. Such an error is still to be avoided, but it is not likely to occur in modern practice, and the powers of amendment are so wide that if the mistake did occur it could be corrected.[2] Where an accused's Christian name and surname were transposed it was held that as he had answered to the name as given he could not afterwards object.[3] It is sufficient to give the accused person the name and place of residence which he gave in his declaration, or, if there is no declaration, the name under which he was committed for trial.[4] When he is in prison at the time of preparing the indictment he is usually designed " prisoner in the prison of . . ."; if on bail, he is designed in accordance with the domicile given in the bail bond.

It is unnecessary to describe the accused, or any other person named in the indictment, as " now or lately " residing at a certain place. These words are held to be implied in all designations.[5] It is only necessary to give the name and place of residence of persons mentioned in the indictment. The trade, profession or occupation is of no consequence, and is often omitted.

[1] 1887 Act, s. 2; 1949 Act, s. 39 (1) and Sched. 12.
[2] 1887 Act, s. 70; 1908 Act, s. 30 and s. 77 (4).
[3] *Poli* v. *Thomson* (1910) 6 Adam 261.
[4] 1887 Act, s. 4; 1908 Act, s. 77 (1).
[5] 1887 Act, s. 13.

Plural accused

6-03   When two or more persons are charged together with committing a crime, it is unnecessary to aver that " both and each or one or other," or " all and each or one or more," of them committed the crime. These alternatives are implied, and are to be read into every indictment or complaint which charges more than one person with crime.[6]

Bodies corporate

6-04   A body corporate is indicted in its corporate name. As to service see infra, para. 7–06.

Accessories

6-05   It is unnecessary to state that a person accused is guilty, " actor or art and part " in any indictment. These words are implied in connection with every statement of charge.[7] There are cases, however, where more detailed specification is requisite.

Certain crimes—rape, for example—are usually committed by one person only. Where more than one are charged, and it is not meant to be implied that both or all have committed the crime, the share taken by the accessories will be explained in the indictment. For example, it might be stated: " You the said A. B. did ravish E. F., and you the said C. D. did aid and abet the said A. B. in committing said crime by (describe act)."

Again, it may be necessary to bring several persons, who are involved in the same crime, to trial on separate indictments. One of them, for example, may have absconded and may not be captured until the others have been sentenced. In such a case it is usual to indicate his association with his companions by some such words as these: " You did, acting along with C. D. and E. F., break into the house, etc." [8]

Instance

6-06   The indictment proceeds in the name of the Lord Advocate. If at the time it is served there is no Lord Advocate in office it may proceed in the name of the Solicitor-General.[9]

Charge

6-07   The actual charge or substance of the indictment is next set forth. The statute [10] gives the proper formulae to be used in regard to most of the commoner crimes. In point of form the charge consists usually of three elements, a statement of the time at which the crime was committed, a statement of the locus, and a statement of the modus. The substance of the libel is treated later.[11]

---

[6] 1887 Act, s. 6.
[7] Ibid., s. 7.
[8] See as an example H.M. Adv. v. Camerons (1911) 6 Adam 456. See also Gordon, 124–126.
[9] See supra, para. 4–03; Sol.-Gen. v. Lavelle (1913) 7 Adam 255; Law Officers Act 1944.
[10] Sched. A. to 1887 Act as amended by Sched. 12, 1949 Act.
[11] Infra, paras. 6–14 et seq.

It is often convenient to use an inventory or schedule where the accused is charged with committing a large number of *similar acts* at different times and places. When this is done, the charge is stated thus: " at the times and places specified in the inventory hereto subjoined "; or " at the times and places specified in the schedule hereto annexed."

When several crimes are charged, *differing in circumstances*, so that an inventory would not be convenient, it is usual to abbreviate the statement of time and place in all charges after the first; for example, " time and place above libelled," or " time above libelled at . . . . . ," or " on . . . . . at the place above libelled."

Signature of prosecutor

6–08   In the High Court the indictment is signed almost invariably by one of the advocates-depute; in the sheriff court the indictment concludes with the words, " By Authority of Her Majesty's Advocate," and is signed by the procurator fiscal.[12] The authority of Her Majesty's Advocate is conveyed to the procurator fiscal in the instruction for trial on indictment.

Citation of documents

6–09   It is unnecessary to set forth in the indictment the fact that the accused person emitted a declaration, or to set forth productions that are to be used against him. It is sufficient that these are entered in the list annexed to the indictment.[13] The labelled productions are referred to in the same manner.

Previous convictions

6–10   Section 39 (1) (*a*) of the 1949 Act prohibits the mention of previous convictions in the indictment and the inclusion of extracts of previous convictions in the list of productions annexed thereto. The section prescribes a procedure regarding previous convictions, which is described later.[14]

Indictments written or printed

6–11   Indictments may be either written or printed, or partly written and partly printed.[15] They are frequently typewritten.

Corrections

6–12   It is desirable to avoid alterations upon an indictment. If corrections have to be made, these are initialled before service by the person who signed the indictment, or who could by law have signed it. Corrections on the service copy are initialled by the person who serves it. After service, corrections cannot be made without the permission of the court, and are treated in the same way as amendments, to be afterwards explained.[16]

---

[12] 1887 Act, s. 2.
[13] Ibid., s. 19.
[14] Infra, paras. 6–32 et seq.
[15] 1887 Act, s. 21.
[16] Ibid.; 1908 Act, s. 30 and s. 77 (4); infra, para. 10–09.

Lists of productions and witnesses

6–13   There are annexed to the indictment lists of the documents and of the articles which are to be produced, and of the witnesses who are to be examined in support of the charge.[17] The list of witnesses contains the name and private address of each person, his occupation not being required, although there is no objection to its being inserted. Police witnesses are normally designed by their rank and force. It is not necessary to qualify the address by saying, " now or lately residing at." It is not an objection to the admissibility of a witness that he has ceased before the date of the trial to reside at the address given, provided he resided there not more than six months previous to the date of trial. It is unnecessary to insert the names of witnesses to the declaration. Witnesses to the declaration or to previous convictions may be examined in regard to these matters without previous notice. This necessity arises where the declaration is to be impugned at the trial under section 69 of the 1887 Act or convictions are to be challenged. As the prosecutor must receive notice of the intention of the accused to make such challenge, he has time to cite the witnesses whom he requires.

Relevancy

6–14   That part of the indictment which contains the ground of the charge against the accused is called the libel. The libel consists of three elements: it must set forth (1) the time, (2) the place of the crime, and (3) the particular facts inferring guilt. In order that an indictment may be relevant, it must meet the statutory requirements as to the specification of time and of place, and it must set forth facts sufficient to constitute a crime.

Specification of time

6–15   Prior to the passing of the 1887 Act the prosecutor had often to take a wide latitude in stating time. The latitude covered three months.[18] This latitude was taken by averring that the accused did a criminal act " on the twentieth day of January 1885, or on one or other of the days of that month, or of December immediately preceding, or of February immediately following." Except as after-mentioned, it is implied in modern practice, when a date is stated in a criminal charge, that it is stated in the above terms.[19] Where the crime is a continuous one extending over a considerable period, or where the prosecutor requires for some sufficient reason to take a wider latitude than three months, the time is expressed thus: " between 1st January 1885 and 30th April 1885, both dates inclusive."

     The principle which governs the allowance of an exceptional time latitude is stated as follows by Alison [20] in a passage which was quoted with approval by Lord Russell in *Ogg* v. *H.M. Advocate* [21]:—" In general,

17 1887 Act, s. 35; cf. 1921 Act, s. 1.
18 Hume, ii. 221; Alison, ii. 251.
19 1887 Act, s. 10.
20 Alison, ii. 256; see Hume, ii. 224; Macdonald, 218.
21 1938 J.C. 152, 154.

6–15 however, it is true of all those cases where an extraordinary latitude in point of time is allowed, that the law allows it unwillingly and from necessity only; and, therefore, that it will not sustain such a latitude where, by due diligence, a more accurate and specific detail could have been given, or where there is nothing appears, either from what is set forth on the face of the libel, or from the nature of the facts charged, to warrant such a departure from the ordinary rule."

There are many cases where an unusual latitude is permissible, e.g. where a series of thefts has been committed by a person in a position of trust [22]; or where, in the case of theft in like circumstances, the thief had an opportunity of taking possession without the fact of his having done so becoming known to the owners [23]; or where sheep are stolen on the hill and a considerable period elapses between the times of counting [24]; or where a long period has elapsed between the date of the crime and the date of trial so that witnesses cannot be expected to remember [25]; or in cases of reset or fraud,[26] especially where continuous acts are averred [27]; or in cases of fraudulent misrepresentation,[28] or of concealment of effects by a bankrupt [29]; or in cases of incest.[30]

An unusual latitude will be allowed in the case of a series of offences against young children.[31] In *H.M. Advocate* v. *A. E.*[32] the accused was charged with having committed incest with his two daughters (respectively aged 8 and 10 years when the offences began) on various occasions, none of which was specified, during periods amounting to two years five months in the one case and two years six months in the other. Lord Justice-Clerk Aitchison allowed the latitudes taken because of the ages of the children at the time when the crimes began and because what the Crown proposed to prove was a course of criminal conduct extending over years and not merely isolated instances of such conduct.

The circumstances which warrant the unusual latitudes may appear ex facie of the indictment, but the prosecutor is not bound to set them forth there.[33] It would appear to be the better practice to do so, at any rate in extreme cases. At the trial the prosecutor must lead evidence to show that the latitude was not unfairly taken.[34] A heavy onus rests on the Crown in such a case, and the presiding judge may require to direct the jury that they must be satisfied that no prejudice has been caused to the accused by

[22] Macdonald, 218.
[23] *H.M. Adv.* v. *Mackenzies* (1913) 7 Adam 189, L.J.-C. at 193.
[24] Macdonald, 218; *Andrew Hempseed* (1832) Bell's Notes 215; *Geo. Douglas* (1865) 5 Irv. 53.
[25] Macdonald, 218; Hume, ii. 223–224; Alison, ii. 257; *Jas. Stewart* (1875) 3 Couper 147.
[26] Macdonald, 218.
[27] *H.M. Adv.* v. *McDonald* (1888) 1 White 593, Lord Trayner at 595; but see *Maguire* v. *H.M. Adv.* (1908) 5 Adam 539.
[28] Macdonald, 218; *Jas. Hill* (1879) 4 Couper 295.
[29] Macdonald, 218; *Wm. Thiele* (1884) 5 Couper 443.
[30] Macdonald, 218; Hume, ii. 222–223; *H.M. Adv.* v. *A.E.*, 1937 J.C. 96.
[31] Macdonald, 218; *H.M. Adv.* v. *A.E.*, supra; *Ogg* v. *H.M. Adv.*, 1938 J.C. 152.
[32] Supra.
[33] 1887 Act, s. 10.
[34] *H.M. Adv.* v. *Mackenzies* (1913) 7 Adam 189.

6-15 the latitude.[35] In *H.M. Advocate* v. *Mackenzies* [36] a person was accused of stealing between July 3, 1907, and April 2, 1913, a book of recipes of chemical secrets belonging to his employers and with making during the same period copies of the recipes with intent to dispose of them for profit. As the Crown proposed to frame a fresh indictment the court did not require to decide whether or not the latitude taken was excessive. Lord Justice-Clerk Macdonald, however, observed:

> " I should myself have expected that a prosecutor proposing to take such a latitude would have set forth facts to indicate his difficulty in being more precise, as, for example, that the accused was in the employment of the owners of the book during the period given, and thus had opportunities of taking possession of it without his having done so becoming known to the owners. And certainly if the case were allowed to go to trial, the prosecutor would have to show by his evidence that the latitude taken was not unfairly taken; and if he failed to do so, his failure might lead to his not being able to obtain a verdict."

If the prosecutor takes a latitude unreasonably, the court may, at the trial, give a remedy to the accused by adjournment of the trial or otherwise, as may seem just.[37]

The statutory provision as to implied latitude applies only to the ordinary case where no difficulty or ambiguity can arise. Suppose an indictment bear that the crime was committed on October 15, the implied latitude covers September, October and November. But where a prosecutor libels two dates, as, for example, when a crime is said to have been committed between October 15 and November 15, the question immediately arises how is the three months' latitude to be calculated. Is it the whole months of October and November with the addition of September or of December or of both these months, or is it a period of three months calculated from the middle of the express period? It was decided in *Creighton* v. *H.M. Advocate* [38] that where a prosecutor libels two dates as the limits within which the crime was committed, he cannot take advantage of the implied latitude allowed by the statute, Lord Stormonth Darling pointing out that it was a misuse of section 10 of the 1887 Act to trust to the implied latitude in any case where to do so might create an ambiguity. The proper course in such a case was to express the latitude which it was desired to take. Where it is alleged that an act has been done on a number of occasions without the particular occasions being specified, it is implied that they are unknown.[39]

The court will be less willing to allow a wide latitude of time where only

---

[35] *H.M. Adv.* v. *A.E.*, supra.
[36] Supra.
[37] 1887 Act, s. 10.
[38] (1904) 4 Adam 356. See also Macdonald, 217.
[39] *Maguire* v. *H.M. Adv.* (1908) 5 Adam 539, L.J.-C. at 544, criticising *H.M. Adv.* v. *Macdonald* (1888) 1 White 593.

one incident is alleged to have occurred within the time than when what is alleged is a course of conduct.[40]

According to Alison,[41] if the accused, " resort to the plea of *alibi*, or make out that time is material for his defence, the prosecutor will be compelled to fix the time more nearly; and if he cannot do so, owing to the lapse of time [between the crime and the charge], that is a disadvantage inherent in his situation, which cannot relieve him from the necessity of obviating the prisoner's defence," or, as Hume [42] puts it, it is a disadvantage " from which he cannot, without injustice to the pannel, be relieved."

Where the exact time is of the *essence of the charge*, the date must be specifically stated, and the statutory implication does not apply. Thus, where it is an essential part of a crime that it was committed upon a certain day of the week (Sunday, for example), or at a certain time of day (as in night poaching), or at a certain period of the year (as in many game and fishery prosecutions), it is necessary to state the exact time.[43]

Specification of place

6-16   As regards place, it has to be kept in view that, as the locus delicti in the ordinary case fixes the jurisdiction of the court, the specification of locus is essential.[44] Such qualifications as " at or near " or " in or near " a particular place, " or in the near neighbourhood thereof " are implied.[45] Prosecutors should adhere to the simple forms authorised by the statute wherever possible and should avoid phrases such as " elsewhere to the prosecutor unknown," unless the circumstances render them necessary.[46]

It is usual, where the spot is outside a burgh, to mention the parish in which it is situated. Where a case is in the sheriff court, it is proper to mention the county, as by doing so it is made manifest that the locus delicti is within the jurisdiction of the court. Where the locus is within a burgh, it is sufficient to mention the street and the burgh, without further specification.[47] If there happen to be two places of the same name in a parish, or two streets of the same name in a burgh, care must be taken to distinguish which is meant.

Great latitude will be allowed in stating the place, where the circumstances require this. In charges of embezzlement and theft, in which it is usually known where the accused person received or found the stolen property, but it is often not known where he appropriated it, and in similar cases, such as reset,[48] the prosecutor is allowed to state the locus delicti in very broad terms. He may even take a whole county.

[40] *R.L.* v. *H.M. Adv.*, 1969 J.C. 40; sub nom. *Littlejohn* v. *H.M. Adv.*, 1970 S.L.T. 21.
[41] Alison, ii. 257.
[42] Hume, ii. 224.
[43] 1887 Act, s. 10; *Drummond* v. *Latham* (1892) 3 White 166; *Macdonald* v. *Patterson* (1894) 1 Adam 366.
[44] Hume, ii. 209; *McMillan* v. *Grant*, 1924 J.C. 13.
[45] 1887 Act, s. 10.
[46] *Gold* v. *Neilson* (1907) 5 Adam 423.
[47] Alison, ii. 260.
[48] *Gold* v. *Neilson*, supra; *Mary Christie or McIntosh* (1831) Bell's Notes 213; *Susan McMillan or Wilkinson* (1835) Bell's Notes 213.

There are certain crimes and offences of which the essence consists in the act being done in a certain place. Under these circumstances the exact locus must be stated, and no latitude is implied.[49] Thus it was held [50] that a summary complaint of loitering " in a close " (without the prefixed adjective " common ") was not a relevant charge under sections 1 and 3 of the Street Betting Act 1906, which enacted: Section 1 (1) : "Any person frequenting or loitering in streets " for betting purposes shall be liable to certain penalties. . . . (4) . . . " ' street ' shall include . . . any public . . . passage. . . ." Section 3: " In Scotland, ' passage ' includes common close. . . ." On the other hand, where a Police Act enacted that every known or reputed thief who was found in any street with intent to commit any crime might be apprehended, and an accused person who was apprehended on a tramway car maintained that he was not thereby on a street, his contention was rejected.[51]

Section 10 of the 1887 Act makes a provision regarding latitude as to place similar to that regarding latitude as to time, viz.: that it is not necessary to set forth in the indictment circumstances which make it necessary to take an exceptional latitude or to state that the particular place is to the prosecutor unknown. In this case also the court, if satisfied that such exceptional latitude is not reasonable, will give such remedy to the person accused by adjournment of the trial or otherwise as seems just.[52]

Where an offence has been committed on or near the boundaries of two jurisdictions, or where the same person has committed several offences in different counties, it is necessary to keep in mind the extensive powers conferred by section 10 of the 1908 Act which apply to procedure by indictment.[53]

The prosecutor in libelling the locus must give the accused person a sufficiently precise definition of it to enable him to prepare his defence. The test of sufficient specification is really fairness and adequate notice of the precise offence charged. These requisites are well illustrated by two cases in which the charge was exceeding the speed limit over a certain distance.[54]

Specification of mode

6-17   This is the operative and crucial part of the indictment. Here the prosecutor must set forth the facts and circumstances of the crime charged. The facts and circumstances so set forth must be such as to constitute a crime known to the law. If such specification be lacking, the indictment is irrelevant. So, an indictment charging an accused with performing an operation on a woman in the belief that she was pregnant, for the pur-

[49] 1887 Act, s. 10.
[50] *Winning* v. *Jeans* (1909) 6 Adam 1.
[51] *Martin* v. *McIntyre* (1910) 6 Adam 252.
[52] 1887 Act, s. 10. See *H.M. Adv.* v. *Mackenzies* (1913) 7 Adam 189; see also supra, para. 6–15.
[53] Supra, para. 1–26. Similar provisions are made for complaints by s. 6 of the 1954 Act.
[54] *Christie* v. *Stevenson* (1907) 5 Adam 382; *Connell* v. *Mitchell* (1909) 5 Adam 641.

pose of causing her to abort, and with attempting to cause her to abort was held irrelevant, in respect that it did not set forth that the woman was at the time pregnant.[55] In another case it was held that an indictment charging the accused with ravishing a woman " while she was in a state of insensibility or unconsciousness from the effects of intoxicating liquor " did not set forth a relevant charge of rape, there being no allegation that the accused had supplied the liquor.[56] In *H.M. Advocate* v. *Smith*, Lord Justice-Clerk Aitchison held that an indictment charging the accused with perjury committed while giving evidence which, although not objected to, was, as the indictment showed, incompetent and should not have been admitted, was an irrelevant indictment.[57]

The prosecutor should adhere as far as possible to the forms given in the 1887 Act, as amended by Schedule 12 to the 1949 Act, which cover practically all the ordinary crimes. The intention of the 1887 Act is that specification is to be avoided as far as possible,[58] and the forms can be adapted to meet most circumstances. Deviation from these may give rise to difficulties, as in *Campbell* v. *McLennan*,[59] where, instead of following the form provided in the Act, the prosecutor brought a charge of theft in the following terms: " Having on 14th November 1887, within the inn of Dunvegan, found in money one pound, you did deny having found the same and did appropriate and thus steal the same." The court held that the charge was irrelevant, Lord McLaren pointing out that everything set out might be true and yet the accused might not be guilty of theft. In a charge of fire raising with intent to defraud insurers it is sufficient to follow the statutory form and unnecessary to aver the making of a claim on the insurance company.[60]

The method of reform adopted by the framers of the 1887 Act was first of all to provide this simplified statutory form and then to go on to provide that all the various embellishments which had formerly appeared in the old indictment were either unnecessary or must be held as implied. The result is that much of the statute is negative rather than positive in effect. In order fully to understand the various improvements it is necessary to keep in mind the old form of indictment.[61] The chief simplifications of the old procedure are as follows:

Nomen juris

6-18   The prosecutor need not state specifically the nomen juris of the crime alleged. It is enough if the facts set forth in the libel are relevant and suffi-

---

[55] *H.M. Adv.* v. *Anderson*, 1928 J.C. 1.
[56] *H.M. Adv.* v. *Grainger and Rae*, 1932 J.C. 40; cf. Gordon, 7–8.
[57] *H.M. Adv.* v. *Smith*, 1934 J.C. 66. See, however, *Angus* v. *H.M. Adv.*, 1935 J.C. 1.
[58] *Bewglass* v. *Blair* (1888) 1 White 574, Lord Rutherfurd Clark at 577. Cf. *Coventry* v. *Douglas*, 1944 J.C. 13.
[59] (1888) 1 White 604. See also *Smith* v. *Sempill* (1910) 6 Adam 348.
[60] *H.M. Adv.* v. *Bell*, 1966 S.L.T.(Notes) 61.
[61] The old form of indictment does not require comment, as its severely logical form makes its scope immediately apparent. The modern form is really a short resume of the crucial facts, the various logical steps whereby these facts are brought within the ambit of the criminal law being implied.

cient to constitute what is recognised by the law of Scotland as an indictable crime.[62] There may be crimes which have no proper nomen juris at all.[63]

Qualifying words

6–19   It is unnecessary to charge an act as done, or omitted to be done, " wilfully," or " maliciously," or " wickedly and feloniously," or " falsely and fraudulently," or " knowingly," or " culpably and recklessly," or " negligently," or " in breach of duty "; or to use such phrases as " knowing the same to be forged," or " having good reason to know," or " well knowing the same to have been stolen." These and similar words and expressions are now implied in every case where their insertion is necessary to make the indictment relevant.[64] They are not to be inserted in a criminal charge unless there is a special reason. So, in a charge of fraud, it is unnecessary to use the words " falsely and fraudulently." On this ground a complaint which charged an advertising agent that he did " pretend " to a female shop assistant that her employer paid yearly for an advertisement in a directory, and " did thus induce " her to pay him 1s. 6d., and did thus defraud her of that amount, was held relevant.[65] It has been held that, in an indictment charging an accused with culpable homicide, it is unnecessary to characterise the acts set forth as having been done " culpably " or " recklessly," the statutory form setting out the facts and concluding " and did kill " being sufficient.[66] In practice, however, these words are inserted, especially where the offence arises from the driving of a vehicle by the accused.

Where a statute defines an offence with the aid of qualifying words it is unnecessary in libelling the offence to insert the statutory qualifying words, as these may be implied. Thus in *Stuart* v. *Clarkson*,[67] where a complaint under section 7 of the Conspiracy and Protection of Property Act 1875, which imposes a penalty on every person who does certain acts "wrongfully and without legal authority," omitted these words, it was held that they were implied under section 8 of the 1887 Act.

6–20   Qualifying words are still required in certain cases.

In charges of fire raising it is necessary to add, " and this you did wilfully," or " and this you did culpably and recklessly," because there

---

[62] 1887 Act, s. 5. *Bewglass* v. *Blair*, supra; *Strathern* v. *Seaforth*, 1926 J.C. 100; *Coventry* v. *Douglas*, 1944 J.C. 13; *Cameron and Ors.* v. *H.M. Adv.*, 1971 S.L.T. 333; but cf. *H.M. Adv.* v. *Grainger and Rae*, 1932 J.C. 40. The old form of indictment was a syllogism in which the major proposition stated that a certain nomen juris was " a crime of a heinous nature and severely punishable." In the minor proposition it was stated that the accused person had committed certain acts which amounted to the crime specified in the major proposition, and that he was therefore liable to suffer the pains of law. See Gordon, 6–8.

[63] As illustrations of unusual crimes, see e.g. *Kerr* v. *Hill*, 1936 J.C. 71; *Gray* v. *Morrison*, 1954 J.C. 31; *Strathern* v. *Seaforth*, supra.

[64] 1887 Act, s. 8. In the old form of indictment it was necessary to set forth every circumstance qualifying the act done by the accused, which it was intended to establish by proof.

[65] *Gallagher* v. *Paton* (1909) 6 Adam 62; see also *H.M. Adv.* v. *Swan* (1888) 2 White 137.

[66] *H.M. Adv.* v. *Parker and Barrie* (1888) 2 White 79.

[67] (1894) 1 Adam 466; cf. *Taylor* v. *H.M. Adv.* (1897) 2 Adam 296.

are two distinct crimes which fall under the general name of fire raising.[68] In like manner, in such charges as malicious mischief, where it is possible that the accused may have had no criminal intent, it is often expedient to say, " you did maliciously and mischievously " do the act charged. There may be other cases where by implying one set of qualifying words one crime would be charged, while if another set were implied, another and a different crime would be charged.[69]

Exceptions, etc.

6–21   By section 34 of the 1949 Act the provisions of section 19 (3) of the 1908 Act are included among the sections which section 77 (4) of that statute makes applicable to procedure on indictment. These provisions are fully discussed in paragraphs 13–50 and 13–51 infra.

As applied to procedure on indictment section 19 (3) is in the following terms—

"Any exception, exemption, proviso, excuse, or qualification, whether it does or does not accompany in the same section the description of the offence in the statute or order creating the offence, may be proved by the accused, but need not be specified or negatived in the indictment, and no proof in relation to such exception, exemption, proviso, excuse, or qualification shall be required on behalf of the prosecution."

Special capacity

6–22   By section 34 of the 1949 Act the provisions of section 19 (5) of the 1908 Act are included among the sections which section 77 (4) of that statute makes applicable to procedure on indictment. These provisions are fully considered in paragraphs 13–52 to 13–54 infra.

As applied to procedure on indictment section 19 (5) is in the following terms—

" Where an offence is alleged to be committed in any special capacity, as by the holder of a licence, master of a vessel, occupier of a house, or the like, the fact that an accused person possesses the qualification necessary to the commission of the offence shall, unless challenged by preliminary objection before his plea is recorded, be held as admitted."

Statutory offences

6–23   Where a contravention of a statute is alleged it is sufficient to aver that the crime was committed contrary to the Act and to refer to the Act and any section founded on without setting forth the enactment in words at length.[70] But it is necessary to specify all such facts and circumstances as form an essential part of the statutory offence; it is not enough to aver only

[68] Macdonald, 81; *H.M. Adv.* v. *Swan*, supra, L.J.-C. and Lord Adam. Cf. *Angus* v. *H.M. Adv.* (1905) 4 Adam 640.
[69] *H.M. Adv.* v. *Swan*, supra.
[70] 1887 Act, s. 9.

some facts or circumstances and leave the rest to be inferred from a knowledge of the contents of the statutory provision referred to.[71] In a charge of
unlawful sexual intercourse with a defective it may be necessary to aver
that the accused knew of the woman's condition.[72] In modern practice the
Act of Parliament alleged to have been contravened is referred to by its
short title, and the particular section of it which creates the offence is
particularly specified: thus, " Contrary to the Night Poaching Act 1828,
section 1." [73]

Descriptions

6–24 Prior to the 1887 Act it was necessary for the prosecutor to insert
qualifying words to cover any possible difficulty that might emerge at the
trial. Thus, all weights and measures were qualified by the words " or
thereby," and no quantity, person, thing, or mode was mentioned without
stating as an alternative some other quantity, person, thing, or mode " to
the prosecutor unknown." In modern practice, the prosecutor states the
exact fact which he intends to prove, and the latitude to which we have
referred is implied by the statute.[74] But the latitude allowed by the
statute does not apply to cases where precision is of the essence of the
charge. So, where an act is a criminal offence only because of the fact
that the person injured is below the age of puberty, the prosecutor should
set forth distinctly the age of the person, and the mere addition of figures
in brackets after the person's name is insufficient.[75]

6–25 In the case of a crime which infers interference with anything—buildings, goods, money or other subject—which is not the property of the
accused, it is unnecessary to state specifically the person to whom such
property belongs.[76] An allegation is implied that such subjects are not the
property of the accused, in all cases where such implication is essential to
the criminality of the charge.[77] Accordingly, in *H.M. Advocate* v.
McLeod [78] a charge in the following terms was sustained as relevant:
" You did . . . break down and remove from its place a quantity of wire-
fencing, part of the boundary fence of the farm of Aignish, Stornoway ";
an objection that the facts did not set forth an indictable offence, as the
fence in question might belong to the accused or he might be acting for the
owner, was repelled.

6–26 To meet the contingency of a person mentioned in the indictment or
in the list of witnesses, etc., having changed his residence, it was necessary
prior to the 1887 Act to qualify all addresses by stating that the person
" now or lately " resided there. It is now sufficient to describe any person
by his name and ordinary address, the alternative being implied.[79]

---

[71] *Tweedle* v. *H.M. Adv.* (1967) 31 J.C.L. 261.
[72] Mental Health (Scotland) Act 1960, s. 96 (1), (2); cf. *H.M. Adv.* v. *Mack*, 1959 S.L.T. 288.
[73] 1887 Act, s. 9.
[74] 1887 Act, s. 11.
[75] *Lockwood* v. *Walker* (1909) 6 Adam 124.
[76] *H.M. Adv.* v. *McLeod* (1888) 2 White 9.
[77] 1887 Act, s. 12.
[78] Supra.   [79] 1887 Act, s. 13.

In the ordinary case it is also sufficient to describe any article in general terms without specifying material; for example, it is proper to say " a watch," not " a gold watch," or " a shawl," not " a silk shawl." But where the crime consists in an act relating to an article of a particular kind, it is still necessary to state that the article was of the nature constituting the crime, e.g., counterfeiting " gold coin " or " silver coin." [80]

It was formerly necessary, in mentioning a sum of money, to specify whether it consisted of gold, notes, silver, copper, Post Office orders, or the like. It is now sufficient to say, e.g. " five pounds fifteen pence of money," without further specification.[81]

When a document is referred to it is sufficient to use a general description, and, if the document is one of the productions, to specify its number in the list.[82]

6-27   In framing an indictment on charges inferring dishonest appropriation of property some special considerations have to be kept in mind. Criminal resetting of property is not limited to the receiving of property taken by theft or robbery.[83] It extends to the receiving of property appropriated by breach of trust and embezzlement, and by falsehood, fraud, and wilful imposition. In an indictment charging the resetting of property dishonestly appropriated by any of these means, it is not necessary to set forth any details of the crime by which the dishonest appropriation was accomplished; but it is sufficient to set forth that the person accused received such property, it having been dishonestly appropriated by theft, or robbery, or breach of trust and embezzlement, or falsehood, fraud and wilful imposition, as the case may be.[84] It must also be kept in mind that it is often difficult to draw an indictment of reset which can be specific and detailed. For instance, in the case of workmen employed in a granary stealing grain and selling it to dealers, it is impossible to specify the particular parcels of grain taken and the exact time at which they were taken. Accordingly when a panel who had been convicted of reset of theft libelled thus: " during the period between 1st July 1907 and 3rd March 1908, in ... on different occasions during said period, the particular occasions being to the prosecutor unknown, you did reset in all 25 lbs. of brass and copper electric and gas fittings and 25 lbs. of solder, the same having been dishonestly appropriated by theft " sought to have the conviction suspended, the court refused to do so,[85] Lord Justice-Clerk Macdonald pointing out that, under the 1887 Act, the prosecutor did not require to aver that the particular articles were to him unknown. He added that he was unable to understand the reasoning of Lord Trayner in *H.M. Advocate* v. *McDonald*,[86] and observed: " Where it is alleged that an

[80] 1887 Act, s. 13.
[81] Ibid., s. 14.
[82] Ibid., s. 15. See *H.M. Adv.* v. *Parker and Barrie* (1888) 2 White 79.
[83] 1887 Act, s. 58.
[84] Ibid. Cf. Gordon, 635–636.
[85] *Maguire* v. *H.M. Adv.* (1908) 5 Adam 539.
[86] (1888) 1 White 593.

act has been done on a number of occasions, without the particular occasions being specified, it is implied that the particular occasions are unknown." [87]

Previous malice

6–28   If the Crown seek to prove previous malice and ill-will towards the victim they must aver that the accused " did previously evince malice and ill-will," [88] unless the malice was evinced only shortly before the incident which forms the subject of the charge. [89]

Previous failure to appear

6–29   If the Crown seek to found on the accused's failure to appear at an earlier diet of trial they should give notice of this in the indictment. This is normally done by an averment that " you being conscious of your guilt did abscond and flee from justice and fail to appear for trial at. . . ." [90]

Alternative charges

6–30   It is also necessary to consider the powers of the jury, which enable them to bring in a verdict convicting the accused of a crime different from that charged in the indictment. [91] This obviates the necessity of inserting in the indictment a number of alternative charges, as was customary in the old practice.

Previous Convictions

6–31   The use of previous convictions as aggravations of a current offence was abolished by section 30 (1) of the 1963 Act. This provision does not, however, prevent the court taking previous convictions into account in considering sentence; section 30 (2) enables the whole of an accused's record to be put before the court instead of, as formerly, only previous convictions for offences cognate with the current offence. It is still open to the procurator fiscal to libel only those parts of an accused's record which he regards as relevant, but he may competently libel his whole record, including previous convictions which led to sentences of probation or absolute discharge. [92] And it is still open to the local authority officer charged with the duty of preparing a social inquiry report to include in his report previous convictions which were not libelled by the procurator fiscal. [93]

It is incompetent to libel a previous conviction which is at the moment under appeal. [94]

[87] 5 Adam 544.
[88] *H.M. Adv.* v. *Flanders*, 1962 J.C. 25.
[89] Cf. *H.M. Adv.* v. *Kennedy* (1907) 5 Adam 347.
[90] *H.M. Adv.* v. *Mulholland*, 1968 S.L.T. 18.
[91] Infra, para. 10–42.
[92] 1949 Act, s. 9.
[93] *Sharp* v. *Stevenson*, 1948 S.L.T.(Notes) 79.
[94] *McCall* v. *Mitchell* (1911) 6 Adam 303.

A previous conviction cannot competently be libelled unless it is legal on the face of it [95] and unless it is of date prior to that of the offence under trial.[96] It must be clear from the notice of previous convictions that the previous conviction libelled applies to the accused.[97] So, in a summary case prior to the 1949 Act, it was held that it was not competent, in a proceeding against the representative of a company as an individual, to libel a previous conviction obtained against the company in its corporate capacity.[98] A previous conviction which has not been included in the notice of previous convictions cannot be taken into account,[99] save that the court may take account of the accused's record as revealed by any social inquiry or other lawful reports in fixing sentence within the maximum permitted having regard to the previous convictions included in the notice.[1]

The former practice of libelling previous convictions on the indictment has been abolished by the 1949 Act, section 39 (1) (a) of which provides: " No mention shall be made in the indictment of previous convictions, nor shall extracts of previous convictions be included in the list of productions annexed to the indictment."

Procedure

6–32   The following procedure is laid down by section 39 of the 1949 Act as amended by the 1963 Act:

If the prosecutor desires to place before the court any previous conviction, he must cause to be served on the accused with the indictment a notice in the form as nearly as may be of Form 1 of Schedule 7. That notice includes a schedule which sets forth particulars of all such previous convictions. Any conviction set forth in that notice is held to apply to the accused unless challenged by him in accordance with the rules set forth in the following paragraph.[2]

6–33   A previous conviction included in the notice of previous convictions may be objected to by the accused on the ground that it does not apply to him or is otherwise inadmissible, provided that written intimation stating the ground of objection is given by him in accordance with the following rules:

    (a) Where the accused pleads not guilty at the first diet this intimation must be given at least five clear days before the second diet:

        (i) In High Court cases to the Crown Agent.

        (ii) In sheriff court cases to the procurator fiscal of the district of the court where the second diet is to be held.[3]

---

[95] *Grant* v. *Allan* (1889) 2 White 261; *Russo* v. *Robertson*, 1951 S.L.T. 408.
[96] *Jess Mitchell or Carr* (1837) Bell's Notes 32; *John Graham* (1842) 1 Broun 445.
[97] *H.M. Adv.* v. *Shedden* (1898) 2 Adam 476; 1887 Act, s. 19.
[98] *Campbell* v. *Macpherson* (1910) 6 Adam 394.
[99] *Adair* v. *Hill*, 1943 J.C. 9.
[1] *Sharp* v. *Stevenson*, supra.
[2] s. 39 (1) (b) and Sched. 7.
[3] s. 39 (1) (c).

(b) When the accused pleads guilty at the first diet no objections to any such conviction can be entertained unless he has given this intimation at least two clear days before that diet to the procurator fiscal of the district of the court to which the accused is cited for that diet.[4]

Under section 31 of 1887 Act

6–34   Where notice is given by the accused under this section of his intention to plead guilty and the prosecutor desires to place before the court any previous conviction, he must cause the foregoing notice of previous convictions to be served on the accused with the indictment. Any conviction set forth in the notice will be held to apply to the accused unless within two days after service of the notice he gives to the procurator fiscal written intimation objecting to such conviction on the ground that it does not apply to him or is otherwise inadmissible.[5]

Laying before court

6–35   Previous convictions must not be laid before the presiding judge until the prosecutor moves for sentence. In that event the prosecutor must lay before the judge a copy of the notice of previous convictions served on the accused under section 39 (1) (b) or section 39 (1) (d), as the case may be.[6]

Proving previous convictions when challenged

6–36   Such previous convictions are proved in accordance with the provisions of section 66 of the 1887 Act, as amended by Schedule 12 to the 1949 Act [7] or the provisions of section 31 of the 1963 Act. This matter is dealt with in paragraphs 10–46 and 10–47 infra.

Amendment of notice

6–37   When the accused has been convicted, it is competent for the court to amend the notice of previous convictions by deletion or alteration to cure any error or defect in it, provided that the amendment does not prejudice the accused.[8]

Entry in record

6–38   Any conviction which is admitted in evidence by the court as contained in a notice served on the accused under section 39 (1), as above described, must be entered in the record of the trial.[9]

[4] s. 39 (1) (c).
[5] s. 39 (1) (d).
[6] s. 39 (1) (e).
[7] s. 39 (1) (f).
[8] s. 39 (1) (ee)—see 1963 Act.
[9] s. 39 (2).

Previous convictions as relevant evidence

6–39   The foregoing provisions do not prevent evidence of previous convictions being led in any case where such evidence is competent in support of a substantive charge.[10]

Irish convictions

6–40   A previous conviction obtained in the Republic of Ireland cannot be libelled.[11]

[10] s. 39 (3); 1887 Act, s. 67; Prevention of Crimes Act 1871, s. 19; *H.M. Adv.* v. *McIlwain*, 1965 J.C. 40.
[11] *Mawhinney* v. *H.M. Adv.*, 1950 J.C. 44.

CHAPTER 7

PROCEDURE PRIOR TO TRIAL

7–01 AFTER the indictment has been prepared and signed, many important steps have to be taken before the trial. Some of these matters arise at an earlier, and some at a later, stage but it will be convenient to consider them in this chapter. In the first place, by service of the indictment, the accused person has to be informed of the charge made against him, and of the nature of the evidence by means of which it is to be supported. The prosecutor has further to see to the lodging of all documents and productions which are to be used at the trial. The agent of the accused has to give notice of any special defence which his client intends to plead. If the accused is not to plead guilty, witnesses for both parties, and a sufficient number of jurors, will have to be cited. Occasionally, valuable evidence is likely to be lost by the death of a witness, and a dying deposition must be taken. It is also necessary at this point to explain the provision made by the legislature to prevent undue delay in bringing accused persons to trial, and to consider the steps to be taken where a witness has been lodged in prison, or has absconded.

Fixing the Diets

First and second diets

7–02 With the exception of special cases falling under section 31 of the 1887 Act, two diets are fixed in all trials upon indictment. These are usually called the first or pleading diet, and the second or trial diet. The first die must not be less than six clear days after the service of the indictment; the second diet not less than nine clear days after the first diet.[1]

The second diet is always called in the court which has jurisdiction to try the accused. In High Court cases it is fixed for Edinburgh or a circuit town; in a sheriff court case it is fixed for the seat of the court which has jurisdiction to try the charge.

The first diet is normally in the sheriff court before which the accused appeared for judicial examination, but the Lord Advocate may direct the first diet to be held at another sheriff court, either in respect of a class of cases or in respect of a particular case. There is no longer any rule requiring the first diet to be held in the sheriff court nearest the prison where the accused is confined.[2]

---

[1] 1887 Act, s. 25.
[2] 1887 Act, s. 26, as substituted by 1963 Act, s. 35.

Citation

Warrant of citation

7–03   When a sitting of the sheriff court, or of the High Court of Justiciary
has been appointed to be held for the trial of persons accused on indictment, the sheriff clerk of the district in which the second diet is to be called,
or the Clerk of Justiciary, according as the trials are to take place in the
sheriff court or High Court, issues a warrant for citation in the form of
Schedule B annexed to the 1887 Act.[3] This warrant authorises officers of
law to cite persons accused, witnesses and jurors. The respective forms of
citation and execution of citation are given in Schedules C, D, E, F and G.
Such warrant, authenticated by the signature of the clerk, or a duly certified
copy of it, is a sufficient warrant to all officers competent.[4]

One warrant suffices for all the trials which are to take place at the
same diet. Where, however, several persons are to be tried on one indictment in the High Court and the first diets are to be called in different
sheriff courts, a separate warrant is necessary for each first diet. A warrant
is not necessary where the accused person has given intimation through his
agent, in terms of section 31 of the 1887 Act, that he intends to plead guilty
and wishes to have his case disposed of at once. The warrant specifies the
date and hour fixed for the trial of the case, and also for the first or
pleading diet.

Service

7–04   Service of the indictment and lists, and of notices or intimations to
persons accused, and citation of witnesses, whether for precognition or
trial, may be made or given by any macer, messenger-at-arms, sheriff
officer, or officer of police.[5] Where the accused is in prison at the time of
service on him, service is made by the governor, deputy-governor, or an
officer of such prison.[6] But where a person who has been released on bail
is subsequently detained in prison on a different charge it is competent to
serve the indictment for the original charge at the domicile of citation given
in the bail bond.[7]

The officer must be duly vested in his office, but it is not necessary for
him to have the warrant of citation in his possession at the time of service.[8]
Where a panel objected that he was not competently before the court,
because the officer who had cited him had never had in his possession or
seen the warrants to cite, it was held that as he had suffered no prejudice
the trial could go on.[9] Failure to serve an indictment is fatal to any
subsequent proceeding and is not cured by the accused's appearance at the
trial.[10]

[3] 1887 Act, s. 23.
[4] Ibid.
[5] Ibid., s. 24.
[6] Ibid.
[7] *Bryson* v. *H.M. Adv.*, 1961 J.C. 57.
[8] Circuit Courts (Scotland) Act 1828, s. 7; Alison, ii. 327.
[9] *H.M. Adv.* v. *Bryson* (1910) 6 Adam 203. See 1887 Act, s. 33.
[10] Cf. *Hester* v. *MacDonald*, 1961 S.C. 370.

A full copy of the indictment and lists is delivered to each accused person, having attached to it a citation in the statutory form furnished in Schedules F and G.[11] The citation is signed by the officer and one witness, except in cases under section 31, where no witness is required. The signature of the prosecutor on the principal indictment must be noted on the copy at the end of the indictment, and of each list. The notice of previous convictions (if any) is served on the accused at the same time (1949 Act, s. 39 (1) (b) and Sched. 7, Form No. 1). The prosecutor may at the trial examine witnesses whose names are not included in the lists lodged by him provided that he obtains leave to do so and provided that written notice containing the names and addresses of the witnesses has been given to the accused not less than two clear days before the jury is sworn to try the case.[12]

7–05 It is desirable that the indictment should be served either upon the accused *personally*, or by leaving it at some place which he has accepted as his domicile of citation. There is seldom any difficulty on these points. If the accused is in prison, he is of course served personally [13]; if he is on bail, his bail bond specifies a place where service is to be made. In the rare cases where he is neither in prison nor on bail, service should be made personally, if he can be found; and if he cannot be found, the copy should be left at his dwelling-house in the hands of a member of the family or a domestic servant.[14] If access to his house cannot be got, the copy is fastened to the most patent door.[15]

Service on bodies corporate

7–06 The procedure as regards service on a body corporate is regulated by section 40 (1) of the 1949 Act, which is in the following terms [15a]—

" In any proceedings on indictment against a body corporate the indictment may be served by delivery of a copy of the indictment with notice to appear attached thereto at the registered office, or, if there is no registered office or the registered office is not in the United Kingdom, at the principal place of business in the United Kingdom of the body corporate.

Where a registered letter containing a copy of the indictment has been sent by post to the registered office or principal place of business of the body corporate, an acknowledgment or certificate of the delivery of the letter issued by the [Post Office] in pursuance of regulations under the [Post Office Acts] shall be sufficient evidence of the delivery of the letter at the registered office or place of business on the day specified in such acknowledgment or certificate."

7–07 Service may also be effected by recorded delivery.[16]

---

[11] 1887 Act, s. 25.   [12] 1921 Act, s. 1.
[13] But see *Bryson* v. *H.M. Adv.*, supra.
[14] Hume, ii. 252; Alison, ii. 329; Citation Act 1555.
[15] Hume, ii. 254; Alison, ii. 332; Citation Act 1555.
[15a] See also Post Office Act 1969.
[16] Recorded Delivery Service Act 1962.

Corrections of errors

7-08   Before service, errors in the principal record and service copies of the indictment may be corrected by deletion or correction duly authenticated.[17] Once, however, the indictment has been lodged with the sheriff clerk of the court of the first diet, it can be amended only by leave of the court. Objections to the service copy must be stated at the first diet, and will not be afterwards entertained.[18]

Productions for Prosecution

7-09   The 1921 Act [19] has made it competent for the prosecutor to put in evidence at the trial productions not included in the lists lodged by him, provided he obtains the leave of the court to do so and has given written notice to the accused not less than two clear days before the day on which the jury is sworn to try the case. This provision, however, does not absolve the prosecution from carrying out the provisions of the 1887 Act with regard to lodging productions.

Record copy of indictment

7-10   The record copy of the indictment must be lodged with the sheriff clerk of the district in which the court of the first diet is situated, on or before the date of service of the indictment. At the same time a copy of the lists of witnesses and productions must be lodged with the sheriff clerk of the district in which the court of the second diet is situated.[20] In practice this is done by lodging a full copy of the indictment and lists.

Other productions

7-11   As regards the other productions, the accused is entitled to see them in the office of the sheriff clerk of the district in which the court of the second diet is situated, or, where that diet is to be in the High Court of Justiciary at Edinburgh, in the Justiciary Office.[21]

7-12   Productions for the prosecution should not be retained in the hands of the procurator fiscal. If, because of their nature, it is impossible to lodge them with the sheriff clerk, they should be lodged in the hands of some person who can hold them as his representative, and this arrangement must permit the accused to have as full and free access to the productions as if they were actually in the hands of the sheriff clerk.[22] It is the proper practice to produce any article referred to in an indictment or complaint where there is no practical difficulty in doing so.[23]

Documents may now be admitted and proof of them obviated by

---

[17] 1887 Act, s. 21.
[18] 1887 Act, s. 33.
[19] s. 1.
[20] 1887 Act, s. 27.
[21] 1887 Act, s. 37.
[22] *Stark & Smith* v. *H.M. Adv.*, 1938 J.C. 170, L.J.-G. at 173.
[23] *Maciver* v. *Mackenzie*, 1942 J.C. 51; *MacLeod* v. *Woodmuir Miners Welfare Society Social Club*, 1961 J.C. 5.

means of a minute of admission in any trial on indictment where the accused is legally represented.[24]

It is usual both in High Court and sheriff court cases to lodge all *documentary* productions for the prosecution, conform to the list annexed to the indictment, along with the record copy indictment. In a sheriff court case the *non-documentary* productions, often called the labelled productions, are, in practice, lodged in the hands of the sheriff clerk of the second diet either at the time of service of the indictment, or more frequently immediately after the first diet; but they may be lodged as late as the day before the second diet.[25] Where it is convenient to do so, it is better to lodge them after the accused pleads not guilty at the first diet.

As regards cases indicted for trial in the High Court of Justiciary, the 1887 Act makes no provision regarding the time for lodging productions, and this matter is accordingly regulated by the practice which existed when the Act was passed and which is expressed in the old form of indictment, viz.: that productions for the prosecution must be lodged " in due time " before the trial. " Due time " means " at such time, according to the circumstances of the case, as allows the panel sufficiently to examine and inspect " the productions.[26] In practice all productions, documentary and non-documentary, are lodged with the clerk of the court of the first diet *before the first diet*. If the agent for the defence makes a written request to the procurator fiscal that the non-documentary productions should be left for his inspection at some convenient court-house other than that of the first diet, they may be left at such place until shortly after the first diet.

Care must be taken when transmitting the non-documentary productions from place to place, that they are conveyed, if possible, by the same officer, in order that continuity of possession may be proved. As they are passed from one person to another, evidence should be preserved by means of written receipts, and if the same officer cannot act throughout, the various transmissions should be proved by witnesses who are named in the list in the indictment.

Where a production consists of a sealed packet, the accused may present a petition to the court craving that the packet may be opened. If he does not do so, he cannot object to the packet having been closed against his inspection.[27]

Effect of section 35 of 1949 Act

7-13   This section facilitates the proof of productions which have been lodged not less than eight days before the second diet, whether in High Court or sheriff court cases. It is considered later.[28]

[24] Criminal Procedure (Scotland) Act 1965.
[25] Act of Adjournal, March 17, 1827; *Craig* v. *Galt* (1881) 4 Couper 541.
[26] Hume, ii. 388–390; 1887 Act, s. 74.
[27] *Adam Lyall* (1811) Hume, ii. 388; Alison, ii. 594.
[28] Infra, para. 18–95.

Notices and Productions for Defence

Special defences

7-14   There are certain special defences which the person accused is not permitted to state unless a plea of special defence is tendered and recorded at the first diet. On cause shown to the satisfaction of the court, a special defence may be received at a later date, but in any case not less than *two clear days* before the second diet.[29]

There is no provision permitting special defences to be lodged at any time later than two clear days before the second diet but later lodging may be competent with the consent of the prosecution.[30] There was at one time a practice of allowing them to be lodged at the trial, the Crown usually offering no objection. Since the introduction of criminal legal aid, however, the statutory requirements have been more rigidly enforced, and defences have even been disallowed where no satisfactory explanation has been given for the delay.[31]

7-15   There is no authoritative list of special defences,[32] but it has been suggested that the accepted categories of special defences are not capable of extension.[33] As understood in modern law a special defence in order to be relevant must set forth facts which, if proved, would lead to acquittal.[34]

Macdonald enumerates the following special defences [35]:

(1) That at the time libelled the person accused was not at the place libelled, but at some other specified place (alibi) [36];

(2) That he was insane at the time when he committed the crime charged [37];

(3) That the crime was not committed by the person accused but by another person, named and designed (incrimination).[38] It is not necessary to give notice of a special defence where the person blamed is a co-accused, although such notice has been given on occasion.[39] Its main result is to make the judge's charge to the jury unnecessarily confusing.[40]

(4) That the crime was committed in self-defence.[41]

(5) That the accused was asleep at the time when he committed the crime charged.[42] But since *H.M. Adv.* v. *Cunningham* [43] it is doubtful whether this is still a proper special defence.

---

[29] 1887 Act, s. 36.
[30] Cf. *Lowson* v. *H.M. Adv.*, 1943 J.C. 141.
[31] *H.M. Adv.* v. *Young and Cater*, Glasgow High Court, Aug. 1966, unreported; see " Criminal Legal Aid," 1967 S.L.T.(News) 237.
[32] See Gerald H. Gordon, " The Burden of Proof on the Accused," 1968 S.L.T.(News) 29.
[33] *H.M. Adv.* v. *Cunningham*, 1963 J.C. 80.
[34] Ibid. In *Adam* v. *MacNeill*, 1971 S.L.T. (Notes) 80, Lord Walker said, " Generally, a special defence is one which puts in issue a fact (1) which is not referred to in the libel, and (2) which if established necessarily results in acquittal of the accused. "
[35] Macdonald, 265. Forms are given in App. C., infra.
[36] Infra, para. 18–02.   [37] Infra, para. 20–16.
[38] Infra, para. 18–02.
[39] e.g. *H.M. Adv.* v. *Peters & Ors.* (1969) 33 J.C.L. 209; cf. *Lee* v. *H.M. Adv.*, 1968 S.L.T. 155.
[40] cf. Gerald H. Gordon, op. cit.
[41] Infra, para. 18–02; for the form of such a defence, see *H.M. Adv.* v. *McGlone*, 1955 J.C. 14.
[42] *Simon Fraser* (1878) 4 Couper 70.   [43] Supra.

Intoxication is not a defence, but it may have the effect of reducing murder to culpable homicide.[44] Neither diminished responsibility nor provocation nor any other plea in mitigation is a special defence, and evidence may be led in the course of the trial of provocation, diminished responsibility, mental weakness, or any other mitigating circumstance, without prior notice.[45] Fairness might be thought to require the defence to give notice of any specific defence, particularly where it is of a medical or technical character, but the current view seems to be that notice should not be given except in the case of an accepted special defence.[46]

It was once thought that special defences were not necessarily limited to those defined. (In one case [47] where a driver of a motor-car was charged with culpable homicide, the following special defence was lodged on his behalf: " The panel pleads not guilty in respect that by the incidence of temporary mental dissociation due to toxic exhaustive factors he was unaware of the presence of the deceased on the highway and of his injuries and death, and was incapable of appreciating his immediately previous and subsequent actions.") But since *Cunningham* v. *H.M. Adv.*[48] this is probably no longer the case.

An objection by the prosecutor to the terms of a special defence is incompetent after a jury has been sworn and the defence read out.[49]

Attack on character of complainer

7–16　　If the person accused intends to attack the character of the person whom he is charged with injuring—if, for example, he is to prove immorality on the part of the woman in a charge of rape, or quarrelsome disposition on the part of the person assaulted—he must give notice of his intention to the prosecutor and to the court.[50] In one murder case notice was given of intention to attack the character of the deceased, but this seems to be unnecessary.[51]

Witnesses and productions for defence

7–17　　The person accused, if he wishes to examine any witnesses, or to put in evidence any productions not included in the lists annexed to the indictment, must give written notice of the names and designations of such witnesses, and of such productions, to the procurator fiscal of the district of the second diet, when the case is to be tried in the sheriff court, or to the Crown Agent where the case is to be tried in the High Court of Justiciary.[52] He must do this at least three clear days before the day on which the jury is sworn to try the case against him. If he is unable to give this

---

[44] See *Kennedy* v. *H.M. Adv.*, 1944 J.C. 171.
[45] *Clark* v. *H.M. Adv.*, 1968 J.C. 53; *H.M. Adv.* v. *Murray*, 1969 S.L.T.(Notes) 85.
[46] cf. Gerald H. Gordon, op. cit.; *H.M. Adv.* v. *Peters and Ors.*, supra.
[47] *H.M. Adv.* v. *Ritchie*, 1926 J.C. 45.
[48] Supra.
[49] *William Crumley* (1871) 2 Couper 27; cf. *H.M. Adv.* v. *Peters and Ors.*, supra.
[50] Infra, para. 18–76.
[51] *H.M. Adv.* v. *Peters and Ors.*, supra. See also *H.M. Adv.* v. *Kay*, 1970 S.L.T.(Notes) 66.
[52] 1887 Act, s. 36.

notice of three days, but can satisfy the court before a jury is sworn of his inability, the court may allow the witnesses to be examined, giving such remedy to the prosecutor, by adjournment or postponement of the trial, or otherwise, as shall seem just.[53] It is competent to take the evidence of witnesses whose names and designations have not been furnished in accordance with the section if the prosecutor takes no objection. The prosecutor, whether in the High Court or sheriff court, is entitled to waive his objection.[54]

The accused is entitled to make use of the witnesses and productions on the Crown list without notice.

A copy, for the use of the court, of every written notice required by section 36 is lodged by the accused with the sheriff clerk of the district of the second diet in a sheriff court case, and with the Clerk of Justiciary in a case before the High Court of Justiciary at Edinburgh. He must do this at or before the second diet.[55]

Recovery of documents

7-18   When documents which the accused requires for the preparation of his defence are in the possession of the Crown or third parties and are not available to him, he is entitled to petition the High Court of Justiciary to grant a commission and diligence for their recovery. As the undernoted cases [56] show, such applications have been repeatedly granted in High Court prosecutions, and in *Downie* [57]—the first reported case—the competency of presenting a petition to the High Court in a sheriff court case was not challenged. Whether in such a case an application can be made to the sheriff does not appear to have yet been decided.

In *Downie* the documents sought to be recovered (apart from an item which was disallowed) were certain books and a ledger in the possession of the Postmaster-General. No question of privilege arose regarding these, but the court continued the petition upon the footing that the petitioner should explain to the Crown authorities for what purpose and to what end these documents were required and that, having learnt this, the Crown authorities would then " be prepared to consider that application on its merits and to deal with it in the generous and fair spirit in which such matters have always been dealt with by the Crown Office." [58]

In *Hasson* v. *H.M. Adv.*[59] the accused was charged with embezzlement and fraud against a Grand Orange Lodge. He lodged a special defence of

---

[53] Ibid.
[54] *Lowson* v. *H.M. Adv.*, 1943 J.C. 141.
[55] 1887 Act, s. 36.
[56] Since 1887 applications have been granted in the following unreported cases: *A. J. Monson,* November 28, 1893; *Pattison,* June 18, 1901; *David Brown,* October 8, 1909 (prosecution under criminal letters; recovery allowed in Barcelona and Scotland); *John Brown Hay,* March 10, 1917; *David Chalmers Anderson,* April 23, 1923; *Alexander Bruce,* January 31, 1928; *Simon Shulman,* June 21, 1928; *Fred. A. Tomlinson and Others,* February 5, 1932. See also Hume, ii. 402, note 3.
[57] *Downie* v. *H.M. Adv.*, 1952 J.C. 37.
[58] Ibid., L.J.-G. Cooper at 40.
[59] 1971 S.L.T. 199.

incrimination in relation to some of the charges. Lord Cameron granted a commission and diligence to recover the minute books, books of accounts and bank statements of a District Lodge of the Order " in order that excerpts may be taken therefrom at the sight of the Commissioner, of all entries relating to or arising out of the matters set out in the indictment showing or tending to show that the money or part of it referred to in charges 3 and 4 was paid to or for the benefit of [the District Lodge] and in particular for paying certain tradesmen's accounts relating to the building or rebuilding of a hall." Commission and diligence was also granted to recover the books and bank statements of the individual named in the special defence "in order to show" that the sums referred to in the relevant charges were paid over to him. In his judgment Lord Cameron criticised a suggestion made in the third edition of this book that *Downie* laid down a general rule taking the decision as to the relevancy of a call in a specification out of the hands of the court and placing it in those of the Crown. His Lordship also criticized the opinion of the late learned editor of that edition: " That in general a statement by the accused's responsible adviser that the document in question is required for the conduct of the defence should be regarded as sufficient." [60] At least an indication in general terms of the relation of the call to the charge and the proposed defence was required.[61]

Objections to Crown witnesses

7–19   The accused must give notice of his intention to object to any misnomer or misdescription of any person named in the indictment, or of any witness in the list of witnesses. The objection must be stated before a jury has been sworn to try the case. If the accused intends to move on this ground for postponement of the trial, or for the exclusion of any witness, he must, at least four clear days before the second diet, give notice to the procurator fiscal of the district of the second diet, in a sheriff court case, or to the Crown Agent, in a High Court case, of his inability to discover who such person named in the indictment is, or to find such witness.[62] On receiving notice, the prosecutor must furnish him with such additional information as will enable him to ascertain who such person is, or to find such witness in time to precognosce him before the trial.[63]

Preparation of Jury List

7–20   The law relating to the constitution of a criminal jury is principally regulated by the Jurors (Scotland) Act 1825,[64] but the Juries Act 1949 has abolished the distinction between special and common jurors and also the right of a landed proprietor to trial by a landed jury. Women are qualified to serve, in virtue of the Sex Disqualification (Removal) Act 1919 and

[60] Renton and Brown's *Criminal Procedure* (3rd ed.), 77.
[61] 1971 S.L.T. at 201.
[62] 1887 Act, s. 53.
[63] Ibid.
[64] See Alison, ii. 376 et seq.

the Jurors (Enrolment of Women) (Scotland) Act 1920. Rules as to the summoning of jurors and the returning of lists of assize are laid down by two Acts of Adjournal,[65] which bring the then existing practice into line with these statutes.

Every person, who is not specially exempted, who is between the ages of twenty-one and sixty years, and who resides in any county in Scotland, is qualified to serve as a juror, provided that at the time of the trial on which he is required to serve, (a) he or she has, and is seised, in his or her own right, of lands or tenements of an estate of inheritance, or for his or her life, within the county or shire, city or place, from whence the jury is to come of the yearly value of £5 at least; or (b) is worth in goods, chattels, and personal estate the sum of £200 sterling at least.[66]

7-21   Many persons are exempted from service by the above-mentioned Act and subsequent statutes. The following are the principal classes[67]:

(1) Peers; (2) judges of the supreme courts and sheriffs[68]; (3) ministers of the Church of Scotland; (4) parochial schoolmasters; (5) advocates, solicitors and procurators in practice; (6) clerks and other officers of any court of justice; (7) jailers and keepers of houses of correction; (8) professors in any university; (9) physicians and surgeons in practice; (10) officers in the Army, Navy or Air Force[69] on full pay; (11) officers of Customs and Excise; (12) messengers-at-arms and other officers of the law[70]; (13) commissioners and other officers and employees of the Inland Revenue[71]; (14) police officers[72]; (15) lighthouse-keepers and their assistants[73]; (16) soldiers of the regular Army or Air Force[74]; (17) dentists, if registered, and if they desire exemption[75]; (18) officers and men of the territorial and army volunteer reserve, or auxiliary air force[76]; (19) factory inspectors[77]; (20) veterinary surgeons[78]; (21) midwives[79]; (22) airport police.[80]

7-22   The names and designations of all persons qualified to serve as jurors are entered in a book made up by the sheriff clerk of the county, and called " the General Jury Book." This volume is open to inspection and examina-

---

[65] Acts of Adjournal for giving effect to the provisions of the Sex Disqualification (Removal) Act 1919, etc., December 6, 1920, and February 2, 1921.

[66] Jurors (Scotland) Act 1825, s. 1.

[67] Authority for these exemptions is to be found in s. 2 of the Jurors (Scotland) Act 1825 unless otherwise stated.

[68] Jurors (Scotland) Act 1825, as amended by Local Government (Scotland) Act 1947.

[69] Air Force (Application of Enactments) (No. 2) Order 1918.

[70] 1825 Act, s. 2.

[71] Inland Revenue Regulation Act 1890, s. 8.

[72] 1825 Act, s. 2, on the basis that they are officers of law. Their specific exemption in the Police (Scotland) Act, 1857 was abolished by the Court of Session Act 1868 along with all other exemptions created subsequent to the 1925 Act.

[73] Juries (Lighthouse Keepers' Exemption) Act 1869.

[74] Army Act 1955, s. 183; Air Force Act 1955, s. 183.

[75] Dentists Act 1957, s. 32.

[76] Auxiliary Forces Act 1953, s. 39.

[77] Factories Act 1961, s. 145 (5).

[78] Veterinary Surgeons Act 1966, s. 24.

[79] Midwives (Scotland) Act 1951, s. 27.

[80] Airports Authority Act 1965, s. 10 (5).

tion by any person on payment of five pence,[81] and from it are selected the jurors to serve on a trial. The names are taken in rotation, and the date on which the juror has been returned to serve is marked on the jury book. Before the book has been completely gone through, the sheriff clerk has to prepare a new one.

Single sex juries

7-23   Section 1 (*b*) of the Sex Disqualification (Removal) Act 1919 provides that the judge before whom a case is or may be held, may, in his discretion, on an application made by the prosecution or the defence, or at his own instance, make an order that the jury shall be composed of men or women only. This means that in the first instance the clerk charged with preparation of the list of assize must include a sufficient number of both sexes to permit of the empanelling of a full jury of either sex.[82]

The procedure to be adopted when either the prosecutor or the person accused wishes a jury of one sex is laid down by the Act of Adjournal, February 2, 1921.[83] The application must be made at the first diet, immediately after the recording of a plea of not guilty, or, where no plea is taken because of preliminary objections held by the sheriff not to be frivolous, then immediately after such objections have been certified or otherwise disposed of by him.[84]

If the second diet is appointed to be held in the sheriff court, and the judge presiding at the first diet is a sheriff having jurisdiction to try the case, he may, if so advised, forthwith deal with the application in the manner in which, as indicated in the next paragraph, it is later provided in the Act of Adjournal that it may be dealt with by the judge of the court of the second diet, or he may at his own instance make an order as to the composition of the jury in accordance with these later provisions, in which case his decision is final; or he may reserve consideration of the question.[85]

In all cases in which an application is made but not dealt with by the presiding judge, the matter must, on the third lawful day after the date of the first diet,[86] be submitted to a High Court judge or, where the second diet is in a sheriff court, to a sheriff having jurisdiction to try the case.[87] The application is disposed of by the judge or the sheriff, as the case may be, summarily in court or in chambers. After such intimation to parties or hearing (if any) as seems just he pronounces an order granting or refusing the application, and his decision is final. If any of the parties (including any person accused in the same indictment as the applicant) gives notice either at the time of making the application or by letter received by

---

[81] 1825 Act, s. 3; Decimal Currency Act 1969, s. 10.
[82] Act of Adjournal, February 2, 1921, I (vi).
[83] Ibid., II–V.
[84] Ibid., II.
[85] Ibid., III.
[86] Where the record copy of the indictment fails to arrive within that time, telegraphic or telephonic communication from the clerk of the court of the first diet regarding the proceedings there will overcome the difficulty: Ibid., IV (ii) (iii).
[87] Ibid., IV.

the Clerk of Justiciary or the clerk of the court of the second diet, as the case may be, before the proceedings are reported to the judge who is to dispose of it, intimating that he desires to be heard in support of or against the application, the judge may not proceed to dispose of the application without giving to this party or his agent such intimation and opportunity of being heard by counsel or agent as the judge considers reasonable. An accused person, however, is not entitled to be personally present at the disposal of an application.[88]

The judge who presides over a trial, may at his discretion, make an order that the jury shall be composed of one sex at any stage prior to the empanelling of the jury, provided that no application has already been made in terms of the Act of Adjournal, as above described, and also provided that there are a sufficient number of men or women (as the case may be) on the assize list and present and available to form a jury of the composition contemplated.[89]

The Act of Adjournal provides [90] that in any case where the jury is to be of one sex, there shall be placed in the boxes or glasses used for containing the slips, the slips containing the names of all the jurors who have been summoned; but in balloting, persons whose names shall be drawn who are not of the required sex shall be passed over; but the jury shall be composed of the fifteen persons of the required sex whose names shall be first drawn and who shall not be successfully challenged. Where the jury is not to be composed of one sex only, the ballot is carried through in the usual fashion without distinguishing between men and women.[91]

Exemption of women

7-24   Any woman summoned to serve on a jury is entitled to apply to be exempted from service on account of pregnancy or other feminine condition or ailment.[92] The citation served on a woman summoned as a juror must have endorsed on it a notice in the form prescribed by the Act of Adjournal informing her of her right to exemption and the steps which she must take to obtain it.[93]

A woman cited to serve as a juror may competently apply to the judge at the trial for exemption because of the nature either of the evidence to be given or of the issues to be tried. The application must be made before the jury is empannelled, and the presiding judge may, at his discretion, grant or refuse it.[94]

Preparation of list of assize

7-25   A list of jurors containing not less than thirty names is prepared from the general jury book under the directions of the Clerk of Justiciary or the

---

[88] Ibid., IV (i).   [89] Ibid., V.
[90] Ibid., VII (i).
[91] Ibid., VII (ii).
[92] Ibid., VIII.
[93] Ibid., IX, and Schedule.
[94] 1919 Act, s. 1 (b); Act of Adjournal, February 2, 1921, X.

7-25 sheriff clerk of the district of the second diet, according as the case is one in the High Court or in the sheriff court. This list contains the names, occupations and addresses of the jurors. The number of jurors on the list varies with circumstances, and the matter is dealt with by the Act of Adjournal, February 2, 1921. The list must contain as nearly as may be an equal number of men and women.[95] The men and women returned must be grouped separately on the list, either by their names being placed in different columns or in some other convenient manner.[96] A husband and wife may not be returned in any case on the same list of assize.[97] The list itself is headed in this form: " List of Assize for the Sitting of the High Court of Justiciary (*or* the Sheriff Court of the Lothians and Peebles) at Edinburgh on the 11th of June, 1954." The list is signed by a High Court judge or by a sheriff of the jurisdiction, as the case may be. On and after the date of service of the indictment it is kept in the office of the sheriff clerk of the second diet. The accused is entitled to have a copy supplied to him on application, free of charge.[98]

It is not necessary to summon all the jurors contained in this list. It is competent to summon such jurors only, commencing from the top of the list of jurors, as may be necessary to ensure a sufficient number for the trial of the cases which remain for trial at the date of the citation of jurors. The number is fixed by the sheriff clerk of the district of the second diet, or by the Clerk of Justiciary, as the case may be. Where some of the jurors are not summoned, their names are placed upon the next list issued, until they have attended to serve.[99]

As already pointed out, the list must, in the first instance, contain a large number of names to meet the contingency of a jury of one sex being required. Once an order to that effect has been pronounced, and it appears that all the cases appointed for trial are to be tried by jurors of one and the same sex, the names of jurors of the other sex may be struck out, and they need not be cited.[1] On the other hand, if no application is made, the clerk of court may proceed to reduce the list by striking out an equal number of each sex, beginning from the bottom of the list for each district. Only the remainder need be cited. If, however, from the terms of any special defence lodged, it appears to the clerk of court that the question of having a jury of one sex may arise, he must take the instructions of a judge competent to try the case before reducing the list.[2]

It sometimes happens, in consequence of death, illness, old age, or other causes, that a number of persons named in the jury list are not available for the trial. There is then danger that after allowing for the challenges, there may not be a sufficient number of jurors present to

[95] Act of Adjournal, supra, I, (i), (ii) and (iii).
[96] Ibid., I (v).
[97] Ibid., I (vii).
[98] 1887 Act, s. 38.
[99] Ibid., s. 39.
[1] Act of Adjournal, supra, VI (i).
[2] 1887 Act, s. 39; Act of Adjournal, supra, VI (ii).

constitute a jury. There is as yet no satisfactory provision for dealing with this contingency, except by placing on the original jury list the names of more jurors than are likely to be needed. At one time some sheriff clerks, in a case of this kind, cited additional jurors and added their names to the list. This is an improper practice, which, if objected to before the jury was sworn, would necessitate the desertion of the diet.[3]

The jurors are cited in virtue of the warrant for citation already described, and in conformity with section 23 of the 1887 Act. They are cited by registered letter or recorded delivery service.

It is necessary to keep in mind that when the High Court of Justiciary holds a court in a town which is not one of the usual circuit towns, the jury is summoned from the general jury roll of the county in which such town is situated. Where the High Court holds sittings in towns which have hitherto been called circuit towns, the jury is summoned from the several counties which compose the circuit.[4]

Failure to attend as juror

7-26   Persons failing to attend when cited as jurors are liable to fines in terms of an ancient statute.[5] In the High Court, however, it is competent to make application for remission of such fines to a Lord Commissioner of Justiciary who considers the excuse offered for non-attendance, and may remit the fine if satisfied of the sufficiency of the excuse.[6]

Prevention of Undue Delay

7-27   The law affords protection to accused persons against the risk of being detained for an unreasonable time without being brought to trial. Under section 24 of the Circuit Courts (Scotland) Act 1828, a return of untried prisoners confined within their jurisdiction is required from sheriffs attending the circuit courts, so that cases of unduly long detention may be brought to the judge's notice.[6a] In addition, an accused may himself accelerate his trial. Statutory provisions for this were made by the Criminal Procedure Act 1701 (also known as the Act 1701, c. 6), but, except in the case of trials for treason, these provisions are repealed, and a new code enacted, by the 1887 Act.[7]

The one hundred and ten day rule

7-28   Any prisoner who is now in prison on a committal until liberated in due course of law, and who has not been served with an indictment within sixty days of committal, is entitled to give notice to the Lord

---

[3] *McArthur* v. *H.M. Adv.* (1902) 10 S.L.T. 310.

[4] 1887 Act, s. 47. See supra, para. 2–03.

[5] Jurors Act 1587.

[6] Act of Adjournal, for regulating the procedure in regard to applications by persons who have been fined for failure to attend in answer to their citations as jurors, etc., March 19, 1925.

[6a] In practice this section is not operated.

[7] 1887 Act, s. 43.

Advocate, through the Crown Agent in Edinburgh, that if he is not served with an indictment within fourteen days of such notice, the prosecutor will be called on to show cause before the High Court of Justiciary why he should not be released from prison. If no indictment is served within such fourteen days, and if the accused presents a note to the court setting forth that he has given notice, and that no indictment has been served, the court appoints the prosecutor forthwith to show cause why the accused should not be released. If cause is not shown to the satisfaction of the court, warrant is granted for the release of the accused at the expiry of three days from the issuing of the order, unless an indictment has been served upon him within that time. If the accused is liberated, it is competent for the prosecutor to raise an indictment against him and to obtain from a judge of the jurisdiction of the second diet, or a judge of the High Court of Justiciary, a warrant authorising the apprehension of the accused and his re-committal to prison to await his trial. In the event of the trial on such indictment not taking place at the second diet or at any adjourned diet, the accused may present a note to the High Court of Justiciary stating the facts. The court, after hearing parties and considering the whole circumstances of the case, may in its discretion (1) order the immediate release of the prisoner, or (2) grant warrant ordering him to be released on a day named in the warrant, unless he shall on or before such day be remitted to the knowledge of an assize on indictment, or (3) may decline to pronounce any order.[8]

Where the accused has been incarcerated for *eighty days*, and an indictment is served upon him, and he is detained in custody after the expiry of such eighty days, then, unless he is brought to trial and the trial concluded within *one hundred and ten days* of the date of his committal until liberated in due course of law, he is forthwith set at liberty, and declared for ever free from all questions or process for the crime with which he was charged.[9]

Where the accused has been liberated from prison after committal until liberated in due course of law, he must not be detained in prison more than one hundred and ten days in all; but unless his trial is brought to a conclusion before the hundred and tenth day of confinement in prison subsequent to committal has expired, he is forthwith set at liberty and declared forever free from all question or process for the crime for which he was committed.

Extension of time

7–29   In any case brought before the High Court of Justiciary under the section it may be shown to the satisfaction of the court that the trial of the person accused ought to be suffered to proceed after the lapse of one hundred and ten days, in respect that the delay is owing to the illness of the accused, the absence or illness of a necessary witness, the illness of a judge or juror, or any other sufficient cause for which the prosecutor is not

[8] 1887 Act, s. 43.
[9] Ibid.

7-29   responsible. If this is done, the court may order the accused to be kept in custody with a view to trial for such further period or periods as may seem just.[10] The power so conferred on the court is not confined to cases in which an application for extension is made before the expiry of the hundred and ten days, but may be exercised even where the accused has already been incarcerated [11] for more than the statutory period.[12]

The court will not exercise its discretion in the prosecutor's favour if the delay is one that he has not taken reasonable steps to avoid. In *H.M. Advocate* v. *Macaulay* [13] the Crown decided to send an accused person committed for trial on October 8, 1891, to be tried at a sitting of the High Court at Dundee which was, on December 19, 1891, fixed for January 29, 1892. By that date the accused would have been incarcerated for eighty days, served with an indictment, detained in custody after the expiry of such eighty days, and the period of one hundred and ten days within which he ought to have been brought to trial would have expired. The court refused a petition presented by the Crown praying for his detention in prison for a period of eight days from the termination of the hundred and tenth day—January 26—on the ground that the Crown were aware on December 19 that the one hundred and ten days must elapse before January 29, that they should, therefore, have made application for a special diet for the disposal of the case, and that in these circumstances the prosecutor was responsible for the delay.

The effect of section 43 was fully considered by a Full Bench in *H.M. Advocate* v. *Bickerstaff*.[14] There a prisoner was committed till liberated in due course of law on December 9, 1924, upon a charge of murder. He was brought to trial upon March 16, 1925, when he was found to be unfit to plead owing to insanity, and was ordered by the court to be detained during His Majesty's pleasure, the diet being deserted pro loco et tempore. On October 22, 1925, the accused was liberated from the asylum in which he had been detained, and was re-arrested on the same day. On October 27 he was again committed; a fresh indictment was served upon him on November 19; and he was brought to trial on December 7, 1925. At the trial, a motion was made in bar of trial, in respect that even if the period of his detention in the asylum was left out of account, he had already been detained in prison for more than one hundred and ten days, and was therefore entitled to be released forthwith. The court held that assuming (but not deciding) that the hundred and ten days fell to be reckoned from the date of the first and not of the second committal, and accordingly that the panel had already been detained in prison beyond the statutory period, it was entitled under section 43 of the 1887 Act to order him to be detained in custody, with a view to trial, for such further period as might seem just. The court also held that, as the delay in prosecuting to verdict had been

---

[10] Ibid.
[11] *H.M. Adv.* v. *Bickerstaff*, 1926 J.C. 65.
[12] *H.M. Adv.* v. *Dickson*, 1949 S.L.T.(Notes) 58.
[13] (1892) 3 White 131.
[14] Supra.

due to the mental illness of the accused, and not to any cause for which the prosecutor was responsible, the case was one for the exercise by the court of its discretionary power.

Computation of the one hundred and ten days

7-30   The hundred and ten days are computed from the date of full committal and not from the date of arrest.[15] Where the accused is successively committed on a number of charges they will be computed separately from the date of committal on each charge, but the court may allow an extension of time on the earlier charges to enable them all to be taken together.[16] Where an accused is fully committed on a charge and then, before being brought to trial on that charge, is sentenced to imprisonment on another charge, the hundred and ten days do not run during the period of that sentence.[17] Conversely, where an accused who is already serving a sentence is committed for trial the hundred and ten days do not begin to run until the expiry of his sentence.[18] As these examples show, section 43, despite the sidenote, " Prevention of delay in trials," applies only to prevent undue detention in custody awaiting trial; it has no application where the accused is not in custody or where his custody is referable to any other warrant or sentence than the committal warrant.

A trial is brought to a conclusion for the purposes of the section when the jury return a verdict, or the Crown accept a plea of guilty, or at latest when the Crown move for sentence. It is therefore competent to continue the case after verdict, e.g. to obtain sentencing reports, beyond the hundred and ten days.[19]

Dying Declarations and Depositions

7-31   When there is danger of material evidence being lost through the death of a witness, either for the prosecution or the defence, previous to trial, it is necessary to take steps for its preservation. This is done by means of dying declarations and dying depositions.[20] The distinction between the two consists in the latter being upon oath and the former not upon oath. A dying declaration may be preserved and proved by oral evidence, just as may any statements of a deceased person, but while such verbal statements may be admissible much will depend on the facts of each case and the circumstances under which the statements spoken to were made.[21] For example, in a trial for murder where the injured party had died before any declaration or deposition could be taken, it was held competent to examine the assistant procurator-fiscal and his clerk as to what the deceased had

[15] *H.M. Adv.* v. *McEwan*, 1953 J.C. 55.
[16] *H.M. Adv.* v. *Dickson*, 1949 S.L.T. (Notes) 58; cf. *H.M. Adv.* v. *Boyle*, 1972 S.L.T. (Notes) 16.
[17] *Wallace* v. *H.M. Adv.*, 1959 J.C. 71.
[18] *H.M. Adv.* v. *Park*, 1967 J.C. 70; 1967 S.L.T.(Notes) 75 (sub nom. *H.M. Adv.* v. *Meechan and Ors.*); see 31 J.C.L. 269; *Hartley* v. *H.M. Adv.*, 1970 S.L.T.(Notes) 6.
[19] *Wallace* v. *H.M. Adv.*, 1955 J.C. 49.
[20] Hume, ii. 407; Alison, ii. 511; *Dickson on Evidence*, paras. 1754–1756; *Walker and Walker on Evidence*, 429.
[21] Lewis, *Law of Evidence in Scotland*, 327.

said while being precognosced for the prosecution regarding the occurrences that had led to his death, reference to the precognition itself being, however, excluded as incompetent.[22] We shall here consider only *written* statements.

If it becomes apparent that an important witness is dying, and there is not time to arrange for his formal deposition, his evidence may be taken down as a declaration in writing by any credible person. The statement concludes with an assertion that it is all truth. If possible, the declaration should be signed by the dying witness. In any case, it must be signed by the person who takes it down and two witnesses present. It is particularly desirable that one of these witnesses should be the medical man in attendance upon the witness. The doctor should be prepared to state that the mind of the dying person was sufficiently clear to enable him to give a reliable statement of fact.

7-32 The conditions which justify taking a dying deposition are these: (1) that the person would be a competent witness in a criminal trial; (2) that he is a material witness; (3) that his life is in danger; (4) that his mind is sufficiently clear to enable him to give reliable evidence; and (5) that he is capable of doing so without danger to his life.

It is important, particularly as the deposition is taken ex parte and no cross-examination of the witness is possible, that it should be taken before the sufferer's mind is weakened by bodily pain or distracted by contemplation of death.[23]

Procedure

7-33 The deposition should be taken by a sheriff who has jurisdiction in the place where it is emitted; but a justice of peace, or burgh magistrate having jurisdiction may take it in an emergency. If the witness is in imminent danger, the magistrate must take the deposition as speedily as possible; but if there is time, the magistrate should first satisfy himself of the necessity for taking a deposition, and of the fitness, mental and physical, of the witness to emit it.

The deposition is usually taken upon a verbal application to the magistrate. The doctor in charge of the case sees the person alone and prepares him for the appearance of the magistrate. If there is time, it is desirable that he should prepare a certificate on soul and conscience that the person is believed to be dying, and is mentally and physically fit to depone. The doctor is present during the examination, both as a witness and to guard against harm to his patient. It is desirable to have as few persons as possible in the room. Two witnesses are necessary, but the magistrate and doctor will suffice. It is advisable to have the sheriff clerk or one of his deputes in attendance to write the deposition, but he should, if possible, be placed out of sight of the witness.

[22] *Francis and Michael Ward* (1869) 1 Couper 186; see supra, para. 5–72.
[23] *Isabella Brodie* (1846) Ark. 45, L.J.-C. Hope at 48.

The magistrate puts the witness on oath and takes down his name, occupation, usual residence, and age, and what he knows of the facts, confining the questions to matters as to which the witness's evidence is essential; and puts any further question suggested by the procurator fiscal, or, if the evidence is taken for the defence, by the accused's solicitor. A previous precognition may be incorporated by reference; but this is not a commendable practice.[24] It is not necessary that the deponent should believe himself to be dying, or even be warned that his life is in danger,[25] nor is it essential that the deposition should bear to be emitted in view of death.[26] At the conclusion it is usual to ask the witness whether he bears any ill-will towards the accused. The magistrate reads over to the witness what has been written, and asks if what he has said is all truth, as he shall answer to God. The witness signs each page, if able; if unable, the fact is stated. The deposition is then signed by the magistrate and witnesses.

The dying deposition or declaration is retained by the procurator fiscal, or, if the deposition has been taken for the defence, by the accused's solicitor, and is entered upon the list of productions for prosecution or defence, and produced at the trial. It is not used unless the deponent dies. The names of the magistrate and the witnesses to the deposition are included in the witness list for prosecution or defence. At the trial these prove the taking of the deposition, and it is then read to the jury and received as the evidence of the deceased witness.

There is not much authority on this subject. The principal authorities are undernoted.[27]

Witnesses in Prison

7–34   When a witness is in prison, it is no longer necessary to present to the sheriff a petition to secure his attendance for precognition or trial.

Since the coming into force of the Prisons (Scotland) Act 1952 (s. 10 (2)), arrangements have been made by the prisons division of the Scottish Home Department with prison governors that, when it is necessary to transfer a person detained in Scotland from one prison to another or from a prison to court for the purpose of giving evidence, a written request for the attendance of the prisoner addressed to the governor of the prison concerned will suffice. Such a request will be made by the Crown Agent or the procurator fiscal according as the case is one for trial in the High Court of Justiciary or the sheriff court. If the prisoner is required for the purposes of the defence, the request to the governor will be made by the accused or his solicitor.

---

[24] *Carl Johan Peterson* (1874) 2 Couper 557.

[25] *H.M. Adv.* v. *Bell* (1835) 13 S. 1179; *Isabella Brodie* (1846) Ark. 45.

[26] *John Stewart* (1855) 2 Irv. 166.

[27] Hume, ii. 407; Alison, ii. 511; *Dickson on Evidence*, paras. 1754–1756; *James Reid* (1831) Bell's Notes 291; *Bell*, supra; *Murdoch McKenzie McIntosh* (1838) 2 Swin. 103; *Isabella Brodie*, supra; *John Stewart*, supra; *Francis and Michael Ward* (1869) 1 Couper 186; *Carl Johan Peterson*, supra.

Absconding Witnesses

7-35   If a witness has absconded, or means to abscond, either party may apply
to the court by petition for warrant to apprehend him.[28] This petition is
supported by a statement on oath that the witness has absconded to avoid
giving evidence. Warrant is granted for the apprehension of the witness
and his committal to prison until the date of trial, unless he finds sufficient
caution for his appearance at the trial.[29] The witness may be proceeded
against for contempt of court and punished accordingly.[30]

English Witnesses

7-36   The citation of witnesses in England is regulated by the Writ of Sub-
poena Act 1805. Service is usually made through the police, and a
reasonable sum of money must be tendered to the witness to defray his
expenses.

[28] Alison, ii. 398; *H.M. Adv.* v. *Bell*, 1936 J.C. 89.
[29] Hume, ii. 375; *H.M. Adv.* v. *Bell*, 1936 J. C. 89.
[30] *H.M. Adv.* v. *Bell* supra.

CHAPTER 8

ACCELERATED TRIAL UNDER SECTION 31 OF THE 1887 ACT

8-01 A PERSON accused is entitled, so soon as he has been committed to prison till liberated in due course of law, to give written notice, through his own procurator or solicitor, to the Crown Agent that he desires to have his case at once disposed of, and intends to plead guilty. This notice is given by a letter addressed to the Crown Agent and signed by the procurator of the accused.[1]

Procedure

8-02 If the plea offered by the accused is to be accepted, an indictment, which is in practice framed upon it, is prepared without any list of witnesses or productions.[2] A copy of this indictment, with a notice in the form of Schedule L, and, if any previous conviction is to be libelled, a notice in terms of section 39 (d) and schedule 7 to the 1949 Act is also served upon the accused person. No witness to the service is required. The accused is cited to a diet not less than four clear days after such notice. If he desires to object to any previous conviction libelled he must, within two days after service upon him of the notice of previous convictions, give written intimation to the procurator fiscal in terms of section 39 (d) of the 1949 Act, as already described.

The diet is called in the sheriff court at which he would have been cited to a first diet. At such diet, if any plea of guilty is tendered which is accepted by the procurator fiscal,[3] he moves for sentence, and the sheriff deals with the case as if the person had pled guilty at a first diet under the ordinary procedure, i.e. the plea is endorsed upon the record copy of the indictment and signed by the accused if he is able to write and also by the sheriff. If the case is one suitable for punishment in the sheriff court, he forthwith pronounces sentence.[4] If the accused does not plead guilty, the diet is, in practice, deserted pro loco et tempore and the procurator fiscal should take instructions from Crown counsel.

Remit to High Court

8-03 If the case is such as can only be tried in the High Court of Justiciary, or is of such an aggravated nature that the sheriff holds that the question

---

[1] 1887 Act, s. 31.

[2] 1887 Act, s. 31; 1949 Act, s. 39 (d) and Sched. 7.

[3] A procurator fiscal is not bound to accept a plea of guilty either in solemn or in summary proceedings (*Peter and Smith* (1840) 2 Swin. 492; *Pattison* v. *Stevenson* (1903) 4 Adam 124; *Kirkwood* v. *Coalburn District Co-operative Society*, 1930 J.C. 38; *Strathern* v. *Sloan*, 1937 J.C. 76). See infra, para. 9–13.

[4] See infra, paras. 10–45 et seq.

of punishment should be disposed of by that court, he remits the accused to the High Court for sentence. It is not competent for the Sheriff to remit for sentence juvenile offenders to whom the provisions of the Children and Young Persons Acts apply so as to make it impossible for the High Court to impose any greater penalty than is open to the sheriff.[5] The interlocutor is written on the principal or record copy of the indictment, and is in the form of Schedule M.[6] The remit is a sufficient warrant to bring the accused, without any further notice, before the High Court of Justiciary for sentence, at any sitting, at any place that may be convenient, as the Lord Advocate may order. The original warrant of committal of such person till liberated in due course of law remains in force until he is brought before the High Court for sentence.

Necessity of strict compliance with procedure

8-04   The procedure laid down by section 31 must be strictly complied with. Where the plea of guilty was signed by the accused but not by the sheriff, the panel on the case coming before the High Court was dismissed from the bar, the diet being deserted simpliciter.[7] In another case where the panel's plea and the remit were written on a copy of the indictment instead of on the principal, the court held that the panel must be discharged on the ground that the sheriff was functus officio and there was no valid remit to the High Court.[8] In the later case of *Pattison* v. *Stevenson*,[9] a panel arrested on a charge of embezzlement offered to plead guilty under section 31 to part of the charge, and an indictment limited to that part was served upon him. He pleaded guilty thereto before the sheriff substitute and was remitted to the High Court for sentence, but, as Crown counsel doubted the relevancy of the indictment, he was liberated without having been brought before the High Court for sentence and was then rearrested on a warrant proceeding upon a charge containing items included in the original charge but omitted from the indictment to which he had pleaded guilty. In refusing a bill of suspension of the warrant brought by the panel the court held that the proceedings did not import any agreement between the panel and the Crown; that at common law the Crown was, subject to the control of the High Court, entitled to abandon an indictment at any time before it was remitted to an assize; that section 31 of the 1887 Act did not contain anything inconsistent with this right; and that the right still subsisted under section 74 of the Act. In the course of his opinion Lord Moncreiff said [10]:

> " According to our law and practice, the prosecutor is not bound to accept a plea of guilty to the whole charge, and is entitled, notwithstanding the plea, to proceed to trial. Further, in this case he might, if

---

[5] *H.M. Adv.* v. *Anderson*, 1946 J.C. 81.
[6] 1887 Act, s. 31.
[7] *H.M. Adv.* v. *Galloway* (1894) 1 Adam 375.
[8] *H.M. Adv.* v. *McDonald* (1896) 3 S.L.T. 317.
[9] (1903) 4 Adam 124.
[10] At 133–135.

he had chosen to do so, have indicted the complainer for the whole £1600, and left the complainer to tender such plea as he thought fit. . . . The case must be considered just as if after the plea was recorded the Sheriff had been prepared himself to pronounce sentence: but the respondent, instead of moving for sentence, had moved to desert the diet *pro loco et tempore.* . . . Before the passing of the Act of 1887 it was quite settled that His Majesty's Advocate was entitled, even after a case had been called in court, to serve a new indictment at his own hand upon the panel during an adjournment, or (in the Sheriff Court) between the first and second diets; subject always to this, that if the second indictment related to the same charges as the first he might be bound before proceeding to trial with the second indictment to judicially abandon the first."

In modern practice the diet is not called in the High Court where there is a defect in the remit. The indictment then falls and a new one is served. In the unreported case of *Robert Bisset McLachlan,* November 3, 1938, a motion by the panel's counsel to call the diet of a case remitted under section 31 was refused by a court of three judges on the ground that the remit had been signed by a depute sheriff clerk and was, therefore, defective, and the same course has been adopted in a number of other unreported cases.

Plea of not guilty

8–05   If the person accused, when brought before the sheriff as above mentioned, pleads not guilty to the charge, or pleads guilty to part thereof, and the procurator fiscal declines to accept such restricted plea, the diet is deserted pro loco et tempore. Thereafter the case proceeds as if no letter had been written.[11]

If the accused person pleads guilty, and has been remitted to the High Court for sentence, he cannot withdraw his plea except on cause shown,[12] it being necessary for him to satisfy the court that his plea was tendered under some substantial error or misconception or in circumstances which tended to prejudice his case.[13] An earlier decision [14] by Lord McLaren to the effect that the plea could not be withdrawn at that stage was disapproved in *Pattison,*[15] Lord Moncreiff pointing out that the criminal law of Scotland, in so far as not inconsistent with the Act of 1887, was still in full force in virtue of section 74. In a number of unreported cases the court has allowed a plea under section 31 to be withdrawn if given under a misapprehension, but exceptional circumstances must be shown.

The cases of *H.M. Advocate* v. *Black* [16] and *H.M. Advocate* v. *Robertson* [17] may be cited as examples of pleas given under misconception suffi-

---

[11] 1887 Act, s. 31.
[12] *Pattison* v. *Stevenson,* supra.
[13] *Paul* v. *H.M. Adv.* (1914) 7 Adam 343.
[14] *H.M. Adv.* v. *Lyon* (1887) 1 White 538.
[15] Supra.
[16] (1894) 1 Adam 312.   [17] (1899) 3 Adam 1.

cient to allow them to be withdrawn in the High Court. In the former the panel pleaded guilty to a charge of incest with his step-daughter having failed to inform his agent that she was illegitimate, and being, therefore, in ignorance of the signification of that fact. In the High Court his counsel asked that he should be allowed to withdraw his plea. The advocate-depute admitted the correctness of the facts as stated for the accused, and lodged a minute withdrawing the libel. The court then allowed the accused to withdraw his plea, and the diet was deserted simpliciter and the panel dismissed from the bar. In the latter case a panel pled guilty under section 31 to a contravention of the Criminal Law (Scotland) Act 1829, s. 3 (vitriol throwing), and was remitted to the High Court for sentence. At that diet his counsel stated that the plea had been tendered in ignorance that the charge inferred the capital penalty, and asked leave to withdraw the plea. The advocate depute stated that he desired to restrict the libel to the common law charge contained therein. The court allowed this to be done.

CHAPTER 9

THE FIRST OR PLEADING DIET

Sheriff Court Cases

9-01 THE procedure where the trial is to take place before the sheriff and a jury will be explained first. The first or pleading diet, as was already stated,[1] may be called in a different court, and even in a different jurisdiction, from that in which the second diet is called. In that event the procurator fiscal of the district in which the first diet is called acts as representing Her Majesty's Advocate. It is competent, however, for an advocate-depute, or the procurator fiscal of the district of the second diet, to appear for the purpose of prosecuting. The sheriff of the first diet, where the sheriff presiding is not the sheriff of the court of the second diet, has all the powers legally exercised by a sheriff at a first diet.[2]

Presence of accused

9-02 Whoever conducts the prosecution must arrange for the person accused being brought from prison, if he is in custody. The procedure begins usually with the sheriff clerk saying: " Call the diet; Her Majesty's Advocate against A. B." The diet is peremptory,[3] and, while it cannot be called, even of consent, *before* the date fixed, the proceedings fall if it is not called *on* that date. This also happens when neither prosecutor nor accused appears. " It is a well-established rule of criminal law that no proceedings can take place in the absence of the prosecutor or of the accused." [4]

Where the accused is a body corporate, it may, instead of appearing by counsel or solicitor in the ordinary way, appear by a representative of the body itself for the following purposes under section 40 (2) of the 1949 Act:

(*a*) Stating objection to the competency or relevancy of the indictment or proceedings;

(*b*) Tendering a plea of guilty or not guilty;

(*c*) Making a statement in mitigation of sentence.

Section 40 (8) defines the expression " representative " as used in the section in relation to a body corporate against whom proceedings on indictment are brought as follows:

" An officer or servant of the body corporate duly appointed by it for the purpose of those proceedings. Such appointment need not be

---

[1] See supra. para. 7-02.
[2] 1887 Act, s. 28.
[3] *Hull* v. *H.M. Adv.*, 1945 J.C. 83; see also infra, para. 10-04.
[4] *Walker* v. *Emslie* (1899) 3 Adam 102, L.J.-C. at 103.

under the seal of the body corporate, and a statement in writing
purporting to be signed by the managing director of, or by any person
having or being one of the persons having the management of the
affairs of the body corporate, to the effect that the person named in the
statement has been appointed the representative of the body corporate
for the purpose of the said proceedings shall be admissible without
further proof as evidence that the person has been appointed."

Presence of prosecutor

9–03   The prosecutor must be personally in court.[5] A procurator fiscal duly
commissioned may act in the absence of the procurator fiscal who instituted the prosecution.[6] In an emergency the court may appoint a person to
act for the procurator fiscal ad interim.[7] " Such an official must be
formally appointed, and must, I think, take an oath or declaration *de
fideli*; but at least he must appear as having an official appointment." [8] A
sentence pronounced in the absence of the prosecutor or his deputy is
invalid.[9]

Failure of accused to appear

9–04   If the accused person has been liberated on bail and fails to appear, the
proper course is for the court, on proof of service, to declare the bail bond,
or the caution deposited for the accused's appearance, to be forfeited, and
a new warrant may be granted for his apprehension and committal to
prison till liberated in due course of law. Service is proved by production
of an execution in the form of Schedule C.[10] The cautioner in the bail bond
may plead objections to the citation as a reason why the bail should not
be forfeited. It is competent to desert the diet pro loco et tempore and
forfeit the bail bond[11]; but as there seems to be an anomaly in deserting
a diet which has never been constituted by the appearance of the accused
person, the preferable course is that which has been indicated. If the
accused person is at liberty without having found bail (which is a rare
case), the court, in addition to granting a warrant for his apprehension and
committal to prison, may impose a moderate fine.[12]

Where a corporate body fails to appear or tender any plea by a representative or by a solicitor or counsel, it is deemed to have tendered a plea
of not guilty.[13]

Representation by solicitor

9–05   In all cases, a solicitor who is entitled to conduct proceedings in the
courts of the district of the second diet is entitled to appear at the first diet

[5] *Walker* v. *Emslie*, supra.
[6] *Macrae* v. *Cooper* (1882) 4 Couper 561.
[7] *Macrae* v. *Cooper*, supra; *Walker* v. *Emslie*, infra; Macdonald, 268.
[8] *Walker* v. *Emslie* (1899) 3 Adam 102, L.J.-C. Macdonald at 103.
[9] Ibid.
[10] 1887 Act, s. 23.
[11] *Morrison* v. *Monro* (1854) 1 Irv. 599.
[12] Hume, ii. 70.
[13] 1949 Act, s. 40 (3).

and to conduct the defence, although he may not be entitled to conduct other law business in the locality of the first diet.[14]

If the accused person does not understand English, an interpreter is sworn to interpret the proceedings to him. It is improper to leave the interpreting to be done by some unofficial person, such as a co-accused.[15] The indictment is then read over to the accused person.

Objections to citation

9–06   Before the accused pleads either guilty or not guilty, he must state any objections to the validity of the citation against him on the ground of any discrepancy between the record copy of the indictment and the copy served on him, or on account of any error or deficiency in the service copy or in the notice of citation. Such objections are not competent at a later diet. No such discrepancy, error, or deficiency entitles the accused to object to plead to the indictment unless the sheriff is satisfied that the same tended substantially to mislead and prejudice him.[16]

So, in *Lloyd* v. *H. M. Advocate*,[17] where an objection that the arrest was without warrant was not stated before the case went to trial it was held that it came too late.

Competency and Relevancy

9–07   Any objections to the competency of the proceedings, or to the relevancy of the indictment, or of the statements made in it, must be made at the first diet.[18] It is only in exceptional cases that objections will be considered at a later stage, viz. (1) where the court is of opinion that gross injustice would be done by refusing to hear the objection,[19] and (2) where the objection is such as to go to the very root of the charge and to make it a fundamental nullity.[20]

When objections are taken it is not necessary to enter on the record copy of the indictment, or in the record, any minute setting forth how such objections were disposed of, except that such objections were sustained or repelled. The minute is signed by the clerk of court.[21]

Prior to 1887, objections to the relevancy of the libel formed an almost invariable step in a criminal trial. Since the passing of the Criminal Procedure Act such objections have become rare in solemn jurisdiction. They are more common in summary jurisdiction, chiefly on account of the varied character of the statutes under which complaints may be brought.

---

[14] 1887 Act, s. 30. This section is in effect superseded by the Solicitors (Scotland) Act 1958, Scheds. 2 and 3, which entitle all solicitors with a practising certificate to practise in all courts.
[15] *Liszewski* v. *Thomson*, 1942 J.C. 55.
[16] 1887 Act, s. 33.
[17] (1899) 2 Adam 637.
[18] 1887 Act, ss. 28, 29.
[19] *H.M. Adv.* v. *Bell* (1892) 3 White 313.
[20] *Sangster* v. *H.M. Adv.* (1896) 2 Adam 182.
[21] 1887 Act, s. 32.

9–08   It is important to distinguish carefully between *objections to competency* and *objections to relevancy*. The distinction is often ignored in practice. The two classes of objections may be distinguished by the general observation that an objection to competency implies that the trial of the accused person before a certain court, or at the instance of a certain prosecutor or upon a certain charge, is not competent; an objection to relevancy implies that the terms of the indictment to which the accused person is asked to plead are not in accordance with the requirements of the law. If successful the former generally puts an end to the whole proceedings; the latter, in the absence of amendment, puts an end to the indictment served. The one is usually fatal; the other in most cases can be cured by amendment, or by the service of a new indictment or complaint.

Objections to competency

9–09   An objection to competency may be taken on any ground which strikes at the right to prosecute. The principal grounds are these:

(a) That the court has no jurisdiction to try the crime charged. This may arise either in respect that the crime has been committed outside the territory of the court; or that its gravity exceeds the powers of trial committed to the court; or that the judge has a material interest in the accused person, or in the question at issue.

(b) That the prosecutor has no title or interest to prosecute. This may arise in the case of a public prosecutor, in respect that his commission does not authorise him to prosecute; in the case of a private prosecutor, in respect that he is neither aggrieved nor injured by the crime charged.

(c) That the charge involves a question of civil right. This is a very complicated question, which arises almost exclusively in summary procedure. It is always a matter of circumstances, and each case has to be judged by itself.

(d) That there has been such irregularity in the prior proceedings as would vitiate any conviction obtainable.[22]

(e) That proceedings in a statutory offence have not been taken within the time limited by the statute for prosecution.

(f) In summary procedure, that the crime charged cannot be tried summarily, or in solemn procedure that it can be tried only summarily.

Objections to relevancy

9–10   A distinction must be drawn at the outset between the relevancy of a criminal libel and the relevancy of a statement contained in a criminal libel. The first raises the question whether the libel as a whole is sufficient in law to justify the court in calling upon the person accused to plead to the charge made in it; the second raises the question whether a particular

---

[22] Cf. *Lloyd* v. *H.M. Adv.* (1899) 2 Adam 637; *McVey* v. *H.M. Adv.* (1911) 6 Adam 503.

allegation in the libel is so distinct and specific that, if proved, it would infer the point sought to be deduced from it, according to the Latin maxim: Frustra probatur quod probatum non relevat.

9–11   The grounds upon which the relevancy of the libel may be objected to are very numerous. The following are some of the principal:

(a) That the libel (whether indictment or complaint) is not in correct form.

(b) That it appears on the face of the libel that an essential preliminary step has been omitted—such as an oath of verity, or the concurrence of the public prosecutor, in cases where either of these is required.

(c) That the libel contains a material error in the name or designation of the prosecutor or the person accused, or in setting forth their respective connection with the case.

(d) That the libel does not set forth facts which constitute either a crime at common law or a contravention of an Act of Parliament applicable to Scotland.

(e) That the libel contains a statement of the charge which is defective or ambiguous in the specification of the time, place or mode of committing the crime charged.

(f) That the libel in a statutory offence does not mention, or mentions inaccurately, the Act of Parliament and the particular section contravened.

(g) That the libel has not been signed, or is signed by the wrong person.

The question whether a particular statement in the libel is relevant or not depends upon the circumstances of each case. It would be useless to attempt to set down here a list of such objections. The principles of relevancy of averment are not in any way different in criminal procedure from what they are in any other form of pleading.

Amendment of indictment

9–12   Very wide powers of amendment are now conferred by statute. These will fall to be considered when explaining the procedure at trial.[23] If, therefore, an objection to relevancy is sustained by the court, the proper course is to amend the indictment, with or without an adjournment, if such amendment will cure the defect. Should this not be possible, the prosecutor will move the court to desert the diet pro loco et tempore. The motion is usually granted. A new indictment can then be prepared and proceedings will be begun de novo.

Plea of Guilty

9–13   If the accused person pleads guilty in whole or in part, and the partial plea (if any) is accepted by the prosecutor, the sheriff pronounces sen-

[23] Infra, para. 10–09.

9-13   tence [24]; or he can adjourn the case to another sitting of his court, with a
view to considering what sentence should be pronounced. He has this
power whether the case is one the second diet of which is to be called in
his own or in another court.[25] Where the second diet is fixed for a different
court, any interlocutor disposing of any preliminary plea, any plea
tendered, any interlocutor adjourning the case, or any sentence pronounced is written on the record copy of the indictment. Where the
plea is one of guilty to the indictment or any part thereof, the accused
person must sign it, if he is able to write. No signature is required where
such plea is tendered by or on behalf of a company.[26] The prosecutor is
not bound to accept a plea of guilty—even to the whole indictment—but
may insist upon the case going to trial.[27] In every case, whether the plea is
one of guilty or not guilty, the sheriff must append his signature to the
plea recorded.[28] The prosecutor's acceptance of the plea is normally
endorsed on the record beside the plea. If a person charged on indictment with any crime or offence tenders a plea of guilty to any other
crime or offence of which he could competently, by virtue of any enactment, be found guilty on the trial of such indictment, and if the plea is
accepted by the prosecutor, it is competent to convict such person of the
crime or crimes to which he has so pled guilty and to sentence him
accordingly.[29]

Where the person accused pleads guilty to only a part of a charge, or to
a minor offence included in the charge, and the prosecutor does not
accept such plea, or where on a plea of guilty to the whole charge the sheriff
considers it expedient in the circumstances, either on the representation of
the accused person or otherwise, that the sentence should be determined by
the sheriff of the district of the second diet, an interlocutor in the form of
Schedule H is written on the record copy of the indictment and signed by
the presiding sheriff.[30]

The sheriff clerk, when the case has been remitted as above mentioned,
records any interlocutors signed, plea tendered, or sentence pronounced.
He does this in the books of court or in a record kept for the purpose.
He then transmits forthwith the record copy indictment to the sheriff clerk
of the district of the court of the second diet.[31]

Where the accused pleads guilty in whole or in part, and the sheriff
holds that any sentence which he can competently pronounce is inadequate,
he may remit the accused to the High Court for sentence.[32]

In all cases where a person accused pleads guilty at the first diet, and is

[24] 1887 Act, s. 28.
[25] Ibid.
[26] 1949 Act, s. 40 (6).
[27] *Peter and Smith* (1840) 2 Swin. 492; *Strathern* v. *Sloan*, 1937 J.C. 76; cf. *Kirkwood* v.
Coalburn District Co-operative Society Ltd., 1930 J.C. 38.
[28] 1887 Act, s. 28.
[29] Law Reform (Miscellaneous Provisions) (Scotland) Act 1940, s. 8.
[30] 1887 Act, s. 28.
[31] Ibid.
[32] 1921 Act, s. 2.

not forthwith sentenced by the sheriff, he is detained in custody until he is sentenced, under the existing warrant of committal.[33] The Lord Advocate has power to consent to the accused being suffered to go at large. Where such consent is given, it is on such conditions as to bail as the Lord Advocate fixes.[34] No unreasonable delay can be allowed to take place between the time of the accused pleading guilty and his being brought up for sentence.[35]

Procedure when plea of guilty not accepted

9–14   The following rules were formulated with regard to such cases by Lord Justice-Clerk Aitchison in *Strathern* v. *Sloan* [36]: (1) The formal entry on the record should not be an entry of not guilty, which is contrary to the fact, but should be to the effect that the panel has tendered a plea of guilty, and that the prosecutor has intimated that he declines to accept the plea. (2) A plea of guilty which is not accepted by the prosecutor must in no circumstances be used against the panel, and must not be disclosed to the jury. In all cases, therefore, under solemn procedure, where a plea of guilty is declined at the first diet, the panel should not be called upon to plead at the second diet, unless in the interval the prosecutor has made up his mind to accept the plea if again tendered. (3) If the prosecutor elects to proceed to trial, and in the course of the trial decides to accept a plea of guilty, he cannot do so unless the panel of new pleads guilty to the offence charged.

Refusal to plead

9–15   If the accused person remains silent, refuses to plead, or makes a statement which is not a direct and unambiguous admission of guilt, or if there is reason to believe that he does not understand what he is being asked to do (for instance, if he is very deaf), the plea is recorded as one of not guilty.[37]

Sentence

9–16   On the plea of guilty being recorded, if sentence is to be pronounced at the same diet, the prosecutor moves for sentence.[38] Unless he does this no sentence can be pronounced. A motion for sentence may be implied from the prosecutor's laying before the court a notice of previous convictions, this being a step he cannot take except when moving for sentence.[39] The accused's solicitor or counsel, or, where the accused is a body corporate, a representative of the body corporate,[40] is then heard in mitigation of

---

[33] 1887 Act, s. 34.
[34] Ibid.
[35] Ibid.
[36] *Strathern* v. *Sloan*, 1937 J.C. 76 at 80; see also *Alexander Main Stirling*, Edinburgh High Court, March 1960, unreported.
[37] *Jas. Currie* (1833) Bell's Notes 231; *Angus Hutton* (1840) ibid.; Macdonald, 278.
[38] See infra, paras. 10–45 et seq.
[39] *Noon* v. *H.M. Adv.*, 1960 J.C. 52.
[40] 1949 Act, s. 40 (2). See supra, para. 9–02.

punishment. At this stage an accused person may lead evidence of good character. This is usually done by reading certificates, but witnesses may be examined if necessary. If an attempt is made to set up a false character, the prosecutor probably can lead evidence to rebut the proof led by the accused.[41]

High Court Cases

9–17   The procedure at the first diet in a case which is to be tried before the High Court of Justiciary is in most respects the same as if the case were to proceed in the sheriff court. The main distinction arises where it is necessary to preserve the right of the High Court to decide legal questions arising in connection with the proceedings, or to pronounce sentence.

If any objection of a preliminary nature is stated by the person accused, whether to the citation or relevancy or otherwise, the sheriff hears the argument. If any objection is made in respect of a discrepancy between the record copy of the indictment and the service copy, or of any error or deficiency in such service copy, or in the notice of citation, and the sheriff is of opinion that such discrepancy, error, or deficiency could not mislead or prejudice the accused person, the accused is called upon to plead guilty or not guilty.[42]

The same course is followed if no preliminary objection is made, or if the sheriff is of opinion that any such objection is frivolous. But if the sheriff holds that a discrepancy, error, or deficiency is one which tended substantially to mislead and prejudice the accused person, or that any other preliminary objection is not frivolous, he endorses upon the record copy of the indictment a certificate in the form of Schedule K. This certificate notes generally the nature of the objections, and states that they are reserved for the consideration of the court at the second diet.[43]

When the accused person is called upon to plead, a certificate of the plea tendered, in the form of Schedule I, is endorsed upon the record copy of the indictment. If the plea is one of guilty to the charge or part thereof, the accused person is required to sign it, if he is able to write. This requirement does not apply in the case of a body corporate.[44] In every case, whether the plea is one of guilty or not guilty, the sheriff must append his signature to the plea recorded.[45]

The sheriff clerk records any certificate of the kind above mentioned. He copies this entry in the books of court, or in a record to be kept for the purpose. He then transmits forthwith the record copy of the indictment to the Clerk of Justiciary.[46] It has already been mentioned that the documentary productions are usually lodged prior to the first diet.

[41] *James Nimmo and James Forsyth* (1839) 2 Swin. 338, Lord Cockburn at 340.
[42] 1887 Act, s. 29.
[43] Ibid.
[44] 1949 Act, s. 40 (6).
[45] 1887 Act, s. 28.
[46] Ibid.

Pleas in Bar of Trial

9-18   A plea in bar of trial must be stated at the first diet.[47] If such a plea is sustained, it effectually stops further procedure. It may be said generally, with regard to pleas of this sort, that if proof is required in their support, the court can hear it without empannelling a jury.

The following are the principal pleas in bar of trial:

9-19   (a) That the accused person is under eight years of age.[48]

9-20   (b) That he is insane at the time of trial, and unable to plead to the libel, or to give instructions for his defence.[49]

9-21   (c) Res judicata. This plea may arise in two ways, viz.:
   (1) On the ground that there has already been a judgment holding a libel in the same form as the indictment and based upon the same facts irrelevant, or
   (2) That the accused person has already tholed an assize—that is to say, that the charge libelled has already been made against him and has been brought to proof.[50]

As regards the first of these grounds for the plea of res judicata it has been held to be incompetent to try a man before the sheriff upon a libel which the sheriff-substitute had decided was irrelevant.[51] On the other hand it is competent to try a man in the High Court on a libel which the sheriff has held to be irrelevant.[52] As regards the second ground, the essence of the plea is that the person tendering it has already been brought to trial and has stood his trial for, or pleaded guilty to, a specific offence duly set out in the indictment or complaint, before a court of competent jurisdiction. An accused cannot plead that he has tholed his assize in respect that an English court has taken his Scottish offence into consideration in sentencing him for an English crime,[53] but his English sentence will be taken into account when the Scottish court deals with him.[54]

The former trial must have been for exactly the same offence,[55] but the plea cannot be avoided by libelling the same facts under a different name, as by charging embezzlement after acquittal for theft.[56] It is not necessary that an accused person should have been actually sentenced if, owing to an error in subsequent procedure, no sentence could have been passed upon him.[57] But there is some authority that in the normal case the plea does not arise until the accused has been convicted and sentenced,[58] and this

[47] 1887 Act, ss. 28 and 29; *H.M. Adv.* v. *Brown* (1907) 5 Adam 312.
[48] Children and Young Persons (Scotland) Act 1937, s. 55. See Macdonald, 271.
[49] Infra, paras. 20–05 et seq.
[50] Hume, ii. 470.
[51] *Longmuir* v. *Baxter* (1858) 3 Irv. 287.
[52] *George Fleming* (1866) 5 Irv. 289.
[53] *Hilson* v. *Easson* (1914) 7 Adam 390.
[54] Ibid., L.J.-G. at 397–398.
[55] *Galloway* v. *Somerville* (1863) 4 Irv. 444; *Glen* v. *Colquhoun* (1865) 5 Irv. 203; *H.M. Adv.* v. *Cairns*, 1967 J.C. 37.
[56] Hume, ii. 466; Alison, ii. 615–616; Macdonald, 272.
[57] *Sarah and Jas. Fraser* (1852) 1 Irv. 1.
[58] Alison, ii. 615, 618.

may be of considerable importance nowadays when sentence often does not follow immediately on conviction. It has been held competent for a burgh fiscal to desert a case pro loco et tempore against a person who has pleaded guilty in order to remit him to the sheriff court in terms of section 55 (4) of the Mental Health (Scotland) Act 1960 after obtaining reports on his mental condition, and for the sheriff thereafter to try him of new on complaint for the same offence.[59]

The assize need not be tholed in Scotland.[60]

If after the previous trial an event has occurred which changes the character of the offence (as, for example, where a trial for assault has taken place and the injured party dies), the plea of res judicata will not exclude an indictment for homicide.[61] Where an accused gives false evidence at his trial he may thereafter be charged with perjury, although proof of the perjury involves proof of his commission of the original offence for which he has been tried. Prosecutions will, however, be taken only rarely in such cases, and perhaps only where the first trial resulted in an acquittal.[62]

If the earlier trial was stopped by some unforeseen accident or by something for which the prosecutor was not responsible, the plea will not avail the accused at a second trial.[63]

9-22   (d) Where a witness is called by the prosecutor as a socius criminis he cannot be charged for the offence in reference to which he depones.[64]

The measure of the indemnity is the libel in support of which he gives evidence. It was formerly thought that the immunity enjoyed by a socius criminis who was adduced as a witness depended on a bargain between the witness and the Crown authorities, but the proper view appears to be that once the socius criminis is tendered as a witness that by itself precludes the Crown from prosecuting him in respect of matters covered by the libel.[65] When thus called, the witness is obliged to answer all pertinent questions even although these may show his own guilt.[66] A person called as a witness in some capacity other than that of a socius, for example as a complainer, is not entitled to immunity.[67]

[59] *Herron* v. *McCrimmon*, 1969 S.L.T.(Sh.Ct.) 37.
[60] *Macgregor and Inglis* (1848) Ark. 49, 60.
[61] Macdonald, 272; *John McNeill* (1826) Shaw 162; *Isabella Cobb or Fairweather* (1836) 1 Swin. 354; *John Stevens* (1850) J. Shaw 287; *Jas. Stewart* (1866) 5 Irv. 310; *Patrick O'Connor* (1882) 5 Couper 206.
[62] *H.M. Adv.* v. *Cairns*, supra.
[63] Hume, ii. 469; Alison, ii. 618–619; cf. *H.M. Adv.* v. *Brown and Foss*, 1966 S.L.T. 341.
[64] Macdonald, 273; *Hare* v. *Wilson* (1829) Syme 373; see also *Jessie McLauchlan* (1862) 4 Irv.App.
[65] *Macmillan* v. *Murray*, 1920 J.C. 13; *McGinley & Dowds* v. *MacLeod*, 1963 J.C. 11.
[66] *Macmillan* v. *Murray*, supra.
[67] *McGinley & Dowds* v. *MacLeod*, supra.

CHAPTER 10

THE SECOND DIET OR DIET OF TRIAL

Legal aid in High Court

10–01 WHERE an application is made for legal aid in a case which is being prosecuted before the High Court that court may grant or refuse the application, or may remit it to the sheriff court to be dealt with there.[1]

Edinburgh solicitor

10–02 It is no longer necessary for an Edinburgh solicitor to be instructed for a trial in Edinburgh High Court where both the accused and his solicitor are from outside Edinburgh.[2]

Calling the diet

10–03 At the calling of the second diet of compearance, whether in the sheriff court of a different district from the first diet, or in the High Court of Justiciary, the clerk of court, on the diet being called, enters in the books of court, or in a record to be kept for the purpose, a transcript of the procedure at the first diet as endorsed on the record copy of the indictment. But if the calling of the second diet is in the same court as that in which the first was called, the case proceeds in ordinary form.[3]

If a body corporate, being the accused, fails to appear by a representative or by counsel or a solicitor, the court must on the motion of the prosecutor, if it is satisfied that the statutory conditions as regards service [4] have been complied with, proceed to hear and dispose of the case in the absence of the body corporate.[5]

Diets peremptory

10–04 " It is a cardinal rule of our criminal procedure that a criminal diet is, and must be made, peremptory, and that, if the diet is not called or duly adjourned or continued on the date in the citation, the instance falls." [6] Failure to observe this rule involves a fundamental nullity, and any conviction which has followed must be quashed.[7] Whether the Crown can thereafter bring a fresh indictment does not appear to have been judicially decided. The first diet may be adjourned to a fixed time up to, but not

---

[1] Act of Adjournal (Rules for Legal Aid in Criminal Proceedings) 1964, rule 6 (1).
[2] (1966) 11 J.L.S. 173.
[3] 1887 Act, s. 40.
[4] 1949 Act, s. 40 (1). See supra, para. 7–06.
[5] Ibid., s. 40 (4).
[6] *Hull* v. *H.M. Adv.*, 1945 J.C. 83, L.J.-C. at 86; Hume, ii. 263, 264; Alison, ii. 343, 344; *Sarah and James Fraser* (1852) 1 Irv. 1; *Edward Tabram* (1872) 2 Couper 259.
[7] *Hull*, supra.

beyond, the second diet, the second diet can be adjourned only by order duly made, or general continuation minute duly executed, on a day fixed for the second diet, and no diet can be adjourned by anticipation before the time fixed for that diet.[8] Any continuation must be to a specified date,[9] and must be recorded in a signed interlocutor.[10]

Preliminary objections

10–05   After the diet has been called, if no motion has been made for an adjournment [11] or if such motion has been made and has been refused, the court disposes of any preliminary objections competently before it. In sheriff court cases no plea in bar or to relevancy may be stated at the second diet unless the plea is in respect of circumstances which have occurred since the first diet or is one which has been reserved by the sheriff at that diet.[12] Accordingly only a limited class of objection falls to be dealt with by the sheriff at the second diet. The High Court, on the other hand, can always review the proceedings at the first diet,[13] and can deal not merely with those pleas which have been reserved by the sheriff for its consideration at the second diet, but also with those of which the sheriff has himself disposed. Moreover, if the accused has pled guilty to the whole or any part of the charge at the first diet, but it is shown at the second diet that such plea was taken to an irrelevant or incompetent charge, or under substantial error or misconception, or under circumstances which tended to prejudice the accused, the court may allow such plea to be withdrawn or modified.[14] In this case the prosecutor may move the court to desert the diet pro loco et tempore, or to postpone the trial to a later date.

Procedure when trial not proceeded with

10–06   Where the second diet has been thus deserted, or where for any reason an indictment is not brought to trial at the second diet, and the court has not postponed the trial or appointed it to be held at a subsequent date at some other sitting of the court, the prosecutor may, at any time within nine clear days after the date of the second diet, give the accused another copy of the indictment having annexed to it a notice in the form of Schedule N to the 1887 Act, requiring him to appear at another diet, in either the High Court or the sheriff court, when that court has jurisdiction, irrespective of the court of the original diet, provided that the notice requires the accused to appear on an induciae of at least nine days, and that on or before the date of the notice a list of jurors is prepared signed and

---

[8] Ibid.

[9] *Frasers*, supra.

[10] *McLean* v. *Falconer* (1895) 1 Adam 564; *MacArthur* v. *Campbell* (1896) 2 Adam 151; *Craig* v. *Tarras* (1897) 2 Adam 344; *Jamieson* v. *Wilson* (1901) 3 Adam 395; *Taylor* v. *Sempill* (1906) 5 Adam 114; *Corstorphine* v. *Jameson* (1909) 6 Adam 154.

[11] Infra, para. 10–10.

[12] 1887 Act, ss. 28, 40; *Smith* v. *Lothian* (1862) 4 Irv. 170.

[13] Ibid., s. 41.

[14] Ibid.

kept by the sheriff clerk of the district to which the notice applies.[15] Further provision for postponement is made by section 41 of the 1949 Act which states that where a sheriff court case is not brought to trial at the second diet, the court may adjourn that diet to a subsequent sitting, provided that a warrant has been issued under section 23 of the 1887 Act for a subsequent sitting within one month of the date of the second diet, and the warrant shall have effect as if the second diet had been originally fixed for the subsequent sitting. On the other hand, where the trial is postponed to a definite date, the adjourned diet is notified to the accused in open court.[16] Where such postponement makes it necessary that the jury for the trial of the case shall be taken from a different list from that of which notice was given, such list is prepared, signed and kept in the office of the proper sheriff clerk within three clear days of the postponed diet.[17]

When the accused has pled guilty at the first diet, any Lord Commissioner of Justiciary in chambers, and without the presence of the prosecutor or person accused, may adjourn the second diet to any other sitting of the High Court of Justiciary.[18]

In the event of a trial being transferred, when there are too few cases for a separate court,[19] or if a sitting of the High Court is dispensed with, such cases as remain for trial may be ordered to be brought up at another court.[20] In either case a notice in the form of Schedule O is served upon each person accused who may have been already cited.[21]

Pleading

10-07   After any preliminary objections have been dealt with the person accused is usually, although not necessarily, asked whether he adheres to his plea as recorded at the first diet. If he pleads guilty, the procedure is the same as if he had pled guilty at the first diet. If he adheres to the plea of not guilty, the case proceeds. It is competent to read the indictment and ask the accused to plead; but in practice, the indictment is not read at the second diet.[21a] It may, however, be noted that the abolition of all references to previous convictions in the indictment by section 39 of the 1949 Act [22] obviates the difficulty which formerly arose with regard to section 67 of the 1887 Act through alluding to previous convictions in the presence of those who had been cited to act as jurors when reading the indictment. Section 67 of the 1887 Act provides that previous convictions against an accused shall not be laid before the jury, nor shall reference be made thereto before the verdict has been returned. It would be fatal to a conviction if such reference were made once the jury had been empannelled, but it

---

[15] Ibid., s. 42.
[16] Ibid., s. 41.
[17] Ibid.
[18] 1887 Act, s. 49.
[19] Supra, para. 2–04.
[20] 1887 Act, s. 48.
[21] Ibid., s. 50.
[21a] But see infra, para. 10–26.
[22] See supra, para. 6–31.

was held that where such reference was made in the presence of the jurors prior to the actual empannelling, the statute was not infringed,[23] even although the jury was actually in the box,[24] the ground for these decisions being the very technical one that the jurors do not become a jury until they have taken the oath. It has also been held [25] that a reference in evidence to an album of police photographs shown to a witness prior to the trial for the purpose of identifying the accused is not a contravention of section 67. In the case in question opinions were expressed that any reference to a previous conviction in contravention of the section must necessarily result in the quashing of the conviction appealed against. This would not apply where the reference was ultroneously included by a witness in answering a proper question.[26]

Where an accused pleads guilty to one of a number of charges in an indictment before the jury are empannelled that charge should not be read to the jury and they should not be asked to return a verdict on it. The plea of guilty cannot be used as evidence to support the remaining charges.[27]

Misnomers and misdescriptions

10–08   Before the jury has been sworn it is necessary to state any objection in respect of misnomer or misdescription of any person named in the indictment, or of any person named in the list of witnesses. No such objection may be admitted as ground for postponing any trial or for excluding any witness, unless the accused person has, at least four clear days before the second diet, given notice to the procurator fiscal of the district of the second diet where notice of trial is given for the sheriff court, or to the Crown Agent where notice of trial is given for the High Court of Justiciary, of his inability to discover who such person named in the indictment is, or to find such witness.[28] In the event of the court being satisfied that notwithstanding such intimation to the prosecutor the accused has not been furnished with such additional information as might enable him to ascertain who such person is, or to find such witness in sufficient time to precognosce him before the trial, the trial may be postponed or adjourned.[29] It has to be observed that in these, and in all cases of necessary adjournment a specified date must be fixed for the adjourned diet, and this date must be entered in the record.[30]

Amendment of indictment

10–09   It is competent at any time prior to the determination of the case, unless the court see just cause to the contrary, to amend the indictment by

---

[23] *White* v. *H.M. Adv.* (1901) 3 Adam 479; *Cornwallis* v. *H.M. Adv.* (1902) 3 Adam 604.
[24] *Cornwallis*, supra.
[25] *Corcoran* v. *H.M. Adv.*, 1932 J.C. 42. See also *Kepple* v. *H.M. Adv.*, 1936 J.C. 76; *Haslam* v. *H.M. Adv.*, 1936 J.C. 82. See also infra, para. 11–42.
[26] Cf. *Deighan* v. *MacLeod*, 1959 J.C. 25; see also *Clark* v. *Connell*, 1952 J.C. 119.
[27] *Walsh* v. *H.M. Adv.*, 1961 J.C. 51.
[28] 1887 Act, s. 53.
[29] Ibid.
[30] *Sarah and Jas. Fraser* (1852) 1 Irv. 1; *Hull* v. *H.M. Adv.*, 1945 J.C. 83; supra, para. 10–04.

deletion, alteration, or addition, so as to cure any error or defect therein, or to meet any objections thereto, or to cure any discrepancy or variance between the indictment and the evidence. Any amendment so made is sufficiently authenticated by the initials of the clerk of court. Such amendment must not change the character of the offence charged. If the court is of opinion that the accused may by such amendment be in any way prejudiced in his defence on the merits of the case, it grants such remedy to the accused by adjournment or otherwise as seems just.[31]

Adjournment and Desertion of Diet

Adjournment

10–10 Every trial must proceed from day to day till concluded, unless the court sees cause to adjourn over a day or days.[32] Adjournment is a matter for the discretion of the court,[33] unless the case is one in which adjournment is prescribed by statute. In one case the court refused an adjournment where the accused's legal aid solicitor withdrew from the case with the consent of the court after the accused had rejected his advice.[34] The adjournment must be made to a specified day, otherwise the libel falls.[35] An adjournment at the second diet ought always to be avoided, if possible. Serious expense and inconvenience may be caused to jurors and witnesses, and there is always the danger of losing valuable evidence in consequence of the delay. Sometimes, however, it is necessary to adjourn.[36] A material witness either for the prosecution or for the defence may be absent, although every effort has been made to secure his attendance,[37] or new and important facts may have been discovered.[38] The criterion to be applied is whether the adjournment is necessary in the interests of justice.[39] An adjournment will be granted to give the defence an opportunity of inspecting Crown productions not made available timeously.[40] On the other hand, in a case where the defence made a motion for an adjournment to allow the panel to prepare his case, on the ground of the multiplicity of Crown witnesses, some of whom were resident in England, and the multiplicity of Crown productions, the request was refused.[41] In one very

---

[31] 1908 Act, ss. 30 and 77 (4). These sections extend the powers of amendment given by s. 70 of the 1887 Act, which were limited to amendment to cure a discrepancy or variance between the indictment and the evidence. Such amendment was not competent after the case for the prosecution was closed, and was not allowed unless the court was satisfied that the discrepancy or variance was not material to the merits of the case and that the accused could not be prejudiced thereby in his defence on the merits.

[32] 1887 Act, s. 55.

[33] Ibid.; cf. *Anderson* v. *Allan* (1868) 1 Couper 4; *Robertson* v. *Duke of Athole* (1869) 1 Couper 348.

[34] *Monteath* v. *H.M. Adv.*, 1965 J.C. 14; cf. *Turnbull* v. *H.M. Adv.*, 1948 S.N. 19; *Thomson* v. *H.M. Adv.*, 1959 J.C. 15.

[35] *Sarah and Jas. Fraser* (1852) 1 Irv. 1; *Hull* v. *H.M. Adv.*, 1945 J.C. 83; supra, para. 10–04.

[36] Macdonald, 279.

[37] *Gardner Niven* (1858) 3 Irv. 204; *W. H. Thomson* (1871) 2 Couper 103; *Vetters* v. *H.M. Adv.*, 1943 J.C. 138.

[38] *Alex. Fletcher* (1847) Ark. 232; *Wm. Wallace* (1855) 3 Irv. 202.

[39] *Vetters* v. *H.M. Adv.*, supra.

[40] Hume, ii. 388.

[41] *Wm. Rodger* (1868) 1 Couper 76.

special case the court, on the motion of the defence, granted a short adjournment to allow the defence to bring a crown witness whose services had been dispensed with by the prosecutor and who had not been cited by the defence, the witness being the signatory of a medical certificate referred to as a production in the indictment.[42] An adjournment will not be allowed to the defence on the ground that a person mentioned in the indictment or in the list of witnesses cannot be found unless four days' notice has been given to the prosecutor in terms of section 53 of the 1887 Act and the defence is still without sufficient information.[43] The refusal of a witness to be precognosced is not a sufficient ground for asking an adjournment.[44]

Desertion pro loco et tempore

10–11   Where a difficulty of a more serious character has emerged, the prosecutor may move the court to desert the diet pro loco et tempore. The granting of this motion is, in the absence of any statutory direction to the contrary, in the discretion of the court.[45] The prosecutor may make this motion at any time before the jury is sworn[46], and where the accused pleads guilty he may be entitled to do so until sentence is moved for.[47] He need not specify his reasons for making the motion.[48] The motion is usually granted without demur, but, if opposed, it may be refused if its granting would involve injustice to the accused.[49] The diet may be deserted by the court at any time. In one case where the panel became ill after the jury had been sworn the court refused to allow the trial to proceed, discharged the jury, and reserved to the prosecutor the right to raise a new libel, meantime on the motion of the accused recommitting her to prison until liberated in course of law. She was subsequently tried by the sheriff.[50] In a recent case in which one of two accused became medically unfit while giving evidence and it was found that he would be unfit for trial for the foreseeable future the court discharged the jury and deserted the diet pro loco et tempore against both accused, reserving to the Crown the right to raise a fresh indictment against either or both.[51]

10–12   The rule of law that desertion of a diet pro loco et tempore brings the libel to an end, with the result that the prosecutor can proceed only by means of a fresh indictment,[52] has been considerably modified by the 1887 Act and the 1949 Act, and is now subject to the following qualifications:

    (a) Where a diet is deserted pro loco et tempore, or is postponed or adjourned, or an order is issued for the trial to take place at a

[42] *Gardner Niven* (1858) 3 Irv. 204.
[43] 1887 Act, s. 53.
[44] *Alex. Fletcher* (1847) Ark. 232.
[45] Hume, ii. 276; Alison, ii. 98, 355.
[46] *Ross and Ors.* (1848) Ark. 481; *John Martin* (1858) 3 Irv. 177.
[47] Cf. *Herron* v. *McCrimmon*, 1969 S.L.T. (Sh.Ct.) 37.
[48] Alison, ii. 356
[49] *Hannah McAtamney or Henry* (1867) 5 Irv. 363.
[50] *Elizabeth McDonald or Hamilton* (1880) 4 Couper 344.
[51] *H.M. Adv.* v. *Brown and Foss*, 1966 S.L.T. 341.
[52] *Collins* v. *Lang* (1887) 1 White 482.

different place from that first given notice of, it is not necessary that a new warrant should be granted for the incarceration of the accused person. The warrant of committal on which such person is at the time in custody continues in force.[53]

(b) Where a second diet has been deserted pro loco et tempore under section 41 of the 1887 Act the accused may be brought to trial on the same indictment if the prosecution follow the procedure laid down in section 42 of that Act.[54]

(c) Where a warrant is in existence under section 23 of the 1887 Act for a subsequent sitting of the court within one month after a second diet at which the indictment was not brought to trial the prosecution may take advantage of the provisions of section 41 of the 1949 Act.[55]

The alternative course of proceeding by means of a fresh indictment is still open to the prosecutor, and, if he chooses to adopt it instead of using the machinery provided by section 42 of the 1887 Act, he does not require to wait until the induciae prescribed by that section have expired.[56]

Desertion simpliciter

10–13   The court may desert a diet simpliciter. The effect of this step is to bring the process to an end.[57] No further procedure can take place upon the existing indictment.[58] As regards the competency of raising a fresh libel upon the same grounds the position is as follows: " Desertion of a diet *simpliciter* on the motion of the prosecutor is an end of all proceedings against the panel for the offence libelled against him." [59] By his motion the prosecutor has raised a bar in the way of further process at his instance and he cannot bring a fresh indictment for the same crime or offence.[60]

Where the diet is deserted otherwise than on the prosecutor's motion (which is unlikely to occur in practice) [61] it would seem that, although there are dicta to the contrary,[62] the prosecutor is not necessarily barred from raising a new libel for the same offence.

Hume states [63] that if the court deserts the diet on account of some objection to the citation, or the form or relevancy of the libel, this is " a special judgment, relative only to that particular process; and it cannot hinder the raising of a new libel in a better form." As an authority

[53] 1887 Act, s. 52.
[54] Supra, para. 10–06.
[55] Ibid.; s. 41 applies only to cases for trial in the sheriff court.
[56] *Wood and Anr.* v. *H.M. Adv.* (1899) 3 Adam 64.
[57] *Collins* v. *Lang* (1887) 1 White 482; *John Hall* (1881) 4 Couper 500.
[58] Ibid.
[59] *John Hall*, supra, L.J.-G. at 508.
[60] *Wm. Leslie* (1788) Hume, ii. 277.
[61] In *G. D. Hamilton*, Glasgow High Court, Nov. 16, 1954, unreported, the judge refused a Crown motion to desert pro loco because of the illness of a witness and instead deserted the diet simpliciter, discharged the jury and assoilzied the accused.
[62] See *Edward Tabram* (1872) 2 Couper 259, Lord Ardmillan at 272; *Collins* v. *Lang*, supra, L.J.-C. at 488.
[63] Hume, ii. 277.

for this proposition he quotes the case of *Buchanan*, June 30 and December 18, 1727. Hume's view is approved by Lord Justice-General Inglis and Lord Justice-Clerk Moncreiff in *John Hall*.[64] In that case it was held by a Full Bench that where the court, on holding a libel irrelevant, refused the prosecutor's motion to discharge the diet pro loco et tempore and dismissed the panel from the bar, the prosecutor was not barred from raising a new libel for the same offence, and both Lord Justice-General Inglis and Lord Justice-Clerk Moncreiff expressed the opinion that the position would have been the same had the court, instead of dismissing the panel, deserted the diet simpliciter.

This further proposition is stated by Hume[65]: " Again, where the Court desert the diet, because the prosecutor is absent at the calling; even this, though it may sometimes, is not however always, or even ordinarily, a bar to a second process at his instance: Because his absence may have been necessary, or at least excusable." In *Edward Tabram*,[66] Lord Justice-Clerk Moncreiff, founding on this passage, advanced the view that, if the court deserts a diet simpliciter in respect of the non-appearance or non-insisting of the prosecutor, the latter will be entitled to proceed with a fresh indictment upon the same grounds, if he is able at the calling of it to support the new instance by proving reasonable cause for his not having insisted in the first.

Postponement of trial

10–14   Apart from desertion of the diet, it is always competent for the court to adjourn the diet,[67] but unless there be some circumstance arising which leads the court to see cause to adjourn over a day or days, every trial must proceed from day to day till concluded.[68] If there is an adjournment, it must always be to a specified time and place, and these must be stated in a written interlocutor duly signed.[69]

This is a strict rule, non-observance of which involves a fundamental nullity,[70] which is unaffected by acquiescence on the part of the accused.[71] It applies even if the adjournment is merely to a later hour on the same day. So, where a sheriff-substitute, having convicted a person, postponed sentence upon him until a later hour in the day without adjourning the diet and, before imposing sentence, heard the evidence in the next case (in which the same person was accused) it was held that the diet in the first case fell when the second diet was called, and the conviction was suspended. Both Lord Justice-Clerk Macdonald and Lord

---

[64] Supra.
[65] Hume, ii. 277.
[66] Supra.
[67] *Wm. Rodger* (1868) 1 Couper 76; *W. H. Thomson* (1871) 2 Couper 103.
[68] 1887 Act, s. 55.
[69] Supra, para. 10–04.
[70] *Hull* v. *H.M. Adv.*, 1945 J.C. 83, 86; *Corstorphine*, infra; *Jamieson* v. *Wilson* (1901) 3 Adam 395; *Taylor* v. *Sempill* (1906) 5 Adam 114.
[71] *Jamieson*, supra; *Taylor*, supra.

Ardwall were of opinion that the position would have been the same had the second case related to a different person.[72]

The rule does not apply where the adjournment is merely for luncheon, as that is not an adjournment in the true sense of the term.[73]

10–15 Sometimes an adjournment is rendered necessary by the illness of the panel. The court will not allow a trial to proceed when, owing to illness, the panel is unable to give instructions for his defence. Where the panel who is taken ill is one of several co-accused, the court will adjourn the diet against them all if it is important that they should be tried at the same diet.[74]

Death or illness of judge

10–16 Section 32 (1) of the 1949 Act makes the following provisions for dealing with such contingency:

> " Where at any sitting of the High Court of Justiciary or of the sheriff court for the trial of cases on indictment the court is unable to proceed owing to the death or illness of the presiding judge, it shall be lawful for the clerk of court—
>
> > (a) in the case where the diet has not been called, to convene the court and adjourn that diet and any other diet appointed for that sitting to a later sitting;
> >
> > (b) in the case where the diet has been called but no evidence has been led, to adjourn the diet or any other diet appointed for that sitting to a later sitting; and
> >
> > (c) where evidence has been led, to desert the diet pro loco et tempore and to discharge the jury;
>
> and any such continuation, adjournment, desertion or other proceeding shall be entered in the record by the clerk of court." [75]

Where the clerk has deserted the diet after evidence has been led, as above described, the Lord Advocate may raise and insist in a new indictment. In such a case if the accused is in custody, it is unnecessary to obtain a new warrant for his incarceration. The warrant of committal on which he is at the time in custody till liberation in due course of law continues in force. If he is at liberty on bail, his bail also continues in force.[76]

[72] *Corstorphine* v. *Jameson* (1909) 6 Adam 154.
[73] *Tocher* v. *H.M. Adv.*, 1927 J.C. 63.
[74] *Agnes Chambers or McQueen and Helen Henderson* (1849) J. Shaw 252. The report states that the diet was continued until the next day, and the jury were discharged. The trial proceeded the following day before another jury chosen from the same list of assize. The panel had taken ill at the original diet as the first witness began to give evidence. Cf. *H.M. Adv.* v. *Brown and Foss*, 1966 S.L.T. 341; *Elizabeth McDonald or Hamilton* (1880) 4 Couper 344.
[75] 1949 Act, s. 32 (1).
[76] Ibid. s. 32 (2).

Separation of Charges and Accused

Separation of charges

10–17   Where there is more than one charge *the* accused may move the court to order the counts to be tried separately. It is in the discretion of the court to grant or to refuse the motion. The test to be applied in every case is whether it is fair to the person or persons accused to put a particular accumulation of charges in one indictment.[77] It is difficult to define the circumstances in which such an action would be fair and legitimate. On the one hand it is the duty of the court to avoid the risk of prejudice to accused persons, particularly in murder cases, but, on the other hand, there may exist between the charges a connection of time or of circumstances or of character which makes it fair and legitimate to put them all in one indictment and to lead evidence in respect of them all together.[78] Crimes may be separated by an interval of time, and yet may be so interrelated by circumstances, or by similarity of character, or by the relevancy of one to the proof of another, that the charges cannot be reasonably separated.[79] Thus, for example, offences which are really successive stages of the same course of criminal conduct are properly tried together.[80] So, a motion for separation of charges was refused by a court of five judges in *H.M. Advocate* v. *Bickerstaff*,[81] a case in which the indictment charged the accused with having, on the same day (1) indecently assaulted one little girl and (2) indecently assaulted and murdered another little girl. At the subsequent trial the Lord Justice-Clerk directed the jury [82] that, in reaching a conclusion upon the second charge, they were neither bound nor entitled to shut their eyes to what they might consider to have been proved under the first charge, because of the close relationship in time, character and circumstances of the incidents relative to each charge. Where, however, charges are less closely allied, prejudice may arise to the accused if they are tried together. Wherever murder is charged it is the duty of the court to prevent prejudice of this kind, and, if there is any risk of the same, to separate the charges. In *H.M. Advocate* v. *McGuinness*,[83] the indictment libelled assault and murder on one date and two charges of assault on an earlier date. In reply to a question from the presiding judge, the advocate-depute stated that he was unable to say that the evidence to be led upon the earlier assaults charged was relevant to the later charges of assault and murder. A motion for separation of charges was accordingly granted.

     It should be said, however, that charges are often tried together where

---

[77] *H.M. Adv.* v. *McGuinness*, 1937 J.C. 37, L.J.-C. at 38; *H.M. Adv.* v. *Bickerstaff*, 1926 J.C. 65; see also Hume, ii. 173; Alison, ii. 238; *John Thomson* (1857) 2 Irv. 747; *Edward Pritchard* (1865) 5 Irv. 88.

[78] *H.M. Adv.* v. *Bickerstaff*, supra, L.J.-G. at 75.

[79] *H.M. Adv.* v. *McGuinness*, supra, L.J.-C. at 38, 39.

[80] *H.M. Adv.* v. *Bickerstaff*, supra, L.J.-G. at 75.

[81] Supra.

[82] Ibid. at 82.

[83] Supra; cf. *Burke and McDougal* (1828) Syme 345.

the only connection between them is that the same person is accused in each. " This is allowed," says Hume, " not only for the sake of doing justice as expeditiously, and with as little expense and trouble as may be to the public, but also (provided it is kept within certain bounds) for the advantage of the pannel; that he may be relieved of the long confinement, and of the anxiety and distress, which would attend a series of successive trials." [84]

It is in the discretion of the court to grant or refuse separation of charges. [85]

Accumulation of accused

10–18 Where two or more persons are charged in the one indictment, the accused may, prior to the empannelling of the jury, make a special motion for separation of the trials. Before discussing this matter, however, it is necessary to consider the circumstances in which different panels may be charged in the same libel.

The accumulation of different accused under one indictment is incompetent if there is no connection between them or their crimes. [86] If, however, there is " an affinity among the pannels, or their crimes " it is proper to try them together. [87] Such accumulation has also been allowed

" wherever there was any natural contingency of the matters charged, as where the several crimes arose out of each other, or were directed towards the same object; or where the several pannels appeared to be in a society for committing crimes of a certain sort; nay, in some instances where the offences were only of the same class, and were not the result of any such confederacy; or where all the pannels were charged with some of the articles in the libel, though not with others." [88]

Separation of trials

10–19 Separate offences which are committed at the same time and contribute to the same result are tried under the same indictment. This practice has been approved in the cases of *H.M. Advocate* v. *Parker and Barrie*, [89] *Matthewson* v. *Ramsay*, [90] and *Morrison* v. *Adair*. [91] The earlier case of *Clelland* v. *Sinclair* [92] is not an authority on this point. " The trial, without separation, of two motorists on one complaint for negligence resulting in the same collision has become recognized as correct procedure." [93]

[84] Hume, ii. 172.
[85] Macdonald, 281.
[86] Hume, ii. 176–177.
[87] Ibid. 177.
[88] Ibid.; *Sangster* v. *H.M. Adv.* (1896) 2 Adam 182.
[89] (1888) 2 White 79.
[90] 1936 J.C. 5.
[91] 1943 J.C. 25.
[92] (1887) 1 White 359.
[93] *Morrison* v. *Adair*, supra, L.J.-G. at 30.

10–19   The matter of separation of trials now falls to be considered. " A motion for separation of trial is very frequently made, but very seldom granted." [94] " It generally requires some specification of peculiar circumstances to render it necessary or desirable." [95]

The matter is one for the discretion of the presiding judge [96] and the appellate court will not recall his decision " unless it appears to be oppressive or is conclusively shown to be entirely wrong." [97] If he considers that a joint trial may result in injustice to any of the accused he should separate the trials.[98] He may also take this step ex proprio motu.[99] His duty is to see that the accused get a fair trial, and it is not always easy. Sometimes it is highly undesirable that one criminal investigation should be taken in one or more stages.[1] It must always be kept in view that separating trials is a very special step. " Persons accused of the joint commission of a crime have no right to insist on a separation of trials; and there is nothing oppressive in refusing a separation, unless it is asked for on some ground which goes to the conditions of fair trial." [2]

It is not per se a sufficient ground for separation of trials that the accused desires to examine a co-accused as a witness,[3] nor is it necessarily enough merely to allege that one accused is dependent on the evidence of the other.[4] The mover of the motion must also satisfy the presiding judge that injustice may result from a refusal to grant separation. In *James Barnet* [5] this motion was granted on a statement by one of the panels' counsel " on his professional responsibility " that material prejudice would arise if all the accused were tried under the same indictment, which admittedly contained two separate and distinct charges. In *McIleer and Mullen* [6] one of two persons accused of the same crime desired the evidence of the other, who, while prepared to plead guilty to the offence, was unwilling also to plead guilty to an aggravation charged against him. The prosecutor having refused to accept the plea, the court, on the statement by McIleer's counsel that there would arise oppression to McIleer if he was denied the evidence of his co-accused, separated the

---

[94] *Sangster* v. *H.M. Adv.* (1896) 2 Adam 182, Lord Moncreiff at 189.
[95] *Robt. Turner and Ors.* (1881) 18 S.L.R. 491, Lord Moncreiff; see also *T. K. Rowbotham and Ors.* (1855) 2 Irv. 89; *Hawton and Parker* (1861) 4 Irv. 58; *Adam Coupland and Wm. Beattie* (1863) 4 Irv. 370.
[96] *Jas. Gibson and Ors.* (1871) 2 Couper 128; *Turner*, supra; *Sangster*, supra; *Collison* v. *Mitchell* (1897) 2 Adam 277; *Gemmell and McFadyen* v. *MacNiven*, 1928 J.C. 5; *Matthewson* v. *Ramsay*, supra; *Morrison* v. *Adair*, supra.
[97] *Morrison* v. *Adair*, supra, Lord Fleming at 32.
[98] Macdonald, 281; *Jas. Barnet* (1831) Shaw 245; *Wm. Cleary and Ors.* (1846) Ark. 7; *T. Clancy and Ors.* (1834) Bell's Notes 183; *McIleer and Mullen* (1869) 1 Couper 390; *Drever and Tyre* (1885) 5 Couper 680; cf. *Robt. Surrage and Ors.* (1820) Shaw 22.
[99] Macdonald, 281.
[1] *H.M. Adv.* v. *Clark*, 1935 J.C. 51; *McAuley* v. *H.M. Adv.*, 1946 J.C. 8; *Greig* v. *Muir*, 1955 J.C. 20.
[2] *Gemmell and McFadyen*, supra, L.J.-G. at 8.
[3] Macdonald, 281–282; *Jane Dempster* (1862) 4 Irv. 143; *Adam Coupland and Wm. Beattie*, supra; *Adam Baxter* (1867) 5 Irv. 351; *McGarth* v. *Bathgate* (1869) 1 Couper 260; *McLeod* v. *Mackenzie* (1888) 2 White 9; *H.M. Adv.* v. *Parker and Barrie* (1888) 2 White 79.
[4] *Marr* v. *Stuart* (1881) 4 Couper 407, L.J.-C. at 415.
[5] (1831) Shaw 245.
[6] (1869) 1 Couper 390.

trials. In *Duncan Gollen and Ors.*[7] and *H.M. Advocate* v. *Turner*,[8] separation of trials was granted to allow the accused to obtain the evidence of co-accused, the Crown consenting to this course.[9] Penuria testium may justify the motion. It was allowed on this ground in *Drever and Tyre*[10] where the master and mate of a ship which had been involved in a collision were indicted together for culpable homicide and the only evidence besides that of the accused as to what took place on the bridge of the vessel at the relevant time was that of the man at the wheel. In another case,[11] however, where the pilots of two colliding ships were charged in the same indictment, separation of trials was refused on the ground that the cases were not readily severable and that no prejudice could arise from their being tried together. The appeal court will intervene where it thinks that the Crown have acted oppressively or improperly in including persons, such as onlookers, in the charge for the purpose of depriving the accused of their evidence, but in ordinary cases will not interfere with the discretion of the trial judge.[12]

The fact that the trial is for perjury is not per se a special cause sufficient to warrant separation.[13]

0-20 Where there are numerous accused it may be convenient to try them in batches. This course was agreed to by the Crown on the suggestion of the court in *H.M. Advocate* v. *Macleod and Ors.*[14]

Conjoining trials

0-21 The converse position to that just discussed may occur, i.e., persons separately indicted for the same offence may, because they consider their defence to be prejudiced by the separation of their trials, desire to be tried together. In such a situation a motion should be made at the second diet of the first of the cases that the indictment should not be remitted to an assize in its existing form, and any of the accused, whether on trial or awaiting trial, can appear for this purpose. The motion will be granted if the court considers that the separation of trials is so prejudicial to any of the accused that a miscarriage of justice may ensue.[15] In *H.M. Advocate* v. *Clark*[16] three employees of a brewery company were charged on one indictment with fraud while acting in concert with each other and with the managing director, who was similarly charged under a separate indictment. At the second diet of the employees' case counsel for the managing director, who was then awaiting trial, craved leave to move that the indictment as it stood should not be remitted to an assize. His application was

---

[7] (1875) 3 Couper 82.
[8] (1881) 18 S.L.R. 491.
[9] See also *H.M. Adv.* v. *Steele and Ors.*, 1958 S.L.T. (Notes) 49, where separation was granted to allow a co-accused to be called as an alibi witness, the Crown not consenting.
[10] (1885) 5 Couper 680.
[11] *H.M. Adv.* v. *Parker and Barrie* (1888) 2 White 79.
[12] *Collison* v. *Mitchell*, supra, L.J-C. at 282; cf. *Kerr* v. *Phyn* (1893) 3 White 480.
[13] *Marr* v. *Stuart* (1881) 4 Couper 407.
[14] (1888) 1 White 554.
[15] *H.M. Adv.* v. *Clark*, 1935 J.C. 51.
[16] Supra. See also *McAuley* v. *H.M. Adv.*, 1946 J.C. 8.

thereupon remitted by the presiding judge to a bench of three judges, before whom counsel renewed his motion. The court granted the motion, holding that, while the court would not, in ordinary circumstances, interfere with the discretion of the Crown, it was nevertheless within its power to disallow procedure which, in its opinion, might lead to a miscarriage of justice, and that, as separate trials might cause prejudice to all the accused, the indictment as it stood should not be remitted to an assize.

Insanity of Accused

10–22   This matter is discussed in a later chapter.[17]

Empannelling the Jury

10–23   The members of the jury are balloted by the clerk of court. Fifteen are chosen.

The names of the jurors summoned to the diet are selected from the list of assize prepared in the manner already described.[18] The names and addresses of the persons summoned are usually called by the clerk of court before the judge takes his seat on the bench. If any fail to answer to their names, these names are again called after the judge takes his seat, and if they are not then present, they are liable to be fined. If a juror fails to answer his citation, and if no reasonable excuse for absence is established on his behalf, he is liable to a fine.[19] The follow-ing are sufficient excuses: (a) That the juror is so ill that he cannot attend without injury to his health; (b) that the juror's age exceeds sixty years; (c) that the juror is exempt from service in virtue of an Act of Parliament.[20] A female juror may, on application to the judge at the trial, be granted exemption from service on the jury by reason of the nature either of the evidence to be given or of the issues to be tried.[21] A medical certificate of illness, or a certificate of age, should be sent to the clerk of court before the date of trial. In the High Court of Justiciary it is competent to apply for remission of fines imposed. In the event of the excuse for non-attendance being held sufficient the application will be granted.[22]

10–24   As each juror is balloted he may be challenged by the prosecutor or the persons accused, each of whom has five peremptory challenges.[23] It is not usual for the Crown to challenge any jurors. Beyond these peremptory challenges, no challenge is allowed unless on special cause shown. A sufficient cause would be insanity, deafness, dumbness, blindness, minority,

---

[17] Infra, paras. 20–05 et seq.

[18] Supra, para. 7–25.

[19] Jurors Act 1587. See *Mitchell* v. *H.M. Adv.*, 1971 S.L.T. (Notes) 82.

[20] Supra, para. 7–21.

[21] Sex Disqualification (Removal) Act 1919, s. 1 (*b*) and relative Act of Adjournal, February 2, 1921. See supra, para. 7–24.

[22] Act of Adjournal, for Regulating the Procedure in regard to Applications by Persons who have been Fined for Failing to Attend in Answer to their Citations as Jurors, etc., March 19, 1925.

[23] Jurors (Scotland) Act 1825, s. 16, as amended by Juries Act 1949, s. 35 and Sched. 3.

relationship, or enmity, on the part of the juror. In one sheriff court case objection was taken to a juror on the ground that she had already served on a jury at the same sitting in a trial concerning an incident which had occurred at about the same time at the same place as that libelled in the indictment and that she might therefore be antagonistic to the accused. The sheriff-substitute repelled the objection, observing that an objection for cause must be an objection personal to the prospective juror.[24]

Where an accused was convicted by the verdict of a jury composed of six special and nine common jurors, and brought a suspension, the suspension was refused on the ground that he could competently have challenged the sixth special juror before the jury was sworn.[25] The same ground of judgment was applied where a suspension was brought because three jurymen had been balloted and served on the jury whose names were not included in the copy of the assize supplied to the accused in terms of the statutory provision.[26]

10–25   Where more trials than one are to be disposed of at a sitting, a jury chosen for any particular trial may, when that trial is disposed of, serve on the trials of other accused, without any new ballot, with the consent of the prosecutor and persons accused. Such jurors must be duly sworn on each successive trial, and the whole of the previous jury must be taken or the fifteen ballot of new.[27] Otherwise a fresh jury is balloted. The consent of the accused need not be his personal consent but may be given on his behalf by the counsel or agent appearing for him even although he is not present at the time. It would appear that, at any rate in the latter case, the consent can be withdrawn at any time before the jury is sworn.[28]

0–26   The jury having been balloted, the clerk of court informs them of the charge against the person accused. He does this in the manner set forth by section 54 of the 1887 Act as substituted by section 3 of the Circuit Courts and Criminal Procedure (Scotland) Act 1925, as amended by Schedule 12 to the 1949 Act, the procedure being as follows: Either the clerk reads the indictment to the jury, substituting the third person for the second, or, if the presiding judge, because of the length or complexity of the indictment so directs, the clerk reads to them a summary of the charge approved by the judge. It is not necessary to lay before the jury copies of the indictment, list of witnesses, or list of productions, but it is competent to the presiding judge, should he think fit, to direct that copies of the indictment without any list of witnesses or of productions appended shall be laid before the jury. It is the practice in every case in the High Court, however, where a summary of the charge or charges is read to the jury, to provide the jury with copies of the indictment, but not of the lists.

The clerk of court then administers the oath to the jury. He asks

---

[24] *H.M. Adv.* v. *Devine* (1962) 78 Sh.Ct.Rep. 173.
[25] *Torri* v. *H.M. Adv.*, 1923 J.C. 52.
[26] *McArthur* v. *H.M. Adv.* (1902) 10 S.L.T. 310.
[27] Jurors (Scotland) Act 1825, s. 18; Act of Adjournal, Sept. 9, 1817; *Daniel* or *Donald Stuart* (1829) Bell's Notes 237.
[28] *Lamont* v. *H.M. Adv.*, 1943 J.C. 21.

them to stand, hold up their right hands, and take the following oath: " You fifteen swear by Almighty God, and as you shall answer to God at the great Day of Judgment, that you will truth say and no truth conceal, so far as you are to pass on this assize." In the case of a juror objecting to be sworn on the ground that he has no religious belief, or that the taking of an oath is contrary to his religious belief, he is permitted to make a solemn affirmation.[29] The following is the form: " I, Thomas Smith, do solemnly, sincerely, and truly declare and affirm that I will truth say and no truth conceal, so far as I am to pass on this assize." After the oath or affirmation is administered, the clerk reads to the jury any special defence lodged on behalf of the accused. The practice of reading a special defence is based on custom only, and its value varies according to the nature of the special defence. A special defence ought always to be read, but failure to do so will not necessarily amount to a miscarriage of justice.[30] The jurors resume their seats and the clerk records their names, occupations and addresses in the record.

Management of jury

10-27   It will be convenient at this place to mention the rules which regulate the management of the jury. After the jury is sworn, no communication on the subject of the trial between a juror and any person can be permitted. But a conviction will not be invalidated because of some trivial remark which can have no influence on the justice of the cause.[31]

If the trial is adjourned from one day to another, it is not necessary that the jury should be secluded during the adjournment, except in any case in which the court may see fit, either ex proprio motu or on the motion of the prosecutor or the person accused, to order that the jury be kept secluded.[32] In such exceptional cases, if the trial lasts more than a day, provision is made for the accommodation of the jury overnight at an hotel under charge of court officials, and they are strictly secluded during the period of the adjournment from all communication whatsoever with any person on the subject of the trial, the clerk of court only having access to, and liberty to communicate with, them in relation to their private affairs.

In one case, in which the circumstances were very special, a conviction was quashed in respect that one juryman in the possession of private information communicated it to his fellow-jurors.[33]

Illness of jurors

10-28   A juror may be taken ill during the trial. Prior to the passing of the Administration of Justice (Scotland) Act 1933, it was incompetent, even

[29] Oaths Act 1888. That Act now also applies where it is not reasonably practicable to swear the juror in the manner appropriate to his religious belief, in which case he must affirm: Oaths Act 1961.
[30] *Moar* v. *H.M. Adv.*, 1949 J.C. 31.
[31] *Smart* v. *H.M. Adv.*, 1938 J.C. 148; Alison, ii. 633; *Dougall and Hamilton* v. *H.M. Adv.*, Dec. 18, 1945, unreported; infra, para. 10-40.
[32] 1887 Act, s. 55.
[33] *Verner* v. *H.M. Adv.*, 1916, 2 S.L.T. 330; see infra, para. 10-39.

with the consent of the accused, to proceed with less than the full number of jurors.[34] Accordingly, if a juror became ill during the trial, the prosecutor had to choose between the alternatives of asking for an adjournment until the juryman recovered [35] or deserting the diet pro loco et tempore,[36] unless the accused consented to the substitution of another juror in place of the absentee.[37] In the last-mentioned event the jury was resworn and the witnesses who had already given evidence deponed again to what had been taken down as their testimony.[38] It was, however, competent for the judge to read over to the jury the notes of evidence instead of having the witnesses testify again.[39]

The above statement must now be read subject to section 19 of the Act of 1933, which is in the following terms:

> " Where in the course of the trial on any indictment any juror chosen to serve on such trial dies, or the court is satisfied that any juror so chosen is, through illness or for any other reason, unfit to continue to serve on the trial, the court may, on application made by or on behalf of the Lord Advocate or an accused, in its discretion, direct that the trial shall proceed before the remaining jurors (if they shall be not less than twelve in number), and where any such direction is given the remaining jurors shall be deemed in all respects to be a properly constituted jury for the purpose of the trial and shall have power to return a verdict accordingly whether unanimous or by majority, provided always that they shall not be entitled to return a verdict of guilty by majority unless eight of their number are in favour of such verdict and if, in any such case, the remaining jurors shall inform the court that less than eight of their number are in favour of a verdict of guilty, and that there is not a majority in favour of any other verdict, they shall be deemed to have returned a verdict of not guilty."

Apart from such a direction trial by fourteen or less jurors would be a nullity, and the prosecutor would appear to be entitled to bring a fresh libel on the ground that the accused had not tholed his assize.[40]

The Trial

Leading of evidence

10–29   After the jury has been sworn, and any special defence, of which notice has been duly given, read to them, the evidence is led.[41] The whole evidence must be taken in the presence of the accused and the jury.[42]

---

[34] *Laird and Hosie* v. *H.M. Adv.*, 1922 J.C. 17; Hume, ii. 469.
[35] *McGarth* v. *Bathgate* (1869) 1 Couper 260.
[36] *Peter Crossan* (1869) 1 Couper 383.
[37] *Denis Lundie* (1868) 1 Couper 86; *H.M. Adv.* v. *McVean* (1903) 10 S.L.T. 648.
[38] *Denis Lundie*, supra.
[39] *H.M. Adv.* v. *McVean* (1903) 10 S.L.T. 648.
[40] Hume, ii. 469. But see *Laird and Hosie* v. *H.M. Adv.*, 1922 J.C. 17.
[41] Evidence in criminal cases is discussed infra, Chap. 18.
[42] *H.M. Adv.* v. *Hunter* (1905) 4 Adam 523; *Aitken* v. *Wood*, 1921 J.C. 84; Hume, ii. 404, 405; Alison, ii. 548; Criminal Justice Act 1587; see also infra, para. 14–72.

Evidence cannot be taken on commission in criminal cases.[43] Once the case for the prosecution is closed, it is incompetent for the prosecutor to call a further witness.[44] The presiding judge may, however, even before both sides have closed their cases recall a witness ex proprio motu in order to clear up ambiguity or obscurity in his evidence,[45] or perhaps even to rectify an omission.[46] It has also been suggested that the judge has a general power to recall in order to ask any question necessary to ascertain the truth.[47] The common law position is not now of paramount importance, since under section 4 of the Evidence (Scotland) Act 1852, the judge may, on the motion of either party, permit any witness who has been examined in the course of the trial to be recalled, although it is probable that a party cannot move for the recall of a witness after closing his case.[48]

The power under the Act is not restricted to clearing up ambiguities, and the witness when recalled is examined by the party calling him and not by the judge.[49] This power has been exercised to allow the Crown to recall a witness in order to ask him to identify the accused.[50]

10-30   Under section 55 (5) of the Mental Health (Scotland) Act 1960 the prosecutor must, if it appears to him that the accused is mentally disordered, bring before the court such evidence as may be available of the accused's mental condition. This is often done after conviction of an accused person in order that the court may proceed in terms of the section.[51]

10-31   The prosecutor conducting the case is not entitled to give evidence as a witness and the fact that he has done so is a good ground for quashing a conviction.[52]

10-32   On the conclusion of the evidence for the prosecution the accused, if he so desires, leads evidence. There is a statutory provision to the effect that, if he is the only witness for the defence as to the facts of the case, he must be called immediately after the Crown case is closed.[53] He is always entitled to lead evidence of good character, but if he does so he is liable to be cross-examined with a view to showing that he has been guilty of offences other than those charged or that he is of bad character.[54] He may, on due notice, attack the character of Crown witnesses.[55]

[43] *H.M. Adv.* v. *Hunter*, supra; Criminal Justice Act 1587.
[44] *Docherty* v. *McLennan* (1912) 6 Adam 700.
[45] *McNeilie* v. *H.M. Adv.*, 1929 J.C. 50; *Davidson* v. *McFadyean*, 1942 J.C. 95; cf. *Collison* v. *Mitchell* (1897) 2 Adam 277; *Saunders* v. *Paterson* (1905) 4 Adam 568; *Docherty* v. *McLennan*, supra.
[46] *Saunders* v. *Paterson*, supra; *Robt. Wilkie* (1886) 1 White 242.
[47] *Collison* v. *Mitchell*, supra; but see *Davidson* v. *McFadyean*, supra.
[48] *Todd* v. *MacDonald*, 1960 J.C. 93. In one case where the accused dispensed with his counsel's services after the latter had intimated that he was calling no evidence it was held that the accused could not call any evidence: *Beatson* v. *H.M. Adv.*, 1949 S.L.T. (Notes) 32.
[49] *Todd* v. *MacDonald*, supra.
[50] Ibid.; see H.M., " Recalling Witnesses in Criminal Cases," 1960 S.L.T. (News) 161.
[51] Infra, paras. 20–19 et seq.
[52] *Ferguson* v. *Webster* (1869) 1 Couper 370; *Grahams* v. *McLennan* (1910) 6 Adam 315. See also infra, para. 18–69.
[53] Criminal Evidence Act 1898, s. 2.
[54] Ibid. s. 1 (*f*); see infra, para. 18–14.
[55] See supra, para. 7–16 and infra, para. 18–76.

Noting of evidence

10-33   The presiding judge must take a note of the evidence.[56] It is now necessary in all trials on indictment for shorthand notes of the proceedings at the trial to be taken.[57] The Act of Adjournal relating to Shorthand Notes taken at Criminal Trials of March 22, 1935, defines " proceedings at the trial " as meaning the whole proceedings, including:

(1) Discussions (a) on any objections to the relevancy of the indictment, (b) in reference to any challenge of jurors, (c) on all questions arising in the course of the trial, with the decisions of the court thereon;

(2) The evidence led;

(3) Any statement by or on behalf of the prisoner, whether before or after the verdict;

(4) The summing up by the judge;

(5) The speeches of counsel or agents;

(6) The verdict of the jury;

(7) The sentence of the court.

Witnesses

10-34   A witness must be sworn or affirmed.[57a] Children under the age of twelve are not sworn but are admonished to be truthful.[58] When a child is between the ages of twelve and fourteen it is a matter for the discretion of the presiding judge whether to swear the child or merely warn him to speak the truth.[59] Dumb witnesses may be sworn through an interpreter, but deaf and dumb persons who do not understand the nature and obligation of an oath are examined through an interpreter [60] without being sworn.[61] A sworn interpreter is employed when witnesses ignorant of English are being examined.[62] If the accused is a foreigner ignorant of the English language an interpreter should be present in court to translate the evidence to him except where his counsel asks that this should be dispensed with and the presiding judge agrees with the request.[63] Failure to provide an interpreter where there is any doubt about the ability of the accused to speak or understand the English language is inconsistent with the proper administration of justice and will invalidate a conviction.[64] An interpreter is pro hac vice an official of the court and does not represent either the prosecution or

[56] Justiciary and Circuit Courts (Scotland) Act 1783; Circuit Courts (Scotland) Act 1828; Criminal Appeal (Scotland) Act 1926. s. 5.

[57] 1926 Act, s. 11 (1) and relative Acts of Adjournal, October 27, 1926 and March 22, 1935.

[57a] Cf. supra, para. 10–26.

[58] Macdonald, 297; Hume, ii. 341; Bishop and Brown (1829) Shaw 213; Robt. Emond (1830) Shaw 230.

[59] Ibid.; Anderson v. Macfarlane (1899) 2 Adam 644.

[60] Macdonald, 297.

[61] Ibid.; John S. Montgomery (1855) 2 Irv. 222; Edward Rice (1864) 4 Irv. 493.

[62] Ibid. The witness must know right from wrong. See Macdonald, 289; Edward Rice, supra; Jas. White (1842) 1 Broun 228.

[63] H.M. Adv. v. Olsson, 1941 J.C. 63; H.M. Adv. v. Kindoreso, 1913 unreported; cf. Rex v. Lee Kun [1916] 1 K.B. 337.

[64] Liszewski v. Thomson, 1942 J.C. 55.

the defence.[65] At common law the evidence of a witness who, before giving evidence, has been present in court without the consent of parties, falls to be rejected,[66] but this rule has been relaxed by section 3 of the Evidence (Scotland) Act 1840,[67] which allows the judge in his discretion to admit the witness where it appears to the judge that such presence was not the consequence of culpable negligence or criminal intent and that the witness has not been unduly instructed or influenced by what took place during his or her presence or that injustice will not be done by his or her examination. The consideration of some specialties of criminal evidence is reserved till a later chapter.[68]

Change of plea

10–35   The accused person may at any stage withdraw his plea and tender a plea of " guilty as libelled," or a modified plea of guilty. If he does so, and the prosecutor accepts such plea, the jury returns, after a formal charge by the presiding judge, a verdict of guilty, in conformity with the plea. In these circumstances the verdict should be recorded thus: " The jury unanimously find the panel guilty as libelled (or as the case may be) in terms of his confession." The prosecutor's acceptance of the plea should be endorsed on the record of proceedings.

Abandonment of prosecution

10–36   If at any stage the prosecutor abandons the trial, the judge directs the jury to return a verdict of not guilty.[69] Following upon the verdict the accused person is assoilzied simpliciter and discharged from the bar.

If, at the conclusion of the Crown evidence, the presiding judge is satisfied that there is no evidence in law to support a conviction, he may, with the consent of the Lord Advocate or his representative who is prosecuting, but not otherwise, withdraw the case from the jury. In the absence of such consent, the judge cannot direct the jury that there is no evidence in law to support a conviction until he comes to charge them at the conclusion of the case.[70]

Reading of declaration

10–37   The last step in the proof for the prosecution is the reading of any declaration emitted by the accused person, upon the charge for which he is under trial or upon a similar impending charge based upon the same facts, if it is considered necessary to produce it. A declaration is evidence only as regards a person who emits it, and is evidence against him, but not in his favour. The accused cannot demand that a declaration be

---

[65] Ibid., Lord Fleming at 58.
[66] Hume, ii. 379; Alison, ii. 542; *Dickson on Evidence*, para. 1599.
[67] See *Macdonald* v. *Mackenzie*, 1947 J.C. 169.
[68] Infra., Chap. 18.
[69] *McArthur* v. *Grosset*, 1952 J.C. 12; *Arch. Phaup* (1846) Ark. 176; cf. *John Craig* (1867) 5 Irv. 523; *Thos. and Peter Galloway* (1836) 1 Swin. 232.
[70] *Kent* v. *H.M. Adv.*, 1950 J.C. 38.

read if the prosecutor objects, but in practice it is read if the accused requests this.[71]

The declaration is received in evidence without being sworn to by witnesses; but it is competent for the person accused, before such declaration is read to the jury, to adduce as witnesses the persons who were present when the declaration was emitted, and to examine them upon any grounds of objection to the reception in evidence of the declaration. He may move the court to refuse to allow the declaration to be read either on grounds appearing on the face of the declaration itself, or on the ground of what has been disclosed in the examination of witnesses above mentioned, or on both of these grounds. Where the accused objects to the declaration, the prosecutor is entitled to examine the witnesses whom the accused might have examined. These witnesses need not be on the list of witnesses.[72]

Speeches

10–38   After the conclusion of the evidence for both parties, the prosecutor and the solicitor or counsel for the defence, if they so desire, address the jury. If the accused does not elect to give evidence on his own behalf, the prosecutor is not permitted to refer to the fact.[73] Such reference, however, is not per se a ground for quashing a conviction.[74] The prosecutor should not make allegations against the accused which are irrelevant or are unsupported by evidence.[75]

Judge's charge

10–39   At the conclusion of the addresses the judge charges the jury.[76]

" The primary duty of the presiding judge is to direct the jury upon the law applicable to the case. In doing so it is usually necessary for him to refer to the facts on which questions of law depend. He may also have to refer to evidence in order to correct any mistakes that may have occurred in the addresses to the jury, and he may have occasion to refer to the evidence where controversy has arisen as to its bearing on a question of fact which the jury has to decide. But it is a matter very much in his discretion whether he can help the jury by resuming the evidence on any particular aspect of the case." [77]

If the judge reviews and comments on the evidence he must take the utmost care to avoid trespassing upon the jury's province as masters of the facts.[78] The judge is entitled to draw the attention of the jury to the fact

[71] Macdonald, 329; cf. Brown v. H.M. Adv., 1964 J.C. 10.
[72] 1887 Act, s. 69.
[73] Criminal Evidence Act 1898, s. 1 (b).
[74] McAtee v. Hogg (1903) 4 Adam 190; Ross v. Boyd (1903) 4 Adam 184.
[75] See Martin v. Boyd (1908) 5 Adam 528; Slater v. H.M. Adv., 1928 J.C. 94.
[76] Justiciary and Circuit Courts (Scotland) Act 1783, s. 5.
[77] Hamilton and Others v. H.M. Adv., 1938 J.C. 134, L.J.-G. at 144.
[78] Simpson v. H.M. Adv., 1952 J.C. 1, L.J.-G. at 3.

10–39 that the accused did not elect to give evidence on his own behalf.[79] Such comment should be made with restraint and only when there are special circumstances which require it. It should in no case be reiterated and emphasised.[80] Where a socius criminis has given evidence for the prosecution the judge must direct the jury that the law regards such evidence with suspicion and that they must specially scrutinize it. If the evidence is crucial failure to give such direction is a ground for quashing a conviction.[81] In a case which arose prior to the 1926 Act [82] the presiding sheriff after summing up handed certain written questions to the jury for their consideration which were not exhaustive of the case. In a suspension it was held that such a practice was not illegal but that it was desirable to adhere to the traditional practice. At that time, however, no appeal could be taken on the ground of misdirection and no record was kept of a judge's charge to a jury in a criminal trial. Accordingly the court, when deciding the appeal, proceeded upon the assumption that the presiding judge had given the jury all the proper directions.

If the judge considers that there is no evidence upon which the jury can legally convict the accused of a charge, he directs them to return a verdict of not guilty upon that charge. Apart from exceptional circumstances, in which the jury's choice may require to be limited by a special direction in law, three verdicts, viz. " guilty," " not guilty " and " not proven," are open to them, and it is proper and desirable that the presiding judge should specifically inform them regarding these verdicts.[83] His failure to do so, however, will not necessarily lead to a conviction being set aside.[84] The judge should explicitly draw the attention of the jury to all the possible verdicts which are in issue in the case,[85] and to the courses they should adopt on the various views of the evidence open to them.[86] It has been held to be a misdirection to refer to the not proven verdict in such a way as to indicate to the jury that they ought to disregard it,[87] but the Appeal Court may quash convictions on this ground only in what they regard as extreme cases.[88] In some circumstances a direction to disregard the not proven verdict may be proper.[89] The jury should be directed as to the majority required for a verdict of guilty,[90] but it is not necessary to direct them as to the majority sufficient for an acquittal.[91] After the

---

[79] *Brown* v. *Macpherson*, 1918 J.C. 3; *Costello* v. *Macpherson*, 1922 J.C. 9; *H.M. Adv.* v. *Hardy*, 1938 J.C. 144.
[80] *Scott (A.T.)* v. *H.M. Adv.*, 1946 J.C. 90.
[81] *Wallace* v. *H.M. Adv.*, 1952 J.C. 78. See infra, para. 18–58.
[82] *Cameron* v. *H.M. Adv.*, 1924 J.C. 101.
[83] *McDermid* v. *H.M. Adv.*, *Neill* v. *H.M. Adv.*, 1948 J.C. 12.
[84] *McDermid*; *Neill*, supra; *Bergson* v. *H.M. Adv* (1970) 34 J.C.L. 270.
[85] *Muir* v. *H.M. Adv.*, 1933 J.C. 46: culpable homicide in a murder trial where diminished responsibility is in issue. Cf. *H.M. Adv.* v. *Kilna*, 1960 J.C. 23.
[86] *Docherty* v. *H.M. Adv.*, 1945 J.C. 89; acquittal in the event of concert not being proved where no evidence against individual accused; cf. *Tobin* v. *H.M. Adv.*, 1934 J.C. 60; *Shaw* v. *H.M. Adv.*, 1953 J.C. 51.
[87] *McNicol* v. *H.M. Adv.*, 1964 J.C. 25; *Hasson* v. *H.M. Adv* (1971) 35 J.C.L. 271.
[88] *Buchan* v. *H.M. Adv* (1968) 32 J.C.L. 114.
[89] *Reid* v. *H.M. Adv.*, 1947 S.L.T. 150.
[90] *McPhelim* v. *H.M. Adv.*, 1960 J.C. 17.
[91] *Mackay* v. *H.M. Adv.*, 1944 J.C. 153; cf. *McPhelim*, supra.

charge the jury may either pronounce their verdict at once, or retire to consider it.[92] Should the next diet be called before the return of this jury, the proceedings therein may, at the discretion of the presiding judge, be interrupted in order either to receive the verdict of this jury and to dispose of the case or to give any further directions they may ask for or to hear any request they may make. If such interruption is allowed by the presiding judge he must direct the jury in the interrupted trial to retire for the period thereof. A minute continuing the diet of the interrupted case is entered in the minute book, and it is sufficient that the diet should be continued to an afterpart of the same day without further specification of time or to the following or a subsequent day as the court may direct. On the interrupted trial being resumed the diet must be called de novo. Similar provisions are made for interrupting trials in order to dispose of pleas of guilty including those in causes remitted under section 31 of the 1887 Act.[93]

Verdict and Sentence

10–40   The jury normally retire to consider their verdict, but need not do so.[94] If they do retire they are inclosed in the charge of a court officer.[95] It is improper for anyone to communicate or be present with the jury after they have retired,[96] but this may not extend to a merely formal inquiry by the clerk of court as to whether the jury have understood the judge's directions.[97] It does not extend to things like the attendance of a doctor on a juror who has taken ill.[98] The jury may return at any stage for further directions or information from the court, and the judge may himself recall them in order to give them a necessary direction omitted from the charge.[99]

    The first duty of the jury is to elect a foreman. Having done this, they proceed to consider their verdict. This may be returned by a majority. A verdict of guilty cannot be returned unless at least eight members of the jury vote for it.[1] It is not necessary for the jury to hear the trial to a finish. They may, at the conclusion of the Crown case, with the consent of the Crown, bring in a verdict in favour of the accused [2] which should be one of not guilty.[3]

    On the return of the jury, if they have retired or, if they have remained in the box, on their being agreed upon their verdict, the clerk of court asks them who speaks for them. The person chosen then rises and states that

---

[92] Justiciary Courts (Scotland) Act 1814, s. 1.
[93] Act of Adjournal relative to Verdicts and Sentences in Criminal Causes, Oct. 13, 1936, as amended by Act of Adjournal (Procedure in Criminal Trials) Amendment 1966.
[94] Justiciary Courts (Scotland) Act 1814, s. 1.
[95] Macdonald, 339.
[96] Criminal Justice Act 1587; Courts Act 1672; Hume, ii. 419–420; Alison, ii. 634–635.
[97] *Brownlie* v. *H.M. Adv.* (1966) 31 J.C.L. 132.
[98] Macdonald, 340; *G. & R. Wilson* (1826) Syme 38, 42.
[99] *Brownlie,* supra.
[1] *L.A.* v. *Nicholson,* 1958 S.L.T. (Sh.Ct.) 17; *McPhelim* v. *H.M. Adv.,* 1960 J.C. 17.
[2] *John Craig* (1867) 5 Irv. 523; *Kent* v. *H.M. Adv.,* 1950 J.C. 38.
[3] *Arch. Phaup* (1846) Ark. 176; *Thos. and Peter Galloway* (1836) 1 Swin. 232, 244; cf. *McArthur* v. *Grosset,* 1952 J.C. 12.

he has been appointed. The clerk asks him if the jury have considered their verdict, and, if so, what it is. The spokesman then announces the verdict. If the jury are not unanimous he must state this fact. Before the verdict is recorded the presiding judge must ask the jury to make any amendment or give any explanation should the verdict require the same,[4] as, after the verdict has been recorded, it cannot be altered or explained.[5] It is recorded by the clerk. After the verdict is recorded it should be read over to the jury and their assent to its recorded terms obtained. Failure to read over the verdict to the jury, although an irregularity which is to be deprecated, does not render the proceedings fundamentally null.[6]

If the verdict is one of not guilty or not proven, the accused is assoilzied simpliciter and dismissed from the bar.

Essentials of verdict

10–41   Three kinds of verdict may, as a rule, be returned—guilty, not guilty, or not proven. The essential qualities of the verdict are:

(a) It must in express terms find the accused guilty or not guilty, or the charge not proven.

(b) Its terms must be consistent with the indictment. A verdict of guilty must infer guilt of the offence of which the accused is convicted. So, in *MacMillan* v. *H.M. Advocate*,[7] it was held that where the charge was embezzlement a verdict of misappropriation was not one of guilty. If, however, the verdict does not deviate from the indictment sufficiently to be inconsistent with it the conviction will stand. Thus a verdict of " wilful fire raising as libelled " upon a charge of " wilfully setting fire " to haystacks has been held good.[8] When the indictment is composed of one charge only or of cumulative charges the proper verdict is the general one of " guilty," and it should be duly recorded as a verdict of guilty as libelled. A general conviction means guilty of all that is charged or a substantial and material part thereof.[9] So, in *Myers* v. *H.M. Advocate*,[10] following *Gold* v. *Neilson*,[11] it was held that a verdict of " guilty of reset " was competent although it referred only to part of the articles libelled in the indictment. The verdict ought to dispose of the whole libel with the exception of any charges which have been departed from. Where a general charge includes several subheads, the proper course is for the jury to return a verdict specifying the subheads in respect of which they

---

[4] *Jas. Alexander* (1823) Shaw 99; *G. & R. Wilson* (1826) Syme 38, 43; *Wm. Hardie* (1831) Bell's Notes 296; *Wm. Harvey* (1833) ibid.; *Wm. Waiters* (1836) 1 Swin. 273.
[5] *Janet Anderson or Darling* (1830) Bell's Notes 295; *Thos. Hunter* (1838) 2 Swin. 1, 15; *McGarry* v. *H.M. Adv.*, 1959 J.C. 30.
[6] *Torri* v. *H.M. Adv.*, 1923 J.C. 52.
[7] (1888) 1 White 572.
[8] *Angus* y. *H.M. Adv.* (1905) 4 Adam 640.
[9] *Gold* v. *Neilson* (1907) 5 Adam 423, L.J.-C. at 431–432.
[10] 1936 J.C. 1.
[11] Supra.

10–41
convict or acquit the accused.[12] Where there are several accused the verdict should deal expressly with each. If it omits to do so, or if where there are several charges it deals with some only and ignores others, it will be held to be an acquittal as regards those persons or charges with which it does not deal. Where the charges are not cumulative but truly alternative a verdict of guilty as libelled is bad and will not warrant any sentence.[13] A verdict of " guilty " is competent in the case of statutory offences capable of being committed in several ways if the manner of executing the offence is not material.[14] If, however, the charge sets forth the various acts which constitute the offence, such a verdict may be bad as failing to specify the precise offence which the jury found proven.[15]

(c) The verdict must be unambiguous.[16] A verdict will not be disturbed because of its form if its meaning is clear.

Thus verdicts have been allowed to stand in the following cases: Where there were two alternative charges and the verdict merely referred to " the alternative charge " (verdict held to apply to the second alternative) [17]; where the presiding judge excluded from the trial one of the charges in the indictment and the jury returned a verdict of " guilty of the crime of fraud as laid before them " [18]; and where, on an indictment for theft, the verdict was " guilty of stealing a part of the articles libelled." [19]

On the other hand, verdicts have been set aside in the following cases: Where the verdict was guilty " of a contravention of the Criminal Law Amendment Act 1885, section 5 " (held that as the section created more than one offence it was impossible to tell from the verdict of the jury of which of these offences the accused had been held guilty) [20]; where the verdict was " guilty of the crime charged aggravated as charged," there being no aggravation libelled [21]; where a panel charged with theft and with being by habit and repute a thief was convicted only of the aggravation [22]; and where, in the case of a charge containing a general charge and several other charges which were only particularisations of it, the jury acquitted the accused of the general charge and convicted him of the remainder.[23]

A verdict which is inconsistent and self-contradictory cannot stand.[24]

---

12 *Young* v. *H.M. Adv.*, 1932 J.C. 63.   13 Infra, paras. 13–65 et seq.

14 Cf. *Scott* v. *Morrison* (1872) 2 Couper 218; *O'Neill, etc.* v. *Campbell* (1883) 5 Couper 305; *Macnaughton* v. *Maddever* (1884) 5 Couper 509; *Shaw* v. *Hart* (1886) 1 White 270; *Maxwell* v. *Marsland* (1889) 2 White 176; *Thomson* v. *Knights* [1947] K.B. 336; *Galletly* v. *Laird*, 1953 J.C. 16; *Hunter* v. *Clark*, 1956 J.C. 59.

15 *De Banzie* v. *Peebles* (1875) 3 Couper 89.

16 As regards summary convictions, see infra, para. 15–11.

17 *Paterson* v. *H.M. Adv.* (1901) 3 Adam 490; cf. *Young* v. *Heatly*, 1959 J.C. 66.

18 *Lloyd* v. *H.M. Adv.* (1899) 2 Adam 637.

19 *Brodie* v. *Johnston* (1845) 2 Broun 559.

20 *Townsend* v. *H.M. Adv.* (1914) 7 Adam 378.

21 *Donald* v. *Hart* (1892) 3 White 274.

22 *Beatson and McPherson* (1820) Shaw 18.

23 *Thos. Hunter* (1838) 2 Swin. 1.

24 *Hamilton and Ors.* v. *H.M. Adv.*, 1938 J.C. 134.

Alternative verdicts

10–42   The provisions of the 1887 Act greatly extended the powers of the jury in regard to the verdict which they may return. These provisions may be summarised thus:

(a) Under an indictment for robbery, or for theft, or for breach of trust and embezzlement, or for falsehood, fraud, and wilful imposition, the accused may be convicted of reset.[25]

So, where an indictment charged the accused with theft of sheep and the jury found the charge of theft not proven, but found the accused " guilty of reset," the verdict was upheld in a suspension, Lord Justice-Clerk Macdonald observing that the indictment would be read, in the light of the 1887 Act, as a charge that the accused did reset these sheep, well knowing them to be stolen.[26]

(b) Under an indictment for robbery, or for breach of trust and embezzlement, or for falsehood, fraud, and wilful imposition, the accused may be convicted of theft.[27]

(c) Under an indictment for theft the accused may be convicted of breach of trust and embezzlement or of falsehood, fraud, and wilful imposition or of reset.[28]

(d) Under an indictment for theft the accused may be convicted of theft, although the circumstances proved amount in law to robbery.[29]

       Section 38 of the 1949 Act provides that in a sheriff court trial the accused may be convicted of another offence in terms of heads (a) to (d) inclusive, notwithstanding that that other offence was committed outside the jurisdiction of that sheriff court. But it must have been committed in Scotland.[30]

(e) Under an indictment charging cumulatively two or more crimes or acts of crime, the accused may be convicted of any one or more of them.[31]

(f) Where any part of an indictment constitutes in itself an indictable crime, and such part is separable, the accused may be convicted thereof.[32]

(g) Under an indictment charging a crime committed with a particular intent, or with particular circumstances of aggravation, the accused may be convicted of the crime without such intent or aggravation.[33]

[25] s. 59.
[26] *Kennedy* v. *H.M. Adv.* (1896) 2 Adam 51.
[27] s. 59.
[28] Ibid.: *H.M. Adv.* v. *Laing* (1891) 2 White 572.
[29] 1887 Act, s. 59.
[30] *Roy* v. *H.M. Adv.*, 1963 S.L.T. 369.
[31] 1887 Act, s. 60.
[32] Ibid.
[33] Ibid.

10-42   (h) Under an indictment which charges a completed crime, the accused may be convicted of an attempt to commit such crime.[34]

(i) Under an indictment charging an attempt to commit a crime, the accused may be convicted of such attempt although the evidence is sufficient to prove the completion of the crime said to have been attempted.[35]

(j) Under an indictment which charges a crime which imports personal injury inflicted by the accused, resulting in death or serious injury to the person, the accused may be convicted of the assault or other injurious act, and also of the aggravation that such assault or act was committed with intent to commit such crime.[36]

(k) Where any act set forth in an indictment as contrary to an Act of Parliament is also criminal at common law, the accused may be convicted of the common law crime.[37]

(l) Under an indictment charging a statutory offence, where the facts proved do not amount to a contravention of the statute, but do amount to a crime at common law, the accused may be convicted of the common law crime.[38]

It is important to remember, when framing indictments, that the last-named provision only applies where the facts which constitute the common law crime are narrated in the indictment. The section does not entitle a prosecutor to lead evidence of facts not charged.

In *Markland* v. *H.M. Advocate* [39] a person was charged with having, while an undischarged bankrupt within the meaning of section 4 of the Bankruptcy, Frauds and Disabilities Act 1884, obtained credit from a firm of bootmakers without informing them of this fact. This statutory charge disclosed no crime at common law. The evidence adduced by the prosecutor negatived the charge, but he was allowed by the sheriff-substitute to lead further evidence of facts not mentioned in the indictment, with the result that a verdict was obtained against the accused of the common law offence of falsehood, fraud and wilful imposition and he was sentenced to a period of imprisonment. The court suspended the conviction, holding that section 62 did not entitle the prosecutor to prove any facts not libelled in the indictment and thereafter obtain a conviction of a common law offence which had not been charged therein.

By virtue of section 9 of the Criminal Law Amendment Act 1885 it is competent on an indictment libelling only a common law charge of rape to return a verdict finding a panel guilty of offences created by sections 3, 4 or 5 of that statute or of indecent assault. It has been held that a conviction of these statutory offences is competent even although the

[34] Ibid., s. 61.
[35] Ibid.
[36] Ibid.
[37] Ibid., s. 62.
[38] Ibid.
[39] (1891) 3 White 21.

indictment does not set forth the statute.[40] But where the common law charge is not one of rape but only of attempt to ravish, section 9 does not apply.[41]

10-43   Under section 31 of the 1949 Act a person may be convicted of, and punished for, a contravention of any statute or order, notwithstanding that he was guilty of such contravention as art and part only.

Jury's right to see productions

10-44   The question whether or not the jury are entitled to see the productions, or any of them, is one for the discretion of the presiding judge.[42] The test is whether such an exercise of discretion is in the interests of justice, and questions of delicacy may arise according to the circumstances of each case.

In an early case,[43] where the accused was charged with forging and uttering a writing purporting to be that of his deceased brother, the court refused to allow the jury to inspect the document alleged to have been forged for the purpose of comparing it with other productions which were admittedly the genuine writings of the deceased. This course was followed shortly afterwards in a case [44] where the charge was one of embezzlement and where the jury had asked to be shown certain receipts alleged to have been granted by the accused, these being productions at the trial. In both cases the reasons for the court's refusal were (1) that it was the duty of the Crown to prove its case by means of evidence which the accused could have an opportunity of testing by cross-examination and that if the jury did not think that the case for the prosecution had been proved in this way they must assume that it had failed, and (2) that by such comparison the jury might easily mislead themselves and the individual jurors might form varying and erroneous conjectures which could not be corrected.

In a later case,[45] however, where the accused was charged with forgery, and the jury, with the permission of the presiding sheriff, took into the jury room when they retired to consider their verdict certain productions in the case and also a tracing made by a witness in the course of his examination to show the difference between two signatures, the court refused to suspend the conviction, holding that what had been done was neither incompetent nor illegal, the matter being one for the discretion of the presiding judge. The cases of *Robertson* and *McGall* were explained by Lord Justice-Clerk Macdonald as being merely decisions to the effect that in particular circumstances it might not be advisable that the jury should

---

[40] *Henry Watson* (1885) 5 Couper 696; *H.M. Adv.* v. *McLaren* (1897) 2 Adam 395; *H.M. Adv.* v. *Barbour* (1887) 1 White 466. A contrary opinion was expressed by L.J.-C. Macdonald in *H.M. Adv.* v. *Henderson* (1888) 2 White 157.

[41] *Townsend* v. *H.M. Adv.* (1914) 7 Adam 378.

[42] *Slater* v. *H.M. Adv.* (1899) 3 Adam 73; *Paterson* v. *H.M. Adv.* (1901) 3 Adam 490; see also *R. M. Beveridge* (1860) 3 Irv. 625.

[43] *J. G. Robertson* (1849) J. Shaw 186.

[44] *Wm. McGall* (1849) J. Shaw 194.

[45] *Slater* v. *H.M. Adv.* (1899) 3 Adam 73.

see the productions and not in any way indicating that this course was incompetent or illegal.

In a subsequent case [46] where the charge was one of sheep-stealing, the sheep were entered in the list of productions, and were penned outside the court during the trial. In a suspension following upon conviction it was averred by the panel that after the close of the prosecution case, his agent had moved the presiding sheriff to allow the jury to examine the sheep and that the sheriff had refused the motion. It was held that the matter was one for the discretion of the sheriff and, as it did not appear from the averments that the motion had been pressed, suspension was refused.

If a production consists of a report which contains hearsay evidence, this must not be allowed to go before the jury. [47]

Motion for sentence

10–45   If the verdict is one of guilty, the prosecutor moves for sentence. If he does not do so, sentence cannot be pronounced. [48] The motion should be made expressly but may be inferred from the prosecutor's actings where he lays previous convictions before the court. [49] The Lord Advocate or his deputes may at any period of the trial of a capital case, and even after verdict, restrict the pains of law to an arbitrary punishment. [50]

Previous convictions

10–46   If previous convictions are libelled, the prosecutor, when moving for sentence, lays before the presiding judge a copy of the notice of previous convictions served on the accused in terms of section 39 (*b*) of the 1949 Act. He cannot do so earlier, [51] nor may any prior mention be made of previous convictions at the trial, unless these have formed part of the competent evidence in support of the charge, in which case they will have been proved along with the rest of the case for the prosecution. [52] It is improper for the prosecutor in moving for sentence to refer to offences not included in the notice of previous convictions. [53]

An extract conviction of a crime committed in any part of the United Kingdom, bearing to be under the hand of the officer in use to give out such extract, is received in evidence without being sworn to by witnesses, [54] and any conviction set out in the notice of previous convictions served on the accused under section 39 (*b*) of the 1949 Act is held to apply to him unless he gives written intimation objecting to such conviction on the ground

---

[46] *Paterson* v. *H.M. Adv.* (1901) 3 Adam 490.
[47] *Grant* v. *H.M. Adv.*, 1938 J.C. 7.
[48] Macdonald, 348; Hume, ii. 470, 471; Alison, ii. 653: *Marion Nicolson or Mailer* (1829) Bell's Notes 300; *Alex. Smith* (1842) ibid.
[49] *Noon* v. *H.M. Adv.*, 1960 J.C. 52.
[50] Macdonald, 349; Hume, ii. 134.
[51] 1949 Act, s. 39 (1) (*e*). See supra, para. 6–35.
[52] 1887 Act, s. 67; 1949 Act, s. 39 (3). See supra, paras. 6–39; 10–07.
[53] *Ramsay* v. *H.M. Adv.*, 1959 J.C. 86.
[54] 1887 Act, s. 66.

that it does not apply to him or is otherwise inadmissible, to the Crown Agent in a High Court case, or to the procurator fiscal of the district of the second diet in a sheriff court case, as already explained.[55] Where such intimation has been given, the Crown may prove the previous convictions according to the provisions of section 66 of the 1887 Act as amended by the 1963 Act, or according to those of section 31 of the 1963 Act. Section 66 of the 1887 Act enables the previous conviction to be proved by witnesses whose names are not on the list of witnesses, and also enables the accused to lead evidence in regard to the alleged conviction. An official of any prison in which the accused may have been confined on such conviction is a competent and sufficient witness to prove the application thereof to the accused, although he may not have been present in court at the trial to which the extract relates. But the prosecutor must prove the application of the conviction to the accused by the ordinary rules of evidence, and where the only evidence led was that of a police constable who was not an official of the prison in which the accused had been confined and had not been present in court when the accused was convicted, it was held that the application of the previous conviction to the accused had not been proved.[56]

10–47   Section 31 of the 1963 Act provides for proof of previous convictions by fingerprints. A certificate purporting to be signed by or on behalf of the Chief Constable of Glasgow or the Metropolitan Police Commissioner, containing particulars relating to a conviction extracted from the criminal records held by these officials and certifying that copies of fingerprints contained in the certificate are copies of prints appearing from those records to have been taken in pursuance of regulations under section 11 of the Prisons (Scotland) Act 1952 or section 16 of the Prison Act 1952 from the person convicted on the occasion of his last conviction is sufficient evidence of that conviction and of all preceding convictions, and that the copies of the prints are copies of those of the person convicted.[57] A certificate signed by or for the chief constable of the police force who apprehended and detained the accused certifying that the prints produced thereon were taken from him while detained is sufficient evidence that the prints are those of the accused,[58] and similar provisions apply to certificates signed by or for prison or remand centre governors in whose institutions the accused has been detained.[59] The necessary link between the prints on criminal records and those taken from the accused on apprehension can then be sufficiently proved by a further certificate signed by or for the Chief Constable of Glasgow.[60]

10–48   Previous convictions against a person accused are not laid before the jury, and no reference can be made thereto in presence of the jury

---

[55] Supra, para. 6–33. For amendment of notice, see supra, para. 6–37.
[56] *McDermott* v. *Stewart's Trs.*, 1918 J.C. 25.
[57] s. 31 (2).
[58] s. 31 (3).
[59] s. 31 (4).
[60] s. 31 (5).

before the verdict is returned.[61] This provision does not prevent the public prosecutor from leading such evidence, where it is competent to lead the same as evidence in causa in support of the substantive charge, or where the person accused leads evidence to prove previous good character.[62]

It is unnecessary for the jury to return a verdict on the subject of previous convictions. The admission of any conviction is a matter for the court. Where the conviction is admitted or proved, the court has power to take it into consideration in awarding punishment.

10–49   Where any person is convicted of any crime and any previous convictions are admitted or are proved against him, the clerk of the court in which sentence is pronounced must enter in the record a statement of the contents of any extract conviction put in evidence, setting forth date, place of trial, court, crime, aggravations (if any), and sentence. Section 39 (2) of the 1949 Act provides that any conviction which is admitted in evidence by the court under section 39 (1) must be entered in the record.

Where the accused is convicted on indictment in the sheriff court of any crime, and an extract of that conviction is subsequently required in evidence, such extract can be issued by the clerk of the court having the custody of the record copy of the indictment, although the plea of the accused may have been taken and the sentence on him pronounced in another court.[63]

10–50   It is still competent in cases of reset to take advantage of the provisions in section 19 of the Prevention of Crimes Act 1871, which enable a prosecutor, on giving seven days' notice in writing to the accused, to prove, after evidence has been led of the accused being found in possession of stolen property, that he has within the immediately preceding five years been convicted of any crime inferring fraud or dishonesty: but recourse is seldom had to this right. Evidence of such prior convictions may be led by the prosecutor whenever he has adduced evidence which, in the opinion of the presiding judge, is sufficient to go to the jury to show that the accused has had the stolen goods in his possession, actually or constructively, at any time after they were stolen.[64]

Adjournment before sentence

10–51   By section 26 of the 1949 Act the power of a court to adjourn the hearing of a case is declared to include power, after a person has been convicted or the court has found that he has committed the offence and before he has been sentenced or otherwise dealt with, to adjourn the case for the purpose of enabling inquiries to be made or of determining the most suitable method of dealing with his case. The court must not, however, for such purpose adjourn the hearing of a case for any single period exceeding three

[61] 1887 Act, s. 67. See supra, para. 10–07.
[62] 1887 Act, s. 67; 1949 Act, s. 39 (3).
[63] 1908 Act, s. 77 (3).
[64] *Watson* v. *H.M. Adv.* (1894) 1 Adam 355.

weeks. Section 47 of the 1963 Act declares for the removal of doubt that a court may defer sentence after conviction for a period and on such conditions as the court may determine.

Remand for inquiry

10–52   Under section 27 of the 1949 Act the court has power to remand persons charged before it with offences punishable with imprisonment for inquiry into their physical or mental condition. This power is without prejudice to the court's power of adjournment under section 26 of that Act. Section 27 (1) provides that, if the court is satisfied that the accused committed the act charged but is of opinion that an inquiry ought to be made into his physical or mental condition before the method of dealing with him is determined, it must remand him in custody or on bail for such period or periods, no single period exceeding three weeks, as the court thinks necessary to enable a medical examination and report to be made. Anyone invoking section 27 must generally put forward sufficient material to enable the court to form an opinion that inquiry ought to be made.[65]

Sentence

10–53   After the previous convictions have been admitted or proved, as the case may be, the accused may state any plea in bar of sentence. These pleas must relate to the sufficiency of the verdict, the powers of the court or the condition of the accused. No plea in bar of judgment grounded on objections to the libel [66] or evidence [67] will receive attention.

The counsel or solicitor of the accused is then heard in mitigation of sentence. At this stage evidence as to previous good character or other mitigating circumstances may be adduced in the same way as at the first diet although evidence of mitigating circumstances may also be led in the course of the trial.[68] At whatever stage it is given it should be in the form of oral evidence on oath.[69] If the accused is not legally represented it is the duty of the presiding judge to ask him if he has anything to say.[70]

Unless he adjourns the case under section 26 of the 1949 Act or remands the accused under section 27 of that statute, the judge then pronounces or formally defers sentence. In all cases, whether in the sheriff court or in the High Court, the sentence to be pronounced is announced by the judge in open court.[71] No sentence can be pronounced outwith the presence of the accused.[72] All sentences are entered in the record in short form. It is unnecessary to read the entry of the sentence from the record.

[65] *H.M. Adv.* v. *Scobie*, 1952 J.C. 96, itself a section 31 case remitted to the High Court for sentence.
[66] Macdonald, 349; *Wm. Allan* (1872) 2 Couper 402.
[67] Macdonald, 349; Hume, ii. 467; Alison, ii. 651.
[68] *Clark* v. *H.M. Adv.*, 1968 J.C. 53; *H.M. Adv.* v. *Murray*, 1969 S.L.T.(Notes) 85.
[69] *Forbes* v. *H.M. Adv.*, 1963 J.C. 68.
[70] In summary procedure failure of the judge to do this will not invalidate a conviction unless the omission amounts to oppression: *Grahams* v. *McLennan* (1911) 6 Adam 315; *Ewart* v. *Strathern*, 1924 J.C. 45.
[71] 1887 Act, s. 57.
[72] Macdonald, 349.

10–54 A valid sentence must contain the following points [73]:

    (*a*) It must be consistent with the law.

    (*b*) It must be consistent with the libel, whether indictment or complaint.

    (*c*) It must state a definite and unambiguous period of imprisonment or amount of fine. Sentences of corrective training and preventive detention under section 21 of the 1949 Act are for definite periods. No fixed period is, however, stated in a sentence of borstal training.

The subject of punishment is treated in Chapter 17.

All sentences, unless qualified, run from the date of pronouncing judgment. If the accused person is already in prison upon a previous sentence, his imprisonment may be made to date from the expiry of such sentence,[74] even when it was imposed in England.[75] A sentence should not normally be imposed to run from the expiry of a current sentence when the second sentence is imposed for an offence known to be outstanding when the first was passed.[76] A sentence of imprisonment should not be made to run from the expiry of a sentence of borstal training.[77] The court in passing sentence of imprisonment or detention in a young offenders institution is obliged to have regard to any time spent by the accused in custody on remand awaiting trial or sentence in determining the length of sentence to be imposed.[78]

Remit to High Court

10–55 The Criminal Procedure (Scotland) Act 1921 provides that in proceedings on indictment in which the second diet is in the sheriff court, where the accused is found guilty by the jury, the sheriff, if he holds that any sentence which he can competently pronounce is inadequate, may remit the accused to the High Court for sentence. Where such a remit is made any inquiries into the accused's mental or physical condition require to be made by the High Court and these matters should not be inquired into by the sheriff.[79]

---

[73] Macdonald, 350, 351.
[74] Macdonald, 357; *John Graham* (1842) 1 Broun 445.
[75] *Grey* v. *H.M. Adv.*, 1958 S.L.T. 147.
[76] Cf. *Kesson* v. *Heatly*, 1964 J.C. 40.
[77] *Scott* v. *H.M. Adv.*, 1964 J.C. 77. For cases on the relationship between the rarely used sentences of preventive detention and corrective training and other sentences, see *Ramsay* v. *H.M. Adv.*, 1959 J.C. 86; *Winning* v. *H.M. Adv.*, 1958 S.L.T. 135; *H.M. Adv.* v. *Miller*, 1954 J.C. 53.
[78] Criminal Justice Act 1967, s. 68.
[79] *H.M. Adv.* v. *Clark*, 1955 J.C. 88.

CHAPTER 11

APPEAL

11–01 UNTIL the passing of the Criminal Appeal (Scotland) Act 1926, all inter-locutors and sentences pronounced by the High Court of Justiciary were final and conclusive, and not subject to review in any circumstances. The finality of the High Court had been upheld by the House of Lords in the case of *Mackintosh* v. *The Lord Advocate*,[1] and was regulated by section 72 of the 1887 Act. This section is not repealed, but is declared by section 17 (2) of the 1926 Act to have effect subject to the provisions of that Act. The result of the 1926 Act is to allow a person convicted in the High Court on indictment to appeal on certain specified grounds to a Court of Criminal Appeal (referred to in this chapter as " the Court ") whose decision is final.[2] There is no appeal available to the Crown against the decision of a High Court judge or jury.

As the Act applies to all trials on indictment, a person convicted on indictment in the sheriff court has the same right of appeal as a person convicted in the High Court. Prior to the passing of the 1926 Act, a person convicted on indictment in the sheriff court could, in certain circumstances, bring a suspension of any conviction, judgment, sentence, or order pronounced by the sheriff. This right has been taken away by the 1926 Act.[3] The result is that appeal in sheriff and jury cases is regulated by the same rules as obtain in High Court cases. The 1926 Act, therefore, gives a uniform right of appeal in all cases falling under solemn procedure. Advocation is not abolished.[4] The High Court also possesses power in the exercise of its nobile officium to reverse the decision of an inferior court or of a judge of the High Court itself where there is no right of appeal, provided that review is not expressly excluded by any relevant statutory provision. The procedure is by way of petition to the High Court.[5] Similar procedure may be available to bring under review any executive order such as one for deportation.[6]

There is no appeal available to the Crown against the verdict of a jury, nor against any decision of a sheriff court in solemn procedure except by way of advocation.[6a]

---

[1] (1876) 3 R.(H.L.) 34.   [2] 1926 Act, s. 17 (1).
[3] Ibid., s. 13.
[4] Ibid., s. 12 (3); see infra, paras. 16–25 et seq.
[5] See e.g. *Wyllie* v. *H.M. Adv.*, 1966 S.L.T. 149 (" appeal " against summary sentence imposed by High Court judge, cf. *Pirie* v. *Hawthorn*, 1962 J.C. 69); *J.P. Hartley, Petnr.* (1968) 32 J.C.L. 191 (" appeal " against order by sheriff disqualifying accused for further legal aid); cf. *MacLeod* v. *Levitt*, 1969 J.C. 16.
[6] See *Haimovici, Petur.*, 1953 S.L.T.(Notes) 49.
[6a] Infra, para. 16–125. An advocation was taken by a private prosecutor against the finding of the sheriff that his indictment was incompetent in *Dunbar* v. *Johnston* (1904) 4 Adam 505.

Quorum

11–02   Three judges form a quorum of the Court for hearing and determining any appeals or other proceedings under the 1926 Act, and for the hearing of cases certified to the High Court of Justiciary by a single judge and appeals by way of advocation from the sheriff court.[7] Certification is a procedure whereby a judge on circuit can refer a point of law for decision by the High Court to avoid making a decision himself. In practice, certification was used to determine preliminary pleas, and there was some doubt whether it could be used to deal, after conviction, with a question as to competency of evidence,[8] a question which can now be dealt with by appeal. Certification of preliminary matters has occurred in recent years.[9] Section 1 of the 1926 Act is widely enough expressed to allow an appeal after conviction on a point already dealt with by certification, but there is no example of such an appeal.

It is competent for a trial in the High Court to be heard by more than one judge,[10] or for additional judges to sit with a trial judge to determine a particular point of law.[11] In such cases appeal is competent after conviction, and will then be heard by a court of greater number than the court which decided the question under appeal.[12]

The opinion has been expressed by three judges that a Full Bench can overrule the decision of a smaller Full Bench.[13] In a summary appeal a Full Bench consisting of seven judges overruled two earlier judgments given by courts of three judges.[14]

Retrospective effect of 1926 Act

11–03   The 1926 Act applied to all persons convicted after 31st October 1926, and did not affect the rights as regards appeal of any person convicted on or before that date.[15] The Criminal Appeal (Scotland) Act 1927 made it possible for the Secretary (now the Secretary of State) for Scotland to exercise the powers conferred on him by section 16 of the 1926 Act of referring cases to the Court in the cases of persons convicted on or before that date.

Legal aid

11–04   It is the duty of the nominated solicitor to consider and advise on the question of an appeal, including if necessary the making of an application for an extension of time or for an interim appeal certificate, and any consequential petition for liberation under the 1926 Act.[16] It is also his

---

[7] 1926 Act, s. 12.
[8] *Sarah & Jas. Fraser* (1852) 1 Irv. 1.
[9] *H.M. Adv.* v. *Cunningham*, 1963 J.C. 80; *H.M. Adv.* v. *Burns*, 1967 J.C. 15.
[10] See *Young* v. *H.M. Adv.*, 1932 J.C. 63.
[11] *H.M. Adv.* v. *Cairns*, 1967 J.C. 37; *Hay* v. *H.M. Adv.*, 1968 J.C. 40.
[12] *Young*, supra; *Hay*, supra.
[13] *Sugden* v. *H.M. Adv.*, 1934 J.C. 103.
[14] *Strathern* v. *Albion Greyhounds (Glasgow) Ltd.*, 1933 J.C. 91. Decisions of the House of Lords are not binding on the Court: cf. *Ritchie* v. *Pirie*, 1972 S.L.T. 2.
[15] s. 19 (2).
[16] Legal Aid (Scotland) (Criminal Proceedings) Scheme 1964, art. 9 (2).

duty, where instructed to appeal and to obtain legal aid therefor, to complete and lodge the statutory notice of appeal or of application for leave to appeal.[17] He should then send the statutory notice with an application for a legal aid certificate (an appeal certificate) to the Supreme Court Committee together with his own views as to whether or not (a) the grounds of appeal are substantial and (b) it is reasonable that legal aid should be granted.[17a] If the Supreme Court Committee are satisfied as to these two requirements they will issue an appeal certificate. Where a person who has not received legal aid in his trial seeks legal aid for an appeal he must obtain a provisional assessment of his financial eligibility from the sheriff clerk.[18] The sheriff clerk will assist him to prepare an application for an interim appeal certificate and this will be granted by the local committee if they are satisfied as to his financial eligibility, and also, where he was originally refused legal aid following on a finding of the court that he has wilfully or deliberately given false information or furnished false particulars,[19] that it would not be unreasonable for him to have the services of an interim solicitor.[20] The interim solicitor then carries out the duties normally carried out by the nominated solicitor. The Supreme Court Committee will then either discharge the interim certificate or, if satisfied as to the grounds of appeal and the applicant's financial eligibility, replace it with an appeal certificate.[21]

Grounds of appeal

11–05   A person convicted on indictment may appeal to the Court as follows:

(a) Without requiring leave of the Court, he may appeal against his conviction on any ground of appeal which involves a question of law alone [22]:

(b) With the leave of the Court or upon the certificate of the judge who presided at the trial that it is a fit case for appeal, he may appeal against his conviction:

   (i) On any ground of appeal which involves a question of fact alone, or

   (ii) On any ground of appeal which involves a question of mixed law and fact, or

   (iii) On any other ground which appears to the Court or to the judge who presided at the trial to be a sufficient ground of appeal.[23]

(c) With leave of the Court he may appeal against the sentence, unless the sentence is one fixed by law.[24]

[17] Ibid., art. 10 (2).
[17a] Ibid., art. 18.
[18] Legal Aid (Scotland) (Criminal Proceedings) Regulations 1964, reg. 7; Act of Adjournal (Rules for Legal Aid in Criminal Proceedings) 1964, rule 8.
[19] Act of Adjournal, supra, rule 10 (3).
[20] Legal Aid (Scotland) (Criminal Proceedings) Regulations 1964, reg. 8 (2) (b).
[21] Legal Aid (Scotland) (Criminal Proceedings) Regulations 1964, reg. 8 (7).
[22] 1926 Act, s. 1 (a).
[23] s. 1 (b).   [24] s. 1 (c).

11–06   Section 18 of the 1926 Act provides that, in the Act, unless the context otherwise requires, ". . . the expression ' sentence ' includes any order of the Court made on conviction with reference to the person convicted or his wife and children, and any recommendation of the Court as to the making of a deportation order in the case of a person convicted and the power of the Court to pass a sentence includes a power to make any such order of the Court or recommendation, and a recommendation so made by the Court shall have the same effect for the purposes of Article 20 of the Aliens Order 1953 [25] as the certificate and recommendation of the convicting Court." [26]

11–07   Section 62 of the Mental Health (Scotland) Act 1960 provides that where a hospital or guardianship order, or an order restricting discharge, has been made by a court in respect of a person charged or brought before it, he may, without prejudice to any other appeal open to him, appeal against the order in the same manner as against a conviction. This section precedes the section dealing with findings of insanity on indictment; the orders made on such findings are called " orders for detention in hospital," and are said to " have the like effect " as certain hospital orders, but they are not hospital orders, and there appears to be no appeal against either a finding of insanity in bar of trial or an acquittal by reason of insanity, or against the subsequent order. [27]

Provisions for Safeguarding Accused Persons Pending Appeal

Preservation of documents

11–08   Any documents, productions, or other things lodged in connection with the proceedings on the trial of any person on indictment who, if convicted, is entitled or may be authorised to appeal under the 1926 Act, are kept in the custody of the court of trial in accordance with rules made by Act of Adjournal for the purpose, for such time as may be provided by the rules, and subject to such power as may be given by the rules for the conditional release of any such documents, productions, or things from that custody. [28]

Availability of forms of appeal

11–09   The Clerk of Justiciary is obliged to furnish the necessary forms and instructions in relation to notices of appeal or notices of application under the Act to any person who demands them, and to officers of courts, governors of prisons, and such other officers or persons as he thinks fit, and the governor of a prison is obliged to cause those forms and instructions to be placed at the disposal of prisoners desiring to appeal or to make any application under the Act, and to cause any such notice given by a

---

[25] See now Immigration Act 1971, s. 6, infra, paras. 17–94 et seq., and relative regulations.
[26] See e.g. *Crolla* v. *Horne*, 1931 J.C. 42.
[27] Such appeals are competent in England: Criminal Appeal Act 1968, ss. 12–16.
[28] s. 10 (2). The rules referred to are laid down by the Act of Adjournal Relative to the Criminal Appeal (Scotland) Act 1926, Oct. 27, 1926, para. 6. See infra, App. D.

prisoner in his custody to be forwarded on behalf of the prisoner to the Clerk of Justiciary.[29]

Postponement of issue of extract convictions

11–10   No extract conviction of any person convicted on indictment may be issued during the period of ten days after the actual day on which such conviction took place save in so far as the same may be required as a warrant for detaining the person under his sentence. In the event of an appeal being taken the issue of the extract is further postponed until the determination of the appeal.[30]

Fines and caution

11–11   Fines which have been paid are retained by the recipient pending the determination of the appeal.[31] If the appellant is successful the fine is refunded to him subject to any order of the Court.[32]

Where a person who has been sentenced to pay a fine, and to imprisonment in default, after conviction on indictment intimates to the judge at the court of trial that he proposes to appeal against his conviction on a point of law, or with the certificate of the trial judge, the judge may order him to find caution for such sum as the judge may think right to prosecute his appeal; and, subject thereto, may also order that payment of the fine shall be made at the final determination of the appeal, if the same be dismissed, to the clerk of the court of trial or otherwise as the Court may then order.[33] If the appellant does not give notice of appeal within ten days from the date of conviction and sentence or pay the fine, the Court may find the caution forfeited and may pronounce against the cautioner decree for such sum as they may think proper, and may issue a warrant for the apprehension of the appellant and may commit him to prison in default of payment of his fine.[34]

Protection of accused's interests and property

11–12   Where upon conviction on indictment of any person of any offence, any disqualification, forfeiture, or disability attaches to such person by reason of such conviction, such disqualification, forfeiture, or disability does not attach for a period of ten days from the date of the verdict or, in the event of a note of appeal or of application for leave to appeal being lodged, until the determination thereof.[35] A like provision is made with regard to any property of the accused which is the subject of the prosecution, any order for the forfeiture or destruction of the same being similarly suspended.[36]

[29] s. 10 (3).
[30] Act of Adjournal, supra, para. 8.
[31] Ibid., para. 5 (a).
[32] Ibid., para. 5 (d).
[33] Ibid., para. 5 (c).
[34] Ibid., para. 5 (e).
[35] Ibid., para. 7 (a).   [36] Ibid., para. 7 (b).

Procedure for Appealing

Time for appeal and mode of appeal

11–13   Where a person convicted desires to appeal to the Court or to obtain the leave of the Court to appeal, he must, within ten days of the date of his conviction in the case of appeal or application for leave to appeal against conviction, or within ten days of the date of his sentence in the case of appeal or application for leave to appeal against sentence, give notice of appeal or of application for leave to appeal.[37] This means that where an accused has been convicted, and the proceedings are adjourned or sentence deferred for more than ten days, he ought to lodge his appeal against conviction before he has been sentenced, but it is understood that this requirement is not insisted on in practice and that an appeal against conviction will be entertained if lodged up to ten days after the final disposal of the case, at any rate if the interval between conviction and sentence is not a lengthy one, as it might be in the case of a deferred sentence. Notice is given by lodging the appropriate note with the Clerk of Justiciary within the due period.[38] Forms for notes of appeal, notes of application for leave to appeal, and notes of application for extension of the time for appealing are prescribed by the Act of Adjournal.[39] These notes, which may be wholly or partly written, typed or printed, may be signed by the appellant or his counsel or agent.[40]

A copy of the note must be sent to the Crown Agent,[41] and, if the court of trial is the sheriff court, also to the clerk of that court [42] who must furnish to the Clerk of Justiciary, according as he may require, either a certified copy of the proceedings or the original record thereof.[43]

The Clerk of Justiciary notifies the Prisons Department of the lodging of the appeal.[44]

11–14   As already stated,[45] leave to appeal may be given by the trial judge by means of a certificate that the case is a fit one for appeal.[46] This certificate may be in the form prescribed by the Act of Adjournal.[47] The judge of the court of trial may, in any case in which he considers it desirable to do so, inform the person convicted before or sentenced by him that the case is, in his opinion, one fit for an appeal under section 1 (b) of the Act, and may give to such person a certificate to that effect.[48]

11–15   Where the appeal is on a question of law, or where, as rarely happens, the trial judge has granted leave to appeal, the appellant presents a note

[37] 1926 Act, s. 4.
[38] Act of Adjournal, para. 2 (a).
[39] Ibid.
[40] Ibid. para. 2 (a) (b).
[41] Ibid., para. 2 (a).
[42] Ibid.
[43] Ibid., para. 2 (d).
[44] Ibid., para. 2 (c).
[45] Supra, para. 11–05.
[46] 1926 Act, s. 1 (b).
[47] Act of Adjournal, para. 4 (a) and Form VII of Schedule.
[48] Act of Adjournal, para. 4 (b).

of appeal to the court. In other cases he presents a note of application for leave to appeal, and is described as the " applicant." Since the single-judge procedure is not in normal use in Scotland there is little difference between appeals and applications except that if an applicant wishes to refer to the notes of evidence at the trial he must first obtain leave to appeal. The notes of evidence are usually not extended until leave has been granted. Where an applicant is granted leave his note of application is deemed to be a note of appeal.[49] It is common to extend the summing-up in both applications and appeals, and where an application can be argued without reference to the notes of evidence the Court often hears a detailed argument and then refuses the application, or treats it as an appeal and grants the appeal.

11–16   The same principles apply to the statement of grounds in appeals and applications. It is the duty of the appellant fully to specify in his note of appeal or note of application for leave to appeal the grounds upon which he maintains that his conviction should be set aside.[50] Proper formulation of these grounds is particularly necessary if an attack is made on the judge's charge, so that the Crown can properly consider and answer the points taken.[51] If a prima facie ground of appeal is not set forth, his application may be refused.[52] Thus, in a case where the only grounds of appeal stated were: " The verdict was contrary to the evidence. The judge misdirected the jury," and counsel for the applicant moved that he should be furnished with a transcript of the presiding judge's charge, both the motion and the application for leave to appeal were refused.[53] Where the ground of appeal is the alleged perjury of a witness, specific circumstances must be averred.[54] Where, however, the grounds of appeal cannot adequately be stated within the time allowed for lodging the application, a supplementary statement setting forth in detail the reasons for the application may be tendered subsequently, subject to the discretion of the Court to receive it before the hearing is allowed to proceed.[55] Where new reasons are substituted for those originally lodged, they should be entirely adequate and substituted without delay.[56] In a case where amended grounds of appeal were lodged a month after the date of the application for leave to appeal and only three days before the hearing of the same, the Court refused to admit the amended grounds.[57] In another case,[58] where an application for leave to appeal against conviction had been presented by an applicant without professional assistance and his counsel moved for a continuation

[49] Ibid., para. 2 (e).
[50] Boyd v. H.M. Adv., 1939 J.C. 6; Reilly and Anr. v. H.M. Adv., 1950 J.C. 52.
[51] Hughes v. McAuley [1949] C.L.Y. 4467.
[52] Boyd, supra; Leighton v. H.M. Adv., 1931 J.C. 1.
[53] Leighton, supra.
[54] Macmillan v. H.M. Adv., 1927 J.C. 62.
[55] Boyd v. H.M. Adv., 1939 J.C. 6. Such amendment has frequently been allowed as, e.g., in Scott (A. T.) v. H.M. Adv., 1946 J.C. 90.
[56] Reilly and Anr. v. H.M. Adv., 1950 J.C. 52.
[57] Fox v. H.M. Adv., 1950 S.L.T. 278. See also Kerr v. H.M. Adv., 1952 J.C. 84; cf. Lee v. H.M. Adv., 1968 S.L.T.(Notes) 25.
[58] Pool v. H.M. Adv., 1951 S.L.T.(Notes) 70.

of the case in order that he might go through the notes of evidence with a view to checking the existing reasons for appeal and to seeing what further reasons might emerge, the Court refused the motion.

The Court is reluctant to receive amended grounds of appeal. They have deplored the practice of submitting entirely inadequate grounds for the sake of bail and following them up with last-minute amendments, a course which deprives the Court of the benefit of the trial judge's comments under section 5 of the Act.[59] The Court have also deprecated the practice of seeking to find in the judge's charge or the notes of evidence grounds of appeal on matters which were not live issues at the trial.[60]

Extension of time

11–17   The time within which an appeal or application for leave to appeal must be made, may be extended by the Court.[61] Such extension, however, will be granted only in cases where the applicant shows reasons excusing him for his non-observance of the statutory limitations and the Crown and third parties are not prejudiced by the delay.[62] Thus an extension was allowed in a case where the prison authorities had failed to inform the applicant that he had a right of appeal until the ten days allowed for that purpose by the 1926 Act had expired, it being admitted that the extension would cause no prejudice to the Crown.[63] An extension was also allowed where the applicants, who were youthful, alleged that their failure to take timeous action had arisen through a misunderstanding between them and their solicitor, they themselves having taken some steps timeously towards an appeal.[64] Where, however, an applicant, who had been duly informed by the prison authorities of the time limit for presenting an application for leave to appeal, instead of himself instructing a solicitor, asked his mother to do so, and, owing to her failure to fulfil this request, the application was not timeously presented, an extension was refused.[65] An extension was also refused in a case where the reason advanced by the applicant for the delay in presenting his application was that after his trial he had been advised by his counsel that he had no grounds of appeal and had not proceeded further in the matter because he did not wish to argue the appeal in person.[66] Again, an extension was refused where two accused alleged that the prison authorities were to blame for not forwarding their applications timeously, there being no substantiation of their statements.[67]

---

[59] *Fox*, supra, *Reilly*, supra.
[60] Ibid.; *Poole*, supra.
[61] s. 4 (1), and Act of Adjournal, para. 2.
[62] *Cockerell* v. *H.M. Adv.*, 1943 J.C. 62; *Casey* v. *H.M. Adv.*, 1948 S.L.T.(Notes) 77.
[63] Ibid. An extension was granted in *Young* v. *H.M. Adv.*, 1946 J.C. 5.
[64] *Ferguson and Others* v. *H.M. Adv.*, 1948 S.L.T.(Notes) 53.
[65] *Spence* v. *H.M. Adv.*, 1945 J.C. 59.
[66] *Scott (J. N.)* v. *H.M. Adv.*, 1946 J.C. 68.
[67] *Padden*; *Seagust* [1949] C.L.Y. 4469.

Bail

11-18   (1) The Court may, if it seems fit, on the application of an appellant, admit the appellant to bail pending the determination of his appeal.[68]

The appellant is in a much less favourable position than an untried prisoner who seeks bail. The latter is said to enjoy a presumption of innocence which involves that, unless good reasons can be shown to the contrary, he has a right to be released on bail if the crime with which he is charged is bailable. But once the prisoner has been convicted, any presumption of innocence is displaced, and the onus is on the applicant thereafter to show cause why, pending any appeal which he may take, he should be released from the prison confinement to which he was sentenced following upon the conviction.[69] So, where an appellant, who had been nine times convicted and had served long terms of imprisonment, and whose prospects of success in his appeal were described by his counsel as being only " at least a possibility," petitioned for interim liberation on bail pending the hearing of the appeal which was shortly due, his petition was refused by the Lord Justice-General and, on appeal, by the Court.[70]

11-19   (2) An appellant who is admitted to bail must, unless the Court otherwise directs, appear personally in court on the day or days fixed for the hearing of his appeal or application for leave to appeal. In the event of the appellant failing so to appear, the Court may decline to consider the appeal or application, and they may dismiss it summarily or may consider and determine it or make such other order as they think fit.[71]

Effect of appeal on sentence

11-20   Section 9 (4) of the 1926 Act as amended by section 30 (1) of the 1949 Act provides as follows:

(1) The time during which an appellant, after admission to bail under section 9 of the 1926 Act, is at large pending the determination of his appeal is not reckoned as part of any term of imprisonment under his sentence.[72]

(2) Imprisonment under the sentence of an appellant who is not in custody shall, subject to any direction which the Court may give to the contrary, be deemed to begin to run or to be resumed as from the date on which he is received into prison under the sentence.[73]

11-21   (3) The time during which an appellant is in custody pending the determination of his appeal shall, subject to any direction which the Court may give to the contrary, be reckoned as part of any term of imprisonment under his sentence.[74]

(4) Imprisonment under the sentence of an appellant who is in custody

---

[68] 1926 Act, s. 9.
[69] *Young* v. *H.M. Adv.*, 1946 J.C. 5.
[70] Ibid.
[71] s. 9 (2).
[72] s. 9 (4) (a).
[73] s. 9 (4) (c).
[74] s. 9 (4) (b).

shall, subject to any direction which the Court may give to the contrary, be deemed to run as from the date on which the sentence was passed by the court of trial.[75] In *Scott (J. N.)* v. *H.M. Advocate* [76] the Court refused to direct that the time during which the accused had been specially treated as an appellant under section 9 of the Act should count as part of his sentence, on the ground that he had made a frivolous application for an extension of time. That case was heard under the original section 9 which provided that time spent in custody during which the appellant was specially treated as an appellant should not count towards sentence unless the Court so ordered, but the Court might exercise its power under the amended section to achieve the same result in similar circumstances. The Court has on occasions since the 1949 Act ordered an appellant's sentence to run from the date of the refusal of a frivolous application or appeal.

References to a prison and to imprisonment include respectively references to a young offenders or borstal institution, detention centre or place of safety and to detention in such institution, centre or place.[77] Any reference to a sentence is to be construed as a reference to a sentence passed by the court of trial or by the Court on appeal as the case may require.[78]

Abandonment of appeal

11-22   At any time after a note of appeal or of application for leave to appeal or of application for extension of time for appealing has been lodged, the same may be withdrawn by the appellant on lodging a note of abandonment in the form provided by the Act of Adjournal.[79] A note of abandonment once lodged cannot be withdrawn,[80] unless perhaps in exceptional circumstances.[80a]

An appellant is held to have abandoned his appeal if no appearance is made by him or on his behalf at the hearing thereof and no written case has been timeously lodged by him.[81]

When an applicant for leave to appeal against sentence escaped from detention before the hearing of his application and could not be found, it was held that the appeal fell to be dismissed.[82]

The Court is not bound to allow an appeal to be abandoned once the hearing has begun, and will not allow an appeal against sentence to be abandoned once it has begun to be heard, where the abandonment is sought in order to avoid an increase in sentence.[83]

---

[75] s. 9 (4) (c).
[76] 1946 J.C. 68.
[77] s. 9 (4) (d), as amended by 1949 Act, and Social Work (Scotland) Act 1968; 1963 Act, s. 2 (2).
[78] Ibid.
[79] Act of Adjournal, para. 13 (a).
[80] *Biondi* v. *H.M. Adv.*, 1967 S.L.T.(Notes) 22.
[80a] cf. *R.* v. *Noble* [1971] 1 W.L.R. 1772.
[81] Act of Adjournal, para. 13 (b).
[82] *Cosgrove* v. *H.M. Adv.*, 1946 S.N. 60; cf. *R.* v. *Jones (Robert)* [1971] 2 Q.B. 456.
[83] *West* v. *H.M. Adv.*, 1955 S.L.T. 425.

Powers of a single judge

11-23   A judge of the Court sitting alone may:

> (*a*) Give leave to appeal;
>
> (*b*) Extend the time within which notice of appeal or of an application for leave to appeal may be given;
>
> (*c*) Allow the appellant to be present at any proceedings in cases where he is not entitled to be present without leave;
>
> (*d*) Admit an appellant to bail.

He exercises these powers in the same manner as they may be exercised by the Court and subject to the same conditions, but, if he refuses an application by an appellant for the exercise of any of the above powers, the appellant is entitled to have the application determined by the Court.[84]

If the application is one of special difficulty the judge may, instead of dealing with it himself, have it sent for hearing by a larger Court.[85]

Representation by solicitors

11-24   In all the proceedings referred to in the preceding paragraph which may take place before a single judge, and in all preliminary and interlocutory proceedings and applications except such as are held before a full Court, the parties thereto may be represented and appear by a solicitor alone.[86]

Hearing of appeal

11-25   The appellant may, if he wishes, present a written case.[87] If he chooses this course, he must intimate to the Clerk of Justiciary four days before the date fixed for the hearing.[88] He must also lodge three copies of his case and argument with the Clerk of Justiciary and send one copy to the Crown Agent.[89] Once the appellant has presented a written case he is not allowed to submit oral argument in addition except with leave of the Court.[90] Unless the Court otherwise directs, the respondent makes his reply orally in the ordinary way.[91]

11-26   An appellant, notwithstanding that he is in custody, is entitled to be present if he desires it, on the hearing of his appeal, except where the appeal is on some ground involving a question of law alone, but, in that case and on an application for leave to appeal and on any proceedings preliminary or incidental to an appeal, is not entitled to be present, except where it is provided by the Act of Adjournal that he shall have the right to be present, or where the Court gives him leave to be present.[92] If the appellant is not present, the decision of the Court is intimated to him by the Clerk of

---

[84] 1926 Act, s. 14.
[85] *Spence* v. *H.M. Adv.*, 1945 J.C. 59.
[86] Act of Adjournal, para. 21 (b).
[87] 1926 Act, s. 4.
[88] Act of Adjournal, para. 12 (a).
[89] Ibid.
[90] Ibid., para. 12 (c).
[91] Ibid., para. 12 (b).
[92] 1926 Act, s. 7; Act of Adjournal, paras. 14 and 17.

Justiciary.[93] It is normal for the appellant to be present. Where he has a right to be present but does not wish to appear, the Court may hear the appeal in his absence.[94]

1-27 The judge who presides at the trial must furnish his notes and also a report giving his opinion on the case or on any point arising therein to the Clerk of Justiciary,[95] who requests these when he receives the appellant's note or application.[96] The report is made to the Court, and, except by leave of the Court or a judge thereof, the Clerk of Justiciary may not furnish any part of it to anyone.[97] The same rule applies when the Secretary of State for Scotland intervenes under section 16 of the Act.[98] The Court or any judge thereof, if they or he see fit, may order the notes of the trial judge to be printed or typed for the use of the Court and the parties.[99]

1-28 The proceedings in trials on indictment are taken down in shorthand, and a transcript may be made for the use of the Court.[1] The accused and any party interested, but no other person, may obtain copies.[2] The term " party interested " is defined by the Act of Adjournal as the prosecutor or the person convicted or any other person named in, or immediately affected by, any order of the trial judge, or any person authorised to act on behalf of an interested party.[3]

1-29 Diets of hearing may be continued by the Court to dates fixed or not fixed.[4]

1-30 Non-compliance with any provision of the Act of Adjournal or with any rule or practice in force under the 1926 Act is not necessarily fatal to the prosecution of an appeal, the matter being one for the discretion of the Court or a judge thereof.[5]

Supplemental Powers of Court

-31 The Court may, if they think it necessary or expedient in the interest of justice, exercise the following powers [6]:

Production of documents and hearing of evidence

They may,

" (a) order the production of any document, or other thing connected with the proceedings, the production of which appears to them necessary for the determination of the case; and

---

[93] Act of Adjournal, para. 19 (a).
[94] *Manuel* v. *H.M. Adv.*, 1958 J.C. 41: the appellant originally intimated a desire to be present but later accepted counsel's advice that this was not in his interest.
[95] 1926 Act, s. 5.
[96] Act of Adjournal, paras. 9 and 10.
[97] Ibid., para. 10 (b).
[98] Ibid., paras. 9 and 10.
[99] Ibid., para. 9.
[1] Supra, para. 10–33.
[2] 1926 Act, s. 11; Act of Adjournal, para. 3.
[3] Act of Adjournal, para. 3 (e).
[4] Act of Adjournal, para. 16.
[5] Ibid., para. 24.   [6] 1926 Act, s. 6 (a)-(c).

(b) if they think fit, order any witnesses who would have been compellable witnesses at the trial to attend and be examined before the Court, whether they were or were not called at the trial, or order the examination of any such witnesses to be conducted in manner provided by Act of Adjournal [7] before any judge of the Court or other person appointed by the Court for the purpose, and allow the admission of any depositions so taken as evidence before the Court; and

(c) if they think fit, receive the evidence, if tendered, of any witness (including the appellant) who is a competent but not compellable witness, and, if the appellant makes an application for the purpose, of the husband or wife of the appellant, in cases where the evidence of the husband or wife could not have been given at the trial except on such an application."

11–32 In its early days the Court took the view that new evidence should be heard if it was material and relevant,[8] but in the leading case, and the first reported one where the Crown opposed the admission of the evidence, the Court laid down a much stricter standard, holding that new evidence would be received only where it could be said that had the jury had the new evidence before it it would have come to a different result, i.e. that if it had convicted with all the evidence before it its verdict would have been liable to be quashed as unreasonable.[9] The Court is clearly very reluctant to receive fresh evidence, and very conscious of its self-imposed duty not to substitute its own view of the facts for that of the jury, and also of the obvious difficulty of making an assessment of the evidence as a whole when it has heard only a part of it. The Court will be particularly reluctant to hear fresh evidence where it is directed to the credibility of the witnesses at the original trial,[10] or to refuting expert opinion given at the trial.[11] On the whole, it seems unlikely that the Court will ever exercise its powers to hear fresh evidence in any but highly exceptional circumstances.[12]

The criterion to be adopted in determining whether to hear fresh evidence is the same whether the matter comes before the Court by way of appeal or by way of reference by the Secretary of State under section 16 (a)

[7] Act of Adjournal, paras. 15, 16.

[8] *Slater* v. *H.M. Adv.*, 1928 J.C. 94; *Lowson* v. *H.M. Adv.*, 1943 J.C. 141; the power was also used in *Lennie* v. *H.M. Adv.*, 1946 J.C. 79.

[9] *Gallacher* v. *H.M. Adv.*, 1951 J.C. 38.

[10] *Higgins* v. *H.M. Adv.*, 1956 J.C. 69; *Thompson* v. *H.M. Adv.*, 1968 J.C. 61; cf. *Meehan* v. *H.M. Adv.* (1970) 34 J.C.L. 132; *H.M. Adv.* v. *Stewart or Temple*, 1971 S.L.T. 193; *Henderson* v. H.M. *Adv.*, 1971 S.L.T. (Notes) 26.

[11] *Alexander Main Stirling*, March 1960, unreported.

[12] See G. H. G., " New Evidence in Criminal Appeals," 1957 S.L.T.(News) 125. The English Court, now the Criminal Division of the Court of Appeal, has now wider powers to hear fresh evidence than has the Scots court, and has also power to order a retrial where an appeal is allowed by reason of fresh evidence received or available to be received by them: Criminal Appeal Act 1968, ss. 7 and 23; Gerald H. Gordon, " Retrials in Criminal Cases," 1971 S.L.T.(News) 169. Even under the Criminal Appeal Act 1907, on which the 1926 Act is based, the English Court took a more liberal view of their powers—see e.g. *R.* v. *Jordan* (1956) 40 Cr.App.R. 152; *R.* v. *Parks* [1961] 1 W.L.R. 1484.

of the Act.[13] Different considerations will apply where the evidence is heard on a reference under section 16 (b).

An application to the Court to hear fresh evidence must be accompanied by the statements sought to be proved and the names and addresses of the witnesses.[14] It appears that the Court will hear the evidence only where they are first of all satisfied, or reasonably satisfied,[15] that if the evidence were credible it would have affected the jury's verdict, and will then, having heard the evidence, determine whether or not it is in their view credible and of sufficient weight to have affected the jury's verdict. They may, perhaps, reject evidence because it conflicts with evidence accepted by the jury and merely repeats evidence of other witnesses, e.g. to an alibi, which was rejected by the jury.[16] In determining whether to hear fresh evidence the Court will take into account its availability at the trial, and will " ask of any appellant who tenders fresh evidence why it was not tendered at the trial." [17] It was said in *Gallacher* v. *H.M. Advocate* [18] that no general rule could be laid down and that " the explanation in any particular case must be viewed, not in the light of any technicality or rule of practice or of procedure, but solely in the light of the dominating consideration that we may order new evidence if we think it necessary or expedient in the interests of justice." [19] One situation in which the Court may hear evidence is where it was wrongly excluded at the trial.[20] Evidence of events subsequent to the trial, such as a confession by a person other than the accused, will not be allowed on appeal.[21]

Taking expert opinion

1–33   The Court may also,

" (d) Where any question arising on the appeal involves prolonged examination of documents or accounts, or any scientific or local investigation, which cannot in the opinion of the Court conveniently be conducted before the Court, order the reference of the question in manner provided by Act of Adjournal [22] for inquiry and report to a special commissioner appointed by the Court, and act upon the report of any such commissioner so far as they think fit to adopt it; and

(e) Appoint any person with special expert knowledge to act as assessor to the Court in any case where it appears to the Court that such special knowledge is required for the proper determination of the case [23];

[13] *Higgins* v. *H.M. Adv.*, supra.   [14] Ibid.
[15] *H.M. Adv.* v. *Stewart or Temple*, supra.
[16] Ibid.
[17] *Gallacher* v. *H.M. Adv.*, supra, L.J.-C. at 45; cf. *Slater* v. *H.M. Adv.*, supra, L.J.-G. at 102.
[18] Supra.
[19] 1951 J.C. 38, L.J.-C. at 45.
[20] *Lowson* v. *H.M. Adv.*, supra.
[21] *Henderson* v. *H.M. Adv.*, 1971 S.L.T.(Notes) 26.
[22] Act of Adjournal, para. 15.
[23] The court refused to take advantage of this provision in relation to psychiatric evidence in *Carraher* v. *H.M. Adv.*, 1946 J.C. 108.

and exercise in relation to the proceedings under this Act any other powers vested in the Court, and issue any warrants necessary for enforcing the orders or sentences of the Court: Provided that in no case shall any sentence be increased by reason of or in consideration of any evidence that was not given at the trial." [24]

Determination of Appeals

11–34   Section 2 (1) of the 1926 Act provides that the Court shall allow an appeal against conviction if they think: (1) that the verdict of the jury should be set aside on the ground that it is unreasonable or cannot be supported having regard to the evidence; or (2) that the judgment of the court before whom the appellant was convicted should be set aside on the ground of a wrong decision of any question of law; or (3) that on any other ground there was a miscarriage of justice. These three grounds, and particularly (2) and (3), are not clearly distinguishable. For example, the unsupportability of a verdict having regard to the evidence may be inseparable from the legal question of the sufficiency or the admissibility of evidence; an error in a summing-up is not " *a wrong decision* of a question of law," but any resulting miscarriage will be appealed against as an appeal on a question of law. The Court is obliged to dismiss any appeal which it is not empowered to allow on any of the three stated grounds. In addition, the Court is entitled to dismiss any appeal even if they decide the point argued in favour of the appellant, if they consider that there has been no substantial miscarriage of justice.[25] This provision, known as " the proviso," presumably applies where the appeal is argued on ground (3) above only where a distinction can be made between a " miscarriage of justice " and a " substantial miscarriage of justice," a distinction which the Court has been able to make in a number of cases.[26]

Verdict unreasonable or unsupportable having regard to evidence

11–35   The Court's attitude to this ground of appeal was established in 1927 in *Webb* v. *H.M. Advocate*,[27] a case in which the appellants had been convicted of assault. The specific grounds on which the appellants sought to maintain their appeal were (a) that the evidence adduced by the Crown was not only insufficient but self-contradictory and unreliable, and (b) that the jury had not given due weight to the evidence adduced by each of the accused to prove an alibi. The Court dismissed the appeal. They approached the verdict of the jury in the same way as the Court of Session approaches the verdict of a civil jury, and indicated that they would interfere only if they thought that the verdict was perverse. It is not enough that the Court disagrees with the verdict, they must find that no reasonable

[24] 1926 Act, s. 6.
[25] 1926 Act, s. 2 (1).
[26] See *Smith* v. *H.M. Adv.*, 1952 J.C. 66; *Mactaggart* v. *H.M. Adv.*, 1934 J.C. 33, Lord Anderson at 36; *Smart* v. *H.M. Adv.*, 1938 J.C. 148; *Moar* v. *H.M. Adv.*, 1949 J.C. 31; infra, paras. 11–42, 11–43.
[27] 1927 J.C. 92.

jury properly instructed could have given that verdict.[28] So far as evidence is concerned, the court has set its face against interfering with the jury's assessment of credibility. There was a suggestion in *Macmillan* v. *H.M. Advocate* [29] that this was subject to special circumstances such as a specific allegation of perjury, but the attitude of the majority of the Court in *Higgins* v. *H.M. Advocate*,[30] suggests that the circumstances will require to be very special indeed before the Court will disturb a jury's assessment of credibility. The Court have frequently asserted that they will not substitute themselves for a jury or re-try the case.[31]

A verdict may be overturned as unreasonable where it is self-contradictory as, for example, where there are two accused, and one is convicted of being art and part with the other while that other is acquitted,[32] or where an accused is convicted on one charge and acquitted on another although the evidence is such that both charges must stand or fall together.[33]

A verdict will not be regarded as unsupported by evidence, provided there is sufficient evidence in law to support it.[34] It is not enough, therefore, that it would have been open to the jury to acquit, either because the case against the appellant was weak or because there was a conflict of testimony, or that the Court might themselves have reached a different conclusion on the evidence.[35] The Court can only set aside a verdict on a question of fact where it is obviously and palpably wrong.[36] A verdict which cannot be supported having regard to the evidence is thus one where the evidence lacks some element which is necessary in law to support the charge [37] or where the evidence is legally insufficient, as where there is no corroboration.[38] In such cases it can be said that the judge misdirected the jury in leaving the evidence to them at all instead of directing them to acquit.

Incompetent or irrelevant indictment

1-36   As no one can be asked to plead to an indictment which is either incompetent or irrelevant, it follows that where the trial judge has wrongly repelled objections to the competency or relevancy of the indictment, a subsequent conviction thereon must be quashed. Even although no objection has been taken to the indictment in the court below, the same

---

[28] *Webb*, supra, L.J.-C. at 95, Lord Ormidale at 97, Lord Anderson at 99, all adopting *Campbell* v. *Scottish Educational News Co., Ltd.* (1906) 8 F. 691, Lord Kinnear at 698. See also *Slater* v. *H.M. Adv.*, 1928 J.C. 94, L.J.-G. at 101–2.

[29] 1927 J.C. 62.

[30] 1956 J.C. 69.

[31] e.g. *Webb*, supra; *Slater* v. *H.M. Adv.*, 1928 J.C. 94, L.J.-G. at 102.

[32] Cf. *Young* v. *H.M. Adv.*, 1932 J.C. 63.

[33] *Hamilton and Ors.* v. *H.M. Adv.*, 1938 J.C. 134.

[34] Cf. *Webb*, supra; but see *Dow* v. *McKnight*, 1949 J.C. 38, Lord Keith at 56.

[35] *Webb*, supra.

[36] The English Court has frequently taken a somewhat wider view of its powers—see especially *R.* v. *Wallace* (1931) 23 Cr.App.R. 32. It is now empowered to allow an appeal where the verdict is " unsafe or unsatisfactory "—Criminal Appeal Act 1968, s. 2 (1) (*a*).

[37] e.g. *Kenny* v. *H.M. Adv.*, 1951 J.C. 104; *Kent* v. *H.M. Adv.*, 1950 J.C. 38.

[38] *Morton* v. *H.M. Adv.*, 1938 J.C. 50.

result will follow if the defect in the indictment is so grave as to make the charge a fundamental nullity.[39] A conviction will also be quashed where the trial court acted in excess of its jurisdiction,[40] where the diet was not properly constituted,[41] or where the verdict was one which was not open on the indictment.

Wrong decision on admissibility of evidence

11–37   Perhaps the most common example of a wrong decision on a question of law is an erroneous decision to admit or reject evidence. What is in issue may be part of a witness's evidence such as evidence of a confession,[42] or a decision whether or not to allow the witness to be called or recalled,[43] or a refusal to allow one party to re-examine or cross-examine a witness.[44]

Withdrawal of defence

11–38   It is a ground of appeal that the judge wrongly withdrew from the jury's consideration a line of defence which ought to have been left to them, such as self-defence,[45] or wrongly withdrew from them the right to convict on a lesser charge such as culpable homicide in a case of murder, or wrongly directed them that certain evidence was insufficient to establish a particular line of defence.[46] These grounds of appeal merge with the ground of misdirection in law. On the other hand a judge is not bound to direct a jury that an alternative lesser verdict is open to them even if asked by either party to do so.[47]

Misdirection by judge

11–39   There is no doubt that misdirection by the presiding judge is a proper ground of appeal, but what constitutes misdirection depends on the facts of each particular case. This gives the Court a fairly wide discretion in determining appeals on this ground, a discretion which may or may not involve explicit reference to the proviso. Misdirection may be in law or on fact; it may consist in telling the jury something which is wrong or in failing to give them an essential direction, in giving them confusing or contradictory directions,[48] or in failing to put the defence case fairly before them.[49] In dealing with appeals on this ground the Court will not examine parts of a summing-up in isolation from the rest but will view the summing-up as a whole against the background of the evidence and arguments in the

---

[39] Supra, para. 9–07.
[40] *Gallagher* v. *H.M. Adv.*, 1937 J.C. 27.
[41] *Hull* v. *H.M. Adv.*, 1945 J.C. 83.
[42] See infra, paras. 18–23 et seq.
[43] e.g. *McNeilie* v. *H.M. Adv.*, 1929 J.C. 50.
[44] *McLeod* v. *H.M. Adv.*, 1939 J.C. 68; cf. *MacKenzie* v. *Jinks*, 1934 J.C. 48; *MacPherson* v. *Copeland*, 1961 J.C. 74.
[45] Cf. *Hillan* v. *H.M. Adv.*, 1937 J.C. 53.
[46] See e.g., *Crawford*, v. *H.M. Adv.*, 1950 J.C. 67; *Kennedy* v. *H.M. Adv.*, 1944 J.C. 171; *Brown* v. *H.M. Adv.*, 1964 J.C. 10.
[47] *Kilna* v. *H.M. Adv.*, 1960 J.C. 23.
[48] *Greig* v. *H.M. Adv.*, 1949 S.L.T.(Notes) 5.
[49] *Scott* (*A. T.*) v .*H.M. Adv.*, 1946 J.C. 90.

trial.[50] The Court is conscious of the danger of analysing a summing-up away from " the living context of the trial." Accordingly, " A Court of Appeal must . . . be constantly on its guard against failing to appreciate what were the vital issues—the matters to which those actively engaged in the trial were directing their attention . . . For that reason, it is our duty to view with confidence and charity the course taken by an experienced Judge in charging a jury. If a charge is to be a good charge, it ought to be one addressed to the fifteen people in the jury-box, and not to the Court of Appeal. A charge, which meticulously covers every theoretical aspect, may be so complicated that the jury's capacity to appreciate what it is being told may be blunted long before the real matters with which it has to deal are reached. On the other hand, a vital and effective charge which brings the relevant issues squarely before the jury may on subsequent analysis be found to have technical weaknesses. No hard and fast rule can be laid down." [51] In *McPhelim*, from which these words are quoted, the Court declined to allow an appeal where the trial judge had failed to direct the jury that they could return a majority verdict and in particular that they could not convict unless eight of them were for guilty, and had also failed to direct them that the onus of proof was on the Crown, although, " from what he did say, [no] reasonable jury could have been in doubt as to what the position was." [52] In this case the consideration that the trial judge was addressing a jury and not an appeal court led to the appeal being dismissed. In other cases it has had the opposite result, and summings-up or statements in summings-up which would have carried a clear meaning to a trained lawyer have been struck down by the court because they were not sufficiently explicit to be clear to a lay jury.[53]

11–40   The following are examples of misdirections in law.

It is a misdirection to give the jury erroneous definitions of the crime charged or of the legal requirements of any specific defence,[54] to direct them that the onus of proof is not on the Crown [55] or to fail to direct them that the onus is on the Crown [56] or to give them an erroneous direction as to the onus of proof which lies on the defence,[57] or to fail to direct them to regard the evidence of an accomplice with care.[58] It is also a misdirection to give them an erroneous direction as to the corroborative force of any evidence,[59] or erroneous directions as to the applicability of the doctrine of recent possession or as to what evidence constitutes a

---

[50] *Muir* v. *H.M. Adv.*, 1933 J.C. 46, Lord Sands at 49; *McPhelim* v. *H.M. Adv.*, 1960 J.C. 17, L.J.-C. at 21; see also *Reynolds* v. *H.M. Adv.*, 1928 S.N. 103; *McEwan* v. *H.M. Adv.*, 1939 J.C. 46; *McCann* v. *H.M. Adv.*, 1960 J.C. 36.

[51] *McPhelim*, supra, L.J.-C. at 21; see also *Reilly and Anr.* v. *H.M. Adv.*, 1950 J.C. 52.

[52] *McPhelim*, supra, at 22.

[53] *Muir* v. *H.M. Adv.*, 1933 J.C. 46; *Tobin* v. *H.M. Adv.*, 1934 J.C. 60; *Docherty* v. *H.M. Adv.*, 1945 J.C. 89.

[54] e.g. *Owens* v. *H.M. Adv.*, 1946 J.C. 119.

[55] *Slater* v. *H.M. Adv.*, 1928 J.C. 94.

[56] *McKenzie* v. *H.M. Adv.*, 1959 J.C. 32; cf. *McPhelim* v. *H.M. Adv.*, 1960 J.C. 17.

[57] *Hillan* v. *H.M. Adv.*, 1937 J.C. 53; *McCann* v. *H.M. Adv.*, 1960 J.C. 36.

[58] *Wallace* v. *H.M. Adv.*, 1952 J.C. 78; see infra, para. 18–58.

[59] *Morton* v. *H.M. Adv.*, 1938 J.C. 50; *Wilkie* v. *H.M. Adv.*, 1938 J.C. 128.

criminative circumstance under that doctrine.[60] Where concert is in issue and the facts are in any way difficult, the judge must give clear and explicit directions on the law of concert, eschewing misleading illustrations [61] and making clear what courses are open to the jury in the event of concert being proved or not.[62] In one extreme case the court allowed an appeal because of a failure to tell the jury in terms that if they found diminished responsibility proved they should bring in a verdict of culpable homicide, although both counsel had so told them.[63] In two cases an appeal was allowed because the judge had discouraged the jury from making use of the not proven verdict.[64] Failure to refer specifically to the not proven verdict is not in itself a misdirection,[65] and in some cases the judge may be entitled to exclude the possibility of a not proven verdict,[66] nor is it necessarily a misdirection to fail to tell the jury that they may bring in a verdict by a majority.[67] In *Russell* v. *H.M. Advocate* [68] the accused appealed against conviction on the ground that the judge had misdirected himself in refusing to sustain a plea in bar of trial.

11–41   It is a proper ground of appeal that the judge misdirected the jury as to the facts of the case. What directions a judge should give on the facts and the extent to which he should go over the evidence in detail depends on the circumstances, including the length and complexity of the trial.[69] The judge is not entitled to trespass on the jury's province as masters of the facts, nor is it enough for him merely to pay lip service to this principle by saying that the facts are for the jury, if he then unduly impresses his own views on them.[70] It is a misdirection to fail to put the defence case properly to the jury,[71] or to give a direction on a vital matter which is inadequate.[72] It is also a misdirection to put the facts before the jury in such a way as to confuse them, or to present something as clearly proved without referring to evidence to the contrary.[73]

Miscarriage of justice

11–42   Appeals have been taken on this ground in relation to irregularities or improprieties in the trial procedure, such as an improper judicial

---

[60] *Christie* v. *H.M. Adv.*, 1939 J.C. 72; *Cameron* v. *H.M. Adv.*, 1959 J.C. 59; *Simpson* v. *H.M. Adv.*, 1952 J.C. 1; *Wightman and Anr.* v. *H.M. Adv.*, 1959 J.C. 44; *Reilly* v. *H.M. Adv.*, 1959 J.C. 59.

[61] Cf. *Greig* v. *H.M. Adv.*, 1949 S.L.T.(Notes) 5; *Docherty*, infra.

[62] *Tobin* v. *H.M. Adv.*, 1934 J.C. 60; *Docherty* v. *H.M. Adv.*, 1945 J.C. 89; cf. *McPhelim*, supra; *Shaw* v. *H.M. Adv.*, 1953 J.C. 51.

[63] *Muir*, supra; but cf. *Kilna*, supra.

[64] *McNicol* v. *H.M. Adv.*, 1964 J.C. 25; *Hasson* v. *H.M. Adv.*, (1971) 35 J.C.L. 271; but cf. *Buchan* v. *H.M. Adv.*, (1968) 32 J.C.L. 114.

[65] *McDermid* v. *H.M. Adv.*, 1948 J.C. 12; see supra, para. 10–39.

[66] *Reid* v. *H.M. Adv.*, 1947 S.L.T. 150.

[67] *Mackay* v. *H.M. Adv.*, 1944 J.C. 153; *McPhelim*, supra, It is now, however, the established practice to tell the jury that they may not convict unless a majority of eight of them are in favour of a guilty verdict—see *McPhelim*, supra, at 22.

[68] 1946 J.C. 37.

[69] See *McPhelim*, supra, L.J.-C. at 22; *Hamilton and Ors.* v. *H.M. Adv.*, 1938 J.C. 134.

[70] *Simpson* v. *H.M. Adv.*, supra, L.J.-G. at 3; cf. *Hamilton and Ors.* v. *H.M. Adv.*, 1938 J.C. 134.

[71] *Scott* (*A. T.*) v. *H.M. Adv.*, 1946 J.C. 90.

[72] *Mills* v. *H.M. Adv.*, 1935 J.C. 77.   [73] *Mills*, supra.

11–42 observation,[74] a conversation between a witness and a juror,[75] failure to read a special defence to the jury,[76] and letting the jury know the accused has pleaded guilty to part of an indictment.[77] Unfairness on the part of the judge or the Crown in the conduct of the trial may also be attacked on this ground. In *Smith* v. *H.M. Advocate* [78] the accused was charged with murder by means of a dagger or other similar instrument. A special defence of self-defence was lodged on his behalf. On the second day of the trial, after all the evidence of fact had been led on behalf of the Crown, the advocate-depute elicited in evidence from the police inspector in charge of the investigation that, in addition to the dagger with which the accused was alleged to have carried out the murder, another small dagger was found in the dance hall where the crime was stated to have been committed. The advocate-depute, in the presence of the jury, said that none of the witnesses apparently attached any importance to the second weapon. The Court were of opinion that this observation might have influenced the jury, but they also considered that, having regard to the whole evidence, no substantial miscarriage of justice had actually occurred and they applied the proviso.

In *McLeod* v. *H.M. Advocate* [79] the only corroboration of the complainer's evidence was a statement elicited by the presiding sheriff from another witness for the Crown after the conclusion of the cross-examination and no further opportunity was given for further cross-examination. The Court allowed the appeal, holding the sheriff's actings to constitute a miscarriage of justice. In *Mactaggart* v. *H.M. Advocate*,[80] a trial for culpable homicide, the prosecutor, without first putting the matter to the witnesses in question, led police evidence to the effect that two earlier Crown witnesses whose evidence had tended to exculpate the appellant had previously made statements to the police directly incriminating him. The Court allowed the appeal on the ground that there had been a substantial miscarriage of justice. In *Lowson* v. *H.M. Advocate* [81] the appellant complained of the presiding sheriff's refusal to allow his witnesses to give evidence, he not having given the appropriate notice to the Crown. The Court exercised their power to hear the witnesses on the ground that the sheriff's refusal had amounted to a miscarriage. It is not clear whether this ground of appeal is appropriate in relation to irregularities occuring prior to the trial, or whether the only relief in such cases is by application to the Secretary of State.[82] Where inadmissible evidence, such as evidence of an accused's previous convictions, emerges at a trial without any decision of the court on its admissibility, an appeal may be brought on the ground

[74] *Bergson* v. *H.M. Adv.* (1970) 34 J.C.L. 270.
[75] *Smart* v. *H.M. Adv.*, 1938 J.C. 148; cf. *Brownlie* v. *H.M. Adv.* (1967) 31 J.C.L. 132.
[76] *Moar* v. *H.M. Adv.*, 1949 J.C. 31.
[77] *Walsh* v. *H.M. Adv.*, 1961 J.C. 51.
[78] 1952 J.C. 66.
[79] 1939 J.C. 68.
[80] 1934 J.C. 33; cf. *Lee* v. *H.M. Adv.*, 1968 S.L.T. 155.
[81] 1943 J.C. 141.
[82] See *Smith* v. *H.M. Adv.* 1952 J.C. 66, L.J.-C. at 74.

that there has been a miscarriage of justice.[83] The inadequacy of the accused's solicitor is not a ground of appeal [84] and the Court is unlikely to allow an appeal on the ground that the trial judge refused the accused an adjournment to obtain another solicitor after he had rejected the one acting for him under the legal aid scheme.[85]

The proviso

11–43   Questions as to the application of the proviso [85a] have sometimes arisen in relation to the wrongful admission or rejection of evidence, or to alleged misdirection of the jury. There can be no general principles as to its applicability since it is essentially a matter related to the particular case. The scheme of the Act is that where the Court hold a verdict to be unreasonable or a decision of the trial judge to be wrong in law, they cannot allow the verdict to stand unless they are able to hold that no substantial miscarriage of justice has occurred. If they have any doubt about this matter, they must allow the appeal.[86] Where evidence has been wrongly admitted, the proviso will be applied if the verdict of guilty was the only reasonable and proper verdict a reasonable jury could have returned on the remaining evidence.[87] The Court has on occasion expressed doubts as to the argument that a conviction can stand despite the wrongful admission of evidence provided there is sufficient admissible evidence to the same effect,[88] for it will be difficult to say that the jury did not proceed on the inadmissible evidence,[89] but has also on occasion applied the proviso where there was ample admissible evidence.[90] Where the inadmissible evidence is such as to create prejudice in the minds of the jury against the appellant the proviso will not be applied.[91] Where what is complained of is the wrongful exclusion of evidence, it will be very difficult for the Court to do otherwise than allow the appeal or themselves hear the evidence.[92]

Where the ground of appeal is misdirection the proviso will be applied if no reasonable jury properly directed could have come to any different conclusion.[93] Generally speaking the proviso will rarely be applied where there has been a material misdirection.[94] In *Tobin* v. *H.M. Advocate* [95] it was said that the Court would apply the proviso in the case of misdirection

---

[83] See e.g. *Corcoran* v. *H.M. Adv.*, 1932 J.C. 42; *Kepple* v. *H.M. Adv.*, 1936 J.C. 76; *Cornwallis* v. *H.M. Adv.*, (1902) 3 Adam 604; *Haslam* v. *H.M. Adv.*, 1936 J.C. 82.

[84] *McCarroll* v. *H.M. Adv.*, 1949 J.C. 10.

[85] *Monteath* v. *H.M. Adv.*, 1965 J.C. 14; cf. *Turnbull* v. *H.M. Adv.*, 1948 S.N. 19; *Thomson* v. *H.M. Adv.*, 1959 J.C. 15.

[85a] Supra, para. 11–34. See also *Smith* v. *H.M. Adv.*, 1952 J.C. 66, supra, para. 11–42.

[86] But cf. *Webb* v. *H.M. Adv.*, 1927 J.C. 92, L.J.-C. at 95–6.

[87] Cf. *Wallace* v. *H.M. Adv.*, 1952 J.C. 78.

[88] *Frank* v. *H.M. Adv.*, 1938 J.C. 17, L.J.-G. at 24; cf. *Foster* v. *H.M. Adv.*, 1932 J.C. 75.

[89] Cf. *Wightman and Anr.* v. *H.M. Adv.*, 1959 J.C. 44; *Forrester* v. *H.M. Adv.*, 1952 J.C. 28.

[90] e.g. *Hopes and Lavery* v. *H.M. Adv.*, 1960 J.C. 104; cf. *Chalmers* v. *H.M. Adv.*, 1954 J.C. 66.

[91] *Kerr* v. *H.M. Adv.*, 1958 J.C. 14.

[92] Cf. *Mackenzie* v. *Jinks*, 1934 J.C. 48; *Brown* v. *H.M. Adv.*, 1964 J.C. 10.

[93] *Burgh* v. *H.M. Adv.*, 1944 J.C. 77, L.J.-C. at 81; *McPhelim* v. *H.M. Adv.*, 1960 J.C. 17.

[94] *Muir* v. *H.M. Adv.*, 1933 J.C. 46; *Mills* v. *H.M. Adv.*, 1935 J.C. 77.

[95] 1934 J.C. 60.

only if they could affirm that with the proper directions the jury would inevitably have reached the same conclusion. This was the case in which Lord Anderson expressed the shrewd suspicion that the jury would have reached the same result if properly directed, but was unable to say that such a result would have been reached, taking into account the fact that the idiosyncrasies of juries are remarkable.[96] In *McKenzie* v. *H.M. Advocate*,[97] the Lord Justice-Clerk adopted the dictum of Viscount Simon in *Stirland* v. *D.P.P.*[98] to the effect that " the provision that the Court of Criminal Appeal may dismiss the appeal if they consider that no substantial miscarriage of justice has actually occurred in convicting the accused assumes a situation where a reasonable jury, after being properly directed, would, on the evidence properly admissible, without doubt convict." [99] The Lord Justice-Clerk referred to this as " a high and exacting test." [1] *McKenzie* [97] itself applied the proviso in a selective fashion. The accused was charged with culpable homicide by reckless driving while drunk, or alternatively with causing death by reckless driving and with driving while unfit through drink. He was convicted on the charge of culpable homicide. The trial judge had failed to direct the jury on onus of proof, and the appeal was upheld, but the proviso was applied to the extent of substituting a verdict of driving while unfit through drink for the verdict of culpable homicide. The maximum prison sentence for the latter offence was then imposed. The proviso is rarely applied in practice.

Powers of court

11-44 In the ordinary case, where the Court allow an appeal against a conviction they quash the conviction and discharge the accused.[2] Where an appeal against conviction is refused the Court may alter the sentence in the same way as if there had been an appeal against sentence.[3] In special cases, however, they may take different steps.

11-45 If it appears to the Court that an appellant, though not properly convicted on some charge or part of the indictment, has been properly convicted on some other charge or part of the indictment, the Court may, instead of allowing or dismissing the appeal, substitute for the verdict found a verdict of guilty on such other charge or part of the indictment, and may either affirm the sentence originally passed or pass such sentence in substitution therefor as they think proper, provided it is warranted in law by the substituted verdict.[4]

11-46 Where an appellant has been convicted of an offence and the jury could on the same indictment have found him guilty of some other offence, and it appears to the Court that the jury must have been satisfied

96 Ibid., at 64.
97 1959 J.C. 32.
98 [1944] A.C. 315; see also *R.* v. *Pink* [1971] 1 Q.B. 508; *Anderson* v. *R.* [1972] A.C. 100.
99 1959 J.C. at 37–38.
1 At 38.
2 1926 Act, s. 2 (2).
3 Ibid., s. 2 (3); *Connelly* v. *H.M. Adv.*, 1954 J.C. 90.
4 1926 Act, s. 3 (1). See e.g. *Cronin* v. *H.M. Adv.*, 1945 S.L.T. 132.

of facts which proved him guilty of that other offence, the Court may, instead of allowing or dismissing the appeal, substitute for the original verdict, a verdict of guilty of that other offence, and pass such sentence in substitution as may be warranted in law for the other offence.[5] The Court must be satisfied that the jurors' minds were applied to the alternative view of the facts, and that they must necessarily have reached a verdict of guilty on that view.[6]

11–47   If the Court are satisfied that the appellant committed the act charged against him but find that he was insane at the time of committing that act they may substitute for the verdict of the jury a verdict of acquittal on the ground of insanity, and may quash the original sentence and make such order for the detention of the appellant as may be made under section 63 of the Mental Health (Scotland) Act 1960 in the case of a person acquitted by a jury on the ground of insanity.[7]

Appeals against Sentence

11–48   On any appeal against sentence the Court may, if they think that a different sentence should have been passed, quash the sentence passed and pass any other sentence warranted in law, whether more or less severe than the original sentence. If they do not think that a different sentence should have been passed, they dismiss the appeal.[8] The Court may not increase a sentence by reason or in consideration of any evidence that was not given at the trial.[9]

A sentence will not be set aside on the ground of excess merely because it is somewhat different from that which the Court would themselves have imposed. To warrant their intervention it must in the absence of other aggravating circumstances go beyond what is necessary and customary in a case of the kind presented.[10]

The Court has used its power to increase sentences on various occasions.[11]

When an accused appeals against sentence on the ground that the trial court failed to obtain any statutorily required information before passing sentence the Court will itself obtain the information and then impose the appropriate sentence.[12]

---

[5] 1926 Act, s. 3 (2). See e.g. *Muir* v. *H.M. Adv.*, 1933 J.C. 46; *Paton* v. *H.M. Adv.*, 1936 J.C. 19; *Willis* v. *H.M. Adv.*, 1941 J.C. 1; *McKenzie* v. *H.M. Adv.*, 1959 J.C. 32; *Bell* v. *H.M. Adv.*, 1947 S.L.T. (Notes) 29; supra, para. 10–42.

[6] *Kent* v. *H.M. Adv.*, 1950 J.C. 38, where the court refused to substitute a verdict of theft for one of embezzlement.

[7] 1926 Act, s. 3 (3), as amended by the Mental Health (Scotland) Act 1960, s. 63 (4).

[8] 1926 Act, s. 2 (4).

[9] Ibid., s. 6.

[10] *O'Reilly* v. *H.M. Adv.*, 1943 J.C. 23; *Moar* v. *H.M. Adv.*, 1949 J.C. 31; cf. *Dewar* v. *H.M. Adv.*, 1945 J.C. 5; *Cawthorne* v. *H.M. Adv.*, 1968 J.C. 32; Macdonald, 363.

[11] e.g. *Sweeney* v. *H.M. Adv.*, 6th Jan. 1944, unreported; *Boyle* v. *H.M. Adv.*, 1949 S.L.T (Notes) 41; *Connelly*, supra; *Morris* v. *H.M. Adv.*, 24 June, 1971, unreported.

[12] *Walsh* v. *H.M. Adv.*, 1961 J.C. 51.

Increase of sentence in appeals against conviction

11–49   Where the appeal is against conviction only the Court have the same powers to reduce or increase the sentence as they have in an appeal against sentence.[13] They may use this power to increase the original sentence even where that was imposed in the sheriff court. In such a case the Court may increase the sentence beyond the maximum which could have been imposed by the sheriff.[14]

Miscellaneous Matters

Frivolous appeals

11–50   If on any notice of appeal against a conviction purporting to be on a ground of appeal which involves a question of law alone it appears to the Court that the appeal is frivolous or vexatious, and that it can be determined without adjourning it for a full hearing, th ey may dismiss the appeal summarily, without calling on any persons to attend the hearing or to appear for the Crown thereon.[15]

Prerogative of mercy

11–51   The Act does not affect the prerogative of mercy, and the Secretary of State for Scotland on the consideration of any conviction of a person on indictment or the sentence passed on a person who has been so convicted, may, if he thinks fit, at any time, and whether an appeal or an application for leave to appeal against such conviction or sentence has or has not previously been heard and determined by the Court, and whether or not the accused has petitioned for the exercise of Her Majesty's mercy [16] either—

" (a) refer the whole case to the Court and the case shall then be heard and determined by the Court as in the case of an appeal under this Act [17]; or

(b) if he desires the assistance of the Court on any point arising in the case with a view to the determination of the petition, refer that point to the Court for their opinion thereon, and the Court shall consider the point so referred and furnish the Secretary of State for Scotland with their opinion thereon accordingly." [18]

Expenses

11–52   On the hearing and determination of an appeal or any proceedings preliminary or incidental thereto under the Act no expenses are allowed on either side.[19]

---

[13] 1926 Act, s. 2 (3).
[14] Connelly v. H.M. Adv., 1954 J.C. 90.
[15] s. 10 (1).
[16] s. 16, as amended by 1949 Act, s. 79 and Sched. 12.
[17] See Slater v. H.M. Adv., 1928 J.C. 94; Higgins v. H.M. Adv., 1956 J.C. 69.
[18] See Gallacher v. H.M. Adv., 1951 J.C. 38, 49n.
[19] 1926 Act s. 8.

Acts of Adjournal

11-53   In pursuance of the powers conferred on it by the Act, and particularly by section 15, the High Court has passed Acts of Adjournal, dated 27th October, 1926, and 22nd March, 1935, to regulate procedure under the Acts. These Acts of Adjournal deal very fully with the various steps of procedure. In view of their importance, they have been printed in the Appendix,[20] and a careful study of them is necessary in order to ensure the proper carrying out of the provisions of the Act itself.

Passive representation

11-54   There is no passive representation in crime or in criminal proceedings.[21] It was held in a summary case,[22] where the appellant was fined £5 and had consigned £10 caution for expenses, and then died after the stated case had been lodged and before the appeal was heard, that his executor could not be sisted in his place.

[20] Infra, App. D.
[21] *Keane* v. *Adair*, 1941 J.C. 77. See Erskine, Inst. iv, 4, 103.
[22] *Keane* v. *Adair*, supra.

Part III

SUMMARY PROCEDURE

CHAPTER 12

JURISDICTION

12–01 THE distinction between solemn and summary criminal jurisdiction and the tests to be applied in determining whether a case should be tried on indictment or on summary complaint have been pointed out in Chapter 3.[1] Original summary criminal jurisdiction is exercised by all the criminal courts in Scotland with the exception of the High Court of Justiciary. The summary criminal courts [2] are:

(1) The sheriff.
(2) Justices of the peace.
(3) Burgh (including the courts of the stipendiary magistrates at Glasgow).
(4) Police.
(5) Bailie of the River Clyde.

12–02 The trial of youthful offenders under sixteen years of age is considered in Chapter 19.

Application of the 1954 Act

12–03 The 1954 Act is the principal regulating statute. It sets forth a uniform system of procedure for all Scottish summary criminal courts.[3] It also makes applicable to summary procedure certain sections of the 1887 Act, section 2 of the Act providing that sections 4 to 15, 58 to 65, 68 and 69 of the Criminal Procedure (Scotland) Act 1887, shall, as set out with modifications in the First Schedule to the 1954 Act, apply to proceedings under the Act.

12–04 The Act, so far as relating to summary procedure, applies to summary proceedings in respect of:

" (a) any offence which might prior to the passing of this Act, or which may under the provisions of this or any Act, whether passed before or after the passing of this Act, be tried in a summary manner;

(b) any offence or the recovery of a penalty,[4] under any statute which does not exclude summary procedure[5];

---

[1] Supra, para. 3–02.
[2] 1954 Act, s. 77.
[3] Ibid.
[4] There is no definition of " penalty " in the 1954 Act. S. 2 of the 1908 Act defined the word as follows:
  " ' Penalty ' shall include a fine and any sum of money which may, under the authority of any statute or order, be recoverable from any person in respect of the contravention

---

For footnote 5, see page 168.

(c) any order *ad factum praestandum,* or other order of court or warrant competent to a court of summary jurisdiction." [6]

of any statutory requirement or prohibition, and any sum which may, under the authority of any statute or order, be recoverable as a penalty or forfeiture, or of which a court has power to order payment, as also the forfeiture of any article where such forfeiture is authorised by statute or order."

S. 2 of the 1908 Act is retained by the 1954 Act only so far as necessary for the interpretation of s. 77 (s. 78 and Sched. 4).

The previous statutory definition of " penalty " given by s. 2 of the Summary Procedure (Scotland) Act 1864 (repealed by the 1908 Act) was as follows:

" ' Penalty ' shall mean any sum of money which may, under the authority of any Act of Parliament, be recovered from any person in respect of the contravention of any statutory requirement or prohibition, and also any sum which may, under the provisions of any Act of Parliament, be recoverable as a penalty or forfeiture whether such sum shall be payable to the party complaining, prosecuting, or suing for the sum, or shall be payable in whole or in part to any other person, or be applicable to any other use, and whether the amount thereof is fixed by such statutory provision, or is so fixed subject to a power to modify or mitigate, or is in the nature of a penalty not exceeding a certain sum, to be awarded by the Court or judge who may take cognizance thereof."

Under s. 2 of the 1864 Act it was held that the following were of the nature of a penalty and recoverable by summary prosecution:

(*a*) Damage for malicious destruction of property in contravention of an Act of Parliament which provided that the offender should be liable to pay the damage caused by his contravention, under pain of imprisonment in default of payment. (*Robertson* v. *D. of Athole* (1869) 1 Couper 348.)

(*b*) Sum due for grazing animals on the land of a neighbour contrary to the provisions of the Winter Herding Act 1686. (*Grant* v. *Hay* (1888) 2 White 6.)

(*c*) Sum sought to be recovered by a local authority from a house owner as his proportion of the cost of constructing a sewer incurred by the local authority under the Public Health (Scotland) Act 1867, s. 24. (*Local Authority of Burgh of Selkirk* v. *Brodie* (1877) 3 Couper 400.) In this case the majority of the Court (Lord Craighill and L.J.-C. Moncreiff) held that the assessment, although a civil debt, was of the nature of a penalty because, in their view, it was recoverable only by summary petition under s. 105 of the Public Health (Scotland) Act 1867 under which imprisonment might be imposed in the event of non-payment. Lord Young dissented strongly and his view appears to be preferable.

A fine imposed under s. 20 of the Public Health (Scotland) Act 1867 for failure to remove a nuisance is not a penalty in any criminal sense but merely a civil compulsitor. (*Lee* v. *Lasswade Local Authority* (1883) 5 Couper 329; *Torrance* v. *Miller* (1892) 3 White 254; cf. *Suburban District Committee of County Council of Midlothian* v. *Maitland* (1894) 1 Adam 325.)

In *Wright* v. *Kennedy,* 1946 J.C. 142, it was held that it was incompetent to appeal to the High Court by stated case against an order for removal of nuisance pronounced in the burgh police court on a petition by a sanitary inspector invoking the provisions of the Public Health (Scotland) Act 1897 in respect (1) (*following Lee* v. *Lasswade Local Authority, supra*) that the proceedings were essentially civil and not criminal in their nature, and (2) that accordingly the 1908 Act had no application to the order pronounced, seeing that the order was not an order made by a court of summary criminal jurisdiction.

(*d*) Money recoverable summarily as compensation under s. 166 (2) of the Merchant Shipping Act 1894 was held not to be a penalty but civil compensation. (*Alexander* v. *James Little & Co.* (1906) 8 F. 841.)

(*e*) Under the 1908 Act it has been held that proceedings for the recovery of penalties under the Plate (Scotland) Act 1836, must be brought under the forms of the 1908 Act, and not in the form of an ordinary action in the Sheriff Court. (*Glasgow Goldsmiths Company* v. *Mackenzie & Co.,* 1912 S.C. 992.)

5 See supra, para. 3–02. S. 9 of the 1954 Act provides that any statutory offence described as a "misdemeanour" or a "crime and offence" may be tried summarily. In such cases the maximum penalty is 3 months' imprisonment or a fine of £100, except where the statute itself specifically provides for a period of imprisonment greater than 3 months or for a specified fine: see 1954 Act, s. 40, as amended by 1963 Act, s. 23 (3).

Summary procedure has been held competent under the following statutes: Winter Herding Act 1686, s. 11—*Grant* v. *Hay,* supra; Plate (Scotland) Act 1836—*Glasgow Goldsmiths Company* v. *Mackenzie & Co.,* supra; Criminal Law Amendment Act 1885—*Clark and Bendall* v. *Stuart* (1886) 1 White 191.

Summary proceedings were also allowed under a private Act, viz. The Glasgow City and District Railways Act 1882, in *The Glasgow City and District Railway Co.* v. *Hutchison and Ors.* (1884) 5 Couper 420.   6 1954 Act, s. 1 (1).

This last subhead refers primarily to the types of application which are described in section 14 of the Act. As its terms indicate, it only applies when the order is competent to a court of summary criminal jurisdiction.[7] It was applied to an order regulating the possession of property of disputed or doubtful ownership pronounced by a magistrate under section 101 of the Glasgow Police Act 1866,[8] and to proceedings for the removal of a checker under section 13 of the Coal Mines Regulation Act 1887.[9] It does not apply to a petition brought by a sanitary inspector under the Public Health (Scotland) Act 1897 for an order for removal of a nuisance.[10]

The Act applies to procedure in all courts of summary jurisdiction in so far as they have jurisdiction in the matters aforesaid.[11]

For the purpose of providing a uniform code for summary criminal procedure and consolidating all existing statutory enactments on the subject the 1954 Act repeals all prior statutory provisions relating to summary criminal jurisdiction and declares that where any statute provides for proceedings being taken under any of these prior provisions such proceedings are to be taken under the 1954 Act.[12]

12–05   The 1954 Act does not interfere with civil procedure as the following case[13] illustrates:

Section 339 of the Burgh Police (Scotland) Act 1892 (as amended by section 104 (2) (5) of the Burgh Police (Scotland) Act 1903) enacts that any person aggrieved by any order of the Commissioners under the Act may appeal either to the sheriff or to the Court of Session and that an appeal against the judgment of the sheriff may be taken to the Court of Session " in terms and subject to the provisions of the Summary Prosecutions Appeals (Scotland) Act 1875." The last named statute provides that appeals shall be taken on stated case to the Court of Session where the cause is of a civil nature. It was held that, notwithstanding the repeal by the 1908 Act of the Summary Prosecutions Appeals (Scotland) Act 1875, an appeal from the judgment of the sheriff might be taken in terms of section 339 of the Burgh Police (Scotland) Act 1892, to the Court of Session under the 1875 Act, the latter statute not being the authority for the appeal but being referred to by section 339 of the 1892 Act merely for purposes of procedure.

12–06   The Dogs Act 1871[14] provides that any court of summary jurisdiction may take cognisance of a complaint that a dog is dangerous, and may make an order " in a summary way " directing the dog to be kept under control or destroyed, and that any person failing to comply with such an order is liable to a penalty. The making of the order is an administrative

---

[7] *Wright* v. *Kennedy*, 1946 J.C. 142, supra, note 2 (*c*).

[8] *Robertson* v. *Burns*, 1943 J.C. 1.

[9] *James Dunlop Ltd.* v. *Calder*, 1943 J.C. 49.

[10] *Wright* v. *Kennedy*, supra.

[11] 1954 Act, s. 1 (1).

[12] Ibid., ss. 1 (2); 78 (1).

[13] *Burgh of Cumnock* v. *Murdoch*, 1910 S.C. 571.

[14] s. 2.

procedure, but the imposition of a penalty for disobeying the order is criminal.[15] Both steps are taken under the 1954 Act.[16]

12–07   Applications for law burrows must, under section 6 (3) of the Civil Imprisonment (Scotland) Act 1882, be disposed of summarily under the provisions of the Summary Jurisdiction Acts. It has, accordingly, been held [17] that judgments in these causes can be reviewed only by means of a stated case under section 60 of the 1908 Act (now section 62 of the 1954 Act).

Revenue proceedings

12–08   The 1954 Act contains no specific provision for revenue or customs offences.[18] Accordingly the right to prosecute summarily under Revenue and Customs Acts rests upon section 1 (1) of the 1954 Act and on the provisions of the statutes themselves. Penalties in excess of those provided by the 1954 Act are authorised in the case of certain offences.[19]

Offences against any of the Inland Revenue or Customs Acts are expressly excepted from the jurisdiction of burgh magistrates by section 454 of the Burgh Police (Scotland) Act 1892.[20]

The only persons entitled to prosecute revenue cases in Scotland are (a) the Lord Advocate, and (b) officers of Inland Revenue acting under the order of the Commissioners.[21] The procurator fiscal may, however, competently prosecute in cases where the revenue concerned in the complaint is not " revenue placed under the care and management of the Commissioners." [22]

Reservation of civil proceedings

12–09   Section 1 (3) of the 1954 Act provides:

> " Nothing in this Act shall extend to any information or complaint or other proceeding under or by virtue of any statutory provision for the recovery of any rate, tax, or impost whatsoever, or shall affect any right to sue for a penalty, or to apply for an order of court or other warrant ad factum praestandum, in the Court of Session or sheriff court, but it shall not be competent to sue for penalties in [a summary cause]." [22a]

[15] *Haldane* v. *Allan*, 1956 J.C. 41; *White* v. *Main* (1897) 2 Adam 348; *Walker* v. *Brander* 1920 J.C. 20.

[16] *Walker* v. *Brander*, supra.

[17] *Mackenzie* v. *Maclennan*, 1916 S.C. 617.

[18] Unlike the 1908 Act, s. 4.

[19] See e.g. Purchase Tax Act 1963, s. 33; Customs and Excise Act 1952, s. 283.

[20] See *Cameron* v. *Sweeney*, 1928 J.C. 34.

[21] See Taxes Management Act 1970, s. 100; Customs and Excise Act 1952, ss. 281 and 291. But see Sheriff Courts and Legal Officers (Scotland) Act 1927.

[22] *Horn* v. *Duckett*, 1929 J.C. 63; cf. *McMillan* v. *Grant*, 1924 J.C. 13, a case dealing with road fund licences. Prosecutions under the Vehicles (Excise) Act 1971, except for breaches of s. 26 thereof (which concern forgery and false information) may be instituted by the Secretary of State for the Environment in any summary court and may be conducted by any person authorised by him. They may also be taken by the procurator fiscal as public prosecutor.

[22a] See Sheriff Courts (Scotland) Act 1971, s. 35.

This section substantially re-enacts provisions contained in section 6 of the 1908 Act and in section 27 of the Summary Procedure (Scotland) Act 1864.[23]

A penalty imposed by statute in respect of failure to execute work in terms thereof may be recovered by civil process.[24] Civil proceedings should be instituted in any case which raises a question of civil right which is unsuitable for determination in a criminal prosecution,[25] or where they are otherwise preferable.[26] The imposition of a statutory penalty does not per se deprive a person injured by the contravention of a common law right to damages against the offender.[27]

12-10 If a complaint raises questions of civil right which cannot suitably be determined in a summary criminal court it should be dismissed,[28] and this course should also be adopted in any case where, although the complaint may not disclose any question of civil right, a prima facie case supporting the same is bona fide put forward by the defence.[29] The 1954 Act applies only to causes brought in compliance with section 1.[30]

Boundaries of jurisdiction

12-11 As the authority of courts of summary jurisdiction is restricted by their territorial boundaries, rules are laid down by section 6 of the 1954 Act to prevent any difficulty which might thus arise. These provisions have already been detailed.[31] It will be convenient, however, to repeat them here:

" (1) An offence committed in any harbour, river, arm of the sea, or other water (tidal or other) which runs between, or forms the boundary of, the jurisdiction of two or more courts, may be tried by any one of such courts.

(2) An offence committed on the boundary of the jurisdiction of two or more courts, or within the distance of five hundred yards of any such boundary, or partly within the jurisdiction of one court and partly within the jurisdiction of another court or courts, may be tried by any one of such courts.

(3) Where an offence is committed on any person or in respect of any property in or upon any carriage, cart, or vehicle employed

---

[23] In *Grant* v. *Hay* (1888) 2 White 6, a decree pronounced in the small debt court for a sum in name of penalties was recalled.

[24] *Lowson* v. *Police Commissioners of Forfar* (1877) 3 Couper 433, Lords Young and Craighill.

[25] *Meiklejohn* v. *Commissioners of Harbour of Fisherrow* (1902) 3 Adam 556.

[26] *Gemmell* v. *Ford* (1887) 1 White 437.

[27] *Clyde* v. *Glasgow City and District Railway Co.* (1885) 12 R. 1315.

[28] *Meiklejohn* v. *Commissioners of Harbour of Fisherrow*, supra; *Dalrymple* v. *Chalmers* (1886) 1 White 37.

[29] *Morrison* v. *Anderson* (1913) 7 Adam 201. On the ground that questions of civil right were raised, convictions were quashed in the following cases—*Stevenson* v. *McDonald* (1855) 2 Irv. 239; *Barlas* v. *Chalmers* (1876) 3 Couper 279; *Blacks* v. *Laing* (1879) 4 Couper 276; *Higgins* v. *Earl of Moray* (1884) 5 Couper 479. A conviction was upheld in *McDonald* v. *White* (1882) 5 Couper 19, while *Lord Lovat* v. *Munro* (1886) 1 White 119, and *Scott* v. *Thomson* (1887) 1 White 398, were sent to trial.

[30] *Wright* v. *Kennedy*, 1946 J.C. 142, L.J.-C. at 147.

[31] Supra, para. 1–26.

in a journey by road or railway, or on board any vessel employed in a river, lake, canal, or inland navigation, such offence may be tried by any court through whose jurisdiction such carriage, cart, vehicle, or vessel passed in the course of the journey or voyage during which the offence was committed, where the side, bank, centre, or other part of the road, railway, river, lake, canal, or inland navigation along which the carriage, cart, vehicle, or vessel passed in the course of such journey or voyage, is the boundary of the jurisdiction of two or more courts, such offence may be tried by any one of such courts.

(4) Where several offences, which if committed in one county could be tried under one complaint, are alleged to have been committed in different counties, proceedings may be taken for all or any of those offences under one complaint before the sheriff of any one of such counties.

(5) Where an offence is authorised by this section to be tried by any court, it may be dealt with, heard, tried, determined, adjudged, and punished as if the offence had been wholly committed within the jurisdiction of such court."

12–12   It has been held in a civil action of damages against a procurator fiscal that, although a complaint issued by him might turn out to have mistaken the locus delicti and so convened the accused to a court which had no jurisdiction to try the offence with which he was charged, the complaint was, nevertheless, a proceeding taken under the 1908 Act within the meaning of section 59 (now replaced by section 75 of the 1954 Act) and not ultra vires of the prosecutor, and that an action for damages would not lie against him in the absence of any averment from which malice on his part could be inferred.[32]

Transfer of fine order

12–13   Under section 44 of the 1954 Act, as substituted by the 1963 Act, Schedule 3, as more fully explained later, where a court of summary jurisdiction in Scotland, or any petty sessions area in England or Wales, has imposed a fine upon a person convicted of an offence, and it appears to the court that he is resident in a place outwith its jurisdiction and within that of another court of summary jurisdiction, the court may order that payment of the fine shall be enforceable in that other court or in that other area by making a transfer of fine order.[33]

Saving of pre-existing powers

12–14   The jurisdiction and powers of all courts of summary criminal jurisdiction except in so far as the same may be altered or modified by any future Act, remain as at the commencement of the Act.[34] Section 24 (2) of the Act provides that where a court has power to take cognisance of an

[32] *Rae* v. *Strathern*, 1924 S.C. 147.
[33] Infra, para. 17–51.
[34] 1954 Act, s. 3.

offence, the penalty attached to which is not defined, the punishment therefor shall be regulated by that applicable to common law offences in that court.

The Sheriff Court
Jurisdiction

12–15 The sheriff [35] has summary jurisdiction in all common law offences except murder, rape, incest and wilful fire-raising. The power to try uttering summarily is affirmed by section 9 (2) of the 1954 Act, and that to try robbery summarily by section 44 of the 1963 Act. The sheriff court has summary jurisdiction in all statutory offences unless expressly or impliedly excluded [36] or unless, perhaps, the minimum punishment provided by the statute exceeds that which it is entitled to impose. [37]

The sheriff can entertain proceedings for recovery of statutory penalties unless his jurisdiction is excluded as above described. [38] Unlike other courts of summary jurisdiction, the sheriff enjoys a universal jurisdiction which is inherent and does not require to be conferred on him per expressum. [39]

12–16 By section 7 (2) of the 1954 Act it is provided that the sheriff shall have a concurrent jurisdiction with every other court within his sheriffdom in regard to all offences competent for trial in such courts. The effect of this provision is that the whole statutory powers and qualifications inherent in the other court are communicated in their entirety to the sheriff. [40] So, where an accused person was charged on a summary complaint in the sheriff court with a contravention of the Finance Act 1910, by selling intoxicating liquor without a licence, and the sale of the liquor was spoken to by one witness only, it was held that in virtue of section 11 of the 1908 Act, which contained the same provision, the sheriff had conferred upon him the statutory right, given to justices of the peace by section 65 of the Excise Management Act 1827, to convict of such an offence upon the evidence of one credible witness. [41]

It will be noted that under a concurrent jurisdiction a case may be tried in either of the courts which possess it, according as it has in the first instance been brought before or taken up by such court. The case, of course, cannot be tried twice. [42]

---

[35] The appointment of sheriffs-principal, sheriffs and honorary sheriffs is regulated by the Sheriff Courts (Scotland) Act 1971. That of procurators fiscal and their deputes and sheriff clerks and their deputes (prosecutors and clerks of court respectively) is regulated by the Sheriff Courts and Legal Officers (Scotland) Act 1927.

[36] 1954 Act, ss. 9 and 24; *McPherson* v. *Boyd* (1907) 5 Adam 247; *Cameron* v. *Macniven* (1894) 1 Adam 346; and see *McMillan* v. *Grant*, 1924 J.C. 13; *Blythswood Taxis Ltd.* v. *Adair*, 1944 J.C. 135; *Clark and Bendall* v. *Stuart* (1886) 1 White 191. An example of a statutory offence which the sheriff cannot try is a third contravention of the Night Poaching Act 1828. See also *Wilson* v. *Hill*, 1943 J.C. 124.

[37] e.g. Coinage Offences Act 1936, s. 9; cf. *Gallagher* v. *H.M. Adv.*, 1937 J.C. 27.

[38] *McMillan* v. *Grant*, 1924 J.C. 13, Lord Sands at 22–3; cf. *Stirling* v. *Dickson* (1900) 3 Adam 252; *Horn* v. *Duckett*, 1929 J.C. 63; supra, para. 3–02; *Chisholm* v. *Black and Morrison* (1871) 2 Couper 49; *Tague* v. *Smith* (1865) 5 Irv. 192.

[39] *McPherson* v. *Boyd* (1907) 5 Adam 247, L.J.-G. at 254.

[40] *Lawrence* v. *Ames*, 1921 J.C. 87.

[41] Ibid.   [42] *Cameron* v. *Macniven*, supra.

The sheriff had jurisdiction to try juveniles in areas where special juvenile courts were set up under the Children and Young Persons (Scotland) Act 1937.[43] The hearings set up by the Social Work (Scotland) Act 1968 are not courts, but the sheriff courts retain jurisdiction over offences committed by children, although that jurisdiction can be invoked only on the instructions of the Lord Advocate.[44]

Powers in common law offences

12-17   Under section 7 of the 1954 Act as amended by section 23 (2) of the 1963 Act, the sheriff, without prejudice to any other or wider powers conferred by statute, has power on summarily convicting any person of a common law offence:

" (*a*) to impose a fine not exceeding one hundred and fifty pounds:
  (*b*) to ordain the accused to find caution for good behaviour for any period not exceeding twelve months and to an amount not exceeding one hundred and fifty pounds, said caution being either in lieu of or in addition to a fine, or in addition to imprisonment as hereafter in this section mentioned:
  (*c*) failing payment of said fine, or on failure to find said caution, to award imprisonment in accordance with section forty-nine of this Act [45]:
  (*d*) to award imprisonment, for any period not exceeding three months."

The total imprisonment which may follow upon a judgment under section 7 must not exceed three months. Care must therefore be taken, in combining caution with fine or imprisonment, to avoid imposing a cumulo period exceeding three months.[46]

The sheriff, however, under the following conditions, has a greater power of summary punishment:

" Where a person is summarily convicted by the sheriff of:

(*a*) a second or subsequent offence inferring dishonest appropriation of property, or attempt thereat, or
(*b*) a second or subsequent offence inferring personal violence,

he may, without prejudice to any wider powers conferred by statute, be sentenced to imprisonment for any period not exceeding six months." [47]

Powers in statutory offences

12-18   The statute which creates the offence must be looked to in order to ascertain what punishment or penalty can be imposed by the sheriff.

[43] *Weir* v. *Cruickshank*, 1959 J.C. 94.
[44] Social Work (Scotland) Act 1968, s. 31 (1), infra, para. 19–03.
[45] See infra, para. 17–36.
[46] *Fairbairn* v. *Drummond* (1836) 1 Swin. 85; *Maguinness* v. *Macdonald*, 1953 J.C. 31; *Fraser* v. *Herron*, 1968 J.C. 1. Cf. *Kesson* v. *Heatly*, 1964 J.C. 40.
[47] 1954 Act, s. 8, as amended by 1963 Act, s. 16.

Section 9 (1) of the 1954 Act provides that any offence described in any statute as a " misdemeanour " or a " crime and offence " may be tried in the sheriff court either by indictment or summarily, and that, if tried summarily, the imprisonment competent on conviction, without prejudice to any wider powers conferred by statute, must not exceed three months.[48]

Inferior Courts of Summary Jurisdiction

Jurisdiction of justice of peace court

12–19   In this court the judges are the justices of the peace for the county, or the county of the city, in which the court is held. Justices of the peace other than those acting ex officio are appointed by the Secretary of State for Scotland.[49] The prosecutors are the fiscals of the peace appointed by the justices at quarter sessions,[50] and the clerks of court are the clerks of the peace appointed by the Secretary of State for Scotland, and their deputes appointed by themselves.

This court exercises a limited summary criminal jurisdiction within its area. The quorum is two justices.[51] Unless specially authorised by statute one justice cannot act judicially.[52] In all other judicial proceedings justices must hear and act together.[53] Convictions should be authenticated by all the justices sitting.[54]

12–20   Under the common law the jurisdiction of the justices is chiefly confined to the preservation of the public peace, and the cases which they can try, viz., breach of peace, minor assaults, petty theft and the like, may all be regarded in the light of offences against the public peace.[55] Certain offences are excepted from the jurisdiction of the justices by section 4 of the 1954 Act. These they can only remit to a higher court under the provisions of section 5. They are further restricted by the provisions of section 3.

12–21   An application for law burrows may still be brought before a justice of the peace, the procedure being now regulated by section 6 of the Civil Imprisonment (Scotland) Act 1882.

12–22   Justices of the peace can try statutory offences only when power to do so is conferred upon them expressly or by implication by the statute which creates the offence. It was held that they had concurrent jurisdiction under section 91 of the Licensing (Scotland) Act 1903 with magistrates in

---

[48] 1954 Act, s. 9 (1). See *Whillans* v. *Hilson* (1909) 6 Adam 129 (held that a person convicted in the sheriff court of an offence against the Night Poaching Act 1828, cannot, if the case is tried summarily, be sentenced to more than three months' imprisonment; and a sentence in excess of that amount restricted thereto).

[49] Transfer of Functions (Justice of the Peace) (Scotland) Order 1955.

[50] Cf. *Rose* v. *Grant* (1853) 25 Sc.Jur. 535.

[51] *Reid* v. *Finlayson* (1730) Mor. 7636; *McKay* v. *Hercules* (1760) Mor. 7637; Justices of the Peace Act 1661; Union with Scotland Amendment Act 1707.

[52] See, e.g., Licensing (Scotland) Act 1959, s. 189 (*e*), as amended by Licensing (Scotland) Act 1962.

[53] *Rex* v. *Forrest* (1789) 3 T.R. 38.

[54] *Williamson* v. *Thomson* (1858) 3 Irv. 295; *Simpson* v. *Reid* (1902) 3 Adam 617.

[55] See *Trotter on Summary Criminal Jurisdiction*, p. 12, and case of *Wilkie*, 10th July, 1798, cited there.

police burghs regarding offences against the Act committed within the burghs by persons resident therein.[56] Justices have jurisdiction under the Salmon Fisheries (Scotland) Act 1868,[57] and they can try offences against the Road Traffic Acts when the maximum penalty is £50, other than offences for which endorsement is competent.[58]

12-23   Justices have power under the Justices of the Peace Act 1661 on complaint of any person being threatened and fearing to be wronged to bind over the party complained against to keep the peace, and a similar right to bind over if credibly informed of appearance of trouble betwixt any parties " except the parties declare upon their consciences that neither of them bear any grudge to the other," as well as all the powers of English Justices as conferred by section 2 of the Union with Scotland Amendment Act 1707, but these powers are never exercised. Scottish justices do not in fact bind over, nor do they sit in Quarter Sessions for judicial purposes.

Jurisdiction of burgh and police courts

12-24   Burgh courts are the courts of the magistrates of royal burghs, but are now assimilated to police courts set up in police burghs.[59] The judges in these courts are the magistrates of the burgh, known as bailies,[60] and other town councillors who have been magistrates of a burgh and are appointed as judges of police.[61] The prosecutors and clerks of court are appointed by the burghs under sections 89 and 90 of the Local Government (Scotland) Act 1947. The clerks are ex officiis legal assessors to the court.[62]

---

[56] *Tasker* v. *Simpson* (1904) 4 Adam 495.

[57] *Gemmell* v. *Hadden and Anr*. (1885) 5 Couper 622.

[58] Road Traffic Act 1962, s. 38; Road Safety Act 1967, Sched. 1; Road Traffic Regulation Act 1967, s. 92.

[59] Burgh Police (Scotland) Act 1892, ss. 5, 454. Edinburgh, Glasgow, Aberdeen, Dundee and Greenock each has its own private Act.

[60] See Local Government (Scotland) Act, 1947, ss. 28–37, as amended by Representation of the People Act 1948.

[61] See Local Government (Scotland) Act 1947, s. 36.

[62] See *Stewart* v. *McDonald* (1901) 3 Adam 532; *Brown* v. *Neilson* (1906) 5 Adam 149. Only the clerk or a deputy or substitute duly authorised to act in his place during the trial can discharge the duties of clerk thereat. (*Stewart* v. *McDonald*, supra; *Brown* v. *Neilson*, supra.) The absence of the clerk of court during a trial is not per se fatal to a conviction, nor is the same invalidated because of the presence, during the clerk's absence, of a substitute who has not been duly authorised so to act (*Stewart* v. *McDonald*, supra). But the substitute must take no active part in the proceedings (ibid.). If he does so, e.g., by giving advice to the magistrate, the conviction will be quashed (*Brown* v. *Neilson*, supra). An assessor need not be a qualified solicitor (*Patrick* v. *Wood* (1905) 4 Adam 648) and he may competently give evidence of a formal nature for the prosecution (ibid.). The same person need not be present throughout the proceedings as clerk of court (*Dunsmore* v. *Threshie* (1896) 2 Adam 202). The clerk is entitled, at any time prior to actual judgment, to advise the magistrate with regard to any point which has been a matter of evidence (*Kelly* v. *Rae*, 1917 J.C. 12).
    Town clerks, depute town clerks and their partners and employees are prohibited from acting as the defence solicitor in the trial of any offence in any police court in the burgh, under the penalty of being thenceforth disqualified from holding any office under the town council and from being a councillor. This disqualification may be removed by the Secretary of State for Scotland on the recommendation of the town council (s. 81, Town Councils (Scotland) Act 1900).
    A clerk of court should not officiate in any case in which he has a personal interest (see *Smith and Tasker* v. *Robertson* (1827) 5 S. 848; *Rex* v. *Essex Justices, ex parte Perkins*

2–25   As already mentioned,[63] the procedure clauses in all general and local Police Acts have been superseded by provisions of the 1954 Act. Subject to these new enactments the jurisdiction and powers of magistrates of the five excepted burghs [64] will be found in their own local Acts, while those of magistrates of the remaining burghs are set forth in section 454 of the Burgh Police (Scotland) Act 1892.[65]

2–26   Magistrates and police judges in burgh or police courts can, within the area of their jurisdiction, try summarily all common law offences which they are empowered to try under the general or local Police Acts applicable to their burgh, their powers, however, like those of justices of the peace, being subject to the provisions of sections 3, 4 and 5 of the 1954 Act.

Magistrates and police judges have, within the limits of their jurisdiction, power to try offences against the Burgh Police (Scotland) Acts and any other statute which gives them such authority, and a like power to entertain summary complaints for the recovery of statutory penalties. They have power to try any offence declared to be punishable on conviction by " a court of summary jurisdiction," but not, unless expressly empowered, to try an offence declared to be punishable on " summary conviction." [66] They may try offences against the Diseases of Animals Act 1950 [67] and their jurisdiction extends to summary complaints for the recovery of penalties incurred through breach of byelaws made by a local authority with regard to offensive trades in virtue of the powers conferred by section 32 (3) of the Public Health (Scotland) Act 1897.[68] A charge of keeping a brothel may be tried under section 403 of the Burgh Police (Scotland) Act 1892, before the sheriff or two police magistrates,

---

[1927] 2 K.B. 475) but is not precluded from acting merely because he is a partner of the fiscal (*Laughland* v. *Galloway*, 1968 J.C. 26). It is improper for an assessor to cross-examine witnesses or aid either party in any way (*Alexander* v. *Boyd*, 1966 J.C. 24; cf. *Johannesson* v. *Robertson*, 1945 J.C. 146).

[63] Supra, para. 12–04.

[64] Supra, n. 59.

[65] S. 454 is in the following terms—" The magistrates of police of a burgh under this Act, or any one or more of such magistrates, except where otherwise provided in this Act, including stipendiary magistrates and sheriffs acting in the police court, shall, within the burgh, have jurisdiction and power to take cognizance of all crimes, offences, and breaches of the police regulations in this Act contained or referred to, or contained in any other Act in force in the burgh, or of any byelaws made in virtue of the provisions of this or any other Act, or of any offence against the Public Parks (Scotland) Act, 1878, or any byelaws made in virtue of the provisions thereof, and of any other crime or offence which is punishable by public general or local statute or common law, and is within the jurisdiction of the magistrates of any royal burgh, and shall have the like jurisdiction within the burgh as any magistrate of a royal burgh, or any dean of guild of a royal burgh, has by the law of Scotland, and all jurisdiction to try offences and award punishment conferred on any justice of the peace, or two justices of the peace, or any magistrate, by any Act, public or local, passed or to be passed, or any byelaws, orders, or regulations made in virtue thereof and in force in the burgh: Provided always that such jurisdiction shall not extend to the trial of offences against any of the Inland Revenue or Customs Acts.

The sheriff shall have power to sit and act in the police court with consent of the magistrates on any special occasion or under any continuing arrangement."

[66] *McPherson* v. *Boyd* (1907) 5 Adam 247.

[67] *McTavish* v. *Neilson* (1903) 4 Adam 303.

[68] *Rae* v. *Hamilton* (1904) 4 Adam 366.

the maximum sentence of imprisonment competent on conviction being
one of sixty days, but, under section 431 of the same Act, this offence
may be tried as a contravention of section 13 of the Criminal Law Amendment Act 1885 before a single police magistrate, who is entitled to impose
a sentence of three months' imprisonment.[69] A magistrate sitting in a
burgh police court can also try an offence against the Immoral Traffic
(Scotland) Act 1902, and can, in virtue of the provisions of section 7 (2) of
the Criminal Law Amendment Act 1912, impose a sentence of six months'
imprisonment therefor.[70] He has also jurisdiction to try charges of
professing to tell fortunes by palmistry with intent to deceive under section
4 of the Vagrancy Act 1824, as amended and made applicable to Scotland
by sections 15 and 17 of the Prevention of Crimes Act 1871.[71]

Offences against the Road Traffic Acts for which the maximum penalty
does not exceed £50 and for which endorsement is not competent, may
be prosecuted in any court of summary jurisdiction which has jurisdiction
at the place where the offence was committed.[72] To this extent, therefore,
burgh magistrates possess criminal jurisdiction under the Acts.

12–27   The court of the bailie of the river and firth of Clyde [73] is now simply
the Marine Police Court at Glasgow. The functions of the river bailie
may be performed by any police court judge in Glasgow.[74]

Jurisdiction of stipendiary magistrates

12–28   Under section 455 of the Burgh Police (Scotland) Act 1892, a stipendiary
magistrate may be appointed in any burgh to which that statute applies.
No such appointment has so far been made, but, under similar provisions
contained in the Glasgow Corporation and Police Act 1895, three stipendiary magistrates have been appointed in Glasgow.

The position of this judge is peculiar. Under the Act appointing
him he is merely a salaried magistrate with legal qualifications exercising,
within the territorial limits of the local burgh and police courts, the
jurisdiction of a magistrate and justice of the peace of Glasgow. But,
by sections 2 and 3 of the Stipendiary Magistrates Jurisdiction (Scotland)
Act 1897, he is empowered, within the same area, also to exercise the
summary criminal jurisdiction of a sheriff. This additional jurisdiction
is obviously unimpaired by the provisions of section 3 of the 1954 Act [75]
(formerly section 7 of the 1908 Act) but the terms of section 4 [76] seem to
imply that, as regards the offences enumerated therein, a stipendiary
magistrate is in the same position as inferior judges other than sheriffs. It

---

[69] *McLaren* v. *Macleod* (1913) 7 Adam 102.
[70] *Hall* v. *Macpherson* (1913) 7 Adam 173.
[71] *Gerald* v. *McIntyre* (1913) 7 Adam 114.
[72] Road Traffic Act 1962, s. 38; Road Safety Act 1967, Sched. 1; Road Traffic Regulation Act
1967, s. 92.
[73] For further details see *Trotter on Summary Criminal Jurisdiction*, p. 20.
[74] Glasgow Police Act 1866, s. 154; Glasgow Corporation Act 1907, s. 42.
[75] See infra, para. 12–29.
[76] Infra, para. 12–30.

has, however, been held [77] that the stipendiary magistrate in Glasgow can entertain a summary complaint under the Milk and Dairies (Scotland) Act 1914, although the statute expressly provides that penalties imposed under it are to be recovered before the sheriff having jurisdiction in the district in which the dairy concerned is situated, and nowhere authorises a prosecution in any other court.[78]

Powers of inferior courts of summary jurisdiction

12–29   Section 3 of the 1954 Act [79] provides that the justice of peace court and justices of the peace, and also any judge of police or burgh magistrate shall, without prejudice to any other or wider powers conferred by statute, be entitled to exercise within their respective jurisdictions power on convicting of a common law offence:

" (a) to award imprisonment for any period not exceeding sixty days;
 (b) to impose a fine not exceeding fifty pounds;
 (c) to ordain the accused (in lieu of or in addition to such imprisonment or fine) to find caution for good behaviour for any period not exceeding six months and to an amount not exceeding fifty pounds.[80]
 (d) failing payment of such fine, or on failure to find such caution, to award imprisonment in accordance with section forty-nine of this Act; provided always that in no case shall the total imprisonment exceed sixty days." [81]

It will be observed:

(a) That this section applies to every court of summary jurisdiction except the sheriff court.
(b) That the powers which it confers upon them relate only to common law offences.
(c) That the section leaves unimpaired any wider powers conferred on them by statute.[82]
(d) That, subject to any differences due to statute, the section makes the powers of sentence of all these courts identical as regards common law offences.

Crimes not triable in inferior courts of summary jurisdiction

12–30   A further limitation of the powers of the inferior courts (other than the sheriff court) is contained in section 4 of the 1954 Act (as amended by the 1963 Act, Schedule 5, which in some respects may be thought to go beyond the limits of the corresponding sections of the Act itself), which provides that:

---

[77] *Torrance and Son* v. *Robertson*, 1946 J.C. 135.
[78] Milk and Dairies (Scotland) Act 1914, ss. 24–25.
[79] As amended by 1963 Act, s. 23.
[80] See 1954 Act, s. 51, and infra, para. 17–52.
[81] For particulars of scale see 1954 Act, s. 49. See also infra, para. 17–36.
[82] See *McLaren* v. *Macleod* (1913) 7 Adam 102, L.J.-G. at 108. Stipendiary magistrates have special statutory power. See supra, para. 12–28.

12–30   " A court of summary jurisdiction other than the sheriff
court shall not have jurisdiction to try, or to pronounce sentence in,
but shall, to the extent and in the manner mentioned in the next
succeeding section, be entitled to take cognizance of,

(1) the case of any person found within the jurisdiction of such
court, and brought before it accused or suspected of having committed at any place beyond the jurisdiction of such court any offence,
or

(2) the case of any person brought before such court accused or
suspected of having committed within the jurisdiction thereof any
of the following offences:

(*a*) murder, culpable homicide, robbery, rape, wilful fire-raising,
or attempt at wilful fire-raising:

(*b*) stouthrief, theft by housebreaking, or housebreaking with
intent to steal:

(*c*) theft or reset of theft,
falsehood, fraud or wilful imposition,
breach of trust or embezzlement,

all to an amount exceeding twenty-five pounds [83];

(*d*) any of the offences specified in the last foregoing paragraph,
or any attempt thereat, where the accused is known to have been
previously convicted of any offence inferring dishonest appropriation of property:

(*e*) assault whereby any limb has been fractured, or assault with
intent to ravish, or assault to the danger of life, or assault
by stabbing:

(*f*) uttering forged documents or uttering forged bank or banker's
notes, or offences under the Acts relating to coinage."

It is not to be deemed a conviction within the meaning of the section
if the accused had been dismissed with an admonition or placed on
probation without any sentence having been subsequently pronounced.[84]

The effect of this section is that inferior courts other than the sheriff
court are (apart altogether from any restriction imposed on them by their
lesser powers of punishment) altogether prohibited from trying any
of the crimes therein enumerated. These courts can take cognisance of
these crimes only to the extent of remitting to the sheriff court in terms
of section 5.

Although section 4 specifies certain offences which cannot be tried or
otherwise dealt with in summary courts, other than the sheriff court,
this does not inferentially confer any right on such courts to try offences
not specially mentioned, and which, from their nature, are inappropriate

---

[83] Thus conferring on the courts concerned jurisdiction in cases of theft by opening lockfast
places.
[84] 1954 Act, s. 4.

for trial in a court other than that of the sheriff. Section 4 does not necessarily apply to attempts to commit any of the specified offences.[85]

Remit to competent court

12–31 Section 5 of the 1954 Act provides as follows:

" If either in the preliminary investigation or in the course of the trial of any offence it shall appear that the offence is one which cannot competently be tried in the court before which an accused is brought, or is one which, in the opinion of the court in view of the circumstances of the case, should be dealt with by a higher court, it shall be lawful for the court to commit the accused to prison for examination for any period not exceeding four days, and the prosecutor shall forthwith give notice of such committal to the procurator fiscal of the district within which such offence was committed, or to such other official as may be entitled to take cognizance thereof, in order that the accused may be dealt with according to law."

These provisions are somewhat similar to the latter part of section 459 of the Burgh Police (Scotland) Act 1892, the earlier part of that section (the whole of which was repealed by the 1908 Act) being now represented by section 5 of the 1954 Act. They enable courts of summary criminal jurisdiction to remit to competent jurisdictions (a) causes which they themselves cannot competently try, and (b) cases which they in their discretion think should be tried by a higher court.

A court may find itself unable competently to try an offence either because the offence has been committed outwith the territorial limits of its jurisdiction or because, although committed within these limits, the offence is of such a nature that the court is prohibited from entertaining it (e.g., because of the provisions of section 4).[86]

12–32 When no complaint has been presented, the remit of a cause is effected by the prosecutor's presenting to the court a petition under section 14 in the form, as nearly as may be, of the form contained in Part I of the Second Schedule setting forth the charge against the accused and craving for a remit and for warrant to commit him to prison. The warrant granting the remit is written on the petition. Once a complaint has been brought, the prosecutor can move for a remit under section 17, but there appears to be nothing in the section to prevent the court at that later stage from acting ex proprio motu or on the motion of the defence.

All remits craved in petitions or granted by warrants must expressly bear to be to competent jurisdictions.[87] Where a person is brought before the court on a petition under section 17 and not on a complaint the court

---

[85] Cf. *Craig*, Criminal Appeal Court, Aug. 1968, unreported: attempted murder indicted in sheriff court.

[86] The section substantially follows s. 459 of the Burgh Police (Scotland) Act 1892, which prescribed remits to the sheriff court alone, and, although not very clearly worded, would seem to be intended to provide for remits only to the sheriff court from the other inferior courts.

[87] *O'Donnell* v. *McKenna* (1910) 6 Adam 242.

may exercise its power to adjourn the case for inquiry under section 21 to give time to ascertain whether the offence of which the person is suspected is within the court's jurisdiction. This is so even where the person is arrested for an offence, such as stealing £400, which is outwith the jurisdiction of the court. In this way a person may be detained for more than four days before being discharged or remitted to the sheriff court.[88] Once the magistrate has determined that the case is outwith his jurisdiction he must immediately remit the suspect to the sheriff court. He cannot both refuse bail on the ground that he has no jurisdiction, and continue for inquiry.[89] Continuation for inquiry cannot exceed seven days except on special cause shown, or in any event twenty-one days.[90] The High Court have reserved their opinion as to whether a bare averment of need for " time for further inquiry " is sufficient cause.[91]

12–33   Section 55 (4) of the Mental Health (Scotland) Act 1960 provides that a court of summary jurisdiction other than the sheriff court shall remit to the sheriff court any person appearing before it charged with an offence punishable by imprisonment if it appears to the lower court that that person is suffering from mental disorder.

Remit to stipendiary magistrate

12–34   Under section 5 of the Stipendiary Magistrates Jurisdiction (Scotland) Act 1897, any magistrate presiding in a police court may remit for trial to a stipendiary magistrate possessing jurisdiction any person brought before him charged with a crime or offence, this provision being without prejudice to the right and duty of the stipendiary magistrate or magistrate sitting in the police court to remit for trial to a higher court any person charged with a crime or offence of a serious nature.

Considerations Determining Appropriate Summary Court for Proceedings

12–35   Assuming that the requisites of territorial jurisdiction are satisfied and there remains a choice of courts in which the prosecutor may bring his complaint, his decision will proceed upon principles similar to those which, as already mentioned,[92] fall to be applied in determining whether a case will be tried according to solemn or summary procedure. Two main considerations must be kept in view:

(1) Whether there is any statutory direction defining the appropriate court, and

(2) The gravity of the offence in view of the powers given to the sheriff court and the other inferior courts respectively by the 1954 Act itself.

[88] *McPhee* v. *Macfarlane's Executor*, 1933 S.C. 163; but see the observations in *Kennedy* v. *Heatly*, 1951 J.C. 118, L.J.-G. at 125. See infra, para. 13–103.
[89] *Kennedy* v. *Heatly*, 1951 J.C. 118.
[90] 1954 Act, s. 21, as amended by 1963 Act, s. 46.
[91] *Kennedy* v. *Heatly*, supra.
[92] Supra, para. 3–02.

Statutory directions

12-36   Statutes which create offences usually prescribe the manner in which they are to be tried. The simple and ordinary case is where a statute specifically gives jurisdiction to a particular court or courts.

Where, however, there is no explicit statutory direction, the case is more difficult. It was pointed out in the Introduction [93] that the jurisdiction of the sheriff court is universal, in contradistinction to the other inferior courts on which jurisdiction must be expressly conferred.[94] It has, however, been held that where an Act imposed penalties on an offender who should be convicted before " a court of summary jurisdiction," that " a " meant " any " and that jurisdiction was expressly conferred on the police court.[95] But where the phrase used in the statute is simply that a person shall be liable " on summary conviction," and there is no reference to a particular court, there is nothing to oust the universal jurisdiction of the sheriff court.[96] Jurisdiction, however, has been conferred on an inferior court by implication.[97]

As already mentioned,[98] section 4 of the 1954 Act prohibits inferior courts other than the sheriff court from trying certain offences.

Gravity of offence

12-37   In the absence of statutory guidance the prosecutor must consider whether the offence can adequately be dealt with by a court of summary jurisdiction other than the sheriff court, in view of the more limited powers of sentence possessed by the former.

[93] Supra, para. 2–10.
[94] *Clark and Bendall* v. *Stuart* (1886) 1 White 191; *McPherson* v. *Boyd* (1907) 5 Adam 247. Supra, para. 2–10.
[95] *Hall* v. *Macpherson* (1913) 7 Adam 173.
[96] *McPherson* v. *Boyd, supra.*
[97] *McTavish* v. *Neilson* (1903) 4 Adam 303.
[98] Supra, para. 12–30.

CHAPTER 13

PROCEDURE PRIOR TO TRIAL

Initiation of Proceedings

13-01 THERE is an important distinction between solemn and summary criminal jurisdiction which strikes one at the outset. In summary procedure there is no petition for warrant to apprehend, and no judicial examination and committal. An accused person is occasionally tried on summary complaint after he has been examined and committed, but this happens only where it was originally intended that such person should be tried upon indictment, and subsequent investigation has shown that the case can be disposed of summarily. This power is reserved by section 77 (4) of the 1908 Act, which has not been repealed by the 1954 Act.

The absence of a preliminary petition materially affects the procedure. It necessitates fuller information before proceedings are begun, because the prosecutor knows that he has to go to trial upon the charge as stated in his complaint. It also calls for careful study of the points suggested for consideration in the Introduction,[1] because the facility and rapidity of summary process may readily lead to hasty prosecution and careless drafting. No one unfamiliar with summary procedure should attempt to prepare a complaint until he has made himself acquainted with the matters discussed in the Introduction and the preceding chapter.

Incidental warrants

13-02 It is sometimes necessary to apply to the court for an incidental warrant or order, prior to the presentation of the complaint, or even where no complaint is to follow. The forms in Part I of the Second Schedule may be taken as typical examples of such applications—to search premises for stolen goods, to destroy diseased meat, to restore stolen property, to remit the accused to another jurisdiction in terms of section 5,[2] or to obtain a warrant to cite witnesses for precognition in terms of section 18 (4) of the 1954 Act. Section 14 provides for such contingencies by enacting that where, prior to the presentation of a complaint, it is necessary to apply to the court for any warrant or order of court as incidental to subsequent proceedings by complaint, or where the court has power to grant any warrant or order of court, although no subsequent procedure by complaint may follow thereon, such application may be by petition at the instance of a prosecutor in the form, or as nearly

---

[1] Supra, para. 3-01.
[2] Supra, para. 12-32.

as may be in the form, contained in Part I of the Second Schedule. Where necessary for the execution of any such warrant or order of court, warrant to break open lockfast places is implied.[3]

Although in the majority of cases the warrant craved in such a petition will be granted as a matter of course, there may be cases where it would be proper that the court should order that intimation of the application be given to any person interested, and afford him an opportunity of being heard, if so advised, before granting or otherwise disposing of it. In such a case the court might order a copy of the petition to be served on such person, with certification that, if he desired to be heard thereon, he would require to attend for that purpose on a day and at a time and place named in the order, and that failing his doing so the order would be granted. Such an order would be served in the usual way by an officer of law, unless in any special circumstances the court prescribed some other method of service.[4]

Prescription

13–03   The time within which proceedings may be instituted is a matter which must be taken into account before preparing a summary complaint, particularly in statutory contraventions.

As regards crimes at common law it is of less moment. There is no limit within which a prosecution for these may be instituted.[5] In practice, however, the question is limited by the impossibility of proving a charge after a considerable interval.

13–04   As regards contravention of statutes, and of orders having statutory authority, the case is different, as, if the statutes and orders do not themselves fix a period within which proceedings in respect of a contravention of their provisions must be instituted, the time-limit prescribed by section 23 of the 1954 Act applies. That section is in the following terms:

> " (1) Proceedings under this Act in respect of the contravention of any statute or order shall, unless the statute or order under which the proceedings are brought fixes any other period, be commenced within six months [6] after the contravention occurred, and, in the case of a continuous contravention, within six months after the last date of such contravention, and it shall be competent in such case in any prosecution to include the entire period during which the contravention has occurred.
>
> (2) For the purposes of this section proceedings shall be deemed to be commenced on the date on which a warrant to apprehend or to cite the accused is granted, if such warrant is executed without undue delay."

---

[3] 1954 Act, s. 14.
[4] See *McLauchlan* v. *Renton* (1910) 6 Adam 378.
[5] *Sugden* v. *H.M. Adv.*, 1934 J.C. 103.
[6] " Month " means calendar month: Interpretation Act 1889, s. 3. See *Farquharson* v. *Whyte* (1886) 1 White 26.

In a case under a statute which required proceedings to be " instituted " within a certain time, it was held that proceedings were instituted when the complaint was tabled and a diet obtained for the disposal of the case.[7]

13–05   In *MacLean* v. *McMahon* [8] a complaint was served on a club under the Food and Drugs (Scotland) Act 1956 within the statutory time-limit of two months. The club intimated after the two months were up that they proposed to prove that the alleged contravention was due to the fault of their barmaid (who had originally been cautioned and charged along with the club secretary) and a complaint was taken against her. It was held to be time-barred, the Crown not having shown that it was impracticable to proceed against her earlier.

Continuing offences

13–06   Where it is an offence to fail to do something at a specific time a continuing failure does not constitute a continuing offence, and the prescriptive period runs from the specified time. Where the offence consists of a failure to do something " forthwith " on the occurrence of some event the prescriptive period begins to run after a reasonable time has followed on the event.[9] In a case relating to a continuous offence [10] it was held that the whole of section 26 of the 1908 Act, including the provision that in the case of a charge of a continuous contravention it shall be competent to include the entire period, is limited in its application to cases in which the statute under which the prosecution is brought fixes no period within which proceedings must be taken.

Special statutory provisions

13–07   The purpose of section 23 is merely to provide a time-limit where none is otherwise provided.[11] Accordingly, if the statute or order creating the offence fixes such time-limit (a) that limit must be strictly followed,[12] even if it is shorter than that prescribed by section 23, and (b) the provisions of section 23 regarding a continuous offence cannot be invoked to eke out an omission by the statute or order to deal with such a circum-

---

[7] *Robertson* v. *Page*, 1943 J.C. 32.

[8] 1960 S.L.T.(Sh.Ct.) 30.

[9] *A. & C. McLennan (Blairgowrie) Ltd.* v. *Macmillan*, 1964 J.C. 1.

[10] *Macknight* v. *MacCulloch* (1909) 6 Adam 144.

[11] Ibid., Lord Low at 31, 32.

[12] The prosecutor cannot take a latitude in his charge, either by implication or otherwise, which will extend back the period fixed by the statute. (*H.M. Adv.* v. *Philp* (1890) 2 White 525.) In that case an indictment for a contravention of s. 5 of the Criminal Law Amendment Act 1885 alleged that the offence was committed on numerous occasions between May 1, 1889 and May 24, 1890. The section provided a time-limit of three months. It was held that the charge was irrelevant in respect that it covered a period beyond the time-limit. Similarly, where a complaint under the Prevention of Cruelty to Children Act 1894, which was served on March 29, 1894, charged the accused with cruelty extending over a period from August 1, 1893, to February 28, 1894, and he was convicted " of the contravention charged," the conviction was suspended on the ground that the period between August 1 and September 28, 1893, was beyond the limitations of six months fixed by the Summary Procedure (Scotland) Act 1864 (*Farquharson* v. *Gordon* (1894) 1 Adam 405). See also *Creighton* v. *H.M. Adv.* (1904) 4 Adam 356.

stance.[13] It is important to note that the section makes the rule as to when proceedings commence apply in all cases unless the statute creating the particular offence prescribes otherwise.

Section 23 is excluded by a considerable number of statutes—e.g. Criminal Law Amendment Act 1922, section 2, as amended by Criminal Law Amendment Act 1928; Mines and Quarries Act 1954, section 163 (3); Food and Drugs (Scotland) Act 1956, section 41 (4); Road Traffic Act 1960, section 244; Protection of Depositors Act 1963, section 23 (4); Ministry of Social Security Act 1966, section 33 (3); Legal Aid (Scotland) Act 1967, section 18 (3); Wireless Telegraphy Act 1967, section 5 (4); Companies Act 1967, section 49 (4). It is not necessary, in a complaint brought under the 1954 Act, to cite the Act which varies the time for proceedings.[14] Where, however, a time-limit runs from the date at which evidence sufficient in his opinion to justify prosecution came to the notice of the Lord Advocate, of which date a certificate by the Lord Advocate is usually conclusive evidence, it is the practice to aver the relevant date in the complaint.[15]

Computation of time

13–08   The time, it will be noticed, is reckoned, not from the date of service of the complaint, but from that of the granting of the warrant to apprehend or cite the accused, provided that the warrant is executed without undue delay,[16] and this rule has been held to apply in all cases unless the statute creating the offence prescribes otherwise.[17] In the case in question a complaint was brought under the Food and Drugs (Adulteration) Act 1928, section 27 (1) of which enacted that in certain circumstances prosecutions " shall not be instituted after the expiration of 28 days " from the time of purchasing a sample. It was held that for the purposes of this section a prosecution is " instituted " when the complaint is tabled and a diet obtained for the disposal of the case.

What constitutes undue delay must be a question of fact in each case. It must not be due to any act for which the prosecutor is responsible. The expression " without undue delay " implies that there has been no slackness on his part and that any delay in execution is due to some circumstance for which he is not responsible, e.g. the conduct of the accused. The point arose in a case prior to the 1908 Act in which the accused was prosecuted for a contravention of the Game Act 1772, committed on August 11, 1884. The complaint and warrant of apprehension thereon were both dated February 7, 1885, but the warrant was not put in force until July 9, 1885. The 1772 Act fixes a time-limit of six

---

[13] *Macknight,* supra.

[14] *Archibald* v. *Plean Colliery Co.,* 1923 J.C. 80.

[15] e.g. Mines and Quarries Act 1954, s. 163 (4); Road Traffic Act 1960, s. 244 (2); Ministry of Social Security Act 1966, s. 33 (3). The Companies Acts contain some special provisions on this matter: see *Lott* v. *MacDonald,* 1963 J.C. 57.

[16] 1954 Act, s. 23; cf. *Aird* v. *MacNab* (1972) 36 J.C.L. 114.

[17] *Robertson* v. *Page,* 1943 J.C. 32.

months. It was held that, no satisfactory explanation of the great delay in the execution of the warrant having been furnished, a conviction fell to be suspended.[18]

Prosecutors

13–09 Summary prosecutors fall into three classes, i.e. (1) public prosecutors of courts, including the procurators fiscal, who are appointed by the Lord Advocate for the sheriff courts,[19] and by the local authority for the police and J.P. courts [20]; (2) other persons prosecuting in the public interest by virtue of an express right conferred by statute, such as inspectors of factories and customs officers; and (3) private prosecutors, i.e., persons prosecuting for a statutory offence which gives an express right to prosecute either to specified classes of persons or to the public at large, or persons held to have a right to prosecute because they are specially injured by the offence or are entitled to all or part of the statutory penalty.[21]

Statutory definition of prosecutor

13–10 " ' Prosecutor ' shall include procurator-fiscal, assistant procurator-fiscal, procurator-fiscal depute, justice of the peace fiscal, burgh prosecutor, and any other persons prosecuting in the public interest, private prosecutor, and complainer, and any person duly authorised to represent or act for any public prosecutor." [22]

These groups are dealt with in the succeeding paragraphs, but the following distinctions may here be noted:

(1) Public prosecutors can act only by themselves or their duly authorised deputies. No other person has any title to sign complaints or appear in court on their behalf.[23] Where, however, the failure of a prosecutor to appear in court has been due to death, disability, or other unavoidable cause, the court has an inherent power to appoint a prosecutor pro hac vice to proceed with the prosecution, in order that the ends of justice may not be defeated.[24] On the other hand, private prosecutors and persons prosecuting in the public interest can employ solicitors to conduct prosecutions on their behalf.[25]

(2) Unlike private prosecutors, persons prosecuting in the public interest do not require to obtain the concurrence of the public prosecutor in complaints at their instance.[26]

---

[18] *Farquharson* v. *Whyte* (1886) 1 White 26.
[19] Sheriff Courts (Scotland) Act 1907, s. 22; now replaced by Sheriff Courts and Legal Officers (Scotland) Act 1927.
[20] Supra, paras. 12–19, 12–24.
[21] *Rintoul* v. *Scottish Insurance Commissioners* (1913) 7 Adam 210; *Lockwood* v. *Chartered Institute of Patent Agents* (1912) 7 Adam 14; cf. *McKinstry* v. *Lanarkshire County Council*, 1962 J.C. 16; *Gerber* v. *British Railways Board*, 1969 J.C. 7.
[22] 1954 Act, s. 77.
[23] 1954 Act, s. 15. See *Thomson* v. *Scott* (1901) 3 Adam 410, L.J.-C. at 419.
[24] *Thomson* v. *Scott*, supra; *Walker* v. *Emslie* (1899) 3 Adam 102, L.J.-C. at 103; *Hill* v. *Finlayson* (1883) 5 Couper 284, L.J.-C. at 206. See also supra, para. 9–03.
[25] 1954 Act, s. 15; *Motion* v. *McGinnes* (1907) 5 Adam 393; *Templeton* v. *King*, 1933 J.C. 58.
[26] 1954 Act, s. 15; *Templeton* v. *King*, supra.

Public prosecutors

13–11   In every court an official is appointed whose duty it is to prosecute all offences competent to be dealt with by the court. In the sheriff court this official is termed the procurator fiscal; in the justice of peace court, the justice of peace fiscal; and in the burgh and police courts, the burgh prosecutor. The term " public prosecutor " denotes this official (besides the Lord Advocate and his deputes).[27] When the term " procurator fiscal " is used without qualification, the public prosecutor of the sheriff court is understood.

All penalties, for the recovery of which in Scotland no special provision has been made by statute or order, may be recovered by the public prosecutor in any court having jurisdiction.[28]

A public prosecutor is not entitled to raise proceedings for an offence committed beyond the limits of his district [29] or to prosecute in a court other than that to which he is attached.[30] Thus the justice of peace fiscal was held not entitled to prosecute in the sheriff court.[31]

Prosecutors in the public interest

13–12   Many statutes confer upon specified officials or bodies the right to prosecute in respect of contraventions of their provisions. For example, inspectors of factories, excise officers and others are given a special title to prosecute. Sometimes a statute provides that prosecutions under it must be brought " with the consent, in writing, of the Secretary of State." In such a case evidence of the consent is unnecessary and incompetent, the statement of the Lord Advocate or of his representative that it has been obtained being sufficient.[32]

13–13   Prior to the 1908 Act the Summary Jurisdiction Acts recognised only two classes of prosecutor, public and private.[33] If a public body had a statutory right to prosecute certain offences and to appoint a qualified person to conduct prosecutions, that person was held to be a public prosecutor.[34] On the other hand, where a person prosecuted in virtue of a statutory power conferred upon himself, he was regarded as a private prosecutor and he required to obtain the concurrence of the public prosecutor unless the statute under which he acted empowered him to bring complaints at his own instance.[35]

13–14   By means of its definition of " prosecutor," which is substantially repeated in section 77 of the 1954 Act,[36] section 2 of the 1908 Act intro-

---

[27] *Wilson* v. *McLaughlin* (1907) 5 Adam 284, Lord Ardwall at 293.
[28] 1954 Act, s. 24.
[29] *McCrone* v. *Sawers* (1835) 13 S. 443. Cf. *Kelso District Committee* v. *Fairbairn* (1891) 3 White 94, and *Rae* v. *Strathern*, 1924 S.C. 147.
[30] *Lockhart* v. *Molison* (1868) 40 S.J. 393.
[31] Ibid.
[32] *Stevenson* v. *Roger* (1914) 7 Adam 571.
[33] *Wilson* v. *McLaughlin* (1907) 5 Adam 284, Lord Ardwall at 293.
[34] *McMurdo* v. *McCracken* (1907) 5 Adam 164; following *Thomson* v. *Scott* (1901) 3 Adam 410.
[35] *Wilson* v. *McLaughlin*, supra; *Motion* v. *McGinnes* (1907) 5 Adam 393.
[36] Supra, para. 13–10.

duced the third class of prosecutor, viz., persons prosecuting in the public interest. In view of the terms of sections 2 and 18 of the 1908 Act (now sections 77 and 15 of the 1954 Act) and of the case of *Templeton* v. *King*,[37] the true position now appears to be that only the official court prosecutors are public prosecutors, and that all other prosecutors prosecuting under statutory authority in the public interest come within the new category, i.e., they can institute complaints without requiring the concurrence of the public prosecutor and they can employ solicitors to prosecute on their behalf. In *Templeton* v. *King* [38] the complaint was at the instance of a person appointed to prosecute " under the Education (Scotland) Acts 1872 to 1928, as read along with the Local Government (Scotland) Act 1929," by a county council which had statutory power to institute proceedings. It was held (1) that the council were entitled to delegate their power to the complainer, and (2) that he was not a private prosecutor in respect that he was prosecuting in the public interest, and, therefore, that he did not require the concurrence of the procurator fiscal, and, further, was entitled to be represented by a solicitor.

Private prosecutors

13–15   Private prosecutions in summary courts for common law offences are virtually unknown. Private prosecutions for statutory offences are fairly common. Several Acts give authority to any member of the public to prosecute. This implies that any member of the public may institute proceedings without setting forth injury suffered, danger incurred, or other substantial interest.[39] The right must be expressly conferred by the statute.[40] The Salmon Fisheries (Scotland) Act 1868 gives any person a right to prosecute for offences against the Act,[41] but limits the right to prosecute for breaches of byelaws made under the Act to District Boards. The Game (Scotland) Act 1772 gives a right of prosecution to the fiscal or any other person who will inform or complain. As regards other statutes a private person having a substantial interest may prosecute if the statute concerned does not expressly or impliedly exclude private prosecution.[42] Prosecutions for trespassing for game by day are conducted by the aggrieved landowner or person with the right to kill game on the land.[43] But the interest must be a substantial one. Where a Parish Council prosecuted, with the concurrence of the procurator fiscal, in respect of offences against the Children Act 1908, the court refused to uphold its title. Lord Justice-General Strathclyde said: " If there

---

[37] 1933 J.C. 58.
[38] Supra.
[39] *Hamilton* v. *Girvan* (1867) 5 Irv. 439; *Hanvy and Orr* v. *Stirrat* (1869) 1 Couper 334; *Kennedy* v. *Cadenhead* (1867) 5 Irv. 539; *Munro* v. *Buchanan* (1910) 6 Adam 234.
[40] *Duke of Bedford* v. *Kerr* (1893) 3 White 493, Lord Adam at 499.
[41] See *Fairley* v. *Fishmongers of London*, 1951 J.C. 14, L.J.-G. at 23; *Hanvy and Orr* v. *Stirrat*, supra; *Kennedy* v. *Murray* (1869) 7 M. 1001.
[42] *Bremridge* v. *Smith* (1902) 3 Adam 565; *Lockwood* v. *Chartered Institute of Patent Agents* (1912) 7 Adam 14. See also *Mackintosh* v. *Weir* (1875) 2 R. 877.
[43] Game (Scotland) Act 1832; Ground Game Act 1880, s. 7; *Russell* v. *Colquohoun* (1845) 2 Broun 572; *Ferguson* v. *McNab* (1885) 12 R. 1083, 1086.

were any patrimonial interests at stake here, the question would be totally different. But I cannot conceive any case in which a public body—whether a Government Department or a Local Authority—entrusted with the administration of an Act of Parliament can be said to be aggrieved or injured by failure to observe the statutory provisions." [44] Private prosecutions have been held competent where the prosecutors were entitled to a portion of the penalties [45]; where the prosecutor had a clear personal interest not only because he might receive part of the penalty as informer, but also because he suffered injury [46]; and where a chartered body had a pecuniary interest because it was entitled to charge registration fees. [47] But a title to prosecute is not set up by implication simply because the Act of Parliament confides to a public department or local authority the duty of administering the Act of Parliament. [48] " Whenever a Public General Act creates an offence, it follows necessarily that the title to initiate and maintain a prosecution in respect of it is vested in the Lord Advocate as the public prosecutor and in him alone—which of course would include those deriving authority from him—unless the Act either expressly or by clear implication confers a title to prosecute upon someone else." [49]

13–16 The right of private prosecution is not confined to individuals but may be exercised by corporate bodies or companies. [50] These may prosecute statutory contraventions where they have authority or an interest to do so. [51] They may also prosecute common law offences committed against themselves in their corporate capacity. [52] Where a corporate body or company prosecutes, the name of one or more of its officials who will be responsible for the conduct of the proceedings in court should be coupled with its own in the instance of the complaint (or, in the case of

[44] *Glasgow Parish Council* v. *Edward* (1914) 7 Adam 486, 490. Cf. *Simpson* v. *Board of Trade* (1892) 3 White 167.

[45] *Glasgow City and District Railway Co.* v. *Hutchison and Ors.*(1884) 5 Couper 420; *Rintoul* v. *Scottish Insurance Commissioners* (1913) 7 Adam 210; Cf. *McKinstry* v. *Lanarkshire County Council,* 1962 J.C. 16, L.J.-C. at 20.

[46] *Simpson* v. *Corporation of Glasgow* (1902) 4 F. 611. See also *Great North of Scotland Railway Co.* v. *Anderson* (1897) 2 Adam 381, where it was held that a railway company had, by implication, a right to prosecute for a contravention of its own bye-laws; *Gerber* v. *British Railways Board,* 1969 J.C. 7. Prosecutions by common informers under local or private statutes are no longer competent: Common Informers Act 1951.

[47] *Lockwood* v. *Chartered Institute of Patent Agents,* supra.

[48] *Simpson* v. *The Board of Trade,* supra; *Glasgow Parish Council* v. *Edward,* supra.

[49] *Inverness-shire C.C.* v. *Weir,* 1938 J.C. 11, L.J.-C. at 14. In that case it was held that the County Council had no authority to prosecute offences against s. 11 of the Restriction of Ribbon Development Act 1935, although that section empowered them to demolish buildings erected in contravention of its provisions. Section 343 of the Local Government (Scotland) Act 1947 which enables local authorities to institute proceedings for the promotion or protection of inhabitants of their area does not confer title to prosecute for offences against local Acts; *McKinstry* v. *Lanarkshire C.C.,* supra. The Secretary of State has the right to prosecute for certain offences against the Vehicles (Excise) Act 1971; see s. 29 of that Act; supra, para. 12–08n.

[50] Macdonald, 213; Alison, ii. 106, 107; *Lockwood* v. *Chartered Institute of Patent Agents,* supra; *J. and P. Coats Ltd.* v. *Brown* (1909) 6 Adam 19.

[51] *Great North of Scotland Railway Co.* v. *Anderson,* supra; *Lockwood* v. *Chartered Institute of Patent Agents,* supra; *Fairley* v. *Fishmongers of London,* 1951 J.C. 14.

[52] Alison, ii. 106, 107.

solemn procedure, the indictment).[53] This was formerly regarded as an imperative requirement,[54] but it has since been held that a summary complaint may be presented at the instance of an incorporated company without the conjunction of any of its officers.[55]

13–17   The question has been mooted whether the representatives of a private prosecutor who has died after instituting the prosecution are entitled to be sisted.[56]

13–18   A person prosecuting in the public interest under a statutory title is not a private prosecutor.[57]

Concurrence of public prosecutor

13–19   Complaints at the instance of private prosecutors for offences at common law, and for statutory offences where imprisonment without the option of a fine is competent, unless otherwise provided in any statute, require the concurrence of the public prosecutor of the court in which they are brought.[58]

This concurrence is usually given as a matter of course on presentation of a complaint regularly prepared and signed. It is not clear what remedy is open in the event of a refusal of concurrence, procedure by criminal letters not being competent in a summary court. The procurator fiscal of the sheriff court is entitled to a fee for his concurrence.

13–20   When a complaint is instituted with the concurrence of the public prosecutor, the fact must be mentioned in the instance, by adding the words, " with the concurrence of C. D., procurator fiscal of court for the public interest." Concurrence is given by a minute signed by the public prosecutor on the complaint in the following terms: (*Place and date*) " I concur in the foregoing complaint.—C. D., procurator fiscal of court." This concurrence will not be given where there are special circumstances which justify refusal, such as great delay in instituting a prosecution, or any element of malice or oppression. If an instance is bad in itself, concurrence by the procurator fiscal does not cure the defect.[59] The concurrence must be given before the complaint is served or executed. The absence of concurrence is a fatal defect, which cannot be remedied by amendment.[60] So, where a prosecution was instituted without the concurrence of the procurator fiscal, and, on objection being taken to the instance, the sheriff allowed the complaint to be amended by the procurator fiscal adding his concurrence, the court held that this was incompetent and set aside the conviction.[61]

---

[53] *Great North of Scotland Railway Co.* v. *Anderson* (1897) 2 Adam 381; *Fairbairn* v. *Lochryan Oyster Fishery Co. Ltd.* (1908) 5 Adam 450.

[54] Hume, ii. 119; Alison, ii. 106, 107; *Aitken* v. *Rennie*, Dec. 11th, 1810, F.C.

[55] *Fairbairn* v. *Lochryan Oyster Fishery Co. Ltd.*, supra.

[56] See *Cathcart* v. *Houston* (1914) 7 Adam 535, where the complainer's trustees were sisted after his death.

[57] *Templeton* v. *King*, 1933 J.C. 58; 1954 Act, s. 15 (4).

[58] 1954 Act, s. 15 (4). See *Kennedy* v. *Cadenhead* (1867) 5 Irv. 539.

[59] *Simpson* v. *The Board of Trade* (1892) 3 White 167. See also *Duke of Bedford* v. *Kerr* (1893) 3 White 493; *McDoull* v. *Irvine*, 1908 S.C. 60.

[60] *Lundie* v. *MacBrayne* (1894) 1 Adam 342.   [61] Ibid.

3-21   A person prosecuting in the public interest under a statutory title does not require the concurrence of the procurator fiscal, not being a private prosecutor.[62]

The Accused

3-22   There is no specific definition of the term " accused " in the Act. It must therefore receive its ordinary meaning, as the person against whom a complaint is directed.[63] Section 2 (1) of the Interpretation Act 1889, provides that, in the construction of every statute relating to an offence punishable on summary conviction, the expression " person " shall, unless the contrary intention appears, include a body corporate.

Bodies corporate

3-23   A company incorporated under the Companies Acts may be proceeded against in England for a common law offence, and there is no reason why the law should be any different in Scotland.[64] No reported example of any such prosecution exists. There is no doubt that a company may be proceeded against in respect of various statutory offences,[65] and, although a sentence of imprisonment is incompetent in the case of such a body,[66] it may be prosecuted even where the penalty provided for the contravention is a fine with the alternative of imprisonment.[67] Section 25 of the 1954 Act provides as follows:

> " With regard to the summary prosecution of offences committed by a company, association, incorporation, or body of trustees, the following provisions shall, without prejudice to any other or wider powers conferred by statute, apply:
>
> (a) proceedings may be taken against the company, association, incorporation, or body of trustees, in their corporate capacity,[68] and in that event any penalty imposed shall be recovered by civil diligence in manner hereinafter provided; or
>
> (b) proceedings may be taken against an individual representative of such company, association, or incorporation, as follows:
>> (i) in the case of an ordinary company or firm, any one of the partners thereof, or the manager or the person in charge

---

[62] *Templeton* v. *King*, 1933 J.C. 58.

[63] *Walker* v. *Brander*, 1920 S.C. 840.

[64] See Gordon, 283–5; *R.* v. *I.C.R. Haulage Ltd.* [1944] K.B. 551; Gower, *Modern Company Law* (3rd ed.), 146–8.

[65] 1954 Act, s. 25. The question whether a limited liability company can competently be convicted of a statutory offence which presumes fraudulent intent was raised, but not decided, in *Galbraith's Stores Ltd.* v. *McIntyre* (1912) 6 Adam 641.

[66] *Fletcher* v. *Eglinton Chemical Co. Ltd.* (1886) 1 White 259.

[67] Ibid.

[68] So, where an unincorporated company trading under the name of " The City and Surburban Dairies " was charged under that name, without the addition of the names of the partners, the complaint was held competent. (*City and Suburban Dairies* v. *Mackenna*, 1918 J.C. 105.)

or locally in charge of the affairs thereof, may be dealt with as if he was the person offending [69];

(ii) in the case of an association, incorporation, or incorporated company, the managing director or the secretary, or other principal officer thereof, or the person in charge, or locally in charge, of the affairs thereof, may be dealt with as if he was the person offending [70];

(iii) the offence shall be deemed to be the offence of such company, association, or incorporation, and a conviction thereof may be libelled as an aggravation [71] of any subsequent offence of the same nature by the same company, association, or incorporation, although the individuals charged and convicted are different." [72]

13–24 It may at first sight seem strange that a body of trustees should in their trust capacity be amenable to the jurisdiction of a criminal court, but, when the wide scope of the Summary Jurisdiction Act is considered, the explanation of this apparent anomaly will be at once seen. Under several Acts of Parliament of an administrative nature, owners of property are liable in penalties for statutory contraventions of a more or less technical nature, and, as such owners may be trustees, it is necessary that there should be some form of process by which these penalties can be recovered. It will be observed, however, that the provisions under subsection (*b*) of this section as to proceedings being taken against an individual representative of a company, association, or incorporation, do not apply to a body of trustees. They must be proceeded against in their corporate capacity, and any penalty imposed recovered, if necessary, by civil diligence against the trust estate.

Mode of prosecuting bodies corporate

13–25 As regards proceedings against a company, association, or incorporation, the prosecutor has a choice: he may proceed against the accused in their corporate capacity, or he may take action against an individual representative. In the former case any penalty, if not paid, will be recoverable by civil diligence; in the latter, the person proceeded against will be liable to imprisonment in the event of non-payment of any penalty imposed. The question of the procedure which is more appropriate will depend on the circumstances of each case. Where the penalties incurred are large, it may, as a general rule, be best to proceed against the accused in their corporate capacity; in other cases, to select

---

[69] See, e.g., *Bean* v. *Sinclair*, 1930 J.C. 31 (manager of omnibus company prosecuted as representing the company).

[70] So, where certain persons were charged with a breach of a Liquor Order in respect that in their capacity as office-bearers and committee of management of a registered club they did " by the hand of A. B., barmaid in the said club," supply exciseable liquor after the authorised hours, the charge was held competent (*Burnette* v. *Mackenna*, 1917 J.C. 20).

[71] Apparently unrepealed, but see 1963 Act, s. 30, supra, para. 6–31.

[72] 1954 Act, s. 25; see infra, para. 13–26.

an individual representative and proceed against him. While in terms a wide choice seems to be given by subsections (i) and (ii) of subsection (b), it will be necessary to ascertain, if possible, the person who is the responsible representative of the company, association, or incorporation. While it would be competent for the court to order recovery of a penalty imposed on an individual representative by civil diligence instead of by imprisonment, such diligence would apparently only be competent against the estate of that individual. The provision in subsection (iii) is important. It prevents the accused, when prosecuted in a corporate capacity through an individual representative, from pleading that a conviction must be treated as personal to the individual convicted.

13–26   In construing subsection (2) (c) of section 28 of the 1908 Act, which was similar to section 25 (b) (iii) of the 1954 Act, it was pointed out that the subsection is confined to proceedings taken against individual representatives of a company. Accordingly, in proceedings against the individual representative of a company for an offence committed by the company, it was held incompetent to libel as an aggravation of the offence a conviction previously obtained against the company in its corporate capacity.[73]

13–27   The provisions for the citation of persons dealt with in a corporate capacity and for recovery of penalties by civil diligence are contained in sections 18 and 50 of the Act.[74] At the proceedings in the inferior court in connection with a complaint, a firm may be competently represented by its manager.[75] In a High Court case, however, in proceedings for review, it was held that a firm of law agents could not be represented in that court by one of its partners and that counsel must be employed.[76]

The Complaint

13–28   Section 13 of the 1954 Act enacts that the forms of procedure under the Act shall be in accordance as nearly as may be with the forms contained in the Second Schedule to the Act. Section 15, however, makes is imperative that all proceedings under the Act for the trial of offences or the recovery of penalties shall be instituted by complaint in the form at nearly as may be of the form contained in Part II of the Second Schedule to the Act.

The forms given in Part II of the Second Schedule[77] illustrate the subject. The general form is applicable equally to both common law and statutory offences, as since the passing of the 1949 Act, section 46 (1) and Schedule 12 of which repealed the requirement of the form provided by the 1908 Act that statutory charges must either specify the enactment fixing the penalty or set forth the penalty, these particulars are not inserted in statutory complaints. In place of this indication of penalty (which was

[73] *Campbell* v. *Macpherson* (1910) 6 Adam 394.
[74] *Infra*, para. 17–46.
[75] *McAlpine & Sons* v. *Ronaldson* (1901) 3 Adam 405.
[76] *Macbeth & Maclagan* v. *Macmillan* (1914) 7 Adam 493.
[77] These include examples of charges.

held to be of the substance of the complaint),[78] section 15 (5) of the 1954 Act provides that the prosecutor must inform the accused of the penalties to which he is liable on conviction by means of a notice in the form as nearly as may be of Form No. 1 of Part III of the Second Schedule to the Act. Where the accused is cited to a diet, this notice must be served on him with the complaint. Where he is in custody a copy of the complaint and notice must be served upon him before he is asked to plead. Section 15 (5) provides that a copy of this notice must be entered in the record of the proceedings.

Heading

13–29   The complaint is headed " Under the Summary Jurisdiction (Scotland) Act, 1954." The particular Act, if the offence be a statutory one, under which the charge is brought should not be added to the heading. Nor should reference be made to any Act conferring jurisdiction on the court to try the offence charged.[79] If the heading has been omitted it may be added by way of amendment.[80]

Next comes the designation of the court and the place of its sitting.

Instance

13–30   The instance is in the form—" The complaint of A. B., Procurator Fiscal (or Burgh Prosecutor) (or other party entitled to prosecute)." A private prosecutor must set forth his full name and designation. He requires the concurrence of the procurator fiscal and he must add the words " with the concurrence of the procurator fiscal of court."[81] Similarly, where the consent or authority of some official such as the Secretary of State is necessary, the fact that it has been obtained must appear in the complaint.[82] The name and official designation of statutory prosecutors must be stated. Where a person other than the public prosecutor has, by public statute, a title to prosecute summary complaints for statutory offences it is not necessary to set out in the complaint the statute giving him his title to prosecute.[83]

Charge

13–31   This runs in the second person, beginning with the accused's name and designation. These should be correctly stated, and, in cases investigated by the police, it is customary for an officer to see the accused person before the complaint is served, inform him of the charge, obtain from him his correct name and designation, and note any explanation which he may wish to make. The accused may be proceeded against under the name and designation which he himself gives. If he is accused in a special

[78] *Logue* v. *Langmuir*, 1938 J.C. 163.
[79] *McLaren* v. *Macleod* (1913) 7 Adam 102.
[80] *Finlayson* v. *Bunbury* (1898) 2 Adam 478.
[81] Supra, para. 13–20.
[82] *Stevenson* v. *Roger* (1914) 7 Adam 571.
[83] *Emslie* v. *Paterson* (1897) 2 Adam 323.

capacity that must be specified.[84] Trivial errors in stating the accused's name or designation will not vitiate the complaint if he appears in answer to it,[85] and, in such a case the necessary correction can be made by way of amendment. If, however, the mistake is of a more serious nature, the safest course is (unless the accused consents to an amendment) to withdraw the complaint and serve of new. The charge is stated in the plainest terms, merely setting forth the act, attempt, or omission of which the accused is alleged to have been guilty, adding, in the case of a statutory contravention, that this was contrary to a particular section of a particular Act of Parliament.[86]

Previous convictions

13-32   Under section 31 (1) of the 1954 Act (as amended by the 1963 Act, Schedule 5), where the prosecutor has decided to lay a previous conviction before the court, this information must be conveyed to the accused by means of a notice in the form as nearly as may be of Form No. 2 or Form No. 3 of Part III of the Second Schedule to the Act, Form No. 2 being applicable where the offence charged is statutory, and Form No. 3 where it is a common law one. Where the accused is in custody the notice must be served on him with a copy of the complaint before he is asked to plead. Under section 31 (1) a copy of such notice must be entered in the record of the proceedings.

13-33   As explained later,[87] no previous conviction can be laid before the judge until he is satisfied that the charge is proved. This rule is strictly enforced. Where three men were charged on a complaint which set forth (1) a charge of theft, and (2) a charge that " being known thieves, having each been convicted as shown in the list annexed," they had been found in a Glasgow street with intent to commit theft by pocket-picking, contrary to a local Act, it was held that under the 1949 Act these two charges should not have been included in the same complaint and that the procedure had prejudiced the accused in their defence on the merits of the first charge by disclosing their previous convictions, and a conviction on that charge was quashed.[88] In another case [89] it was held that reference in a complaint to a penalty exigible for a second offence was an implicit reference to a previous conviction amounting to a fundamental nullity.

Signature

13-34   The complaint concludes with the signature of the prosecutor, or, in the case of prosecutors other than the official court prosecutors, with that of the solicitor representing them.[90] The solicitor who appears

[84] See infra, para. 13–52. As regards representatives of companies, etc., see supra, para. 13–25.
[85] *Poli* v. *Thomson* (1910) 6 Adam 261. See supra, para. 6–02.
[86] See infra, para. 13–49.
[87] Infra, para. 14–65.
[88] *McGregor* v. *Macdonald*, 1952 J.C. 4.
[89] *Bryce* v. *Gardiner*, 1951 J.C. 134.
[90] 1954 Act, s. 15 (2). See supra, para. 13–10.

at the trial need not be the person who signed the complaint.[91] In a prosecution under the Burgh Police Act 1892, the complaint was signed for the burgh prosecutor by an inspector of police who had no written authority to do so, but was merely authorised to do so verbally by the presiding magistrate. It was held that the authority should have been in writing, and the conviction was suspended.[92]

In *Williamson* v. *Macmillan* [93] the complaint was drawn up by the procurator fiscal but signed in his absence by his depute. This depute, who had no concern with or knowledge of, the Crown case, defended the accused at his trial. It was held that the accused had suffered no handicap or injustice, and that the proceedings were competent.

Implied meanings, etc.

13-35   The clauses of the 1887 Act relating to implied meanings and latitudes, alternative verdicts, and previous convictions are applied to summary procedure.[94] As these were explained in Part I, it is only necessary for convenient reference to give here the heads under which they are to be found:

(1) Naming of accused (s. 4), para. 6–02.
(2) Nomen juris (s. 5), para. 6–18.
(3) Plural accused (s. 6), para. 6–03.
(4) Accessories (s. 7), para. 6–05.
(5) Qualifying words (s. 8), para. 6–19.
(6) Quotation of statutes (s. 9), para. 6–23.
(7) Latitude as to time and place (s. 10), paras. 6–15, 6–16.
(8) Quantities, persons, things and modes (s. 11), para. 6–24.
(9) Description of property (s. 12), para. 6–25.
(10) Description of persons and goods (s. 13), para. 6–26.
(11) Money (s. 14), para. 6–26.
(12) Documents (s. 15), para. 6–26. As there is no list of productions annexed to a complaint, it is usual to state that the document " is produced herewith," and to produce it at the first diet and get it marked by the clerk of court.
(13) Charges of dishonesty (s. 58), para. 6–27.
(14) Alternative verdicts (ss. 59–62), para. 10–42.
(15) Previous convictions (ss. 63, 64, 65 and 1954 Act, section 31 (5)), para. 6–31.

Relevancy

13-36   The principles discussed in the chapter dealing with the relevancy of indictments apply equally to complaints.[95] The safe rule in framing complaints for common law offences is strictly to adhere to the statutory

---

[91] *Duke of Sutherland* v. *Douglas* (1907) 5 Adam 416.
[92] *Dunlop* v. *Sempill* (1900) 3 Adam 159.
[93] 1962 S.L.T. 63.
[94] 1954 Act, s. 2 (formerly 1908 Act, s. 5).
[95] *Supra,* paras. 6–14 et seq.

forms. The importance of doing so was emphasised by the court in *Coventry* v. *Douglas*,[96] where it was held, though not without difficulty, that a charge, not stated in the statutory form applicable to attempted theft, but worded thus: " You did insert your hand in said receptacle with intent to steal therefrom " relevantly charged the crime of attempted theft. In *Calder* v. *Mickel*,[97] however, a charge that " you did receive from your daughter a book of clothing coupons . . . the property of A. B. and you did retain the said clothing book as your own property and did thereby steal it " was held to be irrelevant.

13-37   Where the essence of a statutory offence is that the accused acted knowingly, it is advisable that this should be indicated in the complaint if the case is to be tried by a lay magistrate.[98]

13-38   In stating the charge against an accused person, it is competent to use any of the forms contained in Schedule A of the 1887 Act, so far as these are applicable to charges which may be tried summarily, or any of those contained in Part II of the Second Schedule to the 1954 Act.[99] No further specification is required than a specification similar to that given in these forms.[1] So, a charge of indecent exposure in the short form provided by Schedule C of the 1908 Act was held relevant without further specification of the modus of the offence or the circumstances in which it was alleged to have been committed.[2] So, too, a complaint in the appropriate form which charged an assault was held relevant, although it did not set forth (as was the fact) that the accused stood in the relationship of master to the boy assaulted and that the punishment had been administered on account of a school offence, and although it did not allege that the punishment was excessive.[3] So, also, where objection to the relevancy of a complaint charging the accused with perjury was taken on the grounds (1) that, while the complaint set forth that on a certain day in a certain court the accused had made certain false statements in giving evidence in a civil cause then proceeding, it did not describe or define the cause, and (2) that it was not alleged in the complaint that the statements were relevant to the issue of the cause, it was held that the fact that the complaint was in the form prescribed by the Act was a sufficient answer to the objections.[4]

Statutory offences

13-39   Complaints libelling statutory offences must, like those charging common law crimes, fulfil two requirements, viz.: (1) they must relevantly

---

[96] 1944 J.C. 13.
[97] 1947 J.C. 16; cf. *Lawson* v. *Heatly*, 1962 S.L.T. 53. See also *Smith* v. *Sempill* (1910) 6 Adam 348. Questions of relevancy are now rare in the case of complaints dealing with common law offences. As examples see *McShane* v. *Paton*, 1922 J.C. 26; *Brown* v. *Hilson*, 1924 J.C. 1; *Adcock* v. *Archibald*, 1925 J.C. 58.
[98] *Knox* v. *Boyd*, 1941 J.C. 82, Lord Fleming at 85.
[99] 1954 Act, s. 16.
[1] Ibid.
[2] *Poli* v. *Thomson* (1910) 6 Adam 261.
[3] *Brown* v. *Hilson*, supra. But see *McShane* v. *Paton*, supra. Cf. *Gray* v. *Hawthorn*, 1964 J.C. 69.　　　　　　　　　　　　　　　　　　　[4] *Strathern* v. *Burns*, 1921 J.C. 92.

aver facts sufficient to constitute the offence, and (2) they must give the
accused person fair notice of the case which he has to meet.[5] As the
validity of a statutory charge depends solely on the terms of the statute
creating the offence, it is essential that the proper enactment should be
libelled. A complaint is irrelevant if it refers to no statute [6] or to the wrong
statute,[7] or if, while setting forth the correct statute, it either fails to
specify a section at all [8] (unless the statute is so brief as to render such
specification unnecessary [9]) or else libels a section which does not constitute the offence and so gives the accused no notice of the case which he
has to meet.[10] While such mistakes, in respect that they violate the two
fundamental requirements above-mentioned, are fatal to a conviction,[11]
it is thought that, if discovered before the determination of the case,
they may, in most cases, be remedied by amendment of the complaint
with leave of the court under the provisions of section 27 of the 1954
Act, provided that the amendment does not alter the nature of the offence
or prejudice the accused. In *Rendle* v. *Muir* [12] the accused was charged
with possessing drugs contrary to statutory regulations made under the
Dangerous Drugs Act 1920, the relevant section of which made it an
offence to contravene the regulations. At the time of the offence the
Dangerous Drugs Act 1920 had been repealed by the Dangerous Drugs
Act 1951, but the regulations were kept in force by the later Act which
made it an offence to contravene them. It was held that the complaint
was irrelevant but not *funditus null* since the error in libelling the earlier
statute could have been cured by amendment had it been timeously
objected to.[13] Presumably the same reasoning would apply where an
offence created in one statute was repealed and re-enacted in a later statute,
at any rate where the later Act was a consolidating statute re-enacting
the earlier offence in substantially the same terms.

Description of statutory offences

13–40   The description of statutory offences was simplified by section 19 (1)
of the 1908 Act, which provided: " The description of any offence in

---

[5] *Durnion* v. *Paterson*, 1930 J.C. 12, Lord Anderson at 22. Cf. *Tweedle* v. *H.M. Adv.* (1967)
31 J.C.L. 261.

[6] *Hastie* v. *Macdonald* (1894) 1 Adam 505. (Byelaw libelled without any reference to the
statute authorising it.) See also *Sanderson* v. *Robertson*, 1947 J.C. 27 (complaint founded
on non-existent byelaw).

[7] *Lipsey* v. *Mackintosh* (1913) 7 Adam 182 (complaint libelling sections of an Act relating
to entirely different offences from those charged); *Durnion* v. *Paterson*, 1930 J.C. 12 (motor
driver charged under a statute not applicable to his vehicle); *Harris* v. *McClure and
Connell*, 1929 J.C. 96 (charge brought under wrong Revenue Act).

[8] *Hastings* v. *Charles* (1891) 2 White 325; *Whyte* v. *Robertson* (1891) 3 White 245; *Buchanan*
v. *Wilson* (1896) 2 Adam 167; *Bell* v. *Dickie* (1898) 2 Adam 524; *Hotchkiss* v. *McCann*
(1902) 3 Adam 675.

[9] *Buchanan* v. *Wilson*, supra.

[10] See *Macrorie* v. *Bird* (1911) 6 Adam 527.

[11] *Durnion* v. *Paterson*, supra, L.J.-C. at 17; Lord Anderson at 22, 23.

[12] 1952 J.C. 115.

[13] Contrast *Aitkenhead* v. *Cuthbert*, 1962 J.C. 12 where facts alleged to constitute a contravention of two statutory provisions in fact contravened one and the conviction was
quashed.

the words of the statute or order contravened, or in similar words, shall
be sufficient." These words are repeated in section 16 (*a*) of the 1954 Act.
Since the passing of the 1908 Act complaints have proceeded to trial which
would formerly have been held irrelevant. Thus in *Dunn* v. *Mitchell*[14]
a complaint which charged the accused with " driving a motor car
negligently " without specifying wherein the negligence consisted was
held relevant, being in the form prescribed by the 1908 Act. In that case,
however, it was observed by Lord Salvesen[15] that public prosecutors
should, in future, as matter of fair notice to the accused, specify the
particular form of negligence upon which they relied, and in two other
cases[16] the opinion was expressed[17] that there may be cases where mere
re-echoing of the words of a statute will not give the accused fair notice
of the case against him, and that, in such circumstances, the court has
a right to demand further specification. The position has been summed
up as follows by Lord Justice-General Clyde in *Yeudall* v. *William Baird
& Co.*[18]:

> " By subsection (1) of section 19 of the Summary Jurisdiction
> Act, 1908, it is enacted that ' the description of an offence in the words
> of the statute contravened shall be sufficient.' It follows that, since
> this alteration of the law, there are many complaints which must be
> regarded as relevant and sufficient, although they might not have
> passed muster prior to the Act of 1908. It is therefore in vain to quote
> cases decided before the 1908 Act, when the requirements of the law
> in the matter of specification of *modus* were applied rigorously—it
> may be too rigorously—to summary complaints.
>
> I do not, however, mean to cast any doubt upon the opinions
> which have been expressed in cases since the Act of 1908, to the effect
> that, if in the case of a statutory offence some further specification is
> necessary as a condition of fair notice, the Court has the right to
> insist on such further specification as a condition of relevancy."

So far as the reports show, no complaint has yet been dismissed as irrelevant on account of the prosecution's failure to give additional specification. As regards the libelling of sections which create cumulative or
alternative offences, see infra, paras. 13–66 et seq.

13–41   A prosecutor may make his complaint irrelevant by departing from
the statutory form, as the following example illustrates—The Glasgow

---

[14] (1910) 6 Adam 365.
[15] At 374.
[16] *Renton* v. *Ramage* (1910) 6 Adam 266; *Rogers* v. *Howman*, 1918 J.C. 88. In both cases
complaints following the statutory words were held relevant. Another example is *Watson*
v. *Ross*, 1920 J.C. 27, where the complaint in a burgh police court charged the accused
with allowing a motor car to stand in a street longer than was necessary for loading or
unloading goods or for taking up or setting down passengers, contrary to s. 381 (10) of
the Burgh Police (Scotland) Act 1892. The complaint did not allege that any obstruction
was caused. It was held that the complaint was relevant, as it described the offence in
terms of the section.
[17] *Renton* v. *Ramage* (1910) 6 Adam 266, 269–70; *Rogers* v. *Howman*, 1918 J.C. 88, 94.
[18] 1925 J.C. 62, 63. See also *Smith* v. *Moody* [1903] 1 K.B. 56.

Police (Further Powers) Act 1892, section 31, enacts: " That every person who so uses, causes, permits, or suffers to be used any furnace or fire within the city (except a household fire) as that smoke issues therefrom," unless in certain circumstances, shall be liable to certain penalties. The owner of a steam wagon which emitted dense black smoke from its furnace was convicted on a complaint which charged him with using or causing to be used a furnace on the wagon " so that smoke of unnecessary density issued therefrom." It was held that the complaint should have followed the language of the statute, and that the introduction of the words " of unnecessary density " unaccompanied by any statement of a standard of density rendered the complaint irrelevant.[19]

In *MacDonald* v. *Laing*[20] a complaint alleged that the accused was concerned in a game of roulette which was unlawful in respect that it was not in accordance with the conditions specified in section 32 (1) of the Betting, Gaming and Lotteries Act 1963, and set out the three statutory conditions. It was held that the complaint clearly gave notice of intention to prove breach of all three conditions, and was relevant. The court observed that where it was intended to prove only one or two of the conditions, the Crown should libel only the condition or conditions alleged to have been breached.

Specification in statutory offences

13–42   A complaint is not irrelevant merely because it repeats a statutory requirement of " reasonableness " without specifying what is reasonable. In *Marshall* v. *Clark*[21] a Full Bench held relevant a complaint which charged a 'bus conductress with failing to take all reasonable precautions to ensure the safety of passengers, and in particular with failing to keep a proper lookout, and signalling the driver to proceed with the result that a passenger in the act of boarding the vehicle was injured, contrary to the Public Service Vehicles (Conduct of Drivers, etc.) Regulations 1936,[22] without specifying what were reasonable precautions. The court observed that an offence could be created by a regulation using words like " reasonable care " or " reasonable precautions " without further specification, although in a particular case it might be necessary to give such specification in a complaint. There was held to be ample specification in the complaint in *Marshall* v. *Clark*. Lord Justice-Clerk Thomson said of the appellant's argument that it was " on the face of it somewhat startling and

---

[19] *Hemphill* v. *Smith*, 1923 J.C. 23. See also *Grahams* v. *McLennan* (1910) 6 Adam 315. There the accused was charged with contravening s. 381 (41) of the Burgh Police (Scotland) Act 1892, which imposes a penalty on any person who " in vending coals . . . uses any bell . . . to cause annoyance to any inhabitant after being requested by a constable or inhabitant to cease." The complaint did not specify the names of inhabitants said to have been annoyed, and the court doubted its relevancy. The case was decided, however, on other grounds. Contrast *Ronaldson* v. *Williamson* (1911) 6 Adam 519 (complaint alleging nuisance need not state that annoyance was caused to anyone).

[20] 1965 S.L.T. 73.

[21] 1957 J.C. 68, overruling *Allan* v. *Howman*, 1918 J.C. 50, and *Morrison* v. *Ross-Taylor*, 1948 J.C. 74. Cf. *McFadyean* v. *Stewart*, 1951 J.C. 164; *Murray* v. *Sturrock*, 1951 J.C. 90.

[22] Reg. 4 (c).

would appear to accuse an omnipotent parliament of legislative ineptitude [in failing] to point out a standard against which the negligence of the conductress can be measured . . . No doubt in 1918 regulations of this kind were something of a novelty, but since then a good deal of water—some of it pretty muddy—has flowed under Parliamentary bridges and we are now habituated not only to regulations but to legislative enactments of all sorts couched in similar general terms. For myself . . . I feel no particular anxiety that the liberty of the subject will be imperilled or fair trial impeded because an enactment . . . says that a man must take adequate care or reasonable steps and so forth and leaves it to the judge to determine on evidence in what the offence consists." [23]

13–43   Where an accused is charged under an Act making it an offence to loiter with intent to, or to be found about to, commit an arrestable offence, and defining arrestable offence to include a number of offences such as aggravated theft, murder and uttering, it is sufficient to aver in the complaint that he was intending or about to commit " an arrestable offence " and unnecessary to specify which offence he is alleged to have contemplated.[24]

13–44   Where orders or regulations are made in pursuance of a statute and the offence charged is a contravention of such orders or regulations, it is desirable that some reference be made to the orders or regulations on the complaint instead of the complaint just boldly narrating the original statutes.[25] Procedure which is not a necessary preliminary to the charge need not be referred to in the complaint.[26]

13–45   The prosecutor must see that the statute upon which he proposes to ground his charge fits the facts of the case. Thus the General Turnpike Act 1831, section 96 (as incorporated in the Roads and Bridges (Scotland) Act 1878, section 123 and Sched. C), enacted that any person who " shall hang or lay any linen clothes or other such article on any hedge or fence of " a turnpike road should be liable to a penalty. It was held that a complaint which charged the accused with contravening this section by hanging herring fishing-nets on a roadside hedge was irrelevant, as herring fishing-nets did not fall under the category " linen clothes or other such article." [27]

13–46   Complaints must be unambiguous. In *Nimmo* v. *Lees* [28] a complaint under the Sale of Food and Drugs Acts 1875 to 1907 against a grocer set forth that " in response to a demand . . . for one half-pound of butter,

[23] At 75–76. A complaint under the same regulation was held irrelevant in *Reid* v. *MacNicol*, 1958 S.L.T. 42. The allegation there was that the driver failed to take reasonable precautions by failing to stop at a stopping place whereby the complainer stumbled on boarding the 'bus. It was held that the duty of care was owed only to passengers entitled to enter the vehicle and that the complaint failed to specify that the injured person was so entitled.
[24] Vagrancy Act 1824, as applied by Prevention of Crimes Act 1871, as amended by Criminal Law Act 1967; *Phillips* v. *Heatly*, 1964 S.L.T. 163.
[25] *Penrice* v. *Brander*, 1921 J.C. 63.
[26] *Bunton* v. *Miller*, 1926 J.C. 120 (warrant to enter gaming house), following *King* v. *Kidd* (1903) 4 Adam 275 (warrant to enter and search disorderly house). Contrast the provisions of the Poaching Prevention Act 1862.
[27] *Patience* v. *Mackenzie* (1912) 6 Adam 545.
[28] (1910) 6 Adam 279.

you did sell . . . one half-pound of butter which was not of the nature, substance and quality demanded, and was not genuine, as it contained less than 10 per cent. of butter fat, and was margarine." An objection to the complaint on the ground that it was self-contradictory and ambiguous was sustained.

Application of statutes

13–47   Section 16 (*b*) of the 1954 Act provides:

" The statement that an act was done contrary to a statute or order shall imply a statement that the statute or order applied to the circumstances existing at the time and place of the offence, that the accused was a person bound to observe the same, that any necessary preliminary procedure had been duly gone through, and that all the circumstances necessary to a contravention existed." [29]

Section 16 (*b*) goes on to provide that in the case of the contravention of an order, a statement in the terms above mentioned shall imply a statement that the order was duly made, confirmed, published, and generally made effectual according to the law applicable to the same, and was in force at the time and place in question.

With reference to this and the preceding statement from section 16 (*b*) it will be kept in mind that the word " order," as used in the 1954 Act, means " any order, byelaw, rule, or regulation having statutory authority." [30] Section 16 (*b*) relates only to the form of complaint and does not affect the proof of any order. A byelaw not having the probative force of a statute must be proved, even where the prosecution is in a burgh court for contravention of a burgh byelaw. It is proved by the prosecutor putting a copy in evidence at any time before closing his case. [31]

Validity of orders and byelaws

13–48   It is now settled that (although the determination of such a question in a summary process may be inconvenient) [32] any person charged in a court of summary jurisdiction with the contravention of an order or byelaw which has not been declared to have the force of statute may competently challenge the validity of the same either as being ultra vires or on any other competent ground, even although, in the case of a byelaw, the approval of the sheriff and of the Secretary of State has been obtained. [33] Apart, however, from any question of inconvenience arising from the

[29] Cf. *Yeudall* v. *Sweeney*, 1922 J.C. 32.
[30] 1954 Act, s. 77.
[31] *Herkes* v. *Dickie*, 1958 J.C. 51.
[32] *Stewart* v. *Todrick* (1907) 5 Adam 432, Lord McLaren at 542; *Henderson* v. *Ross*, 1928 J.C. 74, L.J.-G. at 77; *Sommerville* v. *Langmuir*, 1932 J.C. 55, L.J.-C. at 59. But see *David Lawson Ltd.* v. *Torrance*, 1929 J.C. 119, L.J.-G. at 121.
[33] *Shepherd* v. *Howman*, 1918 J.C. 78 (government order); *David Lawson Ltd.* v. *Torrance*, supra (byelaw). In this case L.J.-G. Clyde reserved his opinion regarding the position of byelaws declared to have the force of statute. (See also *Forster* v. *Polmaise Patent Fuel Co., Ltd.*, 1947 J.C. 56; *Macdonald* v. *Mackenzie*, 1947 J.C. 122; *Marshall* v. *Clark*, 1957 J.C. 68.)

form of process, this defence is attended with difficulty when it relates to a government order and is advanced in a court of summary jurisdiction other than the sheriff court. In such a case the prosecutor can represent neither the Crown nor the department responsible for making the order, and the proper contradictors are, accordingly, absent.[34] Moreover, " A successful appeal in a stated case on the ground that an Order made by a Government Department was *ultra vires* must depend on this being apparent on the face of the Order or in virtue of the stated facts." [35] Questions of ultra vires are, in any event, plainly unsuitable for determination by lay tribunals, and a prosecutor who has reason to expect this defence should not bring in one of these courts a summary complaint which can equally well be prosecuted in the sheriff court.

Reference to leading sections only

3-49   " Where the offence is created by more than one section of one or more statutes or orders, it shall be necessary to specify only the leading section or one of the leading sections." [36]

As this enactment lessens the amount of specification which it would normally be obligatory on a prosecutor to give when libelling a statutory charge of the type to which it refers, it must be strictly construed.[37] Although the provision appears to contemplate that only one section need be specified, a reference to the forms of statutory charges contained in Part II of the Second Schedule shows that, if the section constituting the offence has been amended by subsequent legislation, the amending statutes and sections must also be specified, and that, where an order or byelaw is alleged to have been contravened, the statutory provision authorising the same must be libelled as well as the order or byelaw.[38]

The section or sections libelled by the prosecutor must be leading sections within the meaning of the enactment.[39] " In my opinion the test in each case for the Court to apply must be whether the complaint on the face of it gives to the person charged fair and reasonable notice of what it is he is charged with, and what offence he is said to have committed; and I do not think that it can be said to be fair notice to select as the sole ground libelled one section of an Act, and to reserve for future introduction and application any number of unlibelled sections, some of which may bear directly on the charge." [40]

---

[34] *Sommerville* v. *Langmuir*, supra, Lord Anderson and L.J.-C. at 59.
[35] Ibid., Lord Hunter at 57, 58. A plea to the relevancy of a complaint on the ground that it proceeds upon an order or byelaw which is ultra vires will, if not stated in the court below, only be considered by the High Court on appeal if the objection arises ex facie of the complaint or of the order or byelaw and amounts to fundamental nullity (*O'Malley* v. *Strathern*, 1920 J.C. 74; *Black* v. *Robertson*, 1954 S.L.T. 329). As an example of a case relating to byelaws where the defence was raised in the stated case to the court, see *Aldred* v. *Langmuir*, 1932 J.C. 22.
[36] 1954 Act, s. 16 (c).
[37] *Macrorie* v. *Bird* (1911) 6 Adam 527, L.J.-C. at 534.
[38] Ibid. The forms are imperative (s. 16).
[39] Ibid., Lord Dundas at 532. Statutes which are only indirectly involved do not require to be libelled. See *Tighe* v. *Wilson* (1912) 7 Adam 46. As to omission of the section, see supra, para. 13-39.   [40] *Macrorie* v. *Bird*, Lord Dundas at 533.

The enactment was considered in *Macrorie* v. *Bird*.[41] In that case the owner of a motor car was charged that he " did deliver a declaration such as is mentioned in the Revenue Act, 1869, section 22, relating to a motor car numbered S.D. 148, wherein the particulars required by said Act to be therein set forth were not fully and truly stated," in that the cylinder measurements were not given, " contrary to said section, whereby you are liable to the penalty of £20." Section 22 neither created an offence nor imposed a penalty, this being effected by section 25 of the same Act. It was held that the section was not " the leading section or one of the leading sections."

Exceptions and qualifications, etc.

13–50   " Any exception, exemption, proviso, excuse, or qualification, whether it does or does not accompany in the same section the description of the offence in the statute or order creating the offence, may be proved by the accused, but need not be specified or negatived in the complaint, and no proof in relation to such exception, exemption, proviso, excuse or qualification shall be required on behalf of the prosecution." [42]

If the statute containing the section which is alleged to have been contravened limits its application by permitting the acts charged to be done by certain persons or in certain circumstances, the accused is entitled to prove, if he can, that he is one of the class so protected, but the prosecutor does not require to anticipate this defence either by negativing it in his complaint or by leading evidence to disprove it.[43] In *McCluskey* v. *Boyd*,[44] where the accused was prosecuted upon a summary complaint for trafficking in exciseable liquor without a certificate, it was held that it was not necessary for the prosecutor to prove that the accused had no certificate. it being for the accused to prove, if he could, that he had one. This case has, however, been much criticised and is no longer of authority.[45] Section 16 (*d*) applies: " where there is first of all a description of an offence . . . and an exception which is something apart from that description. The exception may be in the same section, or subsection, but it must be independent of the description of the offence itself." [46] In *Cruickshank* v. *Smith* [47] it was held that in a charge of fishing by a person " not having a legal right or permission from the proprietor," [48] the prosecutor must prove the lack of right or permission. In *British Transport Commission* v. *Dalgleish* [49] the court was concerned with a provision in section 135 of the Railways Clauses

---

[41] Supra.
[42] 1954 Act, s. 16 (*d*).
[43] *McCluskey* v. *Boyd* (1916) 7 Adam 742; *Chalmers* v. *Speedwell Wire Co.*, 1942 J.C. 42.
[44] Supra.
[45] *British Transport Commission* v. *Dalgleish*, 1955 J.C. 80; *Chalmers* v. *Speedwell Wire Co.*, supra, L.J.-C. at 48; *Cruickshank* v. *Smith*, 1949 J.C. 134, L.J.-C. at 141.
[46] *Muir* v. *Grant and Co.*, 1948 J.C. 42, Lord Carmont at 46.
[47] Supra.
[48] See now Salmon and Freshwater Fisheries (Protection) (Scotland) Act 1951, s. 1.
[49] Supra.

Consolidation (Scotland) Act 1845 that no penalty was recoverable for any offence under the Act unless notice was given by publishing particulars of the offence and penalty in certain ways, and held that such publication must be proved by the prosecutor. In *Chalmers* v. *Speedwell Wire Co. Ltd.*[50] it was held that a summary complaint charging the company with contravening section 13 (1) of the Factories Act 1937, by failing securely to fence transmission machinery, did not require to libel the exception introduced by the words " unless it is in such a position or of such construction as to be as safe to every person employed or working on the premises as it would be if securely fenced " occurring in the sub-section. In *Archibald* v. *Plean Colliery Co. Ltd.*,[51] a clause of exception contained in a regulation made under the Coal Mines Act 1911 was held to be itself a condition prerequisite to the offence and one which the prosecutor required to libel and to negative in proof. In that case, also, as has since been pointed out,[52] the complaint in terms negatived the exceptions which the prosecutor later failed to exclude by evidence. *Archibald* has, however, been the subject of judicial disapproval and has been said to be a special case laying down no general principle.[53]

Nimmo v. *Alexander Cowan & Sons* [54] was an appeal to the House of Lords in a civil action for breach of section 29 of the Factories Act 1961 which provides that every working place " shall, so far as is reasonably practicable, be made and kept safe . . ." It was held to be unnecessary for the pursuer to aver that it was not reasonably practicable to make and keep the place in question safe. Lord Pearson said of section 16 (*d*) of the 1954 Act, " If some enactment *prima facie* requires a stated result to be achieved but provides the defenders with a possible excuse, then it is for the defenders to prove the facts by which they contend that they are excused." [55]

3-51   Their lordships in *Nimmo* also considered the form given in the Second Schedule to the 1954 Act for charges against parents whose children fail to attend school,[55a] which includes an averment that the child failed to attend school without reasonable excuse. Lord Pearson suggested that to be on the safe side this averment should be included by prosecutors, but that no further specification was necessary. He went on to state that no proof of this averment was necessary. The question of proof of this particular issue arose in *Kennedy* v. *Clark* [56] and the High Court held that no onus lay on the prosecutor to prove lack of reasonable excuse. Lord Justice-Clerk Grant observed that another situation in which no such onus lay on the prosecution was the case of persons failing without reasonable

[50] Supra.
[51] 1924 J.C. 77.
[52] *Chalmers* v. *Speedwell Wire Co.*, supra, L.J.-C. at 49.
[53] *Chalmers*, supra, especially Lord Wark at 50; cf. *Nimmo* v. *Alexander Cowan & Sons*, 1967 S.C.(H.L.) 79.
[54] Supra.
[55] At 114.
[55a] Contrary to the Education (Scotland) Act 1946, s. 35.
[56] 1970 S.L.T. 260.

excuse to provide a specimen of breath under section 2 (3) of the Road
Safety Act 1967.[57]

Special capacities

13–52   " Where an offence is alleged to be committed in any special capacity,
as by the holder of a licence, master of a vessel, occupier of a house, or
the like, the fact that the accused person possesses the qualification necessary to the commission of the offence shall, unless challenged by preliminary objection before his plea is recorded, be held as admitted." [57a]

This provision affects proof rather than libelling, but it may be
mentioned here, because it implies that, where a person is to be charged
with committing an offence in a special capacity, the complaint must
state that he was acting in that capacity at the time in question. Unless
the accused at the first calling of the case challenges the statement it will
be held to have been proved. Two cases illustrate this point. In *Smith* v.
Grant [58] a hotel-keeper was charged, as holder of a certificate for his hotel,
with selling liquor outwith permitted hours, in breach of his certificate.
No preliminary objection was taken to the description of the accused
as being the holder of a certificate. The certificate was not produced
at the trial, and no evidence was led regarding its terms. The accused
appealed against his conviction on the ground of the non-production of
the certificate and the failure to prove its terms. The court refused the
appeal, holding that, in terms of section 19 (5) of the 1908 Act, the possession by the accused of a certificate in statutory form must be held as
admitted, and that a breach of the terms of such certificate was necessarily
involved in the sale of liquor outwith permitted hours. Again, in *Thomas
W. Ward Ltd.* v. *Waugh* [59] the accused was charged on a complaint which
set forth that, being the owners of the vessel *Tiger*, then being broken up
in Inverkeithing Bay, they allowed oil to escape from the vessel contrary
to section 1 (1) of the Oil in Navigable Waters Act 1922. The accused,
having been convicted, maintained on appeal that the *Tiger* was not a
vessel within the meaning of that Act. It was held that they were barred
by section 19 (5) of the 1908 Act from maintaining that the *Tiger* was not a
vessel, no preliminary objection having been taken to their description in
the complaint as " the owners of the vessel *Tiger*."

13–53   It was held in *Archibald* v. *Plean Colliery Co.*,[60] where no preliminary
objection was taken by the accused, that the prosecution can waive the
statutory presumption set up by section 16 (*f*). In that case the complaint
charged a colliery company and certain persons in their official capacities
with an infringement of a mining regulation, describing the managing
director of the company as " agent " of the mine. No preliminary objection
was taken by him to this description, but the prosecutor at the trial did not

[57] At 262.
[57a] 1954 Act, s. 16 (*f*).
[58] 1932 J.C. 36.
[59] 1934 J.C. 13.
[60] 1924 J.C. 77.

found on the absence of objection as inferring an admission of agency, and the parties joined issue on the question of agency and led evidence thereon. The sheriff having found it not proven that the managing director was agent of the mine, the prosecutor, on appeal, sought to invoke the provisions of section 19 (5) of the 1908 Act, which are identical with those of section 16 (f). It was held that, as he had not founded on section 19 (5) before the sheriff but had joined issue on the question of agency, he must be held to have waived his right to found on the statutory presumption created by the section. This decision was commented on in *Smith* v. *Ross*,[61] in which its soundness was doubted by Lord Mackay, with whose observations Lord Wark concurred. The observations in *Smith* v. *Ross* are authority that the Crown does not lose the protection of section 16 (f) merely by introducing evidence on the point in issue. They may, however, lose it if they allow the defence to cross-examine or lead evidence on the point, thus creating a situation in which issue is joined between the parties on the capacity in which the accused is charged.[62]

3–54   If the position libelled as being held by the accused does not impose responsibility on him for the offence charged, section 16 (f) does not apply.[63] In *Shiach* v. *Farquhar*[64] the complaint stated that, " being the master or person in charge " of a steam drifter, the accused engaged in illegal fishing, contrary to a certain byelaw made by the Fishery Board for Scotland and to two named statutes. Neither the byelaw nor these Acts imposed vicarious liability upon the master of a vessel for such an offence. The sheriff having acquitted the accused on the ground that it was not proved that he was in charge of the vessel at the time in question, it was held on appeal that, as there was no statutory provision making the master of a vessel liable as such for a contravention of the byelaw, and as the byelaw might be contravened by " any person," the prosecutor could not invoke the provisions of section 19 (5) of the 1908 Act, but was bound to prove that the accused was on board the vessel at the time of the offence. A conviction of the master of a vessel for a contravention of the same byelaw under identical circumstances was, however, upheld in *Smith* v. *Ross*.[65] In that case the complaint (unlike that in *Shiach* v. *Farquhar*, which did not state under what statute the byelaw was made) libelled the byelaw as having been made by the Fishery Board for Scotland under powers conferred on them by the Sea Fisheries (Scotland) Amendment Act 1885. This statute made contravention of such a byelaw an offence under the Sea Fisheries Act 1883, an Act which clearly imposed vicarious liability upon the masters of sea-fishing boats for offences against the Act committed by any person on board.[66] Accordingly, *Shiach* v. *Farquhar* was decided upon the mistaken view that the accused was not vicariously liable for the offence charged. It illustrates, however,

---

[61] 1937 J.C. 65.
[62] Supra, Lord Mackay at 74, Lord Wark at 75. See also *Rendle* v. *Thomson*, 1947 S.L.T. (Notes) 27.
[63] In this connection *Frame* v. *Fyfe*, 1948 J.C. 140 may be referred to.   [64] 1929 J.C. 88.
[65] 1937 J.C. 65.   [66] s. 20 (1).

the position as regards section 16 (*f*) in cases where a qualification has been libelled which is not relevant to the complaint.

Nationality of ship

13–55   In any proceedings under the Merchant Shipping Acts it is unnecessary to produce the official register of the ship referred to in such proceedings in order to prove the nationality of said ship, but the nationality of the ship as stated in the complaint is, in absence of evidence to the contrary, presumed.[67]

This provision also affects proof rather than libelling, but it has to be noted here because it reminds the prosecutor, in proceedings under the Merchant Shipping Acts, to state the nationality of any ship concerned in the charge.

Value of stolen property

13–56   In offences inferring dishonest appropriation of property brought before a court whose power to deal with such offences is limited to cases in which the value of such property does not exceed £10, it is to be assumed, and it is unnecessary to state in the charge, that the value of the property does not exceed said sum.[68]

In view of section 45 of the 1963 Act the reference to £10 should probably have been replaced by a reference to £25, but Parliament omitted to make the appropriate amendment to section 16 (*h*) of the 1954 Act.

Intimation of penalties [69]

13–57   As already mentioned,[70] section 46 (1) of the 1949 Act abolished all references to penalties in a complaint charging a contravention of a statute or order, and section 15 (5) of the 1954 Act, following section 46 (3) of the 1949 Act, provides that the prosecutor must serve on the accused a notice in the form as nearly as may be of Form No. 1 of Part III of the Second Schedule. This form is in the following terms:

> A.B. Take notice that in the event of your being convicted of the charge[s] of contravening (*give reference to the section of Act or Order*) in the complaint preferred against you at my instance you will be liable to the penalties set forth in the said section [*or* in section of the said Act] namely (*set forth shortly the penalties*).
>
> C.D. Procurator Fiscal
[or Burgh Prosecutor]
[or Justice of the Peace Fiscal]
[or E.F. Complainer]
[or G.H. Solicitor for Complainer]
>
> (*Date*)

[67] Ibid. s. 16 (*g*).
[68] 1954 Act, s. 16 (*h*).
[69] Ibid., s. 15 (5) and Second Sched., Part III, Form 1.
[70] Supra, para. 13–28.

The 1954 Act does not give the prosecutor the option which he had under the 1908 Act of either referring to the section or sections imposing the penalties incurred or setting forth shortly the penalties themselves. He must do both now.

Two points may here be noted, viz.:

(1) The heading of the complaint intimating that it is brought under the Summary Jurisdiction Act is sufficient intimation to the accused that the general provisions [71] of that Act apply, e.g., the limitation of the periods of imprisonment, the powers of mitigation, admonition, competency of civil diligence in certain cases, etc. It was therefore unnecessary in former practice to refer in the complaint to any of these sections [72] and the position as regards the notice would appear to be the same.

(2) Under section 48 of the 1954 Act imprisonment in default of payment of a penalty is in every case competent, and that whether the statute imposing the penalty does or does not prescribe any method of recovery, the respective periods of imprisonment being regulated by section 49.

Accordingly, where only a pecuniary penalty is imposed, the notice may conclude thus—" you will be liable to a penalty not exceeding £   , and in default of payment to imprisonment in terms of section 49 of the Summary Jurisdiction (Scotland) Act 1954." [73]

When referring to the section or sections in which the penalties are set forth the prosecutor must be careful to mention the proper sections.[74] When setting forth the actual penalties, he must ensure that they are adequately set out.[75]

13–58 Where the accused is charged with committing a second or subsequent statutory offence for which the penalty exigible exceeds that competent for a first offence, mention of the penalty in the complaint will invalidate any conviction proceeding upon it.[76]

13–59 So, where the penalties were insufficiently set forth in a complaint under the Summary Procedure (Scotland) Act 1864, and the court held that the magistrate had been misled as to his powers of punishment, the conviction was set aside.[77] Again, where a complaint under the Summary Jurisdiction (Scotland) Acts 1864 and 1881 set forth a contravention of two Acts of Parliament, and the prayer craved the court to adjudge the accused " to suffer the penalties provided by the said Acts," but the

---

[71] ss. 40–51, 54–55.
[72] *Macleod* v. *Tarras* (1892) 3 White 339; *MacEwen* v. *Abinger* (1894) 1 Adam 314; *Stewart* v. *Uppleby* (1899) 3 Adam 6.
[73] Subject now to ss. 42–43C of the Act; see 1963 Act, Sched. 5. Infra, paras. 17–37 et seq.
[74] See *Cumming* v. *Frame* (1909) 6 Adam 57; *Galt* v. *Ritchie* (1873) 2 Couper 470; *Holland* v. *Gauchalland Coal Co.* (1867) 5 Irv. 561. *Thomson* v. *Wardlaw*, infra, was decided on the footing that the prayer of the complaint was misleading.
[75] See *Thomson* v. *Wardlaw* (1865) 5 Irv. 45; *Mackenzie* v. *Cadenhead* (1897) 2 Adam 443; *Reids* v. *Miller* (1899) 3 Adam 29. See also *Blains* v. *Rankin* (1892) 3 White 221.
[76] *Bryce* v. *Gardiner*, 1951 J.C. 134.
[77] *Thomson* v. *Wardlaw* (1865) 5 Irv. 45.

body of the complaint contained no reference to penalties, the court held that the complaint was irrelevant, Lord Justice-General Robertson remarking: " The complainer may either name the penalties or he may refer by chapter and section to the enactment which sets them forth. But it will not do to libel two Acts of Parliament, and then bid the accused read them through and find out what he is liable to." [78]

In another case a conviction was suspended because the complaint referred only to the pecuniary penalty to which the accused was liable and did not mention his liability to imprisonment without the option of a fine.[79] Where, however, this objection was taken for the first time during the appeal and did not appear in the bill of suspension, the court held that it came too late.[80] In a later case, a conviction was quashed in respect that the complaint, while specifying the fine to which the accused was liable, failed to state that he was liable to imprisonment in default of payment thereof.[81]

13–60 Convictions have been upheld in the following cases:

> (1) Where a complaint proceeding upon a statute which only prescribed imprisonment as a penalty craved a sentence of fine or imprisonment and to find caution, but the sentence actually pronounced was one of imprisonment only [82];
>
> (2) Where a complaint contained an unwarranted conclusion for expenses, but the conviction did not find the accused liable therefor.[83]

Errors in notices of penalties may be rectified by amendment.[84]

13–61 A disqualification for holding or obtaining a driving licence under the Road Traffic Acts is a penalty, and a statutory notice apprising the accused of his liability to such disqualification is a condition precedent to the power of the court to impose such disqualification. So, where a fine and a disqualification for driving were imposed on a person convicted under section 11 of the Road Traffic Act 1930, who had been served with a complaint and a statutory notice which failed to mention the possibility of such disqualification, the High Court, in a suspension, quashed the disqualification.[85]

13–62 There is no obligation on the prosecutor in the case of a common law offence to libel the Act or Acts of Parliament under which the judge is authorised to pronounce any particular sentence.[86]

---

[78] *Jackson* v. *Stevenson* (1897) 2 Adam 255.
[79] *Mackenzie* v. *Cadenhead* (1897) 2 Adam 443.
[80] *Macleod* v. *Tarras* (1892) 3 White 339.
[81] *Reids* v. *Miller* (1899) 3 Adam 29.
[82] *Chisholm, etc.* v. *Black* (1871) 2 Couper 49.
[83] *Rae* v. *Hamilton* (1904) 4 Adam 366.
[84] 1954 Act, s. 27.
[85] *Coogans* v. *Macdonald,* 1954 J.C. 98 (Full Bench).
[86] *Findlay* v. *Walker* (1908) 5 Adam 408; *McEwen* v. *Abinger* (1894) 1 Adam 314, Lord McLaren at 324.

13–63   Objections to entries in a notice of penalties, such as previous convictions, should not be dealt with until after conviction so as to avoid
bringing the accused's record to the notice of the judge.[87]

Risks attending simplified charges

13–64   There is one general observation to be made upon these abbreviated
forms of charge. They are very convenient in practice, but they are
open to a certain risk. It must be remembered that, although the statement
of certain elements and circumstances essential to the constitution of a
relevant charge is held to be implied in the complaint, this does not relieve
the prosecutor from the necessity of proving these matters at the trial,
except where, in terms of the statute, they are held as admitted. When
they were stated in the complaint, they were kept under the observation of
the prosecutor, and he led proof in regard to them as a matter of course.
Now, however, when they are not mentioned in the complaint, there is
a risk of their being overlooked. The practical lesson is that the prosecutor, before going to trial, must make himself acquainted with all the
facts which it will be necessary for him to prove, irrespective of whether
they are specified in the charge or not.

Cumulative and alternative charges

13–65   When several charges are brought against an accused person in the
same indictment or complaint, they may be libelled cumulatively if they are
such that he can competently be found guilty of them all at the same
time.

In *McCullochs* v. *Rae*[88] a general conviction on a complaint charging a
number of offences which were such that they might have all been committed by the same individual was held valid although the charges were
linked in the complaint by the word " or " and not by " and."

If, however, there are charges which are mutually exclusive (i.e.,
if convicted of one he cannot also be convicted of another) they must
be libelled alternatively.[89] A general conviction in respect of alternative
charges is incompetent.[90]

Where charges have been libelled without stating whether they are
cumulative or alternative, they may be treated as alternative.[91]

13–66   As the court will not convict anyone twice for one and the same crime,
a prosecutor cannot, in general, demand a conviction against an accused
person for more than one offence arising out of the same species facti, or libel
the offences cumulatively as separate crimes.[92] Certain offences against the

---

[87] *Boyd* v. *Gordon* 1968 S.L.T. 269.
[88] (1915) 7 Adam 602. See infra, para. 13–67.
[89] Supra, L.J.-G. at 607–8; *Drummond* v. *Hunter*, 1948 J.C. 109.
[90] Ibid.; *Lang* v. *Walker* (1909) 6 Adam 180. See also infra, para. 15–12.
[91] *Moore & Co.* v. *Wilson* (1903) 4 Adam 231, Lord McLaren at 236.
[92] *Scott* v. *Anderson* (1866) 5 Irv. 285; *Lauder* v. *Brown* (1889) 2 White 348. Cf. *Moore & Co.*
v. *Wilson*, supra and *Harris* v. *Adair*, 1947 J.C. 116, L.J.-C. at 120. See also *Duncan* v.
Smith, 1951 J.C. 1.

13–66 Game Acts,[93] and, possibly, some offences against the Night Poaching Acts,[94] form exceptions to this rule. Also, where a single course of conduct discloses two or more distinct and separate offences, conviction of one of which will not establish conviction of another, it has been held [95] that all the offences may be libelled in one complaint and a conviction obtained in respect of each of them. In the case in question the accused, who had been charged in the same complaint with contravening section 11 and section 15 of the Road Traffic Act 1930 (driving recklessly and driving while unfit through drink) and had been convicted and sentenced in respect of each charge, contended in an appeal that he could not be twice convicted and sentenced in respect of the same course of conduct. It was held that, as the offences with which he was charged were distinct and different offences and as there were sufficient facts in the case to prove each offence independently of the other, the convictions must stand. Moreover, when the means whereby a common law offence was committed also constitute a statutory offence, that offence can be libelled cumulatively with the common law offence, and perhaps must be so libelled if evidence is to be led of its commission.[96] So, where a telegraph clerk and an innkeeper were indicted at common law with defrauding certain persons by placing bets on horse races with them by means of telegrams sent after, but fabricated so as to appear to have been sent before, the races to which they referred, and the accused were respectively charged cumulatively, in addition, with statutory offences of forgery and incitement to forgery under the Post Office Acts, the court held that all the crimes were competently libelled.[97] In that case the law was stated by Lord Justice-Clerk Macdonald as follows: " Where a statutory crime has in fact been committed, it is not the view of the law that the offender should elude punishment for the offence merely because he is also guilty of a common law charge, and here arises the consideration of the distinction between the administration of justice under statute and at common law. In statutory offences the law prescribes an arbitrary punishment up to a certain amount, and under the common law a punishment only limited by the powers given by the law to the particular tribunal trying the case. This being the law, our practice is that where a statutory crime has been committed, as well as a common law crime, it is reasonable and proper that the judge trying the offender should have both these offences brought under his notice in passing sentence." [98] A common

---

[93] Under the Game Laws Amendment (Scotland) Act 1877, s. 11, an accused person who has been prosecuted for a contravention of a Game Act other than a Revenue Game Act can be prosecuted again in respect of the same action or actions in so far as they are offences against any statute relating to the Inland Revenue.

[94] See *Puller and Irvine* (1870) 1 Couper 398, Lord Cowan at 404; and *Moore* v. *Wilson*, supra; Lord McLaren at 236.

[95] *Harris* v. *Adair*, 1947 J.C. 116.

[96] Cf. infra, para. 18–81.

[97] *Wood* v. *H.M. Adv.* (1899) 3 Adam 64. But see *Strathern* v. *Caisley*, 1937 J.C. 118, L.J.-G. and Lord Fleming at 122.

[98] 3 Adam at 71–2.

law charge may also be libelled as alternative to a statutory charge arising on the same species facti.[99]

3-67 Where different offences are created by different sections of a statute it is clearly competent to charge them alternatively. Where one incident involves contraventions of a number of statutory provisions all may be charged cumulatively, at any rate where the facts relevant to each are not precisely the same, and where the offences libelled are not mutually exclusive or impossible of commission by one person at one time.[1] One could hardly charge a man with careless driving and dangerous driving at the same time; one can charge him with careless driving and failing to stop at traffic lights where, for example, he goes through the lights in the presence of crossing traffic which he ought to have seen, but in this type of case where the distinction between the two offences is rather blurred cumulative charges are not viewed with favour.[2] It is common practice, on the other hand, to charge a person cumulatively with unlawfully taking and driving a car, driving without insurance, without a licence, without a test certificate and without lights. Where different offences created by different sections are charged cumulatively, they must be separated out in the complaint, and a separate penalty sought on each.[3]

3-68 Difficulties arise where one section appears to provide for two or more separate offences. The logical principle is that where the section creates one offence and merely specifies different modes of committing it, an accused may be charged with all or some of the modes as one contravention, but where the section creates separate independent offences they must be charged alternatively. Where different modes are charged cumulatively the charge is still one charge of one offence and can attract only one penalty.[4] Unfortunately the cases are confusing and difficult to reconcile.[5]

Perhaps the clearest case is *Gemmell* v. *Weir & Patrick*.[6] The accused there was charged with permitting and suffering drinking and with selling and giving out drink, and was convicted " of the contravention charged." It was held that the conviction was good and was not open to attack as being a general conviction on alternative charges. The various acts alleged were not alternative offences but different modes of committing one offence—acting in breach of the terms of the accused's public house certificate. This case followed *Prentice* v. *Linton* [7] which was a charge of

---

[99] *Archibald* v. *Keiller*, 1931 J.C. 34, Lord Anderson at 41.

[1] Cf. *McCullochs* v. *Rae* (1915) 7 Adam 603, L.J.-G. at 607; *Graham* v. *Waugh*, 1938 J.C. 108.

[2] There is no reported authority on this matter, but the practice has been disapproved from time to time, and the Crown accepted that they could not obtain a conviction on both charges in *Pacitti* v. *Copeland*, 1963 S.L.T. (Notes) 52.

[3] *Aitchison* v. *Neilson* (1897) 2 Adam 284; *Graham* v. *Waugh*, supra.

[4] *Gemmell* v. *Weir & Patrick* (1892) 2 Adam 227.

[5] Cf., e.g. *Murray* v. *MacDougall* (1883) 5 Couper 215 and *Gemmell* v. *Weir & Patrick* (1892) 2 Adam 227; or the latter and *McCullochs* v. *Rae*, supra; or *Connell* v. *Mitchell* (1912) 7 Adam 23 and *Archibald* v. *Keiller*, 1931 J.C. 34.

[6] Supra; cf. *Courage* v. *Smith*, 1960 J.C. 13: " sell or supply " one offence.

[7] (1883) 5 Couper 210.

keeping and managing a brothel and knowingly harbouring prostitutes in contravention of an Edinburgh Police Act.[8] *Gemmell* v. *Weir & Patrick* distinguished the earlier case of *Murray* v. *MacDougall* [9] because there the charges had been of keeping open house, or permitting or suffering drinking, i.e. the modes had been charged alternatively, and so a general conviction " of the contravention " was bad.[10]

Later cases, however, suggest that the use of the word " or " is not conclusive. The real question is not so much the form of the charge as the propriety of a general verdict of guilty " of *the* contravention." Where the alternatives are only modes of the one offence such a conviction is competent.[11] It is competent to convict a person of trespassing in pursuit of game or rabbits,[12] or of driving while unfit through drink or drugs,[13] or of stealing, secreting or embezzling a letter contrary to section 57 of the Post Office Act 1953.[14] In *Connell* v. *Mitchell* [15] a charge of driving " recklessly or negligently " contrary to section 1 of the Motor Car Act 1903 was held to be bad because driving recklessly and driving negligently were separate offences, there being no generic offence of driving of which they could be alternative *modi*.[16] Lord Justice-Clerk Macdonald expressed the opinion that the different types of driving could be charged cumulatively.

13–69   The leading modern case on this question is *Archibald* v. *Keiller* [17] which approved what has become a standard form of charge under the Road Traffic Acts. The accused was charged with driving recklessly and at a dangerous speed contrary to section 11 of the Road Traffic Act 1930, or alternatively with driving carelessly and without due consideration contrary to section 12 of that Act. The propriety of libelling the two sections alternatively was accepted, but it was argued that it was incompetent to charge cumulatively and as one offence the different forms of driving under the respective sections. The defence argument seems to have been that there should have been e.g. a charge of reckless driving and a charge of dangerous driving, each with its own penalty, and it is not surprising that Lord Justice-Clerk Alness found difficulty in understanding the defence objection. Lord Alness and Lord Ormidale rejected this argument, following the dictum in *Connell* v. *Mitchell*.[18] They agreed that reckless driving and driving at a dangerous speed could have been

---

[8] See also *Macnaughton* v. *Maddever* (1884) 5 Couper 509; *Wilson and Others* v. *Renton* (1909) 6 Adam 166; *Graham* v. *Waugh*, supra.

[9] Supra.

[10] Cf. *Duncan* v. *Laing* (1888) 2 White 104.

[11] *McCullochs* v. *Rae*, supra; *Stenhouse* v. *Dykes* (1908) 5 Adam 553; *Drummond* v. *Hunter*, 1948 J.C. 109.

[12] *Morrison* v. *Anderson* (1913) 7 Adam 201; *Maxwell* v. *Marsland* (1889) 2 White 176.

[13] *Thomson* v. *Knights* [1947] K.B. 336; " Drink *And* a Drug," 1953 S.L.T.(News) 129.

[14] *Teesdale* v. *H.M. Adv.* (1896) 2 Adam 137. The phrase " indecent or obscene " is a tautology and a general conviction on a charge of exhibiting " indecent or obscene " articles is competent: *Galletly* v. *Laird*, 1953 J.C. 16, L.J.-G. at 29.

[15] (1912) 7 Adam 23.

[16] See also *Lang* v. *Walker* (1909) 6 Adam 180.

[17] 1931 J.C. 34; cf. *H.M. Adv.* v. *Murray* (1969) 34 J.C.L. 43, repd. on another point, 1969 S.L.T.(Notes) 85.   [18] Supra.

charged separately in one complaint as separate offences, and a separate penalty concluded for for each, but held that it was competent to combine them in one charge, and hardly open to the accused to complain at the prosecutor's leniency in so doing. There are two difficulties in the opinions of these two judges. One is that in addition to following *Connell* they relied on *Gemmell* v. *Weir & Patrick* [19] which was concerned with cumulative modes and not cumulative offences, which suggests that their Lordships were not clear as to that distinction. The other is that despite the agreement of the accused's counsel it is almost inconceivable that a person would be charged in the one complaint with two separate contraventions of the separate parts of either section.[20]

Lord Anderson's opinion is not free from difficulty either, and he too seems to have thought that *Gemmell* was concerned with cumulative offences. More importantly, he spoke of *Connell* as establishing that where a section prescribes a generic offence such as " dangerous driving " and specifies various modes of committing it, these modes are regarded as separate offences which cannot be libelled alternatively. This is difficult not only because of an apparent semantic confusion between offences and modes, but also because *Connell* held that the section there in issue contained distinct offences and not two modes of committing the same offence. It should also be noted that Lord Anderson regarded *Gemmell* as authority that even if it would have been competent to bring two separate charges of reckless and dangerous driving it would have been incompetent to conclude for two penalties. It is now settled law that the various forms of bad driving in each section (be they separate offences or not), may be charged cumulatively, but there would be much to be said for abandoning *Connell* (based as it was on the view that a person driving a car is not therefore versans in illicito) and holding that each of the sections creates one offence of very bad driving and of bad driving respectively.

13–70 It may be noted that although " causing " and " permitting " a statutory contravention are quite distinct, it is common to charge and convict of both cumulatively although only one is proved.[21]

13–71 Where a section which creates only one offence contains subsections which set forth different ways of committing the same, the prosecutor only needs to libel the section.[22]

Oath of Verity

13–72 A few Acts of Parliament introduced into Scotland the English form of a preliminary oath.[23] Where, as preliminary to any procedure, a sworn information is required, it may be sworn to before any judge, whether the subsequent procedure is in his court or in another court.[24]

[19] (1892) 2 Adam 227.
[20] It may be incompetent; *Aitchison* v. *Neilson*, supra; but see *Graham* v. *Waugh*, supra.
[21] See, e.g. *Mackay Bros. & Co.* v. *Gibb*, 1969 J.C. 26.
[22] *Wilson* v. *Renton* (1910) 6 Adam 166; *Stuart* v. *Clarkson* (1894) 1 Adam 446.
[23] See *McDonald* v. *Milne* (1897) 2 Adam 457.
[24] 1954 Act, s. 13 (3).

This removes the doubt which sometimes arose whether the oath of verity in a complaint under the Poaching Prevention Act 1862 could be emitted before a justice of the peace, seeing that the jurisdiction of justices of the peace is in Scotland excluded under the Game Acts.

Where a preliminary oath has to be taken, the justice of peace puts the witness on oath in ordinary form, reads to him the statement of charge, and asks him whether that is true. The witness depones that it is true, and the oath is signed by him and the justice of peace. The omission of the oath, where it is a statutory preliminary, is fatal to the proceedings.[25]

Warrants and Orders

13–73 When a summary complaint has been duly prepared and signed, the prosecutor has to consider whether it is necessary to apply to the court for any warrant or order. If the accused person is merely to be summoned to appear before the court, no warrant is required unless it is necessary to arrange for any special diet. The Act itself is a sufficient warrant for such citation.[26] It is only necessary to lay the complaint before a judge when it is desired to obtain a warrant to apprehend, or a search warrant, or some special order of the court.

13–74 On any complaint under the Act being laid before a judge of the court in which the complaint is brought, such judge has power on the motion of the prosecutor:

" (a) to pronounce an order of court assigning a diet for the disposal of the case to which the accused may be cited as after mentioned:

(b) to grant warrant to apprehend the accused where this appears to the judge expedient:

(c) to grant warrant to search the person, dwelling-house, and repositories of the accused and any place where he may be found, for any documents, articles, or property likely to afford evidence of his guilt of, or guilty participation in, any offence charged in the complaint, and to take possession of such documents, articles or property:

(d) to grant any other order of court or warrant or interim order of court or warrant which may be competent in the circumstances." [27]

Warrants of apprehension and search must be signed by the judge granting them; but all other warrants, orders of court, and sentences may be signed either by the judge or clerk of court. Execution upon any warrant, order of court, or sentence may proceed either upon such warrant, order

[25] *Morris and Boyd* v. *Earl of Glasgow* (1867) 5 Irv. 529.
[26] 1954 Act, s. 18 (1).
[27] 1954 Act, s. 17 (1).

of court, or sentence itself, or upon an extract thereof issued and signed by the clerk of court.[28]

3-75　　In virtue of the definition of " clerk of court " contained in the 1908 Act, section 2, the clerk, if not the principal clerk or his depute, had to be " duly authorised " to exercise the duties of clerk of court; and " duly authorised," having regard to previous decisions, would doubtless be interpreted as meaning duly authorised in writing.[29] " Clerk of court " is not defined in the 1954 Act.

Citation of Accused and Witnesses

3-76　　The 1954 Act itself is a sufficient warrant for the citation of the accused and witnesses in a summary prosecution to any ordinary sitting of the court, or to any special diet fixed by the court, or any adjournment thereof. Such citation is in the form, as nearly as may be, of the appropriate form contained in Part IV of the Second Schedule. In the case of the accused it proceeds on an induciae of at least forty-eight hours, unless in the special circumstances of the case the court fixes a shorter induciae.[30] In the ordinary case the induciae allowed is more than forty-eight hours. Certain statutes prescribe their own induciae. Prior to the passing of the 1908 Act, failure to adhere to the induciae prescribed by such statutes was fatal to the proceedings,[31] but the point has not been considered in the light of the limited powers conferred on the High Court by section 73 of the 1954 Act. Section 26 of the Interpretation Act 1889 provides that service of a document by post is deemed to be effected by properly addressing, preparing, and posting a letter containing the document and, unless the contrary is proved, to have been effected at the time at which the letter would be delivered in the ordinary course of post.

3-77　　There is no warrant for citation until the complaint is signed.[32] The provisions of the 1954 Act regarding the notices to be given to the accused of the statutory penalties and previous convictions have already been considered.[33] Most prosecutors send along with the citation a notice informing the accused of his right to plead by letter under the 1954 Act, but these notices have no statutory authority and must be carefully worded so as to avoid any possibility of misleading the accused.[34] The Act fixes no induciae in the case of witnesses, but they should be given at least forty-eight hours' notice whenever possible. They are not liable to prosecution for failure to attend for precognition unless given twenty-four hours' notice.[35] In the case of the accused the induciae must not be shortened to such an extent as to prejudice his defence.

[28] 1954 Act, s. 13 (2).
[29] 1908 Act, s. 2; *Brown and Bryson* v. *Neilson* (1906) 5 Adam 149.
[30] 1954 Act, s. 18.
[31] *Dunlop* v. *Goudie* (1895) 1 Adam 554; *Laird* v. *Anderson* (1895) 2 Adam 18.
[32] *Stewart* v. *Lang* (1894) 1 Adam 493; cf. *Collins* v. *Lang* (1887) 1 White 482.
[33] Supra, paras. 13–28, 13–32.
[34] *Loughbridge* v. *Mickel*, 1947 J.C. 21.
[35] 1954 Act, s. 33 (4). See infra, para. 13–83.

Modes of citation

13–78   It is to be deemed a legal citation of such accused or witness in terms of sections 2 (2) to 2 (4) of the Act of Adjournal:

" (2) (*a*) if the citation be delivered to him personally or left for him at his dwelling-house or place of business with some person resident or employed therein, or where he has no known dwelling-house or place of business, at any other place in which he may at the time be resident, or

(*b*) where the accused or witness is the master of, or a seaman or person employed in, a vessel, if the citation is left with a person on board thereof and connected therewith, or

(*c*) where the accused is a company, association or corporation, if the citation is left at their ordinary place of business with a partner, director, secretary or other official, or if the company, association or corporation is cited in the same manner as if the proceedings were in a civil court, or

(*d*) where the accused is a body of trustees, if the citation is left with any one of them who is resident in Scotland, or with their known solicitor in Scotland.

(3) It shall be deemed a legal citation of the accused to such a sitting or diet or adjourned sitting or diet [of a summary court], if the citation be signed by the prosecutor and sent by post in a registered envelope or through the recorded delivery service to the dwelling-house or place of business of such accused, or, if he has no known dwelling-house or place of business, to any other place in which he may at the time be resident:

Provided that, if the accused shall fail to appear at a diet or sitting or adjourned diet or sitting to which he has been cited in the manner provided by this subsection, paragraphs (*b*) and (*c*) of section 30 of the Summary Jurisdiction (Scotland) Act 1954, as amended, shall not apply unless it shall have been proved to the court that he received the citation or that the contents thereof came to his knowledge.

(4) The production in court of any letter or other communication purporting to be written by or on behalf of an accused who has been cited in the manner provided in subsection (3) hereof in such terms as to infer that the contents of such citation came to his knowledge, shall be admissible as evidence of that fact for the purposes of the proviso to that subsection." [36]

In the matter of service, the utmost care must be taken to secure that the citation will reach the person for whom it is intended. Personal service wherever practicable should be effected, or, failing this, the citation should be left in the hands of some responsible person, with

[36] Act of Adjournal (Summary Procedure) 1964, ss. 2 (2) and (3). S. 30 (*b*) and (*c*) of the Act deal with disposal in absence and the issue of warrants.

instructions to see to its delivery. Such care is especially necessary in regard to service on board ship.

Objections to citation

13-79 Section 26 (6) of the 1954 Act provides: " It shall not be competent for any person appearing to answer a complaint, or for a solicitor appearing for the accused in his absence to plead want of due citation or informality therein or in the execution thereof." [37] Where, however, the mistake renders subsequent procedure null, appearance by the accused cannot cure the defect.[38] So, in a prosecution under the Burgh Police (Scotland) Act 1892, section 447 of which contains substantially the same provision as that above quoted, it was held a citation upon an induciae of three days to answer to a complaint requiring one of six days was, despite the appearance of the accused, a fatal nullity, as he had never been properly before the court.[39] A conviction in absence resulting from a mistake in citation cannot stand.[40]

13-80 The service copy of the complaint must be substantially accurate. If it contains errors likely to mislead the accused upon a material point a conviction may be set aside.[41] The accused must, however, take objection before pleading to the complaint.[42] It is too late to do so after the leading of evidence has commenced.[43]

Notices of intended prosecution

13-81 Some statutes [44] require a special warning to be given to the accused of the intended prosecution. Such warning must clearly indicate the offence or offences which may be charged. Where only a general warning containing no such indication was given the conviction was quashed.[45]

Citation not essential

13-82 The provisions of section 15 (5) and section 31 (1) (a) of the 1954 Act requiring service to be made on the accused of the complaint along with a special notice (a) where the offence is statutory, and (b) where, in the event of his conviction, a list of previous convictions is to be laid before the court, appear to be the only statutory provisions requiring citation or service of the complaint. Subject to these modifications, it would still

---

[37] Cf. *Armstrong* v. *Stevenson* (1892) 3 White 373; *Stewart* v. *McNiven* (1891) 2 White 627; *Maitland* v. *Neilson* (1892) 3 White 298.

[38] *Laird* v. *Anderson* (1895) 2 Adam 18.

[39] Ibid.

[40] *Waddell* v. *Romanes* (1857) 2 Irv. 611.

[41] See *Stewart* v. *Lang* (1894) 1 Adam 493 (failure to mention alternative crave for imprisonment without the option of a penalty). As examples of non-fatal mistakes see *Chalmers* v. *Webster* (1871) 2 Couper 164 (service copy omitting statement which neither imported a separate offence nor involved a larger penalty); and *Niven* v. *Hart* (1898) 2 Adam 562 (word " strike " occurring in service copy instead of " kick "). Cf. *Boyle* v. *Skeen* (1972) 36 J.C.L. 110.

[42] *Dunsmore* v. *Threshie* (1896) 2 Adam 202.

[43] Ibid.

[44] E.g. Road Traffic Act 1960, s. 241.

[45] *Watt* v. *Smith*, 1942 J.C. 109. In that case dicta of L.J.-G. Clyde in *Taylor* v. *Horn*, 1929 J.C. 111, were approved.

appear to be the law, as laid down in *Kelly* v. *Rae* [46] that it is not essential to the validity of summary prosecutions that the complaint shall in every case be served on the accused, and that service can be dispensed with when the accused has been apprehended in flagrante delicto. [47]

In *Kelly* v. *Rae*, [48] which was decided prior to the 1949 Act and must, therefore, be read subject to the provisions of section 46 regarding statutory offences, the accused, a miner, was arrested on a Saturday in flagrante delicto and taken into custody on a charge of street betting. On Monday he was brought before a magistrate, when the charge was made in his presence. Having pleaded " not guilty," he was released without bail, the trial being fixed for the following Monday. Upon that day the accused and his law agent appeared in court and the complaint was read over to him. After hearing evidence the magistrate convicted. The complaint was never served upon the accused, and no copy of it was given to him or his agent; but no request for a copy was made by either of them. It was held that service was not essential. Apart, however, from any qualification introduced by section 46 of the 1949 Act, the following observations may be made as applying generally. Where the accused is not apprehended in flagrante delicto, he should be served with a copy of the complaint. [49] If he is a person of good character and has a known address it may be oppressive to dispense with service. [50] Further, if the charge is serious, or if the complaint is of a complicated character, absence of service may be an element in bringing about the quashing of a conviction. [51]

Citation for precognition

13-83   The provisions of section 18 of the 1954 Act as to the citation of witnesses apply to the citation of witnesses for precognition by the procurator fiscal or burgh prosecutor, where the judge on the application of such procurator fiscal or burgh prosecutor shall deem it expedient to grant warrant to cite witnesses for precognition in regard to any offence competent for trial in the court of such judge, and whether or not any person has at the time of such application been charged with such offence. Section 33 (4) (as amended by the 1963 Act) enacts that, (*a*) if any witness, after being duly cited in accordance with section 18 fails, without reasonable excuse, after receiving at least twenty-four hours' notice, to attend for precognition by a procurator fiscal or burgh prosecutor at the time and place mentioned in the citation served on him, or (*b*) refuses when so cited to give information within his knowledge regarding any matter relative to the commission of the offence in relation to which such precognition is taken, he shall be liable to the punishment for contempt of

---

[46] 1917 J.C. 12. This case related to a statutory charge.
[47] Ibid.; cf. *Carlin* v. *Malloch* (1896) 2 Adam 98 (a common law charge).
[48] 1917 J.C. 12.
[49] *Carlin* v. *Malloch* (1896) 2 Adam 98; and see *Kelly* v. *Rae*, supra, L.J.-C. at 15.
[50] *Carlin* v. *Malloch*, supra, Lord Trayner at 103; *Kelly* v. *Mitchell* (1907) 5 Adam 268.
[51] See *Ferguson* v. *Brown*, 1942 J.C. 113.

court prescribed by the section, a fine of £25. The prosecutor mould, of course, require to proceed by formal complaint.[52]

Where it is necessary to apply for warrant to cite witnesses in such circumstances, a petition under section 13 or section 14 of the 1954 Act in the form given in Part I of the Second Schedule to the 1954 Act is appropriate, according as to whether or not proceedings have already been commenced.

Service of Complaints, etc.

3–84 Any complaint, warrant, or other proceeding under the 1954 Act may without endorsation be served or executed at any place within Scotland by any officer of law.[53] Such service or execution may be proved either by the oath in court of such officer or by production of his written execution.[54]

3–85 Postal service is proved by written execution in the form of Form 3 of the Schedule to the Act of Adjournal of 6th February 1964, signed by the person who signed the citation, together with the post office receipt for the relative registered or recorded delivery letter.[55]

3–86 A warrant issued in Scotland for the apprehension of an accused may be executed in England and Wales by any constable within his police area.[56] Such warrant and any other warrant under the 1954 Act may also be served or executed in terms of the Indictable Offences Act 1848, the Indictable Offences Act Amendment Act 1868,[57] and the Summary Jurisdiction (Process) Act 1881.[58] Any warrant, order of court, or process to which said Acts apply may, if duly endorsed with a view to service or execution in Scotland, be so served or executed by any officer of law. The Indictable Offences Act 1848 and the Indictable Offences Act Amendment Act 1868 apply for the purposes of the Act to all offences which may be tried by the court issuing any competent warrant order of court, or other process.[59] Reference may be made to what was said on this subject in Part I.[60]

[52] Cf., infra, para. 18–98. Prior to the 1908 Act witnesses could not, in general, be compelled to attend for precognition in summary cases unless a charge had actually been brought (*Forbes* v. *Main* (1908) 5 Adam 503. See supra, para. 5–68).

[53] S. 77 of the 1954 Act (slightly modifying the definition given in s. 2 of the 1908 Act) defines this term thus—" Officer of law " includes chief constable, deputy chief constable, constable, sheriff officer, prison officer, and any person having authority to execute a warrant of court.

[54] 1954 Act, s. 22.

[55] Act of Adjournal 1964, supra, s. 5 (2).

[56] 1963 Act, s. 39 (1).

[57] Indorsation in terms of this Act permits execution of warrants, etc., in the Channel Islands.

[58] Under this statute a warrant endorsed in terms thereof may be executed in England by an officer of either the issuing or the indorsing court. The provisions of this Act will generally be found sufficient for the execution of summary process in England. It has been held that the function of a court of summary jurisdiction in Scotland when indorsing an English process under s. 4 of this Act is purely ministerial. Its duty is to make the indorsation craved if satisfied with the proof of the handwriting of the person issuing the English process, and it has no concern with any questions either as to the jurisdiction of the English Court in issuing the process or as to the relevancy of the statements contained therein (*Murphy* v. *Brooks*, 1935 J.C. 11).

[59] 1954 Act, s. 22.   [60] Supra, para. 5–35.

Arrest of Accused

13–87   The law of arrest, with or without a warrant, was discussed in Part I.[61] It is therefore only necessary to consider in this place the special rules of summary procedure.

It ought to be mentioned that there are special rules applicable to the apprehension of young persons under sixteen years of age. These are explained in Chapter 19.

13–88   A warrant of apprehension or search may be in the form, as nearly as may be, of the appropriate form contained in Part IV of the Second Schedule to the 1954 Act. Any such warrant, where it is necessary for its execution, implies warrant to officers of law to break open all shut and lockfast places. A warrant of apprehension of the accused person in such form as aforesaid implies warrant to search for and to apprehend the accused, and to bring him before the court issuing such warrant, or before any other court competent to deal with the case, to answer to the charge on which such warrant is granted, and, in the meantime, until he can be so brought, to detain him in a police station house, police cell, or other convenient place. A person apprehended under any such warrant or by virtue of the powers possessed at common law, or conferred by statute, must wherever practicable be brought before a court competent to deal with the case either by way of trial or by way of remit to another court, not later than in the course of the first lawful day after he has been taken into custody, such day not being a public or local holiday.[62]

13–89   A warrant of apprehension or other warrant is not required for the purpose of bringing before the court an accused person who has been apprehended without a written warrant, or who attends without apprehension in answer to any charge made against him.[63]

13–90   In any proceedings under the Act, the accused, if apprehended, is, immediately on apprehension, entitled, if he so desires, to have intimation sent to a solicitor, and to have a private interview with such solicitor prior to being brought before the court.[64] Refusal to grant an interview is not per se a bar to further proceedings.[65] When an accused person has been refused an interview with his solicitor his proper course is to bring the matter before the notice of the court at the first calling of the case. The court should then adjourn the diet to a later date to permit of an interview taking place.[66]

Arrest of Witness

13–91 Where a witness, after being duly cited, fails to appear at the diet fixed for his attendance, and no just excuse is offered on his behalf, the court

---

[61] Supra, paras. 5–10 et seq.   [62] 1954 Act, s. 20.
[63] Ibid.
[64] 1954 Act, s. 12. Cf. 1887 Act, s. 17.
[65] *Cheyne* v. *McGregor*, 1941 J.C. 17. Cf. *H.M. Adv.* v. *Fox*, 1947 J.C. 30; *Law* v. *McNicol*, 1965 J.C. 32.
[66] *Cheyne* v. *McGregor*, supra, L.J.-C. at 22. It has been held that after his trial has begun and evidence is being led it is too late for an accused person to ask for an adjournment to obtain legal assistance (*Mackie* v. *Crombie*, 1926 J.C. 29).

may issue a warrant for his apprehension. The court, if satisfied by evidence on oath that a witness is not likely to attend to give evidence without being compelled so to do, may issue a warrant for his apprehension in the first instance.[67] A witness who wilfully fails to attend after being duly cited is deemed guilty of contempt of court and is liable to be punished in accordance with the provisions of section 33 of the 1954 Act.[68]

13–92   A warrant of apprehension of a witness in the appropriate form implies warrant to officers of law to search for and apprehend the witness, and to detain him in a police station house, police cell, or other convenient place until the date fixed for the hearing of the case, unless sufficient security be found to the amount fixed in the warrant for the appearance of such witness at all diets of court.[69]

13–93   The power to issue a warrant for the apprehension of a witness who fails to attend after being duly cited is one which should be exercised with caution. As a general rule it is better not to move for a warrant of apprehension at the time, and before taking any action to ascertain whether there is any reasonable explanation for the non-attendance of the witness. If there is, he should be cited again if the diet has been adjourned. If punishment is not imposed forthwith under section 33 (1) of the 1954 Act upon a witness who wilfully fails to obey his citation, the prosecutor has the right, if he chooses, under section 33 (3), to proceed by summary complaint for contempt of court against him.[70] The power to issue a warrant to arrest and detain a witness likely to abscond is one seldom required in summary procedure, and one which should never be exercised unless in most exceptional circumstances, where it is evident that, unless such a warrant is granted, the ends of justice will be defeated.

Witnesses in England and Wales

13–94   Process may be issued under section 4 (3) of the Summary Jurisdiction (Process) Act 1881 to procure the attendance of a witness from England or Wales where the court is satisfied on oath of the probability that his evidence will be material and that he will not appear voluntarily. The witness is not subject to any liability for failure to obey the process unless a reasonable amount for his expenses is paid or tendered to him.

Legal Aid

13–95   Where an accused appears in custody in the sheriff summary court he is entitled without inquiry into his means to be represented by the solicitor on duty that day under the Legal Aid Scheme (" the duty solicitor ")

[67] 1954 Act, s. 19.
[68] 1954 Act, s. 33. Cf. *Pirie* v. *Hawthorn*, 1962 J.C. 69. See infra, para. 18–98.
[69] 1954 Act, s. 20.
[70] 1954 Act, s. 33 (3). Such a prosecution should be brought within a reasonable time and be dealt with by the judicatory (but not necessarily the same judge) within whose proceedings the contempt was committed (*Petrie* v. *Angus* (1889) 2 White 358). See infra, para. 18–98.

until the conclusion of the first diet at which he is called on to plead or, where he pleads guilty at that diet, until the conclusion of the last subsequent diet fixed for the disposal of his case.[71] The duty solicitor also acts in any application for bail made at the accused's first appearance, and any appeal in connection therewith.[72] Where on any day a duty solicitor is in attendance, as will normally be the case, no one may receive legal aid in respect of the services provided by the duty solicitor except from the duty solicitor unless he has instructed a solicitor on the appropriate list and that solicitor is present and willing to act.[73]

A person who pleads not guilty is not entitled to further legal aid unless the court considers that in all the circumstances of the case it is in the interests of justice that legal aid should be available and grants a legal aid certificate.[74] The same provisions regarding financial eligibility, the continuance of legal aid and the nominated solicitor as apply to persons in solemn proceedings apply to summary proceedings.[75]

If the accused wishes to take a stated case it is the duty of the nominated solicitor to act for him and to take the necessary steps to obtain an interim appeal certificate, and, if that is granted, to continue to act for him, and if an appeal certificate is granted to act in the appeal.[76] Where the appeal is by way of bill of suspension the nominated solicitor will take steps to apply for an appeal certificate, and if that is granted act in the appeal.[77]

Legal aid is not available in inferior courts of summary jurisdiction.

Bail

13–96 As there is no preliminary petition in summary procedure for warrant to apprehend, the question of bail does not usually arise for consideration until the accused person is before the court. As this would lead in many cases to hardship through a person being detained in the police cells on a trifling charge, the provisions of section 13 of the Police (Scotland) Act 1857 and section 471 of the Burgh Police Act 1892, conferring power on police officers to accept bail in certain cases where an accused person has been apprehended without a written warrant, were substantially re-enacted and made generally applicable by section 14 of the 1908 Act. That section is now replaced by section 10 of the 1954 Act, the substance of the provisions of which are as follows:

Bail by police

13–97   Upon the apprehension of any person charged with any offence which may be competently tried before a court of summary jurisdiction other than the sheriff court it is lawful for the chief constable, or other

---

[71] Legal Aid (Scotland) Act 1967, s. 2 (5) (*b*); Legal Aid (Scotland) (Criminal Proceedings) Scheme 1964, art. 8 (3).
[72] Ibid.
[73] Legal Aid (Scotland) (Criminal Proceedings) Scheme 1964, art. 8 (5).
[74] Legal Aid (Scotland) Act 1967, s. 1 (7) (*a*) (ii).
[75] Supra, para. 5–66.
[76] Legal Aid (Scotland) (Criminal Proceedings) Scheme 1964, art. 12.
[77] Ibid., art. 11.

officer of police having charge in absence of the chief constable at any police office or station, to accept of bail or deposit, by a surety or by such person, that such person shall appear for trial before such court, or before the sheriff court, at some time and place to be specified, and at all subsequent diets of court, and to liberate the person so apprehended upon bail being found to an amount not exceeding £20, or upon the deposit of any money or article of value to the amount of the bail fixed. The chief constable, or other officer of police, if deposit be accepted, must immediately enter the same in a book to be kept for the purpose, and grant an acknowledgment for the money or article so deposited, in which acknowledgment the time and place fixed for the accused's appearance must be set forth.

The chief constable or other officer of police may refuse, if he see cause, to accept bail in any shape; and the refusal to accept bail or deposit, and the detention of the person so apprehended until the case of such person is tried in the usual form, does not subject the chief constable or other officer of police to any claim for damages, wrongous imprisonment, or claim of any other kind whatsoever.

It is lawful to liberate any such person without bail, or to discharge him, if the chief constable or other officer deem it proper to do so.

If any person fails to appear in redemption of his bail or deposit, not only may the same be forfeited, but warrant may be granted for his apprehension.

Bail by court

13–98   As explained later,[78] an accused person may be liberated on bail by the court either before or after pleading.[79]

Duration of bail

13–99   Section 51 of the 1954 Act provides that any bail found shall be held to continue in force until the case is finally disposed of, or until the expiry of six months from the date when such bail is found, whichever is earlier, notwithstanding that the diets may have been from time to time continued or deserted pro loco et tempore, or not called.

Forfeiture of bail

13–100   The provisions of section 10 of the 1954 Act have already been noticed. Under section 30 (*d*) of the 1954 Act, where the accused fails to appear at any diet of which he has received intimation or to which he has been cited, the court may, on the motion of the prosecutor, forfeit any bail deposited or found for his appearance.[80] Section 51 prescribes the procedure to be followed where there is default of any payment of bail.

---

[78] Infra, paras. 14–51, 14–56.
[79] 1954 Act, ss. 21, 29 (*d*).
[80] See infra, para. 14–22.

13–101   Section 44 of the 1949 Act empowers a court which has ordered the forfeiture of bail to recall its order. The section is in the following terms:

" Where any court has made an order for the forfeiture of bail it shall be competent for the court, if it is satisfied that it is reasonable in all the circumstances to do so, to recall the order and direct that the bail money forfeited shall be refunded. Any decision of a court under this section shall be final and not subject to review." [81]

Appeal and review

13–102   The provisions of section 37 of the 1963 Act relating to applications to the court to review its decisions on bail [82] apply to summary proceedings.

The procedure for appeals in relation to bail is set out in section 11 of the 1954 Act which incorporates the substance of sections 5–7 of the Bail (Scotland) Act 1888 [83] which had in any event been held to apply to summary proceedings. [84]

Adjournment for Inquiry

13–103   The court, in order to allow time for inquiry or for any other necessary cause, and without calling on the accused to plead to any charge against him, may, from time to time, continue the case for such reasonable time as may in the circumstances be necessary, not exceeding in all a period of seven days, or, on special cause shown, twenty-one days, from the date of the apprehension of the accused, and may liberate him on bail or commit him to prison either without bail or with bail to an amount fixed by such court. No judge is entitled to allow bail in any case which he is not competent to try. [85]

These provisions may be applied by a judge or magistrate for the purpose of allowing further time for inquiry in response to an application presented to him by a prosecutor under section 14 of the 1954 Act. [86] They meet various difficulties which may arise e.g. in a case which may either infer a grave charge or a minor one, according to facts which cannot be ascertained at the moment, or again, where a delinquent is a stranger to the police and it is necessary to institute inquiries about him. Adjournments should not be for longer periods than necessary. They must be granted by signed interlocutor and be to a specified date. [87]

[81] Infra, para. 17–55.
[82] Supra, para. 5–61. As to bail generally, see supra, paras. 5–54 et seq.
[83] See supra, paras. 5–62, 5–63.
[84] *Liddell* v. *Strathern*, 1926 J.C. 107.
[85] 1954 Act, s. 21, as amended by 1963 Act, s. 46.
[86] *McPhee* v. *Macfarlane's Exr.*, 1933 S.C. 163. See supra, para. 12–32. See also *Kennedy* v. *Heatly*, 1951 J.C. 118.
[87] See supra, para. 10–04; infra, paras. 14–51, 14–53 et seq.

CHAPTER 14

PROCEDURE AT TRIAL

Diets of Pleading and Trial

14-01 In summary procedure there is not, as in procedure on indictment, an official pleading diet as distinct from the diet of trial. The accused is asked to plead at the first calling of the complaint in court,[1] and, in certain special cases, the trial may also be held then.[2] In general, however, the accused is tried at an adjourned diet. If the accused is not present at the first calling he can avoid being tried then by exercising his right under section 26 (3) of the 1954 Act to plead not guilty in absence, in which case the trial cannot proceed on that day.[3] Where the accused has been brought before the court on the first diet by apprehension he is entitled, if he makes the request before the prosecutor begins his proof, to an adjournment of not less than forty-eight hours,[4] but the case may proceed to trial at once or on a shorter adjournment if the court considers this necessary to secure the examination of witnesses who otherwise would not be available.[5] The court may from time to time and at any stage of the case, on the motion of either party or ex proprio motu, grant such adjournments as may be necessary for the proper conduct of the case.[6] A motion by the accused for an adjournment must not be oppressively refused.[7]

Adjournment for trial

14-02 Cases may arise where, owing to the distance of their homes from the court, accused persons prefer to be tried at the first diet, but, apart from these cases and those where delay may mean the loss of valuable evidence to either side, it is normally advantageous to hold the trial at an adjourned diet. Questions of relevancy [8] can thereby be disposed of without having to make preparations for the trial, and witnesses need not be brought before they are likely to be required.

The possibility of adjourned diets is provided for by Part IV of the Second Schedule to the 1954 Act, which contains a form which may be appended to the service copy of the complaint and which informs the accused whether, in the event of his pleading not guilty, his trial will take place at an adjourned diet or, if the court does not grant an adjournment,

---

[1] 1954 Act, s. 26.
[2] Ibid. s. 29.
[3] See infra, para. 14–21.
[4] 1954 Act, s. 29 (c).
[5] Ibid.
[6] Ibid. s. 29 (f).
[7] See *MacKellar* v. *Dickson* (1898) 2 Adam 504.
[8] Infra, para. 14–36.

at the first diet. The prosecutor is under no statutory obligation to inform the accused of his above-mentioned right under section 26 (3) of the 1954 Act, or of his right to plead guilty in absence under the same section, but it seems proper that he should do so, and a suitable note is frequently appended to the service copy of the complaint. Care must be taken to see that the wording of the note is not misleading.[9] The officer who serves the complaint should direct the attention of the accused to any note appended to his copy of the complaint. He should advise the accused regarding his right of pleading in absence and should, when the note intimates that the trial is to proceed on the first diet, inform him that any witnesses for the defence must be in attendance then. He can also inform the accused in such a case that, if he does not hear from him to the contrary by a certain date, he will assume that the accused desires to plead not guilty and the prosecution witnesses will be cited.

14-03 While the minimum induciae for citation is forty-eight hours,[10] it is suggested that, where practicable, induciae should be fixed as follows between service and the first diet:

From five to seven days when that diet is to be a pleading diet, and from seven to ten days when it is the diet of trial.

14-04 Section 17 (3) of the 1954 Act provides that where a diet has been fixed in a summary prosecution, it shall be competent for the court, on a joint application in writing by the parties or their solicitors, to discharge the diet so fixed and fix in lieu thereof an earlier or a later diet.

Record

Content and form

14-05 In summary proceedings no list of witnesses or productions is required from either party and the evidence is not taken down in shorthand, the only record being a brief note which the clerk of court is directed to keep by section 38 of the 1954 Act. That section is in the following terms:

" Proceedings in a summary prosecution shall be conducted summarily *viva voce*, and, except where otherwise provided,[11] no record need be kept of the proceedings other than the complaint, the plea, a note of any documentary evidence produced, and the conviction and sentence or other finding of the court:

" Provided that any objections taken to the competency or relevancy of the complaint or proceedings, or to the competency or admissibility of evidence, shall, if either party desires it, be entered in the record of the proceedings."

14-06 As previous convictions and penalties applicable to statutory charges are no longer set forth in the complaint, but are intimated to the accused under section 31 (1) (*a*) and section 15 (5) respectively of the 1954 Act, it is provided (in the case of previous convictions by section 31 (1) (*f*), and in

---

[9] *Loughbridge* v. *Mickel*, 1947 J.C. 21.
[10] 1954 Act, s. 18.
[11] E.g. by ss. 33 and 35 (2).

that of statutory penalties by section 15 (5)) that a copy of any such notice must be entered in the record of the proceedings.

Failure to enter a copy of this statutory notice in the record does not make the proceedings funditus null.[12]

14–07 Where the minutes fail to record the penalty imposed on conviction by a court of summary jurisdiction, it is too late to rectify the omission after an unsuccessful stated case. The High Court must take what appears in the minutes as conclusive of the proceedings in the lower court and, if no penalty there appears, must hold that no penalty has been incurred by the appellant.[13]

14–08 The proceedings may be either in writing or printed, or may be partly written and partly printed, and all forms bearing reference to any antecedent form may be either on the same sheet of paper therewith or on a separate sheet attached to it.[14] They are recorded in accordance as nearly as may be with the forms contained in the Second Schedule to the Act.[15]

14–09 The minutes of procedure are signed by the clerk of court. There is no exact statutory requirement prescribing when the record must be authenticated, but the opinion has been expressed by Lord Justice-Clerk Cooper that it is essential that this should be completed before extract or execution. In the case in question the minutes were not signed until the sixteenth day after the trial, but, in view of the absence of any exact statutory requirement and of the absence of prejudice to the accused, the court declined to quash the conviction.[16]

Witnesses' names

14–10 It is unnecessary to record the names of the witnesses examined. In any case of importance, however, and more especially in any case likely to to be made the subject of an appeal, it is desirable that a record of the names and designations of the witnesses examined should be preserved for future reference. As such a record is not a statutory requisite, errors in the description of the witnesses will not affect the validity of a conviction.

Plea

14–11 Any plea tendered must be noted. Failure to record a plea may be fatal to a conviction.[17] Where, however, the record of proceedings showed that, although the plea of not guilty stated at the first calling of the case was not recorded, the entry relative to the second calling stated that the accused " adhered to the plea of not guilty previously tendered," the court held that the omission to record the plea at the proper time was not fatal to the proceedings.

---

[12] *Bryce* v. *Gardiner*, 1951 J.C. 134.
[13] *Buckley* v. *Frew*, 1953 S.L.T.(Notes) 57.
[14] 1954 Act, s. 39.
[15] 1954 Act, s. 13 (1).
[16] *Furnheim* v. *Watson*, 1946 J.C. 99; cf. *Kelly* v. *MacLeod*, 1960 J.C. 88. See 1954 Act, ss. 13, 58 and 2nd Schedule, Part V.
[17] *Millar* v. *Brown*, 1941 J.C. 12.

A plea of guilty, if accepted, must be authenticated by the signature of the judge or clerk of court,[18] but it was held in one case [19] that failure to authenticate a plea of guilty admitted by the accused to have been given was merely a matter of form, and suspension was refused.

Documentary evidence

14-12   Any documentary evidence produced must be noted, but this applies only to documents actually produced by the witnesses as evidence in the case, and which are competent evidence.[20] What is truly documentary evidence of the character which should be noted is often a question of some difficulty. Before a writing can be used as documentary evidence there must be some fact which the writing proves or tends to prove.[21] Accordingly, documents which are produced merely for the purpose of identification, or in order to refresh the memory of witnesses,[22] or to explain their evidence, are not documentary evidence. The distinction is illustrated by the undernoted cases.[23] Lord McLaren stated as the test: " Is it necessary that the judge should read the contents of the writing produced, or is it only shown to the witnesses for the purposes of identification? " [24] The same judge in a subsequent case pointed out that " the reason for noting is that in case of an Appeal the Court may know the evidence upon which the conviction proceeds, and in case of the Judge refusing to admit the paper that the court may consider whether it was

---

[18] 1954 Act, s. 28.

[19] *Mackay* v. *Patrick* (1882) 5 Couper 132.

[20] *Eastburn* v. *Robertson* (1898) 2 Adam 607; *Marshall* v. *Phyn* (1900) 3 Adam 262; *Reid* v. *Neilson* (1907) 5 Adam 401.

[21] *Jacobs and Anr.* v. *Hart* (1900) 3 Adam 131, L.J.-G. at 141, Lord McLaren at 139–140.

[22] The position regarding documents used by a witness to refresh his memory is as follows: (1) until used they have no evidential value; (2) if used, they form part of the witness' oral testimony and considerations of fairness compel their production; (3) in no case do they constitute documentary evidence within the meaning of s. 38 of the 1954 Act (see cases cited in Note 20 and also *Hinshelwood* v. *Auld*, 1926 J.C. 4, L.J.-G. at 7, 8).

[23] The following documents have been held not to require to be noted as documentary evidence—bank notes stolen by the accused or exchanged by him for stolen notes produced only for identification (*Jacobs* v. *Hart* (1900) 3 Adam 131); receipt produced by witness to explain his evidence and retained by him (*Collison* v. *Mitchell* (1897) 2 Adam 277); plan in possession of witness used by him to explain his evidence (*Marshall* v. *Phyn* (1900) 3 Adam 262; cf. *Slater* v. *H.M.Adv.* (1899) 3 Adam 73, where held that a tracing made by a witness during examination in a trial for forgery to show the difference between two signatures might be shown to the jury although it was not a production); business books used by witnesses to refresh their memory (*Marshall* v. *Phyn*, supra); reports by medical witnesses, referred to by them, though not produced, but the contents of which were covered by their sworn testimony (*Ogilvy* v. *Mitchell* (1903) 4 Adam 237); driving licence handed by accused to sheriff on request and returned after perusal (*Bell* v. *Mitchell* (1905) 4 Adam 661); police book containing charges against the accused, which, during the trial, his agent asked for and was permitted to see, the entries having already been spoken to by police witnesses (*Reid* v. *Neilson* (1907) 5 Adam 401).

It has been held that the following documents require to be noted—letter produced and read to witness during cross-examination as having been written by her (*Avery* v. *Hilson* (1906) 5 Adam 56); plan prepared and produced for the purposes of his case by a prosecutor (*Strachan* v. *Watson* (1893) 1 Adam 55); a return alleged to be false and forming the basis of a charge of contravening the Lands Valuation (Scotland) Act 1854 (*Oliphant* v. *Wilson* (1889) 2 White 403); execution of citation of an accused person who had been tried in absence (*Powdrell* v. *Galloway* (1904) 4 Adam 432).

A bottle of beer has been held not to be documentary evidence (*Collison* v. *Mitchell*, supra).

[24] *Jacobs and Anr.* v. *Hart*, supra, at 140.

properly or improperly rejected." [25] The opinion has been expressed that the noting of documents which are not competent evidence is fatal to a conviction.[26]

Any risk of error in connection with failure to record documentary productions would be obviated if, when a document is produced by a witness, the clerk of court would ask either the prosecutor or the agent for the accused, as the case may be, whether it is desired to make that document a production in the case. In the event of any difference of opinion as to whether or not it is compulsory to treat the document as a production requiring to be put in, the decision of the court should be taken on the point. If the document is put in, it should be at once numbered and initialled by the clerk, and the date of production noted on it. The numbers in the inventory in the record should correspond with the numbers on the documents, and when this is attended to, the nature of the documents may be very shortly noted.

14–13   Prior to the 1908 Act [27] any failure to note a documentary production (as distinct from a trivial error in the recording of it which could not prejudice the accused) [28] was, in general, fatal to a conviction.[29] Such noting is still necessary under the 1954 Act, but its absence is not necessarily fatal, since failure to note productions merely amounts to a technicality, and so does not constitute a valid ground of appeal unless it has prejudiced the accused and so led to a miscarriage of justice.[30]

14–14   The court is not entitled to look at unproved productions when deciding the relevancy of a complaint.[31] The defence are entitled to use documents in cross-examination prior to proving them in the defence case.[32]

Regulations and orders

14–15   The Act lays down that " Any order by any of the departments of state or government, or any local authority or public body made under powers conferred by any statute, or a print or copy of such order, shall when produced in a summary prosecution be received in evidence of the due making, confirmation, and existence of such order without being sworn to by any witness, and without any further or other proof, but without prejudice to any right competent to the accused to challenge any such order as

---

[25] *Ogilvy* v. *Mitchell* (1903) 4 Adam 237, 245.
[26] *Eastburn* v. *Robertson* (1898) 2 Adam 607, L.J.-C. at 615, Lord Trayner at 617.
[27] s. 75.
[28] See, e.g. *Howe* v. *Knowles* (1909) 6 Adam 77.
[29] *Oliphant* v. *Wilson* (1889) 2 White 403; *Strachan* v. *Watson* (1893) 1 Adam 55; *Eastburn* v. *Robertson* (1898) 2 Adam 607; *Avery* v. *Hilson* (1906) 5 Adam 56; *Burns* v. *Williamson* (1897) 2 Adam 308.
[30] *Silk* v. *Middleton*, 1921 J.C. 69; *Ogilvy* v. *Mitchell* (1903) 4 Adam 237, Lord McLaren at 245; 1954 Act, s. 73 (1) (2). *Silk* v. *Middleton* was criticised by Lord Anderson in *Sutherland* v. *Shiach*, 1928 J.C. 49, 53, as effectively striking the requirement of noting out of the Act, but its principle is now well established: see also *Aldred* v. *Miller*, 1925 J.C. 21; *McDonald's Ltd.* v. *Adair*, 1944 J.C. 119; *Cameron* v. *Waugh*, 1937 J.C. 5; *Millar* v. *Brown*, 1941 J.C. 12; *Pennington* v. *Mackenzie*, 1946 J.C. 12; *Furnheim* v. *Watson*, 1946 J.C. 99; *Browning* v. *Farrell*, 1969 J.C. 64.
[31] *Brown* v. *Henry Dougal and Sons*, 1959 J.C. 60.
[32] *Hogg* v. *Clark*, 1959 J.C. 7.

being ultra vires of the authority making it, or on any other competent ground, and where any such order is referred to in the complaint it shall not be necessary to enter it in the record of the proceedings as a documentary production." [33]

It is necessary to produce copies of local byelaws even in a case like *Herkes* v. *Dickie* [34] where the byelaw was one made in 1941 by a burgh licensing court under the Licensing Act 1921 and the case was being heard in the police court of that burgh presided over by a member of the licensing court. It was conceded that byelaws of this kind must be produced unless the enabling Act gives them statutory status. Want of production could not be replaced by judicial knowledge even if the judge had taken part in making the byelaw.

14–16   Orders, etc., which do have statutory status form part of the general law of the land and need not be produced. All statutory instruments fall into this class. In other cases it is a question for the court whether the particular order or regulation does have statutory force. In *Macmillan* v. *McConnell* [35] the court considered an order of the Central Control Board (Liquor Traffic) made under the Defence of the Realm (Liquor Control) Regulations 1915 and held that it did not require to be produced. Lord Justice-Clerk Scott Dickson and Lord Dundas interpreted the regulation that " Every document issued by the Board . . . shall be received in evidence and be deemed to be such an order . . . without further proof unless the contrary is shown " as giving the order statutory force, and so making it part of the general law not requiring proof. Lord Salvesen expressed pleasure at what he called a technical objection being given its quietus. Lord Anderson went so far as to say that logically it should not be necessary to prove even byelaws, but he also expressed some regret at the decision, preferring the practice which had grown up of producing such orders. Lord Johnston and Lord Skerrington were also anxious about the possible effect of the case on an accused's right to fair notice, Lord Johnston suggesting the making of Acts of Adjournal to regulate the position. None has been made, and the 1954 Act repeats the 1908 Act provisions of which Lord Johnston said that the statement that orders " when produced " should be evidence of their due making did not involve an obligation to produce them in the absence of any call for their production by the court or the defence.[36]

Where there is any doubt as to whether an order or regulation has statutory force the prosecutor should produce it if he desires to found on it.

[33] 1954 Act, s. 35 (2).
[34] 1958 J.C. 51.
[35] 1917 J.C 43, overruling *McAvoy* v. *Cameron*, 1917 J.C. 1, and virtually disapproving *Todd* v. *Anderson* (1912) 6 Adam 713.
[36] See also *Brander* v. *Mackenzie* (1915) 7 Adam 609; *Hutchison* v. *Stevenson* (1902) 3 Adam 651.

Objections

14–17   Objections taken to the competency or relevancy of the complaint or the proceedings or to the competency or admissibility of evidence must, if either party desire it, be noted in the record.[37] It was formerly the view of the court that failure to note such objections vitiated the whole proceedings, this opinion being expressed in unqualified terms in *Connell* v. *Mitchell*.[38] Later decisions, however, have followed the line taken in *Silk* v. *Middleton* [39] in regard to documentary productions. So, in *Cameron* v. *Waugh*,[40] where there had been a failure to note objections but these had been noted by the sheriff-substitute and were fully disclosed in a stated case, Lord Justice-General Normand and Lord Moncrieff expressed the opinion (the case being decided on another ground) that the failure to comply with section 41 of the 1908 Act (1954 Act, section 38) was, in the circumstances, a mere matter of form, and, by virtue of section 75 of the 1908 Act (1954 Act, section 73), would not have been fatal to a conviction. Lord Moncrieff distinguished the case from *Connell* v. *Mitchell* on the ground that in *Cameron* v. *Waugh* the objections had been noted by the sheriff-substitute and considered on their merits. What was opinion in *Cameron* v. *Waugh* became decision in *McDonalds Ltd.* v. *Adair*,[41] where the circumstances were the same, stress being laid by the court on the fact that no prejudice to the accused had resulted from the failure to note objections. The appellant claimed that a further objection had been made but neither noted nor referred to by the sheriff. The court held that this objection was not before it, but that it could have been raised in a suspension which might also have included other grounds of appeal.

In *Galletly* v. *Laird*,[42] however, Lord Justice-General Cooper deprecated the tendency to refuse " to visit these irregularities with the extreme penalty of quashing the conviction." His Lordship went on to say that he recognised the futility of punishing a clerk's neglect by releasing a guilty man, but also felt the futility of the High Court uttering repeated exhortations yet condoning " a type of irregularity which involves disregard of a peremptory statutory requirement of manifest value in the due administration of justice." The court asked the Lord Advocate to take steps to see that the clerk did not repeat such acts of negligence.[43]

Objections should be noted in the minutes of procedure themselves and not on a separate paper, although, if the paper is referred to in the minutes, this may suffice.[44]

[37] 1954 Act, s. 38 (formerly 1908 Act, s. 41). In *Frame* v. *Fyfe*, 1948 J.C. 140, the opinion was expressed that s. 41 does not require the noting of objections when the request for noting is made by the successful objector.
[38] (1912) 7 Adam 23.
[39] 1921 J.C. 69.
[40] 1937 J.C. 5.
[41] 1944 J.C. 119.
[42] 1953 J.C. 16.
[43] At 27–28.
[44] See *Connell* v. *Mitchell* (1912) 7 Adam 23.

Correction of errors

14–18   Mistakes in the minutes of procedure may be rectified at any time prior to the execution of sentence,[45] even when the case is before the High Court on appeal.[46] If, however, the sentence has been carried out in whole or in part, the High Court has no power to authorise correction of the minutes and the lower court cannot do so, being functus.[47] So where, during the hearing of an appeal by stated case, it was pointed out to the court that the name recorded in the conviction was different from that of the accused and sentence had not been carried out, the court remitted to the sheriff-substitute to ascertain whether the procedure had been correctly minuted and to make any necessary correction.[48] Where, however, the sentence had been partially executed, the court held that the clerk of court of the lower court could not alter the minutes and that the High Court had no power to remit to him to do so.[49] In *Kelly* v. *MacLeod*[50] the accused was sentenced to imprisonment, disqualified from driving, and had his licence endorsed. Through error only the sentence of imprisonment was recorded contemporaneously. The accused began to serve his prison sentence immediately and his driving licence was taken from him. About a week later, the clerk of court entered the disqualification and endorsement on the minutes of proceedings. It was held that the execution of the sentence imposed had begun when the accused went to prison and that the subsequent correction of the minutes was incompetent. It was held further that as section 58 of the 1954 Act prescribes a time limit for the correction of errors, section 73 of that Act could not be invoked to allow correction at a later date, and accordingly the accused could be required to undergo the sentence of imprisonment but not to suffer disqualification or endorsement. The court held further that a note in the space provided on the front page of the complaint which recorded the accused's name and a sentence of 60 days' imprisonment and disqualification and endorsement had no statutory force, not being part of the record of proceedings but merely something inserted for indexing convenience. Where the minutes omit to specify the penalty imposed, the mistake cannot be rectified after an unsuccessful appeal.[51] Corrections must be authenticated by the initials of the clerk of court.[52] Alterations should be made openly and not by erasure.[53] An unauthenticated alteration may be fatal to a conviction,[54] especially if the correction has been made by means of erasure,[55] but, if such an irregularity is to be made a ground of appeal in a stated case, it must be properly raised in the case, otherwise the court will

---

[45] 1954 Act, s. 58. See also infra, paras. 15–32 et seq.
[46] *Wilson* v. *Brown*, 1947 J.C. 81; cf. *Anderson* v. *Howman*, 1935 J.C. 17.
[47] *Anderson* v. *Howman*, supra.
[48] *Wilson* v. *Brown*, supra.
[49] *Anderson* v. *Howman*, supra.
[50] 1960 J.C. 88.
[51] *Buckley* v. *Frew*, 1953 S.L.T.(Notes) 57.
[52] 1954 Act, s. 58.
[53] See, e.g., *Reids* v. *Miller* (1899) 3 Adam 29 (alteration of sentence).
[54] *Mackenzie* v. *Gray* (1898) 2 Adam 625.
[55] See *Reid* v. *Miller*, supra, L.J.-C. at 34; *White* v. *Jeans* (1911) 6 Adam 489, L.J.-C. at 496–7.

not consider it.[56] Omissions of essential matters from the record are not lightly to be condoned and may be fatal.[57]

Pleading in Absence

14–19 At the time of the calling diet the accused person may be in one of three situations: (a) in custody, in which case the accused has no option but to be present; (b) liberated on bail, deposit or surety, after having been apprehended [58] in which case he may be under an obligation to appear " personally " at all diets in terms of his bond [59]; (c) at liberty, not having been apprehended.

From the point of view of competency, however, the question as to whether he must, or need not, be personally present at the calling diet does not depend upon which of these three positions he occupies, but upon the terms of certain statutory enactments which govern every case, irrespective of the situation of the accused.

14–20 Pleas to competency and relevancy can, in all cases, be tendered on the accused's behalf in his absence in virtue of the provisions of section 26 (2) of the 1954 Act. That subsection is in the following terms:

" (2) Objections to the competency or relevancy of a summary complaint or the proceedings thereon may, in the absence of the accused, be stated by counsel or by a solicitor on his behalf, and where such objections are so stated the provisions of this Act shall apply in like manner as if the accused had appeared and stated the objections."

14–21 Pleas of guilty or of not guilty may be tendered in absence of the accused in terms of section 26 (3)–(6) of the 1954 Act. These subsections are in the following terms:

" (3) Where the accused is not present at a calling of the case in a summary prosecution and either

(*a*) the prosecutor produces to the court written intimation that the accused pleads not guilty or pleads guilty and the court is satisfied that such written intimation has been made or authorised by the accused, or

(*b*) a solicitor, or a person not being a solicitor who satisfies the court that he is authorised by the accused, appears on behalf of the accused and tenders a plea of not guilty or a plea of guilty,

then

---

[56] *Sutherland* v. *Shiach*, 1928 J.C. 49.
[57] *Macdonald* v. *Cuthbert* [1950] C.L.Y. 4662, where the court omitted to record fines and forfeitures.
[58] If the case can be competently tried by an inferior court other than the sheriff court, the accused may be liberated on bail, deposit or surety by the chief constable or other officer in charge of the police station, under s. 10 of the 1954 Act. Or he may have been brought before the court and liberated on bail under s. 21 without having been called on to plead.
[59] For terms of bail bond, see 1954 Act, 2nd Schedule, Part V; infra, App. C., Form 2 (3).

(i) in the case of a plea of not guilty,[60] the provisions of this Act except paragraph (*a*) of section twenty-nine shall apply in like manner as if the accused had appeared and tendered the plea, and

(ii) in the case of a plea of guilty, the court may, if the prosecutor accepts the plea, proceed to hear and dispose of the case in the absence of the accused in like manner as if he had appeared and pled guilty, or may, if it thinks fit, continue the case to another diet and require the attendance of the accused with a view to pronouncing sentence in his presence.

(4) Where in pursuance of paragraph (ii) of the last foregoing subsection the court proceeds to hear and dispose of a case in the absence of the accused, it shall not pronounce a sentence of imprisonment or of Borstal training or of detention in a detention centre, young offenders institution,[61] remand centre, approved school or remand home.[61a]

(5) In this section a reference to a plea of guilty shall include a reference to a plea of guilty to a part only of the charge:

Provided that where such a plea is not accepted by the prosecutor it shall be deemed to be a plea of not guilty.

(6) It shall not be competent for any person appearing to answer a complaint or for a solicitor appearing for the accused in his absence to plead want of due citation or informality therein or in the execution thereof."

Section 77 of the 1954 Act provides that, except where the context otherwise requires, " Borstal training," " detention centre " and " remand centre " shall have the like meanings as in the Prisons (Scotland) Act 1952.

Failure of Accused to Appear

14–22 It may happen that at the calling diet the accused is neither personally present nor competently represented, and has not intimated in writing a plea of guilty or not guilty. In such an event several alternative courses are open to the court under section 30 of the 1954 Act. These are not restricted to this diet, but may be adopted at any diet at which the accused fails to appear. Section 30 is as follows:

" Where the accused in a summary prosecution fails to appear at any diet of which he has received intimation, or to which he has been cited, the following provisions shall apply:

(*a*) the court may adjourn the trial to another diet, and order the accused to attend at such diet, and appoint intimation

---

[60] Cf. *Loughbridge* v. *Mickel*, 1947 J.C. 21.

[61] 1963 Act, s. 2 (2).

[61a] But see 1968 Act, Sched. 2, altering the powers of the sheriff to deal with children: infra, Chap. 19.

thereof to be made to him, which intimation shall be sufficiently given by an officer of law, or by registered letter signed
by the prosecutor and sent by post to the accused at his last
known address, and the production in court of the written
execution of such officer or of the post office receipt for such
registered letter shall be sufficient evidence of such intimation
having been duly given [62];

(b) where the accused is charged with any statutory offence for
which a sentence of imprisonment cannot be imposed [63] in the
first instance, or where the statute founded on or conferring
jurisdiction authorises procedure in the absence of the
accused, the court may, on the motion of the prosecutor and
upon proof that the accused has been duly cited, or has
received due intimation of the diet where such intimation
has been ordered, proceed to hear and dispose of the case
in the absence of the accused. Unless the statute founded
on authorises conviction in default of appearance, proof of
the complaint must be led to the satisfaction of the court.
The court in any case to which this paragraph applies may,
if it shall judge it expedient, allow any solicitor who satisfies
the court that he has authority from the accused so to do,
to appear and plead for and defend him;

(c) the court may grant warrant to apprehend the accused [64];

(d) the court may, on the motion of the prosecutor, forfeit any
bail deposited or found for the appearance of the accused,
or, where the accused has been ordered to attend under a
penalty, may declare such penalty to be forfeited, and such
bail or penalty may, where necessary, be recovered in the
manner provided in section fifty-one of this Act,[65] and in
addition to such forfeiture the court may grant warrant to
apprehend the accused."

Trial in absence

4-23   It will be observed that section 30 (b) of the 1954 Act does not permit
trial in absence in the case of common law crimes—the procedure being
made competent only in two classes of statutory offence, viz.: (1) When
the offence is one for which a sentence of imprisonment cannot be imposed;
(2) When the statute creating the offence, whatever punishment it imposes,
authorises procedure in the absence of the accused person.

4-24   The absent accused may be defended at the trial by a duly authorised
solicitor. Such solicitor or any other authorised person may, of course,

[62] See now also Recorded Delivery Service Act 1962.
[63] It is competent to impose disqualification for holding or obtaining a driving licence in
absence, but it is the practice in many courts to allow an accused an opportunity of making
oral or written representation before disqualifying: see *Sopwith* v. *Cruickshank*, 1959 J.C.
78.
[64] See *Walker* v. *Brander*, 1920 S.C. 840.   [65] See infra, para. 17–54.

tender a plea of guilty under section 26 of the 1954 Act. This section incorporates provisions of section 9 of the Law Reform (Miscellaneous Provisions) (Scotland) Act 1940, which superseded a slightly different provision in section 33 (2) of the 1908 Act. Service of the complaint is proved (a) by the oath in court of the officer who served it; or (b) by production in court of his written execution.[66]

14-25   Trial should not proceed in the absence of an accused person unless the prosecutor is satisfied that the accused has been validly cited to the diet. The court is not bound to deal with an accused person in his absence, even although he has pleaded guilty by letter under section 26, and it should not impose a heavy penalty such as disqualification for driving a motor car without some knowledge of the matter, particularly if the description of the accused in the complaint indicates the possibility of prejudice to the public interest from his disqualification. In such cases the court should often exercise its power of requiring the attendance of the accused.[67] Also the court must be careful if any person claiming authority to do so appears. In one case [68] where the manager of a firm appeared at the calling diet in answer to a complaint against the firm and the sheriff-substitute refused to recognise him as representing the firm and convicted it after trial in the absence of any other representative, the court quashed the conviction, holding that the sheriff-substitute was wrong in refusing to recognise the manager as representing the firm. Two of the judges expressed the opinion that, even if the sheriff-substitute was right upon this point, he ought to have adjourned the trial.

14-26   Where an execution of citation is produced as evidence of citation, it should be noted in the record.[69]

Plea of Guilty

14-27 The most simple form of trial takes place when the accused person is either personally present or is (in a case in which it is competent) represented by an authorised solicitor, or other person, and when he or his representative pleads guilty to the charge. It will be convenient to consider the steps separately.

14-28   Where the accused is present at the first calling of the case in a summary prosecution, and (a) the complaint has been served on him, or (b) the complaint or its substance has been read to him,[70] or (c) he has legal assistance in his defence, he should be asked to plead in common form.[71]

Failure to read the complaint or its substance is not, per se, fatal to a conviction.[72] So, where an accused person had some days prior to the trial been handed a copy of the complaint by the sheriff clerk, it was held that

[66] 1954 Act, s. 22.
[67] *Trotter* v. *Burnet*, 1947 J.C. 151, L.J.-G. at 153–4; cf. *Sopwith* v. *Cruickshank*, supra.
[68] *McAlpine & Sons* v. *Ronaldson* (1901) 3 Adam 405.
[69] *Powdrell* v. *Galloway* (1904) 4 Adam 432.
[70] Under s. 29 of the 1908 Act reading was imperative.
[71] 1954 Act, s. 26 (1).
[72] *Pennington* v. *Mackenzie*, 1946 J.C. 12.

failure to read the complaint or its substance did not invalidate his conviction as there had been no miscarriage of justice within the meaning of section 75 of the 1908 Act (now section 73 of the 1954 Act).[73]

If the accused is a foreigner and does not understand English an interpreter must be obtained.[74]

4–29   If the above requirements of section 26 (1) are fulfilled, the accused is asked by the judge if he pleads guilty or not guilty.[75] It is always competent for the court to continue the case under section 21 of the 1954 Act without calling on the accused to plead.[76] A partial plea of guilty, if not accepted by the prosecutor, amounts to a plea of not guilty.[77] If a partial plea is accepted, a conviction following upon it implies a dismissal of the rest of the complaint.[78] A procurator fiscal is not bound to accept a plea of guilty and may require the court to fix a diet of trial.[79] In that event it is the duty of the court to record the fact that the plea was tendered, and the plea can in no circumstances be used against the accused.[80] In one case the High Court refused to allow on suspension a plea of guilty to be withdrawn, Lord Adam remarking that this was not a case of an accused having been tricked or coerced into pleading guilty to a charge not understood.[81] The court may allow a plea given because of genuine misapprehension to be withdrawn.[82]

Objections to the competency or relevancy of the complaint or proceedings fall to be stated before pleading,[83] but, as such objections will usually be taken when the accused intends to plead not guilty, consideration of them is deferred.

Sentence

4–30   Where the accused pleads guilty to the charge or to any part thereof, and such plea is accepted by the prosecutor, such plea is recorded and signed by the judge or clerk of court. The court thereafter disposes of the case at the same or any adjourned diet.[84]

The accused person does not require to sign his plea, which is authenticated by the signature of the judge or clerk of court. To save double signature, the plea and sentence may be combined: " Compeared the

[73] Ibid.
[74] *Liszewski* v. *Thomson*, 1942 J.C. 55. See also *H.M. Adv.* v. *Olsson*, 1941 J.C. 63. See supra, para. 10–34. It is not enough that the accused is a foreigner. He must also be ignorant of English (*Furnheim* v. *Watson*, 1946 S.L.T. 297, L.J.-C. at 300).
[75] 1954 Act, s. 26 (1).
[76] An inferior court to the sheriff court may remit to that court under s. 9.
[77] *Cochran* v. *Ferguson* (1882) 5 Couper 169, L.J.-C. at 173.
[78] 1954 Act, s. 61.
[79] *Strathern* v. *Sloan*, 1937 J.C. 76. See also *Kirkwood* v. *Coalburn Co-operative Society, Ltd.*, 1930 J.C. 38. See supra, paras. 9–13, 9–14.
[80] *Strathern* v. *Sloan*, supra, L.J.-C. at 80.
[81] See *Spowart* v. *Burr* (1895) 1 Adam 539, Lord Adam at 546.
[82] The circumstances must, however, be very special. See *Williams* v. *Linton* (1878) 6 R. (J.) 12, see also *Sarna* v. *Adair*, 1945 J.C. 141. Cf. supra, para. 8–05.
[83] 1954 Act, s. 26 (1).
[84] Ibid. s. 28. See also 1949 Act, ss. 26, 27.

accused and, in answer to the complaint, pled guilty, and was sentenced to sixty days' imprisonment." [85]

14–31   The whole question of punishment is discussed in Chapter 17.

14–32   If the accused is known or suspected to be mentally disordered, the procedure described in Chapter 20 will be adopted.

Remitted cases

14–33   In courts other than the sheriff court, the duty of remitting to a higher court cases in which the crime charged cannot be tried in the inferior court, in terms of section 4, must be kept in view; and also the power of remitting those cases which the court deems more suitable for trial in a higher court, in terms of section 5.[86]

Previous convictions

14–34   The rules on this subject are discussed separately.[87]

Plea of Not Guilty

Objections to complaint

14–35   The accused may, prior to pleading, state objections to the competency or relevancy of the complaint or proceedings. No such objections can be allowed at any future diet of the case, unless with the leave of the court on cause shown.[88]

The principal preliminary objections were explained in Chapter 9, viz.:

           1. Objections to competency.[89]
           2. Objections to relevancy.[90]
           3. Pleas in bar of trial.[91]

14–36   There appears to be no reason why a sheriff ex proprio motu should not take exception to the relevancy of a complaint. He is not, however, entitled to dismiss the complaint as irrelevant without first allowing the prosecutor to be heard on the question of relevancy.[92] Where the accused person is represented by a solicitor, no review is permitted in respect of such objections, unless these were timeously stated at the trial.[93] Consequently, it is the solicitor's duty to be specially careful that every proper objection to the complaint or proceedings is stated before his client is allowed to plead. In *Walker* v. *Brander* [94] a summary complaint set forth that the accused, " being the owner or person in charge " of a dangerous

[85] 1954 Act, s. 28, 2nd Schedule, Part V.
[86] See supra, para. 12–31.
[87] Infra, paras. 14–65 et seq.
[88] 1954 Act, s. 26 (1).
[89] Supra, para. 9–09.
[90] Supra, para. 9–11.
[91] Supra, paras. 9–18 to 9–21.
[92] *Waugh* v. *Paterson*, 1924 J.C. 52.
[93] 1954 Act, s. 73.
[94] 1920 J.C. 20.

dog, was liable to be ordered to keep it in control. No objection was taken to the relevancy, and the sheriff-substitute pronounced an interlocutor finding that the dog was dangerous and ordering the accused to have it kept under proper control. The accused brought a suspension in which it was maintained that the complaint was irrelevant. The court repelled the objection to the relevancy in respect that while it was well founded, it had not been taken in the sheriff court. The interlocutor was amended under the powers conferred on the court by section 75 of the 1908 Act (now section 73 of the 1954 Act). Where more than one objection is stated to the relevancy of a complaint, the court of first instance should, apart from special circumstances, deal with each objection, so that in the event of an appeal the appellate tribunal may be able to deal with the whole questions in issue.[95] It is not proper for the court to examine a production in order to determine the relevancy of a complaint.[96]

Fundamental nullity

14-37   The rule that objections to the competency or relevancy of the complaint or proceedings must be taken timeously is subject to the exception that if the objection arises ex facie of the complaint or proceedings and is of such a nature as to make a fundamental nullity of the proceedings, the court of review can competently take note of it and will quash the conviction,[97] for the court will not allow a conviction to stand for what is no crime under the law of Scotland or which has been obtained in excess of the lower court's jurisdiction.[98] Accordingly the court can entertain the objection even although it is not raised in the suspension [99] or stated case.[1]

Noting objections

14-38   Objections must be noted in the minutes of proceedings [2] if either party so desires, but, as already explained, failure to do so is not necessarily fatal to a conviction.[3] Noting in a separate paper is probably competent provided that reference is made thereto in the minutes.[4]

14-39   It must be remembered that, if the accused is charged as acting in a special capacity, the fact is held as admitted, unless challenged by preliminary objection before the plea is recorded.[5]

[95] *Robertson* v. *McNamee*, 1950 J.C. 12, L.J.-G. at 15.
[96] *Brown* v. *Henry Dougal and Sons*, 1959 J.C. 90.
[97] *O'Malley* v. *Strathern*, 1920 J.C. 74; *Rogers* v. *Howman*, 1918 J.C. 88; *Sutherland* v. *Shiach*, 1928 J.C. 49, Lord Hunter at 52; *Wilson* v. *Hill*, 1943 J.C. 124; *Blythswood Taxis* v. *Adair*, 1944 J.C. 135; *Coventry* v. *Douglas*, 1944 J.C. 13; *McIlroy* v. *Bell*, 1952 J.C. 92; *Black* v. *Robertson*, 1954 S.L.T. 329; *Rendle* v. *Muir*, 1952 J.C. 115; *Aitkenhead* v. *Cuthbert*, 1962 J.C. 12.
[98] *O'Malley* v. *Strathern*, supra, Lord Mackenzie at 81.
[99] *Walker* v. *Emslie* (1899) 3 Adam 102.
[1] *Sutherland* v. *Shiach*, supra; *Aitkenhead* v. *Cuthbert*, supra.
[2] 1954 Act, s. 38.
[3] Supra, para. 14–17.
[4] *Connell* v. *Mitchell* (1912) 7 Adam 23.
[5] 1954 Act, s. 16 (*f*).

Amendment of complaint

14–40   It is competent at any time prior to the determination of a summary prosecution, unless the court sees just cause to the contrary, to amend the complaint or any notice of penalty or previous conviction relative thereto by deletion, alteration or addition, so as to cure any error or defect therein, or to meet any objections thereto, or to cure any discrepancy or variance between the complaint or notice and the evidence. Such amendment must not change the character of the offence charged. If the court is of opinion that the accused may be in any way prejudiced in his defence on the merits of the case by such amendment it may grant such remedy to him by adjournment or otherwise as it thinks just. An amendment so made is sufficiently authenticated by the initials of the clerk of court.[6]

14–41   An amendment should be engrossed on the complaint at the time when it is allowed.[7] It is too late to do so after sentence has been pronounced.[8] Every amendment must be authenticated by the clerk of court,[9] but, in view of the decisions in *Wilson* v. *Brown*,[10] *Furnheim* v. *Watson*,[11] *Millar* v. *Brown*,[12] *Sutherland* v. *Shiach*[13] and *Silk* v. *Middleton*[14] and of the provisions of section 73 of the Act,[15] it is thought that failure to authenticate amendments is not necessarily fatal to a conviction.[16]

14–42   Subject to the provisions of section 27 the question of whether or not an amendment should be allowed is one for the judge who tries the case, and the court of review will not lightly interfere with the exercise of his discretion, unless it be shown that the public interest or the interest of the accused is affected.[17] While the section gives wide powers of amendment, these are qualified by the provision (similar to that in section 30 of the 1908 Act and section 5 of the 1864 Act) that the amendment must not change the character of the offence charged, the effect of which is not merely to prohibit the substitution of a different complaint but also to forbid the transformation of a complaint which is radically defective in essential particulars into a relevant complaint.[18] In *Stevenson* v. *McLevy*[19] Lord Justice-Clerk Moncrieff observed: " However wide the power of amendment under the Summary Procedure Act may be, it cannot extend to the essential requisites of a criminal charge." In *Macintosh* v. *Metcalfe*[20] Lord McLaren said: " Now, to remedy a defect does not mean to transform into a libel what never was a libel," and, in the same case, Lord

---

[6] Ibid. s. 27.
[7] *Owens* v. *Calderwood* (1869) 1 Couper 217.
[8] Ibid., L.J.-G at 220.
[9] See *Sutherland* v. *Shiach*, supra, Lord Anderson at 53.
[10] 1947 J.C. 81.
[11] 1946 J.C. 99.
[12] 1941 J.C. 12.
[13] Supra.
[14] 1921 J.C. 69.
[15] See infra, paras. 16–13 et seq.
[16] See supra, para. 14–17.
[17] *Cumming* v. *Frame* (1909) 6 Adam 57.
[18] *Stevenson* v. *McLevy* (1879) 4 Couper 196; *Macintosh* v. *Metcalfe* (1886) 1 White 218.
[19] Supra, at 203–4.
[20] Supra, at 224.

Craighill, referring to section 5 of the 1864 Act, said [20a]: " The implication of the clause is that jurisdiction has been disclosed, and it is only upon this assumption that, as I think, the power, or rather the duty, to amend, when that is required, is made applicable, or is rendered competent to the Judge." Jurisdiction is not disclosed if there is no specification of the locus delicti.[21] Such a defect amounts to incompetency within the meaning of section 73 of the 1954 Act,[22] for, without such specification there is no complaint.[23] Amendment is, therefore, incompetent in this case, and, accordingly, in *Stevenson* v. *McLevy* and *Macintosh* v. *Metcalfe*,[24] where the complaints omitted altogether to name the locus of the alleged offence and the sheriff-substitute had allowed them to be amended by inserting the locus, the court held that these amendments were incompetent. A valid instance is also an essential requisite of a charge, and so, in *Lundie* v. *MacBrayne*,[25] the court held that it was incompetent to amend the instance by adding the concurrence of the procurator fiscal after the complaint had been called in court, such addition being competent only before warrant for service had been obtained.

14-43 The following amendments have been allowed:

(1) Adding to a complaint the heading " Under the Summary Jurisdiction (Scotland) Acts, 1864 and 1881, and the Criminal Procedure (Scotland) Act, 1887." [26]

(2) Altering the date of the offence libelled from 8th November to 8th December on discovery of the mistake after the prosecutor's case had been closed, there being no prejudice to the accused, and he having been offered an adjournment and declined the same.[27]

(3) Deleting words which, while not making the complaint irrelevant, were superfluous.[28]

(4) Deleting an incompetent crave for expenses.[29]

(5) Deleting the words " or near " from a complaint charging the accused with committing a certain statutory offence " in or near High Street," the act complained of being only an offence if committed " in any street." [30]

In another case the accused was charged with two separate statutory offences but the prayer of the complaint only asked the court to convict of " the aforesaid contravention." In the course of the prosecution evidence the agent for the accused objected to the relevancy of the complaint in respect that, while two distinct contraventions were charged, the

[20a] At 226.
[21] *Macintosh* v. *Metcalfe* supra.
[22] *McMillan* v. *Grant*, 1924 J.C. 13, L.J.-G. at 22.
[23] *Macintosh* v. *Metcalfe*, supra, L.J.-C. Moncreiff at 224.
[24] Supra.
[25] (1894) 1 Adam 342.
[26] *Finlayson* v. *Bunbury* (1898) 2 Adam 478.
[27] *Matheson* v. *Ross* (1885) 5 Couper 582. Cf. *Jackson* v. *Jones* (1867) 5 Irv. 409.
[28] *James* v. *Earl of Fife* (1880) 4 Couper 321.
[29] *MacKirdy* v. *McKendrick* (1897) 2 Adam 435.
[30] *Ross* v. *Boyd* (1903) 4 Adam 184.

prayer was as stated. The prosecutor having moved for leave to amend the
prayer by adding the letter " s " to the word contravention, the sheriff-
substitute refused the motion, sustained the objection to the relevancy, and
assoilzied the accused from the complaint. It was held, on appeal, that,
under section 5 of the 1864 Act, the sheriff-substitute should have allowed
the amendment.[31]

Where, however, after the sheriff had commenced to give judgment
and had intimated his intention to find the charge not proven, the prosecutor asked leave to amend the complaint, and this request was refused,
the court expressed the opinion, on appeal, that the motion for amendment
came too late.[32]

Abandonment of proceedings

14–44   After a complaint has been served, the prosecutor may abandon proceedings in one or other of the following ways. It is, however, important
to notice the effects of each method, as some infer merely a temporary
abandonment of the proceedings while in others the result is that the charge
itself is abandoned and proceedings finally dropped.

14–45   The prosecutor may find after serving his complaint that there is an
error in it rendering it undesirable to proceed further with it. In such a
case the simplest course is to serve a fresh complaint, preferably for a new
diet, and intimate to the accused at the time of service that the complaint
previously served will not be proceeded with, and that he does not require
to attend at the diet fixed for the hearing of that complaint. That diet will
not be called, the legal effect being that the particular instance drops. The
complainer being master of the instance may call the complaint or he may
not. He cannot be forced to do so. The dropping of the instance by non-
calling has the same effect as desertion pro loco et tempore.

If the accused appears at the diet fixed on the second complaint, no
further procedure in regard to the first complaint is necessary. The
instance has fallen and the complaint itself is at an end. It might, however,
happen that the diet fixed for the second complaint was the same as that
originally fixed for the first. In such a case the only complaint the diet in
which would be called and to which the accused would be asked to plead
would be the second. The effect would, therefore, be the same as that
originally mentioned: the instance in the first complaint would fall, and
the complaint itself would be at an end. It is, however, a good and safe
practice for the complainer when signing a new complaint to minute the
first complaint to the effect that it is withdrawn in respect of the service of
the second complaint. In *Clark* v. *Donald* [33] the agent for the accused
objected to the competency of a complaint at the first diet. On the procurator fiscal's motion the case was continued for two weeks and at the
adjourned hearing the diet was deserted pro loco et tempore. During the

[31] *Macrorie* v. *Crawford* (1906) 5 Adam 32.
[32] *Henderson* v. *Callender* (1878) 4 Couper 120.
[33] 1962 J.C. 1.

two weeks a fresh complaint had been served without any intimation that the first complaint was being given up. When the second complaint called a week after the desertion of the first complaint, the sheriff-substitute sustained a plea as to its competency on the ground that at the time of service of the second complaint the fiscal had not intimated that the Crown did not intend to proceed with the first complaint. The High Court allowed the Crown's appeal without delivering opinions and held that the second complaint was competent.

In *Cochran* v. *Walker* [34] the accused was, on March 5, 1900, charged in the police court with assault, and remitted to the sheriff; but, the procurator fiscal having declined to take up the case, he was on March 6 (having meantime been in prison) again brought up before the police court on a second complaint libelling the same charge, and, on his pleading not guilty, the case was adjourned to March 13. On that date, on his attending for trial, this complaint was not proceeded with, and he was asked to plead to a third complaint charging the same crime of assault, but aggravated by a previous conviction. To this complaint he pled not guilty, and evidence both for the prosecution and defence was led. He was convicted, and presented a suspension, which was refused. Lord Justice-Clerk Macdonald said: " At the adjourned diet on 13th March the prosecutor allowed the previous complaint to drop, and the suspender was asked to plead to a third complaint. All this was quite competent. The same course is followed in all our criminal tribunals from the most summary up to the highest Court in the country. It is always in the power of the public prosecutor to depart from one libel and proceed to charge the accused upon a fresh libel. In the higher Courts the *induciae* must be allowed to run anew in each case, but in the case of a summary complaint there are no *induciae*. But in neither case is any record made of the dropping of the old libel." [34a]

4-46 To refrain from calling the case is also a convenient mode of dropping the complaint when it is ascertained that, owing to the absence of an important witness or owing to the illness of the accused himself, it is impossible to proceed at the diet originally fixed. Where necessary, intimation should be given as early as possible to the accused that his attendance at the diet originally fixed will not be required. It must, however, be carefully kept in view that the effect of not calling the diet is the same as if the court had deserted the diet pro loco et tempore, and, as mentioned in the last paragraph, the prosecutor cannot be forced to call the complaint again. It is a good and safe practice for him to minute the withdrawal on the complaint. If further proceedings are to be taken, a new complaint must be prepared and served.

4-47 Desertion pro loco et tempore is applicable when the accused appears and objections to the relevancy of the complaint are sustained, or when, after the accused has appeared and pled not guilty, it is found impracticable

[34] (1900) 3 Adam 165.
[34a] At 169–170.

to proceed at that diet—owing to the unexpected absence of a material witness or other cause. Although there is no decision exactly on the point, it is thought that, on the analogy of jury trial, the right of the prosecutor to desert the diet pro loco et tempore ceases after he has begun to lead his evidence in causa. It is thought that the right does not cease when a plea of guilty has been tendered and accepted.[35]

Desertion of a diet pro loco et tempore has the effect of bringing the particular complaint to an end. The prosecutor may, however, institute fresh proceedings. " I have always understood, and I believe it is in accordance with the universal practice, that to desert a diet *pro loco et tempore* puts an end to the libel, but, unlike a desertion *simpliciter*, leaves the prosecutor able to defend himself against a plea of *res judicata*, and to bring a new complaint charging the same offence." [36] It is competent for the court to refuse a motion for desertion of the diet pro loco et tempore and at its own hand to dismiss the accused from the bar or to desert the diet simpliciter. The latter would be an extreme course to take, but there is some authority for the view that, even if taken, it would not bar the prosecutor from instituting a fresh complaint.[37]

A prosecutor must take care that new proceedings in respect of a statutory offence are brought within the time limit applicable thereto.

14-48   Where an accused person fails to appear in answer to his citation and the prosecutor does not desire to take advantage of the provisions of section 30 of the 1954 Act, the latter may either (a) desert the diet pro loco et tempore [38] (although this procedure is not suitable to such a case), or (b) move the court for leave to withdraw the complaint (in which case it will be open to him to bring a fresh one), or (c) have a minute written on the complaint stating that the diet has been called and that the accused has failed to appear (in which case no further proceedings can take place upon that particular complaint).

14-49   Where the prosecutor intends to drop, not merely the complaint, but any further proceedings in the case, he moves the court to desert the diet simpliciter, and this has the effect of completely discharging the accused from any further proceedings on the charge libelled.[39]

Remitted cases

14-50   In the justice of peace, burgh, and police courts, it is necessary to keep in mind those cases which have to be remitted to a higher court, whether in terms of section 4 in consequence of their exceeding the powers of trial of

---

[35] Cf. *Herron* v. *McCrimmon*, 1969 S.L.T.(Sh.Ct.) 37.

[36] *Collins* v. *Lang* (1887) 1 White 482, L.J.-C. Moncreiff at 488. In that case a police court diet had been deserted pro loco et tempore and, subsequently a warrant of apprehension of the accused was written on the original complaint, and he was convicted and sentenced upon that complaint. It was held that the procedure was illegal, and the conviction was suspended. See also supra, para. 10–12.

[37] *H.M. Adv.* v. *Hall* (1881) 4 Couper 500.

[38] *Morrison* v. *Monro* (1854) 1 Irv. 599.

[39] *H.M. Adv.* v. *Hall*, supra.

the inferior court, or in terms of section 5 in respect that the court deems them more suitable for trial in a higher court.[40]

Adjournment before pleading

4–51   The court, in order to allow time for inquiry or for any other necessary cause, may, without calling on the accused to plead to any charge against him, from time to time continue the case for such reasonable time as may in the circumstances be necessary, not exceeding in all seven days, or, on special cause shown, fourteen days, from the date of apprehension. The accused may be liberated on bail, or committed to prison with or without bail; but no judge can allow bail in a case which he is not competent to try.[41]

The provisions of section 21 may be utilised to allow time for inquiry in proceedings under section 14.[42] The adjournment must always be to a specified date, and the order granting the same must be duly signed.[43]

Pleading

4–52   All objections to the complaint or proceedings having been taken and disposed of, and the various other points which have been mentioned duly considered, the accused person is asked to plead guilty or not guilty. The procedure where he tenders a plea of guilty, which is accepted by the prosecutor, has been already explained.[44] It only remains to consider the procedure where he pleads not guilty to the charge, or guilty to a part only thereof, and the prosecutor does not accept the partial plea.[45]

Adjournment of trial

4–53   At common law there is inherent in every court a power to adjourn when necessary, the power being one which must be exercised according to the discretion of the judge.[46] A motion for an adjournment is, therefore, an appeal to his discretion,[47] and the High Court will interfere only if the power is oppressively used.[48] Even although both parties concur in the motion, the judge may refuse it, provided that he does not act oppressively.[49] When the accused person has been brought up on short notice, and asks an adjournment for a reasonable cause, the motion should always be granted.[50] But the cause of application must be reasonable and material. A common ground for asking an adjournment is the absence of a witness. A judge is not bound to grant a motion for an adjournment

---

[40] See supra, para. 12–31.
[41] 1954 Act, s. 21.
[42] *McPhee* v. *Macfarlane's Exr.*, 1933 S.C. 163. See also supra, para. 13–103.
[43] See infra, para. 14–53.
[44] Supra, para. 14–30.
[45] 1954 Act, s. 29.
[46] *Bruce* v. *Linton* (1861) 23 D. 85, L.J.-C. at 94; *Carruthers and Ors.* v. *Jones* (1867) 5 Irv. 398, L.J.-C. at 404.
[47] *Robertson* v. *Duke of Athole* (1869) 1 Couper 348.
[48] Ibid.; *Bruce* v. *Linton*, supra; cf. *Mackellar* v. *Dickson* (1898) 2 Adam 504.
[49] *Anderson* v. *Allan* (1868) 1 Couper 4.
[50] See *Ferguson* v. *McNab* (1884) 5 Couper 471; *Reid* v. *Neilson* (1898) 2 Adam 546.

merely because a witness who has been duly cited is absent.[51] He is entitled
to consider whether the proposed evidence is relevant and material and
whether the accused is prejudiced by the witness' absence.[52] For this
purpose the judge may ask the person making the motion what facts
he intends to prove by the absent witness.[53] If the judge is of opinion that
the proposed evidence is irrelevant or immaterial he is entitled to refuse
the motion, and his judgment cannot be reviewed except upon the ground
of malice or oppression.[54]

Every adjournment in a criminal trial must be to a specified time and
place.[55] An adjournment " to a future date " or " to a date to be afterwards fixed " is illegal. There must always be a minute of adjournment
written upon the complaint or in the record of proceedings and signed by
the judge or the clerk of court.[56] Such minute must be signed on the day
on which the adjournment is granted, as, otherwise, the prosecution will
fall at midnight on that date.[57] No minute or record is needed where the
court rises for luncheon.[58]

14–54   When the accused person pleads not guilty, either party may move for
an adjournment, and it will be granted if the court judges it expedient to do
so.[59] The matter is one for the discretion of the court.[60] Where the accused
person has been cited to appear, a note should be attached to his citation
informing him whether the prosecutor intends to proceed to trial at the
first diet, or to adjourn the case for trial at a subsequent diet (Second
Schedule, Part IV).

The court, in adjourning a case for trial, must fix as early a diet as is
consistent with the just interests of both parties.[61] Where the accused
person has not already got a copy of the complaint, the prosecutor must
furnish him with one, if desired by him.[62] This will usually occur where
the accused person has been apprehended, because a citation is always
annexed to a full copy of the complaint.

14–55   Where the accused is brought before the court by apprehension
he is entitled to an adjournment of the case for not less than forty-eight
hours, provided that the request for such adjournment is made before
the prosecutor has commenced his proof. The court must inform the

---

[51] *Haining and Anr.* v. *Milroy* (1893) 1 Adam 86.
[52] Ibid.; *Robertson* v. *Duke of Athole, supra.*
[53] *Haining and Anr.* v. *Milroy, supra.*
[54] *Robertson* v. *Duke of Athole, supra*; *Mackellar* v. *Dickson, supra.*
[55] *Sarah and Jas. Fraser* (1852) 1 Irv. 1. See also *McLean* v. *Falconer* (1895) 1 Adam 564;
MacArthur v. *Campbell* (1896) 2 Adam 151; *Craig* v. *Tarras* (1897) 1 Adam 344; *Jamieson*
v. *Wilson* (1901) 3 Adam 395; *Taylor* v. *Sempill* (1906) 5 Adam 114; *Corstorphine* v.
Jameson (1909) 6 Adam 154; *Hull* v. *H.M. Adv.*, 1945 J.C. 83.
[56] *Craig* v. *Tarras, supra*; *McLean* v. *Falconer, supra*; *MacArthur* v. *Campbell, supra*; *Jamieson* v. *Wilson, supra.* An interlocutor granting an adjournment must do so in specific
terms (*Taylor* v. *Sempill, supra*).
[57] *Taylor* v. *Sempill, supra,* Lord McLaren at 120.
[58] *Tocher* v. *H.M. Adv.*, 1927 J.C. 63.
[59] 1954 Act, s. 29 (*a*).
[60] *Mackie* v. *Crombie*, 1926 J.C. 29, L.J.-C. at 32.
[61] 1954 Act, s. 29 (*b*).
[62] Ibid.

accused of his right to such adjournment. The case may proceed to trial
at once, or on a shorter adjournment than forty-eight hours, if the court
considers this is necessary to secure the examination of witnesses who otherwise would not be available.[63] An absolute duty is laid upon the judge to
inform the accused person in these circumstances of his right to an adjournment, when he pleads not guilty.[64]

14-56   Where the accused is in custody, he may be committed to prison
either without bail or until he finds sufficient bail to appear at such
adjourned diet and at all future diets of the case, and the amount of
such bail must be fixed in the minute of adjournment. The court may
in any case where it judges it expedient, and whether or not the accused
is in custody, instead of fixing bail, appoint the accused to attend at
such adjourned diet under a penalty, not exceeding £10, in case he shall
fail to appear.[65]

14-57   The court may from time to time, and at any stage of the case, on the
motion of either party, or ex proprio motu, grant such adjournments
as may be necessary for the proper conduct of the case.[66] It has been
held that this provision is not imperative, but merely confers on the court
a discretion to grant or refuse an adjournment.[67] In the case in question [68]
an accused person, who had not been apprehended, was cited to appear
in the police court on a charge of contravening the Street Betting Act
1906. Attached to the citation, which was served upon the accused more
than forty-eight hours before the time appointed for the trial, was a copy
of the complaint and a note informing him that the case would proceed at
the hour specified unless an adjournment was granted. After the first
witness for the prosecution had been examined, the accused, who conducted
his own defence, asked for an adjournment in order that he might instruct
a law agent. His application was refused by the magistrates. In a stated
case the court, holding, as above mentioned, that section 32 (6) of the
1908 Act (now section 29 (*f*) of the 1954 Act) was merely an enabling
provision, decided that the magistrates had properly exercised their
discretion in respect that the accused had had ample time before the diet
to instruct a law agent, and in any event that he should have applied for an
adjournment before the trial began.

Section 29 (*f*) of the 1954 Act provides that where from any cause a
diet has to be continued from day to day it shall not be necessary to intimate such continuation to the accused.

14-58   The true criterion for determining whether an adjournment is proper
is the interests of the accused. An adjournment should be granted if there
is a risk of the accused suffering prejudice by his not being informed of

---

[63] 1954 Act, s. 29 (*c*). See *Johannesson* v. *Robertson*, 1945 J.C. 146.
[64] In *Ferguson* v. *Brown*, 1942 J.C. 113, the failure of the sheriff substitute to inform the
accused of their right to an adjournment was one of the grounds upon which the conviction
was quashed.
[65] 1954 Act, s. 29 (*d*) and (*e*).
[66] Ibid., s. 29 (*f*).
[67] *Mackie* v. *Crombie*, 1926 J.C. 29.
[68] Ibid.

his rights, or where irregularities in procedure have occurred which have
prevented the accused from having a full opportunity to prepare his
defence. So, where the effect of a refusal to grant an accused's request
for an adjournment was to deprive him of material evidence and thus deny
him " the normal means of establishing his innocence " his conviction was
set aside.[69] But there must be some risk of substantial injustice, and an
accused will not be allowed to escape by invoking some merely technical
irregularity.[70]

14–59   While in terms of the statute [71] the intimation of a right to adjournment
is only applicable after a plea of not guilty is tendered, there may be cases
in which owing to the age and circumstances of the accused or the serious
nature of the offence, he should, before being asked to plead, be offered an
adjournment in order to permit of his having legal advice as to the plea
which he should tender. Each case must depend on its own circumstances,
but the guiding principle in all should be to see that everyone brought
before a court of justice is treated with justice. The courts will be particularly zealous to safeguard the position of young persons.[72]

Notice of alibi and insanity

14–60   If the accused intends to found on a plea of alibi or of insanity in bar
of trial he is bound to give notice thereof to the prosecutor, with particulars
in the case of alibi as to time and place, and of the witnesses by whom it is
proposed to prove it, prior to the examination of the first witness for the
prosecution. The prosecutor, on such notice being given, and if he so
desires, is entitled to an adjournment of the case.[73]

14–61   It need hardly be said that an accused person is entitled to get from
the prosecutor such information as to time and place as will enable him
to state an alibi if this is his defence. The hours within which the alleged
offence was committed are not mentioned in the complaint unless they
are of the essence of the charge,[74] but, as they may be important for the
defence of alibi, they should, on the accused's request, be disclosed to him.

14–62   Where the trial does not proceed at the diet at which a plea of not
guilty is tendered and the accused is represented by a solicitor at that
diet, notice of the alibi should then and there be given by the solicitor.
This might avoid an inconvenient adjournment at a later stage. Where
the accused has no professional assistance, and there is any reason to
think that his defence may be founded on the plea of alibi, the clerk of
court might point out to him that, if this is his defence, notice requires
to be given; and if such a defence is then stated, the clerk should note

---

[69] *Mackellar* v. *Dickson* (1898) 2 Adam 504.
[70] 1954 Act, s. 73. In *Spowart* v. *Burr* (1895) 1 Adam 539, an informality in procedure which
   did not cause prejudice to the accused was held not to warrant suspension. Cf. *Boyce* v.
   Shaw (1891) 3 White 73, where suspension was also refused.
[71] s. 29.
[72] See e.g. *Mackenzie* v. *McPhee* (1889) 2 White 188; *Reid* v. *Neilson* (1898) 2 Adam 546;
   McGinnes v. *Neilson* (1910) 6 Adam 221. See also *Ferguson* v. *Brown*, 1942 J.C. 113.
[73] 1954 Act, s. 32; Mental Health (Scotland) Act 1960, s. 63 (8).
[74] *Supra*, para. 6–15.

particulars as to time and place and the witnesses by whom it is proposed to establish the defence. Where the accused is brought before the court by apprehension, and there is any reason to anticipate such a defence, the like course might be followed. In such a case an adjournment would generally be necessary to permit of evidence in support of the alibi being led, and also to permit of the prosecutor rebutting that evidence if necessary.

14-63 Where an accused person learns the time of the alleged offence only during the prosecution evidence (the same not being mentioned in the complaint) and wishes to put forward the defence of alibi, it is thought that the court may allow him to do so, provided that his request is made before the prosecutor has closed his proof, so that the latter can, if he so desires, bring evidence to rebut the alibi either then or at an adjourned diet.[75] A case may also be conceived where the accused, in ignorance of the legal provisions relative to notice of alibi, omits to give the necessary notice, and begins to lead proof in support of that plea after the evidence for the prosecution has been closed. In such a case either of two courses would appear to be open to the prosecutor: (1) to object to the evidence being led, or (2) to allow it to be led, trusting to the alibi, if false, being upset by cross-examination.[76] It might be advisable to clarify the situation by specifically giving the court power to grant leave on cause shown to adduce evidence in support of an alibi where the requisite notice has not been given.[77]

14-64 The statute does not provide the particular form in which notice is to be given. Of course, the best and most appropriate form is in writing, but verbal notice is, it is thought, competent. The Act does not, apparently, contemplate that the notice of alibi is to form part of the process or be noted in the record.

---

[75] Otherwise a miscarriage of justice might result. See *Ferguson* v. *McNab* (1884) 5 Couper 471.

[76] The authors thought that if the prosecutor adopted the second course, the court could competently recall any of his witnesses and put to them any questions bearing on the alibi. They based this view on the case of *Collison* v. *Mitchell* (1897) 2 Adam 277, in which L.J.-C. Macdonald expressed the opinion that " the judge was quite entitled to recall a witness and ask him whatever questions might seem necessary to ascertain the facts of the case." This statement was acquiesced in by Lord Kyllachy in *Saunders* v. *Paterson* (1905) 4 Adam 568. In *McNeilie* v. *H.M. Adv.*, 1929 J.C. 50, the court expressed a narrower view, viz., that the judge might recall a witness " for the purpose of clearing up some ambiguity in his evidence which has been disclosed by the course of the trial or otherwise " (L.J.-G. Clyde) or " with a view to clearing up some matter that is doubtful or obscure " (Lord Sands). These later opinions were preferred in the subsequent case of *Davidson* v. *McFadyean*, 1942 J.C. 95. In these circumstances it would appear that the authors' views must now be departed from.

A third alternative course was suggested by the authors in addition to the two above mentioned, viz., that the prosecutor might allow the accused, before proceeding further with his evidence, to furnish particulars of his alibi in the same way as if notice had been timeously given, and then move the court to adjourn the case to a future diet, reserving to the prosecutor the right to lead further evidence at that diet if so advised. Authority for this course was said to be found in s. 32 of the 1908 Act (now s. 29 of the 1954 Act), but that section does not allow a prosecutor who has closed his proof to lead further evidence, and such a proceeding was held to be incompetent in *Docherty* v. *McLennan* (1912) 6 Adam 700. See also *Todd* v. *MacDonald*, 1960 J.C. 93; supra, para. 10-29.

[77] Cf. Criminal Justice Act 1967, s. 11.

Previous Convictions

14–65 The rules applicable to previous convictions have been fully considered.[78] Some special provisions, however, made by section 31 of the 1954 Act, as amended by the 1963 Act, have to be mentioned here.

" (1) Where the accused in a summary prosecution has been previously convicted of any offence and the prosecutor has decided to lay a previous conviction before the court, the following provisions shall have effect:

(a) a notice in the form, as nearly as may be, of Form No. 2 or Form No. 3 of Part III of the Second Schedule to this Act setting forth the previous conviction shall be served on the accused with the complaint where he is cited to a diet and where he is in custody, the complaint and such a notice shall be served on him before he is asked to plead;

(b) the previous conviction shall not be laid before the judge until he is satisfied that the charge is proved [79];

(c) if a plea of guilty is tendered or if, after a plea of not guilty, the accused is convicted the prosecutor shall lay the notice referred to in paragraph (a) of this subsection before the judge, and the judge or the clerk of court shall ask the accused whether he admits the previous conviction, and if such admission is made it shall be entered in the record of the proceedings;

(d) it shall not be necessary for the prosecutor to produce extracts of any previous convictions so admitted;

(e) where the accused does not admit any such previous conviction, the prosecutor unless he withdraws the conviction shall adduce evidence in proof thereof either then or at any other diet;

(f) a copy of any such notice served on the accused under this subsection shall be entered in the record of the proceedings.

(2) A conviction, or an extract conviction of any offence committed in any part of the United Kingdom, bearing to be under the hand of the officer in use to give out such extract conviction, shall be received in evidence without being sworn to by witnesses. An official of any prison in which the accused may have been confined on such conviction shall be a competent and sufficient witness to prove the application thereof to the accused, although such official may not have been present in court at the trial to which such conviction relates. This provision shall be without prejudice to any other

---

[78] Supra, paras. 10–46 et seq.

[79] Cf. *Boyd* v. *Gordon*, 1968 S.L.T. 269 where it was held that a magistrate who had wrongly heard preliminary argument on the competency of a previous conviction contained in the statutory notice should not take the subsequent trial. Objections to the notice should not be heard until after conviction.

competent mode of proving a conviction and the application thereof to the accused.[80]

(3) Where in any court a book of record is kept of the convictions in the court containing the like particulars as are inserted in an extract conviction, and where at the end of each day's proceedings the entries in such book are certified as correct by the judge or clerk of court, such entries shall, in any proceeding in that court, be accepted as evidence of such convictions.

(4) Where the accused in a summary prosecution is convicted of any offence and also of any aggravation by previous conviction, and is again accused of any offence in regard to which such conviction may be competently used as an aggravation, the production of the prior conviction, or an extract thereof, setting forth the particulars of the previous convictions therein libelled, shall be admissible and sufficient evidence to prove against the accused all the previous convictions and aggravations therein set forth.[81]

(6) Nothing in this section shall prevent evidence of previous convictions being led in causa where such evidence is competent in support of a substantive charge." [82]

Previous convictions may now also be proved in terms of section 31 of the 1963 Act.[83]

14-66   It will be observed that the law in regard to the admission and proof of previous convictions, in procedure both on indictment and summary complaint, is put practically on the same footing. In both cases a notice detailing these convictions is served on the accused. In solemn procedure these are held as admitted unless the accused gives notice objecting to them in terms of section 39 of the 1949 Act. In summary procedure the procedure is as follows: An accused person is first asked whether he admits the particular charge against him. If he does so and a notice of previous convictions has been served, the prosecutor lays before the judge a copy of the notice served on the accused, and the accused is then asked

---

[80] Where a single witness is tendered by the prosecution under s. 31 (2) to prove a previous conviction, he must fulfil the statutory requirements. Except in the case of such a witness there is no relaxation of the ordinary rules of evidence. This was pointed out by the court in *McDermott* v. *Stewart's Tr.*, 1918 J.C. 25. In that case the only evidence led to apply a previous conviction to an accused was that of a single witness, a police constable, who was not an official of the prison in which the accused had been confined, and had not been present in court when the accused was convicted. It was held that the evidence was insufficient in law to prove the application of the previous conviction to the accused.

[81] s. 31 (5) is repealed by the 1963 Act.

[82] Where, however, a previous conviction is libelled, not as a substantive charge, but as a circumstance rendering the accused liable to a heavier punishment, it cannot be proved in causa (*Campbell* v. *Kerr* (1911) 6 Adam 550; cf. *Hefferan* v. *Wright* (1910) 6 Adam 321). *Campbell* v. *Kerr* was a prosecution under the Street Betting Act 1906. That statute, which prohibited betting in public places, imposed a certain penalty for a first offence and a larger penalty for a second offence. A complaint charged an accused with a contravention of the Act, and that " such offence is a second offence, you having been previously convicted as in the list annexed, whereby you are liable " to the larger penalty. The accused contended that, as the previous conviction was stated against him in the complaint it had to be proved before the case for the prosecution was closed. The court rejected this view on the ground above mentioned.

[83] Supra, para.10–47.

whether he admits these previous convictions. If he does, the laying of the convictions before the court and the accused's admission are minuted. The former practice of combining the plea of guilty with the admission of previous convictions in one minute as a plea of guilty as libelled is out of keeping with the provisions of section 30 of the 1963 Act whereby previous convictions are no longer libelled as aggravations of the offence. If the accused pleads not guilty to the charge, the charge has first to be established by evidence; and if the accused is found guilty, a copy of the notice served upon him is laid before the judge by the prosecutor, and the accused is then asked whether he admits the previous convictions libelled therein; if he does, this is to be minuted, and the simplest method of doing so will be to add to the finding of the court a finding that the previous convictions are admitted or proved, as the case may be. If the accused denies any previous conviction libelled, proof of such conviction must be led, unless withdrawn by the prosecutor. Such proof may be either at the calling diet of the case, at the diet of trial, or at any adjourned diet. It must be kept in view that, under section 31 (4) of the 1954 Act, previous convictions libelled in an earlier conviction are sufficiently proved by production of that conviction, or of an extract thereof, setting forth the prior convictions. It is essential that great care be taken to set forth accurately in the notice above-mentioned the previous convictions listed therein, and to ascertain whether or not the accused admits their correctness. The provisions of the statute would, it is thought, be sufficiently complied with by the accused being asked whether he has perused the list of previous convictions contained in the notice and is satisfied that it is correct. In the majority of cases the previous convictions will likely be admitted, but if evidence is necessary, a conviction may be proved either by production of the principal conviction or an extract, or a record book of court. The accused should also get every facility for leading evidence to show that the conviction does not apply to him. In addition to the provisions of section 31, it must be kept in mind that the conviction of an individual representative of a company, association, or incorporation is deemed to be the offence of such corporate body, and a conviction thereof may be laid before the court in any subsequent offence of the same nature by the same incorporation, although the individuals charged and convicted are different.[84] But it is not competent to libel a conviction against a company charged in its corporate capacity in a later charge against the same company when charged through an individual representative.[85]

14-67   It will be observed that a conviction or an extract thereof in a summary court is not only evidence of that particular conviction, but also of any other previous convictions libelled which are admitted or proved. It is therefore desirable that a clerk of court issuing an extract of a conviction in a summary court should schedule any such previous convictions.

[84] 1954 Act, s. 25 (b) (iii).
[85] *Campbell* v. *Macpherson* (1910) 6 Adam 394.

14–68 Where a judge considers a previous conviction, he should look at the conviction and the sentence alone and should not take into account the details that led thereto.[86]

Conduct of Trial

14–69 The actual conduct of the trial in a summary case is similar to that in solemn jurisdiction,[87] except that there is no jury and, therefore, no summing-up by the judge. The evidence for the prosecution is led first, but in exceptional circumstances the court may permit witnesses for the defence to be called before the case for the prosecution is closed e.g. where the accused is likely to lose the benefit of the evidence of certain witnesses through delay or other reason as may happen, for example, in maritime causes.[88] In such cases the accused is entitled to lead additional evidence after the close of the prosecution case. When the case for the prosecution is once closed, it is incompetent for the prosecutor to lead further evidence in support of the complaint.[89] It is, however, permissible for the judge, ex proprio motu, at any time to recall a witness for the purpose of clearing up some ambiguity in his evidence which has been disclosed by the course of the trial or otherwise, or with a view to clearing up some matter that is doubtful or obscure.[90] The prosecutor personally conducting the case is not a competent witness,[91] and the fact that he has given evidence is per se a ground for quashing a conviction.[92] Once the case for the prosecution is closed the accused leads what (if any) evidence he thinks fit. The accused may give evidence on his own behalf.[93] At the conclusion of the case for the defence, the prosecutor addresses the court. He is not entitled to comment on the fact that the accused or his or her spouse has not given evidence,[94] but such comment will not invalidate a conviction if the court is satisfied that it did not influence the result of the case.[95] The accused or his agent next addresses the court. Thereafter the court pronounces its finding or adjourns the case to a subsequent date for judgment. Unless the prosecutor consents, the judge is not entitled to end the proceedings before the evidence is complete and the speeches for the prosecution and the defence have been concluded. Where an accused is acquitted without being given an opportunity to lead evidence or address the court, as where the Crown abandon their case, the proper verdict is one of not guilty and not one of not proven.[96] If the finding be one of guilty the

---

[86] *Connell* v. *Mitchell* (1908) 5 Adam 641, L.J.-C. at 646.
[87] Supra, paras. 10–29 et seq.
[88] 1954 Act, s. 29 (*h*).
[89] *Docherty* v. *McLennan* (1912) 6 Adam 700; *Wynn* v. *Lindsay* (1883) 5 Couper 370.
[90] *McNeilie* v. *H.M. Adv*, 1929 J.C. 50, L.J.-G. and Lord Sands at 53; cf. *Davidson* v. *McFadyean*, 1942 J.C. 95.
[91] *Grahams* v. *McLennan* (1910) 6 Adam 315; *Ferguson* v. *Webster* (1869) 1 Couper 370.
[92] Ibid., see supra, para. 10–31.
[93] Infra, paras. 18–07 et seq.
[94] Criminal Evidence Act 1898, s. 1 (*b*). See infra, para. 18–09.
[95] *Ross* v. *Boyd* (1903) 4 Adam 184; *McAtee* v. *Hogg* (1903) 4 Adam 190. As to comment by judge, see infra, para. 18–09.
[96] *McArthur* v. *Grosset*, 1952 J.C. 12.

accused must be given the opportunity of addressing the court before sentence is pronounced.[97]

14–70   The topic of evidence in criminal cases is dealt with in a subsequent chapter,[98] and it must be kept in mind that there are some special provisions enacted by the 1954 Act for use in summary cases.[99]

Irregularities

14–71   There are a number of cases where irregularities or mistakes in conducting the actual trial have come before the High Court. These cases are of a miscellaneous character and may be grouped here.

14–72   It is quite incompetent for any proceedings in a criminal trial to go on outwith the presence of the accused,[1] except, of course, in the cases above mentioned where trial is competent in the accused's absence. So, where a man was charged with assault, it was held a good ground for suspending the conviction that the magistrates had examined the victim's bruises outwith the accused's presence.[2] Where certain entries in books of the accused produced at the trial by the prosecution were held to be false by the sheriff-substitute after a private examination by himself and without any opportunity having been given to the accused to explain them, the conviction was set aside.[3] Nor should a judge examine a locus outwith the presence of the parties.[4] It is incompetent to seek information from a person present in court who has not been tendered as a witness.[5] Where a witness in giving evidence referred to certain notes in his possession it was held that the judge was bound to allow the accused to see them.[6] Where, however, the witness does not use or refer to his notes, their production cannot be compelled.[7] Refusal by the judge to allow a competent cross-examination of a prosecution witness is fatal to a conviction.[8] Where two witnesses give evidence corroborating each other, the fact that the accused did not cross-examine the first does not preclude him from cross-examining the second.[9] Where an accused was without legal representation at her trial and the magistrate informed her that the assessor (who was, in fact, a solicitor) would look after her interests, her conviction was quashed.[10]

14–73   The judge has a discretion as regards admitting or rejecting the testimony of any witness who, before giving evidence, has been present in court during any part of the trial.[11]

---

[97] *Ewart* v. *Strathern*, 1924 J.C. 45.   [98] Infra, Chap. 18.
[99] Infra, paras. 18–101 et seq.
[1] *Aitken* v. *Wood*, 1921 J.C. 84.
[2] Ibid.
[3] *McCann* v. *Adair*, 1951 J.C. 127. See also *Winning* v. *Adair*, 1949 J.C. 91 (Sheriff adjourning trial and perusing scientific text book (conviction quashed)).
[4] *Sime* v. *Linton* (1897) 2 Adam 288.
[5] *Leavack* v. *Macleod* (1913) 7 Adam 87.
[6] *Niven* v. *Hart* (1898) 2 Adam 562.
[7] *Hinshelwood* v. *Auld*, 1926 J. C. 4.
[8] *Mackenzie* v. *Jinks*, 1934 J.C. 48.
[9] *McPherson* v. *Copeland*, 1961 J.C. 74.
[10] *Johannesson* v. *Robertson*, 1945 J.C. 146.
[11] Evidence (Scotland) Act 1840. Infra, para. 18–80.

Information related to sentencing

14–74   It has been held incompetent for the judge after convicting the accused
to obtain evidence from a person in court as to the amount of damage
done by the accused, without calling that person as a witness.[12] While this
may still be the law [13] it is common for oral information as to the accused's
background and character to be given to the court after conviction by
persons who are not called as witnesses. There is, of course, no difficulty
about such information being given by the prosecutor, or by the accused
or his solicitor.[14] Where an accused pleads guilty he cannot deny any
part of the prosecution's statement of facts to the court which constitutes
an essential element of the offence without withdrawing his plea, but if he
denies other circumstances then that denial, unless clearly false, may preclude the court from considering those circumstances in passing sentence.[15]

The prosecutor must always be careful to limit his statement of facts
to the crime to which the accused has pleaded guilty, and not to introduce
matter relevant only to a charge to which a plea of not guilty has been
accepted, such as circumstances connoting reckless driving in a case where
a plea has been accepted to the lesser alternative of careless driving.[16]

[12] *Leavack* v. *MacLeod, supra.*
[13] See *Forbes* v. *H.M. Adv.*, 1963 J.C. 68.
[14] Cf. *Niven* v. *Hart, supra.*
[15] *Galloway* v. *Adair*, 1947 J.C. 7.
[16] Cf. *Galloway* v. *Adair, supra*, where it was held improper to relate circumstances relevant to
reckless driving on a charge of driving at a dangerous speed. See also *Ramsay* v. *H.M.
Adv.*, 1959 J.C. 86; *Steven* v. *Mackenzie*, 1952 S.L.T.(Notes) 18.

CHAPTER 15

DISPOSAL OF CASE

15–01 WHEN an accused person tenders a plea of guilty which the prosecutor accepts, the case is concluded except as regards sentence. Where, however, no such plea is offered, and the case goes to trial, the court must decide on the evidence led by both sides whether or not the accused person is guilty of the charges libelled against him. The conclusions of the court regarding these matters are termed findings.

15–02 There are two findings of the court which result in acquittal. The court may either find the accused not guilty or find the charge not proven.

15–03 There is also a statutory right to acquittal under the 1954 Act. In the trial of any case in a court consisting of more than one judge, if the judges are equally divided in opinion as to the guilt of the accused, the accused must be found not guilty of the charge or part thereof on which such division of opinion exists.[1]

15–04 The finding which results in conviction is one of guilty. It is not competent to pass sentence except upon a plea of guilty which has been accepted by the prosecutor or upon an express finding of guilt.[2]

Forms of Finding and Sentence

15–05 The finding and sentence and orders of court, both as regards offences at common law and under any statute or order, must be entered in the record of the proceedings in the form as nearly as may be of the appropriate form contained in Part V of the Second Schedule to the 1954 Act. The Act is sufficient warrant for all execution thereon, and for the clerk of court to issue extracts containing such executive clauses as may be necessary for implement thereof. When imprisonment forms part of any sentence or other judgment, warrant for the apprehension and interim detention of the accused pending his being committed to prison is, where necessary, implied.[3]

The forms contained in Part V of the Second Schedule must be followed strictly.[4] They require the following particulars to be given in a conviction: (a) place and date of conviction, (b) name of judge or names of judges who pronounced it, (c) the conviction itself, (d) the sentence imposed in consequence of it, and (e) signature of judge or clerk of court.[5]

---

[1] 1954 Act, s. 37.
[2] *Sharp* v. *Todd* (1892) 3 White 154; *Muirhead* v. *McIntosh* (1890) 2 White 473.
[3] 1954 Act, s. 56 (1).
[4] *Paterson* v. *McLennan* (1914) 7 Adam 428.
[5] See 1954 Act, s. 13.

Place and date of conviction

15-06   These must be correctly set forth on the record. The date is an essential part of a conviction.[6] A mistake in it may seriously prejudice the accused's right of appeal [7] and may also affect the measure of the punishment imposed upon him. So, in *McAllister* v. *Cowan* [8] a conviction pronounced on March 19, but not signed till the 22nd, was suspended, and the same course was followed in *Macleman* v. *Duncan*,[9] where the sheriff, having on October 1 intimated to the accused that he found them guilty and that their punishment was a fine with the alternative of imprisonment, dismissed them from the bar, and, on October 3, signed the conviction, which was dated October 1.

15-07   Although in practice the conviction and sentence are announced verbally to the accused by the judge, this intimation does not make them effective. They are pronounced only by the signing of the formal judgment in the record of proceedings.[10] So, where, after a conviction and sentence had been verbally announced but not recorded and signed, a warrant for imprisonment was issued, the conviction and sentence were suspended on the ground that the warrant had been issued illegally, there being at the time of issue no conviction and sentence in existence.[11] But it has been decided in *Rintoul* v. *Stewart* [12] that the voluntary payment of a fine by an accused person following upon intimation of conviction and sentence does not have the same effect. In that case an accused person, who had in such circumstances paid the fine imposed and left the court, was brought back there upon the same day, when the conviction and sentence were signed in his presence. It was held that the signature was legal.

A sentence must be pronounced in open court and, unless the trial is held in his absence, in presence of the accused, but it need not be written out or signed there and then.[13] It is the signing of the formal judgment in the record of proceedings which makes the sentence effective.[14]

Name of judge

15-08   This item calls for no comment other than that the information enables the accused person to know if the judges who tried his case were qualified to do so.[15] The information would also disclose whether the same judge presided throughout the trial.

---

[6] *McAllister* v. *Cowan* (1869) 1 Couper 302, Lord Neaves at 308.

[7] Ibid., L.J.-C. at 308. See also *Macleman* v. *Duncan* (1902) 3 Adam 545, Lord Kyllachy at 548.

[8] Supra. Cf. *Riddell* v. *Stevensons* (1881) 4 Couper 397 (date of conviction wrongly stated on extract).

[9] Supra.

[10] *Cameron* v. *Deans* (1901) 3 Adam 498, L.J.-C. at 501.

[11] *Cameron* v. *Deans*, supra.

[12] (1902) 3 Adam 574.

[13] 1954 Act, s. 57.

[14] *Cameron* v. *Deans* (1901) 3 Adam 498, L.J.-C. at 501.

[15] E.g. in the case of justices of the peace.

Conviction

15–09   The conviction must state either that the accused person pled guilty
or that he was found guilty [16]—whichever is the case. Conviction of part
of a charge implies dismissal of the rest of the charge.[17]

15–10   The power conferred by the 1887 Act, in certain cases, of finding
the accused guilty of a crime different from that with which he is charged
has been extended to summary procedure. By section 2 of the 1954 Act the
provisions of section 59 of the 1887 Act (already noticed) [18] are applied to
summary procedure, as also are the provisions of the 1887 Act [19] with
regard to procedure where more than one crime is charged or where an
accused charged with committing a crime is found guilty of attempt
merely,[20] or where an accused charged with a statutory offence is convicted of a common law crime.[21]

15–11   A conviction must set out clearly and accurately the precise offence
of which it finds the accused person guilty, so that there can be no
dubiety regarding the same.[22] A conviction which is self-contradictory [23]
or ambiguous [24] cannot stand. Thus convictions have been set aside in
the following cases—where an accused person, charged with two separate
offences in the same complaint, was convicted " of the crime charged " [25];
where the conviction bore to be of an offence against the statute libelled,
there being no reference to any section thereof and no specification of
the offence in question [26]; and where the conviction stated that the
magistrate " finds the prisoner guilty of the crime charged, but in respect
it was committed in self-defence dismisses him." [27] If the court finds
only part of the charge proved, the conviction must be specific as to the
extent to which the accused is found guilty. Where several persons are
charged under the same complaint care must be taken to ensure that
no one is convicted of a charge which is not directed against him.[28] So,
where a master charged along with his servant was convicted of an
offence libelled only against the servant, the conviction was quashed.[29]
The conviction must not go beyond the ambit of the complaint.[30]

[16] See 1954 Act, 2nd Schedule, Part V.
[17] Ibid., s. 61.
[18] Supra, para. 10–42.
[19] 1887 Act, s. 60.
[20] Ibid., s. 61.
[21] Ibid., s. 62.
[22] See *McAllister* v. *Douglas* (1878) 4 Couper 29, Lord Young at 36. See also *Graham* v.
Threshie (1888) 2 White 96; *Galbraith* v. *Disselduff* (1895) 2 Adam 4; *Johnstone* v. *Lindsay*
(1907) 5 Adam 192. Cf. *Sharp* v. *Dykes* (1843) 1 Broun 521. All warrants referring to
statutes must quote same accurately. Mistakes may be fatal (*Dunn* v. *Mustard* (1899) 3
Adam 13).
[23] *Mackenzie* v. *Gray* (1899) 2 Adam 625.
[24] *Graham* v. *Threshie*, supra; *Galbraith* v. *Disselduff*, supra; *Johnstone* v. *Lindsay*, supra.
[25] *Johnstone* v. *Lindsay*, supra; but cf. *Young* v. *Heatly*, 1959 J.C. 66.
[26] *Graham* v. *Threshie*, supra.
[27] *Mackenzie* v. *Gray*, supra.
[28] *Galbraith* v. *Disselduff*, supra.
[29] Ibid.
[30] *Donald* v. *Hart* (1892) 3 White 274; *Foley* v. *McHardy* (1893) 3 White 476; *Calder* v.
the Local Authority of Linlithgow (1890) 2 White 472.

Accordingly, where an accused person was convicted of an aggravation not charged in the complaint his conviction and sentence were suspended,[31] and, in another case, a conviction which found the accused guilty of an offence which was neither the offence charged nor an offence against the statute libelled was set aside.[32] It is scarcely necessary to add that a conviction must not find the accused guilty of what is neither a crime nor a statutory offence.[33]

Alternative findings

5-12 The subject of alternative charges has already been considered.[34]

It is evident that a general conviction which proceeds upon a complaint containing proper alternative charges is necessarily ambiguous or self-contradictory, and is, accordingly, bad. There are numerous cases to this effect.[35] As an example *Lang* v. *Walker* [36] may be cited. In that case the accused was charged on a summary complaint under the Street Betting Act 1906, which made it an offence to loiter " in streets or public places " for betting purposes, and gave a separate definition of a street and of a public place. The accused was charged with loitering for the purpose of betting in a certain place described, " being a ' street ' or ' public place ' within the meaning of the Act." He was found guilty as libelled, but the court quashed the conviction on the ground that the conviction was general, while the charge was alternative as to locality. In this case, of course, the locus was of the essence of the offence.

In *Young* v. *Heatly* [37] the complaint contained four charges, each of which referred to a single course of conduct which was charged alternatively as a breach of the peace and a contravention of the Edinburgh Corporation Order Confirmation Act 1933. The minutes recorded that " The Court found the accused guilty of: (1) The first charge; . . .". It was objected that this was incompetent as a general conviction on alternative charges. It was apparent, however, from the stated case that the judge had not found it necessary to consider the alternative charges. In these circumstances the court treated the objection as a sheer technicality, and invoked section 73 of the 1954 Act to reject the argument that the conviction should be quashed as fundamentally irregular. Lord Clyde expressed the view that in solemn procedure the appellant's argument might well have succeeded, and that it would have succeeded even in a summary case had there been any suggestion that there was any ambiguity in the minds of the parties as to what the judge's decision was.

---

[31] *Donald* v. *Hart*, supra.
[32] *Calder* v. *Local Authority of Linlithgow*, supra.
[33] *O'Malley* v. *Strathern*, 1920 J.C. 74. See supra, para. 14–37.
[34] Supra, para. 13–67 et seq.
[35] As, e.g., *Neilson* v. *Stirling* (1870) 1 Couper 476; *De Banzie* v. *Peebles* (1875) 3 Couper 89; *Arthur* v. *Peebles* (1876) 3 Couper 300; *Boyd* v. *McJannet* (1879) 4 Couper 239; *Charleson* v. *Duffes* (1881) 4 Couper 470; *Reaney* v. *Maddever* (1883) 5 Couper 367; *Murray* v. *McDougall* (1883) 5 Couper 215; *Duncan* v. *Laing* (1888) 2 White 104; *Phillips* v. *Auld* (1892) 3 White 105; *Aitchison* v. *Neilson* (1897) 2 Adam 284; *Lang* v. *Walker*, infra; *Connell* v. Mitchell (1912) 7 Adam 23.
[36] (1902) 4 Adam 82.   [37] 1959 J.C. 66.

Form of sentence and extract

15–13   As already mentioned, a sentence must be recorded in the form as nearly as may be of the appropriate form contained in Part V of the Second Schedule to the 1954 Act.[38]

15–14   Where a penalty is paid at the bar it is not necessary for the court to refer to the period of imprisonment applicable to the non-payment thereof.[39]

15–15   Where imprisonment is authorised, an extract of the finding and sentence in the form as nearly as may be of the appropriate form contained in Part V of the Second Schedule is a sufficient warrant for the apprehension and committal of the accused.[40] No such extract is void, or liable to be set aside, on account of any error or defect in point of form.[41] The forms of extract given in the schedule meet all ordinary contingencies, and sufficiently explain themselves.

Cumulo penalties

15–16   Where several charges at common law or under any statute or order are embraced in one complaint, a cumulo penalty may be imposed in respect of all or any of such charges of which the accused is convicted.[42]

The effect of this provision is to dispense with the necessity of specifying a separate penalty for each offence. Care must, however, be exercised when applying it, for the offences may be so disparate that they may require to be considered and penalised separately.[43] Further, a cumulo sentence of imprisonment cannot be imposed if, for one of the offences charged, imprisonment is not competent in the first instance. Thus, where an accused person was found guilty as libelled and was sentenced to imprisonment without the option of a fine under a complaint which charged him (1) with theft of whisky, and (2) with a contravention of the Licensing (Scotland) Act 1903, section 70, for which the penalty prescribed by the statute is a fine not exceeding forty shillings, and, failing payment, imprisonment for a period not exceeding thirty days, it was held in a suspension that the sentence was bad in respect that, quoad the statutory offence, it was disconform to the statute in that it did not give the alternative of a fine. The court, however, exercising its powers under section 75 of the 1908 Act (now section 73 of the 1954 Act), amended the sentence.[44] Certain earlier cases [45] in which it has been held that a conviction is bad altogether, in the case of an offence punishable by statutory penalty, if it does not impose the penalty, do not appear to be consistent with the powers of mitigation

---

[38] See supra, para. 15–05; *Paterson* v. *McLennan* (1914) 7 Adam 428.
[39] 1954 Act, s. 56 (2). Although unrepealed this provision has little application since the passing of the 1963 Act.
[40] 1954 Act, s. 59.
[41] Ibid.
[42] Ibid., s. 56 (3).
[43] *Paisley Ice Rink* v. *Hill*, 1944 J.C. 158.
[44] *McLauchlan* v. *Davidson*, 1921 J.C. 45.
[45] *Gardner* v. *Dymock* (1865) 5 Irv. 13; *Fraser* v. *Neilson* (1903) 4 Adam 139; *Black* v. *Claxton* (1906) 5 Adam 101.

contained in sections 40 and 55 of the 1954 Act and in the statutes relating to the probation of offenders.

5-17   This provision, however, does not empower a court of summary jurisdiction to impose a sentence beyond the limits laid down in the Act. So, where an accused person was sentenced by a sheriff-substitute to nine months' imprisonment in respect of eight charges, a Full Bench, on appeal substituted therefor a sentence of three months' imprisonment.[46]

5-18   It is competent to impose a cumulo fine in excess of the maximum permissible on any particular charge.[47]

Consecutive sentences

5-19   A sentence following on a conviction may be framed so as to take effect on the expiry of any previous sentence which at the date of such conviction the accused is undergoing.[48]

This last provision is applicable to a case in which, while an accused person is in prison undergoing sentence following a conviction in Scotland or England [49] it is found necessary to proceed against him on a charge which from any cause it would be impracticable or inexpedient to delay disposing of until his liberation. In such a case the accused may be brought up for trial, and if convicted his sentence is made to date from the expiry of the previous sentence which he is then undergoing. An extract of the conviction will be furnished to the prison authorities, and on the expiry of the previous sentence he will be detained on the subsequent conviction and sentence.

Where an accused is charged in the same court on the same day with two offences on separate complaints, which could have been put on the same complaint, one sentence should not be made to date from the expiry of the other.[50] In general, a sentence should date from the expiry of one presently being served only when it is for an offence which was committed after the date of the first sentence.[51]

5-20   It may be added that, where two or more sentences are pronounced against the same person under the same complaint they may be made to run either concurrently or consecutively. Where consecutive sentences are imposed by an inferior court their aggregate must not exceed the limit of the court's statutory jurisdiction in respect of a single offence.[52] So, where an accused person, charged with five offences in a police court, was sentenced to twenty days' imprisonment in respect of two of the charges taken together and to twenty days' imprisonment in respect of each of the

---

[46] *Maguiness* v. *MacDonald*, 1953 J.C. 31; see also *Wishart* v. *Heatly*, 1953 J.C. 42; cf. *Kesson* v. *Heatly*, 1964 J.C. 40.

[47] *Wann* v. *Macmillan*, 1957 J.C. 20.

[48] 1954 Act, s. 56 (4).

[49] *Grey* v. *H.M. Adv.*, 1958 S.L.T. 147, a case on indictment in which L.J.-G. Clyde pointed to the absence of any authority for a statement in the 3rd ed. of this book (at p. 273) that a summary sentence could not be made to run from the expiry of an English sentence.

[50] *Kesson* v. *Heatly*, 1964 J.C. 40.

[51] Ibid., L.J.-C. at 158; but cf. *Grey* v. *H.M. Adv.*, 1958 S.L.T. 147.

[52] *Wishart* v. *Heatly*, supra; *Maguiness* v. *MacDonald*, supra.

remaining three charges, the sentences to run consecutively, the High Court, on appeal, substituted therefor a sentence of sixty days' imprisonment in exercise of its powers under section 75 of the 1908 Act (now section 73 of the 1954 Act).[53]

15–21 The rule that where consecutive prison sentences are imposed their aggregate must not exceed the limits of the court's powers in respect of one offence applies whether the offences are all contained in one complaint or are distributed between two complaints heard in the same court on the same day.[54] Where the offences are common law offences the maximum is that laid down by the 1954 Act [55]; where more than one contravention of a statutory provision is involved the maximum is the statutory maximum for a single contravention.[56] It is not clear whether, say, a sentence of 60 days' imprisonment for a common law offence can be made to run consecutively with a similar sentence for a statutory offence for which the maximum penalty is four months.

15–22 A custodial sentence should not be pronounced along with a sentence of probation.[57]

15–23 Where a number of separate fines are imposed on one complaint the alternative imprisonments imposed must not in the aggregate exceed the court's maximum powers of imprisonment. So it is incompetent for a court with power to imprison for only three months on any one charge to impose sentences of £25 or 60 days on each of two charges and order the alternatives to run consecutively.[58] Nor is it competent to impose a sentence of three months' imprisonment on one charge and a fine of £5 or 30 days on another unless the alternative of imprisonment is made to run concurrently with the three months.[59]

In *Fraser* v. *Herron* [60] the accused was convicted of a statutory contravention for which the maximum sentence was three months' imprisonment and a £50 fine. He was sentenced to three months' imprisonment and fined £25 payable in instalments on the conclusion of his sentence. He served the sentence but failed to pay the fine. It was held incompetent to impose an alternative sentence of imprisonment.

Punishment

15–24 The considerations which affect the imposition of punishment and the allowance of time to pay fines are discussed in Chapter 17.

Intimation of sentence to accused

15–25 " Every sentence imposed by a court of summary jurisdiction shall, unless otherwise provided, be pronounced in open court in presence of the accused, but need not be written out or signed in his presence." [61]

[53] *Wishart* v. *Heatly*, 1953 J.C. 42.
[55] ss. 3 and 7.
[57] *Downie* v. *Irvine*, 1964 J.C. 52.
[58] *Williamson* v. *Macmillan*, 1962 S.L.T. 63.
[59] *Duffy* v. *Lakie*, 1962 S.L.T. 30.
[60] 1968 J.C. 1.
[61] 1954 Act, s. 57 (1).
[54] *Kesson* v. *Heatly*, supra.
[56] *Kesson* v. *Heatly*, supra.

The proceedings which can lawfully be taken in absence of the accused have already been noted. If the sentence is one which cannot competently be pronounced in his absence it will be set aside.[62]

Sentence must be unambiguous

15–26   The sentence must be clear and unambiguous.[63] Where several persons are sentenced under the same complaint the punishment inflicted on each must be precisely set forth.[64] It is a fatal ambiguity if, in such a case, the sentence is so worded as to suggest that the failure of one person to pay the fine imposed upon each offender results in the imprisonment of all of them.[65] A sentence which imposes imprisonment without clearly indicating the date from which the same is to run is a fundamental nullity,[66] as also is a sentence which imposes a fine with imprisonment in default of payment thereof within a specified time, and which, at the same time, grants warrant for immediate imprisonment.[67] But the wrongful disqualification of a motorist convicted of a contravention of the Road Traffic Acts, does not vitiate the rest of the conviction.[68] So, where the accused was convicted of a first offence of driving without due care and was disqualified for holding a driving licence for one year, the High Court suspended the sentence only so far as it disqualified the accused for holding a licence.[69]

Any article ordered to be forfeited must be correctly described.[70]

Alteration of sentence

15–27   Section 57 (2) of the 1954 Act provides that it shall be competent at any time before imprisonment has followed on a sentence for the court to alter or modify it; but no higher sentence than that originally pronounced shall be competent.

Section 57 (4) provides that in such a case:

(i) It is not necessary to require the attendance of the accused.

(ii) Without prejudice to its generality the above power shall include in the case of fines which the court has ordered to be paid by instalments:

(a) Power to reduce the amount of any instalment;

(b) Power to allow further time for the payment of any instalment (whether the time for payment thereof has or has not expired);

---

[62] *Watson* v. *Argo*, 1936 J.C. 87.
[63] *Allan* v. *Lamb* (1900) 3 Adam 248; *Watson* v. *Argo*, supra; *Macleman* v. *Middleton* (1901) 3 Adam 353; *Cowans* v. *Sinclair* (1905) 4 Adam 585. See also *Reids* v. *Miller* (1899) 3 Adam 29.
[64] Ibid.
[65] *Macleman* v. *Middleton*, supra; and see opinions in *Allan* v. *Lamb*, supra.
[66] *Grant* v. *Grant* (1855) 2 Irv. 277.
[67] *Morrison* v. *Peters* (1909) 6 Adam 73.
[68] *Anderson* v. *Howman*, 1935 J.C. 17. Cf. *Bell* v. *Mitchell* (1905) 4 Adam 661, and opinion of L.J.-G. Dunedin that orders such as those suspending a licence or disqualifying the accused for obtaining a licence do not form part of the conviction.
[69] *Anderson* v. *Howman*, supra.
[70] See *Rankin* v. *Wright* (1901) 3 Adam 483.

      (c) Power to order payment of the fine, so far as unpaid, by instalments of smaller amount than originally ordered;

      (d) Power to order payment of the fine, so far as unpaid, by instalments at longer intervals than originally ordered.

15–28   This power enables the court to correct mistakes in executorial detail.[71] But sentences cannot be increased under the power.[72] So, where a justice of the peace court had, by mistake, imposed, in default of payment of a fine, a sentence of imprisonment in excess of the maximum allowed by section 48 of the 1908 Act (replaced by section 49 of the 1954 Act), it was held competent for the presiding justice to recall the accused and, sitting alone, to reduce the length of the imprisonment to that maximum.[73] On the other hand, where the same mistake was made and the magistrate sought to correct it by increasing the amount of the fine, it was held that his action was incompetent and that the conviction must be quashed.[74]

15–29   Where the original sentence is incompetent the court may substitute a competent sentence even where it is of greater severity, for the original sentence is void and the second sentence is not an alteration but a de novo imposition.[75]

Signature of sentence

15–30   The sentence must be signed either by the judge or by the clerk of court.[76] The signature of either of them to any sentence is sufficient also to authenticate the findings on which the sentence proceeds.[77]

    In any proceedings in a court consisting of more than one judge, the signature of one judge is sufficient in all warrants or other proceedings prior or subsequent to conviction, although the presence and signature of two or more judges may be necessary to conviction of the offence in respect of which such warrants are granted or procedure takes place. It is not necessary that the judge so signing should be one of the judges trying or dealing with the case otherwise.[78]

15–31   Although the 1954 Act, like the 1908 Act, nowhere expressly prescribes any time limit within which the signature must be appended, it plainly implies that this should be done as soon as reasonably possible, and, in almost every case, a sentence should be signed on the same day upon which it is pronounced.[79]

    The question whether delay in signing a sentence is or is not fatal to it appears to depend upon (a) the length of the delay and (b) the proceedings which have taken place following upon the pronouncement of

---

[71] *Stewart* v. *Uppleby* (1899) 3 Adam 6; *Mackenzie* v. *Allan* (1889) 2 White 253; *Renwick* v. *McDougall* (1913) 7 Adam 91.
[72] 1954 Act, s. 57 (2).
[73] *Renwick* v. *McDougall*, supra.
[74] *McRory* v. *Findlay* (1911) 6 Adam 417.
[75] *Patrick* v. *Copeland*, 1970 S.L.T. 71.
[76] 1954 Act, s. 13 (2).
[77] Ibid. s. 57 (3).
[78] Ibid. s. 60.
[79] *Furnheim* v. *Watson*, 1946 J.C. 99, L.J.-C. at 106.

the sentence in court.[80] It is clear from a series of decisions [81] that the view of the High Court prior to the 1908 Act regarding the legal effect of signature was that expressed by Lord Justice-Clerk Macdonald in *Cameron* v. *Deans*,[82] viz. that conviction and sentence are pronounced, not by their verbal announcement in court, but " by the signing of the formal judgment in the record of proceedings." Accordingly, in cases before the 1908 Act, convictions which bore the date upon which they had been orally announced, but which were signed upon a later date, were suspended,[83] and a warrant which proceeded only upon an oral sentence was held to be invalid.[84] In the more recent case of *Furnheim* v. *Watson*,[85] the sentence was not signed until sixteen days after it had been announced in court, but the accused (who had pleaded guilty to the charge and had, upon being sentenced to a fine or, in default of payment, to a term of imprisonment, obtained a stated case) suffered no prejudice through the delay. Because of the absence of prejudice and also because there was no exact statutory requirement prescribing when the record must be authenticated, the court, while considering the procedure to have been irregular, held that the irregularity was not such as to necessitate quashing the conviction. An argument was submitted on behalf of the prosecutor to the effect that, in virtue of the provisions of sections 41 and 54 of the 1908 Act (now sections 38 and 57 of the 1954 Act), conviction and sentence became effective when pronounced and not when recorded.[86] The court did not find it necessary to decide this point,[87] but Lord Mackay doubted whether the 1908 Act had effected such a change from the old law,[88] and the Lord Justice-Clerk at a later stage in the case [89] expressed the view that it was essential that the authentication of the record should be complete before extract or execution.

Correction of errors in minutes or extracts

15-32   Section 58 of the 1954 Act provides: " It shall be competent to correct any error in the record of the proceedings in a summary prosecution or in the extract of any sentence or order of the court at any time prior to execution thereon, and such correction shall be authenticated by the initials of the clerk of court."

The effect of this section has already been considered,[90] but the following additional observations may be made with special reference to the correction of errors in the recording of convictions or sentences:

---

[80] Ibid.
[81] *McAllister* v. *Cowan* (1869) 1 Couper 302; *Cameron* v. *Deans* (1901) 3 Adam 498; *Macleman* v. *Duncan* (1902) 3 Adam 545; *Rintoul* v. *Stewart* (1902) 3 Adam 574; *Smith* v. *Sempill* (1910) 6 Adam 348.
[82] Supra.
[83] *McAllister* v. *Cowan*, supra; *Macleman* v. *Duncan*, supra.
[84] *Cameron* v. *Deans*, supra.
[85] Supra.
[86] 1946 J.C. at 101.
[87] Supra, Lord Mackay at 102.
[88] Ibid.
[89] At 106.
[90] Supra, para. 14–18.

15-33   The section merely allows errors in recording to be corrected; it does not provide a means of altering convictions or sentences. So, where a conviction wrongly stated the surname of the accused, and the point was taken for the first time during the hearing of a stated case, the High Court declined to exercise its powers of amendment under section 75 of the 1908 Act (now section 73 of the 1954 Act) on the ground that it was not in a position to say that the error was clerical, and remitted the case back to the sheriff-substitute to consider whether correction was possible and, if so, to have it made.[91]

15-34   Once the sentence of a court has been executed that court is functus.[92] Its clerk cannot thereafter alter the minutes and the High Court has no power to remit to him to do so.[93] In *Smith* v. *Sempill*[94] it was held that alteration by the clerk of court of the date of a conviction after sentence had been executed was a matter, not of form, but of substance, and the conviction was quashed.

The High Court may, however, amend a conviction or sentence under the powers conferred on it by section 73 of the 1954 Act. This topic is considered later.[95]

15-35   Errors must be corrected openly and properly authenticated. When a mistake is observed no attempt to erase or change words should be made. The pen should be drawn through the erroneous entry and the corrected entry inserted, the alteration being initialled by the clerk of court. An unauthenticated alteration may be fatal to a conviction. In *Mackenzie* v. *Gray*[96] the record bore that the magistrate " finds the prisoner guilty," but the word " not " had been originally written before the word " guilty," and its deletion was not authenticated. It was held that the conviction must be suspended. And attempts to conceal the alteration by erasing or changing words may be equally fatal. In *White* v. *Jeans*[97] a suspension was brought nine months after the conviction complained of, the ground of complaint being that the minutes of proceedings contained certain erasures and unauthenticated alterations. The court held that the complainers were barred from insisting in the suspension by their delay in bringing it, but the irregularities which they alleged were thus described by Lord Justice-Clerk Macdonald: " The unauthenticated erasure and change of dates appearing in the record of proceedings constitute serious irregularities, and I think erasures as distinguished from mere alterations are always to be looked upon with suspicion, as being intended to conceal something." In *Reids* v. *Miller*[98] two accused persons were convicted, but the warrant of imprisonment was to convey " him " to prison. The word " him " had afterwards been

[91] *Wilson* v. *Brown*, 1947 J.C. 81.
[92] *Anderson* v. *Howman*, 1935 J.C. 17, Lord Anderson at 22; *Kelly* v. *MacLeod*, 1960 J.C. 88.
[93] *Anderson* v. *Howman*, supra, Lord Hunter at 21.
[94] (1910) 6 Adam 348.
[95] Infra, paras. 16-85 et seq.
[96] (1898) 2 Adam 625.
[97] (1911) 6 Adam 489, 497.
[98] (1899) 3 Adam 29, 34.

altered to " them " and was not authenticated. The court quashed the conviction and sentence, Lord Justice-Clerk Macdonald remarking,

> " I wish also to make this observation, that while a mistake of this kind may be corrected within a reasonable time and before effect has been given to the conviction, I do not think it right that a magistrate or clerk should tamper in any way with a conviction after it has been executed. But where such an alteration is permissible, it must be an above-board proceeding and properly authenticated. To turn one word into another word in a covert manner, so as materially to affect a judgment or warrant, can never be justifiable."

As a last example *Dunsire* v. *Bell* [99] may be quoted. There it was sought to remedy a mistake in the sentence by pasting a correct sentence on the top of the original one. The conviction was suspended.

Minuting reasons for sentence

5–36   Certain statutes require the court to minute its reasons for imposing or refraining from imposing certain penalties, for example, sentencing persons under 21 to detention or first offenders to imprisonment, making certain hospital orders, and refraining from disqualifying for driving because of special reasons. In *Winslow* v. *Farrell* [1] the High Court held that the failure to minute the reasons for imprisoning a first offender was a fundamental nullity rendering the sentence incompetent, but themselves exercised their power to impose sentence [2] and passed a sentence of imprisonment for a shorter period than that originally imposed. In *Bruce* v. *Hogg* [3] it was held by a differently constituted High Court that such a failure was " a pure technicality and nothing else," the lower court having been clearly aware that the accused was a first offender and having complied with the necessary provisions for obtaining reports, etc. [4] (The High Court in *Bruce* apparently thought that this had not been the case in *Winslow* v. *Farrell*.)

Omission from record

5–37   In a case relating to salmon poaching where the record omitted to state either the fine imposed or an order for confiscation of nets and other equipment the High Court, on appeal, remitted to the sheriff-substitute to amend the record, but observed that omissions of essential matters from the record were not lightly to be condoned, and might be fatal. [5]

[99] (1908) 5 Adam 625.
[1] 1966 J.C. 13.
[2] 1954 Act, s. 73 (2).
[3] 1966 J.C. 77.
[4] See also *Barr* v. *Herron*, 1968 J.C. 20: failure to minute reasons for making hospital order used as ground for quashing the order. And see infra, para. 16–34.
[5] *Macdonald* v. *Cuthbert* [1950] C.L.Y. 4662.

CHAPTER 16

REVIEW

16-01 THERE are six methods in accordance with which the proceedings of inferior courts may be more or less fully submitted to review:

(1) Appeal to the High Court of Justiciary on a stated case.
(2) Appeal to the High Court of Justiciary on circuit under the Heritable Jurisdictions (Scotland) Act 1746 (now unknown in practice).
(3) Suspension.
(4) Appeal to quarter sessions of the peace (now unknown in practice).
(5) Appeal to the Court of Session as Court of Exchequer.
(6) Advocation.

Stated Case

16-02 Review by stated case was introduced by the Summary Prosecutions Appeals (Scotland) Act 1875 and was adopted and amended by the 1908 Act (now superseded by the 1954 Act) as a uniform method of appeal.

On the final determination[1] of any summary prosecution, either party to the cause may, notwithstanding any provision in any statute excluding review, make application to the court to state a case for the opinion of the High Court. On such application being made, the inferior court, subject to the conditions hereinafter mentioned, is bound to state a case for such opinion.[2]

The provisions of the 1954 Act regulating appeals are, subject to the provisions of the statute, without prejudice to any other mode of appeal competent.[3]

Proceedings where stated case competent

16-03 The words " summary prosecution " are used by section 62 of the 1954 Act instead of the word " cause," which appeared in the corresponding section (60) of the 1908 Act and gave rise to some difficulty. As the word was defined as meaning and including every proceeding brought under the 1908 Act,[4] it was at one time thought that all proceedings purporting to have been taken under that statute might competently be appealed by

---

[1] Appeal by stated case is not competent until the cause has been finally determined and sentence pronounced (cf. *Lee* v. *Lasswade Local Authority* (1883) 5 Couper 329; *Torrance* v. *Miller* (1892) 3 White 254). There is therefore no right to a stated case at the stage at which the court makes a finding of guilt but defers conviction and sentence: *Walker* v. *Gibb*, 1965 S.L.T. 2. The High Court suggested that this should be remedied by Parliament because of the increasing use of sentence deferred as an initial disposal.
[2] 1954 Act, s. 62.
[3] s. 74.
[4] 1908 Act, s. 2.

stated case as soon as they had been finally determined in the inferior court, in other words, that the mere fact that the original proceedings bore to have been brought under the Act rendered the appeal competent. Appeal by stated case was thus competent under the 1908 Act in any proceeding in respect of an order of court competent to a court of summary criminal jurisdiction.[5] The 1954 Act applies generally to proceedings in respect of orders competent to courts of summary jurisdiction, but stated cases, being limited to summary prosecutions, may not be available in relation to some proceedings in respect of orders competent even to courts of summary criminal jurisdiction, if these proceedings are not properly describable as prosecutions. The effect of the change in wording has not been the subject of any reported decision.

Legal aid

6-04   Where a convicted person who has been granted legal aid wishes to apply for a stated case and to obtain legal aid for that purpose the nominated solicitor (or the duty solicitor if he was acting at the time of the conviction), " if he is of opinion that in all the circumstances there are good grounds for an appeal " by stated case, submits a written statement of the grounds with an application for an interim appeal certificate to the local committee.[6] Where the convicted person did not have a legal aid solicitor he may himself submit a statement of ground of appeal and an application for an interim appeal certificate.[7]

6-05   A person who was not legally aided at his trial may apply to the local sheriff clerk for a provisional financial certificate which if granted is transmitted to the local committee with the application for an interim appeal certificate.[8] Unless the committee (in the person of the secretary or a member or members thereof) are reasonably satisfied there are no prima facie grounds for an appeal they will issue an interim certificate. The nominated solicitor, or an interim solicitor, then applies for a stated case and may also apply to the court to take into account that the appellant is legally aided when fixing caution.[9] If the stated case has already been applied for the solicitor merely lodges the interim certificate with the clerk of court when he receives it.[10]

The interim certificate covers the period up to the lodging of an adjusted case with the High Court unless it is discharged earlier.[11] The adjusted case is then forwarded to the Supreme Court Committee with an application for an appeal certificate.[12]

---

[5] *Wright* v. *Kennedy*, 1946 J.C. 142. Cf. *Robertson* v. *Burns*, 1943 J.C. 1; *James Dunlop and Co. Ltd.* v. *Calder*, 1943 J.C. 49.
[6] Legal Aid (Scotland) (Criminal Proceedings) Regulations 1964, reg. 9 (2) (*a*).
[7] Ibid.
[8] Ibid., reg. 7.
[9] Ibid., reg. 9 (5) (*a*).
[10] Ibid., reg. 9 (5) (*b*).
[11] Ibid., reg. 9 (7).
[12] Ibid., reg. 9 (6).

16–06 If the Supreme Court Committee are satisfied that there are substantial grounds for the appeal and that it is reasonable to grant legal aid they replace the interim appeal certificate by an appeal certificate; otherwise they refuse the appeal certificate and discharge the interim appeal certificate.[13] The Committee may require the attendance of the applicant and his solicitor, and the attendance of, or at the discretion of the Committee, a note from, his counsel.[14] If the Committee grant an appeal certificate they will, where appropriate, appoint an Edinburgh solicitor to act along with the nominated solicitor. The certificate covers the period until final disposal of the appeal unless discharged earlier because the Committee decide, after giving the assisted person an opportunity to submit representations, that it appears unreasonable in the light of subsequent developments that legal aid should continue.[15]

16–07 When the stated case is applied for by the prosecutor the local committee will issue an interim appeal certificate on request provided they are satisfied that any necessary provisional financial certificate has been granted.[16] In a subsequent application to the Supreme Court Committee for an appeal certificate the judgment of the court of first instance will be held to show that the applicant has substantial grounds for answering the appeal.

Grounds of appeal

16–08 It is competent to appeal to, and to bring under the review of, the High Court of Justiciary by stated case:

    (1) The relevancy of the complaint;

    (2) Any irregularity in procedure;

    (3) Any alleged error of the court in point of law; and

    (4) Generally any matter which might immediately before the commencement of the 1908 Act have been competently reviewed by suspension, advocation, or appeal under the Heritable Jurisdictions (Scotland) Act 1746, or otherwise.[17]

16–09 Although suspension is the preferable mode of appeal in some cases [18] the grounds on which a stated case may be obtained are so varied as to cover every question which is likely to be submitted to review. They include, for example, objections to the title of the prosecutor, or the jurisdiction of the court, objections that the complaint was time-barred, irregularities in procedure, and refusal to admit or reject evidence.[19] Challenges to the competency or relevancy of the complaint are made by

---

[13] Legal Aid (Scotland) (Criminal Proceedings) Scheme 1964, art. 21; Legal Aid (Scotland) (Criminal Proceedings) Regulations 1964, reg. 8 (7).
[14] Legal Aid (Scotland) (Criminal Proceedings) Scheme 1964, art. 21 (2) (*a*).
[15] Ibid., arts. 22–24.
[16] Legal Aid (Scotland) (Criminal Proceedings) Regulations, reg. 9 (4).
[17] 1908 Act, s. 60, now 1954 Act, s. 62.
[18] Infra, paras. 16–102 et seq.
[19] See e.g. *Thomson* v. *Neilson* (1900) 3 Adam 195; *Clark* v. *Stuart*, 1950 J.C. 8; *Fairley* v. *Muir*, 1951 J.C. 56; *Hogg* v. *Clark*, 1959 J.C. 7; *MacLeod* v. *Woodmuir Miners Welfare Society Social Club*, 1961 J.C. 5.

stated case, including challenges of the validity of any order, byelaw etc. which is not statutory. It may, however, be inconvenient to determine the question of the validity of orders, etc. in a summary proceeding. " In a stated case [the court is] bound by the facts which have been found. . . . A successful appeal in a stated case on the ground that an Order made by a Government Department was *ultra vires* must depend on this being apparent on the face of the Order or in virtue of the stated facts." [20] Issues of competency or relevancy must have been raised at the trial unless it appears ex facie the proceedings that there was a fundamental nullity.[21] The propriety of a general verdict on what may appear to be alternative charges may also be raised in a stated case. Stated cases may also be used to appeal against sentence whether or not there is an appeal against conviction. An appeal against sentence will be upheld only where the sentence is incompetent, or is harsh and oppressive.[22]

Questions of fact and of law

16-10   Unless, perhaps, in some special statutory cases in which a note of the evidence has been taken in virtue of the Act of Parliament alleged to have been contravened,[23] the decision of the inferior judge as to what facts have been proved in the case is final and cannot be reviewed by the High Court.[24] But this finality is confined to his findings in fact. Such findings reach their conclusions in fact directly and not by way of inference from other findings in the case. Findings which, although purporting to be findings in fact, are really legal inferences drawn from other findings, are not binding on the High Court.[25] Assuming that the facts are as the inferior judge has found them, the question remains whether they disclose an offence under the charge,—in other words, " Do the findings in the case entitle the inferior judge to convict? " [26] This question is one of law, and, if put, enables the case to be brought under review,[27] as explained by Lord Young in a case under the 1875 Act [28] as follows:

> " It is almost superfluous to say that I assent to the proposition that we will not interfere with a Judge's decision of a question of fact proceeding upon legal evidence only because we think that he ought, in the exercise of a sound discretion, to have decided otherwise. But

---

[20] *Somerville* v. *Langmuir*, 1932 J.C. 55, Lord Hunter at 57–58; but see e.g. *MacDonald* v. *Mackenzie*, 1947 J.C. 122; *Marshall* v. *Clark*, 1957 J.C. 68.

[21] Supra, para. 14–37; see e.g. *Black* v. *Robertson*, 1954 S.L.T. 329; *Aitkenhead* v. *Cuthbert*, 1962 J.C. 12.

[22] Infra, paras. 16–28; 16–85 et seq.

[23] See *Anderson and Holmes* v. *Cooper* (1868) 1 Couper 18 (Poaching Prevention Act 1862); *Johnston* v. *Robson* (1868) 1 Couper 41 (Tweed Fisheries Amendment Act 1859).

[24] *Cromwell* v. *Renton* (1911) 6 Adam 498, L.J.-C. at 502; *Sommerville* v. *Langmuir*, 1932 J.C. 55, Lord Hunter at 57.

[25] *Fraser* v. *Anderson* (1899) 2 Adam 705; cf. *Robertson* v. *McGinn*, 1955 J.C. 57, Lord Carmont at 63–64. Cf. *Wild* v. *R.* [1971] S.C.R. 101.

[26] *Motion* v. *McFall* (1899) 3 Adam 21, L.J.-C. at 24; *Jenkinson and Inglis* v. *Neilson Bros.* (1899) 3 Adam 88, L.J.-C. at 95; *Kinnear* v. *Brander* (1914) 7 Adam 456, Lord Anderson at 469. See also *Wright* v. *Mitchell* (1910) 6 Adam 287.

[27] *Motion* v. *McFall*, supra; *Fraser* v. *Anderson*, supra; *Davidson* v. *McLeod* (1877) 3 Couper 511, Lord Young at 527.

[28] *Davidson* v. *McLeod*, supra.

the appellant's case, which it is for him to make out, is that the evidence submitted to the Judge is insufficient in law to warrant his decision, or, to express it otherwise, that the facts stated as proved (and which we must assume to have been so) do not, on a right view of the law applicable to them, justify the conviction. If this shall be established to our satisfaction I think the appeal must be allowed, notwithstanding that the conviction is formally a finding of fact, which indeed every conviction necessarily is."

In another case under the 1875 Act [29] the same judge said:

" Now, in order to entitle a party to apply for a case under the statute, he must express his dissatisfaction with the determination of the Judge as erroneous in point of law, and state to the Judge the legal error under which he thinks the Judge is labouring, and must ask the Judge to state a case setting forth the facts, as the Judge holds them to have been proved, which bear upon that alleged legal error. If the Judge says,—' I did not take that view of the law, that was not my view when I convicted,' then there need be no case stated. But if he says,— ' Yes, that is my view of the law,' then he will honestly state a case bringing out the facts, so that this Court may affirm his view on the point of law or reverse it."

Of course, where the real question in a case is one of fact only, the appellant will derive no benefit from formulating a question of law on the above lines beyond that of obtaining a hearing of his appeal.

16–11   The following questions have been held to be questions of fact and not of law:

(1) Whether a man deserted his wife so as to render himself liable to conviction under the Poor Law (Scotland) Act 1845, section 80.[30]

(2) Whether a parent has failed without reasonable cause to provide efficient elementary education for his child under the Education (Scotland) Acts.[31]

(3) Whether, in the sense of section 1 (2) of the Coal Mines Regulation Act 1908, workmen were or were not working in a shift.[32]

(4) Whether a firm of coalmasters charged under section 4 (2) of the Coal Mines Act 1911, had failed to appoint separate under-managers for each of two mines.[33]

(5) Whether a person charged under the Explosives Act 1875, had failed to take due precautions for the prevention of accident from explosions.[34]

---

[29] *Dickson* v. *Linton* (1888) 2 White 51; 15 R.(J.) 76, at 79.
[30] *Motion* v. *McFall*, supra.
[31] *Gair* v. *Black* (1879) 4 Couper 305; *Brown* v. *Frame* (1880) 4 Couper 361; *Gillies* v. *Quigley* (1905) 4 Adam 601; cf. *Mackenzie* v. *Smith*, 1927 J.C. 47. But see *Barr* v. *Smith* (1903) 4 Adam 95.
[32] *Roger* v. *Stevenson* (1912) 7 Adam 52.
[33] *Moore and Co.* v. *Macmillan*, 1921 J.C. 9.
[34] *Dykes* v. *Wm. Dixon Ltd.* (1885) 5 Couper 539.

(6) Whether a person charged under the Sale of Food and Drugs Act 1875, had adulterated an article of food (milk).[35]

(7) Whether a person charged under the Salmon Fisheries (Scotland) Act 1844, had taken sea trout wilfully.[36]

(8) Whether a person charged under the Merchandise Marks Act 1887, with using a trade name belonging to the prosecutor had acted innocently.[37]

(9) Whether a person charged under section 430 of the Burgh Police (Scotland) Act 1892, with making up or exposing for sale goods which were deficient in weight had acted without fraudulent intent.[38]

6-12   The following questions have been held to be questions of law:

(1) Whether, on the facts stated, the accused was guilty of theft.[39]

In *Clyne* v. *Keith* [40] the accused was charged with the theft of 3s. worth of oilcake. It appeared that on the occasion in question he had, while intoxicated, called at a shop where he had previously received goods on credit, wishing to purchase the oilcake, and on the shopkeeper declining to give it to him on credit he walked off with it. On a stated case, it was held that in the circumstances there was no felonious intent, and the conviction was quashed. The question of law was, " Whether in the circumstances stated, the appellant is guilty of the crime of theft? "

In *Fraser* v. *Anderson* [41] the accused was convicted summarily of theft, and obtained a stated case in regard to the facts, which he maintained did not infer felonious intent. The court (*dissentiente* Lord Adam) sustained the appeal, although doubts were expressed by Lord Kinnear as to whether the question was not rather one of fact than of law. In this case the question of law was, " Whether, on the facts stated, an act of theft was committed by the appellant? "

(2) Whether the driving of a motorist constituted negligence within the meaning of section 1 (1) of the Motor Car Act 1903.[42]

In *Waugh* v. *Campbell* [43] the driver of a motor car was charged with driving recklessly and negligently, contrary to the Motor Car Act 1903, section 1. An appeal against the judgment of a sheriff-substitute acquitting him was sustained on the ground that the sheriff-substitute had misdirected himself upon the legal question of what was sufficient to constitute negligence within the meaning of the Act.

(3) Whether a person was a seaman in the sense of the Merchant Shipping Act 1854.[44]

(4) Whether a person charged under the Merchandise Marks Act

[35] *Macleod* v. *O'Neil* (1882) 4 Couper 629; *Todd* v. *Cochrane* (1901) 3 Adam 357.
[36] *Grant* v. *Wright* (1876) 3 Couper 282.
[37] *Jenkinson and Inglis* v. *Neilson Brothers*, supra; cf. *Haddow* v. *Neilson Brothers*, infra.
[38] *Brander* v. *Buttercup Dairy Co.*, 1921 J.C. 19.
[39] *Clyne* v. *Keith*; *Fraser* v. *Anderson*, infra.
[40] (1887) 1 White 356.
[41] (1899) 2 Adam 705.
[42] *Waugh* v. *Campbell*, 1920 J.C. 1; cf. *Sorrie* v. *Robertson*, 1944 J.C. 95.
[43] Supra.
[44] *Thomson* v. *Hart* (1890) 2 White 539.

1887, and found to have acted knowingly but " without intent to defraud," had acted " innocently " in the sense of section 2 (2) of that statute.[45]

Limitations on appeal

16-13   The appeal, however, is qualified by limitations imposed by section 73 of the 1954 Act, which prescribes that:

" (1) No conviction, sentence, judgment, order of court, or other proceeding whatsoever under this Act shall be quashed for want of form, or, where the accused had legal assistance in his defence, shall be suspended or set aside in respect of any objections to the relevancy of the complaint, or to the want of specification therein, or to the competency or admission or rejection of evidence at the trial in the inferior court, unless such objections have been timeously stated at the trial by the solicitor of the accused.

" (2) Save as provided in sections 62 and 71,[45a] no conviction, sentence, judgment, order of court, or other proceeding whatsoever shall be quashed except on the ground of incompetency, or corruption, or malice, or oppression, or unless the High Court shall be of opinion that the accused has been misled as to the true nature of the charge against him or been prejudiced in his defence on the merits, and that a miscarriage of justice has resulted thereby: "

Want of form

16-14   No proceeding will be invalidated through a defect which is merely technical and does not affect its substance.[46] So, the omission of words of style from a conviction will not vitiate it provided that its meaning is clear.[47] In *Paterson* v. *McLennan* [48] the conviction found the accused "guilty" but omitted to comply with the form provided by Schedule E to the 1908 Act by adding the words " as libelled." The subsequent part of the conviction made it clear that the accused had been found guilty of all the offences libelled. The court refused to suspend the conviction. So, also, a clerical error in recording the date of a plea which caused no prejudice and could mislead no one was held not to invalidate the conviction which followed.[49] Again, where the record of proceedings failed to minute a plea of not guilty tendered at the first diet, but it appeared from a subsequent entry that the accused " adhered to the plea of not guilty previously tendered," it was held that the omission to record the plea when tendered

---

[45] *Haddow* v. *Neilson Bros.* (1899) 3 Adam 104; cf. *Jenkinson* v. *Neilson Brothers*, supra.
    From the cases cited on this and the preceding page it will be observed that it is not easy in all cases to distinguish a question of fact from one of law. The case of *McGowan* v. *Langmuir*, 1931 J.C. 10, may also be referred to in this connection.

[45a] This does not mean that an appeal on a ground set out in section 62—supra, para. 16-08, cannot be rejected on the ground that there has been no miscarriage of justice: *Adam* v. *MacNeill*, 1971 S.L.T. (Notes) 80.

[46] See *Silk* v. *Middleton*, 1921 J.C. 69, L.J.-C. at 74.

[47] See *Paterson* v. *McLennan* (1914) 7 Adam 428; *Telford* v. *Fyfe* (1908) 5 Adam 596; *Young* v. *Heatly*, 1959 J.C. 66.

[48] Supra.

[49] *Ogilvy* v. *Mitchell* (1903) 4 Adam 237.

was not fatal.[50] On the other hand, the alteration of the date of a sentence after execution has been held to be a matter of substance.[51] Again, where a clerk of court instead of getting a sentence amended by the authentication of a marginal addition which he had made to it, wrote out and had signed by the magistrate a corrected sentence which was then pasted over the original so as to cover it completely, the court quashed the conviction.[52] In one case two men who had been acting together were tried together but on separate complaints, and it was held that failure to conjoin the charges in one complaint was wrong but that the error was only technical since no prejudice had arisen.[53]

Defective proceedings which may prejudice the accused cannot be regarded as want of form only.[54] " It is our duty in administering the Summary Jurisdiction Act to take care that irregularities of procedure which may prejudice the defence, and which may therefore result in injustice, shall not be allowed to pass." [55]

Objections to complaint or evidence

6–15   The admission of incompetent evidence in the court below may be fatal. The court in applying section 73 should be very careful not to make it possible to use incompetent evidence as an element in consideration of the guilt of an accused person.[56] In *Connell* v. *Mitchell* [57] an objection to the complaint which had been stated in the inferior court was not recorded and there was nothing to show the High Court what it was. This irregularity was held to be sufficient to vitiate the proceedings which followed upon the complaint. In *Cameron* v. *Waugh* [58] two objections to evidence which were not recorded had been noted by the sheriff-substitute and were fully disclosed in a stated case which raised the question whether they had been rightly repelled. The conviction was quashed upon another ground, but the opinion was expressed by Lord Justice-General Normand and Lord Moncrieff that this failure to comply with section 41 of the 1908 Act was in the circumstances a mere matter of form, and, by section 75, would not have been fatal to a conviction, the case of *Connell* v. *Mitchell* being distinguished by Lord Moncrieff as being a case where the irregularity complained of had resulted in the loss of all record of the objection. In *McDonalds Limited* v. *Adair* [59] there was a failure to note two objections to the evidence, but the stated case showed that these had been taken and had been repelled. It was held, following *Cameron* v. *Waugh*, that the omission to note these objections was not fatal to the conviction.

[50] *Millar* v. *Brown*, 1941 J.C. 12.
[51] *Smith* v. *Sempill* (1910) 6 Adam 348.
[52] *Dunsire* v. *Bell* (1908) 5 Adam 625.
[53] *Gilmour* v. *Gray*, 1951 J.C. 70.
[54] See *Cameron* v. *Waugh*, 1937 J.C. 5, L.J.-G. at 9; *Ogilvy* v. *Mitchell*, supra, Lord McLaren at 245.
[55] *Johannesson* v. *Robertson*, 1945 J.C. 146, L.J.-G. at 150.
[56] *Cameron* v. *Waugh*, 1937 J.C. 5, L.J.-G. at 9.
[57] (1912) 7 Adam 23.
[58] Supra.
[59] 1944 J.C. 119. See also *Galletly* v. *Laird*, 1953 J.C. 16, L.J.-G. at 27–28.

16–16   Objections to the competency or relevancy of the complaint should be
intimated at the first calling of the case, and may be stated later only with
leave of the court which may be granted only on cause shown.[60] Objections
to evidence must be made at the time.[61] In cases where the accused has
been represented by a solicitor the High Court will not consider objections
which have not been made timeously.[62] This, however, does not apply
when proceedings in the inferior court are challenged as being fundamentally null.[63] Lack of jurisdiction, for example, is a fatal nullity,[64] and
objections to jurisdiction may be taken for the first time in the High Court.[65]
And it is always competent to maintain on appeal that a charge does not
on the face of it disclose any crime even although the question was not
raised in the inferior court.[66] " Where what is averred does not amount to
a crime or offence, it is the duty of the Court, not only to hold the libel
irrelevant, but also to deny any authority to a conviction which may have
followed upon it." [67]

" Incompetency "

16–17   In *Silk* v. *Middleton* [68] Lord Justice-Clerk Scott Dickson accepted as
apt and appropriate to indicate the meaning of the word " incompetency "
in section 75 of the 1908 Act the following pronouncement of Lord
Justice-General Dunedin in *Robson* v. *Menzies*,[69] a small-debt appeal:

> " I may say at once that I think it is quite impossible to hold that
> under the head of incompetency, you could deal with anything that
> is wrong in the procedure of the case itself. I think that incompetency
> means, and can only mean, an inability in the Court to deal with the
> matter in hand; and I think the reason why the phrase is used—
> ' incompetency including defect of jurisdiction '—is not really to add
> anything, but is merely to look at the matter from another point of
> view. In other words, I think incompetency pure and simple would
> mean any case with which the Court, as a Court, had not power to
> deal."

Views similar to those of Lord Dunedin have been expressed in earlier
cases.[70]

---

[60] 1954 Act, s. 26. See supra, paras. 14–35 et seq.
[61] *Anderson* v. *Macfarlane* (1899) 2 Adam 644. See supra, para. 14–17.
[62] 1954 Act, s. 73 (1); see *Dunn* v. *Mitchell* (1910) 6 Adam 365; *Walker* v. *Brander*, 1920 J.C.
   20; *Penrice* v. *Brander*, 1921 J.C. 23 (objections to relevancy) and *Maciver* v. *Mackenzie*,
   1942 J.C. 51 (objections to evidence). See also *Rogers* v. *Howman*, 1918 J.C. 88, L.J.-G. at
   93; *Coventry* v. *Douglas*, 1944 J.C. 13; *Gilmour* v. *Gray*, 1951 J.C. 70; *McIlroy* v. *Bell*, 1952
   J.C. 92.
[63] *Rogers* v. *Howman*, supra; *O'Malley* v. *Strathern*, 1920 J.C. 74; *Coventry* v. *Douglas*,
   supra; *Rendle* v. *Muir*, 1952 J.C. 115; *Czajkowski* v. *Lewis*, 1956 J.C. 8.
[64] *Wilson* v. *Hill*, 1943 J.C. 124.
[65] *Blythswood Taxis Ltd.* v. *Adair*, 1944 J.C. 135; *Wilson* v. *Hill*, supra.
[66] *Coventry* v. *Douglas*, supra; *Black* v. *Robertson*, 1954 S.L.T. 329; *Rendle* v. *Muir*, supra.
[67] *McDonalds Ltd.* v. *Adair*, 1944 J.C. 119, L.J.-C. at 125–126; *Aitkenhead* v. *Cuthbert*, 1962
   J.C. 12.
[68] 1921 J.C. 69, 74, 75. See also *Mackenzie* v. *McKillop*, 1938 J.C. 91.
[69] (1913) 7 Adam 156, 161.
[70] As, e.g. in *Murchie* v. *Fairbairn* (1863) 1 M. 800, Lord Deas at 804; and *Wilson* v. *Glasgow
   Tramways Co.* (1878) 5 R. 981, Lord Gifford at 993.

Failure to note documentary evidence was held in *Silk* v. *Middleton* [71] not to amount to incompetency within the meaning of section 75 of the 1908 Act. On the other hand, it was held in *McMillan* v. *Grant* [72] (a suspension) that the absence from the complaint of any specification of the locus sufficient at least to determine the jurisdiction of the court did amount to such incompetency.

" Corruption ": " Malice "

6-18 The word " corruption " is used in its natural sense. There is no such thing as " constructive " or " legal " corruption. [73] " Malice " is " malitia," which means wickedness, and it signifies that the judge has pronounced a judgment which is not an honest one given in the course of his duty [74] but one given from some wrong motive, or from caprice.

Oppression

6-19 Oppression arises when something is done in a cause which amounts to unfairness to the accused from which he is entitled to get relief. [75] Differing from corruption and malice, oppression does not require to spring from a dishonest or improper motive. It may be the result of a mere error of judgment and quite unintentional. [76] Actings which are illegal are not, however, necessarily oppressive in the proper sense of the term as thus interpreted by Lord Trayner in *McKenzie* v. *McPhee* [77] " I construe the words ' oppression on the part of the magistrate ' as meaning only any failure of duty on his part, or any straining or abusing of his powers which in the particular circumstances bears with undue or unreasonable weight against the accused." [78]

Oppression: Oral citation

6-20 In *Carlin* v. *Malloch* [79] the opinion was expressed that where a person charged with a police offence has a known place of residence, it is oppressive to bring him before a magistrate without serving upon him a copy of the complaint (unless he is apprehended in flagrante delicto).

Oppression: Refusal of adjournment

6-21 By section 29 (*c*) of the 1954 Act an accused person brought before an inferior court by apprehension who pleads not guilty is entitled to an

[71] Supra.
[72] 1924 J.C. 13. See also *Hefferan* v. *Wright* (1910) 6 Adam 321.
[73] *Adams* v. *Great North of Scotland Railway Co.* (1890) 18 R.(H.L.) 1, Lord Watson at 9, Lord Bramwell at 10; *Robson* v. *Menzies*, L.J.-C. at 95, Lord Kinnear at 98.
[74] *Robson* v. *Menzies*, supra.
[75] *Gordon* v. *Mulholland* (1891) 2 White 576, L.J.-C. at 580.
[76] Ibid; *Robson* v. *Menzies*, supra.
[77] (1889) 2 White 188. In *Rattray* v. *White* (1891) 3 White 89, it was held that a conviction of trafficking in spirits without a licence could not be set aside in a suspension on the ground of oppression where the proceedings were ex facie regular and the real ground of objection to the conviction was an alleged error in law.
[78] *McKenzie* v. *McPhee* (1889) 2 White 188 at 213.
[79] (1896) 2 Adam 98. Cf. *Parr* v. *Henderson* (1879) 4 Couper 252.

adjournment of not less than forty-eight hours, subject to the qualifications contained in the subsection, and the court must inform him of his right.[80]

The 1864 Act made a similar provision,[81] with three differences, viz. (1) the accused's right was unqualified; (2) the right existed whatever the accused's plea, but (3) there was no statutory obligation on the judge to inform him of it. Decisions under that Act proceeded upon the view that the judge was under no obligation in the matter unless the circumstances were such as to create one.[82] Although section 29 (c) applies only where the accused pleads not guilty, failure to offer an accused an adjournment may be an element of oppression even where the subsection does not strictly apply.

16–22   In *Ferguson* v. *Brown*[83] two men of the labouring class were charged with removing and secreting, contrary to Regulation 2B of the Defence (General) Regulations 1939, an imitation gun which was being used by a Home Guard unit in connection with a military exercise. They were taken into custody on a Sunday morning, when they were charged with having removed and taken away the gun, and with having by so doing impaired the efficiency of the services. They remained in custody until Monday morning, when they were brought before the court and the complaint containing the charge of a contravention of the statutory regulation was read over to them, this being the first occasion upon which they were made aware of the exact nature of the charge. Thereafter, without being asked if they wished an adjournment, they were called on to plead and tendered pleas of guilty and were sentenced to imprisonment. They had declined to be represented by a solicitor, not having been informed that they were entitled to the gratuitous services of a solicitor for the poor. In a bill of suspension at their instance it was held (1) that the complaint was irrelevant, and (2) that, since there had been (a) an irrelevant complaint, (b) no legal representation, (c) no service of the complaint before appearance in court, (d) no knowledge on the part of the accused of their right to obtain the services of a solicitor for the poor, and (e) no specific offer to the accused of an adjournment of the diet, there had been such a combination of circumstances as together amounted to oppression within the meaning of section 75 of the 1908 Act, and the conviction and sentence were quashed.

The question remains: Is a breach of the court's statutory duty under section 29 (c) sufficient, per se, to invalidate a subsequent conviction? *Ferguson* v. *Brown*[84] does not supply the answer, but it appears to be clear from other decisions[85] that an irregularity in procedure not amounting to a fundamental nullity—even although it involves a breach of an

---

[80] Supra, paras. 14–55, 14–59.
[81] Summary Procedure (Scotland) Act 1864, s. 11.
[82] See *Reid* v. *Neilson* (1898) 2 Adam 546; *McGinnes* v. *Neilson* (1910) 6 Adam 221; *Pyper* v. *Walker* (1885) 5 Couper 631; *Gardiner* v. *Jones* (1890) 2 White 474. Cf. *Kelly* v. *Mitchell* (1907) 5 Adam 268.
[83] 1942 J.C. 113.
[84] Supra.
[85] E.g. *Silk* v. *Middleton*, 1921 J.C. 69; *Sutherland* v. *Shiach*, 1928 J.C. 49; *Pennington* v. *Mackenzie*, 1946 J.C. 12; *Galletly* v. *Laird*, 1953 J.C. 16.

express statutory provision [86]—will not be regarded as per se fatal to a conviction which follows. The test is—has there been a miscarriage of justice within the meaning of section 73 of the Act? [87] The effect of the irregularity must, therefore, be considered in each case, and, if no prejudice has resulted to the accused therefrom the conviction will not be set aside. Prejudice is obviously not an inevitable consequence of a breach of the duty in question under section 29 (c) (e.g., the accused might be represented by a solicitor). The earlier decisions appear to be useful guides as to what constitutes prejudice in such a case. [88]

6–23   In *Massey* v. *Lamb* [89] it was held that, under section 11 of the 1864 Act, the refusal of an inferior judge to grant a request for an adjournment made by a person charged with a summary complaint, a copy of which had not been served upon him, was a fundamental error which rendered all subsequent proceedings null. In that case the accused was not brought before the court by apprehension, but, a fortiori, the decision would apply had that been the case. Under the 1954 Act, the judge has a limited discretion regarding requests for adjournments made by accused persons brought before him by apprehension in that, if he considers such a course necessary to secure the examination of witnesses who otherwise would not be available, he may refuse the request or grant a shorter adjournment than forty-eight hours.

As regards requests for adjournments other than those made under section 29 (c), the inferior judge has a discretionary power to refuse or grant the same. He must not, however, act oppressively. In *MacKellar* v. *Dickson* [89a] a refusal to grant an adjournment which was necessary to enable the accused to prepare his defence was held to be oppressive, and the same was held in *Ferguson* v. *McNab* [90] regarding a refusal where the adjournment asked for was necessary for bringing witnesses to the trial to prove an alibi.

Oppression: Form of complaint

6–24   In *Walker* v. *Bonnar* [91] a complaint charging the accused with having committed an offence against section 393 of the Burgh Police (Scotland) Act 1892 " along with one or more persons to the complainer unknown " was held to be relevant, but Lord Justice-Clerk Macdonald observed that, if it turned out at the trial that the names were in truth known to the prosecutor, he might not be entitled to a conviction, on the ground that the concealment of his knowledge might be oppressive to the accused.

---

[86] *Pennington* v. *Mackenzie*, supra.
[87] See cases cited supra, paras. 16–14, 16–15.
[88] For examples of situations which might be regarded as prejudicial, see *Pyper* v. *Walker* (1885) 5 Couper 631; *Gardiner* v. *Jones* (1890) 2 White 474; *Reid* v. *Neilson* (1898) 2 Adam 546; *Kelly* v. *Mitchell* (1907) 5 Adam 268.
[89] (1906) 5 Adam 59.
[89a] (1898) 2 Adam 504.
[90] (1884) 5 Couper 471.
[91] (1894) 1 Adam 523.

Oppression: Procedure at trial

16-25   Except in those special cases already noted,[92] no criminal proceedings are competent outwith the presence of the accused.[93] Where, therefore, a magistrate pronounced a deliverance in absence of and without notice to the accused, the proceedings were held to be both fundamentally null and oppressive.[94] It has been held to be oppressive for a magistrate to take a plea of guilty from an accused person during the temporary absence of his counsel and agent.[95]

16-26   An accused person must have a fair trial. There is oppression if the judge refuses to hear competent evidence [96] or to allow the accused to see notes used by a witness to refresh his memory while giving evidence.[97] Whether injudicious remarks by the judge constitute oppression is a question of circumstances in each case.[98]

16-27   Where the accused is not legally represented at his trial it is the duty of the judge to inform him that he is entitled to lead evidence in defence, and to address the court on the evidence which has been led in the case.[99] Where an accused person, unassisted by an agent, has pleaded guilty or has been found guilty, the judge, before pronouncing sentence, ought to afford him an opportunity of making a statement on his own behalf.[1] In neither case is the duty imposed by statute or common law, and it will depend upon the circumstances of each particular case whether its omission amounts to oppression.[2] In *McClung* v. *Cruickshank* [3] the accused tendered a written plea of guilty with an explanation which was inconsistent with guilt. The plea was noted and the case continued for his personal appearance. At the adjourned diet he appeared with a solicitor who asked leave to withdraw the plea. This request was refused and the accused sentenced to imprisonment. It was held on appeal that although the question of allowing a plea to be withdrawn was one for the sheriff's discretion, the sheriff having refused to hear the reason for the motion had in effect not exercised his discretion, particularly in view of the fact that the original plea was ambiguous and tendered without legal advice, and the conviction was quashed.

Oppression: Sentence

16-28   In relation to sentence " oppression means that there has been a disregard of the essentials of justice and the infliction of a penalty which

---

[92] Supra, paras. 14–19 et seq.
[93] *Aitken* v. *Wood*, 1921 J.C. 84.
[94] *Kelly* v. *Rowan* (1897) 2 Adam 357.
[95] *Williams* v. *Linton* (1878) 16 S.L.R. 180.
[96] *Lairds* v. *Neilson* (1905) 4 Adam 537. Cf. *Reid and Son* v. *Sinclair Bros.* (1894) 1 Adam 500 (Small Debt Appeal); Cf. *McLeod* v. *H.M. Adv.*, 1939 J.C. 68 (Refusal to allow further cross-examination after questions asked by judge in jury trial).
[97] *Niven* v. *Hart* (1898) 2 Adam 562.
[98] See e.g. *Macdonald* v. *Mackenzie*, 1947 S.L.T. (Notes) 44; cf. *Bergson* v. *H.M. Adv.* (1970) 34 J.C.L. 270.
[99] *Grahams* v. *McLennan* (1910) 6 Adam 315.
[1] *Ewart* v. *Strathern*, 1924 J.C. 45.
[2] *Grahams* v. *McLennan*, supra; *Ewart* v. *Strathern*, supra.
[3] 1964 J.C. 64; cf. *Nicol* v. *Brown*, 1951 J.C. 87.

is not properly related to the crime of which the party stands convicted, but is either to be regarded as merely vindictive or as having proceeded upon some improper or irregular consideration, or, it may be, upon some misleading statement of facts put before the sheriff by the prosecutor, or the like." [4] The High Court will not interfere with a sentence merely because it is " excessive," but only if it is " harsh and oppressive." [5]

16-29   As examples of cases in which the sentence has been held to be oppressive as being vindictive, *Edward & Sons* v. *McKinnon* [6] and *Macleod* v. *Mackenzie* [7] may be cited. In the former a company and its manager were respectively fined £5,100 and £2,000 by the sheriff-substitute, the company for having, contrary to section 23 of the Finance (No. 2) Act 1940, failed over a considerable period to register as vendors of goods chargeable with purchase tax, and the manager for having, contrary to section 35 (3) of the same Act, on four occasions made statements which were false in material particulars when furnishing information relating to purchase tax. The maximum penalty exigible against the company was £7,200, but its offence was unintentional. The fine imposed upon the manager was the maximum penalty (£500 for each offence), but the information which he gave on the four occasions libelled was substantially the same and he derived no personal benefit from his actings. Moreover, he lost his employment with the company through the episode. The court restricted the company's fine to £150 and the manager's to £500, Lord Justice-Clerk Cooper observing:

> " The heavy penalties so frequently specified in recent statutes, regulations, and orders, ought normally to be regarded as the limit set on the powers of the Court when dealing with the gravest type of offence which the Legislature contemplated as likely to arise in practice. In all proceedings under the Summary Jurisdiction (Scotland) Act 1908 the Court has, in addition, the express power to mitigate the statutory penalty conferred by section 43 of that Act, If that latter power is not used, and if in the early stages maximum, or nearly maximum, penalties are imposed in cases where few or no features of aggravation are present, there is grave risk that, if and when much more serious cases later arise, the Court may find itself powerless to exercise that just discrimination in the award of penalties which is indispensable to the due administration of criminal justice." [8]

In *Macleod* v. *Mackenzie* [9] the sheriff-substitute imposed fines totalling £60 upon a general merchant in a remote village in the Island of Lewis

---

[4] *Stewart* v. *Cormack*, 1941 J.C. 73, L.J.-G. at 77, approved in *Edward and Sons* v. *McKinnon*, 1943 J.C. 156; *W. and A.W. Henderson Ltd.* v. *Forster*, 1944 J.C. 91; *W. and Others* v. *Muir*, 1944 J.C. 128; *Blair* v. *Hawthorn*, 1945 J.C. 17; *Smith* v. *Adair*, 1945 J.C. 103; *Steven* v. *Mackenzie*, 1952 S.L.T. (Notes) 17; *Fleming* v. *Macdonald*, 1958 J.C. 1; *Sopwith* v. *Cruickshank*, 1959 J.C. 78.
[5] *Fleming* v. *Macdonald*, 1958 J.C. 1.
[6] 1943 J.C. 156.
[7] 1947 J.C. 103.
[8] 1943 J.C. at p. 168.
[9] Supra .

who had pleaded guilty to five summary complaints charging him with trifling contraventions of the Goods and Services (Price Control) Act 1941. There was no suggestion that the accused had any dishonest intention, and other goods at his store were undercharged. The court held that the sentences were oppressive and substituted for the fines an admonition under each of the five complaints.

16-30   W. & A. W. Henderson Ltd. v. Forster [10] and Blair v. Hawthorn [11] are cases where the sentence was held to be oppressive as proceeding upon an improper or irregular consideration. In the former, a company which had pleaded guilty to a contravention of section 13 (1) of the Factories Act 1937, was sentenced to a fine of £100—the maximum penalty—by the sheriff-substitute, who stated, inter alia, as a reason for refusing to modify the penalty that, under the section which authorised it, " the whole or any part of the fine may be applied for the benefit of the injured person or his family or otherwise as the Secretary of State determines." It was held that this was an improper and irregular consideration within the meaning of Lord Justice-General Normand's statement in Stewart v. Cormack [12] and that the fine fell to be reduced to £50. In Blair v. Hawthorn [13] a woman, previously of good character, who had pleaded guilty to a charge of stealing from an ordnance depot handkerchiefs to the value of 5s. 6d., was sentenced by the sheriff-substitute to forty day's imprisonment without the option of a fine. In a suspension it appeared from the averments that, while the accused's solicitor was addressing the court in mitigation of sentence, the sheriff-substitute had interjected the remark that she must have been aware of similar cases which had occurred, and of the sentences of imprisonment which had been imposed in many of them. The court, applying Stewart v. Cormack, held that the sentence was oppressive, in respect that a penalty had been inflicted which was not properly related to the gravity of the crime, Lord Justice-General Normand observing that, while it is sometimes proper for a court to take into consideration the frequency of particular crimes in a district, and to inflict an exemplary sentence, it is necessary even in such cases to consider any mitigating circumstances, whereas in Blair the sheriff-substitute appeared to have assumed against the accused that she knew of the similar cases to which he referred.

16-31   In Neil v. Stevenson, [14] a case prior to Stewart v. Cormack, the court reduced the sentence on a similar ground, although they did not actually hold that there had been oppression. The circumstances were that a sheriff-substitute, in passing sentence on an accused who had been convicted of assault for the fourth time, stated that, if the accused was

[10] 1944 J.C. 91.
[11] 1945 J.C. 17.
[12] 1941 J.C. 73.
[13] 1945 J.C. 17.
[14] 1920 J.C. 15. The Court has on several occasions reduced sentences without holding them to be oppressive. See e.g. Girgawy v. Strathern, 1925 J.C. 31, Aldred v. Langmuir, 1932 J.C. 22, Andrew v. Hunter [1948] C.L.Y. 4163 and Scott v. Robertson, [1949] C.L.Y. 4480. See also infra, para. 16-89.

brought back before him on a charge of the same kind, a sentence of six months' imprisonment would be pronounced. Seven months later the same person pleaded guilty to a charge of assault, and the sheriff-substitute sentenced him to six months' imprisonment. In passing sentence the sheriff-substitute referred to his statement on the previous occasion, and stated that he considered it his duty to the public to implement his promise to the prisoner. In a suspension the court, holding that the sheriff-substitute had been unduly influenced by what he had said on the earlier occasion, exercised their power of amendment under section 75 of the 1908 Act by restricting the term of imprisonment to a period of three months.

6–32   As an example of a case where the sentence was influenced by a misleading statement by the prosecutor *Galloway* v. *Adair* [15] may be cited. In that case, which was a prosecution under section 11 of the Road Traffic Act 1930, the accused pleaded guilty to a charge of " driving at a speed which was dangerous to the public." In his statement the prosecutor narrated facts which were relevant to a charge of reckless driving or of driving in a dangerous manner, but irrelevant to a charge of driving at an excessive speed—the only charge libelled. These irrelevant statements influenced the sheriff-substitute, who sentenced the accused to a term of imprisonment and disqualified him from holding or obtaining a driving licence for twelve months. In a suspension the court, holding the sentence to be oppressive, substituted a fine for the imprisonment and reduced the length of the period of disqualification. It is improper to take into account the circumstances of a previous conviction,[16] or any previous conviction which is not properly before the court.[17]

6–33   In *W. and Others* v. *Muir* [18] oppressive sentences which had been pronounced, not as a result of any misleading statement by the prosecutor, but because the facts of the case had not been properly laid before the inferior judge, were quashed by the court in order to avoid a miscarriage of justice. In that case four university students pleaded guilty to a charge of stealing four typewriters from the university premises. They were not separately represented, and the sheriff-substitute, refusing to apply the provisions of section 1 (1) of the Probation of Offenders Act 1907, sentenced each of them to three weeks' imprisonment. In a suspension brought by all of them against their sentences it appeared that two of the accused played a subordinate part in committing the crime, which in their cases could be regarded as partly of the nature of a prank or escapade. The court, holding that, if a miscarriage of justice was to be avoided, it was necessary, without displacing or ignoring the plea of guilty, to differentiate the four cases, applied section 1 (1) of the Act of 1907 to the effect of dismissing the charges against the two accused who had played a subordinate part, and refused the appeal in the other two cases. In *Sopwith* v.

[15] 1947 J.C. 7; cf. *Steven* v. *Mackenzie*, 1952 S.L.T. (Notes) 17.
[16] *Baker* v. *McFadyean*, 1952 S.L.T. (Notes) 70.
[17] *Russo* v. *Robertson*, 1951 S.L.T. 408.
[18] 1944 J.C. 128.

Cruickshank [19] a number of unrelated accused were charged in the sheriff court on the same day on separate complaints with various breaches of the Road Traffic Act. The sheriff-substitute disqualified them all for driving for twelve months. It was held that as the sheriff-substitute had not applied his mind to each case but merely applied an " overhead " disqualification, the disqualifications were oppressive as not being properly related to the offences.

Oppression: Sentence: First offenders

16–34   The question of oppression has frequently been raised in the case of first offenders.

There is nothing, per se, oppressive in imposing a maximum penalty,[20] or even imprisonment,[21] for a first offence although it is now necessary to obtain independent background reports before imposing imprisonment,[22] and imprisonment may be imposed only where no other method is appropriate.[23] Where the sheriff has failed to obtain the requisite reports or omitted some statutory requirement of form, such as the minuting of reasons for imposing imprisonment, the High Court may quash the sentence and release the offender [24] or may itself impose a prison sentence after obtaining any necessary reports.[25] Where the appropriate reports have been obtained it is not in itself harsh and oppressive to impose a more severe sentence than is recommended in the report.[26] In *Stewart* v. *Cormack* [27] the court refused to disturb a sentence of thirty days' imprisonment without the option of a fine which had been passed upon a youth of previous good character who had pleaded guilty to the theft from a motor lorry of some mechanical parts which were not of great value. If the first offence is one which is likely to cause danger to members of the public, the court is not disposed to substitute a fine for a sentence of imprisonment. In *Smith* v. *Adair* [28] the court declined to intervene where the accused had been sentenced to thirty days' imprisonment for a first offence of driving a vehicle while under the influence of drink, Lord Moncrieff remarking that in such a case " it would be a mere misdescription, even in the case of a first offender, to style a sentence of thirty days' imprisonment either harsh or oppressive." It has been held not to be harsh and

---

[19] 1959 J.C. 78.
[20] *Sinclair* v. *Mackenzie*, 1948 S.L.T. (Notes) 23. But see *Edward and Sons* v. *McKinnon*, 1943 J.C. 156, L.J.-G. at 168; *Andrew* v. *Hunter* [1948] C.L.Y. 4163.
[21] *Stewart* v. *Cormack*, 1941 J.C. 73; *Smith* v. *Adair*, 1945 J.C. 103; *Winslow* v. *Farrell*, 1965 J.C. 49; *Bruce* v. *Hogg*, 1966 J.C. 33; *Auld* v. *Herron*, 1969 J.C. 4. But see *Graham* v. *Waugh*, 1938 J.C. 108; *Andrew* v. *Hunter*, supra.
[22] First Offenders (Scotland) Act 1960; *Auld* v. *Herron*, supra. See infra, para. 17–04; supra, para. 15–36.
[23] Ibid.
[24] *Jamieson* v. *Heatley*, 1959 J.C. 22.
[25] *Winslow* v. *Farrell*, supra; *Bruce* v. *Hogg*, supra; *Auld* v. *Herron*, supra.
[26] *Kyle* v. *Cruickshank*, 1961 J.C. 1; *Scott* v. *MacDonald*, 1961 S.L.T. 257; cf. *Farquhar* v. *Burrell*, 1955 J.C. 66.
[27] Supra; cf. *Simpson* v. *Morrison*, 1951 J.C. 82.
[28] 1945 J.C.103.

oppressive to disqualify a lorry driver for driving for twelve months on conviction for having defective brakes.[29]

Oppression: Sentence: One-man company

6–35   In the case of a one-man company, there is nothing per se oppressive in fining both company and director.[30]

Oppression: Caution

6–36   In *Learmonth* v. *Salmon* [31] an applicant for a stated case was called on to find an excessive amount of caution one day before the period allowed for this purpose by section 62 of the 1908 Act was due to expire. He tendered the amount some days later, when the inferior judge refused to state a case in respect that tender had not been timeously made. In a suspension the court quashed the conviction, holding that the inexcusable delay in fixing the amount, and the excessive amount of caution—keeping in view that a month had been allowed within which to pay the fine— amounted to oppression. In *Grant* v. *Forrester* [32] a magistrate upon application for a stated case fixed an amount for caution, but no intimation of this was made to the accused. Thereafter the magistrate refused to state a case on the ground of failure to find caution. It was held that the procedure was inept and the conviction was quashed.

"Misled as to nature of charge": "Prejudiced in his defence on the merits"

6–37   The court cannot interfere on either of these grounds unless it is of opinion that there has been a miscarriage of justice.

Miscarriage of justice

6–38   A miscarriage of justice occurs when a prosecution results in a substantial failure to do justice to the accused person [33] in a matter either of conviction or of sentence.

6–39   As regards conviction there is a miscarriage of justice, not merely in cases where it can be demonstrated that the accused has been found guilty of an offence which he did not commit, but also in those cases in which the conviction is vitiated because of some mistake, irregularity or unfairness in the antecedent proceedings. Where such impropriety is such as to render subsequent procedure incompetent, the conviction will, of course, be set aside on that ground,[34] but, otherwise, the test is whether

---

[29] *Scobie* v. *Brown*, 1959 S.L.T. (Notes) 75.

[30] *Sarna* v. *Adair*, 1945 J.C. 141; cf. *Harrison* v. *Usher*, 1947 S.L.T. (Notes) 18 where eight members of the committee of a club were each fined £3 for selling liquor by the hand of the club secretary without a licence.

[31] 1926 J.C. 103.

[32] 1949 S.L.T. (Notes) 9.

[33] See *Winning* v. *Jeans* (1909) 6 Adam 1, Lord Pearson at 6.

[34] See cases cited supra, para. 16–17. But see also *Mackenzie* v. *McKillop*, 1938 J.C. 91, where, although the court held that the manifest irregularities in the complaint, conviction and sentence amounted to incompetency, they did not quash the conviction, but restricted the same and the sentence, on the ground that the accused had pleaded guilty to the complaint and that there was no dispute as to there having been a contravention of a

and to what extent the accused has suffered prejudice.[35] If the court considers that the impropriety in question was capable of influencing, and might have influenced, the inferior judge to the prejudice of the accused, it will intervene,[36] for a conviction cannot be allowed to stand unless the court is satisfied that no substantial injustice has been done.[37]

16–40   In some cases prejudice is presumed from the nature of the irregularity, and the conviction must be quashed. This rule applies in all cases where evidence has been wrongly excluded, because, as the court of review cannot see the evidence in question, it has no means of judging what its effect would have been had it been admitted.[38] On the other hand, where evidence is said to have been improperly admitted, the court is able to determine whether or not it may have affected the judgment in the case.[39] Prejudice will also be presumed in cases (other than those in which trial in absence is competent) where any part of the trial is conducted outwith the presence of the accused.[40] Prejudice is not presumed from a refusal to grant an accused person a private interview with his law agent upon his apprehension.[41] The position as regards adjournments has already been considered.[42] Failure to provide an interpreter in the case of foreigners with little or no knowledge of English is inconsistent with the proper administration of justice, and their conviction will not be allowed to stand.[43]

16–41   The court will intervene in any case where, from any cause, the sentence is so unfair as to constitute a miscarriage of justice.[44]

---

particular statutory provision which was the main offence charged. And see *Hemphill* v. *Smith*, 1923 J.C. 23, where, although it was held that the complaint was irrelevant, the conviction was not quashed, as it did not appear that the irrelevancy of the complaint had misled or prejudiced the accused.

[35] See e.g. *Pennington* v. *Mackenzie*, 1946 J.C., 12; *Rendle* v. *Thomson*, 1947 S.L.T. (Notes) 27.

[36] *Falconer* v. *Brown* (1893) 1 Adam 96, Lord McLaren at 101.

[37] *Winning* v. *Jeans*, supra, Lord Pearson at 6.

[38] *Winning* v. *Torrance*, 1928 J.C. 79, Lord Anderson at 86; *Falconer* v. *Brown*, supra; *Thomson* v. *Neilson* (1900) 3 Adam 195; *McLean* v. *Skinner* (1907) 5 Adam 376; *Mackenzie* v. *Jinks*, 1934 J.C. 48. In *Clark* v. *Stuart*, 1950 J.C. 8, at p. 11, L.J.-G. Cooper observed that only exceptional circumstances would justify the exclusion of an important chapter of evidence outright, with the effect of placing matters beyond the control of any appellate tribunal, and that the normal and proper course would be to allow such evidence under reservations as to competency. Although there is no provision for recording such evidence it could be incorporated in a stated case. In *MacLeod* v. *Woodmuir Miners Welfare Society Social Club*, 1961 J.C. 5, the sheriff-substitute followed the course suggested in *Clark* v. *Stuart*, allowing the evidence to be led under reservation of its admissibility, and eventually rejected it as incompetent. This enabled the High Court, who held the evidence to be competent, to remit with a direction to convict, but L.J.-G. Clyde said that the proper procedure was to determine the admissibility and competency of evidence when first raised. No reference was made to *Clark* v. *Stuart*. In *Bell* v. *Hogg* (1967 J.C. 49) the *Clark* v. *Stuart* course was adopted and the evidence ultimately held competent by the sheriff and the High Court.

[39] *Winning* v. *Torrance*, supra, Lord Anderson at 86; *Hodgsons* v. *Macpherson* (1913) 7 Adam 118. Where there is ample evidence on which to convict the accused, apart from the evidence complained of, the conviction will not be disturbed. (*Brown* v. *Macpherson*, 1918 J.C. 3: *Waddell* v. *Kinnaird*, 1922 J.C. 40; *Wade* v. *Robertson*, 1948 J.C. 117.)

[40] *Aitken* v. *Wood*, 1921 J.C. 84 (evidence); *Watson* v. *Argo*, 1936 J.C. 87 (sentence).

[41] *Cheyne* v. *McGregor*, 1941 J.C. 17; *cf. Law* v. *McNicol*, 1965 J.C. 32.

[42] Supra, paras. 16–21 et seq.

[43] *Liszewski* v. *Thomson*, 1942 J.C. 55.

[44] *W. and Others* v. *Muir*, 1944 J.C. 128.

Forms of procedure and fees

16–42   A complete course of procedure is prescribed by the 1954 Act; but provision is made for alterations and amendments, if these should be found necessary. The High Court may by Act of Adjournal:

(a) Make rules to give effect to any of the provisions of the Act;

(b) Make rules regulating the procedure under the Act;

(c) Cancel or amend any of the forms under the Act, or provide additional forms;

(d) Fix and regulate the fees payable in the High Court and in the inferior courts in proceedings under the Act.[44a]

The fees payable in the High Court are now regulated by Act of Adjournal,[44b] and the fees payable in the inferior courts are now also set forth in an Act of Adjournal.[44c] Nothing in section 76 affects the regulations enacted by the Courts of Law Fees (Scotland) Act 1895.[45]

16–43   By the Act of Adjournal of March 20, 1909, relative to appeals under section 63 of the 1908 Act, the High Court, in pursuance of the powers conferred on them by section 74 of the 1908 Act, enacted that on and after June 1, 1909, no clerk's fees, court fees, or other fees or expenses shall be exigible from or awarded against an appellant in custody in respect of an appeal to the High Court against the amount of caution fixed or on account of refusal or liberation by a court of summary jurisdiction.

Application for case

16–44   " Application to have a case stated shall be made at the time when judgment is given, or at any time within ten days thereafter, and shall be signed by the appellant or his solicitor, and either written on the complaint or lodged with the clerk of court, and where the latter course is adopted the clerk of court shall enter in the record of the proceedings the date when the application was lodged, and shall thereupon intimate the appeal to the respondent." [46] Prior to the Law Reform (Miscellaneous Provisions) (Scotland) Act 1966, the period allowed was five days.

Intimation by the clerk of court must be given to the respondent personally, notice to his solicitor not being sufficient.[47]

In reckoning the ten days, the date of the determination of the inferior judge is not counted,[48] nor are Sundays and public holidays, it being specifically provided by section 70 that, in computing the period of days in appeals under the Act, Sundays and public holidays shall not be included.

[44a] 1954 Act, s.76.

[44b] Act of Adjournal (Fees in the High Court of Justiciary) 1970.

[44c] Act of Adjournal (Fees in the Inferior Courts) 1972.

[45] 1954 Act, s. 76 (3).

[46] 1954 Act, s. 63 (1), as amended by Law Reform (Miscellaneous Provisions) (Scotland) Act 1966, s. 9.

[47] *Niddrie and Benhar Coal Co.* v. *Young* (1895) 22 R. 413.

[48] *Hutton* v. *Garland* (1884) 5 Couper 274; *Smith* v. *Gray*, 1925 J.C. 8, Lord Anderson at 12.

16–45   While it is obviously desirable that an application for a stated case should actually be lodged before the expiry of the tenth day, it would appear that an application posted on the tenth day is timeous, although it is not received by the clerk of court until later.[49] It would also appear that the application must be in writing.[50] Both of these points were considered in *Smith* v. *Gray*,[51] where an oral application for a stated case was made immediately after conviction, and was recorded in the minutes of procedure. Subsequently a written application signed by the accused's solicitor was posted to the clerk of court on the fifth day (excluding the date of conviction) after the conviction. Objection was taken to the competency of the stated case. The court held that the case failed upon the merits, and neither Lord Justice-Clerk Alness nor Lord Hunter thought it necessary to express a concluded opinion upon the above topic, although the former said that in the circumstances he would be slow to sustain the objection to competency and the latter thought that there had been substantial compliance with the Act. Lord Anderson, however, in view of the general importance of the matter, expressed his opinion thus:

> " In order to satisfy the terms of the section, I am of opinion that an application for a stated case must conform to these three conditions:— (*first*) it must be in writing; (*second*) it must be signed either by the accused or by his law-agent; and (*third*) it must be made within a period of five days after the date on which judgment was pronounced." [51a]

He considered that an oral application recorded in the minutes of procedure was insufficient, because of the absence of the signature of the accused or his law agent, and the consequent non-compliance with the form prescribed by Schedule H of the 1908 Act. As regards the application posted on the fifth day after judgment he said:

> " It was, therefore, timeously dispatched, if not timeously received. It seems to me that the section is to be construed liberally in favour of an accused person who is anxious to have a conviction of which he complains reviewed. So construing it, I have formed the opinion that a written application timeously posted is timeously made in the sense of the Act." [51b]

16–46   Section 9 of the Law Reform (Miscellaneous Provisions) (Scotland) Act 1966 allows the High Court to direct that additional time may be allowed to an applicant to comply with the provisions of section 63 (1). An application for such a direction is made in writing to the Clerk of

---

[49] *Smith* v. *Gray*, supra, Lord Anderson at 12, Lord Hunter at 11; *Charleson* v. *Duffes* (1881) 4 Couper 470. Cf. *Thom* v. *Caledonian Railway Company* (1886) 1 White 248; *Blair* v. *Brown*, 1941 S.N. 30; *Gibson* v. *McKechnie*, 1942 S.N. 69.

[50] *Smith* v. *Gray*, supra, Lord Anderson at 11. See also 1954 Act (2nd Sched. Part VI).

[51] Supra.

[51a] at 11.

[51b] at 12.

Justiciary, stating the grounds for the application. Notification of the application must be made to the clerk of the inferior court, who thereupon transmits the proceedings to the Clerk of Justiciary. The application is dealt with in the same manner as an application for interim liberation, but the High Court has power to dispense with a hearing, and also to make such enquiry relating to the application as the court thinks fit. The High Court may regulate the procedure for such application by Act of Adjournal.

Caution

16–47 " Immediately on an appeal under section sixty-two of this Act being taken the court shall fix a sum to be consigned by the appellant, or for which caution is to be found, to meet any fine and expenses imposed and the expenses of the appeal, and the appellant shall not be entitled to have a case stated unless within five days after the date of his appeal he has made consignation, or found such caution, to the satisfaction of the clerk of court and has also paid the clerk his fees for preparing the case:

Provided that

(i) the court shall have power, in any case where it deems it expedient so to do to dispense with consignation or the finding of caution, and

(ii) a person prosecuting in the public interest shall not be bound to make consignation or to find caution." [52]

The purpose of this section is to allow the appellant five days from the date of his appeal within which to find the money for caution or consignation,[53] and, accordingly, the sum required in either case must be fixed by the inferior court immediately to give him an adequate opportunity of complying with the requirements of the section.[54]

16–48 Where caution or consignation is ordered it is a condition precedent of the appellant's right to have a case stated by the inferior court that he should comply with the order timeously.[55] In the ordinary case, therefore, failure to find caution or to make consignation within the five days allowed by the section is fatal to the appellant. Thus, in a case under the 1875 Act, where an appellant, who had failed to lodge his bond of caution within the three days prescribed by that statute and had been refused a stated case by the sheriff-substitute, presented a note to the High Court asking that the sheriff-substitute be ordained to state a case but averring no special circumstances excusing the delay, the court refused the note.[56]

[52] 1954 Act, s. 64.
[53] *Learmonth* v. *Salmon*, 1926 J.C. 103.
[54] *Mackintosh* v. *Wooster*, 1919 J.C. 15; *Greig* v. *Finlay* (1901) 3 Adam 316.
[55] *Furnheim* v. *Watson*, 1946 J.C. 99, L.J.-C. at 101.
[56] *McGregor* v. *Rose* (1887) 1 White 477.

16–49   Delay in complying with the provisions of section 64 is not, however, invariably fatal to an appellant.

In the first place, he will not be deprived of his stated case if there has been no fault on his part and the delay is due to circumstances outwith his control.[57] In a case under the 1875 Act [58] the applicants were unable to lodge a bond of caution or make consignation or pay the clerk of court's fee within the three days prescribed by the Act, the circumstances being that, although their law agent had done everything in his power to find the magistrate and clerk of court within that period, he had been unable to do so. The magistrate having refused to state a case, the court pronounced an order on him to state and sign one. In *Mackintosh* v. *Wooster* [59] the inferior court did not fix the amount of caution until after five days from the date of the appellant's taking his appeal, and so prevented him from finding caution timeously. He obtained a stated case at the hearing of which the Lord Advocate, who appeared for the respondent, intimated that he did not, in the circumstances, challenge the competency of the appeal. In *Learmonth* v. *Salmon* [60] the court held that the fixing of an excessive amount of caution one day before the expiry of the five days prescribed by the corresponding section of the 1908 Act (section 62) amounted to oppression, and they quashed the conviction.

16–50   In the second place, it would appear that, although the inferior judge has no power to extend the time allowed by section 64 to appellants for obtaining caution or consignation,[61] he may exercise his power under the section of dispensing with caution or consignation even after he has ordered the same and the appellant has failed timeously to comply with the order,[62] thus enabling such appellant to obtain a stated case. As, however, the requirement of caution or consignation is principally in the interests of the respondent to safeguard his claim to expenses in an appeal,[63] it would seem that he is entitled to appear before the inferior judge in order to found upon the appellant's failure to comply with the requirements of section 64 as a reason why a case should not be stated and also to oppose the exercise by the judge of the dispensing power.[64] These steps should be taken in the inferior court. If they are so taken and fail of effect, the respondent may repeat his objections when the case reaches the High Court.[65] There is nothing in section 64 which compels the High Court to hold that a stated case, granted without objection on the part of the respondent to an appellant who has failed to find caution or to make consignation

---

[57] *Mackintosh* v. *Wooster*, 1919 J.C. 15; *Greig* v. *Finlay* (1901) 3 Adam 316; *Thom* v. *Caledonian Railway Company* (1886) 1 White 248, Lord Young at 255; *McGregor* v. *Rose* (1887) 1 White 477, Lord Young at 481. Cf. *Learmonth* v. *Salmon*, 1926 J.C. 103.

[58] Summary Prosecutions Appeals (Scotland) Act 1875, s. 3; *Greig* v. *Finlay*, supra.

[59] Supra.

[60] Supra. Cf. *Grant* v. *Forrester*, 1949 S.L.T. (Notes) 9.

[61] *Furnheim* v. *Watson*, 1946 J.C. 99, L.J.-C. at 102.

[62] Ibid.

[63] Ibid.

[64] Ibid.

[65] Ibid. See also *Thom* v. *Caledonian Railway Company*, supra, Lord Young at 255.

timeously, is, per se, ultra vires of the inferior court and fundamentally null.[66]

6–51 The question of dispensing with caution or consignation is one for the discretion of the inferior judge. Each case must depend on its own circumstances.

Interim liberation

6–52 If the appellant is in custody, the court may, on consignation being made or caution being found as already mentioned, grant interim liberation on such conditions as to caution or otherwise as the court may fix, and may grant a sist of execution, or may dispense with further consignation or caution, or may make any other interim order which the justice of the case may require, or may refuse to grant interim liberation. An application for interim liberation must be disposed of by the court within twenty-four hours after it has been made.[67]

6–53 The appellant, if dissatisfied with the amount of caution fixed, or on refusal of liberation, may, within twenty-four hours after the judgment of the court, appeal thereagainst by a note of appeal written on the complaint and signed by himself or his solicitor. The complaint and proceedings are thereupon transmitted to the Clerk of Justiciary, and the High Court, or any judge thereof, either in court or in chambers, after hearing parties, has power to review the decision of the inferior court, and to grant interim liberation on such conditions as such court or judge may think fit, or to refuse interim liberation.[68]

6–54 In the event of the appellant obtaining interim liberation, and thereafter not proceeding with his appeal, the inferior court has power to grant warrant to apprehend and imprison him for such period of his sentence as at the date of his liberation remained unexpired, said period to run from the date of his imprisonment under such warrant.[69] This warrant may be obtained by the prosecutor in the inferior court on presenting a petition in the form contained in Part I of the Second Schedule.

If at the time of abandonment of his appeal such an appellant is serving a term of imprisonment imposed subsequently to the conviction appealed against, the court from which the appeal was taken has power to order that the sentence relating to that conviction, or the unexpired portion thereof, should run from such date as the court may think fit, provided that it is not later than the expiry of the subsequent sentence.[70]

Consent to setting aside conviction

6–55 Section 72 of the 1954 Act, superseding section 73 of the 1908 Act, provides:

[66] *Furnheim* v. *Watson*, supra, L.J.-C. at 102.
[67] 1954 Act, s. 65.
[68] Ibid.
[69] Ibid.
[70] 1954 Act, s. 65 (4), as added by 1963 Act, s. 32 (1).

" (1) Where an appeal has been taken under section sixty-two of this Act or by suspension or otherwise, and the prosecutor, on the appeal being intimated to him, is not prepared to maintain the judgment appealed against, he may by a minute signed by him and written on the complaint or lodged with the clerk of court consent to the conviction and sentence being set aside, either in whole or in part. Such minute shall set forth the grounds on which the prosecutor is of opinion that the judgment cannot be maintained.

(2) A copy of any minute under the last foregoing subsection shall be sent by the prosecutor to the appellant, and the clerk of court shall thereupon ascertain from the appellant or his solicitor whether he desires to be heard by the High Court before the appeal is disposed of, and shall note on the record whether or not the appellant so desires, and shall thereafter transmit the complaint and relative proceedings to the clerk of justiciary.

(3) The clerk of justiciary on receipt of a complaint and relative proceedings under the last foregoing subsection shall lay them before any judge of the High Court, either in court or in chambers, and such judge, after hearing parties if they desire to be heard, or without hearing parties, may set aside the conviction either in whole or in part and award expenses to the appellant not exceeding five guineas, or may refuse to set aside the conviction, in which case the proceedings shall be returned to the clerk of the inferior court, and the appellant shall then be entitled to proceed with his appeal in the same way as if it had been marked on the date when the complaint and proceedings are returned to the clerk of the inferior court.

(4) Where proceedings are taken under this section, the preparation of the draft stated case shall be delayed pending the decision of the High Court.

(5) The power conferred by this section to consent to a conviction and sentence being set aside shall be exercisable

    (a) where the appeal is by stated case, at any time within ten days after the receipt by the prosecutor of the draft stated case; and

    (b) where the appeal is by suspension at any time within ten days after the service on the prosecutor of the bill of suspension."

16–56   This section provides a shorthand procedure whereby convictions which are untenable and which cannot for palpable reasons be supported may be set aside.[71] Its primary object is to save expense and delay in appeals against such convictions.[72] In a case prior to the 1949 Act, the view was expressed that the proper time for the prosecutor to lodge his minute is when the appeal is intimated to him and that it is an improper practice for prosecutors to defer lodging the minute until they have had an opportunity of perusing the draft stated case.[73]

[71] *O'Brien* v. *Adair*, 1947 J.C. 180, L.J.-G. Cooper at 181.
[72] Ibid.
[73] See opinion of L.J.-G. Cooper in *O'Brien* v. *Adair*, supra.

6-57   Notwithstanding its use of the words " by suspension or otherwise "
the section was held prior to the 1949 Act not to apply to bills of suspension.[74] It is not easy to understand this decision, which was abrogated
by the provisions of section 47 (1) of the 1949 Act which are embodied in
those of the 1954 Act above set forth.

6-58   As a judgment of a competent court cannot be set aside by the High
Court except upon satisfactory grounds of law,[75] the hearing of an appeal
by stated case can be dispensed with only when a decision as to whether
a conviction can be allowed to stand can be reached without the necessity
of considering the questions of law which the case raises.[76] Accordingly,
the procedure provided by section 72 is limited to cases where convictions
are palpably wrong—e.g. " where some fatal flaw in the proceedings has
been discovered or where new facts have come to the prosecutor's
knowledge." [77] In *O'Brien* v. *Adair* [78] the prosecutor endorsed a minute on
the complaint in terms of section 73 of the 1908 Act consenting to the
conviction being set aside " in respect that there is insufficient evidence to
warrant a conviction." The complaint and proceedings were laid before
Lord Justice-General Cooper, who refused in hoc statu to set aside the
conviction on the ground that only the High Court and not the prosecutor
could say whether the inferior judge was entitled to convict. In the course
of his opinion Lord Cooper said, "I am bound by the terms of the section,
and I do not consider that it was intended to authorise the prosecutor to
reverse a Sheriff on a question of law, least of all after consideration
by the prosecutor of a case stated by the Sheriff for the opinion, not of
the prosecutor, but of the High Court." [79]

In *Jensen* v. *Wilson* [80] the parties to a stated case which had been
signed and lodged with the Clerk of Justiciary presented a joint minute
to the court in which they concurred in asking the court to set aside
the conviction. The court held that it could not give effect to the joint
minute without hearing argument against the conviction.

6-59   The maximum sum which might be awarded as expenses under section
73 of the 1908 Act to a successful appellant was £3 3s. It was increased by
section 43 (2) of the 1949 Act to £5 5s. In a case prior to the 1949 Act [81]
the prosecutor intimated that he was not prepared to support the conviction. The appellant having intimated that she desired to be heard, the
appeal was heard in chambers by Lord Justice-Clerk Cooper, who, after
hearing parties, refused in hoc statu to set aside the conviction. The
appellant, having been thereafter successful in the High Court, moved for
expenses upon the ordinary scale, the prosecutor contending that the

---

[74] *Loudon* v. *Torrance* (1916) 7 Adam 762.
[75] *Jensen* v. *Wilson* (1911) 6 Adam 535, L.J.-C. Macdonald at 539.
[76] Ibid.; *O'Brien* v. *Adair*, supra. Cf. *Small* v. *Clark*, 1946 J.C. 133.
[77] *O'Brien* v. *Adair*, supra, L.J.-G. at 181.
[78] Supra.
[79] 1947 J.C. at 182.
[80] Supra.
[81] *Small* v. *Clark*, 1946 J.C. 133. £5 5s. expenses were allowed in *Loudon* v. *Torrance*, supra.

expenses should be limited to those prescribed by section 73. The court, without delivering opinions, awarded £3 3s. of expenses. The soundness of this decision seems open to question.

Preparation of case

16–60   Section 66 of the 1954 Act provides as follows:

" (1) The clerk of court shall, within ten days from an application for a stated case under section sixty-two of this Act, or, when consignation or caution is ordered, within five days from the date when consignation has been made or caution found, prepare a draft stated case, and shall within the said period send the draft to the appellant or his solicitor, and a duplicate thereof to the respondent or his solicitor.

(2) A stated case shall be in the form as nearly as may be of the form contained in Part VI of the Second Schedule to this Act, and shall set forth the particulars of any matters competent for review which the appellant desires to bring under the review of the High Court, and of the facts, if any, proved in the case, and any point of law decided, and the grounds of the decision."

16–61   Section 67 of the 1954 Act provides as follows:

" (1) Within one month after receipt of the draft case under the last foregoing section each party shall cause to be transmitted to the judge against whose judgment the appeal is taken and to the other parties a note of any adjustments he desires to have made on the draft case or intimate that he has no such adjustments to suggest, and if the appellant fails so to do he shall be deemed to have abandoned his appeal, and in any such case the court shall have the like power to grant warrant for his apprehension and imprisonment as is conferred by section sixty-five of this Act.

(2) Within fourteen days after the latest date on which any such adjustments or intimation as aforesaid are or is received the judge against whose judgment the appeal is taken shall (unless the appellant is deemed to have abandoned his appeal) after considering any such adjustments, state and sign the case."

As explained infra, paragraph 16–93, the 1954 Act provides for review by way of suspension where the trial judge is unable to sign a stated case applied for by a convicted person.

Form of case

16–62   The stated case is in the form provided by Part VI of the Second Schedule to the 1954 Act. It ought to set out fully the facts proved.[82] It is improper merely to narrate what the witnesses said, as the inferior court must form its own view of the evidence and state the effect of the evidence

---

[82] *Gordon* v. *Hansen* (1914) 7 Adam 441; *Waddell* v. *Kinnaird*, 1922 J.C. 40; *Jesner* v. *Adair*, 1943 S.N. 25.

in the stated case.[83] Even where the controversy between the parties is confined to some particular point, as, for example, the admission or rejection of a particular line of evidence, the stated case should narrate the facts fully, and should not be confined merely to the questions and answers which were the subject of objection.[84]

16-63 The facts proved should be set forth in the case itself and not in a separate document.[85] It has been held to be an improper practice for a judge to omit findings in fact from the stated case proper and to refer to his annexed judgment, which contained findings in fact and law.[86] The case should not set forth the evidence on which the findings in fact are based.[87] Similarly, the grounds of the decision should be stated distinctly in the stated case,[88] and not in an annexation thereto,[89] there being no warrant in the Act for such annexation.[90] The ground of decision is important when evidence has been disallowed.[91]

16-64 Where a sheriff, for special reasons, imposes disqualification for holding a licence for less than the statutory period when convicting the appellant of an offence against the Road Traffic Acts, the grounds of indulgence should be set forth in the stated case.[92]

Form of question of law

16-65 Where an appellant desires to raise the general issue of whether there was sufficient evidence in law to support the conviction, the question of law should be stated in the following, or similar terms: " On the facts stated, was I entitled to convict (or acquit) the accused ? " A question phrased " On the facts proved ought the Sheriff to have convicted the accused ? " is one " which in ordinary circumstances should not be put " to the court.[93] In commenting on it Lord Justice-Clerk Macdonald said:

> " There are cases where the facts and the law are so inextricably mixed that it may be permissible to put the question of law in this shape; as where a statute provides that certain acts shall constitute an offence where done without ' lawful and sufficient ' excuse, or in cases where the defence depends on the bona fides of the accused. But in this particular case all we have before us is this—that certain

---

[3] *Gordon* v. *Hansen*, supra. Cf. *Coulthard* v. *Mackenzie* (1879) 6 R.1322; *Stenhouse* v. *Dykes* (1908) 5 Adam 553.

[84] *Waddell* v. *Kinnaird*, supra.

[85] *Mackenna* v. *Dunn*, 1918, 2 S.L.T. 66.

[86] Ibid.

[87] *Pert* v. *Robinson*, 1955 S.L.T. 23.

[88] *Lyon* v. *Don Brothers, Buist and Co.*, 1944 J.C. 1, L.J.-G. at 5; *Strathern* v. *Ross*, 1927 J.C. 70, L.J.-C. at 75.

[89] *Cockburn* v. *Gordon*, 1928 J.C. 87, L.J.-C. at 91.

[90] Ibid.

[91] *Falconer* v. *Brown* (1893) 1 Adam 96.

[92] *Campbell* v. *Sinclair*, 1938 J.C. 127, Lord Moncrieff at 128. An accused person who has been duly served with a notice intimating that he is liable to disqualification must state timeously in the inferior court any " special reasons " which he desires to advance for the non-imposition of the disqualification. It is too late to do this in an appeal to the High Court in such a case (*Hynd* v. *Clerk*, 1954 S.L.T. 85).

[93] *Todd* v. *Cochrane* (1901) 3 Adam 357, L.J.-C. at 363; cf. *Boyd* v. *Lewis*, 1959 S.L.T.(Notes) 27.

evidence was led for the prosecution, partly statutory no doubt, and certain other evidence was led for the defence, and we are asked whether, on the whole matter, the Sheriff-Substitute has come to a right conclusion. That is not a case in which we have any power to intervene." [94]

A question in the following terms: " Whether the facts proved warranted a conviction under the Act libelled?" is unsatisfactory.[95] Lord Justice-Clerk Macdonald, with reference to the form of the question, said:

" It is too common for judges in stating cases to put a question of law in this form, but it is not satisfactory. The question of law is not whether the conviction was ' warranted,' but whether the judge has legally pronounced a conviction on the facts found by him. In other words, did he, in holding that the facts proved justified him in convicting, err in applying the law to these facts? If there was nothing illegal in convicting, the question whether a conviction is warranted or not, is one for the judge trying the case." [96]

16–66   Where, however, an appellant wishes to raise a specific legal issue, he must put forward a question of law which precisely defines the issue and not one in mere general terms, as, otherwise, there is no real guarantee that the point taken in the appellate court was a live one in the court below or that the inferior judge had it in view when stating the case.[97] So, where, under the general question " Whether on the foregoing facts the court was entitled to convict the appellant of the offence charged? " it was sought to raise a question of law as to the elements necessary to constitute an offence against the statute libelled, the court held that the point was not properly before it and could not be considered.[98] Similarly, if an appellant wishes to attack a finding in fact on the ground that the inferior judge had no material before him to enable him to make the finding, there must be a question of law specifically raising that issue.[99] A specific question is obviously called for where the issue is whether certain evidence has been improperly admitted or rejected.[1]

---

[94] Ibid. at 363–4.

[95] *Jenkinson* v. *Neilson Bros.* (1899) 3 Adam 88.

[96] Ibid. at 95.

[97] *Drummond* v. *Hunter*, 1948 J.C. 109, L.J.-C. at 113; cf. *Boyd* v. *Lewis*, 1959 S.L.T. (Notes) 27.

[98] *Drummond* v. *Hunter*, supra.

[99] *Rattray* v. *Paterson*, 1954 S.L.T. 107.

[1] In *Waddell* v. *Kinnaird*, 1922 J.C. 40 the question of law was " Whether the evidence above referred to was admissible evidence? " In *Falconer* v. *Brown* (1893) 1 Adam 96, the question was " Whether the Court was right in disallowing the questions put to the witness George Hugh Mackay, by the agent for the accused?" In *Macleod* v. *Woodmuir Miners Welfare Society Social Club*, 1961 J.C. 5 the question was, " Was I right in sustaining the objection made to oral evidence by the sampling officers of the words written on the label of the whisky bottle, without production of the label? " In *Miln* v. *Cullen*, 1967 J.C. 21 it was, " Should I have admitted the evidence of the respondent's reply to the question put to him as to whether or not he was the driver of the car . . . and accordingly have found him guilty . . . ? " In *Bell* v. *Hogg*, 1967 J.V. 49 it was, " Was the evidence of the scientific analysis of the hand-rubbing impressions taken from . . . the appelants admissible? "; cf. *Underwood* v. *Henderson* (1898) 2 Adam 596.

6–67   A question of law: " Were the sentences I imposed excessive? " has been held to be incompetent, as the 1908 Act confers no right of appeal against sentence, except on the ground of oppression.[2]

Record

6–68   On an appeal being taken, the clerk of court must record on the complaint the different steps of procedure in the appeal. Such record is held as evidence of the dates on which the various steps of procedure took place. This provision prevents any dispute as to whether the several steps of procedure have been timeously taken. In appeals the forms of procedure must be in accordance with Part VI of the Second Schedule.[3]

Transmission and intimation

16–69   As soon as the case is signed by the judge against whose judgment the appeal is taken,[4] the clerk of court must send it to the appellant, and must also transmit the complaint, documentary productions, and any other proceedings in the cause to the clerk of justiciary.[5] There appears to be a tendency in modern practice to construe the directive as to the transmission of the case by the clerk of court to the appellant as being a directive to transmit the case to the appellant's solicitor, but the point does not appear to have been the subject of judicial decision.

16–70   Section 67 of the 1954 Act (as amended by the Law Reform (Miscellaneous Provisions) (Scotland) Act 1966, section 9) provides:

> " (4) The appellant shall within ten days after receiving the case send a copy of it to the respondent and cause it to be transmitted to or lodged with the clerk of justiciary together with a certificate by himself or his solicitor that a copy has been sent to the respondent in accordance with the requirement herein before contained.
>
> (5) If the appellant fails to comply with the last foregoing subsection he shall be deemed to have abandoned his appeal, and the court shall have the like power to grant warrant for his apprehension and imprisonment as is conferred by section sixty-five of this Act."

16–71   So far as lodging the case with the Clerk of Justiciary is concerned, it should be noted that established practice requires this to be done by an Edinburgh solicitor who must prepare the appropriate inventory of process and who will be held responsible to the High Court for the proper execution of all matters in connection with the appeal. In effect, this means that non-Edinburgh solicitors must act through Edinburgh correspondents. Procurators fiscal in sheriff courts act through the Crown Agent.

---

[2] *Jesner* v. *Adair*, 1943 S.N. 36. See supra, paras. 16–28 et seq.

[3] 1954 Act, s. 69.

[4] In *Downie* v. *Thomson* (1901) 9 S.L.T. 251, the conviction was quashed of consent because the magistrate who signed the stated case did not sign the conviction.

[5] 1954 Act, s. 67 (3).

So far as notification to the respondent is concerned it was held under the corresponding section of the Summary Prosecutions Appeals (Scotland) Act 1875, that notice of appeal sent to the respondents' agent was not sufficient.[6] Despite this authority modern practice seems to be to permit intimation to solicitors.

16–72   The case and copy thereof should respectively reach the Clerk of Justiciary and the respondent within the statutory ten days. In either case posting within the period is probably sufficient,[7] but otherwise the statutory provisions must be adhered to. The day of reception of the case is not counted as one of the days.[8] Prior to the Law Reform (Miscellaneous Provisions) (Scotland) Act 1966 the High Court applied the time limit strictly.[9]

The High Court has the same power to direct the allowance of additional time to comply with the requirements of section 67 (4) as in the case of section 63 (1). In the case of an application in relation to section 67 (4) notification is not required to the clerk of the inferior court.[10]

Abandonment of appeal

16–73   The appellant may at any time prior to lodging the case with the Clerk of Justiciary abandon his appeal by minute signed by himself or his solicitor, written on the complaint or lodged with the clerk of court, and intimated to the respondent. Such abandonment is without prejudice to any other mode of appeal, review, advocation or suspension competent.[11]

On the case being lodged with the Clerk of the Justiciary the appellant is held to have abandoned any other mode of appeal which might have been open to him.[12] He may, however, in exceptional cases, proceed thereafter by petition to the nobile officium.[13]

Printing

16–74   On lodging the case and the inventory of process with the Clerk of Justiciary it is the duty of the Edinburgh solicitor immediately to uplift the case and the proceedings from the Justiciary Office for printing. It is usual to print the stated case, and to annex to it as an appendix a print of the complaint, record of proceedings, minutes of conviction and sentence, and any documentary productions which are material to the appeal and are referred to in the statement of facts.[14] Fifteen copies of this print should be lodged in the Justiciary Office when the process is returned to

---

[6] *Niddrie and Benhar Coal Company* v. *Young* (1895) 22 R. 413.
[7] Supra; *Smith* v. *Gray*, 1925 J.C. 8; *Charleson* v. *Duffes*, (1881) 4 Couper 470; *Thom* v. *Caledonian Railway Co.* (1886) 1 White 248.
[8] *Cameron* v. *Macdonald*, 1961 J.C. 11.
[9] *Bennett* v. *MacLeod*, 1958 S.L.T. 67.
[10] Law Reform (Miscellaneous Provisions) (Scotland) Act 1966, s. 9; see supra, para. 16–46.
[11] 1954 Act, s. 68 (1). See also supra, para. 16–54.
[12] Ibid., s. 68 (2).
[13] *Patrick McCloy*, Petnr., 1971 S.L.T. (Notes) 32; infra, para. 16–129.
[14] See *Cairney* v. *Patterson*, 1945 J.C. 120.

that office after printing has been carried out. A few prints are usually sent by the appellant to the respondent or his solicitor. In the case of an appeal against a sheriff court procurator fiscal eight copies should be lodged with the Crown Office.

6–75   The case is heard by the High Court on such date as may be fixed by that court.[15]

Powers of High Court

6–76   The following powers as regards appeals by stated case are conferred upon the High Court by section 71 of the 1954 Act:

(a)   To affirm, reverse, or amend the determination of the inferior court; or

(b)   To impose a fine instead of imprisonment, where imprisonment has been awarded; or

(c)   To reduce the period of imprisonment; or

(d)   To reduce any fine imposed by the inferior court; or

(e)   To remit the case back to the inferior court to be amended, and thereafter, on the case being amended and returned, to deliver judgment thereon; or

(f)   To remit the case to the inferior court with their opinion thereon;

(g)   Where an appeal against an acquittal is sustained, the High Court may either convict and sentence the accused or may remit the case to the inferior court with instructions to convict and sentence the accused, who is bound to attend any diet fixed by such court for this purpose.

(h)   The High Court have power to award such expenses both in the High and inferior courts as they may think fit.[16]

(i)   The High Court may remit to any fit person to inquire and report in regard to the facts and circumstances of any appeal, and on considering such report may pronounce judgment.

(j)   In addition, the High Court have the powers of amendment conferred upon them in every kind of appeal by the proviso to section 73 of the 1954 Act, which enacts that the High Court may amend any conviction, sentence, judgment, order of court, or other proceeding, or may pronounce such other sentence, judgment, or order as they shall judge expedient.

6–77   Where the appellant has been granted interim liberation, whether his appeal is under the 1954 Act or otherwise, he must appear personally in court on the day or days fixed for the hearing of his appeal. If he fails to appear, unless the court on cause shown permits the appeal to be heard, he is held to have abandoned it. [17] In the event of the appeal being dismissed or refused in whole or in part, the High Court have power to grant

[15] 1954 Act, s. 71.
[16] The subject of expenses in appeals is dealt with infra, para. 17–101.
[17] 1954 Act, s. 71 (5).

warrant to apprehend and imprison such person for any term, to run from the date of his imprisonment, not longer than the period which at the date of his liberation remained unexpired of the term of imprisonment specified in the sentence brought under review.[18]

16–78   Where at the time his appeal is dismissed or refused the appellant is serving a term of imprisonment imposed subsequently to the conviction appealed against, the High Court has the same power to date the sentence for that conviction or the unexpired part thereof from any date prior to the expiry of the later sentence, as has a summary court under section 65 (4) of the 1954 Act where the appeal has been abandoned.[19]

The exercise by the High Court of the foregoing powers is always subject to the limitations imposed by section 73 of the Act.[20]

Hearing of appeal

16–79   The court will not hear objections which have not been made the subject of questions of law in the stated case, unless the objections are of so serious a character as to indicate fundamental nullity in the proceedings.[21] Objections to the competency of the appeal should be stated before the merits are entered into, otherwise they will be held to have been departed from.[22]

16–80   When a convicted person who has obtained a stated case dies before the hearing of the appeal, his executors cannot be sisted as parties to it, for there is no passive representation in crime or in criminal proceedings.[23] In one case,[24] where a person prosecuting privately under the Solway Fishery Act 1804 died before a case for which he had asked could be stated, the sheriff-substitute, while expressing doubts as to the competency of the course, sisted the deceased's trustees and executors in his place upon their application.

16–81   The court has sustained a conviction which the Crown did not support at the hearing.[25]

Amendment of conviction

16–82   While the court possesses wide powers of amendment under sections 71 and 73, it must not substitute a different conviction for the original,[26] for it has no jurisdiction to retry a case.[27] In *Anderson* v. *Howman*[28] (a suspension) the court refused to exercise its power under section 75 of the

---

[18] 1954 Act, s. 71 (6).
[19] 1954 Act, s. 71 (7), as added by 1964 Act, s. 32 (2); see supra, para. 16–54.
[20] See supra, paras. 16–13 et seq.
[21] *Sutherland* v. *Shiach*, 1928 J.C. 49, Lord Hunter at 52. Cf. *Penrose* v. *Bruce*, 1927 J.C. 79, L.J.-C. at 84 ; *Drummond* v. *Hunter*, 1948 J.C. 109; *Black* v. *Robertson*, 1954 S.L.T. 329. As to fundamental nullities see supra, para. 14–37.
[22] *Thom* v. *Caledonian Railway Co.* (1886) 1 White 248.
[23] *Keane* v. *Adair*, 1941 J.C. 77.
[24] *Cathcart* v. *Houston* (1914) 7 Adam 535. See *Keane* v. *Adair*, supra, at 80.
[25] *McCrindle* v. *McMillan*, 1930 J.C. 56.
[26] *Anderson* v. *Howman*, 1935 J.C. 17, Lord Hunter at 21, Lord Anderson at 22.
[27] *Lipsey* v. *Mackintosh* (1913) 7 Adam 182, L.J.-G. at 189.
[28] Supra.

1908 Act in order to amend a conviction which, it was alleged, had been per incuriam recorded as being under section 12, instead of under section 11, of the Road Traffic Act 1930. In *Monk* v. *Strathern*,[29] an accused person was convicted on a charge of assaulting a constable when engaged in the execution of his duty, contrary to section 12 of the Prevention of Crimes Act 1871. On appeal, the High Court held that, at the time when the assault was committed, the constable was not in the execution of his duty, and consequently that the accused had not been guilty of the statutory offence charged. It was argued on behalf of the prosecutor that under section 75 the court had power to find the accused guilty of an assault at common law and sentence him accordingly. The court held that the case was inappropriate for the application of section 75 and quashed the conviction simpliciter.

6-83   In *Lipsey* v. *Mackintosh*[30] a bookmaker was tried on a complaint charging him with sending by post cards containing invitations to bet " contrary to " certain specified sections of the Betting Act 1853, which dealt with the offence of owning, occupying, or advertising betting houses, and certain sections of the Betting Act 1874, which dealt with the offence of inviting to bet. He was found " guilty as libelled." The court quashed the conviction in respect that the sections of the Betting Act 1853 libelled were not directed against the offence set forth in the complaint but against entirely different offences. It was held further that this was not a case in which the court should amend the conviction under section 75 of the 1908 Act. Lord Justice-General Dunedin said:

> " Here we have the accused found guilty as libelled, that is to say, he is convicted of all and sundry of the offences, some of which, we find, there was no ground of convicting him of at all. If we amended the sentence here we should be retrying the case for ourselves, because we cannot tell what the views of the court were when he was convicted of something of which he had no right to be convicted at all." [31]

In *Duncan* v. *Smith*[32] the court quashed one of two convictions arising out of the same species facti, but did not alter the penalty imposed.

6-84   If, however, the court can, without usurping the functions of the judge of first instance, put a defective conviction or order into proper form by amendment, it will use its powers under section 73.[33] In *Walker* v. *Brander*[34] a summary complaint under the Dogs Act 1871, craved an order on the accused to keep a dog under proper control. The interlocutor making the required order was defective in respect that it did not contain a finding that the accused was the owner of the dog. In his answers to a bill of suspension brought by the accused the procurator fiscal stated that

[29] 1921 J.C. 4.
[30] Supra.
[31] 7 Adam at 188–9.
[32] 1951 J.C. 1.
[33] *Walker* v. *Brander*, 1920 J.C. 20.
[34] Supra.

the sheriff-substitute had found on evidence that the accused was the owner of the dog. The accused did not contradict this statement. The court, exercising its powers under section 75 of the 1908 Act, amended the conviction by inserting the missing finding and refused the suspension.

The question whether the court should exercise its power under section 75 of the 1908 Act to amend defects which amount to incompetency arose in two cases. In *Hefferan* v. *Wright* [35] the complaint, conviction and sentence were incompetent, and the court held that the proper course was to quash the whole proceedings. In the later case of *Mackenzie* v. *McKillop* [36] the complaint, conviction and sentence contained manifest irregularities which the court held to amount to incompetency, but, in respect that there was no dispute that the main offence charged had been committed, —indeed the accused had pleaded guilty to it—the court did not suspend the conviction and sentence, but restricted them in virtue of its powers under section 75.

Amendment of sentence

16–85   Although the 1954 Act confers no express right of appeal against sentence [37] and so leaves to a convicted person as grounds of review of sentence only incompetency and oppression, the power of the court to amend sentences does not seem to be similarly restricted. So far as appeals by stated case are concerned, the combined effect of sections 71 and 73 of the Act appears to be that the court has a discretionary power, at its own hand, to amend or reduce, but not to increase, a sentence.

Amendment of oppressive sentences has already been considered.[38] Whatever be the form of appeal, the court will always amend such a sentence. The same applies in the case of sentences which are incompetent. As Lord Salvesen said in *McCluskey* v. *Boyd*,[39] " There is no better reason for our intervening to reduce a fine than that the Court has exceeded its powers in imposing a fine—exceeded them, I mean, as regards amount. I think it would wholly defeat the intention of section 75 [of the 1908 Act] if we held that the section only applied to what was entirely within the powers and competency of the inferior court."

16–86   If the sentence exceeds the legal maximum the court will reduce it to the appropriate amount. So, in *Whillans* v. *Hilson* [40] and *Hall* v. *Macpherson* [41] sentences of four and six months respectively were reduced to three months—the maximum in each case. Again, where a first offence under section 65 (1) of the Licensing (Scotland) Act 1903, was punished by the infliction of a fine of £100, which was appropriate only to second or subsequent offences, the court reduced the fine to £50, the proper maxi-

[35] (1910) 6 Adam 321.
[36] 1938 J.C. 91.
[37] *Jesner* v. *Adair*, 1943 S.N. 25.
[38] Supra, paras. 16–28 et seq.
[39] (1916) 7 Adam 742, 751; see also supra, para. 15–29.
[40] (1909) 6 Adam 129.
[41] (1913) 7 Adam 173.

mum.[42] In another case,[43] where the accused was sentenced to thirty days' imprisonment in circumstances under which he ought to have had the option of a fine, the court pronounced an appropriate sentence.

5–87 It may be noted that in *McCluskey* v. *Boyd* [44] the court held that it was entitled under section 75 of the 1908 Act to amend the sentence by finding the accused liable in expenses, although the magistrate was not bound, but had a discretionary power, to impose expenses.

5–88 Where a sentence has been incompetently imposed because e.g. of a failure to obtain background reports or to include the reasons for imposing detention, the High Court may quash the sentence and either release the accused [45] or exercise its power to impose sentence itself, sometimes re-imposing the same sentence.[46]

5–89 As regards sentences which are merely excessive the position is now clear.

There are dicta by Lord Justice-General Normand (evidently intended to apply to all cases, irrespective of the manner of the review) to the effect that the High Court is entitled to amend a competent sentence only if it is oppressive.[47] The relevant provisions of the 1954 Act do not seem to necessitate so narrow a view, and, so far as appeals by stated case are concerned, there is some authority against it.[48] But in *Fleming* v. *Mac-Donald* [49] the High Court specifically held that the test to be applied in reviewing a summary sentence was whether it was " harsh and oppressive " irrespective of whether the appeal was by stated case or by bill of suspension.

Remits

5–90 The High Court has frequently remitted cases back to inferior judges in order that additional facts or even questions of law might be stated.[50]

If a motion for such remit is made by one of the parties to a case it should not be granted unless it is accompanied by a precise statement of the additional fact which the inferior judge ought, on the contention of

---

[42] *McCluskey* v. *Boyd* (1916) 7 Adam 742.
[43] *McLauchlan* v. *Davidson*, 1921 J.C. 45. See also *Gray* v. *Morrison*, 1954 J.C. 31 (fine of £10 substituted for sentence of 14 days' imprisonment for a first offence).
[44] Supra.
[45] *Jamieson* v. *Heatly*, 1959 J.C. 22.
[46] *Auld* v. *Herron*, 1969 J.C. 4; *Winslow* v. *Farrell*, 1965 J.C. 49; *Bruce* v. *Hogg*, 1966 J.C. 33.
[47] *Graham* v. *Waugh*, 1938 J.C. 108, 116; *Stewart* v. *Cormack*, 1941 J.C. 73, 76; *Blair* v. *Hawthorn*, 1945 J.C. 17, 27; *Fleming* v. *MacDonald*, 1958 J.C. 1; See also *McCluskey* v. *Boyd* (1916) 7 Adam 742, L. Salvesen at 751.
[48] *Aldred* v. *Langmuir*, 1932 J.C. 22; *Girgawy* v. *Strathern*, 1925 J.C. 31; *Andrew* v. *Hunter* [1948] C.L.Y. 4163; see also *Scott* v. *Robertson* [1949] C.L.Y. 4480.
[49] 1958 J.C. 1, disapproving the contrary view expressed in the third edition of this book at pp. 312–3.
[50] *Macdonald* v. *Mackenzie*, 1947 J.C. 169 (remit for new findings in fact and a new finding in law); *McDonald* v. *Hamilton*, 1954 J.C. 10 (remit to amplify findings with particular reference to nature and sufficiency of corroboration); *Muldoon* v. *Herron*, 1970 S.L.T. 228 (remits to indicate more precisely evidence given by witness in relation to identification of accused); *Girgawy* v. *Strathern*, 1925 J.C. 31 and *Jesner* v. *Adair*, 1943 S.N. 25, may be cited as examples.

that party, to hold proved, and unless a prima facie case is made out for reversing his judgment in view of these additional facts.[51]

In one case [52] the court refused to remit a stated case to be amended with reference to a point which had not been raised before the inferior judge.

16–91   In *Gemmell and McFadyen* v. *MacNiven* [53] the court called for reports both from the sheriff-substitute who tried the case and from the sheriff.

Appeal by prosecutor

16–92   A stated case may be competently used for an appeal against an acquittal.[54]

Appeal where trial judge unable to sign case

16–93   Section 63 (2) of the 1954 Act provides that where a person convicted under the Act has made application thereunder for a stated case and the judge by whom he was convicted dies before signing the case or is precluded by illness or other cause from so doing, it shall be competent for such person to present a bill of suspension to the High Court of Justiciary and to bring under the review of that court any matter which might have been so brought under review by stated case. No comparable right is given to the prosecutor.

Appeal to Circuit Court

16–94   Although still competent, this form of review is now unknown in practice, as the necessity for it is removed by the procedure by stated case, or bill of suspension. It was part of the machinery introduced by the Heritable Jurisdictions (Scotland) Act 1746, which was passed in the year following the rebellion of 1745, with the object of breaking the power of the Highland chiefs and feudal superiors, and is specifically preserved by section 74 of the 1954 Act. Readers are referred to earlier works on procedure for details regarding it.

Suspension

16–95   Suspension is a common law process, restricted to criminal cases,[55] whereby an illegal or improper warrant, conviction or judgment issued by an inferior judge may be reviewed and set aside by the High Court. If the complainer is detained in custody under the warrant or imprisoned under the conviction or judgment, the process becomes one of suspension and liberation. As a remedy, suspension is not open to the prosecutor and is confined to those against whom the warrant, conviction or judgment bears to be directed.

---

[51] *Cairney* v. *Patterson*, 1945 J.C. 120, approving dictum of Lord Skerrington in *Rogers* v. *Howman*, 1918 J.C. 88, at 96.
[52] *Penrose* v. *Bruce*, 1927 J.C. 79.
[53] 1928 J.C. 5.
[54] 1954 Act, s. 62.
[55] *Park* v. *Earl of Stair* (1852) J. Shaw 532.

Legal aid

6-96   Where the nominated solicitor of a person who has been convicted and sentenced, or the interim solicitor of a person who was not legally aided at his trial but has obtained an interim appeal certificate, considers the appropriate method of appeal is by bill of suspension, he submits a draft bill of suspension to the Supreme Court Committee with an application for an appeal certificate and his views as to whether or not (a) the grounds of appeal are substantial and (b) it is reasonable that the appellant be legally aided.[56] This application is then dealt with in the same way as an application accompanied by a stated case.[57]

Competency

6-97   High Court proceedings cannot be suspended.[58] The process was formerly competent in proceedings on indictment in the sheriff court, but, since the passing of the Criminal Appeal (Scotland) Act 1926, it is no longer so, and is now confined to summary procedure.

6-98   As the object of suspension is to secure the annulment of an illegal or improper warrant, conviction or judgment, the process is incompetent where no such order exists, or where it is merely threatened.[59] Thus, where no sentence was signed, it was held that there was nothing to suspend, although a fine had been imposed and paid.[60] For the same reason, suspension is not available to a person who has been illegally detained without an order of court or arrested without a warrant, his remedy being to appeal to the nobile officium of the High Court, that tribunal having an inherent jurisdiction to intervene in extraordinary circumstances in order to prevent injustice or oppression.[61] As the basis of the suspension is the existence of the warrant, conviction or judgment complained of, the process is not rendered incompetent either because no proceedings have followed thereon [62] or because the judgment has been obtempered by the complainer—e.g. by paying the fine or undergoing the imprisonment imposed upon him.[63]

6-99   It has been said that suspension applies to final judgments or determinations only, and cannot be employed during the earlier stages of a case, where advocation, so far as competent, is the appropriate remedy.[64] But incidental warrants which do not form part of the case, e.g. search warrants [65] and warrants to cite witnesses for precognition by the procura-

---

[56] Legal Aid (Scotland) (Criminal Proceedings) Scheme 1964, art. 19.

[57] Supra, para. 16–06.

[58] They can be appealed only under the Criminal Appeal (Scotland) Act 1926, or by petition to the nobile officium, e.g. *Wylie* v. *H.M. Adv.*, 1966 S.L.T. 149.

[59] *Jupp* v. *Dunbar* (1863) 4 Irv. 355; *Lowson* v. *Police Commrs. of Forfar* (1877) 3 Couper 433.

[60] *Jupp* v. *Dunbar*, supra.

[61] *Moncreiff on Review in Criminal Cases*, Chap. V. See supra, paras. 2–06, 11–01.

[62] *Middlemiss* v. *D'Eresby* (1852) J. Shaw 557.

[63] *Bell* v. *Black and Morrison* (1865) 5 Irv. 57; *Russell* v. *Colquhoun* (1845) 2 Broun 572; *Bonthrone* v. *Renton* (1886) 1 White 279; cf. *Milburn*, 1946 S.C. 301.

[64] In the 3rd edn. of this book, at p. 315.

[65] *Bell* v. *Black and Morrison*, supra. Cf. *McLauchlan* v. *Renton* (1910) 6 Adam 378; *Paterson* v. *Macpherson*, 1924 J.C. 38.

tor fiscal [66] may be suspended immediately. So, too, may an order remanding a convicted person in custody for sentencing reports.[67] In view of the disfavour with which advocation is now viewed [68] it is probably the case that any warrant in a criminal proceeding may be appealed by suspension where it involves interference with liberty or property.

16-100 Suspension is not rendered incompetent merely because another mode of review is provided,[69] but, unlike appeal by stated case,[70] it may be effectively excluded by statute. The High Court, however, has an inherent power to entertain a suspension in cases amounting to fundamental nullity or to illegality even although review is expressly excluded [71] or another mode of review provided as the sole one. It may not be competent, however, to review even an excess of jurisdiction in relation to an administrative procedure in an inferior court in connection with a criminal proceeding, such as a petition for restoration of a driving licence.[72]

16-101 As already explained,[73] section 63 (2) of the 1954 Act specially provides that suspension shall be a competent mode of review for a convicted person in any case where the trial judge is unable to sign the stated case for which he has made application.

Appropriateness

16-102 It would appear in view of the terms of section 62 (*d*) of the 1954 Act that appeal by stated case is competent wherever suspension is competent, although " there are certain types of questions . . . which are appropriate only to a stated case, in which we are given the benefit of the considered views of the court of first instance." [74] Suspension " is truly appropriate . . . where the relevant circumstances are instantly or almost instantly, verifiable and the point sought to be raised is raised promptly, a crisp issue of, say jurisdiction, competency, oppression, or departure from the canons of natural justice." [75] Suspension is therefore appropriate when the appeal is based either on defects which appear on the face of the proceedings themselves or on irregular or oppressive conduct on the part of the judge or the prosecutor.[76] In such cases there may be a decided advantage in having ex parte pleadings. On the other hand, when the question for decision by the High Court is whether the inferior judge reached a correct conclusion in law upon the evidence led before him, it is

---

[66] *Forbes* v. *Main* (1908) 5 Adam 503.
[67] *Morrison* v. *Clark*, 1962 S.L.T. 113.
[68] *MacLeod* v. *Levitt*, 1969 J.C. 16; infra, para. 16–128.
[69] 1954 Act, s. 74.
[70] Ibid., s. 62.
[71] *Massey* v. *Lamb* (1906) 5 Adam 59; *Morrison* v. *Peters* (1909) 6 Adam 73; *Clarkson* v. *Muir* (1871) 2 Couper 125; *Mackenzie* v. *McPhee* (1889) 2 White 188; *Bell* v. *McPhee* (1883) 5 Couper 312; *Collins* v. *Lang* (1887) 1 White 482; *MacArthur* v. *Campbell* (1896) 2 Adam 151; *Kelly* v. *Rowan* (1897) 2 Adam 357; *Craig* v. *Tarras* (1897) 2 Adam 344. See also *Mitchell* v. *Morrison*, (1908) 5 Adam 545.
[72] Cf. *MacLeod* v. *Levitt*, 1969 J.C. 16.
[73] Supra, para. 16–93.
[74] *Fairley* v. *Muir*, 1951 J.C. 56, L.J.-G. at 60.
[75] Ibid.
[76] See Hume, ii. 514, 515; Alison, ii. 28–32.

desirable that the court should have an authoritative statement of what the evidence was and of the grounds upon which the judge proceeded.[77] Appeal by stated case is, therefore, the appropriate method of review in such a case.

6–103　　It is a well-established rule that the merits of a conviction cannot be raised in a suspension,[78] and this rule applies in cases other than those where the suspension is brought by a convicted person who has applied for a stated case but cannot proceed thereby owing to the inability of the trial judge to sign it. As already explained,[78a] section 63 (2) of the 1954 Act gives such person the same scope of appeal in his suspension as he would have had in a stated case. Subject to this statutory exception the position is as follows:

6–104　　According to Hume and Alison,[79] suspension was not a competent method of challenging the verdict of a jury as being contrary to the evidence. Hume does not deal specifically with convictions pronounced by inferior judges sitting alone, but he evidently regards these as governed by the same principles as are the verdicts of juries. Alison, however, says,

> " In reviewing the sentences of inferior judges, pronounced without the intervention of a jury, the Court are always in use to consider the weight of the objectionable matter, and not to suspend the sentence on an erroneous legal decision, unless it is in such a material part of the proof as really affects the conviction. If, therefore, enough remains to support the conviction *aliunde*, the alteration of the judgment on one point will not set aside the sentence as to the remainder." [80]

6–105　　It does not appear to have been doubted that, in the ordinary case, suspension was not a competent method of reviewing a conviction on the ground of insufficiency of legal evidence, and that recourse must be had to a stated case. This opinion was clearly expressed by Lord Trayner in *Rattray* v. *White*,[81] and in the later case of *Dunn* v. *Mitchell* [82] a bill of suspension was refused on the ground that a question of fact could not be reviewed in that process. A distinction was, however, drawn where it appeared on the face of the bill of suspension and answers that there was no evidence upon which the inferior judge could legally convict— the court holding that it was entitled to intervene in such cases. In *Lockwood* v. *Walker*,[83] a person convicted of indecent behaviour towards a girl under puberty brought a suspension on the ground, inter alia, that

---

[77] See *O'Hara* v. *Mill*, 1938 J.C. 4, Lord Wark at 7.
[78] *O'Hara* v. *Mill*, supra; *James Y. Keanie, Limited* v. *Laird*, 1943 J.C. 73; *Rattray* v. *White* (1891) 3 White 89, Lord Trayner at 93–94; *Dunn* v. *Mitchell* (1910) 6 Adam 365; *Russell* v. *Paton*, (1902) 3 Adam 639; *Moffat* v. *Skeen*, 1963 J.C. 84; *Rush* v. *Herron*, 1969 S.L.T. 211.
[78a] Supra, para. 16–93.
[79] Hume, ii. 514–515; Alison, ii. 28–32.
[80] Alison, ii. 30.
[81] Supra.
[82] Supra. See *Russell* v. *Paton*, supra.
[83] (1909) 6 Adam 124.

the only evidence regarding the girl's age was her own uncorroborated testimony. In his answers the respondent admitted this, but pleaded that, under section 75 of the 1908 Act, such an objection was not a ground for quashing a conviction. The court, holding that it was not precluded by section 75 from dealing, in a suspension, with a case where the evidence led did not, though accepted, prove the charge made, quashed the conviction. In *Wright* v. *Mitchell*,[84] a person convicted of driving a motor car at a speed exceeding that prescribed by section 9 of the Motor Car Act 1903, brought a suspension on the ground that the method of working the police " trap " was so defective that there was no evidence upon which the sheriff-substitute was entitled to convict him. The respondent admitted the substantial accuracy of the complainer's description of the " trap," but pleaded that the bill was incompetent as being an attempt to have the conviction reviewed upon the merits. The court suspended the conviction. In *McShane* v. *Paton*,[85] a school teacher who had been convicted of an assault upon a pupil brought a suspension on the ground, inter alia, that the facts did not disclose the commission of the offence. An objection (founded on *Rattray* v. *White*[86]) having been taken by the respondent that such a question could be raised only on a stated case, the court repelled the objection and quashed the conviction, being of the opinion that the facts, as admitted by the respondent, disclosed that no assault had been committed.

16–106   The question whether the evidence in the case was sufficient in law to support the conviction was raised by suspension in three more recent cases, *O'Hara* v. *Mill*,[87] *Dawson* v. *Adair*[88] and *James Y. Keanie, Limited* v. *Laird*,[89] in none of which was there complete agreement between the parties as to the material facts. In *O'Hara* v. *Mill*[90] the court emphasised that the appropriate method of raising the question was by stated case, and, although the decisions in *Lockwood* v. *Walker*,[91] *Wright* v. *Mitchell*[92] and *McShane* v. *Paton*[93] were not impugned—being, indeed, distinguished as proceeding upon admitted facts which showed that the convictions were unwarranted—Lord Justice-Clerk Aitchison said that it must not be assumed that the court would again allow the question to be argued in a suspension. In *James Y. Keanie, Limited* v. *Laird*[94] the bill itself was held to be incompetent, and it was laid down that a bill of suspension would not be allowed as a mode of review in cases in which the appropriate method of appeal was by stated case, the practice sanctioned in *Lock-*

---

[84] (1910) 6 Adam 287.
[85] 1922 J.C. 26.
[86] (1891) 3 White 89.
[87] 1938 J.C. 4.
[88] 16th Sept., 1941, unreported.
[89] 1943 J.C. 73. See also *Fairley* v. *Muir*, 1951 J.C. 56.
[90] Supra.
[91] (1909) 6 Adam 124.
[92] (1910) 6 Adam 287.
[93] 1922 J.C. 26.
[94] Supra. See also *Fairley* v. *Muir*, supra.

wood,[95] *Wright* [96] and *McShane* [97] being described by Lord Wark as an "indulgence" which "will not be allowed in future cases."

Lord Wark's dictum was followed in *Fairley* v. *Muir*,[98] where the court refused to allow a suspension on the ground of the admission of incompetent evidence, without any question of disagreement as to the facts.[99] In *Moffat* v. *Skeen* [1] the court held that a bill of suspension was not competent where it disclosed a serious dispute on the facts between the parties as to what was established on the evidence. In *Rush* v. *Herron* [2] the court refused to deal with questions of evaluation and credibility of evidence in a bill.[3]

If the decisions in *Lockwood*, *Wright* and *McShane* mean that an otherwise incompetent process is rendered competent by the parties' agreement upon the evidence, they are, no doubt, illogical. But, then, it is also illogical that both the appellant and the appellate court should have to accept, as an authoritative record of the facts, a version prepared by a person who may have misunderstood or misapplied them; and it is asking much to expect that person in every case to make a frank disclosure of his own blunders. Given a fair-minded prosecutor and the "indulgence," an appellant who had received an unfairly stated case—by no means an unknown occurrence—had yet a chance of presenting the facts of the case properly to the High Court. It is a fact that the "indulgence" has enabled a number of unjust convictions (which might otherwise have stood) to be reviewed on a true statement of the facts and quashed.

6-107   Suspension cannot be used to bring facts before the court which were withheld during the trial, or to obtain probation or other reports.[4]

6-108   Suspension is also subject to the limitations imposed by section 73 of the 1954 Act.[5]

Grounds of appeal

6-109   The following have been recognised as relevant grounds for bringing a suspension. The list is not exhaustive, and must be read subject to the provisions of section 63 (2) of the 1954 Act. [5a]

   (1) Fundamental nullity in the proceedings in respect of some radical defect.[6]

   (2) Oppression.[7]

[95] Supra.
[96] Supra.
[97] Supra.
[98] Supra.
[99] A stated case had originally been sought but the complainer was later advised to drop the case and apply for a bill.
[1] 1963 J.C. 84.
[2] 1969 S.L.T. 211.
[3] It is difficult to see how such a matter could be dealt with at all under any available review procedure.
[4] *Farquhar* v. *Burrell*, 1955 J.C. 66.
[5] Supra, para. 16–13.
[5a] Supra, para. 16–93.
[6] *Collins* v. *Lang* (1887) 1 White 482; *Morrison* v. *Peters* (1909) 6 Adam 73.
[7] *Mackenzie* v. *McPhee* (1889) 2 White 188. See also supra, paras. 16–19 et seq.

(3) No jurisdiction.[8]

(4) No title to prosecute.[9]

(5) Defective citation.[10]

(6) Objections to competency of complaint.[11]

(7) Objections to relevancy of complaint, at any rate where they allege that the charge was funditus null.[12]

(8) Objections regarding admission or rejection of evidence:

　　(a) Admission of incompetent evidence.

　　(b) Rejection of competent evidence.

　　(c) Refusal of competent questions.

In some old cases suspensions were allowed on the ground of admission of incompetent evidence.[13] But in *Fairley* v. *Muir* [14] the court refused to hear an appeal by way of suspension against the admission of allegedly incompetent evidence, partly because such an appeal could not be decided without a narrative of the sheriff's conclusions on the evidence so that the court might discover how important the challenged evidence was.[15] Similar considerations would apply where the appeal was based on the rejection of competent evidence. There is an obiter dictum in *Priteca* v. *H.M. Adv.*[16] that a jury verdict in the sheriff court could be suspended for rejection of competent evidence, and that suspension also lay for admission of incompetent evidence. It may be that questions as to the admissibility of evidence can be raised in a suspension only where they raise " a crisp issue of . . . competency " [17] as where they involve evidence of an accused's character or previous convictions,[18] or some clear act of judicial oppression.[19] But in two clear modern cases appeals of this last kind were taken by stated case.[20]

16–110　　(9) Bad conviction, e.g.:

　　(a) General conviction on alternative grounds.[21]

　　(b) Ambiguous [22] or unintelligible conviction or sentence.[23]

---

[8] *McPherson* v. *Boyd* (1907) 5 Adam 247.

[9] *Duke of Bedford* v. *Kerr* (1893) 3 White 493; *Simpson* v. *Board of Trade* (1892) 3 White 167.

[10] *Stewart* v. *Lang* (1894) 1 Adam 493.

[11] *Hefferan* v. *Wright* (1910) 6 Adam 321. Cf. *Clark and Bendall* v. *Stuart* (1886) 1 White 191.

[12] *Adams* v. *McKenna* (1905) 5 Adam 106; *Smith* v. *Sempill* (1910) 6 Adam 348. See also *Walker* v. *Rodger* (1885) 5 Couper 595. *Jas. Y. Keanie Ltd.* v. *Laird*, 1943 J.C. 73 is authority that a bill of suspension cannot be used to determine a question of relevancy.

[13] *Burns* v. *Hart and Young* (1856) 2 Irv. 571—evidence of accused's character; *Stevenson* v. *Scott* (1854) 1 Irv. 603—evidence of the accused; *McLean* v. *Skinner* (1907) 5 Adam 376—evidence of previous convictions.

[14] 1957 J.C. 56.

[15] L.J.-G. at 60.

[16] (1906) 5 Adam 79.

[17] *Fairley* v. *Muir*, supra, L.J.-G. at 60.

[18] See cases cited in n. 13, supra; *Falconer* v. *Brown* (1893) 1 Adam 96. But in *Deighan* v. *MacLeod*, 1959 J.C. 25, the matter was dealt with by stated case.

[19] *Thomson* v. *Neilson* (1900) 3 Adam 195.

[20] *Mackenzie* v. *Jinks*, 1934 J.C. 48; *McPherson* v. *Copeland*, 1961 J.C. 74.

[21] *Connell* v. *Mitchell* (1912) 7 Adam 23; *Reaney* v. *Maddever* (1883) 5 Couper 367; *Aitchison* v. *Neilson* (1897) 2 Adam 284.

[22] *Macleman* v. *Middleton* (1901) 3 Adam 353; *Reids* v. *Miller* (1899) 3 Adam 29.

[23] *Cowans* v. *Sinclair* (1905) 4 Adam 585.

(c) Conviction where either the sentence itself [24] or the date of the sentence [25] has been altered in the record after its pronouncement.

(d) Conviction or sentence not properly authenticated.[26]

(10) Oppressive [27] or incompetent [28] sentence.

(11) Court either exceeding [29] or failing to exercise [30] its jurisdiction.

(12) Irregularities during trial.[31]

6-111   Suspensions may be brought by persons other than the prosecutor and accused, who are affected by a judgment involving forfeiture of their goods,[32] or perhaps by any other illegal judgment.[33]

Time for bringing suspension

6-112   There is no time-limit for bringing a suspension, but this should be done as soon as possible, as acquiescence in the judgment complained of may be inferred from undue delay.[34]

What amounts to undue delay must always be a question of circumstances and of discretion.[35] In one very special case [36] a delay of four-and-a-half years was held not to bar the suspension, but, as a rule, a delay of only a few months will be fatal,[37] a lapse of eleven weeks having on one occasion been held to be so.[38] If a person says that he is unjustly convicted of a crime it is his duty, as evidence of good faith on his part, to seek redress without delay,[39] and if he voluntarily pays any fine involved, this may be regarded as acquiescence.[40] Where a question of sufficiency of evidence is raised, the appeal should be brought while the evidence is fresh in the mind of the inferior judge. In such a case, however, the

[24] *McRory* v. *Findlay* (1911) 6 Adam 417.
[25] *Smith* v. *Sempill, supra.*
[26] *Simpson* v. *Reid* (1902) 3 Adam 617 (signature by only one of the two magistrates present). As to improper alteration vitiating conviction in essentialibus, see *Clarkson* v. *Muir* (1871) 2 Couper 125.
[27] See, e.g. *Blair* v. *Hawthorn,* 1945 J.C. 17. See also supra, paras. 16–28 et seq.
[28] *Anderson* v. *Begg* (1907) 5 Adam 387.
[29] *McPherson* v. *Boyd* (1907) 5 Adam 247; *Caledonian Railway Co.* v. *Fleming* (1869) 1 Couper 193.
[30] *Muckersie* v. *McDougall* (1874) 3 Couper 54.
[31] *Craig* v. *Steel* (1848) J. Shaw 148; *Sime* v. *Linton* (1897) 2 Adam 288; *Kelly* v. *Mitchell* (1907) 5 Adam 268; *Leavack* v. *Macleod* (1913) 7 Adam 87; *Aitken* v. *Wood,* 1921 J.C. 84; *Johannesson* v. *Robertson,* 1945 J.C. 146; *Loughbridge* v. *Mickel,* 1947 J.C. 21.
[32] *Semple and Sons* v. *Macdonald,* 1963 J.C. 90; *Loch Lomond Sailings Ltd.* v. *Hawthorn,* 1962 J.C. 8.
[33] *Trotter on Summary Criminal Jurisdiction,* 63; *Semple and Sons* v. *Macdonald,* supra, L.J.-G. at 92.
[34] See *Low* v. *Rankine,* 1917 J.C. 39, Lord Anderson at 41–42.
[35] *Watson* v. *Scott* (1898) 2 Adam 501, L.J.-C. at 503.
[36] *Muirhead* v. *McIntosh* (1890) 2 White 473.
[37] See e.g. *McLure* v. *Douglas* (1872) 2 Couper 177 (5 months); *Watson* v. *Scott,* supra (6 months); *Allan* v. *Lamb* (1900) 3 Adam 248 (10 months); *Kelly* v. *Smith* (1904) 4 Adam 466 (14 months); *White* v. *Jeans* (1911) 6 Adam 489 (9 months); *Montgomery* v. *Gray* (1915) 7 Adam 681 (6 months); *Carson* v. *Macpherson,* 1917 J.C. 36 (3 months); *Low* v. *Rankine,* supra (4 months). In *Fairley* v. *Muir,* 1951 J.C. 56, the view was expressed that a delay of two months in bringing a suspension called for an explanation.
[38] *Macfarlan* v. *Pringle* (1904) 4 Adam 403.
[39] *Muirhead* v. *McIntosh,* supra; *Low* v. *Rankine,* supra, Lord Anderson at 41.
[40] *Macfarlan,* supra; *McLure* v. *Douglas,* supra.

appropriate method of redress is not a bill of suspension but an appeal by stated case. If no attempt whatever is made to procure such a case, and a delay of three, four or five months, as the case may be, is allowed to take place, the court will not entertain the bill.[41]

If the question at issue is purely a legal one, and if the offence is a statutory one not involving a moral stigma, acquiescence may not so readily be inferred.[42]

Presentation and service of bill

16-113 The procedure begins with the preparation of a bill of suspension or a bill of suspension and liberation, if the accused is in prison. Forms of these bills will be found in the Appendix.[43] They are signed by counsel or solicitor, and are subsequently lodged in the justiciary office for an order for service, and, where the accused is in prison, an order for interim liberation also.

These preliminary deliverances may be granted by one judge of the High Court,[44] and the bill is, accordingly, presented to a single judge. That judge is not, however, obliged to grant either deliverance. Interim liberation is, as explained below, a matter for his discretion. Further, if he considers that the bill discloses no substantial ground for asking, he may, instead of pronouncing an order for service, remit the case to a quorum of the High Court, who may, if of the same opinion, refuse to pass the bill.[45]

After an order for service has been granted, the bill is served in common form. Any officer of law can serve it.[46] Service is usually proved by a minute of acceptance written upon the bill, and signed by the respondent or his solicitor. The prosecutor is the proper respondent.[47] In relation to service it should be noted that not only must the bill be served on the respondent but the bill and warrant for service must be exhibited to the clerk of the inferior court so that he may transmit the proceedings complained against to the Clerk of Justiciary.

Caution for interim liberation : Printing

16-114 Caution is only ordered if the appellant is in prison and desires interim liberation.

On the bill being presented to a judge of the High Court, he may order the accused, if in prison, to be liberated on his finding caution to such

---

[41] Carson v. Macpherson, supra; Low v. Rankine, supra. Cf. James Y. Keanie Ltd. v. Laird, 1943 J.C. 73.
[42] Adams v. McKenna (1906) 5 Adam 106, Lord McLaren at 112; Low v. Rankine, supra, Lord Anderson at 42.
[43] Infra. App. C, Form 6.
[44] Hume, ii. 514.
[45] Carnegie v. Clark, 1947 J.C. 74, Lord Mackay at 80; Masterton v. Adair, Feb. 22, 1948, unreported; Moncreiff on Review in Criminal Cases, p. 176; Fairley v. Muir, 1951 J.C. 56.
[46] 1954 Act, s. 74 (2).
[47] This is so even where the bill relates to a summary conviction for contempt imposed by the sheriff without any formal complaint: Pirie v. Hawthorn, 1962 J.C. 69; cf. MacLeod v. Speirs (1884) 5 Couper 387, where there was no respondent.

amount as the judge may fix. The accused must in that case personally attend the hearing of the appeal.[48] If he does not do so, he will, unless the court, on cause shown, permits the appeal to be heard, be held to have abandoned the same.[49]

The granting or refusing of interim liberation is a matter for the discretion of the judge, but in practice it is usually granted.

6-115   It is for the complainer to make an inventory of process, lodge his bill with the Clerk of Justiciary, and thereafter uplift the bill and the proceedings and arrange printing. The same arrangements apply to lodging prints as apply in appeals by stated case.[49a]

Hearing of appeal

6-116   The bill is put out for hearing on a date fixed by the High Court. The respondent is not bound to lodge written answers, or even to appear at the hearing, although he usually does both. It must be heard by a bench of at least three judges.[50] It is disposed of by an interlocutor passing or refusing it.

Consent to setting aside conviction

6-117   As already stated,[51] the power conferred by section 72 of the 1954 Act upon the prosecutor to consent to a conviction being set aside is applicable to suspensions and is exercisable at any time within ten days after the service on the prosecutor of the bill of suspension.

Remits

6-118   As the court can deal only with questions of law in a suspension, the general rule is that the facts will not be gone into except so far as they are admitted by the respondent.[52] If, however, it should appear to the court that further ascertainment of fact is required, a remit may be made to the sheriff principal or sheriff to inquire into the matter and report thereon. Such inquiry may be ordered in two cases: (1) where something irregular is disclosed on the face of the proceedings,[53] and (2) where relevant and material averments in the complainer's statement of facts are either denied or not admitted by the respondent in his answers.[54]

6-119   In the first case the court has the record of proceedings to assist it in its decision, but, in the second, the parties' pleadings may be the only guides. In such a case, if the irregularity complained of is not disclosed in the proceedings, inquiry will not be granted unless the complainer

---

[48] 1954 Act, s. 71 (5).
[49] Ibid.
[49]a Supra, para. 16–74.
[50] Hume, ii. 514.
[51] Supra, para. 16–55.
[52] *Russell* v. *Paton* (1902) 3 Adam 639, L.J.-C. at 644; *O'Hara* v. *Mill*, 1938 J.C. 4. See also supra, paras. 16–103 et seq.
[53] *Nardini* v. *Walker* (1903) 4 Adam 174, L.J.-C. at 182.
[54] *Avery* v. *Hilson* (1906) 5 Adam 56; *Renwick* v. *McDougall* (1913) 7 Adam 91; *Ewart* v. *Strathern*, 1924 J.C. 45.

makes out a strong prima facie case of oppression,[55] i.e. relevantly alleges gross and flagrant oppression [56] in statements which the court considers to be probable.[57] In one case,[58] where a sentence of disqualification for driving had been imposed in absence on an accused who had pleaded guilty to a motoring offence by letter the court remitted the case back to the sheriff-substitute to hear what the accused had to say in mitigation. In another case,[59] however, where the accused, who had been served with a complaint and a notice informing him that he was liable to disqualification " unless the Court for special reasons thinks fit to order otherwise," pleaded guilty by letter, but failed to proffer " special reasons " at the relevant date, the High Court refused to remit to the inferior court to consider special reasons advanced in a suspension. In judging probability the court will also have regard to the respondent's answers.[60]

Powers of High Court
16–120 Subject to the limitations imposed by section 73 of the 1954 Act,[6] the court has power:

(a) To pass the bill and suspend the sentence simpliciter, and to order repayment of any fine, penalty, or expenses paid in terms of it; or

(b) To repel the reasons of suspension, refuse the bill, and re-commit the suspender to prison if necessary; or

(c) To amend the conviction and sentence, and to remit to the inferior judge, when necessary, with instructions.

Whatever be the extent of the court's powers of amendment under section 73, there appears to be no reported case in which the sentence has been amended on any ground which did not infer oppression.

16–121 The court awards expenses either in full or modified to a certain sum.[62]
16–122 An objection that the proceedings in the inferior court are funditus null will be entertained by the court even although it is not stated in the bill of suspension.[63]

Appeal to Quarter Sessions
16–123 This method of appeal is now unknown in practice. Details will be found in earlier works on procedure.

Appeal to Court of Session as Court of Exchequer
16–124 This method of appeal may be dismissed with a very brief explanation, as it is restricted to customs and excise prosecutions and is obsolete, and

---

[55] *Nardini* v. *Walker,* supra, Lord Moncreiff at 193.
[56] *Wright* v. *Dewar* (1874) 2 Couper 504; *Russell* v. *Paton,* supra; *Wright* v. *Thomson* (1904) 4 Adam 459.
[57] *Nardini* v. *Walker,* supra, Lord Moncreiff at 183.
[58] *Trotter* v. *Burnet,* 1947 J.C. 151.
[59] *Hynd* v. *Clark,* 1954 S.L.T. 85.
[60] See, e.g. *Nardini* v. *Walker* (1903) 4 Adam 174.
[61] See supra, paras. 16–13 et seq.
[62] Infra, para. 17–101.
[63] *Walker* v. *Emslie* (1899) 3 Adam 102.

therefore has little general interest. It is competent in all cases where, at
the passing of the Exchequer Court (Scotland) Act 1856, a writ of habeas,
or a writ of certiorari, might have competently issued from the Court of
Exchequer to the effect of removing any proceedings before, or warrant
granted by, an inferior court or magistrate to the Court of Exchequer in
order to examination.[64]

Any party aggrieved in such a case may appeal to the Court of Session,
sitting as the Court of Exchequer.

The judgment of the Lord Ordinary may be reclaimed to the Inner
House, and thereafter appealed to the House of Lords.[65]

Advocation

6-125   Advocation is usually regarded as the converse of suspension, in so
far as it is the form of review adopted by the prosecutor, whereas suspension is adopted by the accused person. It takes its name from its *advocating*,
or calling, a case from an inferior court to a superior. But advocation is
not limited to appeals by the prosecutor. The right to use this mode applies
to either party.[66] Its appropriate sphere is review of irregularities in the
preliminary stages of a case.[67] But recourse to advocation is incompetent
until the case is finally determined, unless in very special circumstances.[68]
It is incompetent, alike in solemn and in summary procedure, to review
under a bill of advocation the decision of an inferior court repelling a
preliminary objection to relevancy.[69] Advocation cannot be employed to
obtain a review of the merits.

6-126   The procedure begins with a bill of advocation. It follows the general
course described in a suspension.[70] As most remedies competent under
this process can be more conveniently obtained by means of a stated case,
advocation is used rarely.

6-127   As, however, appeal by stated case is inapplicable to procedure by
indictment, advocation may still be adopted when it is desired to bring
under the review of the High Court a judgment dismissing an indictment
on the ground of irrelevancy or incompetency, or on other grounds of a
like nature. It is not abolished by the 1926 Act.

6-128   Advocation is available where the inferior court dismisses a complaint
as irrelevant [71] or incompetent,[72] or dismisses a case on some other
preliminary ground.[73] It was used in one case where a sheriff ordered a

---

[64] Exchequer Court (Scotland) Act 1856, s. 17.
[65] Exchequer Court (Scotland) Act 1858, s. 20; *Dodsworth* v. *Rijnbergen* (1886) 14 R. 238.
[66] Hume, ii. 510.
[67] *Kinnoul* v. *Tod* (1859) 3 Irv. 501; *Smith* v. *Kinnoch* (1848) Ark. 427; *MacLeod* v. *Levitt*, 1969
   J.C. 16.
[68] *Muir* v. *Hart* (1912) 6 Adam 601. Cf. *Strathern* v. *Sloan*, 1937 J.C. 76; *McFadyean*
   v. *Stewart*, 1951 J.C. 164.
[69] *Aldred* v. *Strathern*, 1929 J.C. 93, following *Muir* v. *Hart*, supra, and *Jameson* v. *Lothian*
   (1855) 2 Irv. 273.
[70] Supra, para. 16-113.
[71] *Duncan* v. *Cooper* (1886) 1 White 43; *Nimmo* v. *Lees* (1910) 6 Adam 279; *McFadyean* v.
   Stewart, supra.
[72] *Dunbar* v. *Johnston* (1904) 4 Adam 505.
[73] *Craig* v. *Galt* (1881) 4 Couper 541; *Macrae* v. *Cooper* (1882) 4 Couper 561.

plea of guilty to be recorded although the prosecutor refused to accept the plea.[74] Advocation is not favourably regarded by the High Court, and it has been described as obsolete.[75] It is not available to review an administrative decision of the sheriff which is alleged to have been made ultra vires, at any rate where the Crown are not a party to the decision, as in the case of a restoration of a driving licence under section 116 of the Road Traffic Act 1960.[76]

Nobile officium

16–129 The High Court exercises a nobile officium to which aggrieved parties may bring petitions where no other mode of review is open.[77] Such petitions may be brought against judgments of inferior courts in statutory matters although the statute does not provide for an appeal, provided it does not declare the inferior courts' decision to be final.[78]

[74] *Strathern* v. *Sloan*, supra.
[75] *MacLeod* v. *Levitt*, 1969 J.C. 16.
[76] Ibid.
[77] E.g. *Patrick McCloy*, Petnr., 1971 S.L.T. (Notes) 32, where a petition was allowed after a stated case had been lodged and abandoned. See also supra, para. 11–01.
[78] *J. P. Hartley*, Petnr. (1968) 32 J.C.L. 191.

Part IV

MISCELLANEOUS MATTERS

CHAPTER 17

PUNISHMENT, OTHER FORMS OF DISPOSAL, AND EXPENSES

Custodial Sentences

Imprisonment

17–01   The only custodial sentence for persons over twenty-one years of age (apart from the obsolescent sentences of preventive detention and corrective training[1]) is imprisonment. Different forms of prison sentence such as penal servitude and imprisonment with hard labour are now abolished.[1a]

The maximum period of imprisonment which can be imposed on indictment in the sheriff court is two years.[2] Prior to the 1949 Act custodial sentences of three years and upwards were sentences of penal servitude which, as the successor to transportation which was itself the successor to capital punishment, could be imposed only by the High Court.

Section 16 of the 1949 Act provides that any enactment conferring power to pass a sentence of penal servitude is to be read as conferring power to pass a sentence of imprisonment. Any statute referring to crimes punishable with transportation is construed as applicable to crimes punishable with penal servitude prior to the 1949 Act.[3] There is no upper limit on the High Court's power to imprison, and sentence may be passed for any fixed period or for life. A life sentence is mandatory in the case of persons convicted of murder,[4] or of offences against the Criminal Law (Scotland) Act 1829[5] at any rate where the Crown do not restrict the penalty sought.[6] A court which passes a life sentence for murder may recommend that the murderer be not released for a stated minimum period.[7] Such a recommendation is not binding on the Secretary of State but will be taken into account in deciding when to release the prisoner. The Secretary of State is, however, obliged to consult the Lord Justice-General and the trial judge if available before releasing on licence a person sentenced to life imprisonment who is recommended for such release by the parole board.[8]

---

[1] Infra, paras. 17–10 et seq.
[1a] 1949 Act, s. 16 (1).
[2] Ibid.
[3] See Penal Servitude Act 1857, ss. 2, 6; Penal Servitude Act 1891, s. 1. The reference in the Prevention of Crimes Act 1871 to theft punishable with penal servitude applies to theft so punishable in 1871—*Gilmour* v. *Gray*, 1951 J.C. 70.
[4] Murder (Abolition of Death Penalty) Act 1965.
[5] Homicide Act 1957, s. 14.
[6] See Criminal Law (Scotland) Act 1829, s. 5.
[7] Murder (Abolition of Death Penalty) Act 1965, s. 1 (2).
[8] Criminal Justice Act 1967, s. 61.

17–02   It may still be the case that offences with a minimum statutory penalty of penal servitude, or of imprisonment for more than two years, cannot be tried in the sheriff court.[9] But the High Court has power to impose a sentence below the statutory minimum.[10]

17–03   A summary court may not impose imprisonment for less than five days,[11] but may, if any police cells or other places certified by the Secretary of State on the application of any police authority (" legalised police cells ") are available, sentence an offender to be detained therein for not more than four days.[12] Such cells may not be used for women unless there is provision for their supervision by women.[13]

Restrictions on imprisonment of first offenders

17–04   The First Offenders (Scotland) Act 1960 (as amended by the 1963 Act) prohibits the use of imprisonment by summary courts for first offenders over the age of twenty-one unless the court is of opinion that no other method of dealing with the offender is appropriate. Appropriateness is to be determined by the method provided in section 1 (2) of the 1963 Act for young offenders,[14] and where the court does imprison it must state and enter in the minutes of proceedings its reason for doing so.[15]

A person is a first offender for the purposes of the Act if he has not since attaining the age of seventeen been convicted of any other offence punishable with imprisonment.[16] Absolute discharge or probation in any court count as convictions for this purpose.[17] No account is to be taken of a previous conviction after the expiry of ten years from its date, excluding any period during which the offender was in custody under sentence in respect of the conviction.[18]

Young offenders

17–05   Section 1 of the 1963 Act, as amended by the 1968 Act,[19] provides that young persons of over sixteen and under twenty-one years of age shall not be sent to prison, but may instead be sentenced to detention in a young offenders institution [20] for a term not exceeding that for which they could have been imprisoned. Sentence of detention in a young offenders institution and not imprisonment must be passed even where the sentence is such that it will continue in force after the detainee has become twenty-one. So a person aged twenty may be sentenced to ten years' detention in a

---

[9] *Gallagher* v. *H.M. Adv.*, 1937 J.C. 27; 1949 Act, Sched. 12, repealing s. 10 of Criminal Procedure (Scotland) Act 1938.
[10] Penal Servitude Act 1891, s. 1 (2).
[11] 1954 Act, s. 47 (1).
[12] Ibid., s. 47 (2)–(4).
[13] Ibid., s. 47 (5).
[14] Infra, para. 17–07.
[15] First Offenders (Scotland) Act 1960, s. 1 (1), (2); 1963 Act, s. 1 (3).
[16] First Offenders (Scotland) Act, s. 1 (3).
[17] Ibid., s. 1 (3A); 1963 Act, s. 17 (1), Sched. 5.
[18] Ibid., s. 1 (3B); 1963 Act, s. 17 (2), Sched. 5.
[19] Sched. 8.
[20] See A. D. Smith, " Young Offenders Institutions in Scotland, " 1968 S.L.T. (News) 17.

young offenders institution and may not be sentenced to imprisonment. But he may be transferred to prison on becoming twenty-one and must be so transferred before reaching his twenty-third birthday.[21] Once transferred, he is treated as if his sentence had been one of imprisonment.[22]

17-06 It is also competent for the Secretary of State to transfer to borstal a person under twenty-one who is detained in a young offenders institution in pursuance of a sentence, after consultation where practicable with the sentencing judge. He will then be treated as if he had been sentenced to borstal on the date of the transfer or, if the unexpired term of his sentence was then less than two years, on a date two years prior to the expiration of that term.[23]

17-07 A court may not impose detention on a young person under section 1 of the 1963 Act unless of opinion that no other method of dealing with him is appropriate. In order to determine whether any other method is appropriate the court must obtain and consider information about the offender's circumstances from a local authority officer [24] or other independent source (and not the Crown or defence [25]) and must also take account of his physical or mental condition.[26] A copy of any report is given to the offender or his solicitor.[27] Where a summary court imposes a sentence of detention in a young offenders institution, it must state and enter in the minutes of proceedings its reason for determining that no other method is appropriate.[28]

Determination of period of sentence

17-08 Section 68 of the Criminal Justice Act 1967 provides that a court in passing sentence of imprisonment or of detention in a young offenders institution shall in determining the period of imprisonment or detention, have regard to any period of time spent in custody by the offender while awaiting trial or sentence.

Detention in precincts of court

17-09 Where a court of summary jurisdiction has power to impose imprisonment on an offender, it may, in lieu of so doing, order that the offender be detained within the precincts of the court, or at any police station, till such hour not later than eight in the evening on the day on which he is convicted as the court may direct. Before making such an order the court must take into consideration the distance between the proposed place of detention and the offender's residence (if known to, or acertainable by, the court)

---

[21] 1963 Act, s. 10.
[22] Ibid.
[23] Prisons (Scotland) Act 1952, s. 32 (1), as substituted by 1963 Act, s. 9 (1).
[24] 1968 Act, s. 27 (6).
[25] *Auld* v. *Herron*, 1969 J.C. 4.
[26] 1963 Act, s. 1 (2). The court is obliged to obtain a report on the accused and consider the information furnished therein, but not to follow any recommendations made by the local authority officer: see *Hogg* v. *Heatlie*, 1962 S.L.T. 39; *Kyle* v. *Cruickshank*, 1961 J.C. 1; *Scott* v. *MacDonald*, 1961 S.L.T. 257.
[27] 1949 Act, s. 10.
[28] 1963 Act, s. 1 (3). As to the effect of failure to do so, see supra, paras. 15–36; 16–34.

and may not make such an order as will deprive the offender of a reasonable opportunity of returning to his residence on the day on which such order is made.[29]

Corrective training and preventive detention

17-10   (a) Corrective Training. This sentence, which is confined to solemn procedure, may, in the circumstances set forth below, be passed in lieu of any other sentence. It is for a term of not less than two nor more than four years [30] and the maximum can be imposed in the sheriff court as well as in the High Court.[31] The general principles upon which sentences of corrective training should proceed are dealt with by Lord Justice-Clerk Thomson in *H.M. Adv.* v. *McErlane*.[32] It is competent where:

(1) a person who is not less than twenty-one years of age:

(a) is convicted on indictment of an offence punishable with imprisonment for a term of two years or more; and

(b) has been convicted on at least two previous occasions since he attained the age of seventeen of offences punishable on indictment with such a sentence; and

(2) the court is satisfied that it is expedient with a view to his reformation and the prevention of crime that he should receive training of a corrective character for a substantial time, followed by a period of supervision if released in accordance with the provisions of the Fifth Schedule to the 1949 Act before the expiry of his sentence.[33]

17-11   (b) Preventive Detention. A sentence of preventive detention can be imposed only by the High Court of Justiciary. Its duration is for such term of not less than five nor more than fourteen years as the court may determine.[34] It is competent where:

(1) a person who is not less than thirty years of age:

(a) is convicted in the High Court of Justiciary [35] of an offence punishable with imprisonment for a term of two years or more; and

(b) has been convicted on indictment on at least three previous occasions since he attained the age of seventeen of offences punishable with such a sentence and was on at least two of those occasions sentenced to borstal training, imprisonment or corrective training.[36] (In this connection a person who has been sentenced to borstal training on summary conviction of an offence is deemed to have been convicted of that offence on indictment [37]) and

---

[29] 1954 Act, s. 46.
[30] 1949 Act, s. 21 (1).
[31] *Mullen* v. *H.M. Adv.*, 1954 J.C. 83.
[32] 1953 J.C. 12. See also *H.M. Adv.* v. *Miller and Others*, 1954 J.C. 53, where the question of sentencing persons who escape during a sentence of corrective training is dealt with.
[33] 1949 Act, s. 21 (1).
[34] Ibid., s. 21 (2).
[35] The High Court can impose a sentence of preventive detention upon a person remitted to it under s. 31 of the 1887 Act: *H.M. Adv.* v. *Churchill*; *H.M. Adv.* v. *Lee*, 1953 J.C. 6.
[36] 1949 Act, s. 21 (2).
[37] Ibid., s. 21 (8).

(2) the court is satisfied that it is expedient for the protection of the public that he should be detained in custody for a substantial time, followed by a period of supervision if released in accordance with the provisions of the Fifth Schedule to the 1949 Act before the expiry of his sentence.[38]

7-12   A person sentenced to corrective training or preventive detention is detained in a prison for the term of his sentence subject to his release in accordance with rules made by the Secretary of State for Scotland under section 35 (6) of the Prisons (Scotland) Act 1952, or the provisions of section 19 of that Act. While so detained offenders must be treated in such manner as may be prescribed by rules made under section 35.[39] A certificate purporting to be signed by or on behalf of the Director of Public Prosecutions that an offence is punishable on indictment in England with imprisonment for a term of two years or more is sufficient evidence of the matter so certified.[40]

7-13   Before sentencing any offender to corrective training or preventive detention, the court must call for and consider a report on the offender's physical and mental condition and his suitability for such a sentence, which report it is the duty of the Secretary of State to cause to be furnished to the court.[41]

If on consideration of such report the court, either ex proprio motu or on the application of either party, thinks it expedient to do so, it may require any person concerned in the preparation of the report or with knowledge of matters dealt with in the report, to appear with a view to his examination on oath on any of the matters dealt with in the report, and such person may be examined or cross-examined accordingly.[42]

A copy of any report so furnished must be given by the clerk of court to the offender or his solicitor at least two clear days before the diet at which the sentence is to be passed.[43]

7-14   Although still competent, sentences of corrective training and preventive detention have fallen into disuse.[44]

Release from prison

7-15   In the normal case a prisoner who has been of good behaviour will be released after serving two-thirds of his sentence, provided the sentence was one of more than thirty days and provided he has served at least thirty days of it.[45]

7-16   Section 59 of the Criminal Justice Act 1967 set up a parole board for Scotland, and section 60 empowers the Secretary of State, on the recommendation of the parole board, to release on licence a person serving a

---

[38] Ibid., s. 21 (2).
[39] Prisons (Scotland) Act 1952, ss. 19, 35. Release on licence may be granted to such offenders: s. 19 (5).
[40] 1949 Act, s. 21 (3).
[41] Ibid., s. 21 (5).
[42] Ibid., s. 21 (6).
[43] Ibid., s. 21 (7).
[44] They have been abolished in England: Criminal Justice Act 1967, s. 37 (1).
[45] Prisons (Scotland) Rules 1952, rule 37.

determinate sentence after a period of twelve months or one-third of his sentence, whichever is the longer. The licence remains in force until the date on which the prisoner would normally have been released on remission. A licensed parolee is subject to recall by the Secretary of State on the recommendation of the parole board,[46] or in certain cases without prior consultation with the board,[47] but the Secretary of State must then refer the case to the board. The prisoner has in both cases a right to make representation to the board who may require his release.[48] Where a licensed parolee is convicted in the High Court or the sheriff court (summarily or on indictment) of an offence punishable on indictment with imprisonment the court may revoke his licence, whether or not it passes any other sentence.[49] A person whose licence is revoked by a court may not be released on parole for a further year or a third of the period for which the licence would have remained in force, whichever is the longer.[50]

17–17   A person sentenced to life imprisonment may be released on licence by the Secretary of State on the recommendation of the parole board.[51] He may be released at any time, but remains under licence for the rest of his life, and the licence may be revoked in the same way as that of an ordinary parolee.[52]

Release from young offenders institution

17–18   Remission[53] and parole[54] apply as they do to imprisonment.

17–19   In addition a person serving a sentence of detention in a young offenders institution for eighteen months or more may instead of being granted remission or parole be released on licence at any time on or after the day when he could have been discharged on remission. This licence remains in force until the expiration of his sentence, and the same recall provisions apply as apply to parolees.[55]

A person detained in a young offenders institution in pursuance of a sentence for a term of six months[56] or more but less than eighteen months[57] is required to be under supervision for twelve months after his release, subject to the Secretary of State's right to discharge the supervision at any time. The person under whose supervision he is and the requirements of his supervision are as specified in a notice of supervision given to him on his release.[58] Such a person may be recalled to a young offenders

---

[46] Criminal Justice Act 1967, s. 62 (1).
[47] Ibid., s. 62 (2).
[48] Ibid., s. 62 (4), (5).
[49] Ibid., s. 62 (8).
[50] Ibid., s. 62 (10).
[51] Ibid., s. 61.
[52] Ibid., s. 62. The Secretary of State must consult with the Lord Justice-General and with the trial judge if available.
[53] Young Offenders (Scotland) Rules 1965, rule 35. Release is subject to s. 12 of the 1963 Act, infra, para. 17–19.
[54] Criminal Justice Act 1967, s. 60 (8) (b).
[55] Ibid., s. 60 (3) (b), (6); supra, para. 17–16.
[56] This period may be reduced to three months by the Secretary of State by Order: 1963 Act, s. 12 (2).
[57] See Criminal Justice Act 1967, Sched. 6.
[58] 1963 Act, s. 12 (1).

institution by order of the Secretary of State if the latter is satisfied that he has failed to comply with any requirement of his supervision notice.[59] Such order lapses at the end of the supervision period unless the offender is then in custody.[60] The period of detention on recall may not exceed three months.[61] A person released after recall remains under supervision until twelve months from his original release, and may be recalled again for a period not exceeding three months less the period of any earlier recall.[62]

Borstal training

–20   Section 20 of the 1949 Act, replacing Part I of the Prevention of Crime Act 1908, provides that a person between sixteen and twenty-one years of age who is convicted on indictment, or summarily by a sheriff or stipendiary magistrate, of an offence punishable by imprisonment may be sentenced to borstal training if " the court is satisfied having regard to his character and previous conduct, and to the circumstances of the offence " that such a sentence " is expedient for his reformation and the prevention of crime." The court must consider a report on the offender's physical and mental condition and his suitability for borstal, which the Secretary of State is bound to furnish.[63] The court may ex proprio motu, or on the application of either party, hear evidence from any person concerned in preparing the report or with knowledge thereof.[64] A copy of the report must be given to the offender or his solicitor two days before the sentencing diet.[65] The provisions of the 1963 Act and the First Offenders (Scotland) Act 1960 which restrict the power to pass sentences of detention on young persons and first offenders [66] do not apply to borstal sentences.[67]

A person who has served any part of a borstal sentence may not be again sentenced to borstal.[68] A borstal sentence is indeterminate, and no term is stated by the court, but the maximum period for which a person sentenced to borstal can be detained is two years.[69]

–21   Where a person detained in borstal is reported to the Secretary of State by the visiting committee as incorrigible or as exercising a bad influence on other inmates of the institution, the Secretary of State may apply to the sheriff within whose jurisdiction the institution is situated to commute the unexpired part of the borstal sentence to detention in a young

[59] Ibid., s. 12 (3). For recall by a court on conviction, see s. 13.
[60] Ibid.
[61] Ibid., s. 12 (4).
[62] Ibid., s. 12 (5).
[63] 1949 Act, s. 20 (3). The report is in fact provided by the governor of the institution to which the offender was remanded for the report.
[64] Ibid., s. 20 (4).
[65] Ibid., s. 20 (5).
[66] Supra, paras. 17–04; 17–07.
[67] *Haggerty* v. *Herron*, 1970 S.L.T. (Notes) 5.
[68] 1963 Act, s. 3. This limitation does not apply in England: see *R.* v. *Noseda* [1958] 1 W.L.R. 793.
[69] 1963 Act, s. 4. There is a six months' minimum in England—Criminal Justice Act 1961, s. 11 (1).

offenders institution. The sheriff may then commute the unexpired part of the sentence to a stated term of detention in a young offenders institution not exceeding that unexpired part. The offender is then treated [70] as if he had been sentenced to detention in a young offenders institution for that term.[71]

Release from borstal

17–22   Persons released from borstal are under supervision for one year following the date of their release.[72] They are under the supervision of such person as is specified in their release notice and subject to any other requirements there specified. The Secretary of State may recall such persons if satisfied that they have failed to comply with any requirement of the release notice. A recall order ceases to have effect at the expiration of one year from the offender's release unless he is then in custody. A person who has been recalled may again be released under supervision.

Where a person under supervision or after recall is sentenced by any court in Great Britain to borstal or corrective training his original sentence ceases to have effect.[73]

Where a person is recalled he is detained in a young offenders institution and not in borstal.[74] The maximum period of detention following recall is three months.[75]

Where a person under borstal release supervision is convicted of an offence punishable with imprisonment the court may make a recall order instead of dealing with him in any other way.[76]

Detention centre

17–23   A person between sixteen and twenty-one years of age who is convicted of an offence punishable in the case of a person over that age with imprisonment may be sentenced to be detained in a detention centre for a fixed term of three months.[77]

It is not competent to make an order rendering a person liable to more than three months' detention in a centre at any one time,[78] so that consecutive sentences of detention are incompetent.

17–24   Where an offender is serving a sentence in a detention centre or has received but not yet begun to serve such a sentence the court may, where otherwise competent, pass sentence of imprisonment or of detention in a young offenders institution for a period not exceeding the aggregate of the maximum period of imprisonment or detention in a young offenders

---

[70] Except for the purposes of section 33 (3), (4) of the Prisons (Scotland) Act 1952 which deal with release supervision and recall.
[71] Prisons (Scotland) Act 1952, s. 32, as substituted by 1963 Act, s. 9 (1).
[72] 1963 Act, s. 4 (2); Prisons (Scotland) Act 1952, s. 33 (3).
[73] Prisons (Scotland) Act 1952, s. 33, as amended by 1963 Act, Sched. 5.
[74] 1963 Act, s. 5 (1).
[75] Ibid., s. 4 (3).
[76] Ibid., s. 6 (1).
[77] 1963 Act, s. 7, as amended by 1968 Act.
[78] 1963 Act, s. 8 (1).

institution which the court could have passed on him together with the unexpired portion of his detention centre sentence, or may sentence him to borstal training. In either case the detention centre sentence ceases to have effect.[79]

7–25   A detention centre sentence may not be passed on a person who has served or is serving a sentence involving his detention for two months or more in a prison or in a young offenders institution, or a borstal sentence, or who has already served a detention centre sentence, unless in each case " the court is of the opinion that, having regard to special considerations arising out of the circumstances of the case and the character of the offender, this method of dealing with him is the most appropriate." [80]

Release from detention centre

7–26   Where it appears to the Secretary of State that a person in a detention centre is unfit therefor for health reasons he may, after consultation where practicable with the sentencing judge, release him under supervision.[81]

Where a person in a detention centre is reported to the Secretary of State by the visiting committee as not amenable to the discipline of the centre for health reasons, the Secretary of State may transfer him to a young offenders institution for a period not exceeding the unexpired portion of his detention centre sentence.[82]

7–27   Detainees in a detention centre are entitled to one-third remission for good conduct, provided they serve at least 30 days and have been sentenced to more than one month.[83]

7–28   A person sent to a detention centre or transferred therefrom to a young offenders institution under section 32 (3) of the Prisons (Scotland) Act 1952 [84] is under supervision for twelve months after his release and bound to comply with any requirement of his supervision notice (which must also name the supervisor), subject to the power of the Secretary of State to discharge the supervision, or cancel or modify any supervision requirement, at any time.[85]

The Secretary of State may order the recall of any such person if satisfied he has failed to comply with any supervision requirement. The recall is to a young offenders institution, and is for a period of fourteen days.[86] A recall order lapses after the end of the twelve months' supervision period unless the offender is then in custody under it. A person may be recalled only once.[87]

---

[79] Ibid., s. 8 (2). This provision would in some cases empower a summary court to pass sentence of nine months' imprisonment or detention in a young offenders institution for common law offences.

[80] Ibid., s. 7 (2).

[81] Ibid., s. 7 (3).

[82] Prisons (Scotland) Act 1952, s. 32 (3), as substituted by 1963 Act, s. 9 (1).

[83] Detention Centre (Scotland) (Amendment) Rules 1969.

[84] Supra, para. 17–26.

[85] 1963 Act, s. 11 (1).

[86] Ibid., s. 11 (2), as amended by 1968 Act.

[87] Ibid.

Fines

17–29   The most ordinary punishment in the case of a minor offence is a fine. The maximum fine for a common law offence imposable in the sheriff summary court is £150, and in other summary courts £50.[88] In statutory offences where the statute provides for a maximum fine that is, of course, the most which may be imposed. Where the statute provides only for imprisonment a summary court may substitute therefor a fine not exceeding one hundred pounds with or without caution for good behaviour.[89]

17–30   In determining the amount of any fine to be imposed a summary court is obliged to take into consideration the means of the offender so far as known.[90]

17–31   There is no limit to the amount of fine which may be imposed on conviction on indictment of a common law crime. Where a statute provides only for imprisonment it is competent instead to imposed a fine related to the maximum period of imprisonment as follows:

Period of imprisonment	Amount of fine
Not exceeding three months	Not exceeding £100
Exceeding three monhs but not exceeding six monthts	„ „ £200
Exceeding six months but not exceeding one year	„ „ £400
Over one year	Such fine as the court may, in its discretion, decide [91]

Payment of fines

17–32   Where a summary court imposes a fine it may order the offender to be searched and any money found on him on arrest or when so searched or when taken to prison or detention centre in default of payment may, unless the court otherwise directs, be applied towards payment of the fine. This power cannot be exercised if the court is satisfied that the money found does not belong to the offender or that its loss will be more injurious to his family than his imprisonment or detention.[92] The procedure is regulated by the provisions of section 8 of the Act of Adjournal (Summary Procedure) 1964.[93]

17–33   A fine may be paid at the bar of the court, but where it is not so paid the court must normally allow the offender at least seven days to pay the fine or the first instalment thereof.[94] Subject to certain exceptions, the court is entitled to allow time for payment whether or not the offender wishes it and may, therefore, when sentencing an offender to

---

[88] 1954 Act, ss. 3 and 7 (1), as amended by 1963 Act, s. 23 (1), (2).
[89] Ibid., s. 40, as amended by 1963 Act, s. 23 (3).
[90] Ibid., s. 41 (1).
[91] 1908 Act, s. 43 (3), as amended by 1963 Act, s. 28.
[92] 1954 Act, s. 41 (2).
[93] See App. D, infra, p. 498.
[94] 1954 Act, s. 42 (1), as substituted by 1963 Act, s. 25.

imprisonment on one charge and a fine on another, postpone the time for paying the fine until after the conclusion of the prison sentence.[95]

Where time to pay is allowed, the court may subsequently allow further time on the offender's application and after giving the prosecutor an opportunity to be heard.[96]

The court may refuse time to pay if the offender appears to have sufficient means to pay forthwith, or does not ask for time to pay, or fails to satisfy the court he has a fixed abode, or if the court is satisfied for any other special reason that no time should be allowed.[97]

7-34   Where a fine is imposed the court may, of its own motion [98] or on application by the offender, order payment to be made by instalments of such amount and at such times as it thinks fit. It is the duty of the court to inform the offender of his right to apply for payment by instalments.[99] Default in payment of any instalment is deemed to be default in payment of a fine of the amount of the unpaid balance of the fine imposed and is dealt with accordingly.[1]

7-35   Where an offender is allowed time to pay the court may, when it imposes the fine or later, order him to be placed under the supervision of such person as the court may appoint to assist and advise him as to payment. A supervision order remains in force so long as any part of the fine is unpaid unless discharged by the court or rendered ineffective by a transfer of fine order under section 44 of the 1954 Act.[2]

Imprisonment in default of payment

7-36   The sanction for default in payment of a fine is imprisonment or such other lawful form of detention in default of payment as is appropriate for a person who is too young to be imprisoned.[3]

The maximum terms of imprisonment, etc. which may be imposed for non-payment of a fine are as follows [4]:

Amount of Sum Imposed	Period of Imprisonment
Not exceeding £2	seven days
Exceeding £2 but not exceeding £5	fourteen days
„ £5 „ „ „ £20	thirty days
„ £20 „ „ „ £50	sixty days
„ £50	ninety days

If in any sentence, or extract sentence, the period of imprisonment inserted in default of payment of a fine or on failure to find caution is in

---

[95] Ibid.; see *Fraser* v. *Herron*, 1968 J.C. 1.
[96] 1954 Act, s. 42 (6).
[97] Ibid., s. 42 (2), as substituted by 1963 Act, s. 25. " Special reason " does not include the nature of the offence: *Barbour* v. *Robertson*, 1943 J.C. 46.
[98] See *Fraser* v. *Herron*, supra.
[99] 1954 Act, s. 43A (1), as substituted by 1963 Act, s. 25.
[1] Ibid., s. 43A (2).
[2] 1954 Act, s. 43B (1)–(3), as substituted by 1963 Act, s. 25. For provisions relating to young offenders, see infra, para. 17–40.
[3] 1954 Act, s. 43C (2), as substituted by 1963 Act, s. 25; 1954 Act, s. 48.
[4] 1954 Act, s. 49 (1), as substituted by Criminal Justice Act 1967, s. 93 (3).

excess of that competent under the above scale, such period of imprisonment is held as being reduced to the maximum period under the scale applicable to such default. The judge who pronounced sentence has power to order such sentence and extract to be corrected accordingly.[5]

The above periods of imprisonment apply to the non-payment of any sum imposed as aforesaid by a court of summary jurisdiction under any statute or order whether or not that statute makes any provision for its recovery, and apply to any statute or order passed before June 1, 1909, notwithstanding that it fixes some other period.[6]

17-37   The power of the court to impose imprisonment in default of payment is considerably restricted by the 1963 Act.

Imprisonment may be imposed at the same time as the fine where the court refuses time to pay, in which case the court must state the special reason for its decision to imprison.[7]

Where time is allowed for payment or payment by instalments is ordered the court cannot, at the same time as imposing the fine, impose imprisonment in the event of future default unless the offender is present, and the court decides, having regard to the gravity of the offence or the character of the offender, or other special reason, that it is expedient to imprison on default without further enquiry, in which case the court must state the special reason for its decision.[8] Where a court does impose imprisonment at the same time as imposing the fine the court may commit the offender to prison at any time if he asks it so to do, notwithstanding that he is not yet in default.[9]

17-38   In the normal case, where imprisonment is not imposed at the same time as the fine, the court may not impose imprisonment unless at some future diet (the " means enquiry " diet) the court enquires into the offender's means in his presence. No such enquiry is necessary, however, where the offender is in prison.[10] The court may secure the presence of the offender at such an enquiry by warrant or citation, and if a cited offender fails to appear may then issue a warrant for his arrest.[11]

The means enquiry court may sentence the offender to immediate imprisonment. It may also exercise the court's general powers to mitigate penalties, to allow further time to pay, to allow payment by instalments, or to alter the terms of any instalment payments already allowed.[12] It will normally impose a period of imprisonment in default of payment on the terms fixed by it. A court is bound to allow an application for further time to pay a fine or instalments thereof unless satisfied that the failure to pay

[5] 1954 Act, s. 49 (3).
[6] 1954 Act, ss. 48 and 49 (4).
[7] 1954 Act, s. 42 (2), as substituted by 1963 Act, s. 25.
[8] 1954 Act, s. 42 (3), as substituted by 1963 Act, s. 25.
[9] 1954 Act, s. 42 (4), as substituted by 1963 Act, s. 25.
[10] 1954 Act, s. 43 (1), as substituted by 1963 Act, s. 25.
[11] 1954 Act, s. 43 (2), (3), as substituted by 1963 Act, s. 25.
[12] 1954 Act, s. 57 (4); supra, para. 15-27.

has been wilful or that the offender has no reasonable prospect of being able to pay if time is allowed.[13]

7–39 Where a supervision order is in force the court may not subsequently impose imprisonment without taking such steps as are reasonably practicable to obtain a report, oral or written, from the supervisor on the offender's conduct and means, and considering any such report in addition to its own means enquiry.[14]

7–40 A court may not order detention in default of payment in the case of a person under twenty-one years of age who has been allowed time to pay unless he has been under supervision, or the court is satisfied that supervision is impracticable, in which case the court must state the grounds for its satisfaction.[15]

7–41 Wherever the court is required to state special reasons for its decision or the grounds on which it is satisfied that it is undesirable [16] or impracticable to place an offender under supervision, the grounds must be entered in the record of proceedings.[17]

Part payment

7–42 Where a person detained for failure to pay a fine imposed by a summary court or on indictment [18] pays part of the fine to the governor of the institution in which he is detained, his term of detention is reduced " by a number of days bearing as nearly as possible the same proportion to the total number of days for which the prisoner is sentenced as the sum so paid bears to the total amount of the fine " [19]; in other words, a person who has served part of the term imposed in default will get credit therefor. This provision applies also to legalised police cells, the money being paid to the officer in charge.[20]

Remission of fine

7–43 Where an offender in borstal or detention centre, or detained under an order made by virtue of section 57 or 58A of the Children and Young Persons (Scotland) Act 1937, or under release supervision from any such place, has not paid a fine imposed on him before his detention, the Secretary of State, after consultation where practicable with the sentencing judge, may remit the fine in whole or part if it appears to him that to do so might assist the rehabilitation of the offender.[21]

---

[13] Act of Adjournal (Summary Procedure) 1964, s. 11 (2); see also 1954 Act, s. 42 (6).
[14] 1954 Act, s. 43B (6), as substituted by 1963 Act, s. 25.
[15] 1954 Act, s. 43B (4), (5), as substituted by 1963 Act, s. 25.
[16] As to which there is no mention elsewhere in the Act.
[17] 1954 Act, s. 43C (1), as substituted by 1963 Act, s. 25, cf. supra. Reasons for not allowing time must be entered in the extract finding and sentence: Act of Adjournal, supra, s. 9.
[18] 1963 Act, s. 27.
[19] 1954 Act, s. 45 (1).
[20] Ibid., s. 45 (2).
[21] 1963 Act, s. 29, as amended by 1968 Act.

Period of imprisonment imposed

17–44   Where an offence is directly punished by imprisonment, the length of the sentence is a matter for the court's discretion. When imprisonment is imposed as an alternative to a fine, the scales laid down by section 49 of the 1954 Act must be kept in mind. If the maximum period fixed by that scale is adopted, the judge has only to decide upon the amount of the fine to be imposed. The 1908 and 1954 Acts provide that the period of imprisonment in default of payment of a penalty is to apply even where the statute imposing the penalty fixes a different period.[22] If, however, the maximum period of imprisonment competent under the scale is in excess of that prescribed by the special statute, it is suggested that the period of imprisonment imposed should be limited to that prescribed by the special statute. This is the view most favourable for the accused, and is not inconsistent with the provisions of the Act, as it will be observed that under the scale the period of imprisonment in default of payment is not to *exceed* the limits fixed by the Act. On the other hand, when by the special statute the period of imprisonment competent in default of payment of a penalty is in excess of that fixed by the scale, it will be necessary to limit the period to that competent under the Act.

17–45   In view of the provisions of section 45 of the 1954 Act it is desirable that the period of imprisonment imposed in relation to the fine should permit of the fine representing an even sum per day. Where a person has been imprisoned in default of payment of any instalment of a fine which he has been ordered to pay by instalments, the sum of the unpaid instalments is deemed to be the fine.[23]

Recovery by civil diligence

17–46   Power to order payment of a fine by civil diligence is preserved by section 42 (5) of the 1954 Act, as substituted by section 25 of the 1963 Act. Such order may be made in any case (1) where the penalty has to be recovered in that manner in terms of the Act,[24] as where proceedings have been taken against a company, association, incorporation, or body of trustees, in their corporate capacity[25]; or (2) where the court thinks it expedient to order a fine to be so recovered.[26] In such cases there are added to the finding of the court imposing such fine the words " and decerns and ordains instant execution by arrestment and also execution to pass hereon by poinding and sale, after a charge of ten free days." Such diligence, whatever the amount of the fine imposed, may be executed in the same manner as if the proceedings were on an extract decree of the sheriff in a summary cause.[26a] Where proceedings by civil diligence under this section are adopted, imprisonment is not thereafter competent.[27] Recovery by civil

[22] 1908 Act, ss. 48, 77 (4); 1954 Act, s. 49 (4).
[23] 1954 Act, s. 43A (2), as substituted by 1963 Act, s. 25.
[24] 1954 Act, s. 50.
[25] Ibid., s. 25 (a).
[26] E.g. *Kinnear* v. *Brander* (1914) 7 Adam 456.
[26a] See Sheriff Courts (Scotland) Act 1971, s. 35 and Sched. 1.
[27] 1954 Act, s. 50 (2).

diligence may be adopted at any time after the imposition of the fine and before the court has imposed imprisonment in default of payments.[28]

Lord McLaren laid down a distinct principle for the guidance of judges in the inferior courts, in the case of *Moffat* v. *Shaw*,[29] where a question arose as to the use of civil diligence in place of imprisonment. His Lordship, speaking of the Vaccination Act 1863, said: " In the enforcement of the penalty the statute requires that the more humane and more effective alternative of imprisonment for a short period should be adopted in preference to the civil remedy of poinding, which might be ruinous to a poor man." Although it is rare for the court to order fines to be recovered from an individual by civil diligence, it may be doubted whether the court would today argue that enforcement by imprisonment is " the more humane and more effective " method of enforcement even where civil diligence might ruin a poor man. In practice, however, the 1963 Act may render the alternative of imprisonment more humane, if less effective, because of the provisions designed to avoid its enforcement.

Person to whom fines are payable

7-47   In summary procedure all fines and expenses imposed under the Act are to be paid to the clerk of court, to be accounted for by him to the person entitled thereto. It is not necessary to specify in any sentence the person entitled to payment of any such fine or expense, unless where it is necessary to provide for the division of the penalty.[30]

This obviates the questions which sometimes formerly arose as to the person to whom payment of a penalty should be directed to be made. The Act does not impose on the clerk of court any obligation to take steps with a view to the recovery of fines. In prosecutions for the Crown in the sheriff court, the responsibility for the collection of the fines and penalties imposed rests upon the sheriff clerk under Exchequer Accounting Regulations.

The provision in regard to division of the penalty applies to prosecutions where the court may order part of the penalty to be paid to the complainer, the balance then going to the Exchequer.

Procedure on indictment

7-48   The provisions for enforcing fines imposed on conviction on indictment are similar to those applying to summary fines, except that the restrictions placed on the imposition of imprisonment by summary courts do not apply.

Payment of fines by instalments is provided for by section 37 of the 1949 Act. Payment by instalments may be ordered at the time the fine is imposed or at any subsequent time. The court may extend the time allowed for payment, reduce the amount of any instalment or allow instalments to

[28] Ibid., s. 50 (3), as added by 1963 Act, Sched. 5.
[29] (1896) 2 Adam 57.
[30] 1954 Act, s. 52.

be paid at longer intervals, all at any time before imprisonment has followed on the sentence, and without requiring the attendance of the accused.[31]

17–49   The maximum periods of imprisonment which may be imposed on default of payment of a fine imposed on conviction on indictment are as follows [32]:

Amount of Fine	Period of Imprisonment
Not exceeding £20	three months
Exceeding £20 but not	
„ £100	four months
„ £100 „ „	
„ £500	six months
„ £500	twelve months.

The provisions of section 45 of the 1954 Act relating to reduction of the period of imprisonment for part payment apply also to fines imposed on indictment.[33]

17–50   Fines imposed on a body corporate are recoverable as if a copy of the sentence certified by the clerk of court were an extract decree of the Court of Session for payment of the fine to the Queen's and Lord Treasurer's Remembrancer.[34]

Transfer of jurisdiction as to person fined

17–51   Where a court of summary jurisdiction has imposed a fine on a person convicted of an offence, and it appears to the court that he is resident outwith the jurisdiction of the court and within the jurisdiction of some other court of summary jurisdiction in Scotland or in any petty sessions area in England or Wales, the court may, if no term of imprisonment has been fixed in default, order the fine to be enforceable there (a " transfer of fine order ").[35]

The order may be made whether or not the offender applies for it.[36]

A transfer of fine order must specify the area or court in or by which the fine is enforceable and, where the court is a court of summary jurisdiction, must specify a sheriff court if the fine was imposed by a sheriff court.[37]

As from the date on which a transfer of fine order is made with respect to any fine, all functions in relation thereto which, if the order had not been made, would have been exercisable under any enactment by the court which imposed the fine or by the clerk of that court cease to be so exercis-

[31] 1949 Act, s. 37 (3). See also Act of Adjournal of June 15, 1950, infra, App. D, p. 497.
[32] 1949 Act, s. 36.
[33] 1963 Act, s. 27; supra, para. 17–42.
[34] 1949 Act, s. 40 (5).
[35] 1954 Act, s. 44 (1), as substituted by 1963 Act, Sched. 3. See also Act of Adjournal (Summary Procedure) 1964, s. 10.
[36] 1963 Act, s. 26 (1).
[37] 1954 Act, s. 44 (2), as substituted by 1963 Act, Sched. 3.

able, and are exercisable instead by the court to which the fine is transferred. These functions include the modification of sentence under section 57 (4) of the 1954 Act.[38]

Caution

7–52   Summary courts have power on convicting of a common law offence to require the offender to find caution for good behaviour for any period not exceeding twelve months in the case of the sheriff court or six months in the case of other courts, and to impose imprisonment on failure to find caution.[39] The maximum amount of caution which may be required is £50 in the case of inferior courts and £150 in the case of the sheriff court.[40]

The provisions of sections 42 (1) and 43 of the 1954 Act relating to the payment of fines and the imposition of imprisonment in default [41] apply equally to caution. Because of the nature of caution there is no provision for finding caution in instalments.

7–53   In summary procedure the following provisions apply with regard to the finding, forfeiture, and recovery of caution:

Caution may be found by consignation of the amount thereof with the clerk of court, or by bond of caution. Such bond may be signed by the mark of the cautioner.

Where caution becomes liable to forfeiture, forfeiture may be granted by the court on the motion of the prosecutor and, where necessary, warrant granted for the recovery thereof.

The court may order any cautioner to be imprisoned in the event of his failing to pay the amount due under his bond within six days after he has received a charge to that effect, and until payment is made, such imprisonment being for the maximum period applicable to the amount of caution in pursuance of section 49 of the 1954 Act or until payment is made, whichever is the less. The court, if it adjudges it expedient, may grant time for payment or may, instead of ordering imprisonment, order recovery of such caution by civil diligence as provided for in section 50 of the Act.

Forfeiture

Bail

7–54   Bail may be found and forfeited, and the like procedure be competent in default of payment thereof as is provided in regard to caution. Any

---

[38] 1954 Act, s. 44 (3), as substituted by 1963 Act, Sched. 3. A transferred fine is enforceable by the court to which it is transferred as if it had been imposed by that court except that where a fine is transferred to an English court, the length of alternative imprisonment is still governed by s. 49 of the 1954 Act—see Magistrates' Courts Act 1952, s. 72B (2); 1963 Act, Sched. 3. Reciprocal arrangements for the enforcement of English fines in Scotland subject to the table of alternative imprisonments in Sched. 3 to the Magistrates' Courts Act 1952, is made by the 1954 Act, s. 44 (4) and the Magistrates' Courts Act 1952, s. 72A; see 1963 Act, Sched. 3; 1954 Act, s. 44 (5); Criminal Justice Act 1967, Sched. 6.

[39] 1954 Act, ss. 3 and 7.

[40] 1963 Act, s. 23 (1) and (2).

[41] Supra, paras. 17–29 et seq.

bail found is held to continue in force until the final determination of the case, or until the expiry of six months from the date when such bail is found, whichever shall first occur, notwithstanding that the diets may have been from time to time continued or deserted pro loco et tempore, or not called. The cautioner is entitled to withdraw his bond of caution at any diet of the court at which the accused appears personally.

Where, instead of being liberated on bail, the accused is liberated under a penalty in the event of his failure to attend at any future diet, and such penalty is declared to be forfeited, the amount thereof may be added to any other penalty subsequently imposed on him, or the court may pronounce a separate finding in respect of such penalty and may grant warrant for the imprisonment of the accused in the event of non-payment thereof.[42]

17-55   Section 44 of the 1949 Act provides as follows:

> " Where any court has made an order for the forfeiture of bail it shall be competent for the court, if it is satisfied that it is reasonable in all the circumstances to do so, to recall the order and direct that the bail money forfeited be refunded. Any decision of a court under this section shall be final and not subject to review."

Instruments and vehicles

17-56   Where a person is summarily convicted of an offence, or is a person in respect of whom a probation order has been made, the court has power to order the forfeiture of any instruments or other articles found in his possession, used or calculated to be of use in the commission of the offence of which he was convicted or on account of which the probation order was made, and, save as otherwise expressly provided in any enactment with regard to the disposal of articles forfeited on conviction of an offence, may order said instruments or articles to be destroyed or otherwise disposed of.[43] Under this provision it is competent to forfeit housebreakers' tools, poachers' nets, and all similar articles, but not, in the absence of special statutory authority, a motor car used as a conveyance to and from the scene of an offence against a fishing statute.[44] The provision applies even when the statute contravened is silent on the subject. It also applies to common law offences.

17-57   Where a person is convicted on indictment of an offence and the sentencing court is satisfied that any property which was in his possession or under his control at the time of his arrest was used or intended by him to be used for the purpose of committing or facilitating the commission of any offence (including the taking of any steps after the commission of the offence for the purpose of disposing of any property to which the offence related or of avoiding apprehension or detection), that property

---

[42] 1954 Act, s. 51.
[43] Ibid., s. 54; 1949 Act, s. 9.
[44] *Simpson* v. *Fraser and Others*, 1948 J.C. 1. See infra, para. 17-58.

is liable to forfeiture, and if forfeited will be disposed of as the court directs.[44a]

Where a person is convicted on indictment of an offence and the sentencing court is satisfied that a motor vehicle was used (by him or by anyone else), for the above purpose, the court may make a similar forfeiture order.[44b]

7–58   Many statutes contain specific provisions for forfeiture. Questions may arise when the goods the court wishes to forfeit do not belong to the accused. Where the forfeiture is expressed to be " in addition to any other penalty," it cannot be levied on goods not belonging to the accused. This was originally the position in relation to using wireless receivers without a licence under section 14 of the Wireless Telegraphy Act 1949.[45] Section 19 of the Salmon and Freshwater Fisheries (Protection) (Scotland) Act 1951 provides that a person convicted of certain offences under the Act is liable to forfeiture of any vehicle or boat used to commit the offence. In one case where a vehicle belonging to a third party was forfeited by the sheriff the third party successfully petitioned the High Court for recall of the forfeiture.[46]

Section 21 (2) of the Sea Fisheries Act 1883 provides that forfeitures under the Act may be destroyed, sold, or disposed of as the court may direct. It has been held to be competent for a court to order forfeiture of fish and gear under this section and to order further that the gear should not be sold back to the accused.[47]

7–59   Where a court has made an order for the forfeiture of an article the court or any justice of the peace may issue a search warrant if satisfied by sworn information that there is reasonable cause to believe that the forfeited article is to be found in any place and that admission thereto has been refused or that such refusal is apprehended.[47a]

Probation Orders

7–60   The Probation of Offenders Act 1907 allowed in certain cases the release of offenders on probation without immediate punishment. This Act is now repealed, along with certain amending statutes, so far as they relate to probation, by the 1949 Act. Probation is now regulated by the 1949 Act, as amended by the 1968 Act.[48] It is applicable in the following circumstances in summary jurisdiction:

(a) The offender must be charged before a court of summary jurisdiction with an offence other than an offence the sentence for which is fixed by law.

[44a] Criminal Justice Bill 1972, cl. 22.

[44b] Ibid., cl. 23.

[45] *J. W. Semple and Sons* v. *MacDonald*, 1963 J.C. 90; s. 11 (4) of the Wireless Telegraphy Act 1967 empowers the forfeiture under the earlier Act of apparatus not belonging to the offender.

[46] *Loch Lomond Sailings Ltd.* v. *Hawthorn*, 1962 J.C. 8.

[47] *Akre* v. *Mathewson*; *Eide* v. *Mathewson* (1966) 31 J.C.L. 49.

[47a] 1963 Act, s. 34.

[48] References to the 1949 Act are references to that Act as so amended.

(b) The court must be satisfied that he committed the offence.

(c) The court must be of opinion, having regard to the circumstances, including the nature of the offence and the character of the offender, that it is expedient to make a probation order.[49]

The court may in these circumstances, without proceeding to conviction, make a probation order, i.e. an order requiring the offender to be under supervision for a period to be specified in the order of not less than one nor more than three years.[50]

17-61   Where any person has been convicted on indictment of an offence (other than an offence the sentence for which is fixed by law) and the court is of the opinion set forth in (c) of the preceding paragraph, the court may, instead of sentencing him, make a probation order.[51]

Contents of orders

17-62   The probation order must be in the form prescribed by Act of Adjournal.[52]

The order must name the local authority area in which the offender resides or is to reside.[53]

Where the offender resides or is to reside within the jurisdiction of the court making the order, that court must in the order provide for the offender to be under the supervision of an officer of the local authority of that area.[54] The court does not nominate any particular officer as it did prior to the 1968 Act.

Where the offender resides or is to reside in a local authority area in which the court making the order has no jurisdiction (other than in England, which case is dealt with by section 7 of the 1949 Act, as explained infra [54a]) the court must name the appropriate court in the area of residence or intended residence and that court shall require the local authority for its area to arrange for supervision of the offender by one of its officers. Where a probationer changes his residence the court may, and if asked to by the officer supervising the probationer must, amend the order by substituting the appropriate area and naming an appropriate court which will enforce the order and require its local authority to arrange supervision.[55]

The court to be named as the appropriate court in such a case must be a court exercising jurisdiction in the place where the offender resides or is to reside and will be a sheriff court, a justice of the peace court or a burgh or police court according as the probation order was made by a sheriff court,

---

[49] 1949 Act, s. 2 (1).
[50] Ibid.
[51] Ibid.
[52] 1949 Act, s. 2 (2), as substituted by 1968 Act, Sched. 8; Act of Adjournal (Probation Orders) 1969.
[53] Ibid.
[54] 1949 Act, s. 2 (2), (4).
[54a] Infra, paras. 17–80 et seq.
[55] Ibid., Sched. 2, para. 2 (1).

a justice of the peace court or a burgh or police court.[56] Where there is no justice of the peace court or burgh or police court, as the case may be, exercising jurisdiction in the area in question, the court to be named as the appropriate court must be the sheriff court.[57]

7–63   A probation order must order the offender to be of good behaviour, to conform to the directions of an officer of the local authority, and to inform the officer of any change of address or employment.[57a]

A probation order may also contain any of the following additional requirements according as circumstances require:

(1) A probation order may require the offender to comply during the whole or any part of the probation period with such requirements as the court, having regard to the circumstances of the case, considers necessary for securing the good conduct of the offender or for preventing a repetition by him of the offence or the commission of other offences.[58] The court may also require security for good behaviour to be given.[59]

(2) A probation order may also include requirements relating to the residence of the offender.[60] Before making an order containing any such requirements, the court must consider the home surroundings of the offender.[61] Where the order requires the offender to reside in any institution or place, the name of the institution or place and the period for which he is so required to reside are specified in the order, and that period may not extend beyond twelve months from the date of the requirement or beyond the date when the order expires.[62]

(3) A probation order may also make requirements regarding treatment of the offender's mental condition. This matter is dealt with later in paras. 17–67 et seq.

Procedure for making orders

7–64   Before making a probation order the court normally obtains a report on the offender's background from a local authority officer. Where any report is made by an officer of a local authority to any court (other than one whose procedure is regulated by rules under section 52 (2) of the Children and Young Persons (Scotland) Act 1937) with a view to assisting the court in determining the most suitable method of dealing with any person in respect of an offence, the clerk of court gives a copy of it to the offender or his solicitor. Where the offender is under sixteen and unrepresented, the copy may be given to his parent or guardian instead of to him.[63] Before making a probation order, the court must explain to the offender in ordinary language the effect of the order.[64] This includes

---

[56] Ibid., Sched. 2, para. 2 (2).
[57] Ibid.
[57a] Act of Adjournal, supra.
[58] 1949 Act, s. 2 (5).
[59] Infra, para. 17–66.
[60] 1949 Act, s. 2 (6).
[61] 1949 Act, s. 2 (6) (a).
[62] Ibid., s. 2 (6) (b).
[63] 1949 Act, s. 10.
[64] 1949 Act, s. 2 (7).

any additional requirements proposed to be inserted therein under section 2 (5) of the 1949 Act (good conduct, etc.) or section 2 (6) of that Act (residence), or under section 3 of the Act (requirement for treatment of offender for mental condition).[65] The court must also explain to the offender that if he fails to comply therewith or commits another offence during the probation period he will be liable to be sentenced for the original offence or, if that offence was tried summarily, to be convicted and sentenced therefor.[66] The court must not make the order unless the offender expresses his willingness to comply with the requirements thereof.[67]

17-65   The clerk of the court by which a probation order is made or of the appropriate court, as the case may be, must cause copies thereof to be given to the local authority officer who is to supervise the probationer, to the probationer, and to the person in charge of any institution or place in which the probationer is required by the order to reside.[68]

Security for good behaviour

17-66   Any court may, on making a probation order under the 1949 Act, if it thinks it expedient for the purpose of the order, require the offender to give security for his good behaviour.[69]

Security may be given by consignation with the clerk of the court or by entering into an undertaking to pay the amount, but not otherwise, and such security may be forfeited and recovered in like manner as caution.[70]

Orders requiring treatment for mental condition

17-67   Orders requiring treatment for mental condition may be made only in accordance with the provisions of section 3 of the 1949 Act,[71] as amended by the Mental Health (Scotland) Act 1960. These are summarised in this and the immediately succeeding paragraphs. Where the court is satisfied, on the evidence of a registered medical practitioner approved for the purposes of section 27 of the Mental Health (Scotland) Act 1960, that the mental condition of an offender is such as requires and as may be susceptible to treatment but is not such as to warrant his detention under a hospital order in terms of Part V of the aforementioned Act, the court may, if it makes a probation order, include therein a requirement that the offender shall submit, for such period not extending beyond twelve months from the date of the requirement as may be specified therein, to treatment by or under the direction of a registered medical practitioner, with a view to the improvement of the offender's mental condition.[72]

The medical witness does not always require to give evidence in court.

---

[65] Ibid., see infra, paras. 17–67 et seq.
[66] 1949 Act, s. 2 (7).
[67] Ibid.
[68] 1949 Act, s. 2 (8).
[69] 1949 Act, s. 8 (1).
[70] Ibid., s. 8 (2); supra, para. 17–53.
[71] Ibid., s. 3 (9).
[72] Ibid., s. 3 (1), (2) as amended by Mental Health (Scotland) Act 1960.

Subject to certain qualifications as to consent, a report in writing as to the mental condition of an offender purporting to be signed by a registered medical practitioner may be received in evidence without proof of the signature or qualifications of the practitioner. The court may, in any case, require that the practitioner be called to give oral evidence, and must do so if requested by the accused.[72a]

Where such a report is tendered other than by or on behalf of the accused a copy of the report must be given to his counsel or solicitor, if any. Where he is not represented its substance must be disclosed to him or, in the case of a child or young person, to his parent or guardian. The accused is entitled to lead evidence in rebuttal.[73]

7–68 The treatment which may be required must be specified in the order and must be one of the following kinds:

(a) treatment as a resident patient in a hospital within the meaning of the Mental Health (Scotland) Act 1960 other than a State hospital;

(b) treatment as a non-resident patient at such institution or place as may be specified in the order; or

(c) treatment by or under the direction of such registered medical practitioner as may be specified in the order.[74]

No specification of the nature of the treatment beyond that contained in the above-mentioned statutory descriptions may be made in the order.[75]

A court must not make a probation order containing a requirement for treatment for an offender's mental condition unless it is satisfied that arrangements have been or can be made for the treatment intended to be specified in the order, and, if the offender is to be treated as a resident patient, for his reception.[76]

While the probationer is under treatment as a resident patient in pursuance of a requirement of the probation order, any officer responsible for his supervision is obliged to carry out the supervision to such extent only as may be necessary for the purpose of the discharge or amendment of the order.[77]

7–69 Where the medical practitioner by whom or under whose direction a probationer is being treated for his mental condition in pursuance of a probation order is of opinion that part of the treatment can be better or more conveniently given in or at an institution or place not specified in the order, being an institution or place in or at which the treatment of the probationer will be given by or under the direction of a registered medical practitioner, he may, with the consent of the probationer, make arrangements for him to be treated accordingly. These arrangements may provide for the probationer to receive part of his treatment as a resident patient in

---

[72a] See infra, para. 20–26

[73] Mental Health (Scotland) Act 1960, s. 57 (2)–(4), applied to 1949 Act by s. 3 (7) of that Act as amended by Mental Health (Scotland) Act 1960.

[74] 1949 Act, s. 3 (2), as amended by Mental Health (Scotland) Act 1960.

[75] Ibid.

[76] Ibid., s. 3 (3).

[77] Ibid., s. 3 (4).

an institution or place notwithstanding that the institution or place is not one which could have been specified in that behalf in the probation order.[78] The treatment so provided is deemed to be treatment to which the probationer is required to submit in pursuance of the probation order.[79]

A medical practitioner who makes such arrangements must give notice in writing to the officer or officers responsible for the supervision of the probationer, specifying the institution or place in or at which the treatment is to be carried out.[80]

Discharge of orders

17–70   A probation order may on the application of the officer supervising the probationer or of the probationer be discharged:

(a) by the appropriate court, or

(b) if no appropriate court has been named in the original or in any amending order, by the court which made the order.[81]

Amendment of orders

17–71   The court by which a probation order was made or the appropriate court may, upon application made by the officer supervising the probationer or by the probationer, by order amend a probation order by cancelling any of the requirements thereof or by inserting therein (either in addition to or in substitution for any such requirement) any requirement which could be included in the order if it were then being made by that court in accordance with the provisions of sections 2 and 3 of the 1949 Act. The court must not, however:

(a) Reduce the probation period, or extend that period beyond the end of three years from the date of the original order.

(b) So amend a probation order that the probationer is thereby required to reside in any institution or place, or to submit to treatment for his mental condition, for any period or periods exceeding twelve months in all.

(c) Insert in the order a requirement that the probationer shall submit to treatment for his mental condition unless the amending order is made within three months after the date of the original order.[82]

If the court by which a probation order was made, or the appropriate court, is satisfied that the probationer proposes to change or has changed his residence from the local authority area named in the order to another local authority area, the court may, and if application is made in that behalf by the officer supervising the probationer, must, by order, amend the probation order by (a) substituting for the area named therein that other area, and (b) naming the appropriate court to which all the powers of the

---

[78] Ibid., s. 3 (5).
[79] Ibid., s. 3 (6) (b).
[80] Ibid., s. 3 (6) (a).
[81] Ibid., s. 4 (1); Sched. 2, para. 1.
[82] 1949 Act, Sched. 2, para. 3. For definition of " appropriate court," see supra, para. 17–62.

court by which the order was made are to be transferred, which court must require the local authority for that other area to arrange for the probationer to be under the supervision of an officer of that authority.[83]

If the probation order contains requirements which in the opinion of the court cannot be complied with unless the probationer continues to reside in the area named in the order, the court will not amend the order as aforesaid, unless, in accordance with the remaining provisions of Schedule 2 to the 1949 Act, it cancels those requirements or substitutes therefor other requirements which can be so complied with.[84]

Where a probation order is so amended as regards the local authority area, the clerk of the court amending it must send to the clerk of the appropriate court four copies of the order together with such documents and information relating to the case as the court amending the order considers likely to be of assistance to the appropriate court, and the clerk of that court must send one copy of the probation order to the local authority of the substituted area, and two copies to the officer supervising the probationer, one of which the officer gives to the probationer.[85]

17-72 Where the probation order which is being thus amended was made by the High Court of Justiciary the foregoing provisions apply subject to the following modifications:

(a) the court does not name an appropriate court, but may substitute for the local authority named in the order the local authority for the area in which the probationer is to reside.

(b) the Clerk of Justiciary sends to the director of social work for the area in which the probationer is to reside three copies of the amending order together with such documents and information relating to the case as is likely to be of assistance to the local authority, and the director of social work sends two copies of the amending order to the officer supervising the probationer, one of which the officer gives to the probationer.[86]

17-73 Where the medical practitioner by whom or under whose direction a probationer is being treated for his mental condition in pursuance of any requirement of the probation order is of opinion:

" (a) that the treatment of the probationer should be continued beyond the period specified in that behalf in the order; or

(b) that the probationer needs different treatment, being treatment of a kind to which he could be required to submit in pursuance of a probation order; or

(c) that the probationer is not susceptible to treatment; or

(d) that the probationer does not require further treatment,
    or where the practitioner is for any reason unwilling to continue

---

[83] 1949 Act, Sched. 2, para. 2 (1).
[84] Ibid., para. 2 (2).
[85] Ibid., para. 2 (3).
[86] Ibid., para. 2 (4). For definition of " appropriate court," see supra, para. 17-62.

to treat or direct the treatment of the probationer, he shall make a
report in writing to that effect to the officer supervising the probationer and the officer shall apply to the court which made the
order or to the appropriate court for the variation or cancellation
of the requirement." [87]

17–74   Where the court which made the order or the appropriate court
proposes to amend a probation order otherwise than:

(a) on the application of the probationer, or

(b) by cancelling a requirement, or reducing the period of any requirement,

or substituting a new local authority area for that named in the order,
it must cite the probationer to appear before it and must not amend the
probation order unless he expresses his willingness to comply with the
requirements of the order as amended. [88]

17–75   On the making of an order discharging or amending a probation order,
the clerk of the court must forthwith give copies of the discharging or
amending order to the officer supervising the probationer; and the officer
then gives a copy to the probationer and to the person in charge of any
institution in which the probationer is or was required by the order to
reside. [89]

Termination of orders by sentence

17–76   Where a probationer is sentenced for the offence for which he was placed
on probation, the probation order ceases to have effect. [90]

Failure to comply with orders

17–77   " (1) If on information on oath from the officer supervising the probationer it appears to the court by which the order was made or to the
appropriate court that the probationer has failed to comply with any of the
requirements of the order, that court may issue a warrant for the arrest of
the probationer, or may, if it thinks fit, instead of issuing such a warrant
in the first instance, issue a citation requiring the probationer to appear
before the court at such time as may be specified in the citation. [91]

(2) If it is proved to the satisfaction of the court before which a
probationer appears or is brought in pursuance of the [above provi-
sions] that he has failed to comply with any of the requirements of the
probation order, the court may:

(a) without prejudice to the continuance in force of the probation
order, impose a fine not exceeding twenty pounds; or

---

[87] 1949 Act, Sched. 2, para. 4.

[88] Ibid., para. 5.

[89] Ibid., para. 6.

[90] 1949 Act, s. 4 (4).

[91] Ibid., s. 5 (1). It is imperative that the correct procedure should be followed: *Roy* v.
Cruickshank, 1954 S.L.T. 217.

       (*b*) (i) where the probationer has been convicted for the offence
for which the order was made, sentence him for that
offence;

          (ii) where the probationer has not been so convicted, convict
him and sentence him as aforesaid; or

     (*c*) vary any of the requirements of the probation order, so how-
ever that any extension of the probation period shall terminate
not later than three years from the date of the probation
order.[92]

(4) A fine imposed under this section in respect of a failure to comply
with the requirements of a probation order shall be deemed for the purposes of any enactment to be a sum adjudged to be paid by or in respect of
a conviction or a penalty imposed on a person summarily convicted." [93]

7–78   A probationer who is required by a probation order to submit to
treatment for his mental condition is not deemed to have failed to comply
with that requirement on the ground only that he has refused to undergo
any surgical, electrical or other treatment if, in the opinion of the court,
his refusal was reasonable having regard to all the circumstances.[94]

Commission of further offence

7–79   Without prejudice to the provisions of section 6 of the 1949 Act
(referred to in the next paragraph) a probationer who is convicted of an
offence committed during the probation period is not on that account
liable to be dealt with under section 5 of the 1949 Act for failing to comply
with any requirement of the probation order.[95]

If it appears to the court by which a probation order has been made or
to the appropriate court that the probationer to whom the order relates has
been convicted by a court in any part of Great Britain of an offence
committed during the probation period and has been dealt with for that
offence, the first-mentioned court or the appropriate court may issue a
warrant for the arrest of the probationer, or may, if it thinks fit, instead of
issuing such a warrant in the first instance issue a citation requiring the
probationer to appear before that court at such time as may be specified
in the citation, and on his appearance or on his being brought before the
court, may, if it thinks fit, sentence him or convict and sentence him in
terms of section 5 (2) of the 1949 Act.[96]

If the warrant for the arrest of a probationer is executed in England,
and the probationer cannot forthwith be brought before the court which
issued it, the warrant will have effect as if it directed him to be brought
before a court of summary jurisdiction for the place where he was arrested;
and that court of summary jurisdiction will commit him to custody or

[92] Ibid., s. 5 (2), as amended by Criminal Justice Act 1967.
[93] 1949 Act, s. 5 (4). S. 5 (3) is repealed by the 1968 Act.
[94] Ibid., s. 5 (5).
[95] Ibid., s. 5 (6).
[96] Ibid., s. 6 (1). See supra, para. 17–77.

release him on bail (with or without sureties) until he can be brought or appear before the court in Scotland.[97]

Where a probationer is convicted by the court which made the probation order or by the appropriate court of an offence committed during the probation period, that court has the like power to deal at the same time with him for the offence for which the order was made as is conferred by section 6 (1) of the 1949 Act as well as for the offence committed during the period of probation.[98]

Transfer of orders between England and Scotland

17-80   Where the court by which a probation order is made is satisfied that the offender has attained the age of seventeen [99] and resides or will reside in England, section 2 (2) of the 1949 Act does not apply to the order i.e. there is no nomination of a local authority area, or officer, or appropriate court. Instead the order must contain a requirement that the offender be under the supervision of a probation officer appointed for or assigned to the petty sessional division in which the offender resides or will reside; and that division must be named in the order.[1]

Where the court in Scotland by which the order was made or the appropriate court is satisfied that the probationer has attained the age of seventeen and proposes to reside or is residing in England, the power of that court to amend the order under Schedule 2 of the 1949 Act [2] includes power to insert the provisions required by section 7 (1) of the 1949 Act (see immediately preceding paragraph). The court may so amend the order without summoning the probationer and without his consent.[3]

If an order so amended is one to which the provisions of the 1949 Act apply by virtue of section 9 of the Criminal Justice Act 1948 (which relates to probation orders under that Act relating to persons residing in Scotland) then, notwithstanding anything in that section or section 7 of the 1949 Act, the order, as from the date of the amendment, has effect in all respects as if it were an order made under section 3 of the Criminal Justice Act 1948, in the case of a person residing in England.[4]

The court by which a probation order is so made or amended must send three copies of the order to the clerk to the justices for the petty sessional division named therein, together with such documents and information relating to the case as it considers likely to be of assistance to the court acting for that petty sessional division.[5]

The provisions of the Second Schedule of the 1949 Act do not apply to an order made or amended under section 7, nor does section 5 (1) of the

---

[97] Ibid., s. 7 (6).
[98] Ibid., s. 6 (2).
[99] See Children and Young Persons Act 1969, Sched. 5, para. 25.
[1] 1949 Act, s. 7 (1).
[2] Supra, para. 17–71.
[3] 1949 Act, s. 7 (2), as amended by 1968 Act.
[4] Ibid., s. 7 (8).
[5] Ibid., s. 7 (7).

Act apply to it.[6] The provisions of the Criminal Justice Act 1948, other than section 8, apply to the order as if it were a probation order made under section 3 of that Act,[7] subject to the following proviso, viz.:

In the application to the order of section 6 of the English Act (which relates to breach of a requirement of a probation order):

(a) section 6 (2) (*a*), (3) (*a*), and (4) (*b*) do not apply.

(b) section 6 (3) (*b*), and (4) (*a*) have effect as if for references therein to a Crown Court and the Crown Court[7a] there were substituted references to a court in Scotland and to the court in Scotland by which the probation order was made or amended under section 7 of the 1949 Act.[8]

7–81 If it appears on information to a justice acting for the petty sessional division or place for which the supervising court (as defined in the Criminal Justice Act 1948) acts that a person in whose case a probation order has been made or amended under section 7 of the 1949 Act has been convicted by a court in any part of Great Britain of an offence committed during the period specified in the order, he may issue a summons requiring that person to appear, at the place and time specified therein, before the court in Scotland by which the probation order was made or, if the information is in writing and on oath, may issue a warrant for his arrest, directing that person to be brought before the last-mentioned court.[9]

7–82 Schedule 5 to the Children and Young Persons Act 1969 adds a new section, section 7A, to the 1949 Act, which provides for the transfer to English juvenile courts of probation orders made on persons under the age of seventeen who reside or will reside in England. The English court on receiving notification of the probation order will either make a supervision order under the Children and Young Persons Act 1969 or dismiss the case.[10]

7–83 Section 9 of the Criminal Justice Act 1948 [11] contains provisions for the transfer of English probation orders to courts in Scotland when the probationer resides there. The court to be specified is a court of summary jurisdiction which, in the case of an order made on indictment, is the appropriate sheriff court. The provisions of the 1949 Act (except sections 5 (2) (*b*) and 6) then apply to the order as if it had been a Scottish order made by the court specified in the order as the appropriate court.

Where the appropriate court is satisfied that the probationer has failed to comply with the probation order it may, instead of dealing with him in any manner authorised by the 1949 Act, commit him to custody or release him on bail until he can be brought before the English court which made the

[6] Ibid., s. 7 (4).
[7] Ibid.
[7a] See Courts Act 1971, Sched. 8.
[8] 1949 Act, s. 7 (4).
[9] Ibid., s. 7 (5).
[10] 1949 Act, s. 7A (4).
[11] As substituted by 1949 Act, Sched. 11.

order. A certificate by the clerk of the Scottish court is evidence of such failure to comply with the requirements of the order as is specified in the certificate.[12]

17–84   English courts cannot make probation orders on persons residing or going to reside in Scotland unless they are sixteen years old or more.[13]

Organisation of probation

17–85   The 1968 Act abolished the system of probation areas, committees and officers which functioned prior to the Act. The duty of providing for the supervision of probationers now falls on the local authority and is carried out by officers of its social work department in accordance with a scheme prepared by the authority of and approved by the Secretary of State.[14]

Absolute Discharge

17–86   In certain circumstances the court may, instead of sentencing an offender, make an order discharging him absolutely.[15] This course is competent where:

(a) A person is convicted on indictment of an offence (other than an offence the sentence for which is fixed by law); or

(b) a person is charged before a court of summary jurisdiction with an offence (other than an offence the sentence for which is fixed by law) and the court is satisfied that he committed the offence; and

(c) in either case the court is of opinion, having regard to the circumstances, including the nature of the offence and the character of the offender, that it is inexpedient to inflict punishment and that a probation order is not appropriate.[16] In summary procedure the court makes this order without proceeding to conviction.[17]

Effects of Probation and Absolute Discharge

17–87   In general, a conviction on indictment of an offence for which an order is made under the 1949 Act placing the offender on probation or discharging him absolutely is deemed not be be a conviction for any purpose other than the purposes of the proceedings in which the order is made and of laying it before a court as a previous conviction in subsequent proceedings for another offence.[18]

This provision, however, does not apply where an offender, being not less than sixteen years of age at the time of his conviction of an offence for

---

[12] Criminal Justice Act 1948, s. 9 (5), as substituted by 1949 Act, Sched. 11.
[13] Criminal Justice Act 1948, s. 9 (9), as added by 1968 Act, Sched. 8.
[14] 1968 Act, s. 27.
[15] 1949 Act, s. 1.
[16] Ibid.
[17] Ibid.
[18] 1949 Act, s. 9 (1), as amended by 1963 Act. This provision does not apply to convictions of employers under the National Insurance (Industrial Injuries) Act 1965, s. 69 (1) or (2), or to the right to use convictions as evidence in civil proceedings under the Civil Evidence Act 1968, s. 11 or the Law Reform (Miscellaneous Provisions) (Scotland) Act 1968, s. 10. See also First Offenders (Scotland) Act 1960, supra, para. 17–04; Immigration Act 1971, s. 6 (3).

which he is placed on probation, is subsequently sentenced under the 1949 Act for that offence.[19]

The conviction of an offender who is placed on probation or discharged absolutely is disregarded for the purposes of any enactment which imposes any disqualification or disability upon convicted persons, or authorises or requires the imposition of any such disqualification or disability.[20]

The provisions mentioned above in sections (a) and (b) are declared not to affect either:

(a) any right of such offender to appeal against his conviction; or

(b) the operation, in relation to any such offender, of any enactment in force at the commencement of the 1949 Act which is expressed to extend to persons dealt with under section 1 (1) of the Probation of Offenders Act 1907,[21] as well as to convicted persons.[22]

7–88   Where a person is absolutely discharged or placed on probation by a summary court the court does not convict him but merely makes a finding that it is satisfied that he committed the offence.[23] He has, however, the same right of appeal against the court's finding as if it were a conviction.[24] Where a person charged with an offence has at any time previously been placed on probation or discharged absolutely in respect of the commission by him of an offence, it is competent, in the proceedings for that offence, to bring before the court the probation order or order of absolute discharge in like manner as if the order were a conviction.[25]

Admonition

7–89   The court may in its discretion, if such course appears to meet the justice of the case, dismiss with an admonition any person found guilty of an offence.[26]

Deferred Sentence

7–90   Section 47 of the 1963 Act gives statutory authority to a well-established practice of deferring sentence after conviction for a period and on such

[19] 1949 Act, s. 9 (1), as amended by 1968 Act.
[20] 1949 Act, s. 9 (2).
[21] S. 1 (1) of this Act (the whole of which is repealed by the 1949 Act) is in the following terms: " Where any person is charged before a Court of Summary Jurisdiction with an offence punishable by such Court, and the Court thinks that the charge is proved, but is of opinion that, having regard to the character, antecedents, age, health, or mental condition of the person charged, or to the trivial nature of the offence, or to the extenuating circumstances under which the offence was committed, it is inexpedient to inflict any punishment or any other than a nominal punishment, or that it is expedient to release the offender on probation, the Court may, without proceeding to conviction, make an order either:
(i) dismissing the information or charge; or
(ii) discharging the offender conditionally on his entering into a recognizance with or without sureties, to be of good behaviour and to appear for conviction and sentence when called on at any time during such period, not exceeding three years, as may be specified in the order."
[22] 1949 Act, s. 9 (3).
[23] 1949 Act, ss. 1 and 2. The finding is a conviction for the purposes of the enactments in n. 18 supra.
[24] 1949 Act, s. 9 (4).
[25] Ibid., s. 9 (5).
[26] 1908 Act, ss. 46 and 77 (4); 1954 Act, s. 55.

conditions as the court may determine. A sentence may be deferred on more than one occasion. Almost all deferred sentences have a condition of good behaviour, and many require repayment of the amount involved in an offence of dishonesty. At the deferred diet the court has the same powers of sentence as it had at the time of conviction, but where the conditions of deferment have been obtempered the court will naturally be more lenient than if they have not, and may merely admonish.[27]

Mitigation of Penalties

17-91   Every court, whether exercising solemn or summary jurisdiction, has power to mitigate the penalties to which an accused person is liable, either at common law or in respect of the contravention of any statute, or of any order, byelaw, rule, or regulation having statutory authority.

17-92   In proceedings, whether on indictment or on complaint, in respect of any statutory contravention which involves imprisonment, the imposition of any pecuniary penalty, the finding of caution for good behaviour or otherwise, either singly or in combination with imprisonment or fine, the court has in addition to any other powers conferred by Act of Parliament the following powers, viz.:

1. To reduce the period of imprisonment.

2. To substitute a fine[28] for imprisonment, either with or without caution for good behaviour, not exceeding the amount and the period competent by law.[29]

(The Merchant Shipping Act 1894, enacted, by section 376 (1) (d), that a seaman lawfully engaged to serve in any fishing boat should, for the offence of wilful disobedience, be liable to imprisonment for any period not exceeding four weeks, and also to forfeit a sum not exceeding two days' wages. It was held competent for a sheriff-substitute to mitigate the sentence prescribed by the 1894 statute by imposing a fine of £10 with the alternative of 28 days' imprisonment.[30])

3. To substitute the finding of caution for a fine or imprisonment.

4. To reduce the amount of any pecuniary penalty.

5. To dispense with the finding of caution.[31]

These powers are subject to two important limitations, viz.:

1. Where any Act carries into effect a treaty, convention, or agreement with a foreign state, and such treaty, convention, or agreement stipulates for a fine of minimum amount, the court is not entitled to reduce the amount of such fine below said minimum.

---

[27] On deferred sentences in practice, see A. D. Smith, " Deferred Sentences in Scotland," 1968 S.L.T.(News) 153.

[28] Not exceeding £100 in the case of a summary court, 1954 Act, s. 40, as amended by 1963 Act, s. 23 (3). For solemn cases see supra, para. 17–31.

[29] 1954 Act, s. 40. See supra, para. 17–52.

[30] *McDonald* v. *Wood and Bruce*, 1950 J.C. 72. But see also *Gallagher* v. *H.M. Adv.*, 193 J.C. 27.

[31] 1908 Act, ss. 43 and 77 (4), as amended by 1949 Act, s. 79 and Sched. 2; 1954 Act, s. 40.

2. They do not extend to proceedings taken under any Act relating to any of her Majesty's regular or auxiliary forces.[32]

Obsolete Penalties

17–93 Sentence of death is now competent only in the case of treason [33] which is governed by English law.[34]

Corporal punishment is no longer competent.[35] Nor are the punishments of outlawry and fugitation.[36] Banishment from all or any part of Scotland was abolished by the Criminal Law (Scotland) Act 1830.[37]

Attainder, corruption of blood and escheat were abolished by the 1949 Act.[38]

Deportation

17–94 Section 3 (6) of the Immigration Act 1971 [39] provides that a person who is not patrial is liable to deportation from the United Kingdom if, after he has attained the age of seventeen, he is convicted of an offence for which he is punishable with imprisonment and on his conviction is recommended for deportation by a court empowered to make such a recommendation.

A person who is found to have committed an offence is regarded as a person convicted of it notwithstanding that the court does not proceed to conviction.[40] In determining whether an offence is one for which a person is punishable with imprisonment no regard is to be had to any enactment restricting the imprisonment of young offenders or first offenders.[41] Recommendations for deportation may thus be made in respect of persons aged seventeen or over who are found to have committed offences punishable with imprisonment in the case of recidivists over the age of twenty-one.

17–95 A person is patrial if he has the right of abode in the United Kingdom.[42] A person has such a right if that person is—

(a) a citizen of the United Kingdom and Colonies by birth, adoption, naturalisation or registration in the United Kingdom, the Channel Islands or the Isle of Man (" the Islands "); or

(b) a citizen of the United Kingdom and Colonies born to or legally adopted by a parent who had that citizenship at the time of the birth or adoption by reason of one of the factors set out in (a)

---

[32] Ibid.

[33] 1887 Act, s. 56; Homicide Act 1957; Murder (Abolition of Death Penalty) Act 1965.

[34] Treason Act 1708. Drawing and quartering were abolished by the 1949 Act, s. 14.

[35] Criminal Justice Act 1948, s. 2.

[36] 1949 Act, s. 15 (2).

[37] S. 10. There was an exception for statutory provisions specifically providing for the punishment of banishment. The last remaining one was the Clandestine Marriages Act 1661, repealed by the Statute Law Revision Act 1964, which provided for banishment furth of Scotland. Banishment overseas was abolished along with transportation by the Penal Servitude Acts 1853 and 1857. For deportation. see infra, paras. 17–94 et seq.

[38] S. 15 (1).

[39] The 1971 Act replaces the Aliens Restriction Act 1914 and the Commonwealth Immigrants Act 1962.

[40] Immigration Act 1971, s. 6 (3).

[41] Ibid.

[42] Ibid., s. 2 (6).

above, or had himself been born to or legally adopted by a parent who at the time of that birth or adoption so had such citizenship; or

(c) a citizen of the United Kingdom and Colonies who has at any time been settled in the United Kingdom and Islands and had at that time while such a citizen been ordinarily resident there for the last five years or more; or

(d) a Commonwealth citizen born to or legally adopted by a parent who was at that time a citizen of the United Kingdom and Colonies by birth in the United Kingdom or the Islands; or

(e) in the case of a woman a Commonwealth citizen who is or has been the wife of a patrial.[43]

A person who was a Commonwealth citizen or a citizen of the Republic of Ireland at the coming into force of the Act and who was then ordinarily resident in the United Kingdom is exempt from liability to a recommendation for deportation if at the time of the conviction he had for the last five years been ordinarily resident in the United Kingdom and Islands.[44]

" Ordinary residence " is a matter of fact and degree in every case.[45] It may be established by residence in breach of the immigration laws.[46] " The last five years " before the material time is to be taken as a period amounting in total to five years exclusive of any time during which the person claiming exemption was detained under a sentence or order made on conviction of an offence in the United Kingdom and Islands [47] (or was unlawfully at large during his sentence, or in England was detained during a period of custody by which the term to be served under the sentence is reduced).[48]

In any question as to whether a person is patrial or is entitled to any exemption the onus of proof lies on the person seeking to prove he is.[49]

17–96   Recommendations for deportation may be made by the sheriff or the High Court but must be made by the court which passes sentence on the offender,[50] so that where a person is remitted to the High Court for sentence only that court can make the recommendation. Where the High Court passes sentence on an appeal it may make a recommendation only where the appeal is against a conviction or sentence on indictment.[51] It is competent to make a recommendation in the case of a person sentenced to life imprisonment.[52]

17–97   No recommendation can be made unless the person concerned is given seven days' notice in writing informing him that patrial persons are not

---

[43] Ibid., s. 2. The section contains some additional subtleties of definition not set out above.
[44] Ibid., s. 7 (1) (c).
[45] R. v. Edgehill [1963] 1 Q.B. 593, 599.
[46] Immigration Act 1971, s. 7 (2).
[47] Ibid., s. 7 (3), 7 (4) (a).
[48] Ibid., s. 7 (4) (c); Criminal Justice Act 1967, s. 67.
[49] Ibid., s. 3 (8).
[50] Ibid., s. 6 (1).
[51] Ibid.
[52] Ibid., s. 6 (4).

liable to deportation, describing the persons who are patrial, and stating the effect of the exemptions from liability to deportation and of the provision regarding the onus of proof.[53]

The court may adjourn under section 26 of the 1949 Act to allow time for such a notice to be given.[54]

7–98 A recommendation for deportation is appealable in the same way as a conviction.[54a]

Expenses

In solemn procedure

7–99 In criminal cases falling under solemn procedure there is no award of expenses except in the rare case of private prosecution, where the private prosecutor may be made liable.[55] The High Court awards expenses only when it is sitting as a court of review.[56] No expenses in appeals are allowed on either side under solemn procedure.[57]

In summary prosecutions

–100 Awards of expenses in summary prosecutions are subject to the following provisions of section 53 of the 1954 Act:

" (a) expenses may be awarded to or against a private prosecutor but shall not be awarded against any person prosecuting in the public interest unless the statute or order under which the prosecution is brought expressly or impliedly authorises such an award [58];

(b) the finding regarding expenses shall be stated in the sentence or judgment disposing of the case;

(c) expenses awarded to the prosecutor shall be restricted to the fees set forth in the Act of Adjournal[58a];

(d) the court may award expenses against the accused without imposing any fine or may direct the expenses incurred by the prosecutor, whether public or private, to be met wholly or partly out of any fine imposed;

(e) expenses awarded against the accused, where the fine or fines imposed do not exceed twelve pounds, shall not exceed three pounds [59]:

Provided that if it appears to the court that the reasonable expenses of the prosecutor's witnesses together with the other

[53] Ibid., s. 6 (2). The High Court has power under s. 6 (7) to make rules by Act of Adjournal to give effect to the provisions of s. 6.
[54] Ibid., s. 6 (2).
[54a] Ibid., s. 6 (5) (b).
[55] Hume, ii. 127; Alison, ii. 113.
[56] H.M. Adv. v. Aldred, 1922 J.C. 13.
[57] Supra, para. 11–52.
[58] See Lockwood v. Chartered Institute of Patent Agents (1912) 7 Adam 14. In MacKirdy v. McKendrick (1897) 2 Adam 435, it was held that an inspector of weights and measures prosecuting under the Food and Drug Acts was a public prosecutor, and that expenses could not be awarded to or against him in a prosecution under these Acts. The 1908 Act provided that no expenses should be awarded to or against anyone prosecuting in the public interest.
[58a] See Act of Adjournal (Fees in the Inferior Courts) 1972.
[59] Tough v. Mitchell (1886) 1 White 79; Stewart v. McNiven (1891) 2 White 627.

expenses exceed the sum of three pounds, the court may direct the expenses of those witnesses to be paid wholly or partly out of the fine;

(f) any expenses awarded shall be recoverable by civil diligence in accordance with section fifty of this Act." [60]

The provision enabling the court to direct the expenses incurred by the prosecutor to be met in whole or in part out of any penalty imposed is specially applicable to prosecutions in which any fines go to Exchequer. although the expenses of prosecution fall on the county. In cases of this nature, where a fine is imposed, it is well for the court to order the expenses to be met out of the fine. The table of fees does not apply where expenses are awarded against a prosecutor, and in such a case the account may be remitted for taxation.[61] Where an Act of Parliament authorises costs to be given against the accused, it is implied that the court has a general power of awarding costs to either party on the view that the power to award costs against the accused being given, it is a fair and equitable inference that the prosecutor may be made liable if he fails in the prosecution.[62] So, in *Todrick* v. *Wilson* [63] it was held that as, under the Cruelty to Animals (Scotland) Act 1850, expenses could by implication be awarded to the prosecutor, they could also be awarded against him.

Where there are several accused, so long as the amount of expenses awarded against each does not exceed the limit allowed, it is immaterial that the cumulo amount of the expenses awarded against all of them exceeds that limit.[64]

Where an award of expenses is excessive but separable from the rest of the sentence, the conviction will be suspended only in regard to expenses.[65]

In proceedings for review

17–101   In stated cases the High Court has power to award such expenses, both in the High Court and in the inferior court, as they may think fit.[66] Expenses usually follow the event,[67] but the conduct of the successful party may induce the court to refuse him expenses.[68] The amount of the expenses awarded does not depend upon the error into which the inferior judge has fallen.[69] Full expenses have been awarded in both courts,[70] and in the High Court only,[71] but the usual practice is to modify the expenses.[72] In

---

[60] 1954 Act, s. 53; *Ross* v. *Stirling* (1869) 1 Couper 336.
[61] *J. and G. Cox Ltd.* v. *Lindsay*, 1907 S.C. 96.
[62] *Todrick* v. *Wilson* (1891) 3 White 28, following *Walker* v. *Bathgate* (1873) 2 Couper 460.
[63] Supra.
[64] *Tough & Ross* v. *Mitchell* (1886) 1 White 79.
[65] *Stewart* v. *McNiven* (1891) 2 White 627.
[66] 1954 Act, s. 71 (3).
[67] Maclaren, *Expenses in the Supreme and Sheriff Courts*, 394.
[68] *Clyne* v. *Keith* (1887) 1 White 356.
[69] *McIntyre* v. *Linton* (1876) 3 Couper 319, Lord Deas at 326.
[70] *Walker* v. *Linton* (1892) 3 White 329.
[71] *Brown and Bryson* v. *Neilson* (1906) 5 Adam 149; *Steuart* v. *Macpherson*, 1918 J.C. 96.
[72] *McIntyre* v. *Linton* (1876) 3 Couper 319; Maclaren, *Expenses in the Supreme and Sheriff Courts*, 394.

suspensions the expenses are usually modified.[73] In one case the court refused to modify in view of the inadequacy of the statutory penalties for the offence charged.[74] Where by statute an accused person may be made liable in expenses the court is entitled if the accused is successful, to award him expenses against the prosecutor.[75] Where a prosecutor consents to a conviction being set aside, the expenses allowed are five guineas.[76]

–102 By statute, if the amount of the expenses found due has not been determined or modified, the account is remitted to the Auditor of the Court of Session to be taxed in the like manner and subject to the same regulations as in the Court of Session.[77] A session fee is not a proper charge.[78]

[73] Ibid.
[74] *Steuart* v. *Macpherson*, supra.
[75] *Walker* v. *Bathgate* (1873) 2 Couper 460; *Todrick* v. *Wilson* (1891) 3 White 28.
[76] 1954 Act, s. 72. See supra, para. 16–59.
[77] Courts of Law Fees (Scotland) Act 1895, s. 3; *Rochiciolli* v. *Walker* (1916) 7 Adam 723.
[78] *Rochiciolli* v. *Walker*, supra.

CHAPTER 18

EVIDENCE

18-01 THE case for the prosecution and for the defence must be established by competent evidence. The rules of evidence cannot adequately be summarised in a work of this kind, but there are a few points of frequent occurrence as to which practitioners desire to have ready reference, and which it will be convenient to consider briefly.[1] It has only to be observed that our remarks, except when they are specially qualified, are equally applicable to both solemn and summary procedure. Some specialties of summary procedure are explained at the conclusion of this chapter.

Burden of proof

18-02   Unless he pleads guilty thereto, every person charged with a crimina offence is presumed to be innocent of the same, and this presumption can be overcome only by evidence relevant to establish his guilt.[2] It follows, therefore, that the burden of proving that the accused committed the crime libelled against him rests upon the prosecutor throughout the trial.[3] The standard required is proof beyond reasonable doubt.[4] This onus is not transferred or affected by any common law defence pleas other than insanity and diminished responsibility. Although the matter is not altogether clear, partly because of a failure to distinguish between the evidential and the persuasive burden of proof,[5] the position probably is that there is no duty on the Crown to refute any specific defence until it is raised in evidence by the accused or arises out of the evidence led for the Crown, but that once a specific defence, whether or not technically " special," has been raised, it is for the Crown to exclude it beyond reasonable doubt.[6] Although it will normally be difficult to establish a defence like self-defence or alibi unless the accused gives evidence there is no reason in principle why this should not be done.[7]

Where the defence plead insanity or diminished responsibility the onus, i.e. the persuasive burden, is on them.[8] The position where insanity is raised by the Crown is not clear.[9]

---

[1] See Lewis, *Law of Evidence in Scotland*, pp. 284 *et seq.*

[2] *Slater* v. *H.M. Adv.*, 1928 J.C. 94; cf. *Woolmington* v. *Director of Public Prosecutions* [1935] A.C. 462.

[3] *Lennie* v. *H.M. Adv.*, 1946 J.C. 79, 80; *Owens* v. *H.M. Adv.*, 1946 J.C. 119, 124.

[4] *McKenzie* v. *H.M. Adv.*, 1959 J.C. 32, L.J.-C. at 36–37.

[5] See *Cross on Evidence* (3rd ed.), 68; *Brown* v. *Rolls Royce Ltd.*, 1960 S.C. (H.L.) 22; G. H. Gordon, " The Burden of Proof on the Accused," 1968 S.L.T.(News) 29; for some Scottish decisions see *Owens*, supra (self-defence); *Lennie*, supra; *Dickson* v. *H.M. Adv.*, 1950 J.C. 1 (alibi).

[6] This means, incidentally, that a jury can always acquit on the accused's uncorroborated evidence: *Owens*, supra; cf. *McNeill* v. *Ritchie*, 1967 S.L.T. (Sh.Ct.) 68.

[7] See *Blair* v. *H.M. Adv.* (1968) 32 J.C.L. 48.

[8] *H.M. Adv.* v. *Braithwaite*, 1945 J.C. 55; *H.M. Adv.* v. *Mitchell*, 1951 J.C. 53.

[9] *H.M. Adv.* v. *Harrison* (1968) 32 J.C.L. 119.

" Where the burden of proof is on the accused, it is enough if he brings evidence that satisfies [the jury] of the probability of what he is called upon to establish." [10]

Although the burden of proof in a criminal case is always upon the prosecution,[11] cases may occur in which the proved facts raise a presumption that the accused has committed the offence libelled, and in which, if he fails to put forward an explanation sufficient to create in the minds of the jury (or judges in summary cases) a reasonable doubt as to his guilt, they will be entitled to draw an inference of guilt against him.[12]

One common example of a state of facts entitling a jury to convict in the absence of explanation is where the accused is found in possession of recently stolen property in what are called criminative circumstances. It is going too far to say that recent possession creates a presumption of guilt or shifts the persuasive burden, for the requirement of " criminative circumstances " itself shows that all that is involved is a state of facts from which it is reasonable to infer guilt.[13]

Admission or rejection of evidence

3–03   It must be pointed out that, as criminal procedure affects the liberty and reputation of the lieges, the rules of evidence applicable to it are more strict than those applicable to civil procedure. From this it follows that the admission of incompetent, or the rejection of competent, evidence, where such admission or rejection may possibly have led to an erroneous decision, is absolutely fatal to a conviction. This rule applies whether the error has been committed by admitting or rejecting witnesses or productions, or by allowing or disallowing questions.[14]

The effect of the incompetent admission or rejection of evidence which is not vital to the charge varies with the circumstances of each case. In a case [15] where a railway servant, convicted of theft, appealed against the conviction on the ground that evidence of statements made by him to a stationmaster and two constables was wrongly admitted, it was held that the evidence was rightly admitted, but Lord Salvesen expressed the opinion that even if the evidence in question had been improperly admitted, the conviction would not fall to be quashed, as it did not appear that the conviction depended on that evidence. Lord Ormidale

---

[10] *H.M. Adv.* v. *Mitchell*, 1951 J.C. 53, L.J.-C. at 53–54; *Robertson* v. *Watson*, 1949 J.C. 73, L.J.-G. at 88; *H.M. Adv.* v. *Braithwaite*, 1945 J.C. 55, L.J.-C. at 58; *Carraher* v. *H.M. Adv.*, 1946 J.C. 108, Lord Russell at 113. See also *R.* v. *Carr-Briant* [1943] K.B. 607; *Hendry* v. *Clan Line Steamers*, 1949 S.C. 320.

[11] *Lennie*, supra; *Owens*, supra.

[12] See *H.M. Adv.* v. *Hardy*, 1938 J.C. 144.

[13] See G. H. Gordon, op. cit., especially at pp. 40–43. The principal cases on the so-called doctrine of recent possession are *Christie* v. *H.M. Adv.*, 1939 J.C. 72; *Fox* v. *Patterson*, 1948 J.C. 104; *Simpson* v. *H.M. Adv.*, 1952 J.C. 1; *Brannan* v. *H.M. Adv.*, 1954 J.C. 87; *Cryans* v. *Nixon*, 1955 J.C. 1; *Wightman and Anr.* v. *H.M. Adv.*, 1959 J.C. 44; *Cameron* v. *H.M. Adv.*, 1959 J.C. 59.

[14] *Kerr* v. *Mackay* (1853) 1 Irv. 213; *Burns* v. *Hart and Young* (1856) 2 Irv. 571; *Falconer* v. *Brown* (1893) 1 Adam 96; *Grant* v. *H.M. Adv.*, 1938 J.C. 7; *Frank* v. *H.M. Adv.*, 1938 J.C. 17.

[15] *Waddell* v. *Kinnaird*, 1922 J.C. 40.

expressed an opinion to the contrary. In the earlier case of *Brown* v. *Macpherson*[16] it was held that where there was sufficient evidence against the accused apart from the evidence the competency of which was in dispute, the court was not entitled to set aside the conviction. This principle was applied in the later case of *Wade* v. *Robertson*.[17] But where one part of a charge was held to be irrelevant by the court of review, a conviction was suspended on the other part on the ground that it was at least probable that the accused had been prejudiced by the admission of evidence on the irrelevant part.[18]

Primary and secondary evidence

18-04   The *best evidence* must always be led. It is necessary, if possible, to produce the eye-witnesses of actions, the persons who made statements, and the principal documents to which reference is made. Sometimes it is impossible to do this. The persons may be dead, or the documents may have been destroyed. In such a case, the death or destruction is first proved. It is then competent to adduce witnesses who can prove statements made by the deceased persons, or produce copies of the destroyed documents and depone to their accuracy. Secondary evidence may be led about articles which it is not reasonably practicable to produce at a trial.[19] Statements made outwith the presence of the accused person by someone who is alive but is not adduced as a witness cannot be received, even on proof that the person who made the statements has fled the country.[20] Evidence taken on commission is incompetent in criminal trials.[21] It is also incompetent to take the evidence of a witness as concurring with that of a previous witness.[22]

Admissions

18-05   Apart from express statutory permission no fact can be established in a criminal trial by admissions on the part of the accused. This arises from the consideration that a person accused of crime is not in a position to make admissions with safety to himself. So where admissions which were without statutory warrant were made by the accused's agent the conviction was set aside.[23]

Certain admissions, however, are now authorised by statute.

As regards trials on indictment the Criminal Procedure (Scotland) Act 1965 provides that where an accused is legally represented it shall not be necessary for either that accused or the prosecutor to prove any fact which is admitted by the other, or to prove any document whose terms and

[16] 1918 J.C. 3.
[17] 1948 J.C. 117.
[18] *Winning* v. *Jeans* (1909) 6 Adam 1.
[19] *MacLeod* v. *Woodmuir Miners Welfare Society Social Club*, 1961 J.C. 5; *Maciver* v. *Mackenzie*, 1942 J.C. 51.
[20] *H.M. Adv.* v. *McConnell* (1887) 1 White 412; *H.M. Adv.* v. *Monson* (1893) 1 Adam 114.
[21] *H.M. Adv.* v. *Hunter* (1905) 4 Adam 523; Criminal Justice Act 1587.
[22] *Cafferty* v. *Cheyne*, 1939 J.C. 1.
[23] *Tullis* v. *Millar* (1899) 3 Adam 3.

application are not in dispute between them. They may also agree to accept a copy of any document as equivalent to the original.[24] An admission or agreement is made by lodging a minute signed in the case of an admission by the prosecutor or by the counsel or solicitor acting for the accused, and in the case of an agreement by the prosecutor and such counsel or solicitor.[25] Once the minute is signed and lodged with the clerk of court, the facts and documents admitted or agreed are deemed to have been duly proved and any copy agreed to be accepted as equivalent to an original will be so accepted.[26]

As regards summary procedure, section 36 of the 1954 Act provides as follows:

" (1) It shall not be necessary in any summary prosecution for either party to lead proof of any fact which is admitted by the opposite party, or to prove any documents the terms and application of which are not in dispute, and copies of any documents may, by agreement of the parties, be accepted as equivalent to the originals:

Provided that this subsection shall not apply unless the accused has legal assistance in his defence.

(2) Admissions or agreements under the last foregoing subsection may be made by lodging with the clerk of court a minute signed by the person or persons making the same or by his or their counsel or solicitor, and any facts and documents so admitted or agreed shall be accepted as if they had been duly proved."

18–06 A plea which has been tendered and rejected cannot be founded on by the prosecutor.[27] Nor may reference be made in the course of a trial on any charge to any other charge in the same indictment to which the accused has pleaded guilty.[28]

Evidence of Accused and Spouse of Accused

18–07 At common law the accused is not a competent witness at his trial. Prior to the Criminal Evidence Act 1898 the accused could give evidence only where there was a specific statutory provision allowing him to do so. These provisions were all superseded by the 1898 Act and any accused who gives evidence now gives it as a witness under that Act.[29]

The Act makes every person charged with an offence a competent witness for the defence at every stage of the proceedings, whether he is charged solely or jointly with any other person.[30] An accused may be called only on his own application[31]; he cannot be called as a witness for a

---

[24] S. 1 (1).
[25] S. 1 (2).
[26] S. 1 (3).
[27] *Cochran* v. *Ferguson* (1882) 5 Couper 169; *Brown* v. *Macpherson*, 1918 J.C. 3; *Strathern* v. *Sloan*, 1937 J.C. 76.
[28] *Walsh* v. *H.M. Adv.*, 1961 J.C. 51.
[29] 1898 Act, s. 6; *Charnock* v. *Merchant* [1900] 1 Q.B. 474.
[30] 1898 Act, s. 1.
[31] Ibid., s. 1 (a).

co-accused, although he may take the opportunity of being called as a witness for himself to give evidence in favour of a co-accused. By doing so he will, of course, render himself open to cross-examination as to his own part in the offence.

It is not necessary for an accused to be included in the list of defence witness in trials on indictment,[32] and he is not normally so included.

The accused is a competent witness " at any stage," including the " trial within a trial " held to determine the admissibility of evidence.[33] Where the accused is called in the ordinary way as a defence witness he should be called immediately after the Crown case is closed if he is the only defence witness to the facts of the case.[34]

18–08   An accused is not entitled to make an unsworn statement from the dock; if he wishes to make a statement he must give evidence.[35]

He gives his evidence on oath or affirmation in the ordinary way, and, unless the court orders otherwise, does so from the witness box.[36] If he gives false evidence he may be subsequently charged with perjury.[37]

Nothing in the Act makes the accused compellable to disclose any communications made by his spouse during the marriage.[38]

18–09   The prosecution may not comment on the failure of an accused to give evidence,[39] but such comment is not fatal to a subsequent conviction where it does not influence the result of the case.[40] If any comment is made it is the duty of the judge to check the prosecutor and, if there is a jury, to tell them to disregard it. Comment in a jury trial without judicial reproof may be fatal to the conviction.[41]

It is open to the presiding judge to comment on an accused's failure to testify, and it may sometimes be his duty to do so.[42] Unjustifiable and repeated comment may, however, amount to a misdirection as constituting a failure to put the defence case fairly to the jury.[43] A judge in a summary case may take the accused's failure to give evidence into account in arriving at a guilty verdict.[44]

---

[32] *Kennedy* v. *H.M. Adv.* (1898) 2 Adam 588.

[33] e.g. *Manuel* v. *H.M. Adv.*, 1958 J.C. 41.

[34] 1898 Act, s. 2; *R.* v. *Smith (Joan)* [1968] 1 W.L.R. 636. There is force in the comment in *Walker and Walker on Evidence*, p. 381, that to enforce this section by refusing to allow the accused to testify, "seems drastic." There is no reported example of its enforcement in Scotland, and it may have been enacted because of English rules about the order of speeches—see E. Griew, "The Order of Defence Evidence " [1969] Crim.L.R. 347.

[35] *Gilmour* v. *H.M. Adv.*, 1965 J.C. 45. He may, of course, make a speech where he is representing himself.

[36] 1898 Act, s. 1 (*g*).

[37] *H.M. Adv.* v. *Cairns*, 1967 J.C. 37.

[38] 1898 Act, s. 1 (*d*). See infra, para. 18–22.

[39] Ibid., s. 1 (*b*).

[40] *Ross* v. *Boyd* (1903) 4 Adam 184; *McAttee* v. *Hogg* (1903) 4 Adam 190.

[41] *Ross* v. *Boyd*, supra.

[42] *Brown* v. *Macpherson*, 1918 J.C. 3; *H.M. Adv.* v. *Hardy*, 1938 J.C. 144. Comment may also be made by a co-accused who is affected by the silent co-accused's line of defence: *R.* v. *Wickham* (1971) 55 Cr.App.R. 199.

[43] *Scott (A.T.)* v. *H.M. Adv.*, 1946 J.C. 90.

[44] *Brown* v. *Macpherson*, supra.

Cross-examination of accused as to character

8–10   Section 1 (e) of the 1898 Act provides that the accused may be asked any question in cross examination, notwithstanding that it would tend to incriminate him as to the offence charged. It appears that this subsection permits only questions tending to connect the accused directly with the crime charged, and does not permit all questions which tend to incriminate merely in the sense that the answers would tend to persuade the jury of the accused's guilt.[45] A question prohibited by section 1 (f) cannot be allowed by section 1 (e).[46] Section 1 (f) provides that

> " A person charged and called as a witness in pursuance of this Act shall not be asked, and if asked shall not be required to answer, any question tending to show that he has committed or been convicted of or been charged with any offence, other than that wherewith he is then charged, or is of bad character, "

unless certain conditions are satisfied.

What is prohibited is the asking of improper questions, and even an unanswered question may provide good ground for quashing a conviction.[47] It is accordingly the practice for prosecuting counsel who wish to take advantage of any of the exceptions to the prohibition to ask leave of the judge to do so.

8–11   The prohibition is said to be absolute, subject only to the statutory exceptions,[48] which must be strictly construed.[49] But it does not apply to questions asked in examination-in-chief.[50] More importantly, it applies only to evidence " tending to show " the accused's bad character, and it has been held that where that character is already before the jury, whether as the result of competent prosecution evidence, or of evidence given by the accused himself in examination-in-chief, cross-examination does not tend to show to the jury what is known to them already, even if it reveals it in greater detail.[51] Nor does the prohibition apply where the accused pleads a defence available only to someone who has not been previously charged, as in the case of a person pleading error as to the age of the girl in a charge under section 5 of the Criminal Law Amendment Act 1885 as amended by section 2 of the Criminal Law Amendment Act 1922,[52] although where this is the sole ground for cross-examination it should presumably be restricted to the statutory requirements of the defence. An accused is not liable to be cross-examined as to character merely because

---

[45] *Jones* v. *D.P.P.* [1962] A.C. 635, Lord Reid at 662–663.
[46] Ibid.
[47] *Barker* v. *Arnold* [1911] 2 K.B. 120. The ordinary rules regarding timeous objections in summary trials apply—*Andersons* v. *McFarlane* (1899) 2 Adam 644, but the judge is entitled to disallow the question ex proprio motu: Lewis, *Law of Evidence in Scotland*, 305; cf. *Cook* v. *Cook* (1876) 4 R. 78. See also *Stirland* v. *D.P.P.* [1944] A.C. 315.
[48] *Maxwell* v. *D.P.P.* [1935] A.C. 309; *Jones* v. *D.P.P.*, supra.
[49] *Jones* v. *D.P.P.*, supra.
[50] Ibid., Lord Reid at 663.
[51] *Jones* v. *D.P.P.*, supra.
[52] *Maxwell* v. *D.P.P.*, supra, at 321.

such cross-examination is directed to disproving some matter on which he has given evidence.[53]

" Character " means both actual disposition and general repute.[54]

" Charged " means " charged in court." [55]

18–12   The questions prohibited by section 1 (*f*) may be asked, and if asked must be answered, in four cases, provided that they are relevant according to the ordinary rules of evidence, and provided the judge does not exercise his discretion to disallow them on the ground that they would be unfair or unduly prejudicial.

18–13   (i) Where " the proof that he has committed or been convicted of [another] offence is admissible evidence to show that he is guilty of the offence wherewith he is then charged." [56] This exception relates to proof of a specific offence, and would apply where the previous conviction was an essential part of the offence, as in the case of breaches of provisions applying to known thieves, or of driving while disqualified [57]; it probably also applies where there is a specific statutory provision rendering evidence of previous conviction admissible, as in the case of reset.[58] In so far as evidence of similar facts is relevant or competent, it could be introduced under this exception.[59] On the other hand, where part of the evidence against the accused only incidentally involves a previous conviction, as where he is identified by articles left at the scene of the crime which were issued to him a few hours earlier on his discharge from prison,[60] this exception would not allow cross-examination as to that conviction. But such cross-examination would be permissible because it would not be struck at by the initial prohibition of section 1 (*f*) since it would not be tending to show anything the jury had not already heard during the Crown case.

18–14   (ii) Where the accused has put his own character in issue by asking Crown witnesses questions with a view to establishing his good character, or by himself leading evidence of his good character.[61] Cross-examination in reliance on this exception may be disallowed either as prejudicial, or because it is irrelevant. It has been held irrelevant to the disproof of good character to show that an accused who swore that he had never been charged with forgery had been questioned by his employer about a suspected forgery,[62] or to show that an accused had been previously acquitted of a similar offence to that for which he was being tried.[63] Such evidence

---

[53] *Jones* v. *D.P.P.*, supra; cf. *Stirland* v. *D.P.P.* [1944] A.C. 315, Visc. Simon L.C. at 326.
[54] *Stirland* v. *D.P.P.*, supra; *Malindi* v. *The Queen* [1967] 1 A.C. 439; *R.* v. *Selvey* [1970] A.C. 304.
[55] *Stirland* v. *D.P.P.*, supra.
[56] 1898 Act, s. 1 (*f*) (i).
[57] See 1887 Act, s. 67; 1949 Act, s. 39 (3); 1954 Act, s. 31 (6).
[58] Prevention of Crimes Act 1871, s. 10.
[59] *Maxwell* v. *D.P.P.*, supra, at 318.
[60] e.g., *H.M. Adv.* v. *McIlwain*, 1965 J.C. 40, where this point did not arise. See (1965) 29 J.C.L. 286.
[61] 1898 Act, s. 1 (*f*) (ii).
[62] *Stirland* v. *D.P.P.*, supra, at 327.
[63] *Maxwell*, supra.

might, however, be relevant if directed, for example, to what the accused did or said on the prior occasion.[64]

3-15 (iii) *Where the nature or conduct of the defence has been such as to involve imputations on the character of the prosecutor or prosecution witnesses.*[65]

This is the only part of section 1 (*f*) which has been the subject of reported decision in Scotland, and the Scots courts have interpreted it differently from the House of Lords.[66] The object of the exception is seen in Scotland as being that if the general credit of the prosecution witnesses is assailed, it is only fair that the accused's credit be similarly assailed. "The principle seems to be that it is unfair that an accused with a bad record should stand safe in the box while blackguarding the witnesses who testify against him."[67] A distinction is drawn between attacks which arise inferentially from questions necessary to enable the accused fairly to establish his defence, and attacks on the general character of the witnesses.[68] The former do not deprive the accused of the protection of the prohibition in section 1 (*f*), the latter do. In *O'Hara* v. *H.M. Adv.*[69] the accused was charged with assaulting two constables; he pleaded provocation and self-defence, and cross-examined one of them to show that he had been under the influence of drink and had been the aggressor. It was held that this did not fall within the exception, and that the accused could not be cross-examined on his record. In *Fielding* v. *H.M. Adv.*[70] the accused was charged with extorting money from the complainer by threatening that if he were not paid the complainer would be robbed as he had been some months previously. The complainer was cross-examined as to whether on this previous occasion he had been engaged in an illegal activity. It was held that this cross-examination was not necessary to establish the accused's defence, relating as it did to an event some six months earlier than the crime charged, and that the accused could accordingly be cross-examined as to character.

The House of Lords have refused to distinguish between imputations necessary to the conduct of the defence and those not so necessary, and have held that any imputations render the accused liable to be questioned as to his record, with the sole exception of imputations limited to establishing a defence of consent on a rape charge.[71] A mere denial of the charge or of statements by the prosecution witnesses is not an imputation on their character even if emphatically embodied in an allegation that they are liars,[72] but an allegation that the police acted unfairly in obtaining a

---

[64] Ibid., at 320.
[65] 1898 Act, s. 1 (*f*) (ii).
[66] *R.* v. *Selvey*, supra, Visc. Dilhorne at 338, pace Lord Guest at 352; see R. L. C. Hunter, "Imputations on the Character of Prosecution Witnesses," 1968 J.R. 238.
[67] *O'Hara* v. *H.M. Adv.*, 1948 J.C. 90, L.J.-C. at 98.
[68] Ibid., at 99.
[69] Supra.
[70] 1959 J.C. 101.
[71] *R.* v. *Selvey*, supra.
[72] Ibid.; *R.* v. *Rouse* [1904] 1 K.B. 184.

confession would come within the exception in England [73]: it has never been so treated in Scotland.

Both countries rely on the discretion of the judge to refuse to allow even permissible cross-examination to avoid unfairness in the application of this exception, but such discretion is more necessary in England. In *O'Hara* Lord Justice-Clerk Thomson said that the judge " may feel that even though the position is established in law, still the putting of such questions as to the character of the accused person may be fraught with results which immeasurably outweigh the result of questions put by the defence, and which make a fair trial of the accused person almost impossible. On the other hand, in the ordinary and normal case he may feel that, if the credit of the prosecutor or his witnesses has been attacked, it is only fair that the jury should have before them material on which they can form their judgment whether the accused person is any more worthy to be believed than those whom he has attacked." [74] In *Fielding* [70] the fact that the judge had warned the defence of the dangers they ran in their cross-examination of the complainer was regarded as relevant to the appeal court's refusal to interfere with the trial judge's refusal to disallow the cross-examination of the accused.

18–16   (iv) Where the accused has given evidence against any other person charged with the same offence.[75] The House of Lords has held that the co-accused against whom evidence has been given has a right to cross-examine as to character, and that the judge has no discretion to refuse to allow him to do so.[76] It has also been held that any evidence which would rationally have to be included in any summary of the evidence in the case which, if accepted, would warrant the conviction of the other accused, is evidence against him for the purpose of this exception, whatever its motive, " whether it is the product of pained reluctance or of malevolent eagerness," whether given with regret or relish.[77]

This exception has not been discussed in any reported Scots case.

It is not clear whether the exception applies where the accused witness had given evidence against a person other than the person seeking to bring out his character, or where the evidence relied on by the cross-examiner had been given in other proceedings. The Crown may rely on this exception but the judge has a discretion to refuse to allow them to do so.[78]

The other person must be charged with the same offence, and not merely with an offence connected with the same incident.[79]

---

[73] e.g., *R.* v. *Clark* [1955] 2 Q.B. 469; *R.* v. *Jones* (1923) 17 Cr.App.R. 117.
[74] 1948 J.C. 90, 97. For an example of the use of the discretion, see *H.M. Adv.* v. *Deighan*, 1961 S.L.T. (Sh. Ct.) 38.
[75] 1898 Act, s. 1 (*f*) (iii).
[76] *Murdoch* v. *Taylor* [1965] A.C. 574.
[77] *Ibid.*, Lord Morris of Borth-y-Gest at 584.
[78] *Murdoch* v. *Taylor*, supra.
[79] *R.* v. *Roberts* [1936] 1 All E.R. 23. But see *R.* v. *Russell* (*George*) [1971] 1 Q.B. 151— consecutive possessions of forged notes the " same " offence.

Evidence of co-accused

–17   One accused may not call a co-accused as a witness.[80] When, however, one of two or more co-accused gives evidence his evidence is evidence in the case, available like any other evidence, for or against all the accused.[81]

It is clear that where one co-accused gives evidence which involves another that other may cross-examine him.[82] There is some authority that one co-accused has no locus to cross-examine another where that other has not given evidence tending to incriminate him,[83] but this rule is applied very loosely in practice. Where cross-examination is allowed it is not restricted to the incriminating part of the witness's evidence and may be used to obtain additional evidence favourable to the cross-examiner.[84] There is, indeed, one situation in which accused B has a duty to cross-examine accused A even if A's evidence does not in any way involve B. That is where A gives evidence before B and it is B's intention to give evidence incriminating A. B has a duty to put this incriminating evidence to A in cross-examination to give the latter a chance to refute it.[85]

The prosecution are entitled to cross-examine last, after the co-accused.[86] It is not, however, regarded as proper for the prosecution to use their right to cross-examine one accused as a way of turning him into a witness against another accused. It may be, therefore, that if A is charged with an offence on his own as well as with one in concert with B, and gives evidence only in respect of the former, the prosecution cannot cross-examine as to the latter, while B may have no right to cross-examine at all.[87]

–18   The rule that an accused may be called only on his own application applies only to an accused at his own trial. Where A and B are charged with the same offence but are tried separately, each is a competent witness for prosecution or defence at the trial of the other.[88] He may be questioned like any other witness subject to his right not to answer incriminating questions when called as a defence witness or otherwise not protected by immunity.[89] Where A and B are charged together but A pleads guilty, or

---

[80] 1898 Act, s. 1 (e) requires only that he be called on his own application, but it is incompetent at common law for one accused to call another—see *Dickson on Evidence*, paras. 1563–1566; *Morrison* v. *Adair*, 1943 J.C. 25. The position is different in England—*R.* v. *Rowland* [1910] 1 K.B. 458.

[81] This, at any rate, is the situation in practice, whatever the common law rule may be about evidence by a witness for one accused not being evidence against another—*Walker and Walker on Evidence*, p. 387.

[82] *Hackston* v. *Millar* (1906) 5 Adam 37; *Young* v. *H.M. Adv.*, 1932 J.C. 63.

[83] *Gemmell and McFadyen* v. *MacNiven*, 1928 J.C. 5. The law in England now is that the co-accused is always entitled to cross-examine whether or not the witness incriminates him: *R.* v. *Hilton* [1971] 3 W.L.R. 625, applying dicta in *Murdoch* v. *Taylor, supra.*

[84] *Young, supra*, L.J.-G. at 74; *Morrison* v. *Adair*, 1943 J.C. 25.

[85] *Lee* v. *H.M. Adv.*, 1968 S.L.T. 155.

[86] *Walker and Walker on Evidence*, p. 385.

[87] Ibid., pp. 386–387. Cf. *R.* v. *Rowland, supra.*

[88] *Bell and Shaw* v. *Houstoun* (1842) 1 Broun 49; *Dickson on Evidence*, paras. 1563–1564. On separation of trials to allow one accused to call another see *supra*, para. 10–19.

[89] See *McGinley and Dowds* v. *MacLeod*, 1963 J.C. 11. See *infra*, para. 18-58, on the evidence of accomplices.

the charges against him are dropped, B may call him as a witness,[90] even if he has not been included in the list of defence witnesses.[91]

Evidence of spouse of accused

18–19   At common law the spouse of an accused person was not a competent witness for the defence.[91a] He or she was a compellable witness for the prosecution where the accused was charged with an offence against him or her, otherwise he or she was incompetent. For the purpose of this rule the term " offence against " was not restricted to offences of personal injury to the other spouse, but extended to false accusation [92] and to offences against property including theft [93] and the forgery of the spouse's signature on a cheque.[94]

18–20   Under the Criminal Evidence Act 1898 this rule is unchanged, but the spouse of an accused is rendered a competent witness " for the defence " on the application of that accused.[95] The right to comment on the failure of a spouse to give evidence is limited in the same way as the right to comment on the failure of the accused himself to do so.[96] If the spouse is to be called she should be included in the list of witnesses.[97] The position of the evidence of the spouse of one accused as evidence against a co-accused is probably the same as that of any other witness.[98] The Act may allow one accused to lead the spouse of another as a witness, but it is difficult to see how that other can apply for his spouse to be called for his co-accused in the Scottish setting.

18–21   There are a number of offences in relation to which the accused's spouse may be called as a witness for the prosecution or defence (presumably the defence of a co-accused) [99] without the accused's consent.

In all these cases the spouse is a competent but not a compellable witness.[1]
They are:

(i) Offences against the Criminal Law Amendment Act 1885.[2]
(ii) Bigamy.[3]
(iii) Incest in respect of a child.[4]

---

[90] *Thomson* v. *H.M. Adv.* (1892) 3 White 321; *Agnes Wilson and Ors.* (1860) 3 Irv. 623; *Dickson on Evidence*, para. 1564; cf. *Boal and Cordrey* [1965] 1 Q.B. 402.
[91] See *Walker and Walker on Evidence*, p. 386.
[91a] Cf. *Hawkins* v. *U.S.*, 358 U.S. 74 (1958).
[92] *Elliot Millar* (1847) Ark. 355.
[93] *Harper* v. *Adair*, 1945 J.C. 21.
[94] *Foster* v. *H.M. Adv.*, 1932 J.C. 75.
[95] 1898 Act, ss. 1 and 1 (*c*).
[96] Ibid., s. 1 (*b*).
[97] Ibid., s. 5.
[98] See supra, at n. 81.
[99] See *Cross on Evidence*, 3rd ed., 151; cf. *Walker and Walker on Evidence*, p. 377.
[1] *Leach* v. *R.* [1912] A.C. 305; *Walker and Walker on Evidence*, p. 378.
[2] 1898 Act, s. 4 and Sched.
[3] Criminal Justice Administration Act 1914, s. 28 (3).
[4] Criminal Procedure (Scotland) Act 1938, s. 11, applying the 1898 Act to offences in Sched. 1 to Children and Young Persons (Scotland) Act 1937.

(iv) Sexual offences against mental defectives contrary to section 96 of the Mental Health (Scotland) Act 1960.[5]

(v) Contraventions of sections 12–15, 22 and 23 of the Children and Young Persons (Scotland) Act 1937.[4]

(vi) Any offence involving bodily injury [6] to a child.[4]

(vii) Contraventions of section 25 of the Children and Young Persons Act 1933.[7]

(viii) Offences against the Immoral Traffic (Scotland) Act 1902.[8]

(ix) Offences against sections 4, 5 and 6 of the Conspiracy and Protection of Property Act 1875.[9]

(x) Offences against the National Insurance Act 1965, and the National Insurance (Industrial Injuries) Act 1965.[10]

(xi) Offences against the Ministry of Social Security Act 1966.[11]

(xii) Offences against sections 2 and 5 of the Industrial Injuries and Diseases (Old Cases) Act 1967.[12]

Matrimonial communings

-22   The 1898 Act preserves the common law right to refuse to give evidence of matrimonial communings [13] and most of the later Acts provide expressly that the witness shall not be compellable to disclose these.[14] It has been held [15] that the privilege of non-disclosure belongs to the witness and that he or she may therefore give evidence of communings without the consent of the accused, but it may be doubted whether this should be so, since the person in need of protection is the accused and not the witness.[16]

Evidence of Statements by Accused

Judicial statements

-23   Nothing short of a judicial admission of guilt by his pleading guilty in open court will serve of itself to convict a person accused of crime; but to a certain extent his pretrial statements are admissible in evidence.

Statements in a valid judicial declaration are evidence against their maker. The accused is not entitled to have the declaration read as evidence in his favour,[17] but if a request is made by the accused it is rarely

---

[5] 1898 Act, Sched., as amended by Mental Health (Scotland) Act 1960, s. 96 (5).

[6] This includes lewd practices—*H.M. Adv.* v. *Lee*, 1923 J.C. 1; and attempted murder even if the child was untouched—*H.M. Adv.* v. *Macphie*, 1926 J.C. 91.

[7] Children and Young Persons Act 1933, s. 26 (5).

[8] Criminal Law Amendment Act 1912, s. 7 (6).

[9] Conspiracy and Protection of Property Act 1875, s. 11.

[10] National Insurance Act 1965, s. 94 (6); National Insurance (Industrial Injuries) Act 1965, s. 68.

[11] Ministry of Social Security Act 1966, s. 33 (6).

[12] Industrial Injuries and Diseases (Old Cases) Act 1967, s. 11 (5).

[13] 1898 Act, s. 1 (*d*).

[14] But not the Criminal Justice Administration Act 1914, the Children and Young Persons Act 1933, or the Criminal Law Amendment Act 1912.

[15] *H.M. Adv.* v. *H.D.*, 1953 J.C. 65; *Rumping* v. *D.P.P.* [1964] A.C. 814; *Walker and Walker on Evidence*, p. 380.

[16] See *Rumping* v. *D.P.P.*, supra, Lord Reid at 833–834; Gerald H. Gordon, " The Evidence of Spouses in Criminal Trials," 1956 S.L.T.(News) 145.

[17] *Elizabeth Kennedy or Potts* (1842) 1 Broun 497.

refused.[18] If there are two or more declarations and one is read, all must be read.[19] The declaration of one accused is not as a rule evidence against a co-accused.[20]

Statements made by an accused on oath in previous proceedings, civil or criminal, or, for example, at a fatal accident inquiry are also admissible.[21]

Statements to police officers: general considerations

18-24   The law regarding the circumstances under which statements made by persons to the police will be admissible as evidence against their makers is not easy to state either shortly or with any confidence. The law's suspicion of such statements rests on a number of factors. Historically, the interrogation of suspects was part of the function of the sheriff at the judicial examination, and no business of the police.[22] The duty of the police was simply to bring the suspect to the sheriff, although if he said anything on the way, and especially if he said anything when informed of the charge on which he was being arrested, that would usually be admissible.[23] Once judicial examination ceased to be a normal method of obtaining information from accused persons, and as the importance of detective officers increased, emphasis came to be laid on the necessity of protecting the suspect from any unfair treatment by the police. This seems to have been of much greater importance than the fear that the adduced confession might be false, perhaps because that danger was thought to be avoided by the requirements of the law of corroboration. The suspect was to be protected, not merely against physical injury or intimidation, but against cross-examination, against being offered inducements to confess, against sharp practices, even against the possibility of confession because of a misapprehension of what was happening.[24] Each case had to be judged on its own facts to determine whether there was any unfairness, but the general attitude of the courts has varied from time to time, the high-water mark of

---

[18] Macdonald, 329; cf. *Brown* v. *H.M. Adv.*, 1964 J.C. 10.

[19] *Thos. Loch* (1837) 1 Swin. 494.

[20] *Geo. Milne* (1866) 5 Irv. 229.

[21] *Banaghan* v. *H.M. Adv.* (1888) 1 White 566; *McGiveran* v. *Auld* (1894) 1 Adam 448.

[22] See e.g. *John Millar* (1859) 3 Irv. 406; *H.M. Adv.* v. *Smith* (1901) 3 Adam 475; *Hodgsons* v. *MacPherson* (1913) 7 Adam 118; see also Gerald H. Gordon, "Institution of Criminal Proceedings in Scotland" (1968) 19 N.I.L.Q. 249. In *John Millar*, supra, Lord Neaves said, at 408–409, "The duties of an officer are very clear. He goes to apprehend the accused and to state the charge against him, and then the panel is put on his guard not to commit himself. The officer's duty then is to take him before a magistrate. I think it was very ill-advised and wrong on the part of the superintendent of police to commence the conversation by asking the panel why he did not run away. Drawing the lad on in that way was most unjust. It would entirely subvert the course of justice if police officers were to be allowed, by nicely-contrived questions, to entrap prisoners into a confession."

[23] *H.M. Adv.* v. *Smith*, supra; *John Martin* (1842) 1 Broun 382; *Helen Hay* (1852) 3 Irv. 181. There are some cases where evidence was admitted somewhat reluctantly in circumstances which might later have been thought improper: see Bell's Notes, 244–245; *Gracie* v. *Stuart* (1884) 5 Couper 379; *Agnes Christie or Paterson* (1842) 1 Broun 388. See also *Lewis* v. *Blair* (1858) 3 Irv. 16. The earlier cases are reviewed in *Waddell* v. *Kinnaird*, 1922 J.C. 40, itself a case where the decision to admit the evidence, diss. Lord Ormidale, is mildly surprising.

[24] See e.g. *H.M. Adv.* v. *Olsson*, 1941 J.C. 63; *H.M. Adv.* v. *McSwiggan*, 1937 J.C. 50.

what might be called the " anti-police " approach being reached in Lord
Justice-Clerk Cooper's observations in *H.M. Adv.* v. *Rigg* [25] where he
said, " I am bound to say that I have viewed with growing uneasiness and
distaste the frequency with which in recent years there have been tendered
in support of prosecutions alleged voluntary statements said to have been
made to the police by persons charged, then or subsequently, with grave
crime." Lord Cooper said of the statement in that case, which he described
as a detailed precognition of the accused extending to upwards of seven-
hundred words, " To my mind, it is quite incredible that such a statement
could have been taken from any person, least of all from a person of the
age and apparent experience and condition of the accused, as a truly
spontaneous and voluntary statement in the sense in which that expression
has been used in the decisions, or without such interrogation as would in
common experience be indispensable to the taking of such a detailed
precognition." [26] Perhaps the most extreme example of a case in which an
apparently genuine and truthful confession was rejected is *H.M. Adv.* v.
Campbell,[27] where the accused offered to make a statement to the press on
payment of money, and the press told the police of this offer. The police
then arranged that when the reporter met the accused in a public-house
he should be accompanied by a policeman disguised as a photographer. At
the public-house the accused repeated his request for money, and, on being
reassured about this, proceeded to make his statement. This statement
was held to be inadmissible as having been obtained by a trick. It was held
that it was the duty of the police officer to reveal himself and to caution
the accused before the statement was made. This situation must be distinguished from that where the police use a trick to overhear statements
made during the actual commission of a crime such as blackmail; the latter
statements seem to be regarded as clearly admissible.[28]

The suspicious approach to police statements is most authoritatively
embodied in *Chalmers* v. *H.M. Adv.*,[29] although the facts there were
somewhat special. In recent years there has been less suspicion of the
police and a growing realisation of the necessity of admitting the results of
police investigation. The court must see that the standards of fairness have
been adhered to, but fairness does not mean merely fairness to the accused,
it involves fairness to the public interest as well.[30] Here, as in questions of
evidence obtained by search, the court must balance the interest of the
citizen to be protected and the interest of the state to secure that necessary
evidence is not withheld on formal or technical grounds.[31]

8–25   Detailed consideration of the law probably still requires separate
discussion of three periods of time in the investigation of a criminal

---

[25] 1946 J.C. 1, 3.
[26] Ibid., at 4–5.
[27] 1964 J.C. 80. Contrast the English cases of *R.* v. *Stewart* [1970] 1 W.L.R. 907 and *R.* v.
Keeton (1970) 54 Cr.App.R. 267.
[28] *Hopes and Lavery* v. *H.M. Adv.*, 1960 J.C. 104.
[29] 1954 J.C. 66.
[30] *Miln* v. *Cullen*, 1967 J.C. 21.
[31] *Lawrie* v. *Muir*, 1950 J.C. 19; *Bell* v. *Hogg*, 1967 J.C. 49.

charge. The first is that of preliminary investigation where no one is under any particular suspicion. The second is that where the maker of the impugned statement is under suspicion, but has not yet been charged, or rather (since it would be improper to allow the police to postpone the actual charge in order to obtain further evidence from the suspect) where the police are not yet in a position in which they can and should charge him. This stage might be described as that where the accused is a suspect but not yet a chargeable suspect. The third stage begins when he is charged or becomes chargeable.

Statements to police officers at stage of preliminary investigations

18–26   In investigating a crime the police are entitled to ask questions of anyone, and all citizens have a duty to assist them, although no one can be compelled to answer any questions. Any statements made at this stage are not rendered inadmissible because the maker is subsequently placed on trial for the offence under investigation.[32] An example of this stage is where the police believe that one of a group of people was involved in a crime but do not suspect any particular person; they may question all the members of the group, and if one of them is the offender his statements during this preliminary questioning will be admissible.[33] Once suspicion has crystallised on any particular person, the investigation probably moves into the second stage. Another example of the first stage is what happens when the police exercise their power to stop someone seen carrying goods in suspicious circumstances and question him as to the origin and nature of the goods. The police can probably ask questions in this situation until they have some grounds for suspecting the goods to be the proceeds of a particular crime.[34]

It is not necessary at this stage of the investigation to caution any person that he need not answer any questions, or that any answers he does make may be used in evidence. It may be, indeed, that in some circumstances a failure to make an explanation at this stage can be evidence against the accused at his trial. This would be particularly so where the charge was one of reset and the accused declined to explain his possession of the property.[35]

Statements to police officers at stage of suspicion

18–27   The modern law on this stage of investigation stems from *H.M. Adv.* v. *Aitken*,[36] where Lord Anderson stressed the need to protect a person suspected of but not charged with a crime. Lord Anderson did so in order to point out that while it was settled law that a voluntary statement made

---

[32] *Bell* v. *H.M. Adv.*, 1945 J.C. 61; *Chalmers* v. *H.M. Adv.*, 1954 J.C. 49.
[33] *Bell*, supra; cf. *Brown* v. *H.M. Adv.*, 1966 S.L.T. 105; *Thompson* v. *H.M. Adv.*, 1968 J.C. 61.
[34] See *Costello* v. *MacPherson*, 1922 J.C. 9; cf. *Bell* v. *Hogg*, supra.
[35] See *Cryans* v. *Nixon*, 1955 J.C. 1; *Fox* v. *Patterson*, 1948 J.C. 104, 109; cf. *Wightman and Anr.* v. *H.M. Adv.*, 1959 J.C. 44.
[36] 1926 J.C. 83.

by someone who had been charged was admissible, it did not follow that a voluntary statement made by someone not yet charged was equally admissible. For the uncharged suspect lacked certain rights enjoyed by the charged person, since the latter was entitled to be cautioned that any answer to the charge might be used against him, to have the advice of a solicitor, and to elect to make a statement before a magistrate should he so wish. In these circumstances, if he did elect to make a statement the statement might truly be regarded as voluntary; an election to make a statement without these safeguards required to be more closely investigated. The fact that the accused had been a suspect was, however, only one circumstance among a number which led his Lordship to reject a statement made by him to the police.[37] The accused was a sixteen year old boy who was " detained on suspicion " of murdering his grandmother; he was physically ill and mentally confused, his solicitor had not been admitted to advise him, and he had been questioned for about an hour before he offered to make his statement. It seems, too, that although cautioned when questioned he was not cautioned again before making the statement.

In *Aitken*, and in other cases,[38] the accused was said to be detained on suspicion. But although this aspect of the law was stressed in *Bell* v. *H.M. Adv.*[39] there is no such category as that of detainee under suspicion. The fact that the suspect is in the police station is a circumstance to be taken into account in assessing the fairness of the police behaviour, and the voluntariness of any statement made, but the important factor is not that the accused is detained, but that he is a suspect.[40]

-28 The leading case on the stage of suspicion is *Chalmers* v. *H.M. Adv.*[41] Although, strictly speaking, much of the opinions in this case are obiter, the case was heard by a Full Bench convened to consider the law relating to confessions, and is therefore of high authority. The accused was a sixteen year old boy who was charged with murder and robbery. The crime was committed on 24th July and the accused was questioned by the police on 26th July and 7th August as to his movements at the time of the crime. Further information given by other witnesses to the police on 13th August cast doubt on the truth of the accused's statements, and he was brought from his bed to the police station at about 11 a.m. on 15th August. He was there cautioned, and cross-examined on his earlier statements for about five minutes during which he was reduced to tears. He was cautioned again, was offered but declined the presence of his father and a solicitor, and made a statement. The Crown did not seek to adduce this statement

---

[37] Some observations in *Adair* v. *McGarry*, 1933 J.C. 72, suggest that at that time it was normal for the police to interrogate suspects, even after arrest—see L.J.-C. at 79, Lord Hunter at 84.

[38] See especially *Bell* v. *H.M. Adv.*, 1945 J.C. 61.

[39] Supra.

[40] See *Chalmers* v. *H.M. Adv.*, 1954 J.C. 66, L.J.-G. at 75, 78–79, L.J.-C. at 82; *Miln* v. *Cullen*, supra.

[41] 1954 J.C. 66. See A. D. Gibb, " Fair Play for the Criminal " (1954) 66 J.R. 199.

18-28   which was thus ex concessione unfairly obtained. After making his statement the accused was questioned as to the whereabouts of the deceased's
purse, and at about 11.45 a.m. he took the police to a cornfield where the
purse was hidden. The accused was detained for a further two hours or so
while his father was summoned; he was then cautioned and charged, and
replied, " I did it. He struck me."

The trial judge held that while in the police station the accused was a
suspect and that his interrogation was improper. He held, however, that
evidence of the visit to the cornfield was competent provided it did not
include any statements made during the trip, and also held that the answer
to the caution and charge was admissible.

On appeal, it was held that the evidence of the visit to the cornfield was
inadmissible because it was " part and parcel of the same transaction as the
interrogation, and, if the interrogation and the ' statement ' which emerged from it are inadmissible as ' unfair,' the same criticism must attach to
the conducted visit to the cornfield." [42] It should be noted that the court
also regarded the visit as equivalent to a statement, as being merely a
dramatic way of replying to the question, " Where is the purse? " Since a
verbal reply would have been inadmissible, so was the act of taking the
police to the purse. It is arguable that this part of *Chalmers* has no reference to the situation where a suspect says in an inadmissible answer to
police questioning that the stolen goods are hidden, say, under the floor
boards in his attic, and the police give evidence that they found the stolen
goods in that place. Such evidence may well be admissible, whether or not
the accused's statement is known to the court. If the police in *Chalmers* had
merely produced the purse, that evidence, to quote Lord Cooper, " would
have carried them little or no distance in this case towards implicating the
appellant. It was essential that the appellant should be linked up with the
purse, either by oral confession or by its equivalent." [43] The situation may
be different where the whereabouts of the property themselves incriminate
the accused.[43a]

Lord Cooper regarded the answer to the caution and charge as too
closely linked to the earlier police actings to be admissible, especially
as the answer might not have been the same had the police limited their
earlier questioning to eliciting admissible evidence, but he did not make
that a ground of judgment.

On the general point the view of the court in *Chalmers* on the position
of suspects can be summed up in two different statements, one by Lord

[42] L.J.-G. at 76.
[43] Ibid. It was not argued that the finding of the purse rendered the earlier statement credible
and therefore admissible: cf. *Cross on Evidence* (3rd ed.), 263–266. See also *The Queen*
v. *Wray* [1971] S.C.R. 272.
[43a] In the United States evidence obtained as a result of an unlawful search or of interrogation after an unlawful arrest is excluded as the fruit of unlawful conduct: *Wong Sun* v.
U.S. 371 U.S. 471 (1963). This principle may well not apply to evidence obtained following on questioning the answers to which are inadmissible in Scotland since, (a) there is a
general discretion to admit real evidence irregularly obtained: supra, para. 5–26; infra.
para. 18–94, and (b) it is not clear that such questioning is in itself unlawful.

-28 Cooper and one by Lord Justice-Clerk Thomson, with both of which the remaining judges appear to have agreed. Lord Cooper said,

> " The theory of our law is that at the stage of initial investigation the police may question anyone with a view to acquiring information which may lead to the detection of the criminal; but that, when the stage has been reached at which suspicion, or more than suspicion, has in their view centred upon some person as the likely perpetrator of the crime, further interrogation of that person becomes very dangerous, and, if carried too far, e.g., to the point of extracting a confession by what amounts to cross-examination, the evidence of that confession will almost certainly be excluded." [44]

Lord Thomson said,

> " But there comes a point of time in ordinary police investigation when the law intervenes to render inadmissible as evidence answers even to questions which are not tainted [by bullying, pressure, third degree methods and so forth]. After the point is reached, further interrogation is incompatible with the answers being regarded as a voluntary statement, and the law intervenes to safeguard the party questioned from possible self-incrimination. Just when that point of time is reached is in any particular case extremely difficult to define— or even for an experienced police official to realise its arrival. There does come a time, however, when a police officer, carrying out his duty honestly and conscientiously, ought to be in a position to appreciate that the man whom he is in process of questioning is under serious consideration as the perpetrator of the crime. Once that stage of suspicion is reached, the suspect is in the position that thereafter the only evidence admissible against him is his own voluntary statement." [45]

Because of its greater explicitness and its less qualified terms, the views of Lord Thomson were fairly commonly accepted as representing the law.[46] Police officers continued to talk of questioning under caution, but the admissibility of the replies to such questioning rested in the main on lack of objection. *Chalmers* suggested that either an accused was a suspect, in which case any answers to questions were inadmissible, or he was not a suspect, in which case a caution was unnecessary. To give a caution out of a desire to be supererogatorily fair might be dangerous since it might be interpreted by the court, as in *Chalmers* itself, as evidence that the accused was indeed under suspicion. In any event, if Lord Strachan was correct, cautioning did not help, since the caution " is not a preliminary which will regularise an interrogation by a police officer, it is a warning that should be given before a voluntary statement is received. Where a person is detained

[44] 1954 J.C. at 78.
[45] At 81–82.
[46] And not only by Scots lawyers: see *Culombe* v. *Conn.*. 367 U.S. 568, 589 (1961); *Miranda* v. *Arizona*, 384 U.S. 436, 488 (1966).

on suspicion the police are not entitled to cross-examine him, whether they give a caution or not." [47]

18-29   Whichever view of *Chalmers* was taken the general message of the case was clear—the courts would look with great suspicion on admissions by suspects, and in cases of doubt might be expected to reject them. More recent cases, however they may be analysed in detail, clearly show a change in attitude. [48] The courts will now look with sympathy on the need of the police to ask questions in detecting and bringing home guilt to offenders, and in cases of doubt the courts may be expected to admit statements made in response to questioning which does not smack of unfairness, whether because it is oppressive, or is of the nature of cross-examination, or involves threats, inducement or trickery. The mechanics of this change have been twofold. They have involved some redefinition of the stage of suspicion, and also a rejection of the notion that the existence of suspicion is in itself a paramount consideration. Recent cases adopt Lord Cooper's view of *Chalmers*, and emphasise its tentative and pragmatic aspects.

18-30   In *Chalmers* the police evidence was that when they brought Chalmers to the police station to check his statement in the light of their further information, they were " inclined to suspect " that he might have some connection with the crime. According to Lord Thomson, a person was a suspect when he was " under serious consideration as the perpetrator of the crime." [49] In *Brown* v. *H.M. Adv.*,[50] the accused was one of a number of people who had been in the company of the murdered girl, and as such was taken to the police station, cautioned, and asked by the police for an account of his movements. He gave them an account. Later the same day the police checked his statement with that of other witnesses and noticed some discrepancies. The police then returned to the accused, told him that there were discrepancies, and that they were going to question him further. He immediately broke down and said, " I kill't her." He was then cautioned and charged, and he showed the police where he had hidden the girl's purse and the murder weapon. All this evidence was held to be admissible. Lord Justice-General Clyde said, " The police at this stage had obviously not reached the point of eliminating all other possible suspects and of treating the appellant as the only suspect . . . they were still in the process of investigating who committed the crime. The appellant at that stage was only one of the possible persons who might have committed the crime. He was not the only suspect." [51] Lord Migdale said that what the police were doing was still " dealing with preliminary matters in that they were still in course of interviewing a number of people, including no doubt some who had nothing to do with the crime." [52] But Lord Cameron referred

---

[47] 1954 J.C. at 69.
[48] See J. W. R. Gray, " *Chalmers* and After: Police Interrogation and the Trial within a Trial," 1970 J.R. 1.
[49] 1954 J.C. at 82.
[50] 1966 S.L.T. 105.
[51] 1966 S.L.T. at 108.
[52] Ibid.

to the police officer's evidence that when he went to " ' clarify the discrepancies ' his general suspicions had ' crystallised ' so that in his mind a measure of suspicion of guilt of this murder did point to the appellant." [53] And Lord Cameron himself described the accused as being an " object of close suspicion."

In *H.M. Adv.* v. *McPhee* [54] Lord Cameron admitted a statement taken when the accused was, in the words of the police, " a mild suspect," although the accused had not been cautioned at the time at which he blurted out his admission.

–31   In *Miln* v. *Cullen* [55] the police arrived by chance at the scene of an accident involving a lorry and a car. The lorry driver pointed out the car driver to the police and the police formed the opinion that the car driver was unfit to drive through drink. The police approached the car driver and asked him, without any caution, if he was the driver. The sheriff-substitute held his affirmative reply to be inadmissible, but was overruled on appeal. While Lord Strachan was prepared to assume, and indeed the Crown conceded, that the car driver was a suspect, Lord Justice-Clerk Grant was satisfied that the facts fell well short of the *Chalmers* suspicion stage, and that the case " had never got beyond the investigation stage." [56] Lord Wheatley also felt that the degree of suspicion was rather tenuous since it rested on the unsupported statement of the lorry driver who was an interested party. One is left with the impression that Lord Wheatley was not happy with the Crown's concession. On the other hand his Lordship said that in circumstances where the police had already in their possession information clearly pointing to the commission of an offence, and the only further point in the enquiry was to establish the identity of the perpetrator, a question without caution designed to extract an admission of identity would not be equally unobjectionable.

–32   In *Thompson* v. *H.M. Adv.*[57] the accused was one of a number of persons questioned in connection with the murder of his grandmother. His own account of his movements was checked with the statements of other witnesses who gave a different account and he was placed in a room in a police station, partly at least because he could not go back home to his grandmother's house where police investigations were in process. He was not under arrest and his continued presence in the station was of a quasi-voluntary nature. As it happened his account of his movements was correct and that of the witnesses wrong. He was left in the room in the station having a desultory conversation with a detective about their respective families. At about 7.15 a.m., by which time Thompson had been with the detective for about three hours, and had had no sleep for twenty-four hours, and just after some talk about the grandmother, Thompson

[53] Ibid. at 109.
[54] 1966 S.L.T. (Notes) 83.
[55] 1967 J.C. 21.
[56] At 26.
[57] 1968 J.C. 61.

blurted out, " It was either her or me." The detective, who apprehended that a confession or an admission was about to be made, fetched a chief detective inspector who cautioned the accused and took his statement. This was held to be admissible as being voluntarily given and properly taken. In the course of his charge to the jury Lord Wheatley said, " Once a person has become a suspect and further questioning is going to take place he must be warned that he is under no obligation to answer any question the result of which might be to incriminate him," [58] which clearly implies the admissibility of statements made by suspects questioned after caution. He also told the jury that " if the police in the course of a very difficult and serious investigation have got to keep asking questions and probing and probing and probing then as long as they are doing that fairly having regard to their task and their duty, and that nothing unfavourable or unfair to the accused was done either by word or by deed or by trickery, then, of course, anything that they can elicit is normally competent and acceptable evidence." [59] The admissibility of the confession was upheld on appeal. Lord Justice-General Clyde added that there was neither precedent not practice for the defence suggestion that the police should have obtained a solicitor for the accused, saying that there was no need to obtain a solicitor until after arrest.[60]

18–33   The retention of the category of suspect no doubt has the advantage of avoiding a direct conflict with the full bench decision in *Chalmers*, but if stressed it masks the appreciable change in the law represented by the later cases. In any event, if the category of suspect is to be so narrow as to exclude a person suspected on uncorroborated evidence, there will be little if any distinction between a suspect and a chargeable suspect: and the *Chalmers* rules and restrictions are not required in the case of the chargeable suspect.[61]

18–34   The later cases can also be interpreted as representing a return to something like the position in *Aitken*.[62] That the accused was, on any definition, a suspect is a circumstance to be taken into account, but no more. In particular it does not in itself preclude questioning, under caution if this seems appropriate, but in some cases without caution. In *Brown* v. *H.M. Adv*.[63] Lord Cameron said, " I know of no authoritative decision in the law of Scotland which lays down that once a person has become suspect he may not thereafter be questioned by the police at all, or that if they do question him the answers which he makes may not be given in evidence." He relied on what Lord Cooper had said in *Chalmers* as establishing the contrary,

---

[58] Transcript of judges' charge, p. 26.
[59] Ibid., 27–28.
[60] 1968 J.C. 65. Contrast *Miranda* v. *Arizona*, 384 U.S. 436 (1966).
[61] See also *Barry Dean Ashington*, Edinburgh High Court, February 1968, unreported; see (1968) N.I.L.Q. 261. The accused was found in Ireland in possession of articles belonging to the murdered girl, whose body was discovered in a sleeping bag in his tent in Edinburgh. He gave an account of his meeting with her, under caution, until he said, "When I woke up next morning and saw what had happened," at which stage he was cautioned and charged.
[62] 1926 J.C. 83.
[63] 1966 S.L.T. 105, 109.

and added, " It is also clear that not all answers to all questions addressed to a person under concentrated suspicion are necessarily inadmissible." [64]

In *H.M. Adv.* v. *McPhee* [65] the same judge said that " the mere fact that an accused person may have come under suspicion of complicity in the crime," was not in itself sufficient to require the cessation of questioning. In *Miln* v. *Cullen* [66] Lord Strachan said,

> " Both the argument and the objection appear to assume that, if a person is under suspicion, it is unfair for a police officer to ask him any material question without first cautioning him. In my opinion that is not an accurate representation of the law ... the mere fact that a suspected person is asked a question by a police officer before being cautioned is not in itself unfairness. The whole circumstances must be taken into account, and the test in every case is whether in the particular set of circumstances there has been unfairness on the part of the police."

In the same case Lord Wheatley said,

> " Even at the stage of routine investigations, where much greater latitude is allowed, fairness is still the test, and that is always a question of circumstances. It is conceivable that even at that stage a question might be asked or some action might be perpetrated which produced an admission of guilt from the person being interviewed, and yet the evidence might be disallowed because the circumstances disclosed an unfairness to that person. At the other end of the scale, it is wrong to assume that, after a person has been cautioned and charged, questioning of that person is no longer admissible." [67]

3-35   Both in *Chalmers* [68] and in *Brown* [69] the court declined to lay down rules for determining the admissibility of statements to the police, relying on the test of fairness and holding that each case depends on its own facts. The attitude of the courts in the later cases appears to be that evidence obtained by fair questioning of a non-chargeable suspect is admissible. *Chalmers* and *Rigg* [70] were distinguished in *Brown* because in the earlier cases there was an element of unfairness and cross-examination, the statement in *Rigg* being described as taken by a police officer " desperate " to find out who had last seen the victim. [71] In *Brown* it was stressed that there was no suggestion of bullying by the police or of pressure to confess, or that the police were in any way cross-examining the accused. There was in fact no questioning at all in *Brown*, but that was only because it was

[64] At 110.
[65] 1968 S.L.T. (Notes) 83.
[66] 1967 J.C. 21, 27.
[67] At 30. The reference to questioning a person who has been cautioned and charged seems to have been directed to questioning designed merely to clear up ambiguities in voluntary statements.
[68] 1954 J.C. 66.
[69] 1966 S.L.T. 101.
[70] 1946 J.C. 1.
[71] *Brown* v. *H.M. Adv.*, supra L.J.-G. at 108.

unnecessary, and the decision must have been the same had there been questioning, provided it was not unfair questioning. The admissibility of a statement does not depend on whether the detective officer's aspect is frightening enough to provoke a breakdown by his mere confrontation of the accused, or mild enough to require to be supplemented by some polite questions.[72] What is excluded is evidence obtained by " interrogation," or anything " approaching cross-examination or pressure or deception of any kind by the police." [73]

Statements to police officers after charge

18–36   On arrest the prisoner is informed of the charge against him and cautioned. Whatever may once have been the case, caution is now an invariable accompaniment of formal arrest. In almost all cases an answer made to the caution and charge will be admissible, even if it is one which reveals A's bad character.[74] Where, however, the caution and charge follow on an improper interrogation, the reply may be excluded as having been tainted by the earlier impropriety or influenced by things said during the earlier questioning.[75] No adverse inference may be drawn from an accused's silence when charged.[76]

18–37   After having been charged the prisoner's status changes, and if the police thereafter ask him any questions about the offence on which he has been charged his answers will not be admissible in evidence.[77] This prohibition extends to answers to questions about information subsequently obtained by the police, even where that information indicates that the original charge will be extended, for example, by an increase in the number of allegedly stolen goods.[78] The law is very jealous of the right of the charged prisoner. In H.M. Adv. v. Lieser [79] one detective asked a question of another in the presence of the accused and the accused, believing that the question was addressed to him, answered it in an incriminating way. The answer was held inadmissible. In Wade v. Robertson [80] the police visited the accused and showed him a bottle of whisky which they had recovered from his house, and cautioned him. Before they could ask any questions, he made an admission, which was held to be inadmissible.

18–38   There have been suggestions that the police should not even receive a spontaneous statement voluntarily offered by a charged prisoner, but

---

[72] Cf. Wade v. Robertson, 1948 J.C. 117, 120.
[73] Miln v. Cullen, 1967 J.C. 21, Lord Strachan at 27.
[74] See H.M. Adv. v. McFadyen, 1926 J.C. 93, where the answer was "The idea is ridiculous, it is big things I go in for." Another answer which has passed into legend is, "I'll plead guilty if it's a summary."
[75] Chalmers v. H.M. Adv., 1954 J.C. 66.
[76] Robertson v. Maxwell, 1951 J.C. 11; Wightman and Anr. v. H.M. Adv., 1959 J.C. 44; Hall v. The Queen [1971] 1 W.L.R. 298.
[77] Stark and Smith v. H.M. Adv., 1938 J.C. 170; Wade v. Robertson, 1948 J.C. 117.
[78] Stark and Smith, supra.
[79] 1926 J.C. 88.
[80] Supra.

should instead take him before a magistrate there to make a declaration,[81] but this is clearly not the law.[82]

3–39 To be admissible the statement must be voluntary and spontaneous and not elicited by questions—although questions may be asked for the limited purpose of elucidating difficulties and ambiguities.[83] The accused should be cautioned before being allowed to make a statement.[84] He should not be invited, encouraged, or induced to make any statement, for example by a promise that if he does confess his father will be released from custody or that if he does not, his father will be implicated in his offences. The fact that without inducement an accused confesses because of his fear that others may be implicated does not vitiate the confession.[85] The statement will not be admitted if it appears that the accused did not fully understand what he was being charged with.[86] The accused should be offered the chance of consulting with his lawyer, but failure to bring this right to his notice is not necessarily fatal to the admissibility of any statement made.[87] It is improper to elicit or read a confession by one accused in the presence of his co-accused, in order to make that confession evidence against the co-accused.[88]

The general test is always whether the statement was (a) fairly taken and (b) voluntarily and spontaneously given, the element of fairness sometimes being used as a test of voluntariness.[89]

In one case where an accused who was on bail made an admission to a police constable concerned with the case in the course of a conversation in the street the court had no difficulty in admitting this as a voluntary statement, although it was made without caution.[90]

In *H.M. Adv.* v. *Keen*,[91] a police officer was not allowed to give evidence of what he had heard prisoners shouting to each other when in the cells after arrest.[92]

[81] *H.M. Adv.* v. *Christie*, Glasgow High Court, November 1961, unreported; see D. B. Smith, "A Note on Judicial Examination," 1961 S.L.T.(News) 179; *H.M. Adv.* v. *McSwiggan*, 1937 J.C. 50; Lord Kilbrandon, "Scotland: Pre-trial Procedure," in "The Accused" (ed. J. A. Coutts) 64.

[82] *H.M. Adv.* v. *Aitken*, 1926 J.C. 83; *H.M. Adv.* v. *Cunningham*, 1939 J.C. 61; *Manuel* v. *H.M. Adv.*, 1958 J.C. 41; *Miln* v. *Cullen*, 1967 J.C. 21, Lord Wheatley at 30.

[83] Cf. *Manuel* v. *H.M. Adv.*, supra; *Miln* v. *Cullen*, supra.

[84] *Cunningham*, supra; *Manuel*, supra.

[85] *Manuel*, supra.

[86] *H.M. Adv.* v. *Olsson*, 1941 J.C. 63, where the accused was a Swede who made his statement without the assistance of an interpreter; *H.M. Adv.* v. *McSwiggan*, 1937 J.C. 50, where the accused in answer to a charge of committing incest with his sister whereby she became pregnant, detailed the contraceptive precautions he had taken and added, "and that is the way I cannot be responsible for her condition," the accused being described as mentally "not very bright."

[87] *Cunningham*, supra; *H.M. Adv.* v. *Fox*, 1947 J.C. 30; *Law* v. *McNicol*, 1965 J.C. 32. Article 8 (1) of the Legal Aid (Scotland) (Criminal Proceedings) Scheme 1964 provides that when the duty solicitor receives intimation that "a person has been taken into custody" on a charge of murder or culpable homicide and that his services are required, he shall visit and advise him, and act for him.

[88] *Stark and Smith*, supra; *H.M. Adv.* v. *Davidson*, 1968 S.L.T. 17.

[89] See *Manuel* v. *H.M. Adv.*, supra, at 48.

[90] *Smith* v. *Lamb* (1888) 1 White 600. [91] 1926 J.C. 1.

[92] This case may be compared with *H.M. Adv.* v. *Campbell*, 1964 J.C. 80, and with *Peter Campbell*, Glasgow High Court, November 1965, unreported, see infra, para. 18–42.

Statements to persons other than the police

18–40 Statements made to prison officers are comparable to statements made to the police (save that prison officers should probably not receive confessions at all, but send for a magistrate or perhaps for the police).[93]

18–41 The rules relating to investigation by the police do not apply to the same extent to investigations made by or on behalf of employers.[94] This is so even where, as in the case of the Post Office, the investigation is carried out by means of an interrogation by officials employed as security officers. Such officials appear not to be in any way inhibited by the law in interrogating suspects, provided they act without duress, persuasion, or inducement, and provided the proffered statements were voluntarily made.

18–42 Statements made by an accused person other than those dealt with above are usually admissible. So, although a police officer cannot give evidence of what he overheard the accused say in the cells, there is nothing to prevent a fellow-prisoner giving evidence of a conversation with the accused.[95] Statements by the accused to friends and acquaintances before or after arrest are admissible. This presumably also applies to statements made to the press.[96] The position of private enquiry agents has not been discussed.

18–43 Voluntary statements have been considered in the following cases:

(a) Statements to magistrates and prosecutors-fiscal are inadmissible as they must be put in the form of a declaration.[97]

(b) Statements to the legal adviser of the accused are confidential and cannot be admitted without the accused's consent.[98]

(c) Although in one case [99] a voluntary statement made verbally to a clergyman was admitted as evidence, the position regarding statements to clergymen is not clear.[1]

(d) Statements to relatives and to private individuals, even if made in answer to questions, may competently be proved, provided they are not extracted [2] and the person in question is not acting in any official capacity.[3]

Thus, in a murder trial a statement made voluntarily by the accused to a police surgeon who was examining the body of the deceased in order to ascertain the cause of death was admitted,[4] but a statement made by a

---

[93] *John Proudfoot* (1882) 4 Couper 590; *Catherine Beaton or Bethune* (1856) 2 Irv. 457; *May Grant* (1862) 4 Irv. 183.

[94] *Waddell* v. *Kinnaird*, 1922 J.C. 40; *Morrison* v. *Burrell*, 1947 J.C. 43. Cf. *Philip Turner and Peter Rennie* (1853) 1 Irv. 284.

[95] *Peter Campbell*, Glasgow High Court, November 1965, unreported.

[96] Cf. *H.M. Adv.* v. *Campbell*, 1964 J.C. 80; *H.M. Adv.* v. *Cairns*, 1967 J.C. 37, where the Crown presumably intended to lead evidence of a statement made to the press.

[97] *Macdonald*, 314; *Dickson on Evidence*, para. 349; *Robt. Emond* (1830) Bell's Notes 243; *Hendry and Craighead* (1857) 2 Irv. 618.

[98] *Walker and Walker on Evidence*, pp. 414–416; *H.M. Adv.* v. *Parker*, 1944 J.C. 49.

[99] *Isobel Cuthbert* (1842) 1 Broun 311.

[1] *Macdonald*, 315; *Dickson on Evidence*, para. 1684; *Janet Hope or Walker* (1845) 2 Broun 465; *McLaughlin* v. *Douglas and Kidston* (1863) 4 Irv. 273; *David Ross* (1859) 3 Irv. 434.

[2] *Macdonald*, 315; *Dickson on Evidence*, para. 345.

[3] *May Grant* (1862) 4 Irv. 183; *H.M. Adv.* v. *Parker, supra* (statement made to brother while in prison admissible).

[4] *H.M. Adv.* v. *Duff* (1910) 6 Adam 248.

woman charged with child murder to the wife of a police constable to whose house the accused had been brought after arrest was rejected.[5]

(e) The admissibility of statements made to officials other than police officials depends on the circumstances of each case.[6] It does not seem to be a matter of competency so much as of fairness.[7]

A statement made by a person in the navy to his superior officer was rejected as not being voluntary,[8] as were statements made to a Kirk Session in response to questions,[9] and a confession of parentage of an incestuous child extorted by an inspector of poor.[10]

(f) Expressions uttered during sleep have been admitted,[11] but the propriety of so doing is open to very serious question.[12]

Objections to admissibility of statements

8-44   Where a statement alleged to have been made by the accused is challenged at his trial, evidence of the circumstances of its taking, including any evidence by and for the accused, should be led outwith the presence of the jury.[13] The judge must then decide whether to admit the evidence. If he does so decide the trial is resumed before the jury and the Crown evidence as to the taking of the statement led again before them. The accused may lead his evidence on this matter with the rest of the evidence for the defence. The jury are then entitled to consider both whether the statement was voluntary and whether they regard it as reliable. In *Chalmers*[14] Lord Justice-Clerk Thomson rejected the suggestion that the judge should direct the jury whether the statement was voluntarily made, describing the situation as one in which logic must yield since, " It is impossible to ask a jury to accept as an item of evidence a statement made by an accused while preventing it from considering the circumstances under which it was made." [15]

This trial-within-a-trial procedure has been followed since *Chalmers* and can presumably be abandoned only after a full bench of seven or more judges overrule this aspect of *Chalmers*. or when the matter has been dealt with by legislation. In *Thompson* v. *H.M. Adv.*,[16] however, the court expressed disapproval of the procedure. Lord Justice-General Clyde said that experience had revealed undesirable features in it. It led to the repetition of evidence and therefore lengthened trials and it allowed the reconstruction of evidence for the second " trial " without the jury being able to

---

[5] *May Grant*, supra.
[6] Macdonald, 314.
[7] Ibid.
[8] *Turner and Rennie* (1853) 1 Irv. 284.
[9] *Isobel Cuthbert*, supra.
[10] *Robertson and Bennet* (1853) 1 Irv. 219.
[11] *Dickson on Evidence*, para. 351; *Robt. Emond* (1830) Bell's Notes 243.
[12] Macdonald, 315; cf. *Patrick Connolly Meehan*, Petnr., 1969 S.L.T. (Notes) 90.
[13] *Chalmers* v. *H.M. Adv.*, 1954 J.C. 66.
[14] Supra.
[15] At 83; contrast the English position where voluntariness is a question for the judge alone: *R.* v. *Burgess* [1968] 2 Q.B. 112; *Chan Wei Keung* v. *The Queen* [1967] 2 A.C. 160.
[16] 1968 J.C. 61.

test the consistency of the evidence heard by them with that led in their absence. Lord Clyde said that if the jury had to decide whether the confession was voluntary it was difficult to justify a separate trial before the judge alone. He suggested that the evidence should be led before the jury and that the judge should then direct them to disregard it if he thought the confession was not shown to have been freely and voluntarily given.

Where inadmissible evidence is led of a statement by the accused the conviction will be quashed unless it is supported by sufficient other evidence.[17]

Duty to give information to police

18-45   Some statutes impose a duty on persons, who may include the perpetrators of the offence being investigated, to give information to the police.[18] Statements made by virtue of these provisions are admissible even when incriminating.[19]

The most important of these provisions in practice is section 232 of the Road Traffic Act 1960 which makes it an offence to fail to give certain information when required " by or on behalf of a chief officer of police." [20] It is not necessary that the requiring constable be authorised to make the inquiry in question, it is sufficient for a chief constable to post a notice authorising all his force to exercise the powers contained in section 232 on his behalf.[21]

Admissibility of statements in trial on different charge

18-46   If A makes an admission in relation to one charge, can that statement be used in his trial on another charge arising out of the same species facti? Where the first charge is a more serious one, the statement can be used.[22] Where the more serious charge is the second one the position is not quite so clear. In *H.M. Adv.* v. *Cunningham* [23] a statement on a charge of assault to the danger of life was admitted in a subsequent trial for murder, but in the earlier case of *James Stewart*,[24] the court refused to admit a declaration on a charge of assault to the danger of life in a subsequent trial for murder. In *McKie* v. *H.M. Adv.*[25] the accused was medically examined on a charge of driving while unfit through drink under the elaborate safeguards provided for such cases, and the court allowed the evidence of the examination to be received in his subsequent trial for

[17] *Brown* v. *Macpherson*, 1918 J.C. 3; *Waddell* v. *Kinnaird*, 1922 J.C. 40; *Chalmers* v. *H.M. Adv.*, supra.

[18] E.g. Road Traffic Act 1960, ss. 225, 226, 228, 229, 231, 232; Vehicles Excise Act 1971, s. 27; Official Secrets Act 1920, s. 6.

[19] *Foster* v. *Farrell*, 1963 J.C. 46. Cf. Weights and Measures Act 1963, s. 49, which reserves the right not to incriminate oneself.

[20] See *Foster* v. *Farrell*, 1963 J.C. 46.

[21] *Gray* v. *Farrell*, 1969 S.L.T. 250.

[22] *MacDougall* v. *Maclullich* (1887) 1 White 328 (assault and mobbing reduced to breach of the peace); *Willis* v. *H.M. Adv.*, 1941 J.C. 1 (murder reduced to culpable homicide).

[23] 1939 J.C. 61.

[24] (1866) 5 Irv. 310.

[25] 1958 J.C. 24.

culpable homicide, on what seem to have been general grounds of public policy. In *McAdam* v. *H.M. Adv.*[26] a statement made on a charge of assault to severe injury was allowed in a trial for attempted murder. In that case the test of fairness to the accused was described as being singularly unhelpful in matters of this kind. It was held that the statement was admissible only if each charge fell into the same category, for example, dishonesty or personal violence, and if each covered *substantially* the same facts. Accordingly, a reply to a charge of assault could be used in a trial for aggravated assault, culpable homicide, " or even non-capital murder (which is essentially now a form of aggravated assault)." [27] In *H.M. Adv.* v. *Graham* [28] the court rejected a statement made on a charge of assault causing grievous bodily harm in a trial for capital murder, but in *H.M. Adv.* v. *Taylor* [29] a statement on a charge of murder was admitted by Lord Wheatley in a trial for capital murder and robbery on the ground that the offences there all fell into a single category.

Res gestae

8-47   Subject to the foregoing remarks, it may be said generally that all statements made by the accused at the time of the offence may be proved.[30] If the statements are connected with the crime in some relevant way they are admissible as being part of the res gestae. The general rule that hearsay is inadmissible suffers an exception in the case of the accused, whose statements may be proved although not reduced to writing.[31] Thus, a narrative dictated before the crime by the accused to a friend, in order that the latter might embody it in a letter, was admitted in evidence, although the letter written was not produced.[32] Statements indicating malice antecedent to the acts charged may be proved by the prosecutor, on giving fair notice in the indictment.[33] So expressions indicating murderous intent, uttered by the panel two years before a murder, have been allowed to be proved,[34] and, in another murder case, proof of threats made fourteen days prior to the murder was admitted.[35] Statements indicating malice uttered a short time after the offence may also be proved.[36] Thus, words used by the accused twenty-four hours after a murder, betraying anger against the murdered woman, were held to be competent evidence against him, as matter arising de recenti, and, in fact, forming part of the res gestae.[37]

[26] 1960 J.C. 1.
[27] Ibid, L.J.-G. at 4.
[28] 1958 S.L.T. 167.
[29] 1963 S.L.T. 53.
[30] Macdonald, 305 et seq.
[31] Ibid. 311.
[32] *Mary Downie* (1865) 5 Irv. 202.
[33] Macdonald, 306; *H.M. Adv.* v. *Flanders*, 1962 J.C. 25; cf. *H.M. Adv.* v. *Kennedy*, infra.
[34] *David Ross* (1859) 3 Irv. 434.
[35] *H.M. Adv.* v. *Kennedy* (1907) 347; not followed in *Flanders*, supra.
[36] Macdonald, 306.
[37] *John Stewart* (1855) 2 Irv. 166.

Statements by the accused are not evidence in his favour.[38] Thus, although, in charges of rioting, it may be proved that the accused, before the outbreak, had addressed the people, instigating and inciting them to lawless acts,[39] a prisoner so charged was not permitted to lead evidence that prior to the riotous assembly he had advised certain individuals to have nothing to do with it.[40] So, also, where a woman was charged with child murder, she was not allowed to put her own letters in evidence in order to prove that she was ignorant of the probable date of conception and that her confinement came suddenly upon her.[41] Where, however, what is said by the accused is part of the res gestae, it may be proved, not as proof of the facts, but for the purpose of showing that he had from the outset denied guilt, or told a consistent tale.[42]

Evidence of Co-accused and Accomplices

18–48   The right of an accused person to cross-examine a co-accused whose testimony tends to incriminate him has already been noticed.[43] The following points may also be mentioned:

18–49   1. Where two or more persons are charged jointly they may put up (a) a joint defence, or (b) separate defences, which may be inconsistent or conflicting. In the first case, the evidence of each on his own behalf is evidence against all, because their case is one and indivisible.[44] The second case, is more difficult. If the testimony of one accused when called as a witness on his own application does not tend to incriminate another accused it is arguable that the prosecutor alone has the right to cross-examine.[45] If, however, the evidence in chief does tend to incriminate a co-accused, that person has a right to cross-examine, for the evidence is admissible against him, as, also, is the evidence elicited by the prosecutor in cross.[46]

18–50   2. Each of several co-accused can give evidence on his own behalf, but one accused cannot as long as the case is sub judice call a co-accused to give evidence on his behalf unless the trials have been separated.[47]

18–51   3. The prosecutor may call one of several co-accused as a witness, but he cannot afterwards prosecute him for the crime.[48]

18–52   4. Where several accused are charged jointly the prosecutor is not entitled to adduce as a witness against any of them a person who is incompetent as a witness for the prosecution against one of them.[49]

---

[38] Macdonald, 316; Hume, ii. 401; *H.M. Adv.* v. *Macleod and Ors.* (1888) 1 White 554.
[39] *Donald Macrae and Ors.* (1888) 1 White 543.
[40] *Alex. Macleod and Ors.* (1888) 1 White 554.
[41] *H.M. Adv.* v. *Scott* (1892) 3 White 240.
[42] Macdonald, 316; *Neil Moran and Ors.* (1836) Bell's Notes 285; *John Forrest* (1837) 1 Swin. 404; *Jane Pye* (1838) 2 Swin. 187; cf. *Brown* v. *H.M. Adv.*, 1964 J.C. 10.
[43] Supra, para. 18–17.
[44] *Young* v. *H.M. Adv.*, 1932 J.C. 63, L.J.-G. at 72.
[45] Macdonald, 337; *Gemmel and McFadyen* v. *MacNiven*, 1928 J.C. 5; see supra, para. 18–17.
[46] Macdonald, 337, 338; *Young* v. *H.M. Adv.*, supra, L.J.-G. at 74.
[47] Macdonald, 291; Criminal Evidence Act 1898, s. 1 (*a*).
[48] *Todd* v. *Priestly* (1905) 4 Adam 605, L.J.-C. at 607; supra, para. 9–22.
[49] Macdonald, 337; Alison, ii. 533.

8-53   5. Where several persons are brought to trial and the evidence of a co-accused is desired, the only course open to the other accused is to move that the trials be separated.[50] It is in the discretion of the Court to grant or refuse this motion.[51]

8-54   6. Where the trials have been separated the accused who is under trial may examine the other accused provided that he has given notice to the prosecutor.[52]

8-55   7. Where one accused pleads guilty, and the plea is accepted, he is a competent witness for the prosecutor or for the other accused.[53] The proper course is either to sentence him or to delay sentence and order him to be detained in custody until called for examination.[54]

8-56   8. If no motion is made to separate the trials, and no plea tendered, one accused, against whom during the trial the charge is departed from but in respect of whom a verdict of acquittal has not been returned, cannot be examined in exculpation of another accused as of right.[55]

8-57   9. Where the prosecutor gives up the case against any of the persons accused, such person may be allowed to be examined as a witness for those still under charge if the court see fit to allow the examination.[56]

Evidence of accomplices

8-58   Where part of the evidence against an accused consists of that of an accomplice, it is necessary for the judge to warn the jury that they must regard the accomplice's evidence with special care (cum nota).[57] No special words are necessary; it is enough to make plain to the jury the need for careful scrutiny of the accomplice's evidence.[58] The rule rests on the idea that an accomplice may have an interest to blame someone else for the crime in which he was involved, but it applies whether or not the accomplice has already been dealt with for the offence, and therefore whether or not he is acquiring immunity from prosecution by giving evidence. A person is an accomplice if he has been charged with the same offence as the accused, or if he admits his guilt of that offence when giving evidence.[59] For the purposes of this rule thief and resetter are treated as

---

[50] Macdonald, 291; *Margt. McFadyen and Ors.* (1857) 2 Irv. 599; *John Nicolson and Ors.* (1887) 1 White 307.

[51] Macdonald, 291; *Sangster* v. *H.M. Adv.* (1896) 2 Adam 182; *Morrison* v. *Adair*, 1943 J.C. 25. See also supra, para. 10–19.

[52] Macdonald, 291; *Bell and Shaw* v. *Houston* (1842) 1 Broun 49; *Thomson*, infra; *Mitchell and Ors.* (1887) 1 White 321. Notice is, of course, not necessary in summary trials. But the co-accused should not remain in court during the evidence or he may be rejected as incompetent on that ground: infra, para. 18–80.

[53] *Todd* v. *Priestly* (1905) 4 Adam 605; *Bell and Shaw* v. *Houston*, supra; *Thomson* v. *H.M. Adv.* (1892) 3 White 321; Macdonald, 291.

[54] Macdonald, 291; *Brown and Macleish* (1856) 2 Irv. 577; *Agnes Wilson and Ors.* (1860) 3 Irv. 623.

[55] *Margt. McFadyen and Ors.* (1857) 2 Irv. 599; Macdonald, 291.

[56] Macdonald, 291, 292; *Thos. Henderson and Ors.* (1850) J. Shaw 394; *Nicolson*, supra.

[57] *Dow* v. *McKnight*, 1949 J.C. 38; *Wallace* v. *H.M. Adv.*, 1952 J.C. 78.

[58] *Slowey* v. *H.M. Adv.*, 1965 S.L.T. 309.

[59] *Wallace* v. *H.M. Adv.*, supra; *H.M. Adv.* v. *Murdoch and Ors.*, 1955 S.L.T.(Notes) 57. For the limitations of the meaning of socius criminis, see *McGinley and Dowds* v. *MacLeod*, 1963 J.C. 11; *Slowey* v. *H.M. Adv.*, supra.

accomplices in one offence.[60] Failure to give the necessary warning will
normally lead to the quashing of the conviction unless there is sufficient
other evidence in the case to support it, or perhaps unless the evidence of
the accomplice is not material.[61] The jury are entitled to believe the evidence of the accomplice once they have been duly warned, and it is competent to convict on the evidence of two accomplices, uncorroborated by any
other evidence.[62] Before the rule can be applied it must be clear that the
witness is an accomplice, a socius criminis; mere suspicion of his involvement does not oblige the court either to give the warning or to enquire into
the facts to determine whether the suspicion is well founded. In the absence of an actual conviction against the witness he will probably not be
treated as a socius criminis unless he admits his complicity in evidence. It
has been suggested that the Crown should draw the court's attention to the
need for a warning in appropriate cases.[63]

   The rule does not apply to one of a number of co-accused giving evidence on his own behalf,[64] or even giving evidence which incriminates his
co-accused.[65] Indeed, to give a warning in such a case is improper, since
it prejudices the accused who gives evidence [66] and who is entitled to be
treated like any other witness and to have the benefit of the presumption of
innocence.[67] Although it is wrong to direct the jury that they must as a
matter of law view cum nota that part of an accused's evidence which
incriminates his co-accused it is apparently not wrong to suggest that they
may wish so to view it.[68] The rule requiring a warning applies to witnesses
called by the Crown, and therefore not to co-accused; it probably does not
apply to other defence witnesses either.[69]

Corroboration

18-59   " By the law of Scotland, no person can be convicted of a crime or a
            statutory offence, except when the Legislature otherwise directs,
            unless there is evidence of at least two witnesses implicating the
            person accused with the commission of the crime or offence with
            which he is charged." [70]

   This rule does not require every circumstance to be proved by two
witnesses.[71] The basic requirement is that the offence be brought home to

[60] Dow v. McKnight, supra; Brown v. McPherson, 1918 J.C. 3; Wallace v. H.M. Adv., supra;
     Murdoch and Ors., supra.
[61] Wallace v. H.M. Adv., supra; Slowey v. H.M. Adv., supra.
[62] Dow v. McKnight, 1949 J.C. 38; Brown v. McPherson, 1918 J.C. 3.
[63] Murdoch and Ors., supra.
[64] Martin v. H.M. Adv., 1960 S.L.T. 213.
[65] Slowey v. H.M. Adv., 1965 S.L.T. 309; McGuinness v. H.M. Adv., 1971 S.L.T.(Notes) 7.
[66] Martin, supra.
[67] Martin, supra; Slowey, supra.   [68] McGuinness, supra.
[69] Cf. Slowey, supra.
[70] Morton v. H.M. Adv., 1938 J.C. 50, at p. 55. See also Dickson on Evidence, para. 1807;
     Lockwood v. Walker (1909) 6 Adam 124; Harrison v. Mackenzie, 1923 J.C. 61; Townsend
     v. Strathern, 1923 J.C. 66.
[71] Hume, ii. 384–386; Alison, ii. 551; Scott v. Jameson (1914) 7 Adam 529; Gillespie v. Mac-
     millan, 1957 J.C. 31; see " Corroboration of Evidence in Scottish Criminal Law " 1958
     S.L.T.(News) 137; W. A. Wilson, " The Logic of Corroboration " (1960) 76 S.L.R. 101.

the accused by evidence from at least two sources. Only essential circumstances require to be separately corroborated. It has been held necessary to corroborate the age of the complainer in a charge of unlawful carnal knowledge [72]; the identity of the accused [73]; the identity of a vessel charged with illegal trawling [74]; the accused's knowledge of the falsity of representations in a charge of fraud. [75] It is not necessary to corroborate essential matters of procedure, such as that the accused was duly informed of his rights before submitting to medical examination on a charge of driving while unfit through drink. [76] It is not necessary in a charge of theft by housebreaking or by opening lockfast places to corroborate that the house or place was locked. [77] Where the accused is found in possession of allegedly stolen goods the theft is sufficiently proved by the uncorroborated evidence of the owner that these were his goods and were stolen. Where the goods are not recovered the fact that the articles libelled in the indictment as stolen were stolen must be proved by corroborated evidence. [78] In all these cases it is of course also necessary to lead corroborated evidence implicating the accused in the theft. It is unnecessary to lead evidence of a post-mortem dissection from two doctors in homicide cases, but this is regarded as the proper practice, although the cause of death can be proved without a post mortem at all. [79] It may be that the only fact of which one can say that it must always be corroborated is the identity of the accused, which is seen as being in a different category from any other fact in issue. [80]

Identification of accused

8–60   The simplest cases are those where there are two eye-witnesses to the accused's involvement in the offence. In that situation the Crown must merely ensure that the accused is properly identified in court by the two witnesses. This is normally done by having the witnesses point him out as he sits in the dock. It is not enough for a witness to say that he saw the accused commit the crime and name him; he must point him out. [81] This rule does not, of course, apply to trials in absence where the accused must be linked with the offence in some other way. [82] Evidence that a witness identified the accused at an earlier stage, for example at an identification parade, [83] or at the scene of the crime, [84] may be sufficient. So if, as in

[72] *Lockwood* v. *Walker* (1910) 6 Adam 124.
[73] *Morton* v. *H.M. Adv.*, 1938 J.C. 50; cf. *Burrows* v. *H.M. Adv.*, 1951 S.L.T.(Notes) 70.
[74] *Harrison* v. *Mackenzie*, 1923 J.C. 61.
[75] *Townsend* v. *Strathern*, 1923 J.C. 66.
[76] *Farrell* v. *Concannon*, 1957 J.C. 12; cf. Road Safety Act 1967, s. 2 (1); *MacLeod* v. *Nicol*; *Torrance* v. *Thaw*, 1970 S.L.T. 304.
[77] *Richard Cameron* (1839) 2 Swin. 447; *James Davidson* (1841) 2 Swin. 630.
[78] *McDonald* v. *Herron*, 1966 S.L.T. 61.
[79] *Brown* v. *H.M. Adv.*, 1964 J.C. 10.
[80] *Morton*, supra; *Gillespie* v. *Macmillan*, supra, L.J.G. at 37.
[81] *Bruce* v. *H.M. Adv.*, 1936 J.C. 93; *Wilson* v. *Brown*, 1947 J.C. 81, 96.
[82] Cf. *Wilson* v. *Brown*, supra.
[83] *Walker & Walker on Evidence*, 406; cf. Macdonald, 325; Alison, ii. 627.
[84] *McGaharon* v. *H.M. Adv.*, 1968 S.L.T.(Notes) 99.

McGaharon v. *H.M. Adv.*,[85] two police constables can point out the accused as the person identified to them on an earlier occasion by a witness, and the witness gives evidence that the person he earlier identified to the police constables was the perpetrator of the crime, that is equivalent to a direct identification by one witness. It must, of course, be corroborated by another identification, direct or indirect, or by other facts and circumstances.

In *McGaharon* [85] the eye-witnesses stated that they were unable to identify the accused in court because of lapse of memory. In *Muldoon* v. *Herron* [86] neither of the two witnesses to a disturbance identified the accused in court, being apparently afraid to do so. One of them gave evidence similar to that in *McGaharon,* while the other denied that the accused were involved in the disturbance or that she had ever identified them to the police. However she also gave evidence (or so the High Court inferred from the stated case and additional reports on the evidence made by the sheriff at the court's request) that she had identified the perpetrators of the disturbance to the police. The police gave evidence that both witnesses had identified the accused to them shortly after the disturbance. A Full Bench endorsed *McGaharon,* and held (diss. Lord Wheatley) that in the case of the second witness the sheriff was entitled to reject her denials, and that the result of that was to leave her evidence in the same state as that of the first witness. Applying *McGaharon* the majority of the court accordingly upheld the conviction. It should be stressed that the decision depended on the fact that the second witness's evidence included a statement that she had pointed out the culprits to the police: without that essential link, the police evidence of her earlier identification would have been no more than hearsay.[87]

18–61   Identification of the accused need not be by persons who have seen him, it may be by persons who have heard him and recognised his voice.[88]

An accused may also be identified by fingerprint evidence, or by evidence of a palm print or footprint, and it is competent to convict on the basis of such evidence alone.[89] The evidence of two witnesses to the presence of the fingerprint and the evidence of two experts that it is identical with fingerprints made by the accused in the presence of two witnesses is treated as equivalent to the identification of the accused at the scene by two eye-witnesses and not as evidence all deriving from one source, the fingerprint. This is the case whether the finding of the print, the taking of the print from the accused, and the identification of the two prints, are spoken to by the same two witnesses or not. It is not altogether clear to what extent evidence of handwriting is sufficient identification.[90]

[85] Supra.
[86] 1970 S.L.T. 228.
[87] L.J.-C. at 232; Lord Cameron at 238.
[88] *McGiveran* v. *Auld* (1894) 1 Adam 448; *Burrows* v. *H.M. Adv.*, 1951 S.L.T.(Notes) 69.
[89] *H.M. Adv.* v. *Rolley,* 1945 J.C. 155; *Hamilton* v. *H.M. Adv.*, 1934 J.C. 1.
[90] See *Richardson* v. *Clark*, 1957 J.C. 7; it was held sufficient in *Camilleri* v. *MacLeod* (1965) 29 J.C.L. 126; but see *Walter Scott Ellis*, Edin. High Court, Feb. 1965, unreported.

18-62   Where the accused is identified by one eye-witness the Crown must produce evidence of some circumstance or circumstances corroborating the identification. The circumstance must be such as to connect the accused with the crime, but the degree of connection required will vary with each case. The corroborating evidence need probably not in itself point unequivocally to guilt.[91]

Corroboration of a confession

18-63   The making of a confession need not itself be corroborated.[92] A confession alone, irrespective of how many witnesses speak to its making, is insufficient. This is so even when it is contained in a judicial declaration.[93] Again, any number of confessions are insufficient to convict, since a witness cannot corroborate himself. The amount of evidence needed to corroborate a confession depends on the circumstances of the case and especially on the circumstances and reliability of the confession.[94] An indisputably genuine confession may in some circumstances be corroborated by evidence that the accused was one of a number of persons at the locus, or perhaps that he was the registered owner of the vehicle involved in the incident out of which the charge arose.[95]

18-64   Where the accused makes a circumstantial confession describing, for example, where he buried the body or hid the stolen goods,[96] evidence that the body or goods were found where the confession indicated can corroborate the confession.[97]

Circumstantial evidence

18-65   Where the evidence is wholly circumstantial the only general principle is that the law requires a minimum of two circumstances, each spoken to by one witness,[98] although it will not be often that convictions are obtained without a little more than this.[99] It has been held that where one police constable gives evidence that he started a stop-watch as the accused's car passed him and another gives evidence that he started his stop-watch as the car passed him a measured distance ahead of the first constable, the two constables corroborate each other, and the accused's speed is proved by comparison of the watches.[1]

In one case evidence was led of the activities of a tracker dog to link

---

[91] Cf. *Sinclair* v. *Clark*, 1962 J.C. 57; *Sinclair* v. *MacLeod*, 1964 S.L.T. 197.
[92] *Mills* v. *H.M. Adv.*, 1935 J.C. 77; *Innes* v. *H.M. Adv.*, 1955 S.L.T.(Notes) 69.
[93] Macdonald, 334; *Dickson on Evidence*, para. 339; Hume, ii. 324; Alison, ii. 578–579; *Duncan and McKenzie* (1831) Bell's Notes, 239; *Thomas Hunter* (1838) 2 Swin. 1; *Banaghan* v. *H.M. Adv.* (1888) 1 White 566.
[94] *Sinclair* v. *Clark*, supra.
[95] *Sinclair* v. *Clark*, supra; *Sinclair* v. *MacLeod*, supra; cf. *Foster* v. *Farrell*, 1963 J.C. 46.
[96] *Manuel* v. *H.M. Adv.*, 1958 J.C. 41; *Allan* v. *Hamilton*, 1972 S.L.T.(Notes) 2.
[97] *Manuel*, supra; *Connolly* v. *H.M. Adv.*, 1958 S.L.T. 79; *Allan* v. *Hamilton*, supra; Alison, ii, 580.
[98] Cf. *Gillespie* v. *MacMillan*, 1957 J.C. 31.
[99] Cf. *Houston* v. *Leslie*, 1958 J.C. 8.
[1] *Gillespie* v. *MacMillan*, supra; cf. *Houston* v. *Leslie*, supra; but see " Corroboration of Evidence in Scottish Criminal Law," 1958 S.L.T.(News) 137; W. A. Wilson, "The Logic of Corroboration" (1960) 76 S.L.R. 101.

the accused with the crime through an article left by him at the scene. There was some corroboration in the form of an admission by the accused that he had been near the scene of the crime dressed and equipped to commit it, but no admission that he had committed it. The evidence was held to be sufficient.[2] A charge of careless driving may be proved by evidence of marks on the road in the absence of any eye-witness evidence as to the driving of the car at all.[3] Evidence that a vehicle travelling at right angles to the accused's car crossed traffic lights at green and collided with the accused's car, in the absence of any evidence that the lights were not operating normally at about the time of the accident, is sufficient to prove that when the accused crossed the lights they were at red for him.[4]

Where proof of the charge depends on measurements made by instruments it is necessary to prove but probably not, despite the elaborate practice in trials for speeding, to corroborate every element of the proof of the accuracy of the instruments.[5]

The rule in Moorov

18–66   Where the accused is charged with a series of similar offences, closely linked in time [6] and circumstances, the evidence of one witness as to each offence will be taken as mutually corroborative, each offence being treated as if it were an element in a single course of conduct.[7] This rule, known as the rule in *Moorov*,[8] was thought at one time to be limited to sexual offences and to be explained by the difficulty of obtaining corroboration in such cases, but it has been applied to bribery,[9] to assault [10] and to reset.[11] The offences must all form the subject of charges before the jury; evidence may not be led of any uncharged incidents, or even of charges in the indictment to which the accused has pled guilty.[12] It has been held that evidence of sodomy and evidence of incest are not mutually corroborative [13]; it has also been held that while a charge of lewd and libidinous practices may be corroborated by evidence of incest, at least where the incest was preceded by similar lewd acts, evidence of lewd practices does not corroborate a charge of incest.[14]

[2] *Patterson* v. *Nixon*, 1960 J.C. 42; cf. *R.* v. *Lindsay* (1970) N.Z.L.R. 1002.
[3] *Ryrie* v. *Campbell*, 1964 J.C. 33.
[4] *Pacitti* v. *Copeland*, 1963 S.L.T.(Notes) 52.
[5] See *Grierson* v. *Clark*, 1958 J.C. 22; *Farrell* v. *Simpson*, 1959 S.L.T.(Sh.Ct.) 23.
[6] See *H.M. Adv.* v. *A. E.*, 1937 J.C. 96; *Ogg* v. *H.M. Adv.*, 1938 J.C. 152; *H.M. Adv.* v. *Cox*, 1962 J.C. 27.
[7] Hume, ii, 385; Alison, ii, 551; *Dickson on Evidence*, paras. 1807–1810; *H.M. Adv.* v. *Bickerstaff*, 1926 J.C. 65, 82; *H.M. Adv.* v. *McDonald*, 1928 J.C. 42; *Moorov* v. *H.M. Adv.*, 1930 J.C. 68; *H.M. Adv.* v. *A. E.*, supra; *Ogg* v. *H.M. Adv.*, supra; *Burgh* v. *H.M. Adv.*, 1944 J.C. 77; *H.M. Adv.* v. *McQuade*, 1951 J.C. 143; *McCudden* v. *H.M. Adv.*, 1952 J.C. 86; *Harrison* v. *Clark*, 1958 J.C. 3; cf. *Michlek* v. *Michlek*, 1971 S.L.T.(Notes) 50.
[8] 1930 J.C. 68.
[9] *H.M. Adv.* v. *McQuade*, supra.
[10] *McCudden* v. *H.M. Adv.*, supra.
[11] *Harris* v. *Clark*, supra.
[12] *Walsh* v. *H.M. Adv.*, 1961 J.C. 51.
[13] *H.M. Adv.* v. *Cox*, 1962 J.C. 27.
[14] *H.M. Adv.* v. *Brown*, 1969 J.C. 72.

Statutory exceptions to need for corroboration

8–67   Several Acts of Parliament [15] provide that persons accused of contravening their provisions may be convicted on the evidence of one credible witness. In these cases one witness whom the court believes is enough,[16] even although there is no penuria testium and others might have been called,[17] and even although the prosecutor calls two witnesses, only one of whom supports the charge.[18] Where a statute gives power to the justices to convict on the testimony of one witness, the same power is impliedly conferred on the sheriff if the complaint is brought before him under section 7 (2) of the 1954 Act.[19]

Miscellaneous Rules

Witness's name must be on list of witnesses

18–68   This rule, which applies to solemn procedure only, does not apply to the case of the accused giving evidence on his own behalf.[20] The rule is subject to the provisions of the Criminal Procedure Act 1921, which makes it competent for the prosecutor, but only with the leave of the court, to examine a witness not included in the lists lodged by him, provided that written notice containing the proposed witness's name and address has been given to the accused not less than two clear days before the trial.

Witnesses who are not in the lists lodged may be examined to prove previous convictions [21] and incidental matters such as the competency of a witness,[22] the lodging of a production or the execution of a citation.[23] Any question as to the accused's declaration may similarly be dealt with.[24] The accused may, at the desire of the court, examine a witness in causa, though not included in the list.[25] The court may, on cause shown before the jury is sworn, allow the accused to examine witnesses not on the lists,[26] and, even where such cause has not been shown, may, at least with the consent of the prosecutor, allow such witnesses to be examined.[27]

Prosecutor and counsel as witness

18–69   A public prosecutor conducting a case may not be examined as a witness, and the fact that he has been is a good ground for quashing the

[15] e.g. Salmon and Freshwater Fisheries (Protection) (Scotland) Act 1951 and the earlier Salmon Fisheries Act 1868 (as to which, see *Jopp* v. *Pirie* (1869) 1 Couper 240); Game (Scotland) Act 1832 (*Lees* v. *Macdonald* (1893) 3 White 468); Poaching Prevention Act 1862 (*Anderson* v. *Macdonald*, infra); Road Traffic Act 1960, s. 14 (*Sutherland* v. *Aitchison*, 1970 S.L.T.(Notes) 48). See also *Gerber* v. *British Railways Board*, 1969 J.C. 7.
[16] *Anderson* v. *Macdonald* (1910) 6 Adam 229; *Manson* v. *Macleod*, 1918 J.C. 60.
[17] *Jopp* v. *Pirie* (1869) 1 Couper 240.
[18] *Coventry* v. *Brown*, 1926 J.C. 20.
[19] *Lawrence* v. *Ames*, 1921 J.C. 87.
[20] Criminal Evidence Act 1898, s. 5.
[21] 1887 Act, s. 35.
[22] Macdonald, 338; *Thos. Mackenzie or McKenna* (1869) 1 Couper 244 (medical witnesses not on list examined as to state of mind of a witness on list).
[23] Circuit Courts (Scotland) Act 1828, s. 7.
[24] 1887 Act, s. 69.
[25] Macdonald, 338; *Smith and Campbell* (1855) 2 Irv. 1, 40.
[26] 1887 Act, s. 36.
[27] *Lowson* v. *H.M. Adv.*, 1943 J.C. 141; Macdonald, 338.

conviction.[28] If he is not actually conducting the case he is a competent witness.[29] A defence solicitor or counsel is, on the other hand, a competent witness for his client.[30] Witnesses should not be present in court prior to giving evidence, but the court has a discretion to allow a witness to give evidence although he has heard the evidence of other witnesses.[31] The court cannot refuse to hear evidence from the accused's agent or counsel on this ground.

Expert witnesses

18–70   There are special rules for expert witnesses. For example, medical men, who are called to give their opinion on the facts, may of consent be, and usually are, permitted to remain in court while witnesses to the facts are giving evidence.[32] The court has, however, a discretion in this matter and it may refuse to grant the privilege,[33] both where the accused opposes [34] and where he asks for [35] the same. An expert witness should be excluded from the court during the evidence of other experts [36] at any rate while they are giving their opinions.[37] An expert witness who has been in court during the previous part of the trial cannot be examined on the facts of the case, but only on matters of opinion.[38]

Mentally disordered witnesses

18–71   A witness may be rendered inadmissible by reason of mental disorder. whether occurring at the time of the incident he witnessed, at the time of the trial, or between the incident and the trial,[39] if the mental illness is such as to affect his capacity as a witness.[40] Inability from weakness of intellect to understand and take an oath or to have any notion of a future state has been held to disqualify witnesses,[41] but in one case [42] Lord McLaren expressed the opinion that an imbecile or weak-minded person who was unable to understand the taking of an oath, might be examined if " shown to be capable of making a correct and truthful statement respecting facts as to which he or she is not likely to be mistaken." In one case [43] the court

---

[28] *Ferguson* v. *Webster* (1869) 1 Couper 370; *Grahams* v. *McLennan* (1910) 6 Adam 315.
[29] *Mackintosh* v. *Wooster*, 1919 J.C. 15. See supra, para. 10–31.
[30] *Campbell* v. *Cochrane*, 1928 J.C. 25; Macdonald, 294.
[31] Macdonald, 294; infra, para. 18–80.
[32] Macdonald, 295; *H.M. Adv.* v. *Laurie* (1889) 2 White 326.
[33] Macdonald, 295.
[34] *Alex. Dingwall* (1867) 5 Irv. 466.
[35] *Andrew Granger* (1878) 4 Couper 86.
[36] Macdonald, 295; *Edward W. Pritchard* (1865) 5 Irv. 88. See also *Dickson on Evidence*, para. 1761; Alison, ii. 544–5; *Alex. McKenzie* (1827) Syme 158; *Braid* (1834) 6 S.J. 220; *Chas. Donaldson* (1836) Bell's Notes 269; *Alex. Murray* (1858) 3 Irv. 262; *Alex Milne* (1863) 4 Irv. 301. See also *Madeleine Smith* (1857) 2 Irv. 641.
[37] *Mackenzie*, supra; *Donaldson*, supra; cf. *Madeleine Smith*, supra.
[38] Macdonald, 295; *Jas. Newlands* (1833) Bell's Notes 269; *Eliz. Jeffray* (1838) 2 Swin. 113.
[39] *Walker & Walker on Evidence*, 375–376; Macdonald, 288; Hume, ii. 340; *Dickson on Evidence*, para. 1552; Alison, ii. 435–436; *T. Meldrum* (1826) Syme 30.
[40] Macdonald, 288; *Dickson on Evidence*, para. 1551; *Skene Black* (1887) 1 White 365.
[41] Macdonald, 289; *John Murray* (1868) 5 Irv. 232; *Hugh McNamara* (1848) Ark. 521 (when the witness tendered was unable to take the oath or to have any notion of a future state).
[42] *Skene Black*, supra.
[43] *Neil and Gollan* (1858) 3 Irv. 93.

refused to receive a witness who had lost the power of speech and could only indicate an affirmative or negative answer to the questions put, on the ground that there was no proof that, as alleged, the cause of the incapacity was paralysis, or that, if it was, it had not affected the mind.

Defects which do not render a witness non compos mentis, e.g. a memory impaired by old age, only affect credibility.[44] Compulsory detention in a mental hospital is not per se a ground of disqualification.[45] In one case [46] a person who was a patient in a lunatic asylum was examined, but the presiding judge warned the jury that his evidence, although not incompetent, must be received with great caution. In another case,[47] where an attendant in a lunatic asylum was charged with the culpable homicide of a patient, Lord Low allowed the evidence of an epileptic patient who was insane and subject to delusions, but warned them that, as it was impossible to say how much of the witness's evidence was a reliable statement of facts and how much the production of a diseased mind, they could not safely proceed upon it except in so far as it was corroborated by other witnesses.

When a witness is objected to on the ground of mental incapacity the party adducing him may call medical evidence to prove his capacity to understand and give evidence, and the other party may then do likewise to prove the reverse.[48] The names of these witnesses need not be in the lists lodged.[49] The presiding judge then decides the matter upon the medical (and other, if any) evidence before him regarding the state of mind of the witness.[50]

Deaf and dumb witnesses

18–72   These are admissible although they have no education and can converse only by gestures.[51] They may be examined through a sworn interpreter provided they are not inadmissible by reason of mental defect.[52] Their evidence may be taken in the deaf and dumb alphabet or other signs through an interpreter.[53] Where a witness was dumb but not deaf he was sworn and answered questions in writing.[54] Whether or not the witness is sworn depends on his mental capacity.[55] If the accused is deaf and dumb an interpreter will be provided for him.[56]

---

[44] *Dickson on Evidence*, para. 1551; Macdonald, 288–289. Cf. *Nicholson* v. *McAlister* (1829) 7 S. 743; *Riley* v. *McLaren* (1853) 16 D. 323.

[45] *Dickson on Evidence*, para. 1551; Macdonald, 288–289; *Littlejohn and Gall* (1881) 4 Couper 454; *H.M. Adv.* v. *Mackenzie*, supra; *Sheriff and Mitchell* (1866) 5 Irv. 226, supra.

[46] *Littlejohn and Gall*, supra.

[47] *H.M. Adv.* v. *Stott* (1894) 1 Adam 386.

[48] As examples, *Skene Black* (1887) 1 White 365, and *H.M. Adv.* v. *Stott* (1894) 1 Adam 386, may be referred to.

[49] *Thos. McKenzie or McKenna* (1869) 1 Couper 244.

[50] *Black*, supra; *Stott*, supra.

[51] Macdonald, 289; *Farquhar & McGregor* (1833) Bell's Notes 245; *J. S. Montgomery* (1855) 2 Irv. 222; *Geo. Howison* (1871) 2 Couper 153.

[52] Macdonald, 289; *Dickson on Evidence*, paras. 1555–1556; Alison, ii. 436–437.

[53] *Walker & Walker on Evidence*, p. 376; *Robert Reid* (1835) Bell's Notes 246.

[54] *Geo. Howison*, supra.

[55] *Alex Martin* (1823) Shaw 101; *Edw. Rice* (1864) 4 Irv. 493; *J. S. Montgomery*, supra.

[56] Macdonald, 270; Hume, i. 45; *David Smith* (1841) Bell's Notes 231; *Donald Turner* (1861) 4 Irv. 93; *H.M. Adv.* v. *Wilson*, 1942 J.C. 75, 80.

Children

18-73   Children, however young, may be examined if they have sufficient intelligence to understand the obligation to speak the truth.[57] The judge must satisfy himself of this by examination of the child, and, if he considers it necessary, of others.[58] No age limit is fixed by the law.[59] In one case [60] the evidence of a child of three-and-a-half years was admitted after evidence had been led as to what it had said at the time of the offence, but in an earlier case the evidence of a child of three years was rejected.[61] The child's age at the time of the trial is more material than that at the time of the crime, unless the child is very young and the interval between these dates is a long one.[62] The question whether an oath should be administered to a young witness is a question within the discretion of the judge,[63] but children under the age of twelve are not normally sworn, while those over fourteen are.[64]

Reference to prior statements

18-74   It is competent to ask a witness whether on any specified occasion he made a statement pertinent to the issue different to the one made in the witness-box, and, if he denies it, to prove the fact.[65] This rule does not apply to statements made in formal precognitions.[66] A witness cannot be referred to his precognition with a view to confirming his evidence,[67] but he may be cross-examined regarding statements made in a judicial declaration.[68] A witness is entitled to have his signed precognition destroyed before he gives evidence at the trial.[69] It seems that it is incompetent to prove statements made by a witness after he has given evidence in order to discredit his testimony.[70] If it is sought to discredit a witness by reference to a previous statement he should be asked if he made the earlier state-

---

[57] *Walker & Walker on Evidence*, pp. 374–375; Macdonald, 285–286; *Dickson on Evidence* para. 1543; Hume, ii. 341; Alison, ii. 443; Bell's Notes 246–247 (cases of *J. H. Pirie* (1830); *Matthew Baillie* (1830); *John Buchan* (1833); *Jos. Hempson* (1839)); *Walter McBeth* (1867) 5 Irv. 353.

[58] Macdonald, 286; *Dickson on Evidence*, para. 1548.

[59] Macdonald, 286.

[60] *Janet Miller* (1870) 1 Couper 430.

[61] *John Thomson* (1857) 2 Irv. 747. This case was somewhat special.

[62] Macdonald, 286; *Dickson on Evidence*, para. 1547; Hume, ii. 342; Alison, ii. 435.

[63] *Andersons* v. *McFarlane* (1899) 2 Adam 644.

[64] *Walker & Walker*, supra.

[65] Evidence (Scotland) Act 1852, s. 3.

[66] *Kerr* v. *H.M. Adv.*, 1958 J.C. 14; *McNeilie* v. *H.M. Adv.*, 1929 J.C. 50; *Binnie* v. *Black*, 1923 S.L.T. 98; *O'Donnell* v. *McGuire* (1855) 2 Irv. 236; Macdonald, 310; *Walker & Walker on Evidence*, p. 368. A different view was formerly taken, as in *Inch* v. *Inch* (1856) 18 D. 997; *Peter Luke* (1866) 5 Irv. 293; *Alice Robertson* (1873) 2 Couper 495. Statements made to the police in the course of their investigations and not embodied in formal precognition may not be confidential. See Macdonald, 310–311; *Gilmour* v. *Hansen*, 1920 S.C. 598; *Hall* v. *H.M. Adv.*, 1968 S.L.T. 275; *H.M. Adv.* v. *Stark*, 1968 S.L.T.(Notes) 10; see also *Shearer* v. *McLaren*, 1922 S.L.T. 158; *Connolly* v. *N.C.B.*, 1953 S.C. 376.

[67] Macdonald, 311; *J. G. Robertson and Ors.* (1842) 1 Broun 152, 190.

[68] *Agnes Wilson* (1860) 3 Irv. 623.

[69] Hume, ii. 381; Alison, ii. 534–535; Macdonald, 298.

[70] Macdonald, 311; *La Motte* v. *Jardine* (1791) 3 Pat.App. 197; *Begg* v. *Begg* (1887) 14 R. 497; cf. *Anderson* v. *Gill* (1858) 20 D. 1326; 3 Macq. 180.

ment [71] and asked before evidence is led of that statement.[72] This rule may lead to difficulties in criminal cases because of the absence of any right in the Crown to lead evidence in replication,[73] so that the Crown can discredit a defence witness only by leading him themselves.[74]

Insulting or annoying questions

8-75   A judge may disallow a question which he is satisfied is not put bona fide but is merely intended to insult and annoy the witness. Before doing so, however, he should ascertain whether the questioner intends to follow up his question by evidence, and he should, in a summary case, see that the ground of his refusal is noted in the record.[75]

Attacks on witness's character

8-76   As already explained,[76] notice is necessary before the accused is entitled to attack the character of a witness. A distinction, however, falls to be drawn between witnesses who are persons whom the accused is charged with injuring and witnesses who are not.[77]

The accused may prove that a complainer (for example in an assault case) was of a quarrelsome disposition,[78] but he may not normally prove specific acts of violence committed by him.[79] The judge has, however, a discretion to allow such questioning in the interests of justice as in one case [80] where the Crown averred previous malice and ill-will and the accused pled self-defence. A prosecutor is entitled to put a general question as to the peaceable disposition of the injured person [81] or as to the respectability of females alleged to have been abused,[82] even where no notice of attack has been given by the defence.[83] It has been indicated that such questions should not be put before the complainer has given evidence.[84] In cases of injuries to women, e.g. rape, it is competent for the accused to attack the woman's character for chastity by putting questions to herself, or to prove her general bad repute at the time of the alleged offence.[85] He may also prove that the woman yielded her person to himself shortly before then.[86] But he is not permitted to prove individual acts of

[71] *Gall* v. *Gall* (1870) 9 M. 177; *Mactaggart* v. *H.M. Adv.*, 1934 J.C. 33.
[72] A contrary decision was given in *Wm. Common* (1860) 3 Irv. 632, but this was doubted in *Kerr* v. *H.M. Adv.*, 1958 J.C. 14.
[73] *Common*, supra; *McNeilie* v. *H.M. Adv.*, 1929 J.C. 50.
[74] *Walker and Walker on Evidence*, p. 367.
[75] *Falconer* v. *Brown* (1893) 1 Adam 96.
[76] Supra, para. 7–16.
[77] Macdonald, 309.
[78] *Jas. Blair* (1836) Bell's Notes 294; *Jas. Irving* (1838) 2 Swin. 109.
[79] *Irving*, supra; *Margt. Shiells or Fletcher* (1846) Ark. 171.
[80] *H.M. Adv.* v. *Kay*, 1970 S.L.T.(Notes) 66.
[81] *Robt. Porteous* (1841) Bell's Notes 293; Macdonald, 309.
[82] *Malcolm Maclean* (1829) Bell's Notes 294; *Duncan McMillan* (1833) and *Robertson Edney* (1833) Bell's Notes 293.
[83] *Robt. Porteous* (1841) Bell's Notes 293; *John McMillan* (1846) Ark. 209.
[84] *John McMillan*, supra.
[85] *Jas. Reid and Ors.* (1861) 4 Irv. 124; *Forsyth and Ors.* (1866) 5 Irv. 249; Macdonald, 309; *Dickson on Evidence*, para. 14; Hume, ii. 413; Alison, ii. 530, 630.
[86] *Walter Blair* (1844) 2 Broun 167; *Dickie* v. *H.M. Adv.*, infra.

unchastity on her part with other men,[87] although it may be that such proof
would be competent if the acts in question occurred just before and
practically on the same occasion as the crime charged, on the ground that
they formed part of the res gestae.[88] It is a question of circumstances
whether evidence of subsequent conduct is competent.[89] In one case
evidence was allowed of an act of immorality on the same day as, and
subsequent to, the offence charged, but general proof of subsequent
character was disallowed.[90]

18-77   The general character of other witnesses cannot be inquired into,
except where it is alleged to be so degraded as to affect credibility.[91]
Thus the prosecutor may not ask if a witness is an inoffensive person, there
being no indication of an intention to show the contrary,[92] nor may
he ask questions as to the general character of an exculpatory witness.[93]
Again, the accused is not allowed to prove the bad character of a com-
panion of the injured party in a rape case.[94] In one case,[95] where a
witness was asked whether from her knowledge of two young witnesses
she could " place any reliance on their recollections," or whether they
were " veracious boys," the question was disallowed. It is, however,
competent to prove that the witness has committed a crime when this
is relevant to his credibility,[96] but this can only be done by his own
admission or by the production of an extract conviction.[97]

A witness may be cross-examined on any matter affecting credibility.[98] It is competent to ask a woman if she is a prostitute [99] and to
inquire of any witness whether he stands indicted for, or has been
convicted of, a crime.[1] It is also competent to ask a witness whether
his evidence is being given under pressure, e.g. because of threats made
by friends of the accused.[2] It is not, as a rule, competent to bring evidence
to contradict a witness regarding matters relating to his former life and
outside the res gestae.[3]

---

[87] *David Allan* (1842) 1 Broun 500; *Jas. Reid and Ors.*, supra; *Dickie* v. *H.M. Adv.*, infra.
See also Hume, i. 304, Note 1. See, however, *McFarlane* (1834) 6 S.J. 321, and opinion
of L.J.-C. Hope in *Walter Blair*, supra, at 171.

[88] *Dickie* v. *H.M. Adv.* (1896) 2 Adam 331, L.J.-C. at 338; *Jas. Reid and Ors.* supra, Lord
Neaves at 129; Macdonald, 309.

[89] Macdonald, 309; *Hugh Leitch* (1838) 2 Swin. 112.

[90] *Hugh Leitch*, supra.

[91] Macdonald, 310; *Dickson on Evidence*, para. 1621.

[92] *Robt. Porteous* (1841) Bell's Notes 293; Macdonald, 310.

[93] *Thos. Wight* (1836) 1 Swin. 47; Macdonald, 310.

[94] *Webster and Ors.* (1847) Ark. 269; Macdonald, 310.

[95] *Thos. and Peter Galloway* (1836) 1 Swin. 232. But a similar examination was allowed of a
mother regarding her child in *John Buchan* (1833) Bell's Notes 293. See also *Malcolm
Maclean* (1829) Bell's Notes 294; Macdonald, 310.

[96] Macdonald, 310; cf. *Walter Blair* (1844) 2 Broun 167.

[97] Ibid.; *Dickson on Evidence*, para. 1618.

[98] Macdonald, 310; *Walker & Walker on Evidence*, p. 365.

[99] Cf. *Webster and Ors.*, supra; *Walker & Walker on Evidence*, p. 366.

[1] Macdonald, 310.

[2] *Manson* v. *H.M. Adv.*, 1951 J.C. 49; *Brown and Henderson* (1832) Bell's Notes 267; *Clark
and Greig* (1842) 1 Broun 250; Macdonald, 310.

[3] *Jas. Reid and Ors.* (1861) 4 Irv. 124; Macdonald 310.

Order of examination of witnesses

3–78   As already mentioned, the evidence for the prosecution is heard first and the evidence (if any) for the defence immediately thereafter.[4] After being examined by the party adducing him, a witness may be cross-examined by the other party. Leading questions are competent in cross-examination,[5] but not in examination-in-chief [6] unless the witness gives evidence against the party calling him (which usually means he has gone back on his precognition) or shows a reluctance to answer questions.[7] The prohibition of leading questions does not apply to facts leading up to or incidental to the facts which the witness is called to prove.[8] Under the provisions of section 4 of the Evidence (Scotland) Act 1840, the party against whom a witness is called and examined may examine the witness in causa as well as in cross. Further, if the prosecutor calls a witness whose name is on both lists the accused must exhaust his examination both in cross and in causa when the witness is called for the prosecution.[9] After cross-examination, the party adducing the witness may re-examine him, but, once the re-examination is closed, any question which either party or a juryman may wish to ask must be put through the court.[10] The presiding judge may, ex proprio motu, question the witness himself, but if he elicits any new matter thereby, he must allow the party adversely affected to cross-examine upon it.[11] Witnesses must be called to give their evidence at the proper stage of the case. Where evidence might be adduced according to section 20 of the Criminal Law Amendment Act 1885, " at every stage " it was held that these words meant at every stage at which the production of evidence is competent.[12]

Recall of witnesses

3–79   Neither the prosecutor nor the defence may adduce evidence after their case is closed.[13] Section 4 of the Evidence (Scotland) Act 1852 entitles the judge on the motion of either party to recall any witness. The witness so recalled is examined by the party requesting his recall, and the questions asked are not limited to clearing up ambiguities in his evidence. In one case [14] the prosecutor was allowed to recall a witness in order to repair his omission to ask him to identify the accused. It seems that a witness cannot be recalled under the Act on the motion of a party whose case has been closed.

---

4 Supra, paras. 10–29 et seq.
5 Macdonald, 299; *Thos. Mure or Muir* (1858) 3 Irv. 280.
6 Macdonald, 299; *Dickson on Evidence*, para. 1771; Alison, ii. 545; *Bishop* v. *Bryce*, 1910 S.C. 426; *McKenzie* v. *McKenzie*, 1943 S.C. 108.
7 *Walker & Walker on Evidence*, pp. 364–365; cf. *Frank* v. *H.M. Adv.*, 1938 J.C. 17.
8 *Dickson on Evidence*, para. 1772; Alison, ii. 545–546.
9 Macdonald, 300; *Robt. Wilkie* (1886) 1 White 242.
10 Macdonald, 299; *Dickson on Evidence*, para. 1763.
11 Macdonald, 299; *McLeod* v. *H.M. Adv.*, 1939 J.C. 68.
12 *Clark and Bendall* v. *Stuart* (1886) 1 White 191.
13 *Docherty and Graham* v. *McLennan* (1912) 6 Adam 700; *McNeilie* v. *H.M. Adv.*, 1929 J.C. 50; *Davidson* v. *McFadyean*, 1942 J.C. 95; *Robt. Wilkie*, supra.
14 *Todd* v. *MacDonald*, 1960 J.C. 93.

At common law the judge may recall a witness at any stage. This recall is allowed only for the purpose of clearing up ambiguities,[15] and the witness is examined by the judge, subject to the right of any party to cross-examine on any evidence elicited by the judge.[16] There is some authority that the judge may ask the witness any questions necessary to ascertain the truth,[17] but it has been disapproved in later cases.[18]

It has been suggested [19] that the repeal by section 5 of the Evidence (Scotland) Act 1852 of any law inconsistent or at variance with the Act means that the Crown is entitled to proof in replication for the purpose of discrediting a witness under section 3 of the Act. But there is no authority for such a suggestion, and the consistent refusal of the courts to read section 3 itself as meaning what it says in relation to precognitions gives little ground for supposing that the suggestion will be accepted.

A practice seems to be growing up whereby a recalcitrant witness who has been detained for prevarication will be allowed to purge his contempt by returning to the witness box to contradict his earlier protestations of ignorance.

Presence of witnesses in court

18–80   The case of expert witnesses has already been considered.[20] As regards witnesses to the facts, these should not be in court before their own turn to give evidence arrives.[21]

It is not imperative to reject a witness because he has been in court without permission during the examination of other witnesses.[22] He may competently be examined, but only in the discretion of the court, and that discretion can be exercised only after the court is satisfied with regard to certain matters, viz.: that the presence of the witness was not the consequence of culpable negligence or criminal intent, that the witness has not been unduly instructed or influenced by what took place during his or her presence, and that injustice will not be done by his or her examination.[23] It is for the party tendering the witness so to satisfy the court if the witness is objected to.[24] Further, where it is apparent to the judge that a witness is present in court, it is pars judicis for him to raise the question himself.[25]

The evidence of a solicitor engaged in the case cannot be objected to on the ground that he has been in court.[26] Where a second trial takes

---

[15] Davidson v. McFadyean, 1942 J.C. 95; Todd v. MacDonald, supra; McNeilie v. H.M. Adv., 1929 J.C. 50; Docherty and Graham v. McLennan (1912) 6 Adam 700.
[16] Cf. McLeod v. H.M. Adv., supra.
[17] Collison v. Mitchell (1897) 2 Adam 277; Saunders v. Paterson (1905) 4 Adam 568.
[18] Davidson v. McFadyean, supra; Docherty and Graham v. McLennan, supra; cf. McNeilie v. H.M. Adv., supra; Todd v. MacDonald, supra.
[19] Macdonald, 302.
[20] Supra, para. 18–70.
[21] Hume, ii. 379; Alison, ii. 542; Docherty and Graham v. McLennan, supra.
[22] Evidence (Scotland) Act 1840, s. 3.
[23] Ibid. See also Macdonald v. Mackenzie, 1947 J.C. 169.
[24] Macdonald v. Mackenzie, supra, Lord Jamieson at 176; Ryan v. Paterson (1972) 36 J.C.L. 111.
[25] Ibid.
[26] Campbell v. Cochrane, 1928 J.C. 25; Evidence (Scotland) Act 1840, s. 3; Evidence (Scotland) Act 1852, s. 1; supra, para. 18–69.

place with reference to the same facts, a witness thereat cannot be objected to on the ground that he heard evidence of other witnesses at the first.[27]

Evidence of crimes not charged

–81   It is not competent to lead evidence of any crime not libelled in the indictment either as a specific charge, or as a specific averment [28] in which case it must be relevant evidence of the crime charged.[29] This rule does not apply in certain common situations, such as the leading of evidence that an accused thief sold the stolen goods as his own without a charge of defrauding the buyer, where the facts all form part of one general species facti although they could be broken up into separate offences. Nor does it apply to otherwise competent and relevant evidence of an accused's previous conviction where what is in issue is not his commission of the uncharged crime but his having been convicted of it.[30]

It is competent to lead evidence of the completion of a crime in a charge of attempt,[31] or evidence of penetration on a charge of assault with intent to ravish.[32]

Hearsay

–82   As a general rule, hearsay, being only secondary evidence, cannot be received.

There are, however, several special exceptions to this rule.

–83   1. Statements by the accused may be proved,[33] provided of course that they are not evidence of a crime which is not charged or otherwise libelled.[34]

Certain statements by an accused person have already been considered.[35] In addition to these it is competent to prove statements made by him on oath in a civil process [36] or when a witness in exculpation of a person charged with the same offence.[37] And, in a trial for perjury, a previous deposition by him which is relevant evidence of the offence charged may be proved.[38] It is not, however, competent to prove a statement made on oath by a bankrupt at a compulsory examination in his sequestration at his subsequent trial for embezzlement of the funds to which the examination related.[39]

---

[27] Macdonald, 295; *Dickson on Evidence*, para. 1599; *Peter Heughan* (1810) Hume, ii. 379; Alison, ii. 489, 490.

[28] *H.M. Adv.* v. *Joseph*, 1929 J.C. 55; *Griffen* v. *H.M. Adv.*, 1940 J.C. 1; *Edw. Pritchard* (1865) 5 Irv. 88; *H.M. Adv.* v. *Monson* (1893) 1 Adam 114; cf. *Cameron* v. *Waugh*, 1937 J.C. 5. But see *Gallagher* v. *Paton* (1909) 6 Adam 62—evidence of other fraudulent statements to other people on same day as fraud charged allowed to prove mens rea.

[29] *H.M. Adv.* v. *Joseph*, supra.

[30] See supra, para. 18-13; see also *H.M. Adv.* v. *McIlwain*, 1965 J.C. 40; 29 J.C.L. 286.

[31] 1887 Act, s. 61; *Muldoon* v. *H.M. Adv.*, 1967 S.L.T. 237.

[32] *Muldoon* v. *H.M. Adv.*, supra.

[33] Macdonald, 311. See supra, para. 18-47.

[34] Macdonald, 311; *J. G. Robertson & Ors.* (1842) 1 Broun 152; *Jas. Cumming, John Grant and Ors.* (1848) J. Shaw 17.

[35] Supra, paras. 18-23 et seq.

[36] *Banaghan* v. *H.M. Adv.* (1888) 1 White 566; *McGiveran* v. *Auld* (1894) 1 Adam 448.

[37] *Eliz. Edmiston* (1866) 5 Irv. 219.

[38] *Thos. Bauchop* (1840) 2 Swin. 513.

[39] *A. G. Fleming* (1885) 5 Couper 552.

18–84   2. Where the question at issue as regards a particular statement is not whether it was true, but whether it was made, evidence of it is admissible.[40] Evidence of conversation in a brothel is admissible to prove the character of the house.[41]

18–85   3. Hearsay is sometimes admitted to prove incidental points, e.g. that a person is dead. In such a case prima facie proof is sufficient unless the opposite party disputes the fact.[42] The accused cannot competently prove threats made by a third party against the injured party unless he has lodged a special defence that the third party committed the crime.[43]

18–86   4. Evidence will be admitted of statements which form part of the res gestae, that is to say, things said which form part of what occurred at the time of the crime or immediately after it, and are either interwoven or intimately connected with the acts done, although not necessarily contemporaneous with them. The person who said these things, if alive, must be called as a witness, or accounted for.[44]

18–87   5. Evidence is admissible of statements made by the person wronged or injured by the crime, if these were made not more than a few hours after the crime, while his feeling on the subject was fresh.[45] A wider latitude has to be allowed in cases of rape.[46]

18–88   6. The statement of a child witness, made de recenti after the crime, is received for the purpose of checking the evidence he gives at the trial.[47]

18–89   7. Hearsay is admissible when it becomes the best evidence. If a deceased person, who would have been a competent witness, has made a statement which would have been competent evidence, that statement may be proved.[48] The death must be proved in the first instance. It has been suggested that the same principle should apply to the case of a person who, since he made the statement, has become hopelessly insane.[49] Dying depositions have already been considered.[50] Serious illness or absence of a witness from the country will not admit proof of his statement.[51] In such cases the only remedy is to delay the trial until the person can attend as a witness. Evidence on commission is incompetent.[52]

---

[40] *Walker & Walker on Evidence*, p. 396; *Dickson on Evidence*, para. 247; *Coles* v. *Homer and Tulloh* (1895) 22 R. 716.

[41] *McLaren* v. *Macleod* (1913) 7 Adam 110.

[42] Macdonald, 317; *Dickson on Evidence*, para. 269.

[43] Macdonald, 317; *Robt. Rouatt* (1852) 1 Irv. 79; cf. *Paul Cavalari* (1854) 1 Irv. 564.

[44] Macdonald, 316; *Dickson on Evidence*, para. 254; Hume, ii. 406; Alison, ii. 517, 518; cf. *Wm. Harvey* (1835) Bell's Notes 292.

[45] Macdonald, 317; *Dickson on Evidence*, 258; *Neil Moran* (1836) 1 Swin. 231; *Peter Kelly* (1829) Bell's Notes 288.

[46] Macdonald, 317; *Dickson on Evidence*, para. 261; Alison, ii. 514. Such evidence goes only to credibility.

[47] Macdonald, 317; *John Stewart* (1855) 2 Irv. 166, 179.

[48] Macdonald, 318; *Dickson on Evidence*, paras. 266–267; Hume, ii. 407–410; Alison, ii. 511–515; *Jas. Reid* (1831) Bell's Notes 291; *McCormacks* (1831) ibid.; *Thos. Hunter* (1838) 2 Swin. 1.

[49] *Dickson on Evidence*, para. 268.

[50] Supra, para. 7–31.

[51] See Macdonald, 318, and cases of *H.M. Adv.* v. *McConnell* (1887) 1 White 412; *H.M. Adv.* v. *Monson* (1893) 1 Adam 114; and *Glyn* v. *Johnston and Co.* (1834) 13 S. 126, cited there.

[52] *H.M. Adv.* v. *Hunter* (1905) 4 Adam 523.

3–90   8. Where a witness gives evidence that he identified the criminal to the police shortly after the crime but cannot or will not identify him as the accused in court, police evidence of the earlier identification is not hearsay.[53]

3–91   9. Evidence of a statement heard over the telephone or transmitted through a microphone is equivalent to evidence of a statement heard directly.[54] In *Hopes and Lavery* v. *H.M. Adv.*[55] evidence was transmitted by microphone to a tape recorder. The tape when played over was very indistinct and evidence was given of a transcript reconstructed from the tape by a stenographer after repeated playings of the tape. The court had doubts as to whether this was admissible, particularly as the stenographer, although she had some experience in transcribing tapes, was not an expert. It was suggested that the jury should not take the tape to the jury room to try to decipher it themselves. The proper course was thought to be to lead evidence from someone skilled in reading tapes. Lord Clyde indicated that evidence of statements heard on a clear tape might be equivalent to direct evidence of hearing the statement.[56]

3–92   10. The Criminal Evidence Act 1965 [57] provides in certain cases for proof of facts by recourse to business records. Section 1 of the Act is as follows:

> " 1.—(1) In any criminal proceedings where direct oral evidence of a fact would be admissible, any statement contained in a document and tending to establish that fact shall, on production of the document, be admissible as evidence of that fact if—
>
> (a) the document is, or forms part of, a record relating to any trade or business and compiled, in the course of that trade or business, from information supplied (whether directly or indirectly) by persons who have, or may reasonably be supposed to have, personal knowledge of the matters dealt with in the information they supply; and
>
> (b) the person who supplied the information recorded in the statement in question is dead, or beyond the seas, or unfit by reason of his bodily or mental condition to attend as a witness, or cannot with reasonable diligence be identified or found, or cannot reasonably be expected (having regard to the time which has elapsed since he supplied the information and to all the circumstances) to have any recollection of the matters dealt with in the information he supplied.
>
> (2) For the purpose of deciding whether or not a statement is admissible as evidence by virtue of this section, the court may draw any reasonable inference from the form or content of the document in

---

[53] *Muldoon* v. *Herron*, 1970 S.L.T. 228; *McGaharon* v. *H.M. Adv.*, 1968 S.L.T.(Notes) 99.
[54] *McGiveran* v. *Auld* (1894) 1 Adam 448; *Hopes and Lavery* v. *H.M. Adv.*, 1960 J.C. 104.
[55] *Supra.*
[56] At 110.
[57] Passed as a result of *Myers* v. *D.P.P.* [1965] A.C. 1001.

which the statement is contained, and may, in deciding whether or not a person is fit to attend as a witness, act on a certificate purporting to be a certificate of a fully registered medical practitioner.

(3) In estimating the weight, if any, to be attached to a statement admissible as evidence by virtue of this section regard shall be had to all the circumstances from which any inference can reasonably be drawn as to the accuracy or otherwise of the statement, and, in particular, to the question whether or not the person who supplied the information recorded in the statement did so contemporaneously with the occurrence or existence of the facts stated, and to the question whether or not that person, or any person concerned with making or keeping the record containing the statement, had any incentive to conceal or misrepresent the facts.

(4) In this section " statement " includes any representation of fact, whether made in words or otherwise, " document " includes any device by means of which information is recorded or stored and " business " includes any public transport, public utility or similar undertaking carried on by a local authority and the activities of the Post Office."

Fingerprints, etc.

18–93　At common law the police are entitled, without a warrant, to take the fingerprints of a person apprehended on a criminal charge but not yet committed to prison. This right is not affected by the Prisons (Scotland) Act 1952, and relative regulations.[58] It is not exercisable in the case of a person who has not been apprehended.[59]

An accused person may competently be convicted upon fingerprint evidence alone.[60]

Other bodily peculiarities, such as bite marks, are comparable to fingerprints.[61] Handwriting evidence is not as highly regarded as evidence of fingerprints but there has been at least one case where the accused was convicted on such evidence.[62]

Admissibility of irregularly obtained evidence

18–94　It has been held by a Full Bench that an irregularity in the method by which evidence has been obtained does not necessarily make that evidence inadmissible in a criminal prosecution. There is no absolute rule governing the matter, the question whether any given irregularity ought or ought not to be excused depending in each case upon the nature of the irregularity and the circumstances in which it was committed, an important consideration always being whether the admission of the evidence will be fair to the

[58] *Adair* v. *McGarry*, 1933 J.C. 72.
[59] *Adamson* v. *Martin*, 1916 S.C. 319.
[60] *Hamilton* v. *H.M. Adv.*, 1934 J.C. 1; *H.M. Adv.* v. *Rolley*, 1945 J.C. 155.
[61] *Hay* v. *H.M. Adv.*, 1968 J.C. 40.
[62] *Camilleri* v. *MacLeod* (1965) 29 J.C.L. 126; see *Richardson* v. *Clark*, 1957 J.C. 7; *Walter Scott Ellis*, High Court, Feb. 1965, unreported.

accused. No distinction can be drawn in this matter between a prosecution for a statutory offence and a prosecution for a common law crime.[63]

Proof of productions in solemn procedure

8–95   Section 35 of the 1949 Act provides as follows:

" Where, in any proceedings on indictment, a person who has examined a production is adduced to give evidence with regard thereto and the production has been lodged at least eight days before the second diet, it shall not be necessary to prove that the production was received by him in the condition in which it was taken possession of by the procurator fiscal or the police and returned by him after his examination of it to the procurator fiscal or the police unless the accused, at least four days before the second diet gives to the Crown Agent, where he is cited to the High Court of Justiciary for the second diet, or to the procurator fiscal of the district to the court of which he is cited for the second diet, where the case is to be tried in the sheriff court, written notice that he does not admit that the production was received or returned as aforesaid."

Proof of exceptions, etc. in solemn procedure

8–96   The provisions of section 19 (3) of the 1908 Act (identical with section 16 (d) of the 1954 Act) are applied to procedure on indictment by section 34 of the 1949 Act in the terms set forth supra, para. 6–21.

Proof of special capacity in solemn procedure

8–97   The provisions of section 19 (5) of the 1908 Act (identical with section 16 (b) of the 1954 Act) are applied to procedure on indictment by section 34 of the 1949 Act in the terms set forth supra, para. 6–22.

Contempt of Court by Witnesses

8–98   If any witness in a summary prosecution wilfully fails to attend after being duly cited, or unlawfully refuses to be sworn, or after the oath has been administered to him refuses to answer any question which the court may allow, or to produce documents in his possession when required by the court, or prevaricates in his evidence, he is deemed guilty of contempt of court, and is liable to be summarily punished forthwith for such contempt by a fine not exceeding £25, or by imprisonment for any period not exceeding twenty days. Where such punishment is summarily imposed, the clerk of court enters in the record of the proceedings the act or acts constituting the contempt and the statements forming the prevarication. The prosecutor may, if he prefers to do so, proceed by way of formal

---

[63] *Lawrie* v. *Muir*, 1950 J.C. 19. See also *H.M. Adv.* v. *McGuigan*, 1936 J.C. 16; *McGovern* v. *H.M. Adv.*, 1950 J.C. 33; *Fairley* v. *Fishmongers of London*, 1951 J.C. 14; *H.M. Adv.* v. *Turnbull*, 1951 J.C. 96; *H.M. Adv.* v. *Hepper*, 1958 J.C. 39; *Bell* v. *Hogg*, 1967 J.C. 49; *Hay* v. *H.M. Adv.*, 1968 J.C. 40. See also supra, paras. 5–24 et seq.

complaint for such contempt, where such summary punishment as above mentioned is not imposed.[64]

The same penalty as is above mentioned is incurred by any witness who, after being duly cited in accordance with section 18 of the Act, (a) fails, without reasonable excuse, after receiving at least twenty-four hours' notice, to attend for precognition by a procurator fiscal or burgh prosecutor at the time and place mentioned in the citation served on him, or (b) refuses when so cited to give information within his knowledge regarding any matter relative to the commission of the offence in relation to which such precognition is taken.[65]

18–99   Every court has power at common law to punish summarily acts in contempt of its authority,[66] such as, for example, defiant or insulting language to the judge [67]; a witness,[68] or a juror,[69] or the accused[70] appearing in a state of intoxication; witnesses breaking out of the room in which they were enclosed prior to their examination [71]; etc. The court may also punish persons who attempt to pervert the course of justice, e.g. by failing to attend court when cited as a witness,[72] or accused, provided the failure is wilful,[73] or by refusing to take the oath,[74] or by granting false certificates of character,[75] or by wilfully parting with a document after having been cited as a haver to produce it,[76] or by whispering to a witness under examination,[77] or by intimidating a witness.[78] A witness in a jury trial who prevaricates may be dealt with at common law for contempt of court. It is not infrequent for such witnesses to be detained until the conclusion of the trial, or until they purge their contempt by giving evidence without prevarication. Those who remain in contempt may be summarily sentenced for contempt by the judge.

The High Court will intervene where a judge has punished an offender oppressively.[79] Where the sentence was imposed by a High Court judge it may be brought under review by petition to the nobile officium.[80] The immediate withdrawal of the words complained of is a matter to which the court will have regard when considering whether a sentence is oppressive.[81]

[64] 1954 Act, s. 33, as amended by 1963 Act.
[65] Ibid.
[66] Hume, ii. 138; Gordon, Chap. 50.
[67] *Robt. Clark or Williamson* (1829) Shaw 215.
[68] *John Allan* (1826) Shaw 172; *Jas. Wemyss* (1840) Bell's Notes 165.
[69] *Eliz. Yates* (1847) Ark. 238.
[70] *Alex. MacLean* (1838) 2 Swin. 185.
[71] *Innes and McEwan* (1831) Shaw 238; Bell's Notes 165.
[72] *H.M. Adv.* v. *Bell*, 1936 J.C. 89; *Petrie* v. *Angus* (1889) 2 White 358.
[73] *Pirie* v. *Hawthorn*, 1962 J.C. 69.
[74] *Wylie & Anr.* v. *H.M. Adv.*, 1966 S.L.T. 149.
[75] *Nimmo and Forsyth* (1839) 2 Swin. 338.
[76] *L.A.* v. *Alex. Galloway* (1839) 2 Swin. 465.
[77] *Wm. Smith* (1714) Hume, ii. 140.
[78] See *Forkes* v. *Weir* (1897) 5 S.L.T. 194.
[79] *Lawrie* v. *Roberts & Linton* (1882) 4 Couper 606. Cf. *Milburn*, 1946 S.C. 301; *Wylie and Anr.*, supra.
[80] *Wylie and Anr.*, supra.
[81] Ibid.

–100   The word " prevarication " is not easily defined. " It is a loose and indefinite term, which may mean many different things short of perjury; the general idea which it conveys is manifest unwillingness candidly to tell the whole truth, fencing with questions in such manner as to show reluctance to disclose the truth, and a disposition to conceal or withhold it." [82]

The provision in section 33 (2) of the 1954 Act that, where offenders are dealt with and punished forthwith, the clerk of court shall record the act or acts constituting the contempt and the statements forming the prevarication, is obviously intended to secure an accurate record of the matter should the case be appealed. In *Soutar* v. *Stirling* [83] a sentence which found the witness " guilty while under examination on oath of prevarication and wilfully concealing the truth " was quashed for lack of specification. In a later case [84] under the Police Act 1850, section 360, which gave magistrates the power to imprison for prevarication, and provided that " the sentence awarding such imprisonment shall set forth the nature of such offence," it was held, following the case of *Soutar* v. *Stirling*,[83] that the " nature of the offence " was not sufficiently set forth by the words " having wilfully concealed the truth and having persisted in such concealment after having been duly cautioned."

The power of dealing summarily with persons who commit contempt of court should be exercised with caution.[85] It will be observed that where the court does not itself deal with an offender, the prosecutor may proceed at his own instance by a formal complaint.[86]

Special Provisions in Summary Procedure

Administration of oath to same witness

–101   Where a witness is examined upon oath in any case in which the accused is charged with an offence under any statute, and where the same witness is examined at the same diet in subsequent cases against the same or different persons accused of offences under the same statute, it is not necessary for the judge to administer the oath to the witness in the subsequent cases, but it is sufficient that the judge reminds him in each case that he is still on oath.[87]

This procedure is convenient in such cases as prosecutions under the Education Acts, where a teacher or school attendance officer has to be called in each of a number of cases.

Defence witnesses

–102   Provision has been made to meet the difficulty which sometimes arises in maritime and other cases where the evidence of a witness for the defence

---

[82] *MacLeod* v. *Speirs* (1884) 5 Couper 387; Lord Young at 405. See also *Nicholson* v. *Linton* (1861) 4 Irv. 115; *Adam Baxter & Ors.* (1867) 5 Irv. 351.
[83] (1888) 2 White 19.
[84] *Blake* v. *Macdonald* (1890) 2 White 477. But see *MacLeod* v. *Speirs* (1884) 5 Couper 387.
[85] *Blake* v. *Macdonald* (1890) 2 White 477, Lord Young at 479. See also *Lawrie* v. *Roberts & Linton* (1882) 4 Couper 606.
[86] 1954 Act, s. 33 (3).   [87] Ibid., s. 34

will be lost if he is not examined at once. The power is sparingly used, because it is obviously inexpedient for both sides that witnesses for the defence should be examined before evidence has been heard in support of the charge. The court is empowered, in any case where it considers such a course expedient, to permit any witness for the defence to be examined prior to evidence for the prosecution having been led or concluded. In any such case the accused is entitled to lead additional evidence after the case for the prosecution is closed.[88]

Proof of official documents

18–103   " Any letter, minute, or other official document issuing from the office, or in the custody of any of the departments of state or government in the United Kingdom the production of which in evidence is required in any summary prosecution, and which according to the rules and regulations applicable to such departments may be competently produced, shall, when produced, be received as prima facie evidence of the matters contained in it without being produced or sworn to by any witness and a copy thereof bearing to be certified by any person having authority to certify the same shall be treated as equivalent to the original, and no proof of the signature of the person certifying such copy, or of his authority to certify it shall be necessary." [89]

Any order by any of the departments of state or government or any local authority, or public body, made under powers conferred by any statute, or a print or copy of such order, is, when produced in a summary prosecution, received in evidence of the due making, confirmation, and existence of the order, without being sworn to by any witness, and without any further or other proof. This is, however, without prejudice to any right competent to the accused to challenge any such order as being ultra vires of the authority making it, or on any other competent ground. Where any such order is referred to in the complaint, it is not necessary to enter it in the record of the proceedings as a documentary production.[90]

The foregoing provisions are deemed to be in addition to, and not in derogation of, any powers of proving documents conferred by statute, or existing at common law.[91]

Defence productions may be used in cross-examining Crown witnesses before the productions have been themselves proved.[92]

Proof of exceptions, etc.

18–104   An accused person is entitled to prove any exception, exemption, proviso, excuse, or qualification applicable to an offence under a statute or

---

[88] 1954 Act, s. 29 (*h*).
[89] Ibid., s. 35 (1); *Hunter* v. *Herron*, 1969 J.C. 64.
[90] Ibid., s. 35 (2). See supra, paras. 14–15 et seq.
[91] Ibid., s. 35 (3).
[92] *Hogg* v. *Clark*, 1959 J.C. 7.

order; but no proof in relation to such matter is required on behalf of the prosecution.[93]

Proof of special capacity

3-105   Where an offence is alleged to have been committed by the accused while acting in a special capacity, as holder of a licence, master of a vessel, occupier of a house, or the like, the fact that he possesses that qualification is held as admitted without proof, unless it is challenged by preliminary objection before his plea is recorded.[94]

Proof of nationality of ship

3-106   The nationality of any ship as stated in a complaint under the Merchant Shipping Acts is, in the absence of evidence to the contrary, presumed without proof, and it is no longer necessary to produce the official register of the ship.[95]

[93] 1954 Act, s. 16 (*d*).   Similar provisions in 1908 Act, s. 19 (3), are applied to solemn procedure by 1949 Act, s. 34.   See supra, para. 6–21.
[94] 1954 Act, s. 16 (*f*).   Similar provisions in 1908 Act, s. 19 (5), are applied to solemn procedure by 1949 Act, s. 34.   See supra, para. 6–22.
[95] 1954 Act, s. 16 (*g*).   See supra, para. 13–55.

CHAPTER 19

PROVISIONS RELATING TO CHILDREN

19-01 THE law relating to children who are alleged to have committed offences is governed by the Children and Young Persons (Scotland) Act 1937 as amended by the Social Work (Scotland) Act 1968 ("the 1937 Act"), and by the Social Work (Scotland) Act 1968 ("the 1968 Act") itself. A "child" for the purposes of these Acts is a person who has not attained the age of sixteen years.[1] The provisions of the Acts relating to child offenders apply also to persons over sixteen but under eighteen years old who are subject to a supervision requirement under Part III of the 1968 Act and to certain other persons under eighteen brought before a children's hearing under Part V of that Act.[2]

A child alleged to have committed an offence may be dealt with by prosecution or by the machinery of reporter and hearing set up by Part III of the Social Work (Scotland) Act 1968. Section 38 (2) of the 1968 Act requires police officers making reports on children to the appropriate prosecutor in terms of section 17 (1) (b) of the Police (Scotland) Act 1967 to make a report also to the appropriate reporter. The child will be dealt with by the reporter only if the prosecutor decides not to prosecute. In practice, as a result of administrative directions, most cases involving children which come to the knowledge of the police will be reported only to the reporter; some cases reported to the prosecutor and reporter will not in fact be taken up by the prosecutor but be sent by him to the reporter; while a few serious offences will be prosecuted. Generally speaking the seriousness of an offence will not be a reason for prosecution unless the offence is bad enough to merit proceedings on indictment. Summary proceedings will, however, have to be taken where the prosecutor thinks that either disqualification for driving or the forfeiture of any article is appropriate, since these penalties cannot be imposed by a hearing. The provision of the 1937 Act that cases where a child was alleged to have offended along with an adult had to be dealt with by an ordinary court is repealed by the 1968 Act.[3] Whether such a child is dealt with by an adult court along with his older accomplice or is referred to a reporter is now a question for the discretion of the prosecutor and therefore all such cases will be reported by the police to the prosecutor. Where a child and an adult are both prosecuted the court has power under section 56 of the 1968 Act to remit the child to a children's hearing for disposal if he is found guilty.

[1] 1968 Act, s. 30 (1); Sched. 2, para. 1.
[2] Ibid.
[3] Sched. 2, para. 10.

Every court dealing with a child brought before it is obliged to have regard to his welfare, and to take steps in a proper case to remove him from undesirable surroundings.[4]

I. Prosecution of Child Offenders

Arrest

19-02 The general law of arrest applies to children as to any other suspected persons.

Where someone who is apparently a child is arrested and cannot be brought forthwith before a sheriff summary court [5] a police officer of the rank of inspector or above or the officer in charge of the police station to which he is brought is obliged to inquire into the case, and may liberate the child on an obligation being entered into by him or his parent or guardian that he will attend at the hearing of the charge, or on bail being found for his attendance in a sum fixed by the officer. The police officer is bound to liberate the child unless the charge is of homicide " or other grave crime," or it is necessary in the interests of the child to remove him from association with any reputed criminal or prostitute, or the officer has reason to believe that his liberation would defeat the ends of justice.[6]

Where an arrested child is not liberated he must be detained in a place of safety other than a police station until he is brought to court unless the police officer concerned certifies that such detention is impracticable, or unsafe because of the child's unruly character, or inadvisable because of his state of health or bodily or mental condition. Any certificate must be produced to the court when the child appears there.[7]

A " place of safety " is " any residential or other establishment provided by a local authority, a police station, or any hospital, surgery or other suitable place, the occupier of which is willing temporarily to receive a child." [8]

Where a child is arrested the arresting constable or the officer in charge of the police station to which he is brought must warn the child's parent or guardian, if he can be found, to attend at the court where the child will appear.[9]

Title to prosecute

19-03 No child may be prosecuted for any offence except on the instructions of the Lord Advocate, or at his instance, and no court other than the High Court of Justiciary and the sheriff court has jurisdiction over a child for an offence.[10] These provisions apply whether or not the offence occurred before the coming into force of Part III of the 1968 Act on April 15, 1971.[11]

---

[4] 1937 Act, s. 49 (1).
[5] 1968 Act, Sched. 2, para. 2.
[6] 1937 Act, s. 40 (1); see also infra, para. 19-36.
[7] Ibid., s. 40 (2).
[8] 1968 Act, s. 94; Sched. 8, para. 10.
[9] 1937 Act, s. 42 (2).
[10] 1968 Act, s. 31 (1).
[11] Ibid., s. 31 (2).

It is conclusively presumed that no child under the age of eight years can be guilty of any offence.[12]

Notification of prosecution

19-04   Where a child is to be brought before a court the chief constable of the area where the offence is alleged to have been committed is obliged to notify the local authority in whose area the court sits of the day and hour when and the nature of the charge on which the child is to appear.[13] Where a local authority receive such notification they are obliged to make such investigations and render available to the court a report containing such information as to the child's home surroundings as appear to them will assist the court in disposing of the case. The report must also contain information provided by the appropriate education authority on the child's school record, health and character.[14]

19-05   The parent or guardian of a child charged with an offence may, and if he can be found and resides within a reasonable distance will, be required to attend all the court proceedings against the child unless the court is satisfied that such a requirement would be unreasonable.[15] The parent or guardian who is to attend is the one having actual possession and control of the child. Where, however, that is not the father, the father may also be required to attend.[16] Where the child has already been removed from the custody or charge of a parent by a court order that parent's attendance is not required.[17]

Court procedure

19-06   Juvenile courts have been abolished by the 1968 Act so that a child charged summarily appears in the sheriff summary court. Proceedings against a child on indictment follow the normal pattern. Summary proceedings are commenced on the instructions of the Lord Advocate by complaint at the instance of the procurator fiscal, and continue in accordance with the 1954 Act.[18] There are, however, special provisions governing the procedure of summary courts when dealing with a child. These provisions do not apply when the child has been charged with an offence jointly with a person who is not a child.[19]

19-07   The sheriff must sit in a different building or room from that in which he usually sits or on different days from those on which other courts in the same building are doing criminal business.[20]

The court must take what steps are possible to prevent children attending the court from mixing with one another. This should be done by

[12] 1937 Act, s. 55.
[13] 1937 Act, s. 43 (1) as substituted by 1968 Act, Sched. 2, para. 5.
[14] 1937 Act, s. 43 (2), substituted as above.
[15] 1937 Act, s. 42 (1). He need not be formally cited; it is enough that he has reasonable notice: *White & Ors.* v. *Jeans* (1911) 6 Adam 489; *Montgomery* v. *Grey* (1915) 7 Adam 681.
[16] Ibid., s. 42 (4).
[17] Ibid., s. 42 (5).
[18] Act of Adjournal (Summary Proceedings) (Children) 1971, paras. 3, 4.
[19] 1937 Act, s. 50, as substituted by 1968 Act, Sched. 2, para. 10.
[20] 1937 Act, s. 52 (1); 1968 Act, Sched. 2, para. 11.

holding separate sittings or fixing different hours for the different cases
and types of cases before it, or where this is not possible by using extra
waiting rooms or providing an attendant in the waiting room or rooms.[21]

Arrangements must also be made to prevent children detained in
police stations, or being taken to or from a criminal court, or waiting
before or after their appearance at court, from associating with an adult
(other than a relative) charged with any offence other than one on which
the child is jointly charged, and to ensure that a female child shall be under
the care of a woman while being detained, or conveyed, or waiting.[22]

9–08 No person may be present at the sitting without the special authorisa-
tion of the court except members and officers of the court, parties to the
case, their solicitors and counsel, witnesses and other persons directly
concerned in the case, and bona fide journalists.[23]

9–09 Where the child is not represented by solicitor or counsel his parent or
guardian is entitled to assist him in his defence, including the examining
and cross-examining of witnesses. Where the parent or guardian cannot
be found or reasonably required to attend any other relative or responsible
person may be allowed by the court to take his place. [24]

9–10 The following procedure is laid down for cases where a child is brought
before a court charged with an offence [25]:

" (1) The Court shall explain to the child the substance of the
charge in simple language suitable to his age and understanding, and
shall then ask the child whether he admits the charge.

(2) If the child has been brought before the Court on apprehension,
the Court shall inform him that he is entitled to an adjournment of
the case for not less than 48 hours.

(3) If the child does not admit the charge the Court may adjourn
the case for trial to as early a diet as is consistent with the just interest
of both parties, and in that event shall give intimation or order intimation to be given of such adjourned diet to such child and his parent or
guardian: but the Court may proceed to trial forthwith if the Court
considers this to be advisable in the interests of the child or to be
necessary to secure the examination of witnesses who would not
otherwise be available.

(4) (a) At the trial of the case the Court shall hear the evidence
of the witnesses in support of the charge. At the close of the
evidence-in-chief of each witness the witness may be cross-
examined by or on behalf of the child.

(b) If, in any case where the child is not represented by solicitor or counsel or assisted in his defence as provided by this Act
of Adjournal, the child, instead of asking questions by way of

---

[21] Act of Adjournal (Summary Proceedings) (Children) 1971, para. 9.
[22] 1937 Act, s. 39.
[23] 1937 Act, s. 52 (1).
[24] Act of Adjournal (Summary Proceedings) (Children) 1971, para. 5.
[25] Ibid., para. 6.

19–10 cross-examination, makes assertions, the Court shall then put to the witness such questions as it thinks necessary on behalf of the child and may for this purpose question the child in order to bring out or clear up any point arising out of any such assertions.

(5) At the close of the case for the prosecution, the Court shall tell the child that he may give evidence or make a statement, and the evidence of any witness for the defence shall be heard.

(6) Where the Court is satisfied, after trial or otherwise, that the child has committed an offence, the Court shall so inform the child and,

(*a*) he and his parent or guardian, or other person acting in accordance with this Act of Adjournal, shall be given an opportunity of making a statement;

(*b*) the Court shall obtain such information as to the general conduct, home surroundings, school record, health and character of the child as may enable it to deal with the case in his best interests, and shall if such information is not fully available consider the desirability of remanding the child for such inquiry as may be necessary;

(*c*) the Court shall take into consideration any report which may be made or obtained by a local authority in pursuance of section 43 of the Act of 1937;

(*d*) any written report of a local authority, education authority, or registered medical practitioner may be received and considered by the Court without being read aloud, provided that

(i) the child shall be told the substance of any part of the report bearing on his character or conduct which the Court considers to be material to the manner in which he should be dealt with;

(ii) the parent or guardian, or other person acting in accordance with this Act of Adjournal, shall, if present, be told the substance of any part of the report which the Court considers to be material as aforesaid and which has reference to his character or conduct, or the character, conduct, home surroundings or health of the child; and

(iii) if the child or his parent or guardian, or other person acting in accordance with this Act of Adjournal, having been told the substance of any part of any such report, desires to produce evidence with reference thereto, the Court, if it thinks the evidence material, shall adjourn the proceedings for the production of further evidence, and shall, if necessary, require the attendance at the adjourned hearing of the person who made the report;

(*e*) if the Court acting in pursuance of this paragraph of the Act of Adjournal considers it necessary in the interests of the child, it may require the parent or guardian, or other person acting in accordance with this Act of Adjournal, or the child, as the case may be, to withdraw from the court.

(7) The Court shall thereupon, unless it thinks it undesirable to do so, inform the parent or guardian, or other person acting in accordance with this Act of Adjournal, of the manner in which it proposes to deal with the child and shall allow the parent or guardian, or other person acting in accordance with this Act of Adjournal, to make a statement."

The court may from time to time and at any stage of a case remand a child for information to be obtained with respect to him,[26] as well as for any other purpose permitted by the 1954 Act.

Committal to place of safety

9-11 Where a court remands or commits for trial a child who is not liberated on bail the child is normally not committed to prison but to the local authority in whose area the court sits for them to detain him in a place of safety chosen by them for the period of remand or until liberation in due course of law. A child over fourteen years of age may be committed to prison if the court certifies that he is of so unruly a character that he cannot be safely committed to the local authority or of so depraved a character that he is not a fit person to be detained in a place of safety.[27]

A committal to the local authority under the above provisions may be varied, or, in the case of a child over the age of fourteen who proves to be unruly or depraved, revoked, by the court which made the order or by any sheriff summary court having jurisdiction in the place where the original court sat, and if the order is revoked the child may be committed to prison.[28]

Disposal of Child Offenders

9-12 Although the provisions of the 1937 Act setting up juvenile courts have been repealed by the 1968 Act [29] parts of section 53 of the 1937 Act referring to juvenile courts remain in force, and presumably apply to summary courts hearing charges against children. Thus a court dealing with someone believed to be a child may continue to deal with him although it is discovered that he is not a child.[30] Further, where a child is remanded for information to be obtained about him any court acting for the same place may in his absence extend the period of remand provided he appears before a court at least once in every twenty-one days, and may deal with him finally once the information is obtained. Where the original remanding court made a finding that the child was guilty of the offence the disposing

[26] Ibid., para. 8.
[27] 1937 Act, s. 41 (1) as substituted by 1968 Act, Sched. 2, para. 4 (1).
[28] 1937 Act, s. 41 (2).
[29] 1968 Act, Sched. 2, para. 10.
[30] 1937 Act, s. 53 (1).

court need not hear any evidence of the offence except in so far as it considers such evidence will assist in determining how to deal with him.[31]

19–13　　The terms " conviction " and " sentence " are not used in relation to children dealt with summarily. Instead the terms " finding of guilt " and " order made upon a finding of guilt " are used. Any reference in any enactment to persons convicted, conviction or sentence is in the case of a child construed as including a reference to a person found guilty of an offence, a finding of guilt or an order made upon such a finding.[32]

Non-custodial sentences

19–14　　A court may deal with a child by way of absolute discharge, admonition, probation order or fine in the same way as it could deal with an adult on a similar charge before it. Where a child is ordered to pay expenses in addition to a fine the amount of expenses awarded may not exceed the amount of the fine.[33]

Where a child would if he were an adult be liable to imprisonment for non-payment of a fine or expenses the court may, if it considers that none of the other methods by which the case may be legally dealt with is suitable, order him to be detained for such period of not more than one month as it specifies in a place chosen by the local authority for the area in which the court sits.[34]

Where a child has been allowed time to pay a fine by a summary court detention cannot be ordered unless he has been placed under supervision in respect of the fine or unless the court is satisfied, on grounds which must be stated by the court, that supervision is impracticable.[35]

19–15　　The court may order the parent or guardian of the child to give security for his co-operation in securing the child's good behaviour. The order may not be made without giving the parent or guardian an opportunity of being heard except where he has been required to attend and has failed to do so.[36] Any sum ordered to be paid on forfeiture of the security is recoverable by imprisonment or civil diligence.[37] The court may not impose a fine on the parent or guardian.[38]

Custodial sentences

19–16　　Where a child is convicted on indictment and the court is of opinion that no other legally available method is suitable it may sentence him to be detained for a specific period. The child will then be liable to be detained during that period in such place and on such conditions as the Secretary of State may direct.[39]

---

[31] Ibid., s. 53 (4).
[32] 1937 Act, s. 63 (1).
[33] 1937 Act, s. 63 (2).
[34] 1937 Act, s. 58; 1968 Act, Sched. 2, para. 15.
[35] 1954 Act, s. 43B (4), (5), as inserted by 1963 Act, s. 25.
[36] 1937 Act, s. 59 (3).
[37] Ibid., s. 59 (4).
[38] 1968 Act, Sched. 9; repealing 1937 Act, s. 59 (1).
[39] 1937 Act, s. 57 (2); for release on licence see Criminal Justice Act 1967, s. 61.

Where a person convicted of murder appears to the court to have been under eighteen at the time of the offence he is sentenced to be detained during Her Majesty's pleasure, and is liable to be detained in such place and under such conditions as the Secretary of State may direct.[40]

9–17 A child found guilty of an offence in the sheriff summary court may be committed for such period of not more than two years as is specified by the court to such a place as the Secretary of State may direct for the purpose of undergoing residential training, and the child is liable during that period to be detained in that place subject to such conditions as the Secretary of State may direct.[41]

Children detained under section 57 or section 58A of the 1937 Act are deemed to be in legal custody while so detained.

9–18 The Secretary of State is empowered to order the transfer to a specified residential establishment of a child with respect to whom he is authorised to give directions under section 57 (2) of the 1937 Act and also of a person under the age of eighteen who is detained in borstal. The order may specify the period of detention which must not extend beyond his nineteenth birthday or the date on which his detention would otherwise have expired.[42]

Remits to hearings

9–19 Where a child who is not subject to a supervision requirement imposed by a hearing is found guilty of an offence the court may, instead of dealing with the case itself send it to the reporter of the local authority to arrange for its disposal by a hearing or for the purpose of obtaining advice from the hearing as to the treatment of the child.[43] Where the court obtains such advice it may either deal with the case itself or remit it to the reporter for disposal by a hearing.[44]

Where a child found guilty in a court is subject to a supervision requirement the court is obliged to ask the reporter to arrange for a hearing to give advice on his treatment. It may then deal with him itself or remit him to the reporter for disposal by a hearing.[45]

In the case of a person over the age of sixteen who is not within six months of being eighteen and is not subject to a supervision order, a summary court may ask the reporter to arrange for a hearing to give advice as to his treatment. The court may then dispose of the case or, if the hearing have so advised, remit it to the reporter for disposal by a hearing.[46]

A person over the age of sixteen who is remitted to the reporter under section 57 (1) of the 1968 Act is thereafter dealt with as a child.[47]

[40] 1937 Act, s. 57 (1), as substituted by Murder (Abolition of Death Penalty) Act 1965, s. 1 (5); for release on licence see Criminal Justice Act 1967, s. 61.
[41] 1937 Act, s. 58A (1), as substituted by 1968 Act, Sched. 2, para. 16.
[42] 1937 Act, s. 62.
[43] 1968 Act, s. 56 (1).
[44] Ibid., s. 56 (2).
[45] Ibid., s. 56 (3).
[46] Ibid., s. 57 (1).
[47] Ibid., s. 57 (2).

19-20   Where a case has been remitted by a court to the reporter for disposal
by a hearing the court's jurisdiction over the case ceases and the case
stands referred to a hearing.[48] A certificate by the clerk of the court that
the accused pleaded or was found guilty of the offence is conclusive evidence of the commission of the offence for the purpose of the remit.[49]

19-21   The provisions for remit and advice do not apply where the offence is
one the sentence for which is fixed by law.[50]

Breach of probation

19-22   Paragraph seven of the Act of Adjournal (Summary Proceedings)
(Children) 1971 makes the following provisions for dealing with a child
brought before a court upon information given on oath that he has failed
to comply with any of the requirements of a probation order:

" In any case where a child is to be brought before a Court upon
information given on oath that he has failed to comply with any of
the requirements of a probation order, the following procedure shall
be followed, viz. :

(1) The person under whose supervision the child has been placed
shall immediately upon making oath as aforesaid give intimation of the fact to the procurator fiscal.

(2) The citation (if any) requiring the appearance of the child shall
be accompanied by a notice giving the reasons for the issue of
such citation and stating in what respects it is alleged that any
one or more of the requirements of the order has or have not
been complied with by him, and in any case where the child
has been apprehended without prior citation such notice shall
be handed to him in court.

(3) The Court shall explain to the child in simple language suitable
to his age and understanding the effect of the notice and shall
then ask him whether he admits having failed to comply with
the requirements of the order as alleged: provided that where
the notice has been handed to the child in court, the Court
may, if it thinks it desirable, adjourn the proceedings for 48
hours before so interrogating him.

(4) If the child does not admit the alleged failure to comply with
the requirements of the order, the proceedings shall thereafter
be conducted and the matter shall be determined by the Court
in like manner as if the same were a matter which had arisen
for determination upon the original complaint."

Presumption and Determination of Age in Prosecutions

19-23   Section 103 of the 1937 Act provides that where a person charged with
an offence is brought before a court otherwise than as a witness and it

[48] Ibid., s. 56 (4); see infra, para. 19–104.
[49] Ibid., s. 56 (5).
[50] Ibid., s. 56 (6).

appears to the court that he is a child, the court shall make due inquiry as to his age, having regard to the definition of " child " in section 30 (1) of the 1968 Act, and take such evidence for that purpose as may be forthcoming during the case. No order or judgment of the court will be invalidated by any subsequent proof that his age was not correctly stated to the court or that the court was not informed at the material time that he was subject to a supervision requirement under the 1968 Act or that his case had been referred to a hearing under Part V of that Act.[51] The age presumed or declared by the court to be the person's age is deemed to be his true age for the purposes of the 1937 Act.[52] Where it appears to the court that the person's age is seventeen or over he is deemed not to be a child for the purposes of the 1937 Act.[53]

Restriction on Publicity of Court Proceedings

9-24   No newspaper report of any summary proceedings in a sheriff court in respect of an offence by a child may reveal the name, address or school, or include any particulars calculated to lead to the identification, of any person under the age of seventeen [sic] concerned in the proceedings either as the person against or in respect of whom the proceedings are taken or as being a witness, nor may any picture be published of any such person.[54] This requirement may be dispensed with in whole or in part by the court or the Secretary of State in any case if satisfied it is in the interest of justice to do so.[55]

9-25   No child under the age of fourteen years (except an infant in arms) may be present in court during the trial of any other person or during any proceedings preliminary to such trial, except in so far as his presence is required as a witness or otherwise for the purposes of justice. Any child who is present when his presence is forbidden must be ordered to be removed.[56]

9-26   Where a child is called as a witness in any proceedings relating to conduct contrary to decency or morality, only members or officers of court, parties and their counsel or solicitors, persons otherwise directly concerned in the case and bona fide journalists may be present in court during the child's evidence.[57]

9-27   The court is entitled to restrict the reporting of any such proceedings so as to prevent the publication of information or pictures revealing the identity of any person under seventeen years of age concerned in the proceedings.[58]

[51] 1937 Act, s. 103 (1), (1A); 1968 Act, Sched. 8, para. 9 (2).
[52] 1937 Act, s. 103 (1).
[53] Ibid.
[54] 1937 Act, s. 54 (1); this provision does not apply to proceedings where a child is charged jointly with an adult; 1937 Act, s. 50.
[55] Ibid.
[56] 1937 Act, s. 44.
[57] Ibid., s. 45.
[58] Ibid., s. 46.

II. Proceedings under Part III of the 1968 Act

19–28   The main purpose of Part III of the 1968 Act was to remove juvenile delinquents from the courts and to deal with them instead in a social welfare context; to see them not as criminals, or as persons guilty of offences for which they were responsible and so deserved punishment, but as persons in need of care, as socially deprived persons, deserving of support from social welfare agencies.[59] These agencies are organised within local authority departments of social work set up in counties and large burghs under the 1968 Act.[60] Part III of the 1968 Act deals specifically with children in need of compulsory measures of care, children who before the coming into force of that Part of the Act on April 15, 1971, would have been dealt with by juvenile or other courts.

Functions formerly carried out by the courts are now shared between specially constituted bodies called " children's hearings " and the courts. The place of the prosecutor in cases dealt with by hearings is now taken by an official called the reporter.

Children's panels and children's hearings

19–29   A children's panel has been formed for every local authority area (or group of areas).[61] It is made up of members appointed by the Secretary of State in such numbers as he considers appropriate. The Secretary of State also appoints a chairman and deputy chairman for each panel.[62] Members hold office for a period specified by the Secretary of State but may be removed by him at any time.[63] The names and addresses of panel members are open for public inspection.[64]

Sittings of children's hearings are constituted from the panel, each hearing consisting of a chairman and two other members. Each hearing must contain at least one man and one woman.[65] The selection of any hearing is made by the chairman, or in his absence the deputy chairman, of the panel, either directly or by standing arrangements made in consultation with the reporter and such panel members as the chairman may think fit.[66] The hearings sit in accommodation provided by the local authority, which need not be in its own area but which must be " dissociated " from criminal courts and police stations.[67]

The reporter

19–30   The reporter is appointed by the local authority. He may be a full-time or part-time official. The authority may also appoint deputy reporters.[68]

---

[59] See Report of Interdepartmental Committee on Children and Young Persons (Scotland) 1964, Cmnd. 2306: the " Kilbrandon Report."
[60] See " Social Work and the Community," Cmnd. 3065, 1966.
[61] 1968 Act, s. 33 (1): the relevant local authorities are counties and large burghs.
[62] Ibid., Sched. 3, para. 1.
[63] Ibid., para. 2.
[64] 1968 Act, s. 33 (3).
[65] 1968 Act, s. 34 (1), (2).
[66] Children's Hearings (Scotland) Rules 1971, rule 5 (1).
[67] 1968 Act, s. 34 (3).
[68] 1968 Act, s. 36 (1).

A deputy reporter has the same powers and duties as a reporter under the various procedural regulations made under the Act.[69] The reporter must be selected by the local authority from a list of suitable applicants compiled by the Secretary of State after advertisement by the local authority. If an advertisement produces no suitable applicants or none of the suitable applicants is acceptable to the local authority the Secretary of State may order re-advertisement.[70] A reporter may not be removed by the local authority or required to resign or be employed in any other capacity than as a reporter, except with the consent of the Secretary of State.[71] It would seem that the Secretary of State cannot himself remove a reporter from office. These provisions for protecting the security of tenure of the reporter do not apply to deputy reporters, whose tenure of office is governed by the Local Government (Scotland) Act 1947, as indeed is that of the reporter so far as not inconsistent with section 36 of the 1968 Act.[72]

The Act says nothing as to the qualifications of the reporter. He need not be legally qualified.

-31   The functions of the reporter are to arrange children's hearings,[73] and to investigate and take action on any information he receives about children likely to be in need of compulsory measures of care.[74] He is the most important person in the scheme of Part III of the 1968 Act since the decision whether or not to bring a child before a children's hearing as in need of compulsory measures of care rests entirely with him. There is no central authority such as Crown Office to exercise any control over or ensure any uniformity among reporters. So far as children coming to his notice as alleged offenders are concerned he has to take account both of whether the offence can be proved and of whether the offender is in need of compulsory care. In making his decision he has thus to consider not merely or even principally the nature or gravity of the offence (since cases where the offence is of paramount importance will be dealt with by the prosecutor), but the welfare and needs of the particular child, bearing in mind his personality, and his educational, family and other environmental circumstances. The leaflet entitled " To Tell You About the Children's Hearing," issued, with the authority of the Children's Hearing (Scotland) Rules 1971, to persons required to attend hearings,[74a] tells its readers that " the children's hearing are meeting to talk over your difficulties solely so that they can decide how you might best be helped."

The jurisdiction of the hearings

-32   There are no provisions regarding the territorial jurisdiction of a children's hearing. Normally they will deal with matters occurring within

---

[69] Children's Hearings (Scotland) Rules 1971, rule 2; Reporter's Duties and Transmission of Information, etc. (Scotland) Rules 1971, rule 2; Act of Sederunt (Social Work) (Sheriff Court Procedure Rules) 1971, rule 2.
[70] 1968 Act, s. 36 (2), (3).
[71] Ibid., s. 36 (4), (5).
[72] 1968 Act, s. 36 (7).   [73] 1968 Act, s. 36 (1).
[74] Ibid., s. 37 (1); 38 (1).
[74a] Children's Hearings (Scotland) Rules 1971, Forms 1–3.

the area of the local authority for which they sit. Where, however, any hearing are satisfied that a particular case could be better considered by a hearing in another local authority area they may ask their reporter to arrange with the reporter of that other area for a hearing in that area to dispose of the case.[75] A transfer of this kind can be made only with the consent of the reporter of the area to which it is wished to transfer the case.[76] Where a case is transferred the second hearing may proceed on the basis of any ground of referral accepted or established for the case at the first hearing.[77]

19-33   A child may be brought before a hearing on any of the following grounds, which are set out in section 32 (2) of the 1968 Act:

" (a) he is beyond the control of his parents; or

(b) through lack of parental care he is falling into bad associations or is exposed to moral danger; or

(c) the lack of care as aforesaid is likely to cause him unnecessary suffering or seriously to impair his health or development; or

(d) any of the offences mentioned in Schedule 1 to the Children and Young Persons (Scotland) Act 1937 has been committed in respect of him or in respect of a child who is a member of the same household; or

(e) the child, being a female, is a member of the same household as a female in respect of whom an offence which constitutes the crime of incest has been committed by a member of that household; or

(f) he has failed to attend school regularly without reasonable excuse; or

(g) he has committed an offence; or

(h) he is a child whose case has been referred to a children's hearing in pursuance of Part V of this Act."

This chapter is concerned only with ground (g). It is to be noted that the Act speaks of committing an offence and not of being guilty of an offence. It may therefore be argued that a child under the age of eight years, who is conclusively presumed to be incapable of being guilty of an offence [78] may nonetheless be dealt with by a hearing for committing an offence. It is submitted, however, that the phraseology of the 1968 Act reflects merely its sponsors' rejection of the terminology of the criminal law, and does not require either a hearing or a court to find that a child who cannot be guilty e.g. of an offence of theft, nonetheless committed theft. If Parliament had meant this to happen it could have done so by referring not to the commission of an offence but to the commission of what would if committed by a person of the age of eight years or over have been an offence.

[75] 1968 Act, s. 54 (1).
[76] Ibid.
[77] Ibid., s. 54 (2).
[78] 1937 Act, s. 55.

The reporter's decision

Where a reporter receives information of a case which may require to come to a children's hearing, he has three courses of action open to him among which he must decide after such initial investigation as he thinks necessary.[79]

-34   He may decide to take no further action, and in that event may if he thinks it proper to do so inform the child and his parent, and his own informant, or any of them.[80] There may thus be cases where the child and his parent are never aware that the child has been under consideration by the reporter.

He may refer the case to the local authority with a view to their making arrangements for the advice, guidance and assistance of the child and his family under Part II of the 1968 Act which deals mainly with the promotion of social welfare on a voluntary basis.[81]

He may refer the case to a hearing for consideration of compulsory measures of care.[82]

-35   If the reporter decides to take no further action or to refer the case to the local authority to be dealt with under Part II he may not subsequently refer the child to a hearing in relation to the same facts.[83] Whatever the reporter's decision he is obliged to keep a record of it, and where his informant was the local authority or a police officer, to notify the local authority or the appropriate chief constable.[84] But it is not clear what is to be included in the record, or on what basis or criterion a hearing may reject a case on the ground that it is based on facts which have already formed the subject of a decision not to take proceedings.   Nor, strangely enough, is there any provision preventing a reporter or a hearing from dealing with a child who has been dealt with by way of prosecution, or any provision entitling a child who is prosecuted to plead that his case has already been disposed of by a hearing. A reporter will not, however, in practice take action in any case which has been taken up by a prosecutor unless and until the prosecutor drops proceedings and the matter is referred to the reporter. Even then, it is hardly conceivable that the reporter would take up, say a case of homicide, in which the Crown had ordered no further proceedings, but such an action would not be incompetent.

Most information relating to offences will come to the reporter from the police who are obliged to report to him children alleged to have committed offences.[85]

---

[79] 1968 Act, ss. 38, 39. Throughout Part III of the 1968 Act, and the relevant subordinate legislation, " parent " includes a guardian: 1968 Act, s. 30 (2).

[80] 1968 Act, s. 39 (1).

[81] Ibid., s. 39 (2).

[82] Ibid., s. 39 (3).

[83] Ibid., s. 39 (5).

[84] Reporter's Duties and Transmission of Information, etc. (Scotland) Rules 1971, rule 3 (2); he must also record the name and address of all his informants: ibid., rule 3 (1).

[85] 1968 Act, s. 38 (2).

Arrested children

19–36   Where an arrested child is not liberated by the police under section 40 of the 1937 Act and it is decided (presumably by the police acting in accordance with the Lord Advocate's instructions as to the reporting of cases concerning children, or by the procurator fiscal) not to proceed with the charge against him the police must inform the reporter of the local authority of the area in which the child is being held, and the child may continue to be detained in a place of safety [86] until the reporter has decided what to do with him.[87]

Where a reporter decides that compulsory measures of care are not necessary the child is released.[88] A child may not be detained under section 40 of the 1937 Act for more than seven days.[89]

The reporter may authorise the person in charge of the place of safety to liberate the child if he is satisfied that further detention is unnecessary in his interest and if he has no reason to believe the child will run away during the investigation of the case.[90] Notification of liberation is given to the person in charge of the place of safety in a prescribed form [91] and to the child's parent.[92]

19–37   When the reporter considers the child is in need of compulsory measures of care and does not order his interim liberation he must whenever practicable arrange a hearing not later than in the course of the first lawful day after the commencement of the child's detention,[93] and the child may not continue to be detained under section 40 after the day on which that hearing sit.   Presumably the requirement that the reporter provide any hearing with certain documents three days before the hearing [94] does not apply to a hearing of this kind under section 37 (4) of the 1968 Act.

If the hearing called under section 37 (4) cannot dispose of the case and are satisfied that further detention is necessary in the child's interest, or have reason to believe he will run away during the investigation of his case, they may issue a warrant for his detention in any place of safety for up to twenty-one days. Such a warrant may be renewed on one occasion for up to another twenty-one days on cause shown by the reporter.[95]

19–38   Where a reporter receives information about a child who has not been arrested he may ask a hearing to issue a warrant for the child's apprehension if this is necessary to secure his appearance at the hearing of his case.[96] The hearing may also issue such a warrant of their own motion. The warrant may be executed as if it were a warrant issued by a court of

---

[86] Which may include a police station.
[87] 1937 Act, s. 40 (3), as inserted by 1968 Act, Sched. 2, para. 3 (3).
[88] Ibid., s. 40 (4) (a).
[89] Ibid., s. 40 (4) (c).
[90] Reporter's Duties and Transmission of Information, etc. (Scotland) Rules 1971, rule 4 (1).
[91] Ibid., Sched.
[92] Ibid., rule 4 (2).
[93] 1968 Act, s. 37 (4), (5).
[94] Children's Hearings (Scotland) Rules 1971, rule 6.
[95] 1968 Act, s. 37 (4).
[96] 1968 Act, s. 40 (3), (4).

summary jurisdiction.[97] It is authority for bringing the child before a hearing and for his detention in a place of safety.[98] A child arrested under such a warrant may not be detained on that warrant after the day on which a hearing first sit to hear his case, or for a period exceeding seven days.[99] Where a child arrested on such a warrant cannot be brought immediately before a hearing the reporter must wherever practicable arrange for a hearing to sit not later than the first lawful day after his arrest.[1]

-39   Where a hearing is arranged to consider the case of a child who has been detained, under section 37 (4) or section 40 (6) of the 1968 Act, the reporter must give the child notification of the hearing in the form of Form I of the Children's Hearings (Scotland) Rules 1971 as soon as possible before the hearing. This requirement is laid down by rule 7 (1) of the above Rules which goes on to provide that where the notification cannot be given in writing the reporter may notify the child orally that he is required to attend the hearing and of its date, time and place. Similar provisions apply to the notification of hearings of this kind to parents.[2] Notice of the grounds of referral need not be given at this stage unless the reporter wishes the case to be disposed of without a further hearing.[3] In any event a hearing under section 37 (4) of the 1968 Act may not proceed to dispose of the case unless the reporter provides them with a report of a local authority on the child and his social background.[4]

Where a hearing are considering the issue or renewal of a warrant under section 37 (4) they must give the child, his parent, and any representative attending the hearing, an opportunity of being heard.[5] The child and/or his parent are entitled to a copy of any warrant issued.[6]

Notification of hearings

-40   In the ordinary case, where the child is not detained, the reporter discharges his obligation to secure the attendance of a child at a hearing by sending him a notification of the hearing seven clear days before the hearing.[7] At the same time he must give notice of the hearing to any parent who has a duty to attend the hearing or to any parent who has a right so to attend, indicating whether or not his attendance is required, provided always that the parents' whereabouts are known.[8] Forms of notification are given in the Schedule to the Children's Hearings (Scotland) Rules 1971.

[97] Ibid., s. 40 (9).
[98] Ibid., s. 40 (4).
[99] Ibid., s. 40 (5).
[1] Ibid., s. 40 (6).
[2] Children's Hearings (Scotland) Rules 1971, rule 8 (4).
[3] The duty to give notice of grounds of referral refers to hearings under s. 39 (3), but not specifically to hearings under ss. 37 (4) or 40 (6): see Children's Hearings (Scotland) Rules 1971, Part IV.
[4] Children's Hearings (Scotland) Rules 1971, rule 21.
[5] Ibid., rule 23 (1).
[6] Ibid., rule 23 (2).
[7] Ibid., rule 7 (2).
[8] Ibid., rule 8.

Statement of grounds of referral, etc.

19–41   Where the hearing are to proceed to deal with the case under section 42 of the 1968 Act the reporter must give a statement of the grounds for the referral of the case to the child and, if his whereabouts are known, to his parent, seven clear days before the hearing or, if the child is in detention, as soon as practicable before the hearing.[9] This statement will normally be served with the notification of the hearing.

The statement of grounds is in the form as nearly as may be of Form 4A of the schedule to the Children's Hearings (Scotland) Rules 1971 and states the facts on the basis of which the referral is made. The statement of facts constituting the alleged offence must be as specific as a complaint under the 1954 Act and, unlike a complaint, must specify the nature of the offence in question.[10] The examples of offence given in the schedule are as follows:

" that on (*date*) between the hours of (   ) and (   ) (*state time*) at (*place*) he (*here specify the facts constituting the offence*) contrary to section (   ) of the Burgh Police (Scotland) Act 1892."

" that on (*date*) between the hours of (   ) and (   ) (*state time*) at (*place*) he stole (*specify the facts constituting the further offence*) being an offence of theft."

19–42   The reporter is also required to notify the members of the hearing seven, or at least three, days before the hearing and to supply them with certain documents including a copy of a local authority report on the child and his social background and a copy of the grounds for referral of the case.[11] Any documents supplied are to be returned to the reporter after the hearing. He must also inform the director of social work for the area in which the hearing sit.[12] When the reporter has arranged a hearing to consider the disposal of a child he requests a report on the child and his social background from the local authority who have a duty to supply the report which may contain information from any such person as the reporter or the local authority may think fit.[12a]

Procedure at Hearing
Presence of child

19–43   Normally the child is present during the hearing of his case but the hearing may consider all or part of a case in the absence of the child if they are satisfied that it would be detrimental to his interests to be present.[13] The leaflet, " To Tell You About the Children's Hearing," [13a] says, more generally, " [The hearing] may wish to talk to you or your parents separ-

---

[9] Ibid., rule 14.
[10] Ibid., rule 15.
[11] Ibid., rule 6 (1).
[12] Reporter's Duties and Transmission of Information, etc. (Scotland) Rules 1971, rule 5.
[12a] 1968 Act, s. 39 (4).
[13] 1968 Act, s. 40 (2).
[13a] Supra, para. 19–31.

ately, and may ask you to go outside while they talk to your parents."
The hearing have no right to talk to the child outwith the parent's
presence.[14]

Non-appearance warrant

-44   Where a child fails to attend any hearing of his case the hearing may on
cause shown by the reporter or of their own motion issue a warrant for his
apprehension if satisfied that this is necessary.[15] Such a warrant is the
same in effect and is followed by the same procedure as a warrant for the
apprehension of a child in order to secure his attendance at a hearing.[16]

Presence of parents and representative

-45   A parent has a right to attend at all stages of a hearing who are considering the case of his child,[17] and is obliged so to attend unless the hearing are satisfied that it would be unreasonable to require his attendance or
that his attendance would be unnecessary to the consideration of the case.[18]
It is not clear if these provisions prevent the members of the hearing retir-
ing to consider a case, or discussing it, at any time outwith the parent's
presence. A failure by a parent to attend as required is an offence carrying
a fine of £50 on summary conviction.[19]

"Parent" means either or both parents in the case of a legitimate
child, adopters in the case of an adopted child, and the mother of an
illegitimate child.[20] "Parent" includes a guardian.[20a]

-46   Both the child and his parent [21] attending a hearing may be accompanied by a representative. Child and parent may be represented separately
or by the same person. The representative is present to assist in the discussion of the case with the hearing.[22] A chairman may exclude a representative if the hearing are satisfied, of their own accord or on the motion of
child, parent or reporter, that the representative is persisting in behaviour
which disrupts the proceedings or is otherwise likely to be detrimental to
the child.[23]

The representative may or may not be legally qualified. A hearing may
therefore take place without the presence of any legally qualified person.
The child and his parents will not normally be in a position to know
whether any of the elaborate regulations laid down for the proceedings
have been disregarded, a factor which will reduce the number of appeals
from hearings. Legal aid is not available in proceedings before a hearing.

[14] 1968 Act, s. 41 (1).
[15] Ibid., s. 40 (1), (4).
[16] Supra, para. 19–38.
[17] 1968 Act, s. 41 (1).
[18] Ibid., s. 41 (2). See also infra, para. 19–57.
[19] Ibid., s. 41 (3).
[20] Ibid., s. 94.
[20a] Ibid., s. 30 (2).
[21] Quaere both parents.
[22] Children's Hearings (Scotland) Rules 1971, rule 11 (1), (2).
[23] Ibid., rule 11 (3).

Privacy of hearings

19-47   Children's hearings are private and apart from the child, his parent and their representative, members of the Council on Tribunals or the Scottish Committee thereof, and bona fide journalists, no one may be present unless his presence is necessary for the proper consideration of the case being heard or he is permitted to be present by the chairman.[24] Clearly the reporter's presence is necessary, and presumably the same is true of the social worker or workers who prepare the report on the child under section 39 (4) of the Act, although there is no explicit reference to them. The leaflet " To Tell You About the Children's Hearing " [24a] says that " the reporter and a social worker, possibly the one who has already had talks with you " will be present.

The chairman is obliged to take all reasonable steps to ensure that the number of persons present at any one time is kept to a minimum.[25] He may, however, permit the following persons to be present:

(a) the chairman and members of the Children's Panel Advisory Committee for the local authority area of the children's hearing and the clerk of the local authority;

(b) any members or possible members of children's panel whose attendance is required at children's hearings for the purpose of their training as members of children's hearings, and their instructors;

(c) any student engaged in formal education or training in social work or any person engaged in research relating to children who may be in need of compulsory measures of care;

(d) any other person whose presence at the sitting may in the opinion of the chairman be justified by special circumstances; and

(e) any clerk, interpreter, janitor, messenger or other person whose attendance in a like executive capacity is required or expedient for the proper conduct of the proceedings of the children's hearing.[26]

The procedure at a hearing, except in so far as otherwise provided, is at the discretion of the chairman.

Presumption and determination of age

19-48   When a person is brought before a hearing they must make inquiries as to his age, and if it appears that he is a child, they then proceed with the case. No decision or requirement made by the hearing will be invalidated by any subsequent proof that his age was not correctly stated, and the age presumed or declared by the hearing to be his age is deemed his true age for the purposes of Part III of the 1968 Act.[27] Where it appears that the person before the hearing is sixteen or over he is deemed not to be a child except as the Act otherwise provides.[28]

[24] 1968 Act, s. 35.
[24a] Supra, para. 19–31.
[25] 1968 Act, s. 35 (2).
[26] Children's Hearings (Scotland) Rules 1971, rule 12.
[27] 1968 Act, s. 55.
[28] Ibid.

Consideration of grounds of referral

–49   Before considering the case the chairman must explain to the child and his parent the grounds stated by the reporter for the referral in order to discover whether they are accepted in whole or part by the child and parent.[29] He should also explain the purpose of the hearing to them.[30]

Where the child and his parents, if present, accept the grounds for referral the hearing proceeds. Where the grounds are accepted in part the hearing may proceed on the grounds so far as accepted if they consider this proper.[31] The acceptance of an absent parent is not necessary to enable the hearing to proceed.[31a]

–50   There is no provision for any amendment or adjustment of the grounds for referral. If, therefore, a child appears on an allegation of theft and offers to accept an allegation of reset it appears that the hearing cannot proceed to deal with him but must direct the reporter to apply to the sheriff, whereupon the reporter may abandon the referral and perhaps take a fresh referral on the ground of reset.[32]

–51   Where the grounds for referral are not accepted in whole or the hearing does not agree to proceed on a partial acceptance, the reporter is directed to apply to the sheriff for a finding as to whether the disputed grounds are established.[33] It is not clear whether the acceptance or non-acceptance of grounds for referral is part of " the discussion of the case " in which a representative is entitled to assist child and parent.

–52   Where the hearing are satisfied the child is for any reason incapable of understanding the chairman's explanation of the grounds of referral, or where it appears that the explanation is not understood by the child, the hearing must either discharge the referral or direct the reporter to apply to the sheriff for a finding.[34]

Consideration of case

–53   Where the hearing are empowered to deal with the case they go on to consider it. During such consideration they are obliged to:

" (a) consider a report of a local authority on the child and his social background, and any judicial remit or other relevant document and any relevant information available to them;

(b) consider any report the submission of which has been requested by the manager of the residential establishment in which the child is required to reside;

(c) discuss the case with the child, parent, and representative if attending the hearing;

---

[29] Ibid., s. 42 (1).
[30] Children's Hearings (Scotland) Rules 1971, rule 17 (1).
[31] 1968 Act, s. 42 (2) (*a*), (*b*).
[31a] Ibid., s. 42 (8).
[32] See Act of Sederunt (Social Work) (Sheriff Court Procedure Rules) 1971, rule 7; cf. infra. para. 19–77.
[33] 1968 Act, s. 42 (2) (*c*).
[34] Ibid., s. 42 (7).

(d) endeavour to obtain the views of the said child and his parent, if attending the hearing, on what arrangements with respect to the child would be in the best interests of the child." [35]

19-54   The chairman must inform the child and his parent of the substance of any reports, documents and information mentioned in rule 17 (2) (a) (but not of any report requested by the manager of the residential establishment) if it appears to the chairman that this is material to the disposal of the case and that its disclosure would not be detrimental to the interests of the child.[36] Nothing is said about informing their representative. The leaflet " To Tell You About the Children's Hearing " [36a] says loosely, " [The hearing] will tell you what is in the social worker's report if they think it would be helpful to do so," which misrepresents the position to the detriment of the child and his parents.

There is no procedure for challenging or proving any statement in any report.

Adjournment of hearing

19-55   A hearing may be adjourned at any time provided it sits again on the same day.[37]

A hearing may at any time be continued to a later date for further investigation of the child and his history,[38] and where the hearing have reason to believe that the child may not attend at the continued hearing or any other proceedings arising from the case they may issue a warrant requiring his detention in a place of safety for up to twenty-one days.[39] Such a warrant may be renewed once only for up to twenty-one days on cause shown by the reporter.[40] Presumably a fresh warrant can be issued on each occasion on which a hearing sit to consider the case and continue the case for further investigation.

19-56   A hearing may require a child to attend or reside at any clinic, hospital or establishment for up to twenty-one days for the purpose of further investigation [41] and may issue a warrant under section 40 (7) if he fails to comply with the requirement.

Disposal of Case

Form of disposal

19-57   The Children's Hearings (Scotland) Rules 1971 provide that after the hearing have completed their consideration and made their decision the chairman, before the end of the hearing at which the decision was made,[42]

---

[35] Children's Hearings (Scotland) Rules 1971, rule 17 (2).
[36] Ibid., rule 17 (3); cf. Act of Adjournal (Summary Proceedings) (Children) 1971, para. 6 (6) (d), supra, para. 19–10.
[36a] Supra, para. 19–31.
[37] Children's Hearings (Scotland) Rules, rule 9 (2).
[38] Ibid., rule 10; 1968 Act, s. 43 (3).
[39] 1968 Act, s. 40 (7).
[40] Ibid., s. 40 (8).
[41] 1968 Act, s. 43 (4).
[42] Quaere if the hearing can hear, say, four cases, and then issue all four decisions after the fourth case.

must inform the child, parent and any representative of the decision and the reasons for the decision, and of their rights to appeal to the sheriff and to receive a written statement of the decision.[43] The parents' right to be present at all stages of the case is limited to the " consideration " of the case [44] and so does not cover the " making " of a decision. But there is no guidance as to how consideration and making are to be distinguished.

The chairman is obliged to provide a signed report of the hearing's decision and their reasons as soon as may be after the hearing.[45] The child and his parent are entitled to obtain a copy of this report from the reporter.[46] Where a child or parent was not present at the hearing the reporter must notify the absent child or parent of the decision, of the right to a copy of the statement of reasons, and of the right of appeal to the sheriff.[47]

Powers of disposal

9-58   A hearing may dispose of a case by discharging the referral if they decide that no further action is required.

9-59   If they do not discharge the referral but decide that the child is in need of compulsory measures of care, they may make a supervision requirement. Such a requirement either requires the child to submit to supervision in accordance with such conditions as they may impose, or requires him to reside in a named residential establishment [48] and to be subject to such conditions as they may impose.[49]

9-60   A " non-residential " supervision requirement may include a condition as to the child's place of residence in a place other than a residential establishment. The place may be in England or Wales.[50]

9-61   The Reporter's Duties and Transmission of Information etc. (Scotland) Rules 1971 empower the local authority to provide temporary accommodation for twenty-one days between the making of a supervision requirement and the child's reception in any place in which the requirement provides he is to reside. Where they cannot make arrangements for his reception in twenty-one days a hearing must sit to review the requirement, if possible within the twenty-one days.[51]

9-62   A " residential " requirement must have regard to the child's religious persuasion.[52]

---

[43] Children's Hearings (Scotland) Rules 1971, rule 17 (4).
[44] 1968 Act, s. 41 (1).
[45] Children's Hearings (Scotland) Rules 1971, rule 9 (3).
[46] Ibid., rule 18 (1).
[47] Ibid., rule 18 (2).
[48] A " residential establishment " is " an establishment managed by a local authority, voluntary organisation or any other person, which provides residential accommodation for the purposes of this Act, whether for reward or not ": 1968 Act, s. 94 (1). It may be an institution known before April 15, 1971 as an approved school and since then as a List D establishment.
[49] 1968 Act, s. 44.
[50] Ibid., s. 44 (1).
[51] Rule 12.
[52] 1968 Act, s. 44 (2).

19–63   Where in any case it seems that the education authority may need to exercise its function of ascertaining whether the child is under a disability,[53] the hearing will send a report to that effect to the education authority concerned.[54]

19–64   The effect of a supervision requirement is to place the child in the care of the local authority for the area for which the hearing sit, for most of the purposes set out in Part II of the Act, including the right to assume parental rights in certain circumstances.[55] Where, however, the performance of any function under Part II requires or would be facilitated by a change in the supervision requirement the authority must seek a review of the requirement.[56]

19–65   The hearing may not deal with the child by admonition or fine, or in any other way than by discharge or supervision requirement. They may, however, postpone the operation of a supervision requirement.[57] Nothing is said as to whether the postponement must be to a specific date or may be subject to conditions, or as to how this form of suspended sentence is to be activated or prevented from coming into force.

19–66   A supervision requirement, unless discharged or varied on review, lasts till the child is eighteen.[58]

Applications to Sheriff

19–67   Where the child or either parent disputes the grounds for referral or the child cannot or does not understand them the hearing may discharge the referral. If they do not discharge it they must direct the reporter to apply to the sheriff for a finding as to whether the grounds are established.[59]

Where such a direction is given the chairman will inform the child and his parent of the purpose of the application to the sheriff.[60] The hearing may exercise their right to order the child's detention under section 40 (7) of the Act to ensure the child's attendance before the sheriff.

Arrangements for hearing application

19–68   The reporter issues an initial notification of the application to the sheriff to the child and parent, telling them that they will be told of the time and place of the hearing of the application later.[61]

The reporter is obliged to lodge his application with the sheriff clerk within seven days of the direction.[62] The sheriff clerk then assigns a diet

---

[53] See Education (Scotland) Act 1962, s. 63.
[54] 1968 Act, s. 44 (4).
[55] 1968 Act, ss. 40 (5), 16–18, 20, 24–26, 28, 29.
[56] Ibid., s. 44 (5).
[57] 1968 Act, s. 44 (3).
[58] 1968 Act, s. 47 (2). Where a child subject to a supervision requirement reaches the age of sixteen the reporter must inform the chief constable of the police area in which the local authority area is situated and of that in which the child resides: Reporter's Duties and Transmission of Information etc. (Scotland) Rules 1971, rule 8.
[59] 1968 Act, s. 42 (2), (7); the sheriff is presumably one having (civil?) jurisdiction in the area for which the children's hearing sit, but the Act is silent on this.
[60] Ibid., s. 43 (3).
[61] Children's Hearings (Scotland) Rules 1971, rule 16; Forms 5 and 6.
[62] Act of Sederunt (Social Work) (Sheriff Court Procedure Rules) 1971, rule 4 (1).

and issues a warrant.[63] The diet must be within twenty-eight days of the lodging of the application.[64]

On the issue of the warrant the reporter cites the child by serving a copy of the application and warrant with citation attached.[65] He must as soon as possible also intimate the diet to any parent whose whereabouts are known by serving on him a copy of the application and warrant with citation attached.[66] Executions of citations or intimations under rule 6 of the Act of Sederunt [67] are made in accordance with Form 5 of the Schedule to the Act of Sederunt. Citation or intimation is made on an induciae of not less than forty-eight hours, or seventy-two hours in the case of postal citation.[68]

9–69   The warrant assigning the first diet or the warrant for any continued diet are warrants for citation of witnesses and havers.[69] Citation or intimation to any person is sufficiently made if it is:

(a) delivered to him personally; or

(b) left for him at his dwellinghouse or place of business with some person resident or employed therein; or

(c) where it cannot be delivered to him personally and he has no known dwellinghouse or place of business, left for him at any other place at which he may at the time be resident; or

(d) where he is the master of, or   seaman or person employed in, a vessel, left with a person on board thereof or connected therewith; or

(e) sent by post, in a registered or recorded delivery letter, to his dwellinghouse or place of business, or if he has no known dwellinghouse or place of business to any other place in which he may at the time be resident.[70]

9–70   Citation of witnesses on behalf of the child or his parents may be made by a sheriff officer or, in the case of postal citation, by a solicitor.[71]

9–71   Warrants of citation, intimation or service may be executed in any sheriffdom without endorsation by the local sheriff clerk,[72] and may be signed by the sheriff clerk.[73]

Representation and legal aid

9–72   A child or his parent may be represented at any diet at which the sheriff hears an application.[73a] This right of representation is expressed to be " without prejudice to their right of legal representation," so that presum-

---

[63] Ibid., rule 5.
[64] 1968 Act, s. 42 (4).
[65] Act of Sederunt (Social Work) (Sheriff Court Procedure Rules) 1971, rule 6 (1); Form 3.
[66] Ibid., rule 6 (2); Form 4.
[67] Supra.
[68] Ibid., rule 17.
[69] Ibid., rule 18 (1); Form 11 is a form for execution of such citations.
[70] Ibid., rule 19 (2).
[71] Ibid., rule 20.
[72] Ibid., rule 22.
[73] Ibid., rule 23.
[73a] 1968 Act, s. 42 (4).

ably anyone may represent child or parent before the sheriff and perhaps, as before the children's hearing, they may be separately represented.

19–73 A child or his parent may be given legal aid for the purposes of the application if the sheriff is satisfied (a) that legal aid is necessary in the interests of the child [74] and (b) after considering the financial circumstances of the child, or of the child and his parent, as the case may be, that the expenses of the case cannot be met without undue hardship to the child or, as the case may be, to the parents or the dependants of either.[75]

The legal aid provisions are comparable to those for legal aid in criminal proceedings. Applications for legal aid are made in writing to the sheriff clerk and heard by the sheriff in chambers.[76] Although the Legal Aid (Scotland) Act 1967 talks only of financial eligibility and " the interests of the child " [77] the Act of Sederunt (Legal Aid) (Children) 1971 provides that the sheriff shall grant legal aid if satisfied on financial grounds " and that it is in the interests of justice that legal aid should be made available," [78] which is an importation of a condition applied by the Legal Aid (Scotland) Act 1967 to legal aid in criminal proceedings.[79] Where parent or child have other sources of assistance in litigation legal aid will not be given.[80]

The sheriff may disqualify a person for continuance of legal aid on the ground of misconduct, as he may in the case of criminal proceedings.[81]

Hearing of application

19–74 An application under section 42 is heard summarily [82] and in chambers.[83] The hearing of the application is begun with evidence tendered by or on behalf of the reporter.[84] At the end of the reporter's case the sheriff may either hold that a prima facie case has not been made out (as to which he can presumably hear submissions on behalf of the child or parent) or tell the child and his parent or representative that they may give evidence or make a statement (presumably an unsworn statement not subject to cross-examination) and call witnesses.[85] The sheriff may hear evidence in the absence of the child but not of his parent or representative where the nature of the case or of the evidence renders this course suitable in the interests of the child.[86] It will be only rarely that evidence relating to an offence will be led in the absence of the child, but it is competent for this

[74] Legal Aid (Scotland) Act 1967, s. 1 (6A), inserted by 1968 Act, Sched. 4.
[75] Ibid., s. 2 (2).
[76] Act of Sederunt (Legal Aid) (Children) 1971, para. 4 (1).
[77] S. 1 (6A) (b).
[78] Para. 4 (4).
[79] Legal Aid (Scotland) Act 1967, s. 1 (7) (a) (ii).
[80] Act of Sederunt (Legal Aid) (Children) 1971, para. 4 (2).
[81] Ibid., para. 8; cf. supra, para. 5–66. Detailed provision for legal aid is made in the Legal Aid (Scotland) (Children) Regulations 1971 and the Legal Aid (Scotland) (Children) Scheme 1971. The general framework is similar to that for legal aid in criminal proceedings.
[82] Act of Sederunt (Social Work) (Sheriff Court Procedure Rules) 1971, rule 26.
[83] 1968 Act, s. 42 (4).
[84] Act of Sederunt (Social Work) (Sheriff Court Procedure Rules) 1971, rule 8 (1).
[85] Ibid., rule 8 (2).
[86] Ibid., rule 8 (3).

to be done. The sheriff may also hear the child's evidence or statement in the absence of the parent if satisfied that in the special circumstances it is proper to exclude the parent. If he does this he must inform the parent of any allegation made by the child and give him an opportunity to refute it.[87] This again is unlikely to occur in relation to an offence.

Subject to the requirement of section 42 (4) of the 1968 Act that applications must be heard within twenty-eight days the sheriff may continue the case for such reasonable time as he may consider necessary.[88]

9–75 Where a child fails to attend before the sheriff he may grant a warrant for his apprehension, which warrant is authority to bring him before the sheriff and for his detention in a place of safety until the application can be heard. Such a warrant is not effective to detain the child for more than seven days or beyond the disposal of the application.[89]

9–76 Where the ground of referral is an offence the sheriff is directed to apply to the evidence the standard of proof required in criminal procedure.[90] Apart from this the legislation is silent as to what rules are to be applied to what is notionally a civil proceeding designed to determine whether a particular person has committed an offence. Since the purpose of the referral to the sheriff in such cases is to protect the rights of the child it would be reasonable to apply the general rules of criminal evidence such as the rule [91] that the " accused " is not obliged to give evidence and so cannot be called as a witness on behalf of the reporter.

Disposal of application

9–77 Where the sheriff holds that none of the grounds of referral in respect of which the application was made has been established he dismisses the application and discharges the referral.[92] It is open to the reporter, at any stage before the application is determined, to abandon all or part of the application by lodging a minute or by motion at the hearing and by intimating the abandonment to the child and his parent. The sheriff will then dismiss the application and discharge the referral in so far as it relates to any ground which has been abandoned.[93]

9–78 Rule 10 of the Act of Sederunt (Social Work) (Sheriff Court Procedure Rules) 1971 provides that where the grounds of referral are alleged to constitute an offence or attempted offence the sheriff may find on the facts that any offence established by the facts has been committed. This is presumably intended to serve the same purpose as section 60 of the 1887 Act, and enables the sheriff to find that parts of the facts alleged have been established and constitute an attempt at the offence charged or an offence other than that charged. It would seem, however, that where a ground of

---

[87] Ibid., rule 8 (4).
[88] Ibid., rule 9.
[89] 1968 Act, s. 42 (3).
[90] Ibid., s. 42 (6).
[91] Whose preservation may be envisaged by rule 8 (2) of the Act of Sederunt (Social Work) (Sheriff Court Procedure Rules) 1971.
[92] 1968 Act, s. 42 (5).
[93] Act of Sederunt (Social Work) (Sheriff Court Procedure Rules) 1971, rule 7.

referral alleges that the child " stole " an article the sheriff has no power to find that he reset it, or obtained it by fraud, although on an allegation of robbery it might be open to him to find that theft was committed. All these suggestions assume that the facts on which the sheriff proceeds must be facts stated in the statement of grounds of referral. And it is submitted that this must be so, as otherwise the requirement that facts be specified would be pointless. There is no provision for amending the statement of facts either before the sheriff or elsewhere.

19–79 Where the sheriff is satisfied that any ground has been made out he remits the case to the reporter to arrange for a children's hearing to consider and determine the case.[94]

19–80 The sheriff gives his decision orally at the conclusion of the hearing of the application, and a copy of his interlocutor is sent by the sheriff clerk to the child and his parent and to the reporter.[95] The reporter then issues the appropriate notifications for the child and his parent and representatives, if any, to attend a children's hearing which will proceed to consider and determine the case on the ground of referral established before the sheriff in accordance with the Children's Hearings (Scotland) Rules 1971 and sections 43 and 44 of the 1968 Act.

Appeals

19–81 Quite apart from applications to the sheriff to determine disputes of fact as to the grounds of referral, there is an appeal to the sheriff from any decision of a children's hearing, including a decision to grant or renew a warrant of arrest or detention,[96] or to make a requirement of residence at a clinic etc., for investigation under section 43 (4) of the Act.

Form of appeal to sheriff

19–82 The child or his parent may take an appeal any time within three weeks of the date of the decision appealed against [97] in the form as nearly as may be to Form 6 of the Schedule to the Act of Sederunt (Social Work) (Sheriff Court Procedure Rules) 1971.[98]

The forms suggest that the grounds of appeal against a disposal under section 44 may be that the measures prescribed are not appropriate, or may be based on a point of law or on grounds of irregularity. Appeals against warrants or a section 43 (4) requirement are on the ground that they are unnecessary. The forms of course require specification of the point or facts founded of or of the reasons for claiming that the warrant or requirement was unnecessary.

19–83 The reporter may lodge answers to the appeal, of which he must serve a copy on the child and his parent.[99] The reporter must lodge with

---

94 1968 Act, s. 42 (6).
95 Act of Sederunt (Social Work) (Sheriff Court Procedure Rules) 1971, rule 16.
96 1968 Act, s. 49.
97 1968 Act, s. 49 (1).
98 Rule 12 (1); there are separate forms for appeals against disposal, appeals against a warrant, and appeals against a requirement under s. 43 (4) of the Act.
99 Act of Sederunt (Social Work) (Sheriff Court Procedure Rules) 1971, rule 12 (3).

the sheriff clerk all reports and statements available to the hearing along
with the reports of their proceedings and the reasons for their decision.[1]

-84   The sheriff clerk must assign a diet for the appeal as soon as practicable
and issue a warrant in the form of Form 7 of the Schedule to the rules[2] and
send a copy of the appeal and the warrant to the reporter.[3] An appeal
against the issue of a warrant must be disposed of within three days of being
lodged, otherwise the warrant ceases to have effect.[4]

Suspension of supervision requirements

-85   Where an appeal is taken against a decision of a children's hearing
relating to a supervision requirement, the child or parent may apply " to a
children's hearing " (Quaere " to any children's hearing ") for a suspension
of the requirement. The reporter will then forthwith arrange for a hearing
to consider the application.[5] The decision of that hearing does not seem
to be appealable, or at any rate not so as to ensure the hearing of that
appeal before the appeal against the requirement. If the appellant does
not attend the hearing of his application it is treated as abandoned.[6]

Legal aid

-86   Legal aid is available in these appeals in much the same way as it is in
applications for a finding as to whether a ground for referral has been
established.[7] Where legal aid has been given in an application the child or
his parent continue to be regarded as financially eligible for legal aid for an
appeal. The appeal is otherwise treated as a distinct proceeding from such
an application.[8] Legal aid is available for an appeal against the detention
of a child in a place of safety pending the disposal of his case without any
enquiry into means.[9]

Hearing of appeal by sheriff

-87   The appeal, which is heard summarily [10] in chambers,[11] opens with a
statement from the appellant or his representative.[12] The sheriff may then
" examine " the reporter and the authors or compilers of any reports or
statements.[13] Presumably he does this in discussion and not by calling
them as witnesses. Where a ground of appeal is an alleged irregularity in
the conduct of a case the sheriff may proceed on any facts stated in the
appeal which are admitted by the reporter, and otherwise must hear

[1] 1968 Act, s. 49 (2).
[2] Act of Sederunt (Social Work) (Sheriff Court Procedure Rules) 1971, rule 13.
[3] Ibid.
[4] 1968 Act, s. 49 (7).
[5] Ibid., s. 49 (8).
[6] Children's Hearings (Scotland) Rules 1971, rule 20 (5).
[7] Supra, para. 19–73.
[8] Act of Sederunt (Legal Aid) (Children) 1971, para. 2 (c).
[9] Legal Aid (Scotland) Act 1967, s. 2 (5A), inserted by 1968 Act, Sched. 4; cf. Act of Sederunt
(Legal Aid) (Children) 1971, para. 3.
[10] Act of Sederunt (Social Work) (Sheriff Court Procedure Rules) 1971, rule 26.
[11] 1968 Act, s. 49 (1).
[12] Act of Sederunt (Social Work) (Sheriff Court Procedure Rules) 1971, rule 14 (1).
[13] 1968 Act, s. 49 (3).

evidence by or on behalf of the appellant, and any evidence of the reporter and of any witnesses called by the parties.[14] No guidance is given as to the rules of evidence or standard of proof to be applied. The sheriff may exclude the child but not his parent or representative during the examination of an author or compiler of a report or at any other stage if he thinks the child should not be present.[15] His power to exclude a parent while a child is giving evidence or making a statement in an application is applied " with necessary modifications " to an appeal.[16]

A sheriff may call for further reports to assist him in deciding an appeal [17] and may for that purpose or for any other necessary cause, on the motion of either party or on his own motion, adjourn the appeal for a reasonable time.[18] He may also adjourn the appeal to allow the child or his parent or a representative to lead evidence with regard to information disclosed to them in the course of the appeal.[19] This is in a way a strange rule as there appears to be no provision anywhere else allowing the child or his parent to lead any evidence with regard to the contents of any information laid before a children's hearing in reports or otherwise.

Disposal of appeal by sheriff

19–88   The sheriff's decision is given orally either at the conclusion of the appeal or on an appointed day.[20]

Where an appeal fails the sheriff confirms the decision of the hearing.[21]

The sheriff must allow an appeal if he is satisfied that the decision of the children's hearing is not justified in all the circumstance of the case.[22] He then recalls the warrant in the case of an appeal against the issue of a warrant, and otherwise may remit the case to a children's hearing for their consideration, or discharge the child from any further proceedings on the ground for the referral of the case.[23] Where he remits a case for reconsideration the sheriff must issue a note of the reasons for his decision, which is transmitted to the reporter and the appellant.[24]

Appeal to Court of Session

19–89   An appeal lies to the Court of Session by way of stated case on a point of law or in respect of any irregularity in the conduct of the case, at the instance of a child and/or his parent or of a reporter, from any decision of the sheriff. This is the only appeal competent from the sheriff.[25] An application for a stated case must be made within twenty-eight days of the

14 Act of Sederunt (Social Work) (Sheriff Court Procedure Rules) 1971, rule 14 (2).
15 Ibid., rule 14 (3).
16 Ibid., rule 14 (4); supra, para. 19-74.
17 1968 Act, s. 49 (3).
18 Act of Sederunt (Social Work) (Sheriff Court Procedure Rules) 1971, rule 15 (1).
19 Ibid., rule 15 (2).
20 Ibid., rule 16 (1).
21 1968 Act, s. 49 (4).
22 Ibid., s. 49 (5).
23 Ibid.
24 Act of Sederunt (Social Work) (Sheriff Court Procedure Rules) 1971, rule 16.
25 1968 Act, s. 50 (1).

sheriff's decision.[26] There may thus be in the course of any case an application to the sheriff for a finding of fact on the ground of referral, an appeal to the Court of Session against that finding, a disposal by the hearing, and an appeal to the sheriff and from him to the Court of Session on the disposal. Such a course of events is, however, very unlikely. The sheriff must prepare a draft stated case within fourteen days of application and send a copy to the parties.[27] The sheriff may require the reporter to return to the sheriff clerk any relevant report or statement which has been returned to the reporter after an appeal.[28] Any party desiring the stated case to be adjusted must return his copy of the case with his adjustments to the sheriff within fourteen days of being sent the draft case.[29] As soon as possible after the return of the copies or, if none is returned, within fourteen days of the issue of the draft the sheriff states and signs his case and delivers it to the appellant.[30] It is then for the appellant to intimate and lodge the case in terms of rule 277 of the Rules of Court.[31]

90 The court may hear all or any of the proceedings in chambers.[32]

91 On deciding the appeal the court remits the case to the sheriff to proceed in accordance with such directions as the court gives.[33]

92 No appeal lies to the Court of Session against a decision of a children's hearing imposing a supervision requirement where the only ground of appeal is that the treatment prescribed is inappropriate for the child.[34] This does not prevent an appeal on the ground that the treatment is, as a matter of law, inappropriate for any child, e.g. because it involves corporal punishment.

93 It has been suggested [35] that the Court of Session can deal only with points of law or irregularities arising before the sheriff. But section 50 (1) talks about an appeal from the sheriff on a point of law or any irregularity *in the conduct of the case*, and it seems clear that the purpose of the provision is merely to prevent an appeal to the Court of Session on any point of fact such as the accuracy of any report, or the sheriff's finding that the ground of referral had been made out unless that finding was based on error of law or irregularity. The same author states boldly that a gross irregularity in the proceedings before the hearing is not appealable even to the sheriff " whose concern seems to be to determine whether the decision of the hearing is justified." [36] But there is no limitation of the possible grounds of appeal under section 49, and the Act of Sederunt (Social Work)

[26] Ibid., s. 50 (2).
[27] Rules of Court, rule 289A (1).
[28] Ibid., rule 289A (2).
[29] Ibid., rule 289A (3).
[30] Ibid., rule 289A (4).
[31] Ibid., rule 289A (5).
[32] Ibid., rule 289A (7).
[33] 1968 Act, s. 50 (3).
[34] 1968 Act, s. 50 (4).
[35] John P. Grant, " Juvenile Justice: Part III of the Social Work (Scotland) Act 1968," 1971 J.R. 149, 172–173.
[36] Ibid., p. 173.

(Sheriff Court Procedure Rules) 1971 clearly envisages appeals on the ground of irregularity or on points of law.[37]

19-94 Legal aid is available for appeals to the Court of Session if there is substantial ground for the appeal and legal aid is regarded as reasonable in the particular circumstances of the case, and the appellant is financially eligible therefor.[38]

Procedure on remit to hearing after appeal

19-95 Where a case is remitted by the sheriff to a children's hearing after an appeal to the sheriff and/or the Court of Session the reporter then issues the normal notifications and arranges a children's hearing to reconsider the case which proceeds, on the basis of the decision of the appellate court, in the same way as an initial hearing.[39]

19-96 There is a right of appeal to the sheriff against the decision reached by a children's hearing after reconsideration by them of a case remitted to them by the sheriff after an appeal under section 49 or 50 of the 1968 Act, and that appeal is governed by the same provisions as appeals against an initial decision, except that it must be taken within seven days of the decision.[40] Presumably the sheriff's decision on this appeal is appealable to the Court of Session as a decision of the sheriff in terms of section 50 (1) of the 1968 Act.

Review Proceedings

19-97 One of the principal features of the 1968 Act is the provision it makes for the continuing supervision of a child who has been dealt with by a children's hearing. This continuing supervision is exercised by means of review proceedings.

All supervision requirements are liable to at least annual review, and any supervision requirement which is not reviewed within a year of its making or its last continuance ceases to have effect at the end of the year.[41]

The child or his parent may require a review at the end of any of the following periods: (1) three months from the initial making of the requirement; (2) three months from the date of a review which varied a previous requirement; or (3) six months from the date of a review which merely continued a previous requirement.[42]

A local authority may require a supervision requirement to be reviewed at any time.[43] Where a local authority consider that any supervision requirement should cease or should be varied they must refer the case to their reporter for review by a hearing which may terminate the requirement, or continue or vary it.[44] Part of the function of the local authority is

[37] Rule 14 (2); Form 6A.
[38] Legal Aid (Scotland) Act 1967, ss. 1 (6A) (c); 2 (3) (e); 2 (4) (d); all inserted by 1968 Act, Sched. 4.
[39] Children's Hearings (Scotland) Rules 1971, Part IV.
[40] 1968 Act, s. 51 (2).
[41] 1968 Act, s. 48 (3).
[42] Ibid., s. 48 (4).
[43] Ibid., s. 48 (2).
[44] Ibid., s. 47 (1).

to enforce the Act's provision that no child shall continue to be subject to a supervision requirement for any time longer than is necessary in his interest.

–98   The 1968 Act provides that in review applications by a local authority the hearing may make any such supervision requirement as may be made under section 44 [45] and provides generally that in disposing of a case on review section 44 shall apply.[46] A review hearing may therefore vary a supervision requirement by imposing additional conditions, or by changing a non-residential requirement into a residential one, whether or not it is asked to do so by the local authority, child or parent who sought the review. Although the Act does not specifically say so, a review hearing requested by a child or parent can presumably terminate an order in the same way as a review hearing requested by the local authority.

Arrangement of review hearings

–99   Review hearings are arranged by the reporter at the request of child, parent or local authority.[47] Where the review is requested by the child or his parent they are entitled to at least seven days' notice of the hearing.[48] The rules do not provide for notification of other review hearings to the child unless a previous hearing has determined that the attendance of the child will be necessary or expedient,[49] which is a reversal of the approach of section 40 of the 1968 Act which requires a child's presence unless the children's hearing dealing with the matter think it would be detrimental to his interests to be present. The parent is entitled to the same notification as in the case of an initial hearing.[50]

Conduct of review hearings

100   A review hearing is conducted in the same way as an initial hearing.[51] Since, however, there are no " grounds for referral " at a review there is no provision for any remit to a sheriff to settle any disputed facts. There is indeed no machinery at all for determining any dispute as to the circumstances on the basis of which the review is sought.

101   A review decision is subject to appeal in the same way as any other decision by a hearing.[52] Where, however, the sheriff is satisfied that an appeal against a requirement made at a review is frivolous he may order that no appeal against a decision to continue that requirement on a subsequent review shall be made for a period of twelve months following on the order.[53]

[45] Ibid., s. 47 (1); supra, paras. 19–58 et seq.
[46] Ibid., s. 48 (6).
[47] Ibid., s. 48 (5).
[48] Children's Hearings (Scotland) Rules 1971, rule 7 (2) (b).
[49] Ibid., rule 7 (2).
[50] Ibid., rule 8; supra, para. 19–40.
[51] Ibid., Part IV, especially rules 17 and 18; supra, paras. 19–53; 19–57.
[52] 1968 Act, s. 49.
[53] Ibid., s. 49 (6).

Miscellaneous Matters

Termination of supervision requirements

19–102   All supervision requirements cease to have effect when the child reaches the age of eighteen.[54] Within three months before that time the local authority must refer the case to the reporter so that a hearing may advise whether the child still requires supervision and guidance, and if they do so advise the authority must provide such supervision and guidance as the child is prepared to accept.[55]

The Secretary of State may terminate a supervision requirement at any time if satisfied that this should be done having regard to the circumstances of the case and the needs of the child.[56]

Transfer of child in cases of urgency

19–103   Where a child is required to reside in any place by a supervision requirement he may be transferred by a director of social work to another place if this is urgently necessary in the interests of the child or of other children in the former place.[57] The case of any child so transferred must be reviewed by a hearing within seven days of his transfer.[58] The child and his parent are entitled to written or oral notification of the review hearing as soon as possible before its occurrence.[59] The hearing itself proceeds like any other review hearing.[60]

Hearing of remits from sheriff

19–104   Where a court remits a person convicted or found guilty of an offence to a reporter for disposal by a hearing under sections 56 (1) (*a*), 56 (2), 56 (3), or 57 of the 1968 Act [61] the court ceases to have any jurisdiction over the child and " his case shall stand referred " to the hearing.[62] The rules regarding notification of the hearing to the child and his parent presumably apply as if the hearing were on an initial referral.[63] The hearing proceeds as if it were a hearing on an initial referral on accepted or established grounds.[64] There is the usual appeal to the sheriff and the Court of Session against the hearing's decision. What is not clear is what appeal lies against the conviction or finding of guilt by the court. A stated case cannot be brought under the 1954 Act until the case is finally determined [65]: is it finally determined when the court's jurisdiction ceases, when the

---

[54] Ibid., s. 47 (2).
[55] The power to guide and supervise arises from Part II of the 1968 Act. The procedure before the hearing is governed by Part V of the Children's Hearings (Scotland) Rules 1971.
[56] 1968 Act, s. 52.
[57] 1968 Act, s. 44 (6).
[58] Ibid., s. 44 (7).
[59] Children's Hearings (Scotland) Rules 1971, rules 7 (1) (*b*), 8 (4).
[60] Ibid., rules 13, 17, 18.
[61] Supra, paras. 19–19 et seq.
[62] 1968 Act, s. 56 (4).
[63] Children's Hearings (Scotland) Rules 1971, rule 7 (2) (*a*); 1968 Act, s. 56 (4).
[64] Ibid., Part IV.
[65] Supra, para. 16–02.

hearing come to a decision under section 44 of the 1968 Act, or when a supervision requirement imposed by the hearing comes to an end, which may not be for nearly ten years? Can a stated case under the 1954 Act be taken to the High Court before, concurrently with, or after, an appeal to the sheriff or the Court of Session under the 1968 Act? Can one appeal the sheriff's decision if the hearing discharge the referral under section 43 of the 1968 Act? Or is the appropriate remedy to take a bill of suspension before the case reaches a children's hearing?

-105 Where a court refers a case for advice under sections 56 (1) (b), 56 (3), or 57 of the 1968 Act, the child and his parent are entitled to the same notification as in the case of an initial hearing.[66] Where child, parent or representative are present the chairman begins the hearing by explaining the purpose of the hearing.[67] The hearing then consider the case, and (a) consider the reference by the court, any supervision requirement to which the child is subject, the report of a local authority on the child and his social background, and any other relevant document or any relevant information available to them; (b) discuss the case of the child and afford to the child, parent and representative, if attending the hearing, an opportunity of participating in the discussion and of being heard on the case; and (c) endeavour to obtain the views of the child and his parent, if attending the hearing, on what arrangements with respect to the child would be in his best interest.[68] The child and his parent are entitled to be informed by the chairman of the substance of any reports, documents or information considered by the court if he thinks this is material to the advice that will be given and that its disclosure would not be detrimental to the interests of the child.[69]

The hearing then determine what advice they will give. There is no provision for informing the child or his parent or any representative of what this advice is.

Absconding children

-106 Where a child absconds from a place of safety or from the control of a person under whose control he has been placed by a supervision requirement or by virtue of rules relating to his conveyance to a residential establishment or elsewhere, he may be arrested without warrant in any part of the United Kingdom or Channel Islands.[70] Where after his arrest the occupier of the place of safety or the person in whose control he was placed cannot or will not have him back, he will be detained in another place of safety pending the reporter's decision as to whether he may be in

[66] Children's Hearings (Scotland) Rules 1971, rules 7 (2) (c), 8.
[67] Ibid., rule 19 (2).
[68] Ibid., rule 19 (3).
[69] Ibid., rule 19 (4).
[70] 1968 Act, s. 69. Rule 13 of the Reporter's Duties and Transmission of Information etc. (Scotland) Rules 1971 provides that a child being conveyed to any place in which he is required to reside by a supervision requirement may be placed under the control of any person authorised by the local authority, which person has all the powers, protections and privileges of a constable for this purpose.

need of compulsory measures of care or until he can be brought before a hearing.[71] A hearing must be arranged within seven days and the child may not be detained under section 69 of the 1968 Act after the hearing have met or in any event for more than seven days.[72]

The rules for notification of this hearing are the same as those for a hearing under section 40 (6).[73] The hearing proceeds as an ordinary hearing for consideration of his case or review, as the case may be.[74]

English orders

19–107 Part V of the 1968 Act makes provisions for the transfer of jurisdiction over children between Scottish children's hearings and English juvenile courts. An English court may notify a supervision or probation order to the reporter of the local authority for the area in which the child resides or proposes to reside, and the reporter then arranges in the normal way for a hearing to consider and determine the case.[75] The notification of the order by the English court is conclusive evidence of its existence in relation to the child[76]; and the order ceases to have effect once the hearing dispose of the case.[77]

Mentally disordered children

19–108 Where a hearing, after considering a case, think that an application for admission to hospital or guardianship under Part IV of the Mental Health (Scotland) Act 1960 should be made to the sheriff in respect of the child, they make a report to the mental health officer concerned.[78] A hearing have no power themselves to make any order under the 1960 Act.

Expenses

19–109 The local authority are obliged to pay travelling and subsistence expenses to the child, his parent and any one representative of either, where such expenses have in the opinion of the authority been reasonably incurred to enable the child, parent or representative to attend a hearing. Expenses are not paid where they amount to less than fifteen new pence.[79]

No expenses are awarded in respect of any proceedings in the sheriff court[80] or in the Court of Session.[81]

Authentication of documents

19–110 All documents authorised or required to be issued by a hearing or by the chairman of a hearing are authenticated by the chairman or, if he is not

---

[71] 1968 Act, s. 69 (3).
[72] Ibid., s. 69 (4).
[73] Supra, para. 19–39; Children's Hearings (Scotland) Rules 1971, rule 7 (1) (d).
[74] 1968 Act, s. 69 (3).
[75] 1968 Act, s. 73 (1).
[76] Ibid., s. 73 (2).
[77] Ibid., s. 73 (3).
[78] Ibid., s. 46 (1).
[79] Children's Hearings (Scotland) Rules 1971, rule 29.
[80] Act of Sederunt (Social Work) (Sheriff Court Procedure Rules) 1971, rule 24.
[81] Rules of Court, rule 289A (9).

available, by a member of the hearing. Documents authorised or required to be made by a reporter are authenticated by the signature of the reporter or a person duly authorised by him, and the same applies to the certification of copies as true copies of documents issued by a reporter.[82]

Notifications

-111   Any written or oral notification authorised or required under the Children's Hearings (Scotland) Rules 1971 to be given by a reporter may be given by a reporter or a person duly authorised by him, or by a police officer.[83]

Any written notification to a child or parent may be:

(a) delivered to him in person; or

(b) left for him at his dwelling-house or place of business or where he has no known dwelling-house or place of business, at any other place in which he may at the time be resident; or

(c) where he is the master of, or a seaman or other person employed in, a vessel, left with a person on board thereof and connected therewith; or

(d) sent by post in a registered or first class service recorded delivery letter to his dwelling-house or place of business.[84]

Restrictions on reporting of proceedings

-112   No newspaper or broadcast report of any proceedings under the 1968 Act in any hearing or in the sheriff court or Court of Session may reveal the name, address or school or include any particulars calculated to lead to the identification of any child concerned, nor may any picture of a child concerned be published.[85] This requirement may be dispensed with by the Secretary of State in the interests of justice.[86]

---

[82] Children's Hearings (Scotland) Rules 1971, rule 26.
[83] Ibid., rule 27 (1).
[84] Ibid., rule 27 (2).
[85] 1968 Act, s. 58; contravention of this provision is an offence punishable on summary conviction with a fine of £150.
[86] Ibid., s. 58 (3).

CHAPTER 20

MENTAL DISORDER IN RELATION TO
CRIMINAL PROCEDURE

20–01 IN criminal procedure the question of an accused person's mental condition is important for several reasons: (*a*) a person cannot be tried upon a criminal charge when he is insane, (*b*) a person who commits a crime while insane cannot be convicted of, or sentenced for, it, (*c*) a person who is mentally disordered may be dealt with under the Mental Health (Scotland) Act 1960 instead of being sentenced in the normal way. Mental disorder means mental illness or mental deficiency however caused or manifested.[1]

Pre-Trial Procedures

20–02 Where the procurator fiscal has any reason to believe that an accused is suffering from mental disorder he has him examined by doctors. In solemn procedure the reports of these doctors are transmitted with the rest of the precognition to Crown Office; in summary procedure the procurator fiscal considers them himself, and acts accordingly. In minor cases, where the local authority mental health officer is prepared to make an application for the accused's admission to hospital under the non-criminal provisions of the Mental Health (Scotland) Act 1960, the procurator fiscal may decide to take no proceedings or no further proceedings. It was at one time not uncommon for comparable steps to be taken in serious cases, such as the murder of children by mentally disturbed mothers, but recent practice tends to deal with such cases by court proceedings.

Section 55 (5) of the 1960 Act lays upon the prosecutor in any court before which a person is charged with an offence a duty to bring before the court such evidence as may be available of the mental condition of any person who appears to the prosecutor to be possibly suffering from mental disorder.

20–03 Section 55 (4) of the 1960 Act provides that where a person is charged before a court of summary jurisdiction other than a sheriff court with any act or omission constituting an offence punishable by imprisonment, and it appears to the court that he may be suffering from mental disorder, the court must remit him to the sheriff court in the manner provided by section 5 of the 1954 Act.[2] The sheriff court may then make a hospital order under section 55 of the 1960 Act in the same way as it can in respect of persons charged before it, or may deal with the accused in any way which would have been competent to the remitting court.

---

[1] 1960 Act, s. 6.
[2] *Supra*, para. 12–31; see *Herron* v. *McCrimmon*, 1969 S.L.T.(Sh.Ct.) 37.

0–04   Section 54 (1) of the 1960 Act provides that any court remanding or committing for trial a person who appears to be suffering from mental disorder may commit him to a hospital instead of remanding him in custody. In order to commit the accused to hospital the court must be satisfied that there is a hospital available for his admission, and also that he is suffering from mental disorder. Evidence of mental disorder must be either written or oral evidence from a medical practitioner,[3] not necessarily one specialising in mental illness. If the responsible medical officer of the hospital, which must be specified in the committal warrant, is satisfied that the accused is suffering from a mental disorder which would warrant his compulsory admission to hospital in the ordinary way under Part IV of the Act, the accused will be detained in hospital for the period of remand or until liberated in due course of law. The responsible medical officer must examine any person sent to his hospital under this section and report the result to the court. If that report is to the effect that the accused is not so mentally disordered as to warrant his compulsory admission the court may then commit him to any prison or other institution, or otherwise deal with him according to law.[4]

The responsible medical officer is any medical practitioner on the staff of the hospital authorised to act as such by the Board of Management.[5]

Insanity

Insanity in bar of trial

0–05   Insanity at the time of trial is a bar thereto if it prevents the accused from being able rationally to plead or to instruct his defence,[6] or, in the words of Lord Justice-General Dunedin,[7] " prevents a man from doing what a truly sane man would do and is entitled to do—maintain in sober sanity his plea of innocence, and instruct those who defend him as a truly sane man would do." It is sufficient to justify a finding that a panel is incapable of instructing his defence that, although sane in ordinary matters, he is insane in regard to the particular subject-matter of the charge which is made against him.[8]

Unfitness to plead may result from mental illness or defect, or from other causes, preventing the accused instructing his defence.[9]

0–06   The plea is generally taken by the defence, in which case it must be stated at the first diet,[10] but the question may also be raised by the prosecu-

---

[3] 1960 Act, s. 54 (4).

[4] 1960 Act, s. 54 (3).

[5] 1960 Act, ss. 53 (1) (*a*), 111 (1).

[6] Hume, ii. 143; Alison, i. 659; Bell's Notes 4; Macdonald, 9, 10, 271; Gordon, 330–332.

[7] *H.M. Adv.* v. *Brown* (1907) 5 Adam 312, 343.

[8] *H.M. Adv.* v. *Sharp*, 1927 J.C. 66, following *Archibald Miller* (1874) 3 Couper 16, and *H.M. Adv.* v. *Alex. Robertson* (1891) 3 White 6.

[9] See Gordon, 330–332, 352–353; *Barr* v. *Herron*, 1968 J.C. 20; see 32 J.C.L. 113. *H.M. Adv.* v. *Breen*, 1921 J.C. 30, is no longer of authority. Hysterical amnesia does not constitute a plea in bar of trial—*Russell* v. *H.M. Adv.*, 1946 J.C. 37; *H.M. Adv.* v. *Kidd*, 1960 J.C. 61. See also *H.M. Adv.* v. *Brown and Foss*, 1966 S.L.T. 341.

[10] 1887 Act, ss. 28 and 29; and see *H.M. Adv.* v. *Brown* (1907) 5 Adam 312.

tor,[11] and the court may, if it sees cause, ex proprio motu investigate whether the accused is a proper subject for trial or not.[12]

20-07   It has been held by a Full Bench that where a question is raised as to whether a person charged under an indictment is mentally capable of pleading, the court, both at common law and under the Lunacy (Scotland) Act 1857, had power either (a) to hold a preliminary inquiry as to the mental condition of the accused before calling on him to plead, or (b) to call on the accused to plead, leaving it to the jury at the trial to say whether he was capable of pleading.[13]

20-08   The normal procedure is by preliminary inquiry. If the court holds a preliminary inquiry and determines that the accused is fit to plead the question of his fitness should not be put again to the jury.[14] Where the Crown are in possession of evidence of the accused's unfitness to plead it is their duty to raise the question before the court.[15]

The evidence at the preliminary investigation normally consists of evidence led by the defence from two psychiatrists who have examined the accused, usually on the instructions of the Crown. There is a view that it is improper for the psychiatrists to read each other's reports before giving their own opinions.[16]

20-09   The fact that the accused is a deaf mute unable to communicate or to understand the proceedings is a good ground for a plea in bar of trial, but the only two reported cases concerning deaf mutes resulted in their being allowed to plead and being ultimately acquitted.[17]

In one case a plea of insanity in bar of trial was sustained where the accused was at the time of the trial enjoying a lucid interval, he being, however, still at that time capable of being certified as a lunatic.[18]

20-10   There is some authority that under the Lunacy (Scotland) Act 1857 a finding of insanity could be made at any time during the trial and the accused then detained under that Act [19] but in the one reported case of a prisoner becoming insane during his trial the Crown moved to desert simpliciter and the accused was found not guilty. His relatives who were present in court took charge of him and he was dismissed.[20] Section 63 (1) of the 1960 Act provides that if in the course of the trial of any person on indictment it appears to the jury that he is insane, the court should record a finding to that effect, and proceed to deal with him in the same way as with someone found insane in bar of trial. But in one reported case since

11 H.M. Adv. v. Alex. Robertson (1891) 3 White 6; H.M. Adv. v. Brown, supra; Macdonald, 271.
12 John Warrand (1825) Shaw 130; Wm. Douglas (1827) Shaw 192; John Barclay (1833) Bell's Notes 4; Mary Paterson (1842) 1 Broun 200.
13 H.M. Adv. v. Brown, supra. See also H.M. Adv. v. Wilson, 1942 J.C. 75.
14 Russell v. H.M. Adv., 1946 J.C. 37.
15 H.M. Adv. v. Brown (1907) 5 Adam 312; H.M. Adv. v. Wilson, 1942 J.C. 75; H.M. Adv. v. Alex. Robertson (1891) 3 White 6.
16 H.M. Adv. v. Cameron, 1946 S.N. 73.
17 Jean Campbell (1817) Hume, i. 45; H.M. Adv. v. Wilson, 1942 J.C. 75.
18 Flynn v. H.M. Adv. (1910) 6 Adam 251.
19 See Alex Milne (1863) 4 Irv. 301, 331.
20 H.M. Adv. v. Walsh, 1922 J.C. 82.

the Act the court on the motion of the Crown deserted the diet pro loco et tempore against a mentally unfit accused and his fit co-accused, reserving to the Crown the right to raise a fresh indictment.[21]

0–11 Section 63 (9) of the 1960 Act provides that where it appears to a court that it is not practicable or appropriate to bring an accused before it for the purpose of determining whether he is unfit to plead, then if no objection is taken by or on behalf of the accused, the court may proceed with the case in his absence.

Disposal of persons insane in bar of trial

0–12 Where the court directs a finding of insanity in bar of trial, either on a plea in bar of trial or on its appearing to the jury that the accused is insane, the court makes a hospital order detaining the accused in a State hospital (i.e. Carstairs) or such other hospital as for special reasons the court may specify.[22] Such an order operates as an order committing the accused to the hospital together with an order restricting his discharge without limitation of time. Where the accused is already in the hospital when the order is made he is deemed to be admitted in pursuance of and as of the date of the order.[23] The order remains in force until the restriction is lifted by the Secretary of State who must first be satisfied that it is no longer required for the protection of the public.[24] While the order is still in force the Secretary of State may discharge the accused from hospital by warrant. If this discharge is an absolute one the restriction order falls, but it does not fall if the discharge is conditional, and a patient conditionally discharged may be recalled so long as the restriction order remains in force.[25] When a restriction order is in force in respect of any patient he may not be granted leave of absence or transferred without the consent of the Secretary of State,[26] and if he escapes or fails to return to the hospital he may be taken into custody and returned at any time.[27]

Insanity in bar of trial in summary proceedings

0–13 The law relating to insanity in bar of trial applies in the sheriff summary court as it does to trials on indictment. Where the court is satisfied that the accused is insane it must record a finding to that effect and the reason for that finding.[28] The court then makes a hospital order in terms of section 55 (1) of the Act.[29] It is not competent to make a guardianship order in the case of a person found insane in bar of trial or to deal with him in any other way than by hospital order.[30]

[21] *H.M. Adv.* v. *Brown and Foss*, 1966 S.L.T. 341.
[22] 1960 Act, s. 63 (1), (3).
[23] Ibid., s. 63 (1), (5).
[24] Ibid., s. 61 (1).
[25] Ibid., s. 61 (2), (3).
[26] Ibid., s. 60 (3) (*b*).
[27] Ibid., s. 63 (3) (*c*). That is to say he cannot earn his discharge like any other patient by remaining at liberty for twenty-eight days; see s. 36.
[28] 1960 Act, s. 63 (7); see *Barr* v. *Herron*, supra.
[29] Ibid., ss. 63 (7), 55 (2).
[30] *Barr* v. *Herron*, supra.

20–14   The accused in a summary prosecution cannot found on insanity in bar of trial unless he has given notice of his intention to do so, and of the witnesses he proposes to adduce in support of his plea, before the first witness for the prosecution is called. Where notice is given the prosecutor is entitled to an adjournment.[31] Presumably, the plea may still be taken by the Crown or the court at any time.

Effect of finding of insanity in bar of trial

20–15   A person dealt with as insane in bar of trial either on indictment or summarily has not tholed his assize and may be put on trial should he recover sanity.[32]

Acquittal on the ground of insanity

20–16   A person who commits a crime while irresponsible as a result of any mental or pathological condition may not be convicted. Instead he is acquitted on a special verdict which states that the jury find that he committed the act charged, but that he was insane at the time, and that they therefore acquit him on the ground of insanity.[33] Although defences of this kind usually rest on what is normally thought of as insanity, the plea extends to any form of mental or pathological disorder, and where an accused wishes to plead such disorder in exculpation he must lodge a special defence of insanity.[34] An accused is irresponsible on the ground of insanity if his reason was overpowered by some mental disorder and he was thereby rendered incapable of exerting his reason to control his conduct and reactions.[35]

20–17   Where a jury declare that a person has been acquitted by them on the ground of insanity the court makes the same order as it would have made had the accused been found to be insane in bar of trial, that is to say, it orders his detention in a State hospital or, if there are special reasons, in some other specified hospital, and his discharge is restricted without limitation of time.[36] Where a person is charged in the sheriff summary court with an act or omission as an offence and the court would have power on convicting him to make a hospital order under section 55 (1) [37] then, if it is satisfied that he did the act or made the omission charged, it may if it thinks fit make such an order without convicting him.[38] This means that where a person is acquitted on the ground of insanity in the summary court he may be dealt with by an ordinary hospital or guardianship order or, if the court thinks it appropriate, may be dealt with by a hospital order with a restriction on his discharge with or without limitation of time, and may be committed to any hospital, including a State hospital, chosen by the court,

---

[31] 1960 Act, s. 63 (8).
[32] *H.M. Adv.* v. *Bickerstaff*, 1926 J.C. 65.
[33] 1960 Act, s. 63 (2); *H.M. Adv.* v. *Mitchell*, 1951 J.C. 53.
[34] *H.M. Adv.* v. *Cunningham*, 1963 J.C. 80; cf. *Clark* v. *H.M. Adv.*, 1968 J.C. 53.
[35] *H.M. Adv.* v. *Kidd*, 1960 J.C. 61, 70; Gordon, Chap. 10.
[36] 1960 Act, s. 63 (3), (5).
[37] Infra, para. 20–19.
[38] 1960 Act, s. 55 (3).

provided that in the case of an order restricting discharge the provisions of section 60 [39] are satisfied.

Hospital Orders on Convicted Persons

0–18   Prior to 1949 the law was that if the accused was responsible and convicted he was punished; if he was irresponsible he was not convicted but was acquitted and committed to a mental hospital. Where, therefore, a person was convicted of culpable homicide by reason of diminished responsibility the only course open to the court was to impose a sentence; it could not commit him to hospital. The only exception to this was a special power provided by section 24 of the Criminal Justice (Scotland) Act 1949 [40] to order the detention in a hospital of mental defectives convicted of offences.[41] The 1960 Act replaces and extends this power, and makes it possible for a hospital order to be made in the case of a mentally disordered person who has been convicted of an offence. The court in such a case, given the appropriate medical evidence, has a discretion to deal with the accused in the ordinary way or by making a hospital order.

0–19   Section 55 (1) of the 1960 Act provides that where a person is convicted in the High Court or sheriff court of an offence punishable with imprisonment, other than an offence the sentence for which is fixed by law, such as murder, the court may in certain circumstances make a hospital order. Before the court can make such an order it must be satisfied on the written or oral evidence of two medical practitioners, one of whom must be a practitioner approved by a Regional Hospital Board as having special experience in the diagnosis or treatment of mental disorder, that the offender is suffering from mental disorder of a certain nature or degree. The nature or degree is expressed as being that which would in the case of a person under the age of twenty-one years warrant his admission to hospital or his reception into guardianship under Part IV, the civil part, of the Act. What this means is that a person who is suffering from mental illness of any kind, including a persistent disorder manifested only by abnormally aggressive or seriously irresponsible conduct, may be dealt with by a hospital order on conviction of an imprisonable offence whatever his age; and similarly that a mental defective whose mental deficiency is not such that he is incapable of living an independent life or of guarding himself against serious exploitation may be dealt with on conviction by way of a hospital order whatever his age.[42] In addition, the court must be of opinion, having regard to all the circumstances, including the nature of the offence and the character and antecedents of the offender, and to the

[39] Infra, para. 20–25.

[40] Replacing the more complicated s. 9 of the Mental Deficiency and Lunacy (Scotland) Act 1913 which avoided a technical conviction where an order was made; see *H.M. Adv.* v. *Breen*, 1921 J.C. 30; *H.M. Adv.* v. *Gordon*, 1921 J.C. 67.

[41] See e.g. *George Dunn*, Glasgow High Court, December 1952; reported on another point sub nomine *Shaw* v. *H.M. Adv.*, 1953 J.C. 51.

[42] 1960 Act, ss. 55 (1) (*a*); 23 (1).

other available methods of dealing with him, that the most suitable method of disposing of the case is by an order under the section. If these conditions are satisfied the court may make a hospital order authorising the admission to and detention in such hospital as may be specified by the court, or in the case of a guardianship order make an order placing the accused under the guardianship of a specified local health authority or of any other person approved by a local health authority.

Where the sheriff remits a case to the High Court for sentence the power to make an order is to be exercised by the High Court.[43]

20–20   The court may not make an order committing the accused to any hospital unless it is first satisfied that the hospital is available for his admission thereto within twenty-eight days of the making of the order [44] and may not make a guardianship order unless satisfied that the guardian is willing to receive the accused.[45]

Form of hospital orders

20–21   The order must specify the form of mental disorder, being mental illness or mental deficiency or both, from which the offender is found to be suffering. The court is not empowered to make an order unless each of the medical practitioners who give evidence describes him as suffering from the same form of mental disorder, whether or not either of them describes him as also suffering from the other.[46] That is to say, a court cannot make an order in respect of a person who is diagnosed by one medical witness as suffering from mental illness, and by the other as suffering from mental defect, unless one of the witnesses agrees that he is also suffering from the condition diagnosed by his colleague.

Other powers of court when making hospital orders

20–22   Where the court exercises its power to make a hospital order it may not pass any sentence of imprisonment or impose a fine or make a probation order in respect of the offence on which the hospital order is made. " Sentence of imprisonment " is deemed to include any order for detention.[47] The court may, however, make any other order which is competent to it, so that it can, for example make an order disqualifying the offender for holding or obtaining a driving licence.

Effect of hospital orders

20–23   The effect of an order under section 55 made without restriction on the accused's discharge is similar to the effect of a compulsory order made under the civil provisions of the Act. A number of differences between the two types of order are set out in the Second Schedule to the Act, but the only important ones are that the patient's nearest relative has no power to

---

[43] Ibid., s. 55 (1).
[44] Ibid., s. 55 (6).
[45] Ibid., s. 55 (8).
[46] Ibid., s. 55 (9).
[47] Ibid., s. 55 (10).

order his discharge, and that the provisions requiring renewal of authority for the detention or guardianship of psychopaths and high grade mental defectives who have reached the age of twenty-five, do not apply to persons admitted under section 55 orders.[48]

Detention in State hospital

0-24 Section 55 hospital orders will normally order the detention of the patient in an ordinary mental hospital. He may be ordered to be detained in a State hospital if the court is satisfied on the evidence of the medical practitioners which is taken into account under the section that he requires treatment under conditions of special security on account of his dangerous, violent or criminal propensities, and cannot be suitably cared for in a hospital other than a State hospital.[49] Section 55 orders naming the State hospital are rarely made except by the High Court. They are, however, quite commonly made by the High Court following on conviction for culpable homicide on the ground of diminished responsibility.

Restriction on discharge

0-25 A court making a hospital order under section 55 may in certain circumstances make a further order that the accused's discharge from hospital should be restricted, either without limit of time or during such period as may be specified in the order. A restriction on discharge may be imposed where it appears to the court, having regard to the nature of the offence, to the antecedents of the accused, and to the risk that as a result of his mental disorder he would commit offences if set at large that such a restriction is necessary for the protection of the public.[50] A restriction order cannot be made unless the medical practitioner approved by the Regional Hospital Board who gives evidence in the section 55 proceedings gives such evidence orally.[51]

A section 55 order committing the accused to a State hospital with an unlimited restriction on his discharge has the same effect as an order under section 63.[52] Such a form of section 55 order is commonly made in the case of persons convicted of culpable homicide on the ground of diminished responsibility, so that the net effect of such a conviction in such cases is the same as that of an acquittal by reason of insanity.[53]

Evidence of mental disorder

0-26 Evidence under section 55 may (subject to section 60 (1)) consist entirely of written evidence, and a report in writing purporting to be signed by a medical practitioner may be received in evidence without proof of the

---

[48] Ibid., ss. 58 (3); 43; 23 (2); 40.
[49] Ibid., s. 55 (7).
[50] Ibid., s. 60 (1).
[51] Ibid., s. 60 (2).
[52] Supra, paras. 20–12; 20–16. A limited order has the same effect for the period of its duration. Both are subject to the Secretary of State's powers under s. 61.
[53] See *H.M. Adv.* v. *Harrison* (1968) 32 J.C.L. 119; *H.M. Adv.* v. *Gordon* (1967) 31 J.C.L. 270.

signature or the qualifications of the practitioner. The court may, however, require in any case that the practitioner be called to give oral evidence.[54]

Where a written report is tendered in evidence other than on behalf of the accused, the accused's counsel or solicitor is entitled to receive a copy of the report, and where the accused is not represented the substance of the report must be disclosed to him or, if he is a child, to his parent or guardian if the latter is present in court. In either case the accused is entitled to require that the practitioner be called to give oral evidence, and is also entitled to call evidence to rebut the Crown evidence. The court is entitled to adjourn the case if it thinks that further time is necessary in the interests of the accused to consider the report.[55] The accused may also have arrangements made for himself to be examined by a medical practitioner for the purpose of rebutting the evidence contained in any report lodged with the court.[56]

Alteration of hospital orders by Secretary of State

20-27   Where the court makes an order under section 55 and within the period of twenty-eight days which may pass before the accused is transferred to hospital it appears to the Secretary of State that because of emergency or other special circumstances it is not practicable for him to be received into the hospital specified in the order, the Secretary of State may give directions for his admission to another appropriate hospital.[57] This may give the Secretary of State a right to transfer a person to the State hospital although the court ordered his detention in an ordinary hospital.

Orders on Persons in Custody

Transfer orders

20-28   Where it appears that a person committed in custody awaiting trial or sentence is suffering from mental disorder warranting his admission into hospital under Part IV of the Act, the Secretary of State may apply to the sheriff for an order that he be removed to and detained in a specified hospital other than a private hospital, and the sheriff, if satisfied by medical reports, may make the order.[58] One of the reports must be by a doctor approved for the purposes of section 27 of the Act by the Regional Hospital Board as having special experience in the diagnosis or treatment of mental disorders.   The order must specify whether the patient is suffering from mental illness or mental defect, and both doctors must agree that he suffers from one of these even if one of them also thinks he suffers from the other.[59] Such an order, which is called " a transfer order," ceases to have effect if the accused is not in fact admitted into the hospital within fourteen days of the order.[60] A transfer order has the same effect

54 1960 Act, s. 57 (2).
55 Ibid., s. 57 (3).
56 Ibid., s. 57 (4).
57 Ibid., s. 59 (2).
58 Ibid., s. 65 (1).
59 Ibid., s. 65 (4), (5); cf. supra, para. 20–21.
60 Ibid., s. 65 (2).

as a hospital order with an unlimited restriction on discharge.[61] A transfer order under section 65 ceases to have effect if the proceedings against the accused are dropped, or when his case is disposed of.[62] This, of course, does not prevent a disposing court making an order under section 55 or section 63 where appropriate.[63] Where a transfer order is in force and the Secretary of State is notified by the responsible medical officer before the accused is brought back to court that he no longer requires treatment, the Secretary of State may by warrant direct that he be sent to any place where he might have been detained but for his removal to hospital, and on his arrival at such place the transfer order ceases to have effect.[64] Where a transfer order ceases to have effect because the proceedings against the accused have been dropped, or because he has been dealt with by the court otherwise than by a sentence of imprisonment or other detention or a hospital or guardianship order, the patient continues to be liable to be detained in the hospital as if he had been admitted there in pursuance of an ordinary application under Part IV of the Act on the date at which the transfer order ceased to have effect.[65]

Transfer directions

20–29   The Secretary of State also has power to make what is called " a transfer direction " in respect of certain classes of persons who are found to be suffering from mental disorder established by evidence of the same kind as is required by section 65 of the Act. The classes of persons affected are those serving sentences of imprisonment and suffering from mental disorder of a kind which would warrant their admission under section 55, and civil prisoners and aliens detained in pursuance of the immigration laws who are suffering from mental disorder of a nature or degree warranting their admission under Part IV of the Act.[66] A transfer direction has the same effect as a hospital order,[67] but the Secretary of State may by warrant direct that the patient be subject to restrictions on discharge.[68] The patient is entitled to appeal to the sheriff to cancel a transfer direction within three months of his transfer to a hospital thereunder, and if it is cancelled he is then remitted to any prison or other institution in which he might have been detained.[69] Where the patient has been made subject to a transfer direction with restriction of discharge and the responsible medical officer notifies the Secretary of State that he no longer requires treatment, the Secretary of State may by warrant direct that he be remitted to any prison or institution in which he might have been detained.[70] A restriction

---

[61] Ibid., s. 65 (3).
[62] Ibid., s. 68 (1).
[63] Ibid.
[64] Ibid., s. 68 (2).
[65] Ibid., s. 68 (3).
[66] Ibid., s. 66 (1), (2).
[67] Ibid., s. 66 (4).
[68] Ibid., s. 67. A " direction restricting discharge " has the same effect as an order restricting discharge under s. 60.
[69] Ibid., s. 66 (5).
[70] Ibid., s. 69 (1).

of discharge in a transfer direction applies only for the period during
which the patient would have been liable to be detained in prison etc. if
the transfer direction had not been given.[71] When it ceases to have effect
the patient is entitled to be discharged unless he is in need of continued
detention in hospital.[72]

Appeals

20–30   Section 62 of the 1960 Act provides that an accused may appeal against
a hospital order, guardianship order, or order restricting discharge in the
same manner as he may appeal against a conviction. Neither this Act nor
the 1926 Act, however, gives the accused any right to appeal against an
order made under section 63 of the 1960 Act.

20–31   The Criminal Appeal Court has the same powers as the trial court
would have had if in any case it substitutes an acquittal on the ground of
insanity for a conviction.[73] There appears to be no specific power in the
1926 Act to entitle the Appeal Court to make a finding that the accused
was unfit to plead. If a convicted accused successfully appeals against the
lower court's finding that he was fit to plead it may be that the Appeal
Court's only course is to quash the conviction.[74] Nor is there any specific
provision in either the 1926 Act or the 1960 Act to entitle the Appeal
Court to make an order under section 55 of the 1960 Act in substitution
for a sentence imposed by the trial court, unless an order under section
55 is to be regarded as a sentence in terms of section 2 (4) of the 1926 Act.

[71] Ibid., s. 69 (2).
[72] Ibid., s. 69 (3), (4), (5).
[73] 1926 Act, s. 3 (3); 1960 Act, s. 63 (4).
[74] Cf. *Russell* v. *H.M. Adv.*, 1946 J.C. 37.

CHAPTER 21

LIABILITY OF JUDGES, CLERKS OF COURT, AND PROSECUTORS TO ACTIONS OF DAMAGES AGAINST THEM

Judges of the supreme court

21–01   Judges of the supreme court are immune from all action at law for damages for anything done by them when sitting in their judicial capacity.[1] Lord Justice-Clerk Macdonald stated the principle on which this immunity is based, as follows [2]:

> " Such Judges are the King's Judges directly, bound to administer the law between his subjects, and even between his subjects and himself. To make them amenable to actions of damages for things done in their judicial capacity, to be dealt with by Judges only their equals in authority and by juries, would be to make them not responsible to the King, but subject to other considerations than their duty to him in giving their decisions, and to expose them to be dealt with as servants not of him but of the public. Accordingly the remedy in this case, if they flagrantly offend against duty, is not by proceedings in any Court, but only by addresses to the Crown from the Houses of Parliament."

Sheriffs

As sheriffs are also the Sovereign's judges, the same principle applies.[3]

Inferior judges

21–02   As explained below, inferior judges, other than sheriffs, enjoy the protection given by section 75 of the 1954 Act in the exercise of their judicial functions under that statute.

21–03   At common law any claim to immunity on their part cannot be based on the fact of immunity of the Queen's judges, as they are not appointed by the Queen.[4] Nevertheless, they have, in common with all judges, an absolute privilege with respect to words uttered by them, in the course of judicial proceedings, with reference to the case before them.[5] Further, in the absence of malice and want of probable cause on their part, they are not liable in damages for any mistake or informality in the exercise of their judicial functions.[6]

---

[1] *Haggart's Trs.* v. *Hope*, 1st June, 1821, F.C., (1824); 2 Sh.App. 125; *Harvey* v. *Dyce* (1876) 4 R. 265; *Scott* v. *Stansfield* (1868) L.R. 3 Ex. 220; *Primrose* v. *Waterston* (1902) 4 F. 783.
[2] *McCreadie* v. *Thomson*, 1907 S.C. 1176, 1182.
[3] *Harvey* v. *Dyce*, supra.
[4] *McCreadie* v. *Thomson*, supra.
[5] *Primrose* v. *Waterston* (1902) 4 F. 783.
[6] *Malonie* v. *Walker* (1841) 3 D. 418.

459

21-04   The position where an inferior judge has acted ultra vires is not quite clear. In *McCreadie* v. *Thomson*,[7] which was decided before the passing of the 1908 Act, it was held that a person who had suffered imprisonment under a sentence pronounced by a magistrate in excess of his jurisdiction did not require to aver malice and want of probable cause in an action of damages against the magistrate because the latter's act had been entirely ultra vires.[8] In view of dicta in the more recent case of *McPhee* v. *Macfarlane's Executor* [9] it is doubtful if *McCreadie* v. *Thomson* would now be decided as it was. It may be that a magistrate who acts ultra vires will not in every case be protected by section 75 of the 1954 Act, but, if he merely misconstrues his powers under that statute, he does not deprive himself of the protection of the section.

Prosecutors

21-05   The common law recognises that a public prosecutor, while discharging his public duties, occupies a position of high privilege. The Lord Advocate enjoys an absolute privilege in connection with proceedings on indictment, even where the ground of complaint is failure to serve the indictment.[10] This privilege extends also to procurators fiscal acting in proceedings on indictment, as they always do, on the authority of the Lord Advocate.[11] A procurator fiscal acting without that authority, e.g. in proceedings on petition, presumably does not share in the privilege. The position of a procurator fiscal in a summary prosecution taken on instructions from the Lord Advocate is so far undecided.[12] In normal summary proceedings, taken in the name, and on the authority of, the procurator fiscal or other inferior prosecutor, the prosecutor is not liable in damages to anyone whom he has prosecuted unless he can be shown to have acted maliciously and without probable cause.[13] This rule applies even although the offence charged is found not to have been committed.[14] A private prosecutor taking proceedings in the interest for which they were intended to be used enjoys a similar protection.[15] He loses this when he uses his powers in an improper interest.[16]

Statutory protection of inferior judges and officials

21-06   The position regarding inferior judges (other than sheriffs [17]) and officials is now crystallised in section 75 of the 1954 Act which provides that:

---

[7] 1907 S.C. 1176; cf. *Strachan* v. *Stoddart* (1828) 7 S. 4 (where a similar decision was given in the case of a grossly illegal and irregular warrant); and *Pollock* v. *Clark* (1829) 8 S. 1.

[8] In *Strachan* v. *Stoddart*, supra, at 6, Lord Pitmilly expressed the view that malice was not the groundwork of an action of damages laid on a grossly illegal warrant and did not therefore require to be averred.

[9] 1933 S.C. 163.

[10] *Hester* v. *MacDonald*, 1961 S.C. 370; Hume, ii. 135; Alison, ii. 92; *Henderson* v. *Robertson* (1853) 15 D. 292, L.J.-C. at 295; *McMurchy* v. *Campbell* (1887) 14 R. 725, Lord Young at 728.

[11] *Hester* v. *MacDonald*, supra.

[12] See *Hester* v. *MacDonald*, supra, L.P. at 379.

[13] *Walker on Delict*, 876.

[14] *Glegg on Reparation*, 3rd edn. 183.

[15] *Cook* v. *Spence* (1897) 4 S.L.T. 295.

[16] *Strang* v. *Strang* (1849) 11 D. 378.   [17] 1954 Act, s. 75 (4).

" (1) No judge, clerk of court, or prosecutor in the public interest shall be found liable by any court in damages for or in respect of any proceeding taken, act done, or judgment, decree, or sentence pronounced under this Act, unless

(a) the person suing has suffered imprisonment in consequence thereof; and

(b) such proceeding, act, judgment, decree, or sentence has been quashed; and

(c) the person suing shall specifically aver and prove that such proceeding, act, judgment, decree, or sentence was taken, done, or pronounced maliciously and without probable cause.

(2) No such liability as aforesaid shall be incurred or found where such judge, clerk of court, or prosecutor shall establish that the person suing was guilty of the offence in respect whereof he had been convicted, or on account of which he had been apprehended or had otherwise suffered, and that he had undergone no greater punishment than was assigned by law to such offence.

(3) No action to enforce such liability as aforesaid shall lie unless it is commenced within two months after the proceeding, act, judgment, decree, or sentence founded on, or in the case where the Act under which the action is brought fixes a shorter period, within that shorter period."

21-07   The effect of the section is to impose four conditions before such an action is competent.[18] (1) The common law is specifically declared, and a pursuer must aver both malice and want of probable cause. (2) The person suing must have suffered the real injury of imprisonment. If the punishment has been a fine, it is implied that sufficient reparation may be obtained by procuring the quashing of the conviction and the repayment of the fine. (3) The proceeding complained of must have been quashed. And (4) the action of damages must be commenced within two months after the proceeding complained of, unless a shorter period is fixed by the special statute under which proceedings were taken. Failure to aver facts and circumstances from which, if proved, malice and want of probable cause can be inferred, has been held fatal to the relevancy of an action against a procurator fiscal. In Rae v. Strathern [19] a father, resident in Midlothian, was arrested and detained in prison on a charge at the instance of the procurator fiscal of Lanarkshire, purporting to be brought under the 1908 Act, of neglecting his child contrary to the Children Act 1908. He was tried in the sheriff court of the county of Lanark, where the child was living with its mother, and acquitted. In an action of damages at his instance against the procurator fiscal, on the ground that the proceedings were ultra vires of the 1908 Act in respect that the place of the alleged

---

[18] Graham v. Strathern, 1924 S.C. 699, Lord Anderson at 724.
[19] 1924 S.C. 147. See also Beaton v. Ivory (1887) 14 R. 1057; McPherson v. McLennan (1887) 14 R. 1063.

offence was in Midlothian and not in Lanarkshire, the court held that the proceedings were not ultra vires and that the action was excluded by section 59 of the 1908 Act in respect that there was no averment of an oblique motive or of facts and circumstances from which malice could be inferred. The questions whether the pursuer had suffered " imprisonment " and whether the proceedings had been " quashed " were mooted but not decided.[20]

21–08   If the defender in an action of damages invokes the protection of this section, he must have been proceeding under the Act.[21] If he has acted outwith the sphere of his jurisdiction,[22] or if he proceeds without a warrant or on a warrant from a judge who is not qualified to grant it,[23] or if he purports to prosecute on a charge which does not set forth " any known offence either statutory or at common law, but some indifferent or ludicrous act inferring no legal consequences of any kind," [24] he cannot claim the statutory privilege. In fact, in such cases malice might well be presumed.[25] In *Graham* v. *Strathern* [26] a bank teller brought an action against a procurator fiscal, averring that the defender, knowing that the pursuer was not guilty of reset, had charged him, ostensibly under the 1908 Act, with reset of certain coins, and had obtained a warrant for his arrest. The pursuer further averred that he had been detained in custody in the bank until the coins were handed over and had then been immediately released. He averred that these proceedings were taken, not in order to prosecute him for the crime of reset, but solely to concuss him into surrendering the coins which the defender desired for the purpose of prosecuting the thief. It was held that the pursuer's averments at most instructed that the proceedings, which were ex facie regular and competent under the 1908 Act, had been taken maliciously by the defender; that in the circumstances the proceedings did not on that account cease to be proceedings under the Act; and that as the pursuer had not suffered imprisonment and the proceedings against him had not been quashed, the action was excluded by section 59.

---

[20] *Rae* v. *Strathern,* supra.
[21] *Graham* v. *Strathern,* 1924 S.C. 699.
[22] *McCrone* v. *Sawers* (1835) 13 S. 443.
[23] *Bell* v. *Black and Morrison* (1865) 3 M. 1026; *Hester* v. *MacDonald,* 1961 S.C. 370, L.P. at 381; cf. *Robertson* v. *Keith,* 1936 S.C. 29.
[24] *Ferguson* v. *McNab* (1885) 12 R. 1083, L.P. at 1089.
[25] Cf. *Graham* v. *Strathern,* 1924 S.C. 699, L.J.-C. at 718.
[26] Supra.

SYNOPSIS OF SOLEMN PROCEDURE

TABLE I.—SHERIFF AND JURY TRIAL WHEN ACCUSED IN PRISON

BRANCH 1.—BOTH DIETS IN SAME COURT

Note.—The sections referred to are those of the 1887 Act, unless where otherwise stated

1971.

Monday,	June	7.	Petition and warrant to arrest issued (s. 16). Accused arrested.
Tuesday,	,,	8.	Declaration (if desired by accused) and committal for further examination (s. 17).
Wednesday,	,,	16.	Committal for trial.

Should as a general rule be within eight days from declaration.

Copy petition and warrants served on accused.

Monday,	July	19.	Case reported to Crown Office.

No fixed period for this, but should be as early as possible after committal for trial.

Thursday,	,,	22.	Case returned for trial by sheriff and jury.
Friday,	,,	23.	Indictment prepared by P.F. First and second diets arranged for.
Monday,	,,	26.	Warrant of citation of accused, witnesses, and jurors obtained from sheriff clerk (s. 23). Jury list made up by sheriff clerk (s. 38 as amended by Sched. 3, Juries Act 1949). Accused entitled on application to have copy supplied free of charge.
Tuesday,	,,	27.	Indictment served (ss. 24 and 26) and, if necessary, notice of previous convictions (1949 Act, s. 39 (1) (*b*) and Sched. 7, Form 1). Indictment lodged with sheriff clerk (s. 27 as amended by 1949 Act, Sched. 12).
Tuesday,	Aug.	3.	First diet (six clear days after service). Any objections to relevancy, etc., to be stated and minute signed by clerk stating that such objections sustained or repelled (ss. 28, 32, 33). Any special defence tendered (s. 36).

Note.—A special defence may be lodged not later than two clear days before second diet, if accused can at that diet show cause to the satisfaction of the court for such defence not being lodged at first diet (s. 36).

Plea of not guilty and any special defence recorded and signed by sheriff (s. 28).

Saturday, Aug. 7. Last day (five clear days before second diet) for accused giving written intimation to P.F. of any objections to previous convictions (1949 Act, s. 39 (1) (*b*), (*c*)).

Saturday,   ,,   7. Last day (four clear days before second diet, and following day being Sunday) for notifying P.F. of inability to find any person or witness named in indictment (s. 53).

Monday,   ,,   9. Last day (three clear days before second diet) for giving written notice to P.F. of witnesses for and productions for defence (s. 36).

            Copies of written notices to be lodged with sheriff clerk (s. 36).

> *Note.*—If before jury sworn accused can show that he was unable to give full three days' notice in regard to any witness or production, the court may permit such witness to be examined or production put in, but shall give such remedy to prosecutor by adjournment or postponement of trial or otherwise as shall seem just (s. 36).

Tuesday,   ,,   10. Last day (two clear days before second diet) for P.F. giving notice to accused of names and addresses of witnesses not on Crown list whom he desires, with leave of the court, to examine at the trial (1921 Act, s. 1).

Friday,   ,,   13. Second diet (nine clear days after first diet). Trial. Prisoner intimates adherence to plea of not guilty (Circuit Courts (Scotland) Act 1828, s. 12; Sheriff Courts (Scotland) Act 1853, s. 34).

            Jury balloted—fifteen persons. Prosecutor and accused each five peremptory challenges (Jurors (Scotland) Act 1825, s. 16, as amended by the Juries Act 1949). They may challenge any number of jurors on cause shown.

            Clerk states charge (or, if judge so directs, reads a summary thereof), swears jury and reads any special defence (Circuit Courts and Criminal Procedure (Scotland) Act 1925, s. 3 ; 1887 Act, s. 67, 1949 Act, s. 39).

            Evidence for prosecution led.

                  ,,   for defence led.

            Speeches for prosecution and defence.

            Judge charges jury.

            Verdict. Prosecutor moves for sentence. Previous convictions (if any) laid before judge (1949 Act, s. 39). Sentence (s. 57). Sheriff may remit to High Court for sentence (1921 Act, s. 2).

BRANCH 2.—FIRST DIET IN DIFFERENT COURT FROM THAT OF SECOND DIET

> Procedure same as in Br. 1 up to service of Indictment.
>
> The 1887 Act required the first diet to be in the court nearest the prison in which the accused was confined or in that of his domicile of citation (s. 26). This provision was repealed by s. 35 of the 1963 Act and replaced by a provision that the first diet should be in the same court in which the accused appeared for judicial examination unless the Lord Advocate otherwise directs. In most sheriff and jury cases now, therefore, the first and second diets will be in the same court.

1971.

Tuesday,   July 27. Indictment served (ss. 24 and 26).

Indictment lodged with sheriff clerk of court of first diet, and copy indictment lodged with sheriff clerk of court of second diet (s. 38).

Jury list, etc., as in Br. 1 made up by sheriff clerk of court of second diet.

Tuesday,   Aug. 3. First diet.

Procedure same as at first diet in Br. 1, with the following modifications :—

(a) The P.F. of the district of the first diet acts as representing Her Majesty's Advocate, unless an A.D. or P.F. of district of second diet, appears to prosecute (s. 28).

(b) The clerk records any interlocutor signed and plea tendered not only on the indictment but also " in the books of court " of the first diet or " in a record to be kept for the purpose."

(c) Immediately after the first diet the clerk transmits the indictment to the sheriff clerk of the court of the second diet.

> Procedure thereafter the same as in Br. 1. Objections to previous convictions are intimated to P.F. of district of second diet (1949 Act, s. 39 (1) (c)).

TABLE II.—SHERIFF AND JURY TRIAL WHERE ACCUSED IS LIBERATED ON BAIL

(BAIL (SCOTLAND) ACT 1888)

1971.

Monday,   June 7. Petition and warrant to arrest issued (s. 16). Accused arrested.

Tuesday,   „ 8. Declaration (if desired by accused) and commitment for further examination (s. 17).

Application for bail may be made at this stage.

Accused has no right of appeal against refusal or amount fixed, but P.F. has, if bail granted, right of appeal (Bail Act, s. 5).

Wednesday, June 16. Committed for trial.

> *Note.*—If accused liberated on bail prior to this, he may be indicted without being committed for trial (s. 18).

Application for bail made and granted.

The Bail Act contains the following provisions :—

(*a*) Application must be disposed of within twenty-four hours from presentation of petition, otherwise accused is entitled to liberation (s. 2).

(*b*) Amount of bail to be sufficient in opinion of magistrate to secure accused's appearance at all diets (s. 4).

(*c*) Either party may appeal against deliverance—the accused in respect of the refusal of bail, or the amount being excessive; the prosecutor in respect of the granting of bail, or the amount being inadequate (s. 5). It is also open to the accused to apply to the sheriff to review his decision, provided he has not appealed to the High Court (1963 Act, s. 37).

(*d*) The appeal is disposed of by the High Court or any Lord Commissioner of Justiciary in court or in chambers.

(*e*) When the prosecutor appeals, the accused if he has found bail, must be liberated after seventy-two hours (or in the Outer Hebrides or Orkney and Shetland, ninety-six hours) from the time of his application being granted, unless his further detention is ordered by the High Court pending consideration of the appeal. In computing hours, Sundays, public fasts, and general or court holidays are not included.

> Procedure after bail has been found will be as in Table I., Br. 1, except that service will be at the domicile of citation as fixed in accused's bail bond; and if he fails to appear either at the first or second diet or any other diet fixed for his appearance his bail will be forfeited and warrant granted for his apprehension.

TABLE III.—SHERIFF AND JURY TRIAL WHERE ACCUSED PLEADS GUILTY AT
FIRST DIET

BRANCH 1.—BOTH DIETS IN SAME COURT

> Procedure the same as in Table I., Br. 1, up to the first diet.

1971.

Tuesday, July 6. First diet.

Plea of guilty tendered, recorded, and signed by prisoner and judge.

Sentence pronounced then or at adjourned diet.

Sheriff may also remit to High Court for sentence (1921 Act, s. 2).

> *Note.*—If previous convictions challenged, accused must give written intimation of such challenge to P.F. by two clear days before first diet, and P.F. may at such diet lead proof of such convictions, and accused may lead rebutting evidence (s. 66 as amended by 1949 Act, Sched. 12; 1949 Act, s. 39 (1) (*b*) (*c*)).

BRANCH 2.—FIRST DIET IN DIFFERENT COURT FROM THAT OF SECOND DIET

Procedure the same as in Table I, Br. 1, up to the first diet.

1971.

Tuesday, July 6. First diet (s. 28).

Plea of guilty tendered, recorded and signed by prisoner and judge.

Sentence pronounced then or at adjourned diet; or

Case may be adjourned to second diet in order that the sheriff of the court of that diet may pronounce sentence (s. 28, Sched. H.). Sheriff may also remit to High Court for sentence (1921 Act, s. 2).

> The rest of the procedure at the first diet will be as set forth in Table I., Br. 2.
>
> As to challenge of previous convictions, see note to Br. 1, supra. Objections must be intimated to P.F. of district of first diet (1949 Act, s. 39 (1) (*b*) (*c*)).

TABLE IV.—PLEA UNDER SECTION 31

1971.

Monday, June 7. Petition and warrant to arrest (s. 16). Accused arrested.

Tuesday, ,, 8. Declaration (if desired by accused) and committal for trial (s. 17).

Letter from agent of accused addressed to Crown Agent (but given to P.F.), stating that accused intends to plead guilty and desires his case to be disposed of in terms of s. 31 as early as possible.

Case transmitted to Crown Agent, with short
report on facts of case.

Wednesday, June 9. Case returned to be proceeded with under s. 31.

Indictment prepared. (No list of witnesses or
productions.) Diet fixed in consultation with
sheriff clerk.

Indictment served, with notice attached in terms
of Sched. L., and also a notice in terms of Form
1, Sched. 7 of 1949 Act of any previous convictions which prosecution desires to place before
the court. (No warrant of citation required.)

Friday,   „   11.   Last day (two days after service of indictment)
for challenge of previous convictions by accused
(1949 Act, s. 39 (1) (d).

Monday,   „   14.   Diet for plea (at least four clear days after service).
Plea tendered, recorded and signed by accused
and sheriff.

Sentence will be pronounced by sheriff, unless the
case is such as can be tried only in the High
Court, or unless from the nature of the case he
thinks it desirable or necessary to remit the
case to the High Court for sentence, in which
cases an interlocutor in terms of Sched. M. will
be written on the indictment.

If the case falls to be disposed of in a court different from that in which the accused was committed for trial, the procedure will be as above;
and if sentence is pronounced in the sheriff
court, the procedure will as nearly as may be
follow that set forth in Table III., Br. 2.

If the accused pleads not guilty P.F. deserts diet
and accused is detained on original committal
warrant. He may now apply for bail.

TABLE V.—CASE TRIED IN HIGH COURT OF JUSTICIARY

Procedure the same as in Table I., Br. 1, up to
date when case reported to Crown Office. If
bail is applied for, Crown counsel should be
consulted thereon.

1971.

Monday,   June 28.   Indictment drafted by Crown counsel.
Friday,   July 2.   Proof print sent to P.F. for revisal.
Monday,   „   5.   Proof print returned revised.
Friday,   „   9.   Warrant of citation issued by Clerk of Justiciary
(s. 23, Sched. B.).

List of jury prepared under directions of clerk of
justiciary, and kept in office of sheriff clerk of
second diet (s. 38, as amended by Sched. 3,
Juries Act 1949).

Monday, July 12. Indictment served.

Indictment and documentary productions lodged with sheriff clerk of court of first diet (s. 27).

Other productions may either be lodged with clerk of first diet, or retained in district to which the case belongs, as may be most convenient for parties interested.

Monday, „ 19. First diet (s. 29).

Procedure similar to that in Table I., Br. 1; but—

(a) If plea of guilty in whole or in part tendered, it will be dealt with at second diet, and sentence then pronounced.

(b) If accused on bail and fails to appear, this will be minuted, but the forfeiture of his bail bond will be dealt with at second diet.

(c) If any objections to relevancy, etc., stated which sheriff considers should be reserved for the consideration of the High Court, he endorses on indictment certificate in terms of Sched. K. Copy of this certificate kept in books of court or in record kept for the purpose.

(d) Immediately after first diet indictment and documentary productions will be transmitted to Clerk of Justiciary; other productions will also be then lodged with him, if trial is to be in Edinburgh; or, if at a circuit town in the office of the sheriff clerk of that town.

Friday, July 23. Last day (five clear days before trial) for intimation to Crown Agent of objections to previous convictions (1949 Act, s. 39 (1) (b) (c)).

Saturday, „ 24. Last day (four clear days before trial) for notice to Crown Agent of inability to find any person or witness mentioned in indictment (s. 53).

Last day (three clear days before trial, allowing for Sunday intervening) for notice to Crown Agent of witnesses and productions for defence (s. 36).

Copies of all written notices to be lodged with clerk of justiciary for use of court.

See note, Table I., Br. 1.

Monday, „ 26. Last day (two clear days before second diet) for P.F. giving notice to accused of names and addresses of witnesses not on Crown list whom he desires, with leave of the court, to examine at the trial (1921 Act, s. 1).

Thursday, July 29. Second diet. Trial.

Transcript made of procedure at first diet in books of court or in a record to be kept for the purpose.

Other procedure same as at second diet in a sheriff and jury trial. See Table I., Br. 1.

APPENDIX B

SYNOPSIS OF SUMMARY PROCEDURE

Note.—The sections referred to are those of the Summary Jurisdiction (Scotland) Act, 1954, unless where otherwise stated.

TABLE I.—ACCUSED CITED

BRANCH 1.—CASE PROCEEDING TO TRIAL

1971.

Monday, June 7. Complaint prepared (ss. 15, 16).

> Act sufficient warrant for citation to any ordinary sitting of court or to any special diet fixed by court (ss. 17, 18, 2nd Sched., Part IV.). In some cases complaint sent to clerk of court for warrant to cite: supra, para. 13–04.

Tuesday, „ 8. Complaint served (ss. 18, 22) along with notice of previous convictions (if any) which the prosecutor has decided to lay before the court (s. 31 (1) and 2nd Sched., Part III, Forms 2 and 3) and, where the complaint includes any statutory charge, a notice of penalties thereunder (s. 15 (5) and 2nd Sched., Part III, Form 1).

> *Induciæ* at least forty-eight hours, unless in special circumstances the court fixes a shorter induciae (s. 18).

There should be annexed to the copy of complaint served a note in terms of 2nd Sched., Part IV, intimating whether first diet merely for pleading or a diet for trial. A note may also be annexed informing the accused of his rights of pleading in absence under s. 26. Such note must not be worded so as to mislead the accused into omitting to take timeous steps to challenge the competency or relevancy of the complaint (*Loughbridge* v. *Mickel*, 1947 J.C. 21).

Monday, „ 14. First diet (s. 26).

Any objections to relevancy, etc., should be now stated (s. 26).

> Objections may be met by amendment of complaint if character of offence not altered (s. 27).

Plea of not guilty tendered (ss. 29, 26).

Case adjourned to 17th for trial (s. 29).

> (*a*) Minute of adjournment must be signed by judge or clerk (s. 13).
>
> (*b*) Court may order accused to attend adjourned diet under a penalty (s. 29 (*e*)).

471

If defence *alibi*, or if insanity pleaded in bar of trial, notice should now be given to prosecutor (s. 32; Mental Health (Scotland) Act 1960, s. 63 (8)).

Tuesday, June 15. Witnesses cited (s. 18).

> Although no fixed induciae for citation of witnesses, they should receive at least forty-eight hours' notice unless the court fixes a shorter induciae.

Friday, „ 18. Trial (s. 29).
Evidence for prosecution and defence led.

> In special circumstances, evidence for defence may be led prior to that for prosecution (s. 29 (*h*)).

See s. 35 as to evidence of official documents, and s. 36 as to admissions by parties.

Finding (s. 56). Where this is one of guilty prosecutor lays before the judge any notice of previous convictions libelled and, where the complaint includes any statutory charge, a copy of the notice of penalty thereunder served on the accused under s. 15 (5). The judge or clerk of court will then ask accused if he admits these previous convictions, and, if so, fact will be recorded (s. 31 (1) (*c*)). The court may adjourn the case for the purpose of enabling inquiries to be made or of determining the most suitable method of dealing with it (1949 Act, s. 26) or may remand the accused for inquiry into his physical or mental condition (1949 Act, ss. 27, 28).

It is unnecessary to produce extracts of convictions admitted (s. 31 (1) (*d*)).

Proof of any conviction not admitted may be led either at the diet of trial or at any adjourned diet (s. 31 (1) (*e*)).

Record (s. 38) only necessary of—

(*a*) Complaint.

(*b*) Plea.

(*c*) Note of any documentary evidence produced.

(*d*) Conviction and sentence or other finding of court.

(*e*) Objections to competency or relevancy of complaint or proceedings, or competency or admissibility of evidence (if either party desires that a note of such objections be taken).

(*f*) Copy of any notice served on accused under s. 31 (1).

(g) Copy of any notice served on accused under s. 15 (5).

Sentence (s. 56).

Sentence signed by judge or clerk authenticates findings on which it proceeds (ss. 15, 57).

Penalties may be mitigated (s. 40).

Implements, etc., forfeited (s. 54).

> Where the sentence is a fine, time to pay must be allowed except for special reasons (s. 42 (2)), and alternative of imprisonment may not be pronounced when fine imposed except for special reasons (s. 42 (3)). Reasons must be entered in record (s. 43 C). The court must inform offender of right to pay by instalments when fine imposed (s. 43 A).
>
> The alternative of imprisonment is usually imposed at a means court convened after failure to pay (s. 43).

Expenses (s. 53 and Act of Ajournal 1972).

Forms of finding and sentence (s. 56).

Sentence may be modified prior to imprisonment thereon (s. 57).

Correction of errors in minutes or extracts (s. 58).

Extract (s. 59 and 2nd Sched., Part V.).

BRANCH 2.—PLEA OF GUILTY AT FIRST DIET

Procedure same as in Br. 1 up to first diet.

1971.

Monday, June 14. First diet (s. 26).

Plea of guilty tendered (s. 28).

Plea recorded and signed by judge or clerk of court (s. 28).

Plea and sentence may be combined, in which case one signature is sufficient to authenticate both (s. 28).

After intimation of plea of guilty prosecutor lays before the court notice of previous convictions (if any), and the judge or clerk of court then asks the accused if he admits correctness of such convictions; if so, admission entered in record (s. 31 (1) (c)). Court may adjourn case under s. 26 of the 1949 Act, or remand accused under ss. 27, 28 of that Act.

Unnecessary to produce extracts of convictions admitted (s. 31 (1) (d)).

If any conviction denied, proof may be led at same or adjourned diet (s. 31) (1) (e)).

Where the complaint includes any statutory charge, the prosecutor also lays before the judge a copy of the notice of the statutory

penalties thereunder already served on the
accused under s. 15 (5).

Sentence pronounced at same or adjourned diet
(s. 28).

Minute of adjournment must be signed.

For sentence, etc., see Br. 1.

BRANCH 3.—ACCUSED FAILING TO APPEAR
Procedure same as in Br. 1 up to first diet.

Monday,   June 14.   Accused fails to appear (s. 30).
                       The court may—

(1) Adjourn to another diet, of which intimation to be given to accused (s. 30 (a)).

Intimation sufficiently given either by officer or
by registered letter or recorded delivery signed
by prosecutor. Production of officer's execution or of post-office receipt for letter sufficient
evidence of intimation.

Or

(2) Grant warrant of apprehension and forfeit
any bail, etc. (s. 30 (c), (d)); or

(3) If accused charged with statutory offence
for which a sentence of imprisonment
cannot be imposed in first instance, or if
procedure in absence otherwise competent under statute, proceed in absence
(s. 30 (b). See s. 26 (3), and

(a) Plea of guilty may be tendered by a solicitor
or other authorised person (s. 26).

In such circumstances it is desirable to have plea
signed by person tendering it.

(b) On proof that accused has been duly cited
or received due intimation of diet, proof
may be led in absence, and solicitor may,
with permission of court, appear for and
defend accused. Proof must be led unless
statute permits of conviction in default
(s. 30 (b)).

Proof of service may be given either by oath in
court of officer or by his written execution
(s. 22).

TABLE II.—ACCUSED ARRESTED

BRANCH 1.—CASE PROCEEDING TO TRIAL

1971.

Monday,   June 7.   Accused arrested (ss. 17, 20).
                      If offence of a minor character, and arrest
                      not under warrant on a complaint, bail may
                      be accepted by officers of police (s. 10).

Tuesday,   June   8.   Prisoner brought before court (s. 20).

> No warrant required for this purpose where prisoner in custody or appears voluntarily (s. 20).
>
> To allow time for inquiry or otherwise, case may be adjourned for a period not exceeding seven days or on special cause shown fourteen days, without accused being asked to plead, and he may be liberated on bail or committed to prison without bail. Judge not to allow bail in case he is not competent to try (s. 21). Accused, charged on complaint under the Act, may appeal to High Court where bail is refused or where he is dissatisfied with amount of bail fixed.   He may also apply to original court for review (1963 Act, s. 37).   Prosecutor may appeal if dissatisfied with the granting of bail or with the amount fixed (s. 11).
>
> Where the complaint includes any statutory charges, the accused must, before being called on to plead, be served with the complaint and a notice of the penalties applicable to these charges (s. 15 (5) and 2nd Sched., Part III, Form 1). Where any previous convictions are libelled the accused must, before being asked to plead, be served with the complaint and a notice of these convictions (s. 31 (a) and 2nd Sched., Part III, Forms 2 and 3).

Plea of not guilty tendered (s. 29).

Accused entitled to an adjournment of at least forty-eight hours. Court to inform accused of his right to adjournment (s. 29 (c)). Where case is adjourned prosecutor must, if requested by accused, furnish him with copy of complaint if he has not already got one (s. 29 (b)).

> In special circumstances requiring dispatch, adjournment may be for shorter period than forty-eight hours (s. 29 (c)).

Case adjourned to 10th inst., and accused meantime committed to prison, bail being fixed in minute of adjournment (s. 29 (d)).

> Bail may be refused (s. 29 (d)).
> Accused may be ordered to attend under a penalty not exceeding £10 (s. 29 (e)).

Thursday,   „   10.   Trial (s. 29).

> Procedure same as in Table I, Br. 1.

BRANCH 2.—PLEA OF GUILTY AT FIRST DIET

1971.

Monday,   June   7.

> Procedure same as in Br. 1 up to this diet. Thereafter procedure as in Br. 2 of Table I.

TABLE III.—REVIEW

(ss. 62–74)

BRANCH 1.—APPEAL BY STATED CASE

1971.

Friday,   June 18. Conviction and sentence.
                          Fine imposed, with alternative of imprisonment.
                          Fine paid.

Wednesday,   „   30. Last day for application to have case stated
                          (s. 63 (1) as amended by Law Reform (Misc.
                          Prov.) (Scotland) Act 1966, s. 9 which also
                          empowers High Court to allow further time).

> Period ten days after 18th (s. 63 (1)).
> Sunday 20th and 27th not included (s. 70).
> Public Holidays not included (s. 70).

Intimation of application to be given to respondent by clerk of court (s. 63 (1)).

Court fixes sum to be consigned or for which
caution is to be found to meet any fine and
expenses of appeal (s. 64).

> Court may dispense with consignation or caution,
> and person prosecuting in public interest not
> bound to make consignation or find caution
> (s. 64).

Tuesday,   July 6. Last day (five days after appeal) for consignation
                          or caution, and for payment of clerk's fees
                          preparing case (s. 64).

Monday,   „   12. Last day (five days from consignation or caution)
                          for completion by clerk of draft case. Draft to
                          be given to appellant or his solicitor, and dupli-
                          cate to respondent or his solicitor (s. 66).

Friday,   Aug. 13. By this date (one month after receipt of draft
                          case) each party must cause to be transmitted
                          to the judge against whose judgment the appeal
                          is taken and to the other parties a note of any
                          adjustments he desires to have made on the
                          draft case or intimate that he has no such
                          adjustments to suggest (s. 67 (1)).

> If the appellant fails so to do, he shall be deemed
> to have abandoned his appeal, and in any such
> case the court shall have the like power to grant
> warrant for his apprehension and imprison-
> ment as is conferred by s. 65 (Ibid.).

Monday,   Aug. 16. Case stated and signed by judge after considering
                          any adjustments (unless the appellant is deemed
                          to have abandoned his appeal (s. 67 (2)).

> If the judge dies before signing the case or is pre-
> cluded by illness or other cause from so doing,
> it is competent for the appellant to present a bill
> of suspension to the High Court of Justiciary
> and to bring under the review of that Court any
> matter which might have been so brought
> under review by stated case (s. 63 (2)).

Case sent to appellant, and proceedings transmitted to Clerk of Justiciary (s. 67 (3)).

Saturday, Aug. 28. Last day (ten days after receipt of case excluding Aug. 17 as date of receipt: *Cameron* v. *MacDonald*, 1960 S.L.T. 10, assuming that case still to apply) for appellant sending copy of case to respondent and transmitting case through Edinburgh solicitor to Clerk of Justiciary, with certificate of intimation having been made to respondent (s. 67 (4)).

> If the appellant fails so to do, he may be deemed to have abandoned his appeal, and the High Court shall have the like power to grant warrant for his apprehension and imprisonment as is conferred by s. 65 (s. 67 (5)), but the High Court may afford further time (Law Reform (Misc. Provn.) (Scotland) Act 1966, s. 9 (1); *cf. Bennett* v. *Macleod*, 1958 S.L.T. 67).
>
> Appellant may at any time prior to lodging case with Clerk of Justiciary abandon appeal by minute written on complaint or lodged with clerk of inferior court (s. 68 (1)).

On case being lodged with Clerk of Justiciary, any other mode of appeal held to be abandoned (s. 68 (2)).

> It is usual to print stated case with appendix containing copy of the proceedings and any written productions referred to in the statement of facts and material to the case (see *Cairney* v. *Patterson*, 1945 J.C. 120).

Thursday, Oct. 14. Case heard by High Court (s. 71).

High Court may—

(*a*) Affirm, reverse, or amend determination of inferior court.

(*b*) Substitute fine for imprisonment, reduce period of imprisonment, reduce fine.

(*c*) Remit case back for amendment, and on case being amended and returned deliver judgment.

(*d*) Remit case to inferior court with opinion thereon.

(*e*) Where appeal is against acquittal, convict and sentence, or remit case back for conviction and sentence.

(*f*) Award such expenses either in High or inferior court as they think fit.

(*g*) Remit to any fit person to inquire and report in regard to facts and circumstances, and on considering such report pronounce judgment.

> A conviction, judgment, etc., is not to be quashed for want of form, or, where accused has had legal assistance in his defence, in respect of objections not stated in inferior court, or unless

for incompetentency, corruption, or malice, or unless High Court of opinion that accused misled as to nature of charge or prejudiced in his defence on merits, and that a miscarriage of justice has resulted. Court may amend any conviction, sentence, etc., or pronounce such other sentence as they shall judge expedient (s. 73).

Despite the terms of s. 73, the High Court will always set aside any conviction, etc., which are ex facie fundamentally null. (See, e.g., *Wilson* v. *Hill,* 1943 J.C. 124; *Blythswood Taxis Ltd.* v. *Adair,* 1944 J.C. 135; *Coventry* v. *Douglas,* 1944 J.C. 13; *Black* v. *Robertson,* 1954 S.L.T. 329.)

Friday,   Oct. 15.   Process returned to inferior court along with copy interlocutor of disposal.

BRANCH 2.—APPEAL BY STATED CASE WHEN APPELLANT IN CUSTODY

1971.

Friday,   June 18.   Conviction and sentence.

Imprisonment without option of fine.

Application to have case stated.

Intimation by clerk to respondent (s. 63 (1)).

Court fixes sum to be consigned or for which caution is to be found to meet expenses of appeal (s. 64).

> Court may dispense with such caution or consignation (s. 64).

Saturday,   „ 19.   Consignation made or caution found and clerk's fees for case paid (s. 64).

Court, on application of appellant, fixes sum to be consigned or for which caution is to be found in respect of interim liberation or refuses to grant interim liberation (s. 65 (1)).

> Application must be disposed of within twenty-four hours after it is made (s. 65 (2)).

Appellant, being dissatisfied with amount of caution fixed or refusal of interim liberation, appeals to High Court (s. 65 (2)).

> Note of appeal to be written on complaint.

Proceedings transmitted to Clerk of Justiciary.

Thursday,   „ 24.   Parties heard in High Court.

Sum fixed by inferior court reduced and case remitted back.

Interim liberation refused or caution found for same and case remitted back.

Friday,   „ 25.   Caution found for sum fixed by High Court, and liberation granted.

> Procedure thereafter similar to that under Br. 1; but (*a*) if appellant does not proceed with his appeal he may, under warrant of inferior court, be imprisoned for such period of his sentence as at the date of his liberation remained unexpired; and (*b*) if he fails to attend at the hear-

ing of his case in the High Court, and the
appeal is dismissed, he may, under warrant of
the High Court, be imprisoned for a like period.

BRANCH 3.—APPEAL WHERE PROSECUTOR CONSENTS TO CONVICTION BEING
SET ASIDE

Friday,   June 18.   Conviction and sentence.

Application to have case stated.

Intimation thereof given by clerk to respondent
(s. 63 (1)).

Court fixes sum to be consigned by appellant or
for which caution to be found (s. 64).

Wednesday,   „ 30. Last day (ten days after receipt by him of draft
stated case) for prosecutor to consent to con-
viction and sentence being set aside (s. 72 (5)).
His consent is given by a minute signed by him
and written on the complaint or lodged with
the clerk of court (s. 72 (2)). He must send
a copy of the minute to appellant (s. 72 (2)).

Clerk of court ascertains from appellant or his
solicitor whether he desires to be heard (s. 72
(2)).

Transmits complaint and proceedings to Clerk of
Justiciary.

Thursday,   July 1. Case placed before judge in chambers and conviction set aside (s. 72 (3)).

Expenses not exceeding £5 5s. may be awarded
to appellant (s. 72 (3)).

Judge may refuse to set aside conviction, in which
case proceedings are returned to clerk of
inferior court, and appeal proceeds as if marked
on date of return.

This summary method of getting a conviction set
aside is also applicable to appeal by suspension
or otherwise.

This procedure is considered by L.J.-G. Cooper
in *O'Brien* v. *Adair*, 1947 J.C. 180.

FORMS OF PROCEDURE

1. JUDICIAL EXAMINATION

DECLARATION

At Edinburgh, the —— day of —— Nineteen hundred and — In
    presence of R. L., Esquire, Sheriff of the Lothians and Peebles,—
COMPEARED a prisoner, attended by E. F., Solicitor, Edinburgh, his
    agent, and the charge against said prisoner being read over and
    explained to him, and he being judicially admonished and
    examined thereanent:
DECLARES:—My name is A. B. I am twenty-three years of age. I am
    unmarried. I am a labourer, and reside at 81 High Street, Edin-
    burgh. I have to say in answer to the charge of Theft which has
    been read over to me, that I was at my mother's house, No.—
    Sauchiehall Street, Glasgow, at the time when the theft is said to
    have been committed. All which I declare to be truth. A. B.
R. L.

The foregoing Declaration, written (so far as not printed) by G. H.,
Sheriff Clerk Depute of Midlothian, was, on the date which it bears, freely
and voluntarily emitted by the therein-designed A. B. while in his sound
mind and sober senses; and on being read over was adhered to by him,
and subscribed by him and, in his presence, by said Sheriff, before
these witnesses, the said G. H., and J. K., and L. M. [*design them*].

(Signed) G. H., Witness.

(,,   ) J. K., Witness.

(,,   ) L. M., Witness.

2. BAIL

(1) PETITION FOR BAIL

EDINBURGH, [*date*].

UNTO THE HONOURABLE THE SHERIFF OF THE LOTHIANS AND PEEBLES
The PETITION of A. B. [design],

HUMBLY SHEWETH,—

That he has been committed to the Prison of Edinburgh, therein to
remain until liberated in due course of Law, upon a Petition at the
instance of J. G. B., Procurator Fiscal of Midlothian, for the public
interest, charging the Petitioner with the crime of Theft,[1] conform to
Copy Petition and Warrant of Committal produced herewith.

That the Petitioner is innocent of the said crime.

That the said crime is bailable.

---

[1] Where more than one crime is charged these should be stated.

May it therefore please you Lordship to liberate the Petitioner on his finding bail to the satisfaction of the Clerk of Court to such amount as your Lordship shall appoint.

According to Justice, etc.,
E. F.,
Pror. for Petitioner.

(2) NOTE OF APPEAL: RENEWAL OF APPLICATION FOR BAIL AFTER REFUSAL OF BAIL BY SHERIFF AND BY HIGH COURT OF JUSTICIARY ON APPEAL

UNTO THE RIGHT HONOURABLE THE LORD JUSTICE-GENERAL, LORD JUSTICE-CLERK AND LORDS COMMISSIONERS OF JUSTICIARY:

NOTE OF APPEAL
for
A. B. [design], Appellant,
for Liberation on Bail

HUMBLY SHEWETH,—

(1) That on [*date*] the Appellant was committed to prison to be detained till liberated in due course of Law on a Petition at the instance of the Procurator Fiscal at [*place*] charging him with [*here state crime or crimes*] he having been apprehended and detained in custody from [*date*].

(2) That on [*date*] the Sheriff of —— at [*place*] refused his Petition for his liberation on bail.

(3) That an Appeal was taken from the said decision of the Sheriff to the High Court of Justiciary and was heard on [*date*].

(4) That at the hearing of said Appeal, Counsel for the Crown opposed the granting of liberation on bail to the Appellant on the ground that [*here state shortly the ground*]. Lord —— dismissed the said Appeal from the said decision of the Sheriff.

(5) That no Indictment has been served on the Appellant and a date has not been fixed for his trial on said charge(s).

(6) That there has now been a material change in the circumstances since the Appellant's prior Application for bail, and Appeal, were refused. [*Here state the particulars relative to the Appellant and the circumstances justifying the Note of Appeal.*]

Therefore the Appellant prays your Lordships to grant warrant for his liberation, so far as detained on said charge(s), on his finding bail to the satisfaction of the Clerk of Court at [*place*] to such amount as your Lordships shall appoint.

According to Justice, etc.
(Signed by Counsel).

(3) BAIL BOND

I, M. N. [*design him*], considering that A. B. [*design*] has been brought before the Sheriff of the Lothians and Peebles for judicial examination under a Petition at the instance of the Procurator Fiscal of Midlothian relative to the crime of Theft as therein set forth, and has been admitted to bail on finding caution as after mentioned, do hereby judicially BIND and OBLIGE myself, my Heirs, Executors, and Successors, as Cautioners

and Sureties, acted in the Sheriff Court Books of Midlothian, for the said
A. B. that he shall, when desired, appear at all Diets to which he may be
cited for further examination on said charge; and also that he shall
appear personally, and answer any and every Indictment or Complaint
which may be served upon him with reference to the said charge, at any
time and place to which he shall be lawfully cited within the space of six
months from the date hereof, and at all Adjournments or Continuations
of the Diets of Court, aye and until the said Charge shall be finally disposed of, or the said period of six months has fully expired, and that
under the penalty of —— pounds; and I, the said A. B., hereby appoint
the Sheriff Clerk's Office, Edinburgh [*or other place, such as his Solicitor's
office*], as a domicile at which I may be lawfully cited; declaring that any
and every citation left for me there shall be as effectual as if delivered to
me personally: And we consent to the registration hereof in the said
Sheriff Court Books, or others competent for preservation and execution.
In Witness Whereof, etc.

(4) CERTIFICATE BY JUSTICE OF PEACE

I, P. Q., one of Her Majesty's Justices of the Peace for the County of
the City of Edinburgh, hereby certify the within-designed Cautioner to be
habit and repute responsible for the sum of —— pounds contained in
the within Bond.

Given under my hand at Edinburgh this —— day of —— Nineteen
hundred and —   P. Q., J.P.

Note.—This certificate may be dispensed with if the amount of bail is
consigned with the Bond, or if the Clerk of Court is satisfied of the
sufficiency of the Cautioner.

3. NOTICES OF (1) SPECIAL DEFENCE AND (2) PLEA IN BAR OF TRIAL

(1) ALIBI

Graham, for the panel, states that the panel pleads not guilty, and
specially, and without prejudice to said plea, that on the afternoon of
[*day and date*] from three until half-past five o'clock, between which times
the alleged crime is believed to have been committed, he was in the public-
house in College Street, St. Andrews, occupied by C. D., in company with
E. F. and G. H., who are to be called as witnesses for the defence.

THOS. GRAHAM.

(2) SELF-DEFENCE

Graham, for the panel, states that the panel pleads not guilty, and
specially and without prejudice to said plea, that on the occasion libelled
he was acting in self-defence, he having been assaulted by the said C. D.[1]

THOS. GRAHAM.

(3) INSANITY AT THE TIME OF CRIME

Graham, for the panel, states that the panel pleads not guilty and
specially, and without prejudice to said plea, that at the time the alleged

[1] See *H. M. Adv.* v. *McGlone*, 1955 J.C. 14.

$\dfrac{\text{crime is}}{\text{acts are}}$ said to have been committed by the panel, he was insane and therefore not responsible for his actions.

THOS. GRAHAM.

(4) CRIME COMMITTED BY ANOTHER PERSON

Graham, for the panel, states that the panel pleads not guilty and specially and without prejudice to said plea, that the sums set out in the Indictment if embezzled were embezzled not by the panel but by [*name and designation of person*] and that any entries alleged to be false if made by the panel were made by him on the instructions of the said A. B. to whose authority the panel was subject.

(5) NOTE OF PLEA OF INSANITY IN BAR OF TRIAL

Graham, for the panel, states that the panel is presently insane and unfit to plead to the Indictment or to instruct his defence.

THOS. GRAHAM.

4. DYING DEPOSITION

At Edinburgh, and within the Royal Infirmary there, the —— day of —— Nineteen hundred and — years. In presence of R. L., Esquire, Sheriff-Substitute of the Lothians and Peebles, compeared J. G., Carpenter, 110 Lothian Road, Edinburgh, and he having been solemnly sworn by the Sheriff-Substitute to tell the truth, depones as follows:—[*Take in statement*]; and declares that owing to weakness he cannot at present write; all which is truth as he shall answer to God.

R. L., Sheriff.

G. H., Witness.
J. K., Witness.

The foregoing Deposition, written on the two preceding pages by G. H., Sheriff Clerk Depute of Midlothian, was of the date which it bears freely and voluntarily emitted by the therein-designed J. G. while in his sound mind and sober senses, and after having been sworn as aforesaid; and the same is now signed in his presence by the said Sheriff after it had been read over to him, as he declared he could not at present write. All in presence of G. H. and J. K. [*design them*].

R. L.

G. H., Witness.
J. K., Witness.

Note.—If the witness is able to sign his name, substitute the following words:—" and the same on being read over was adhered to by him, and was subscribed by him and the said Sheriff-Substitute in his presence, before these witnesses, G. H., and J. K." [*design them*].

5. PETITION TO APPREHEND ABSCONDING WITNESS

That PETER SMITH, 52 Rose Street, Edinburgh, who is a material witness for the Prosecution in an Indictment at the instance of the Right Honourable ——, Her Majesty's Advocate, against A. B., Prisoner in the Prison of Edinburgh, charging him with the crime of theft, has absconded from the dwelling-house at 52 Rose Street, Edinburgh, aforesaid, occupied by him, without leaving any information as to the place at which he may be found, in order, as your Petitioner has good reason to believe, to avoid giving evidence at the trial of said Indictment before a Sheriff and Jury, to be held within the Sheriff Court-House at Edinburgh on —

May it therefore please your Lordship to examine on Oath Andrew Smith, a Constable of the Edinburgh City Police, as to the facts above set forth, and to Grant Warrant to Officers of Law to search for and apprehend the said Peter Smith, and bring him before you for examination in the premises, and thereafter to commit him to the Prison of Edinburgh, therein to be detained until the trial of the said A. B., or until the said Peter Smith finds sufficient caution acted in the Books of Court for his compearance at the said trial to bear witness as aforesaid.

According to Justice,

J. G. B., P.-F.

At Edinburgh, the — day —— The Sheriff having considered the foregoing Petitition and examined on Oath Andrew Smith, a Constable of the Edinburgh City Police, in support of the application, Grants Warrant to Officers of Law to search for and apprehend the said Peter Smith, and if necessary to detain him in a police station house, police cell, or other convenient place, and bring him for examination, and, if necessary for the execution of the foresaid purpose, Grants Warrant to open all shut and lockfast places.   R. L.

6. Suspension

BILL OF SUSPENSION AND LIBERATION

UNTO THE RIGHT HONOURABLE THE LORD JUSTICE-GENERAL, LORD JUSTICE-CLERK AND LORDS COMMISSIONERS OF JUSTICIARY

BILL OF SUSPENSION AND LIBERATION FOR *A. B.*, presently Prisoner in the Prison of   —Complainer;

against

C. D., Procurator-Fiscal, Sheriff Court [*place*] [*or, Burgh or other Prosecutor*]—Respondent;

HUMBLY MEANS AND SHEWS your Servitor, *A. B.*—Complainer—

That the Complainer is under the necessity of applying to your Lordships for suspension of a pretended conviction and/or sentence dated on or about the — day of——, whereby *W. G.*, Esquire, Sheriff at [*place*] [*or, Magistrate or Justices*] found the Complainer guilty of [*here describe the crime or offence*] as charged in a Summary Complaint at the Respondent's instance, and therefore ordained the Complainer to be removed from the Bar and to be imprisoned in the Prison of——, for a period of——from the date of the said conviction and sentence, most wrongously and unjustly, as will appear to your Lordships from the annexed statement of facts and Note of Pleas in Law;

That the Complainer, having been imprisoned in the Prison of——, under the foresaid conviction and sentence, also prays for liberation. He

is desirous of obtaining *interim* liberation without caution; but, if necessary, he is willing to find caution in common form to return to prison and
undergo the remainder of his sentence in the event of this Bill being ultimately refused.

  Therefore the Complainer prays your Lordships to grant Warrant for
    serving a copy of this Bill and deliverance thereon on the said
    C.D., the Respondent; and further to Grant Warrant ordaining the
    Clerk of the Sheriff [*or other Court*] at——, to transmit the whole
    proceedings complained of to the Clerk of Justiciary; to suspend
    the said pretended conviction and/or sentence *simpliciter*; and to
    ordain the Complainer to be immediately set at liberty, if not
    already liberated *ad interim*, and to find the Complainer entitled
    to expenses; in the meantime to grant *interim* liberation as
    craved; or to do otherwise or further in the premises as to your
    Lordships may seem proper.

According to justice, etc.,
[*Signed by Counsel or Solicitor.*]

Statement of Facts for Complainer

  (Here follow in numbered articles averments of those facts upon which
the Complainer intends to found his pleas in law.)

Pleas in Law for Complainer

  (Here follow the pleas upon which the Complainer founds his crave to
have the proceedings set aside.)

APPENDIX D

ACTS OF ADJOURNAL

ACT OF ADJOURNAL

RELATIVE TO THE CRIMINAL APPEAL (SCOTLAND) ACT 1926 (16 AND 17 GEO. V. CAP. 15)

At Edinburgh, the Twenty-seventh day of October Nineteen hundred and twenty-six

Present—

THE RIGHT HONOURABLE THE LORD JUSTICE-GENERAL.
THE RIGHT HONOURABLE THE LORD JUSTICE-CLERK.
THE HONOURABLE LORD ORMIDALE.
THE HONOURABLE LORD HUNTER.
THE HONOURABLE LORD ANDERSON.
THE HONOURABLE LORD SANDS.
THE HONOURABLE LORD BLACKBURN
THE HONOURABLE LORD ASHMORE, and
THE HONOURABLE LORD FLEMING.

The Lord Justice-General, Lord Justice-Clerk, and Lords Commissioners of Justiciary, by virtue of the powers conferred upon the Court by the Criminal Appeal (Scotland) Act 1926, hereinafter referred to as the Act, and, in particular, by section 15 thereof, do hereby ENACT AND DECLARE as follows:—

1. The Clerk of Justiciary is hereinafter referred to as " the Clerk," and this expression shall mean and include the Principal and Assistant Clerks of Justiciary and any person duly authorised to perform the duties of Principal Clerk or Assistant Clerk of Justiciary.

2. (*a*) Notes of (1) Appeal against conviction or sentence ; (2) Application for leave to Appeal against conviction or sentence; and (3) Application for extension of time within which, under the Act, Notes of Appeal or Application for leave to Appeal shall be given, shall be wholly or partly written, typed, or printed, and shall be signed by the appellant or applicant or his Counsel or Agent. Said Notes, which may be in the Forms I.–VI. contained in the Schedule hereto, shall, save as is hereinafter provided, be lodged with the Clerk within the prescribed period for Appeal or Application for leave to Appeal or any extension thereof granted by the Court, and the appellant or applicant shall immediately after lodging a Note of Appeal, a Note of Application for leave to Appeal or a Note of Application for extension of time as aforesaid, send a copy of the Note lodged to the Crown Agent, and also, if the Court of Trial was a Sheriff Court, to the Clerk of that Court.

(*b*) Where, on the trial of a person entitled to Appeal or make Application for leave to Appeal under the Act, a plea of insanity in bar of conviction has not been affirmed by the Jury, any Note required by this Act of

486

Adjournal to be signed by the appellant or applicant himself may be signed by his Counsel or Agent, or other person authorised to act on his behalf, and may be lodged with the Clerk by such Agent or other person authorised as aforesaid.

(*c*) On an Appeal being lodged and on an Application for leave to Appeal being granted, the Clerk shall give notice to the Prison Commissioners for Scotland.

(*d*) In the case of an Appeal or Application for leave to Appeal against a conviction obtained or sentence pronounced in a sheriff Court, the Clerk of the Court of Trial shall furnish to the Clerk a certified copy of the proceedings at the trial, or shall forward to him the original record of the proceedings, as may be required by the Clerk.

(*e*) Where the Court has, on a Note of Application for leave to Appeal, given an applicant leave to appeal, it shall not be necessary for such applicant to lodge any Note of Appeal, but the Note of Application for leave to Appeal shall in such case be deemed to be a Note of Appeal.

3. (*a*) The shorthand writer shall sign the shorthand notes taken by him of any trial or proceeding and certify the same to be complete and correct shorthand notes thereof, and shall retain the same unless and until he is directed by the Clerk to forward a transcript of such shorthand notes to him.

(*b*) The shorthand writer shall, on being directed by the Clerk, furnish to him for the use of the Court a transcript of the whole or of any part of the shorthand notes taken by him of any trial or proceeding in reference to which an appellant has appealed under the Act.

(*c*) The shorthand writer shall also furnish to a party interested in a trial or other proceeding in relation to which a person may appeal under the Act, and to no other person, a transcript of the whole, or of any part of the shorthand notes of any such trial or other proceeding, on payment by such party interested to such shorthand writer of his charges on such scale as the Treasury may fix.

(*d*) A party interested in an Appeal under the Act may obtain from the Clerk a copy of any documentary production lodged by or for any other party to the Appeal, upon payment therefor of the charges thereof on the scale referred to in the preceding sub-section.

(*e*) For the purposes of this section, " a party interested " shall mean the prosecutor or the person convicted or any other person named in, or immediately affected by, any order made by the judge of the Court of Trial, or other person authorised to act on behalf of a party interested, as herein defined.

(*f*) Whenever a transcript of the whole or of any part of such shorthand notes is required for the use of the Court, such transcript may be made by the shorthand writer who took and certified the shorthand notes or by such other competent person as the Clerk may direct.

(*g*) A transcript of the whole or any part of the shorthand notes relating to the case of any appellant which may be required for the use of the Court shall be typewritten and certified by the person making the same to be a correct and complete transcript of the whole or of such part, as the case may be, of the shorthand notes purporting to have been taken, signed and certified by the shorthand writer who took the same.

(*h*) Repealed by Act of Adjournal, dated March 22, 1935, and new provisions enacted—post p. 494.

4. (*a*) The certificate of the Judge of the Court of Trial that the case is a fit case for appeal may be in terms of Form VII. of the Schedule.

(*b*) The Judge of the Court of Trial may, in any case in which he considers it desirable to do so, inform the person convicted before or sentenced by him that the case is, in his opinion, one fit for an appeal to the Court under s. 1 (*b*) of the Act, and may give to such person a certificate to that effect.

5. (*a*) Where a person has, on his conviction on indictment, been sentenced to payment of a fine, and, in default of payment to imprisonment, the person lawfully authorised to receive such fine shall, on receiving the same, retain it until the determination of any appeal in relation thereto.

(*b*) If a person sentenced to payment of a fine remains in custody in default of payment of the fine he shall be deemed, for all purposes of the Act or of this Act of Adjournal, to be a person sentenced to imprisonment.

(*c*) Where any person has been convicted on indictment and is thereupon sentenced to the payment of a fine, and, in default of such payment, to imprisonment, and he intimates to the Judge of the Court of Trial that he is desirous of appealing against his conviction to the Court, either upon grounds of law alone, or with the Certificate of the Judge of the Court of Trial upon any grounds mentioned in s. 1 (*b*) of the Act, such Judge may, by order entered on the Record, appoint such person forthwith to find caution for such sum as such Judge may think right to prosecute his appeal; and, subject thereto, may also so order that payment of the said fine shall be made at the final determination of the appeal, if the same be dismissed, to the Clerk of the Court of Trial or otherwise as the Court may then order.

(*d*) An appellant who has been sentenced to the payment of a fine, and has paid the same in accordance with such sentence, shall, in the event of his appeal being successful, be entitled, subject to any order of the Court, to the return of the sum or any part thereof so paid by him.

(*e*) If an appellant to whom sub-section (*c*) of this section applies does not pay the fine or lodge a Note of Appeal upon grounds of law alone, or with the Certificate of the Judge of the Court of Trial upon any grounds mentioned in s. 1 (*b*) of the Act, within ten days from the date of his conviction and sentence, the Clerk shall report such omission to the Court or any Judge thereof, who, after such notice as they or he may deem advisable, may find that the foresaid caution has been forfeited, and may pronounce against the Cautioner, decree for such sum as they or he may think proper, and may issue a warrant for the apprehension of the appellant and may commit him to prison in default of payment of his fine, or may make such other order as they or he may think right.

6. (*a*) All documents and other productions produced at the trial of a person convicted on indictment shall be kept for the period of ten days after the actual day on which such conviction took place in the custody of the Court of Trial in such manner as it may direct, and, failing direction, such custody shall be in the hands of the Sheriff Clerk of the District of the Court

of the second diet to whom the Clerk of Court shall hand them over at the close of the trial, unless otherwise ordered by the Court on a Note of Appeal or Application for leave to Appeal being lodged, and if within such period of ten days or any extension thereof authorised by the Court a Note of Appeal or of Application for leave to Appeal has been lodged under the Act, they shall be so kept until the determination thereof; provided that the Judge of the Court of Trial may, on cause shown, grant an order authorising any of such documents or productions to be released, on such conditions as to custody and return, as he may deem it proper to prescribe.

(b) All such documents or other productions so retained in custody or released and returned shall, under supervision of the custodian thereof, be made available for inspection and for the purpose of making copies of documents or productions to an appellant or applicant who has lodged a Note of Appeal or of Application for leave to Appeal or to his Counsel or Agent, and to the Crown Agent and the Procurator-Fiscal or his Deputes.

(c) In case no Note of Appeal or Application for leave to Appeal is lodged within such period of ten days or extension thereof as aforesaid, all such documents and productions shall be dealt with as they are in use to be dealt with according to the existing law and practice at the conclusion of a trial.

7. (a) Where, upon conviction on indictment of any person of any offence, any disqualification, forfeiture or disability attaches to such person by reason of such conviction, such disqualification, forfeiture or disability shall not attach for the period of ten days from the date of the verdict against such person nor, in the event of a Note of Appeal or of Application for leave to Appeal being lodged under the Act, until the determination thereof.

(b) Where, upon a conviction on indictment, any property, matters, or things the subject of the prosecution or connected therewith, are to be or may be ordered to be destroyed or forfeited, the destruction or forfeiture or the operation of any order for destruction or forfeiture thereof shall be suspended for the period of ten days after the date of the verdict in the trial, and, in the event of a Note of Appeal or of Application for leave to Appeal being lodged under the Act, shall be further suspended until the determination thereof.

8. No extract conviction of any person convicted on indictment shall be issued during the period of ten days after the actual day on which such conviction took place save in so far as the same may be required as a warrant for the detention of the person convicted under any sentence which shall have been pronounced against him nor, in the event of a Note of Appeal or of Application for leave to Appeal being lodged under the Act, until the determination thereof.

9. The Clerk, when he has received a Note of Appeal, or a Note of Application for leave to Appeal, or a Note of Application for extension of time as aforesaid, or when the Secretary of State for Scotland shall exercise his powers under s. 16 of the Act, shall request the Judge of the Court of Trial to furnish him with a copy of his notes of the proceedings at the trial, certified by him, and such Judge of the Court of Trial shall thereupon furnish the same to the Clerk in accordance with such request, the Court or

any Judge thereof, if they or he see fit, may order the said notes to be printed or typed for the use of the Court and the parties.

10. (*a*) When the Clerk has received a Note of Appeal or of Application for leave to Appeal or for extension of time as aforesaid, or when the Secretary of State for Scotland shall exercise his powers under s. 16 of the Act, he shall request the Judge of the Court of Trial to furnish him with a Report in writing, giving his opinion upon the case generally, or upon any point arising upon the case of the appellant or applicant, and the Judge of the Court of Trial shall furnish the same to the Clerk in accordance with such request. When making a request for such Report the Clerk shall send to the Judge of the Court of Trial a copy of the Note of Appeal or Note of Application for leave to Appeal or Note of Application for extension of time as aforesaid, or any other document or information which he shall consider material or which the Court at any time shall direct him to send or with which such Judge may request to be furnished, to enable such Judge to deal in his Report with the appellant's or applicant's case generally or with any point arising thereon.

(*b*) The Report of the Judge shall be made to the Court, and except by leave of the Court or a Judge thereof, the Clerk shall not furnish to any person any part thereof.

11. (*a*) When the Court fixes the date for the hearing of an Appeal, or of an Application for leave to Appeal or for extension of time for lodging Notes of Appeal or of Application for leave to Appeal which it is proposed to dispose of by the Court, the Clerk shall give notice to the Crown Agent and to the Agent of the appellant or applicant, or to the appellant or applicant himself if he have no known Agent, and the latter shall thereupon lodge three copies (typed or printed) of the said Appeal or Application for the use of the Court.

(*b*) Where it is proposed that the powers of the Court shall be exercised by a single Judge under the provisions of s. 14, one copy only of the Application to be disposed of shall be lodged by the Agent of the applicant for the use of the Judge.

12. (*a*) If an appellant or an applicant for leave to Appeal desires to present his case and his argument in writing instead of orally he shall intimate this desire to the Clerk at least four days before the diet fixed for the hearing of the Appeal or Application for leave to Appeal, and, at the same time, shall lodge with the Clerk three copies of his case and argument; at the same time, he shall also send a copy thereof to the Crown Agent.

(*b*) Unless the Court shall otherwise direct, the respondent, in a case to which this section applies, shall not make a written reply to the case and argument in writing, but shall reply orally thereto at the diet fixed for the hearing of the Appeal or Application for leave to Appeal.

(*c*) Unless the Court shall otherwise allow, an appellant or an applicant for leave to Appeal who has presented his case and argument in writing shall not be entitled to submit in addition an oral argument to the Court in support of the Appeal or Application for leave to Appeal.

13. (*a*) An appellant or applicant at any time after he has lodged a Note of Appeal or of Application for leave to Appeal, or of Application for

extension of time as aforesaid, may abandon his Appeal or Application by lodging with the Clerk notice of abandonment thereof, which may be in terms of Form VIII. of the Schedule, and on such notice being lodged the Appeal or Application shall be deemed to have been dismissed by the Court.

(*b*) Where no appearance is made by or on behalf of an appellant or applicant at the diet appointed for the hearing of an Appeal or Application for leave to Appeal and where no case or argument in writing has been timeously lodged, the Court shall dispose of the Appeal or Application for leave to Appeal as if it had been abandoned by the appellant.

14. (*a*) When an Application or Applications have been dealt with by a Judge of the Court, under s. 14 of the Act, the Clerk shall notify to the applicant the decision in terms of Form IX. of the Schedule. In the event of such Judge refusing all or any of such Applications, the Clerk on notifying such refusal to the applicant shall forward to him Form X. of the Schedule hereto, which Form the applicant shall fill up and forthwith return to the Clerk. If the applicant does not desire to have his said Application or Applications determined by the Court as fully constituted for the hearing of Appeals under the Act, or does not return within five days to the Clerk Form X. duly filled up by him, the refusal of his Application or Applications by such Judge shall be final. If the applicant desires that his said Application or Applications shall be determined by the Court as fully constituted for the hearing of Appeals under the Act and is not legally represented, he may be present at the hearing and determination by the Court of his said Application; provided that an applicant who is legally represented shall not be entitled to be present without leave of the Court.

When an applicant duly fills up and returns within the prescribed time to the Clerk Form X. expressing a desire to be present at the hearing and determination by the Court of the Applications mentioned in this section, such Form shall be deemed to be an Application by the applicant for leave to be so present, and the Clerk, on receiving the said Form, shall take the necessary steps for placing the said Application before the Court. If the said Application to be present is refused by the Court, the Clerk shall notify the applicant ; and if the said Application is granted, the Clerk shall notify the applicant and the Governor of the Prison wherein the applicant is in custody and the [Scottish Prisons Department]. For the purpose of constituting a Court of Appeal the Judge who has refused any such Application may sit as a member of such Court, and take part in determining such Application.

(*b*) A Judge of the Court sitting under the provisions of s. 14 of the Act may sit and act wherever convenient.

15. (*a*) The evidence of any witnesses ordered to be examined before the Court or before any Judge of the Court or other person appointed by the Court shall be taken in accordance with the existing law and practice as to the taking of evidence in criminal trials in Scotland. The appellant or applicant and the respondent or Counsel on their behalf shall be entitled to be present at and take part in any examination of any witness to which this section relates.

(*b*) When an Order of Reference is made by the Court under s. 6 (*d*) of the Act, the question to be referred and the person to whom as Special Commissioner the same shall be referred shall be specified in such Order. The Court may in such Order, or by giving directions as and when they from time to time shall think right, specify whether the appellant or respondent or any person on their behalf may be present at any examination or investigation or at any stage thereof as may be ordered under s. 6 (*d*) of the Act, and specify any and what powers of the Court may be delegated to such Special Commissioner, and may require him from time to time to make *interim* Reports to the Court upon the question referred to him, and may, if the appellant is in custody, give leave to him to be present at any stage of such examination or investigation, and may give directions to the Clerk that any Report made by such Special Commissioner shall be made available to the appellant and respondent or to Counsel or Agent on their behalf, and that they shall be entitled to have copies thereof made if they so desire.

16. The Court or any single Judge exercising the powers of the Court under s. 14 of the Act may continue the hearing of any Appeal or Application to a date, fixed or not fixed, and any Judge of the Court, or other person appointed by the Court to take additional evidence, may fix any diet of proof necessary for that purpose.

17. When an appellant or applicant is entitled or has been granted leave to be present at any diet (1) before the Court or any Judge thereof or (2) for the taking of additional evidence before a person appointed for the purpose under s. 6 (*b*) of the Act, or (3) for an examination or investigation by a Special Commissioner in terms of s. 6 (*d*) of the Act, the Clerk shall give timeous notice to the [Scottish Prisons Department], in terms of Form XI. of the Schedule, which notice shall be sufficient warrant to the said Commissioners for transmitting the appellant or applicant in custody from prison to the place where said diet or any subsequent diets are to be held and for reconveying him to prison at the conclusion of the said diet and any subsequent diets. The appellant or applicant shall appear at all such diets in ordinary civilian clothes.

18. The [Scottish Prisons Department] shall, on notice under the preceding section from the Clerk, cause from time to time such sufficient number of male and female warders to attend the Sittings of the Court as, having regard to the list of Appeals thereat, they shall consider necessary.

19. (*a*) On the final determination of any Appeal under the Act or of any matter under s. 14 of the Act the Clerk shall give notice of such determination to the appellant or applicant if he is in custody and has not been present at such final determination, to the Clerk of the Court of Trial, and to the [Scottish Prisons Department].

(*b*) [*No longer applicable.*]

(*c*) The Clerk shall in all cases of Appeal or of Application for leave to Appeal from a conviction obtained or sentence pronounced in the High Court of Justiciary, note on the margin of the record of the trial the fact of an Appeal or Application for leave to Appeal having been taken and the result of the Appeal or Application for leave to Appeal, and, in the case of an Appeal or Application for leave to Appeal taken against any conviction obtained or sentence pronounced in the Sheriff Court, the Clerk shall notify the Clerk of the Court of Trial of the result of said Appeal or Application, and it shall be the duty of the Clerk of the Court of Trial to enter on the margin of the record of the trial a note of such result.

20. (*a*) The Clerk shall keep a Register, in such form as he thinks right, of all cases in which he shall receive a Note of Appeal or Note of Application for leave to Appeal under the Act, which Register shall be open for public inspection at such place and at such hours as the Clerk, subject to the approval of the Court, shall consider convenient.

(*b*) The Clerk shall also take the necessary steps for preparing, from time to time, a list of cases to be dealt with by the Court, and shall cause such list to be published in such manner as, subject to the approval of the Court, he shall think convenient for giving due notice to any parties interested, of the hearing of such cases by the Court.

(*c*) Where an appellant or applicant is in custody and has obtained leave or is entitled to be present at the hearing and determination of his Appeal or Application, the Clerk shall notify the appellant or applicant, the Governor of the Prison in which the appellant or applicant then is, and the [Scottish Prisons Department] of the probable day on which the Appeal or Application will be heard. The [Scottish Prisons Department] shall take steps to transfer the appellant or applicant to a Prison convenient for his appearance before the Court, at such reasonable time before the hearing as shall enable him to consult his legal adviser, if any.

21. (*a*) Except where otherwise provided in this Act of Adjournal, any application to the Court may be made by the appellant or respondent as the case may be or by Counsel on his behalf, orally or in writing, but in regard to such applications if the appellant is unrepresented and is in custody and is not entitled or has not obtained leave to be present before the Court, he shall make any such application by forwarding the same in writing to the Clerk, who shall take the proper steps to obtain the decision of the Court thereon.

(*b*) In all proceedings before a Judge under s. 14 of the Act, and in all preliminary and interlocutory proceedings and applications except such as are heard before the full Court, the parties thereto may be represented and appear by an Agent alone.

22. Subject to the provisions of s. 14 of the Act and without prejudice thereto, preliminary and interlocutory proceedings incidental to any appeal or application may be disposed of by a single Judge.

23. When the Court has heard and dealt with any Application under the Act or this Act of Adjournal, the Clerk shall (unless it appears to him unnecessary so to do) give to the applicant (if he is in custody and has not been present at the hearing of such Application) notice of the decision of the Court in relation to the said Application.

24. Non-compliance with the provisions of this Act of Adjournal, or with any rule of practice for the time being in force under the Act, shall not prevent the further prosecution of an Appeal or Application if the Court or a Judge thereof consider it just and proper that such non-compliance be waived or remedied by amendment or otherwise. The Court or a Judge thereof may, in such manner as they or he think right, direct

the remedy of such non-compliance, and upon the same being remedied accordingly the Appeal or Application shall proceed.

25. Sittings of the Court (including Sittings in Court of Session Vacation and Sittings of a Judge of the Court under s. 14 of the Act) shall be arranged to be held as may from time to time be directed by the Lord Justice-General whom failing by the Lord Justice-Clerk.

26. Save in so far as herein provided for no Clerk's fees, Court fees, or other fees or expenses shall be exigible from or awarded against an appellant or applicant in respect of an Appeal or Application under the Act.

27. In computing the period of days in appeals and other applications under the Act and this Act of Adjournal, Sundays and public holidays shall not be included.

28. The Clerk may, with the sanction of the Lord Justice-General and the Lord Justice-Clerk, vary the forms appended to this Act from time to time as may be found necessary for giving effect to the provisions of the Act.

29. This Act of Adjournal shall come into operation on the first day of November, 1926, and shall be printed and published in the *Edinburgh Gazette*.

J. A. CLYDE, *I.P.D.*

ACT OF ADJOURNAL

To

REGULATE PROCEDURE RELATIVE TO SHORTHAND NOTES TAKEN AT CRIMINAL TRIALS, UNDER SECTION 11 (1) OF THE CRIMINAL APPEAL (SCOTLAND) ACT 1926, HEREINAFTER REFERRED TO AS " THE ACT."

At Edinburgh, the Twenty-second day of March,
Nineteen hundred and thirty-five

Present—

THE RIGHT HONOURABLE THE LORD JUSTICE-GENERAL.
THE RIGHT HONOURABLE THE LORD JUSTICE-CLERK.
THE HONOURABLE LORD BLACKBURN.
THE RIGHT HONOURABLE LORD MORISON.
THE HONOURABLE LORD FLEMING.

The Lord Justice-General, Lord Justice-Clerk, and Lords Commissioners of Justiciary, considering that it has been found necessary for the determination of some Appeals to the High Court of Justiciary sitting as a Court of Criminal Appeal under the Act, to have a transcript of the shorthand notes of every part of the proceedings in the Court of Trial, do hereby ENACT AND DECLARE as follows :—

1. That for the purpose of section 11 of the Act, the expression " Proceedings at the trial " shall mean the whole proceedings, including discussions (*a*) on any objection to the relevancy of the Indictment ; (*b*) in reference to any challenge of jurors ; and (*c*) on all questions arising in the course of the trial—with the decisions of the Court thereon—the

evidence led at the trial, any statement made by or on behalf of the prisoner, whether before or after verdict, the summing up by the Judge, the speeches of Counsel or Agent, the Verdict of the Jury and sentence by the Judge.

2. That the entry in the Minute Book of the Court of Trial which shall be signed by the Clerk of Court shall be in the following terms, viz. :—

" The Court directed that the whole proceedings in this case (*or*) in all the cases set down for trial at this Sitting, be taken down in shorthand and appointed Mr.   , Shorthand Writer [*address*] to do so, and the declaration *de fideli administratione officii* was administered to him."

3. That sub-section (*h*) of section 3 of the Act of Adjournal—under the Act—dated the 27th day of October, Nineteen hundred and twenty-six, is hereby repealed.

4. This Act of Adjournal shall come into operation on the date hereof and shall be printed and published in the *Edinburgh Gazette*.

J. A. CLYDE, *I.P.D.*

ACT OF ADJOURNAL

RELATIVE TO VERDICTS AND SENTENCES IN CRIMINAL CAUSES.[1]

At Edinburgh, the Thirteenth day of October,
Nineteen hundred and thirty-six
Present—

THE RIGHT HONOURABLE THE LORD JUSTICE-GENERAL.
THE RIGHT HONOURABLE THE LORD JUSTICE-CLERK.
THE RIGHT HONOURABLE LORD MORISON.
THE HONOURABLE LORD FLEMING.
THE HONOURABLE LORD MONCRIEFF.
THE HONOURABLE LORD MACKAY.
THE HONOURABLE LORD PITMAN.
THE HONOURABLE LORD WARK.

The Lord Justice-General, Lord Justice-Clerk, and Lords Commissioners of Justiciary, by virtue of the powers conferred upon the Court by an Act passed in the Third Session of the Second Parliament of King Charles the Second, entitled, " Act concerning the Regulation of Judicatories " and "The Criminal Procedure (Scotland) Act 1887," 50 & 51 Vict., c. 35.

Do hereby ENACT AND DECLARE that from and after the passing hereof, the following provisions shall have effect, viz. :—

I. When in any criminal trial the jury shall have retired to consider their verdict, and, owing to delay in returning their verdict or for other sufficient reason, the diet in another criminal cause has been called, it shall be lawful to interrupt the proceedings in such other cause (*a*) in order to receive the verdict of the jury in the preceding trial, and thereafter to dispose of the cause either by passing sentence upon the panel, or by postponing sentence, or by assoilzing the panel, as the case may be, (*b*) to

[1] As amended by Act of Adjournal (Procedure in Criminal Trials Amendment) 1966.

give a direction to the jury in the preceding trial upon any matter upon which the jury may wish a direction from the judge or to hear any request from the jury regarding any matter in the cause, as, for example, to make available any production for examination by the jury, provided always as follows :—

(1) That whether in any cause interruption shall be allowed shall be a matter in the discretion of the judge who presides at the trial ;

(2) That in no case shall the verdict of the jury in the preceding trial be returned, or sentence in the event of a verdict of guilty be imposed upon the panel, or any direction be asked or given, or any request be heard or granted, in the presence of the jury in the interrupted trial, but in every case such jury shall be directed to retire by the presiding judge ;

(3) That in the case of any such interruption a minute of continuation of the diet of the interrupted trial shall be entered in the Minute Book of the Court, and it shall be sufficient that the minute should bear that the diet be continued until an afterpart of the same day without further specification of time or to the following or a subsequent day as the Court may direct, and on the interrupted trial being resumed the diet shall be called *de novo* ;

II. Where in any cause the diet of which has not been called, the panel shall intimate through his counsel to the Clerk of Court that he is prepared to tender a plea of guilty as libelled or such qualified plea as the Crown is prepared to accept, or where a cause is remitted to the High Court for sentence in which the panel has pleaded guilty under sec. 31 of the Criminal Procedure (Scotland) Act 1887, any trial (other than a trial for murder) then proceeding may be interrupted for the purpose of receiving such plea or dealing with said remitted cause and pronouncing sentence or otherwise disposing of any such cause ; provided always :—

(1) That in the case of any such interruption an entry will be duly made in the Minute Book of the Court continuing the diet of the interrupted cause to an afterpart of the same day without further specification of time or to the following or a subsequent day as the court may direct ;

(2) That in any such interposed cause the plea of the panel shall not be tendered or accepted, nor sentence passed in the presence of the jury in the cause then proceeding, but said jury if not already retired shall be directed by the presiding judge to retire.

W. G. NORMAND, *I.P.D.*

ACT OF ADJOURNAL

RELATIVE TO THE CRIMINAL JUSTICE (SCOTLAND) ACT, 1949

At Edinburgh, the Fifteenth day of June,
Nineteen hundred and fifty

Present—

THE RIGHT HONOURABLE THE LORD JUSTICE-GENERAL.
THE RIGHT HONOURABLE THE LORD JUSTICE-CLERK.
THE HONOURABLE LORD CARMONT.
THE HONOURABLE LORD RUSSELL.
THE HONOURABLE LORD KEITH.

The Lord Justice-General, Lord Justice-Clerk, and Lords Commissioners of Justiciary, by virtue of the powers conferred upon the High Court of Justiciary by section 37 (4) of The Criminal Justice (Scotland) Act, 1949 do hereby ENACT as follows :—

1. Where a Court imposes a fine on a person convicted on Indictment such person may apply to that Court for an order for payment of the fine by instalments, and where, either at the time said fine was imposed or at any subsequent time, such an order has been made, may at any time thereafter before imprisonment has followed on the sentence apply to that Court to vary the order.

2. An application, other than one made at the time the fine was imposed, shall be made in the case of a fine imposed in the High Court of Justiciary (whether at Edinburgh or on Circuit) to the Clerk of Justiciary, and in the Sheriff Court to the Sheriff Clerk of the Court by which the fine was imposed ; and such application may be accompanied by a statement in writing setting forth the reasons therefor and any proposals the applicant may have for the payment of the fine by instalments or for variation of the order for payment of the fine by instalments, as the case may be.

3. Where an application has been made as aforesaid, the Clerk of Justiciary or Sheriff Clerk, as the case may be, shall lay it before any Judge or the Sheriff Principal or any Sheriff of the Court which imposed the fine, either in Court or in Chambers ; and the said Judge or Sheriff Principal or Sheriff may dispose of the application without requiring the attendance of the accused.

4. The determination of any such application shall be entered in the Minutes of Proceedings of the trial by the Clerk of Court ; and where an application is made to a Sheriff Court which is not the Court having custody of the record copy indictment and such Minutes, the Sheriff Clerk shall obtain the same from the Court having custody thereof, and shall, after the application has been disposed of, return the record copy Indictment and Minutes to that Court.

5. This Act of Adjournal may be cited as the Act of Adjournal Fines on Indictment (Payment by Instalments), 1950.

6. This Act of Adjournal shall come into operation on the date hereof and shall be forthwith printed and published in the *Edinburgh Gazette*.

And the Lords Appoint this Act of Adjournal to be recorded in the Books of Adjournal.

T. M. COOPER, *I.P.D.*

1964 No. 249 (s. 20)

ACT OF ADJOURNAL (SUMMARY PROCEDURE) 1964

Made Sixth February, Nineteen hundred and sixty-four
Coming into Operation, Second March Nineteen hundred and sixty-four
At Edinburgh, the Sixth day of February, Nineteen hundred and sixty-four
Present—
> THE RIGHT HONOURABLE THE LORD JUSTICE-GENERAL
> THE RIGHT HONOURABLE THE LORD JUSTICE-CLERK
> THE HONOURABLE LORD CARMONT
> THE HONOURABLE LORD STRACHAN
> THE HONOURABLE LORD GUTHRIE
> THE HONOURABLE LORD MIGDALE
> THE RIGHT HONOURABLE LORD WHEATLEY
> THE HONOURABLE LORD WALKER
> THE HONOURABLE LORD CAMERON

The Lord Justice-General, Lord Justice-Clerk and Lords Commissioners of Justiciary, by virtue of the powers conferred upon them by section 76 of the Summary Jurisdiction (Scotland) Act 1954 as amended, and of all other powers competent to them in that behalf, do hereby ENACT as follows—

1. The Act of Adjournal relative to the Criminal Justice Administration Act 1914 (4 & 5 Geo. 5. c. 58) and the Act of Adjournal relative to the Criminal Procedure (Scotland) Act 1938 (1 & 2 Geo. 6. c. 48) are hereby repealed.

2.—(1) The citation of the accused and witnesses in a summary prosecution to any ordinary sitting of a summary court or to any special diet fixed by a summary court or to any adjourned sitting or diet of such court shall be effected as provided in this section.

(2) It shall be deemed a legal citation of the accused or a witness to such a sitting or diet or adjourned sitting or diet as is mentioned in the last foregoing subsection—

(*a*) if the citation be delivered to him personally or left for him at his dwelling-house or place of business with some person resident or employed therein, or where he has no known dwelling-house or place of business, at any other place in which he may at the time be resident, or

(*b*) where the accused or witness is the master of, or a seaman or person employed in, a vessel, if the citation is left with a person on board thereof and connected therewith, or

(*c*) where the accused is a company, association or corporation, if the citation is left at their ordinary place of business with a partner, director, secretary or other official, or if the company, association or corporation is cited in the same manner as if the proceedings were in a civil court, or

(*d*) where the accused is a body of trustees, if the citation is left with any one of them who is resident in Scotland or with their known solicitor in Scotland.

(3) It shall be deemed a legal citation of the accused to such a sitting or diet or adjourned sitting or diet as is mentioned in subsection (1) hereof, if the citation be signed by the prosecutor and sent by post in a registered envelope or through the recorded delivery service to the dwelling-house or place of business of such accused, or, if he has no known dwelling-house or place of business, to any other place in which he may at the time be resident:

Provided that, if the accused shall fail to appear at a diet or sitting or adjourned diet or sitting to which he has been cited in the manner provided by this subsection, paragraphs (*b*) and (*c*) of section 30 of the Summary Jurisdiction (Scotland) Act 1954, as amended, shall not apply unless it shall have been proved to the court that he received the citation or that the contents thereof came to his knowledge.

(4) The production in court of any letter or other communication purporting to be written by or on behalf of an accused who has been cited in the manner provided in subsection (3) hereof in such terms as to infer that the contents of such citation came to his knowledge, shall be admissible as evidence of that fact for the purposes of the proviso to that subsection.

3. The citation of a probationer to appear before a court of summary jurisdiction in terms of section 5 (1) or section 6 (1) of the Criminal Justice (Scotland) Act 1949 shall be effected in like manner, *mutatis mutandis*, as the citation of an accused to a sitting or diet of a summary court.

4.—(1) The citation of an offender to appear before a court of summary jurisdiction in terms of section 43 (2) (*a*) of the Summary Jurisdiction (Scotland) Act 1954, as amended, shall be effected in like manner, *mutatis mutandis*, as the citation of an accused to a sitting or diet of a summary court:

Provided that the citation shall be signed by the clerk of the court before which the offender is required to appear, instead of by the prosecutor, and provided also that the forms contained in Part IV of the second schedule to the Summary Jurisdiction (Scotland) Act 1954, shall not apply to such citation.

(2) The citation of such an offender shall be in the form, as nearly as may be, of Form 1 contained in the Schedule hereto.

(3) If the citation of such an offender shall have been effected by an officer of law, the written execution, if any, of that officer of law shall be in the form, as nearly as may be, of Form 2 contained in the Schedule hereto.

5.—(1) When the citation of any person other than a witness is effected by post in terms of any of the preceding sections hereof, the *induciae* shall be reckoned from twenty-four hours after the time of posting.

(2) It shall be sufficient evidence that a citation has been sent by post in terms of any of the preceding sections hereof, if there is produced in court a written execution, signed by the person who signed such citation and in the form, as nearly as may be, of Form 3 contained in the Schedule hereto, together with the post office receipt for the relative registered or recorded delivery letter.

6.—(1) A warrant of apprehension issued by a court of summary jurisdiction in terms of section 43 (2) of the Summary Jurisdiction (Scotland) Act 1954, as amended, shall be in the form, as nearly as may be, of Form 4 contained in the Schedule hereto.

(2) The Minute of procedure in relation to an enquiry into the means of an offender under section 43 of the Summary Jurisdiction (Scotland) Act 1954, as amended, shall be in the form, as nearly as may be, of Form 5 contained in the Schedule hereto.

7.—(1) When a court of summary jurisdiction shall have made an order in terms of section 43B (1) of the Summary Jurisdiction (Scotland) Act 1954, as amended, placing an offender under the supervision of another person, a notice shall be sent by the clerk of the court to such offender in the form, as nearly as may be, of Form 6 contained in the Schedule hereto.

(2) The person appointed to supervise such an offender shall communicate with him with a view to assisting and advising him in regard to payment of the fine, and unless the same or any instalment thereof shall have been paid to the clerk of the court within the time allowed by the court for payment, the person so appointed shall report to the court without delay after the expiry of such time, as to the conduct and means of the offender.

8.—(1) When a court of summary jurisdiction which has adjudged that a sum of money shall be paid by an offender, shall consider that any money found on the offender on apprehension or after he has been searched by order of the court, should not be applied towards payment of such sum, the court shall make a direction in writing to that effect which shall be written on the extract of the sentence which imposes the fine, before the same is issued by the clerk of the court.

(2) An accused may make an application to such a court either orally or in writing, through the governor of the prison in whose custody he may be at the time, that any sum of money which shall have been found on his person should not be applied in payment of the fine adjudged to be paid by him.

(3) A person who alleges that any money found on the person of an offender is not the property of the offender, but belongs to such person, may apply to such court either orally or in writing for a direction that such money should not be applied in payment of the fine adjudged to be paid, and the court after inquiry may so direct.

(4) A court of summary jurisdiction which has adjudged that a sum of money shall be paid by an offender, may order the attendance in court of the offender if he is in prison, for the purpose of ascertaining the ownership of money which shall have been found on his person.

(5) A notice in the form, as nearly as may be, of Form 7 contained in the Schedule hereto, addressed to the governor of the prison in whose custody an offender may be at the time, signed by the judge of a court of summary jurisdiction shall be a sufficient warrant to the governor of such prison for conveying the offender to the court.

9. In all cases where time is not allowed by a court of summary jurisdiction for payment of a fine, the reasons of the court for not so allowing time shall be stated in the extract of the finding and sentence as well as in the finding and sentence itself.

10.—(1) Where a court of summary jurisdiction makes a transfer of fine order under section 44 of the Summary Jurisdiction (Scotland) Act 1954 as amended, the clerk of the court shall send to the clerk of the court specified in the order a notice in the form, as nearly as may be, of Form 8 or Form 9 contained in the Schedule hereto, or in the case of a further transfer of fine order, of Form 10 contained in the Schedule hereto, and shall at the same time send to that clerk a statement of the offence of which the offender was convicted, and of the steps if any which shall have been taken to recover the fine, and shall give him such further information if any as, in his opinion, is likely to assist the court specified in the order in recovering the fine.

(2) In the case of a further transfer of fine order the clerk of the court which shall have made the order shall send to the clerk of the court by which the fine was imposed a copy of the notice which shall have been sent to the clerk of the court specified in the order.

(3) The clerk of the court specified in a transfer of fine order shall, as soon as may be after he has received the notice prescribed in subsection (1) above, send an intimation to the offender in the form, as nearly as may be, of Form 11 contained in the Schedule hereto.

(4) The clerk of the court specified in a transfer of fine order shall remit or otherwise account for any payment received in respect of the fine, to the clerk of the court by which the fine was imposed, and if the sentence shall have been enforced otherwise than by payment of the fine, he shall inform the clerk of that court how the sentence was enforced.

11.—(1) An application by an offender for further time in which to pay a fine adjudged to be paid by him by a court of summary jurisdiction, or of instalments thereof, shall be made to that court, except in a case where a transfer of fine order shall have been made under section 44 of the Summary Jurisdiction (Scotland) Act 1954, as amended, or under section 72A of the Magistrates' Courts Act 1952, as amended, in which case the application shall be made to the court specified in the transfer order, or to the court specified in the last transfer order where there is more than one transfer.

(2) A court to which an application is made under the last foregoing subsection shall allow further time for payment of the fine or of instalments thereof, unless it is satisfied that the failure of the offender to make payment has been wilful or that the offender has no reasonable prospect of being able to pay if further time is allowed.

(3) An application made under this section to a court of summary jurisdiction in Scotland may be made orally or in writing.

12. The Second Schedule to the Summary Jurisdiction (Scotland) Act 1954 shall be amended as follows—

(1) In Part IV by adding after the words " police constable " occurring at the end of the form for citing an accused, the words (" *or* Prosecutor)."

(2) In Part V by deleting the forms from the words " Fined £................
(or £........................each) " which occur opposite the marginal note
" Fine " to the words " months thereafter, and in default................
days' imprisonment further," which occur opposite the marginal
note " Imprisonment and caution," together with the relative
marginal notes, and by substituting therefor the following forms
and relative marginal notes:—

Fine, time allowed   Fined £........................, (or £........................each),
.... days allowed for
payment.

or

Fine, imprisonment   Fined £........................, (or £........................each),
imposed for future   .... days allowed for
default   payment. For the reason stated below
.... days' imprisonment
(or .... days' imprisonment each) imposed in default of payment
within time allowed.
(Here state reason)

or

Fine, no time to pay   Fined £........................, (or £........................each),
and in default of payment........................
.... days' imprisonment. For the
reason stated below, no time allowed for
payment.
(Here state reason)

or

Caution   To find £........................ caution for good
behaviour, ... days
allowed for finding such caution.

13. The forms in the Schedule annexed hereto shall be in supplement of
the forms contained in the Second Schedule to the Summary Jurisdiction
(Scotland) Act 1954, and may be used with such variations as circumstances
may require for the purposes of the aforesaid Act, or, so far as they relate
to summary jurisdiction or procedure, of the Criminal Justice (Scotland)
Act 1949 or the Criminal Justice (Scotland) Act 1963.

14. This Act of Adjournal may be cited as the Act of Adjournal
(Summary Procedure) 1964, and shall come into operation on 2nd March
1964.

And the Lords appoint this Act of Adjournal to be recorded in the
Books of Adjournal, and to be published in the *Edinburgh Gazette*.

(Sgd.)   J. L. Clyde,
I.P.D.

SCHEDULE

FORMS OF PROCEDURE PROVIDED BY THIS ACT OF ADJOURNAL

FORM 1

To (name and designation)

In respect that in the..Court, you were on the...............................day of..................................19.........., sentenced to pay a fine of £........................... (or ordered to find caution for £........................... for good behaviour) and.............................days were allowed for payment (or to find caution); and in respect that the said fine (or part of the said fine amounting to £........................) has not been paid (or caution for £........................ has not been found) within the time allowed, you are ordained to appear personally on (date) at.............................noon in the ....Court at (address) for an enquiry into your means under section 43 of the Summary Jurisdiction (Scotland) Act 1954, as amended.

FORM 2

I, ..., Officer of Law, upon the .... day of ....19........., did lawfully cite (name and designation as in the citation) to appear personally before the.............................. Court at .... on.................................. at.............................. noon, for an inquiry into his means, under section 43 of the Summary Jurisdiction (Scotland) Act 1954, as amended. This I did by delivering a copy of the citation to the said (state how served upon accused, whether personally or left at dwelling-house or otherwise).

....C.D. Police Constable.

FORM 3

I, ..., Procurator Fiscal (or other person who has signed the citation) did lawfully cite (name and designation as in the citation) to appear personally before the............................. Court at .... on at .... noon, to answer to a complaint at my instance (or at the instance of.............................) charging him with (state offence) (or for an enquiry into his means under section 43 of the Summary Jurisdiction (Scotland) Act 1954, as amended). This I did by posting a citation to him in a registered letter (or through the recorded delivery service) addressed to him at his dwelling-house (or place of business) as follows:—

The post office receipt for the said registered (or recorded delivery) letter accompanies this execution.

FORM 4

(Place and Date) In respect that in the.............................. Court, ... (name and designation) on the.............................day of.................................19........., was sentenced to pay a fine of £................ (or ordered to find caution for £................ for good behaviour) and .... days were allowed for payment (or to find caution); and in respect that the said .... has failed to pay the fine (or part of the said fine amounting to £........................) (or find the caution) within the time allowed, the court grants warrant for the apprehension of the said .... for the purpose of his being brought before the court for an enquiry into his means under section 43 of the Summary Jurisdiction (Scotland) Act 1954, as amended.

FORM 5

(Place and Date) ...., Sheriff (or Magistrate).

Compeared the accused for enquiry into his means. After enquiry, the Court, in relation to the fine imposed on the accused on ...., 19........., imposed as an alternative to the payment of the said fine .... days' imprisonment to commence forthwith or allowed payment of the said fine to be made within.............................days from this date, (or as the case may be).

FORM 6

To (name and designation)

In respect that a fine of £................ was imposed upon you by the.............................. Court at................ on.............................and the said fine (or the balance of £................

of the said fine) remains unpaid, you are hereby given notice that you were this day by order of the said Court placed under the supervision of (*name*), Probation Officer, (*or* other designation) for so long as the said fine remains due and unpaid or until further order of the Court.

FORM 7

To the Governor of the Prison of .... Take notice that the attendance of (*name*), presently in your custody, is required at .... on...at.......................................noon.

(Sheriff or Magistrate).

FORM 8

TRANSFER OF FINE ORDER (within Scotland)

Under section 44 of the Summary Jurisdiction (Scotland) Act 1954, as amended·
In the...Court, at.., (*name*) was on the........................... day of..................................19..........., convicted of (*offence*) and was sentenced to pay a fine of £................ (said fine to be paid by weekly (*or* monthly*) instalments of .... the first instalment to be paid on (*date*)), and the said fine (*or* the balance of the said fine as shown in the statement annexed hereto) is still unpaid and no term of imprisonment has been fixed in the event of a future default in payment of the sum in question:

And as it appears that the said (*name*) is now residing at ....: a transfer of fine order is hereby made in pursuance of section 44 of the Summary Jurisdiction (Scotland) Act 1954, as amended, transferring to .... Court (*insert name of a court of summary jurisdiction for the area in which the offender is now residing*), and to the Clerk thereof with respect to the said fine all the functions referred to in the said section.

(Sheriff or Magistrate).

Statement referred to

Fine   £.........................
Instalment(s) paid to date of transfer   £........................

Balance due £.........................

In instalments of £.........................
(Signed by Clerk).

FORM 9

TRANSFER OF FINE ORDER (to England or Wales)

Under section 44 of the Summary Jurisdiction (Scotland) Act 1954, as amended.
In the........................... ....Court, at..........................., (*name*) was on the........................... day of.................................. 19..........., convicted of (*offence*) and was sentenced to pay a fine of £................ (said fine to be paid by weekly (*or* monthly) instalments of.............................. the first instalment to be paid on (*date*)), and the said fine (*or* the balance of the said fine as shown in the statement annexed hereto) is still unpaid and no term of imprisonment has been fixed in the event of a future default in payment of the sum in question: And as it appears that the said (*name*) is now residing at............................... ....:

A transfer of fine order is hereby made in pursuance of section 44 (1) (*b*) of the Summary Jurisdiction (Scotland) Act 1954, as amended by section 26 and Schedule 3 of the Criminal Justice (Scotland) Act 1963, transferring to............................... (*insert name of the Magistrates' Court acting for the Petty Sessions area in which the offender is resident*) and to the clerk of the said Court with respect to the said fine, all the functions referred to in the said section 44.

(Sheriff or Magistrate).

Statement referred to

Fine   £.........................
Instalment(s) paid to date of transfer   £........................

Balance due £.........................

In instalments of £.........................
(Signed by Clerk).

FORM 10

FURTHER TRANSFER OF FINE ORDER

Under section 44 of the Summary Jurisdiction (Scotland) Act 1954, as amended.

In the................................Court at................................(*or* the Magistrates' Court acting for the Petty Sessions area of................................in the County of................................), (*name*) was on the................................day of................................ convicted of (*offence*) and was sentenced to pay a fine of £.................... (said fine to be paid by weekly (*or* monthly) instalments of...................., the first instalment to be paid on (*date*)).

By virtue of a transfer of fine order dated the................................day of ....19............, the function of the last mentioned court and the clerk thereof with respect to that sum are exercisable by this................................Court at................................and the clerk thereof:

And the said (*name*) has not yet paid the said fine (*or* has paid £.................... in part payment but has still to pay a balance of £.................... as shown in the statement annexed hereto):

And as it appears that the said (*name*) is now residing at................................ outwith the jurisdiction of this court:

A further transfer of fine order is hereby made in pursuance of section 44 of the Summary Jurisdiction (Scotland) Act 1954, as amended by Section 26 and Schedule 3 to the Criminal Justice (Scotland) Act 1963, transferring to................................ (*insert name of a court of summary jurisdiction or the Magistrates' Court for the area in which the offender is now resident*) and to the Clerk thereof all the functions referred to in the said section with respect to the sum(s) due (or balance of the sums due).

(Signed by Judge).

Statement referred to

(1)	Fine	£....................
(2)	Any sums paid before transfer of fine to this Court	£....................
(3)	Instalment(s) paid to this Court to date of this further transfer	£....................
(4)	Balance remaining due	£....................
	In instalments of	£....................

(Signed by Clerk).

FORM 11

NOTICE TO OFFENDER OF TRANSFER OF FINE ORDER

In the................................Court at................................

To (*name and designation*)

On the................................day of................................19............, you were convicted by................................Court at................................and were sentenced to pay a fine of £.................... (said fine to be paid by weekly (*or* monthly) instalments of ....the first instalment to be paid on (*date*)), and the said fine has not been fully paid.

Notice is hereby given to you that in consequence of a transfer of fine order made by ....Court on the................................day of................................ 19............, the enforcement of the said fine or balance thereof due by you as shown in the statement annexed hereto, has become a matter for this Court.

Payment of the instalments (*or* balance) due by you should therefore be made within the time (*or* times) ordered, by post or personally to me (*Clerk of court and address*). If you cannot pay forthwith (*or* by................................day of.................... ....19............) (*expiry of time allowed for payment*) you should at once make an application for further time to be granted. Such an application should be made either in person to this Court or by letter addressed to me stating fully why you are unable to pay the sum due.

(Signed by Clerk).

Note

Any communication sent by post must be stamped. Cash should not be sent in an unregistered envelope.

Statements referred to

Fine	£.............
Instalment(s) paid to date of transfer	£.............
Balance due	£.............
In instalments of	£.............

FORM 12

DIRECTION OF COURT AS TO MONEY FOUND ON OFFENDER

(Section 41 (2) of the Summary Jurisdiction (Scotland) Act 1954)

The Court directed that the money found on the person of *(name of offender)* should not be applied to payment of the fine of £...................imposed upon him on ....19.........

FORM 13

ORDER OF DETENTION IN PRECINCTS OF COURT

(Section 46 of the Summary Jurisdiction (Scotland) Act 1954)

The Court ordered the accused to be detained within the precincts of the Court *(or* police station) until *(state time)* of this day.

FORM 14

ORDER FOR DETENTION IN POLICE CUSTODY NOT EXCEEDING FOUR DAYS, INSTEAD OF IMPRISONMENT

(Section 47 (2) of the Summary Jurisdiction (Scotland) Act 1954)

The Court ordered the accused to be detained in the custody of the Police, at *(place)* for the space of *(time)*.

FORM 15

ORDER FOR EXTENSION OF TIME FOR PAYMENT OF FINE

(Section 42 (6) of the Summary Jurisdiction (Scotland) Act 1954 as amended)

The Court having considered the application of the accused for extension of time for payment of the foregoing fine allowed payment to be made within................................ days from this date.

(Sgd.) *J. L. CLYDE,*
I.P.D.

INDEX

ABSOLUTE DISCHARGE,
appeal against, 17–88
child, of, 19–14
effect of, in subsequent proceedings,
17–04, 17–87, 17–88, 17–94

ACCELERATED PROCEDURE UNDER
SECTION 31 OF THE 1887 ACT,
abandonment of charge, 8–04
diet,
desertion of, 8–02, 8–04, 8–05
place of, 8–02
failure to comply with procedure,
8–04
indictment,
form of, 8–02
service of, 8–02
induciae, 8–02
notice of intention to plead guilty,
8–01
plea of guilty, 8–02
withdrawal of, 8–05
plea of not guilty, 8–05
previous convictions, 8–02
sentence,
imposition of, 8–02
motion for, 8–02
remit for, 8–03, 8–04, 10–39
juvenile offenders, 8–03
substitution of fresh indictment, 8–04
warrants unnecessary, 7–03
withdrawal of plea, 8–05

ACCESSORY,
averment of art and part implied,
6–03, 6–05
directions by judge as to responsibility
of, 11–40
evidence of, 9–22, 10–39, 11–40,
18–58
immunity of, for giving evidence,
9–22
reference to, in charge, 16–24
statutory offences, in, 10–43
trial of, with co-accused, 10–18,
10–21, 16–14

ACCUSED,
absence of,
at empanelling jury, 10–25
at first diet, 9–04
at hearing of plea of insanity in
bar of trial, 20–11
at trial, 10–53, 14–23 et seq., 16–25
summary proceedings, in, 13–78,
14–19 et seq., 14–46, 14–48,
14–72, 16–25, 16–40
accumulation of, 10–18
admissions by, see EVIDENCE
appearance of, cures lack of citation,
13–79, 14–21
batches, trial in, 10–20

ACCUSED—cont.
body corporate as, see BODY COR-
PORATE
character of, evidence as to, 9–16,
10–32, 10–53, 18–10 et seq., and
see WITNESS
condition of, remand for inquiry into,
10–52, 19–10
consent of, to trial by existing jury,
10–25
death or illness of, 7–29, 10–15,
20–10
declaration by,
making of, 5–44, 5–45
objections to, 10–37
reading of, 10–37, 18–23
definition of, in summary proceedings,
13–22
description of,
in complaint, 13–31
in indictment, 6–02 9–11
duty of,
to appear at appeal, 11–19, 11–23,
16–77, 16–114
to give notice of witnesses, 7–17
to give notice of special defence,
7–01, 7–14, 14–60
to give notice of productions, 7–17
to give notice of plea in bar of
trial, 9–18, 14–60, 20–14
to give notice of attack on character of witness, 7–16, 18–76
to give notice of alibi in summary
case, 14–60
to give information under statute,
18–45
evidence by, 10–32, 18–07 et seq.,
and see WITNESS
comment on absence of, 10–38,
10–39, 14–69, 18–09
evidence for, 10–32, 14–69
identification of, 10–29, 18–60 et seq.
identification parade, 5–24, 18–60,
and see EVIDENCE
illness of,
before trial, 7–29
during trial, 10–11, 10–15, 20–10
immunity from prosecution, 5–71,
9–22
judicial examination of, 5–44 et seq.
liberation of,
on bail, see BAIL
on instructions of Crown Office,
5–67
pending appeal under 1926 Act,
11–18
pending summary appeal, 16–52 et
seq., 16–113, 16–114
under penalty, 14–56, 17–54
perjury by, 9–21, 18–08
refusal to plead, 9–15

507

PROSECUTOR—*cont.*
expenses against, 17–99 *et seq.*
justice of peace court, in, 12–19
limit of jurisdiction of, 12–12, 13–11, 21–07
non-acceptance of plea by, 8–05, 9–13, 9–14, 14–21, 14–29, 14–52
private,
  body corporate as, 13–16
  interest to prosecute, 4–04, 13–15 *et seq.*
  liability of, to action for damages, 21–05
  member of public as, 4–04, 13–15
  representative of deceased prosecutor, 13–17
  solemn procedure, 4–01, 4–04
  statutory offences, in, 13–15
  summary procedure, 4–06, 13–09, 13–15 *et seq.*
public,
  appointment by court ad interim, 9–03, 13–10
  concurrence of in private prosecution, 4–04, 4–06, 9–11, 13–13 *et seq.*, 13–19 *et seq.*
  duty of, in considering charge, 3–01
  liability of, to actions for damages, 21–05 *et seq.*
  solemn procedure, in, 4–01
public interest, in, under various statutes, 13–12 *et seq.*, 13–18, 13–21
reference by,
  to failure of accused or spouse to give evidence, 10–38, 14–69, 18–09
  to offences on which accused not convicted, 14–74, 16–32
  to previous convictions not libelled, 10–46
right of, to adjournment on plea of alibi, 14–60, 14–62
speech by, 10–38, 14–69
summary proceedings, in, 13–09 *et seq.*
summary case, preparation of, by, 13–01
title of, objection to, 9–09, 13–20, 16–109
witness, as, 10–31, 14–69, 18–69

PUNISHMENT,
absence of accused, imposable in, 14–25
admonition, 17–89
banishment, 17–93
borstal training, *see* BORSTAL TRAINING
capital, 1–04, 17–93
corporal, 17–93
corrective training, 10–54, 17–01, 17–10, 17–12 *et seq.*
cumulo penalties, 12–17, 15–16 *et seq.*
deportation, *see* DEPORTATION
detention centre, *see* DETENTION CENTRE
disqualification for driving, 13–61, 16–32, 16–33
fine, *see* FINES
first offenders, of, 17–04

PUNISHMENT—*cont.*
forfeiture of articles and vehicles, 17–56 *et seq.*, *and see* FORFEITURE
imprisonment, *see* IMPRISONMENT
legalised police cells, 17–03
mitigation of penalties, 15–27, 17–91, 17–92
notice of penalty, 13–57, *and see* NOTICE OF PENALTY
obsolete penalties, 17–93
penal servitude, 17–01
persons under twenty-one, of, 17–05 *et seq.*
powers of High Court, 1–04, *and see* HIGH COURT OF JUSTICIARY
powers of inferior summary courts, 12–29, *and see* INFERIOR COURTS
powers of sheriff,
  in solemn procedure, 1–04, 2–08, 17–01
  in summary procedure, 12–17, 15–21, 17–29, *and see* SHERIFF COURT
power of summary court to modify, 15–27
preventive detention, 10–54, 17–01, 17–11 *et seq.*
second or subsequent offence, increased powers on, 12–17
young offenders institution, *see* YOUNG OFFENDERS INSTITUTION
witness, of, for contempt, 18–98, 18–99
See also SENTENCE

RELEVANCY. *See* COMPLAINT; INDICTMENT; OBJECTIONS.

REMAND,
for inquiry into condition of accused, 10–52, 19–10 *et seq.*
of person appearing mentally disordered, to hospital, 20–04
REMAND CENTRE, 5–49, 14–21

REMIT,
cases involving children, *see* CHILDREN
incidental application for, in summary cases, 13–02
person appearing mentally disordered 12–33, 20–03
sentence, for,
  after trial, 10–55
  at first diet, 9–13
  in cases under s. 31 of 1887 Act, 8–03 *et seq.*
to competent court, from inferior summary court, 12–31 *et seq.*, 14–33, 14–50
to sheriff, 3–01n., 12–30, 12–31, 14–45, 14–50
  accused mentally disordered, 12–33, 20–03
  where no complaint, 12–32
to stipendiary magistrate, 12–34

REVIEW OF SUMMARY PROCEEDINGS—
cont.
methods of—cont.
appeal to Court of Exchequer,
16–01, 16–124
appeal to quarter sessions, 16–01,
16–123
appropriateness of bill of suspension or stated case, 16–102 et seq.
suspension, see BILL OF SUSPENSION
stated case, see STATED CASE
questions of fact, on, 16–10, 16–11
questions of law, on, 16–10, 16–12
sentence, appeal against, 16–09, et
seq., 16–28, 16–67, 16–85 et seq.,
16–110, 16–119
absolute discharge, 17–88
amendment of sentence, 16–85 et
seq.
excessive sentence, 16–41, 16–67,
16–89
facts not properly before judge,
16–33
failure to minute reasons, 15–36,
16–34, 16–88
failure to obtain statutory reports,
15–36, 16–34, 16–88
first offenders, by, 16–34
"harsh and oppressive," 16–28 et
seq., 16–67, 16–85
improper account taken of previous
conviction, 14–74, 16–32
incompetent sentence, 15–36, 16–34,
16–85, 16–86, 16–88
misleading statement by prosecutor,
16–32
one-man company, 16–35
probation order, 17–88
unrecorded sentence, 14–18, 15–37
unsigned sentence, 15–31

SEA, OFFENCES AT, 1–12 et seq.
Coinage Offences Act 1936, under,
1–13
Fishery Acts, under, 1–12
" territorial waters," 1–12, 1–14
Wireless Telegraphy Act 1949, under,
1–14
SEARCH,
forfeited articles, for, 17–59
irregular, 5–28 et seq., 18–94
good faith of searcher, 5–28
invasion of privacy, 5–28, 5–31
urgency, 5–28, 5–30
use of evidence obtained by, 5–26,
5–28, 5–31, 18–94
person, of,
before arrest, 5–24, 5–25
on arrest, 5–24
physical examination, 5–24
use of force, 5–25
with warrant, 5–25, 5–28
without warrant, 5–24
statutory provisions, 5–27
urgency, 5–24

SEARCH—cont.
premises, of,
with warrant,
articles not in warrant, 5–31
before arrest, 5–28
execution of warrant, 5–31
specific articles, for, 5–31
statutory provisions, 5–29
without warrant,
before arrest, 5–28
on arrest, 5–28
statutory provisions, 5–30
urgency, 5–28
procurator fiscal, by, 5–28
vehicles and vessels, of, 5–30
warrant, see WARRANT
with consent, 5–31
See also POLICE.
SECRETARY OF STATE,
appointment of children's panels by,
19–29
approval of appointment and removal
of reporters by, 19–30
consent of, to summary proceedings,
13–12
duty to furnish reports,
on suitability for borstal training,
17–20
on suitability for corrective training and preventive detention,
17–13
powers of,
in relation to mentally disordered
prisoners, etc., 20–28, 20–29
to allow publication of proceedings
against children, 19–24, 19–112
to direct child detainees, 19–17
to vary hospital order, 20–27
recall by,
of borstal licensee, 17–22
of parolee, 17–16
of person released from detention
centre, 17–28
to young offenders' institution,
17–19, 17–22, 17–28
reference by, to court under 1926 Act,
11–51
release by,
from detention centre, 17–26
from life imprisonment, 17–01,
17–17
on parole, 17–01, 17–16, 17–17
remission of fine by, 17–43
supervision orders, discharge or variation of, by, 17–19, 17–28
supervision requirement under 1968
Act, discharge of, by, 19–102
transfer by,
from borstal to young offenders
institution, 17–21
from detention centre to young
offenders institution, 17–26
from young offenders institution to
borstal, 17–06
to residential establishments, 19–18
SECTION 31 PROCEDURE. See ACCELERA-
TED PROCEDURE UNDER S. 31 OF
1887 ACT.